Historical Sketch of the Progress of Discovery, Navigation, and Commerce, from the Earliest Records to the Beginning of the Nineteenth Century

By

William Stevenson

A
General History And Collection Of
Voyages And Travels
Volume 18
Editor
Kerr, Robert, 1755-1813

The Echo Library 2006

Published by

The Echo Library

Echo Library
131 High St.
Teddington
Middlesex TW11 8HH

www.echo-library.com

Please report serious faults in the text to complaints@echo-library.com

ISBN 1-40683-043-7

PREFACE

THE curiosity of that man must be very feeble and sluggish, and his appetite for information very weak or depraved, who, when he compares the map of the world, as it was known to the ancients, with the map of the world as it is at present known, does not feel himself powerfully excited to inquire into the causes which have progressively brought almost every speck of its surface completely within our knowledge and access. To develop and explain these causes is one of the objects of the present work; but this object cannot be attained, without pointing out in what manner Geography was at first fixed on the basis of science, and has subsequently, at various periods, been extended and improved, in proportion as those branches of physical knowledge which could lend it any assistance, have advanced towards perfection. We shall thus, we trust, be enabled to place before our readers a clear, but rapid view of the surface of the globe, gradually exhibiting a larger portion of known regions, and explored seas, till at last we introduce them to the full knowledge of the nineteenth century. In the course of this part of our work, decisive and instructive illustrations will frequently occur of the truth of these most important facts,— that one branch of science can scarcely advance, without advancing some other branches, which in their turn, repay the assistance they have received; and that, generally speaking, the progress of intellect and morals is powerfully impelled by every impulse given to physical science, and can go on steadily and with full and permanent effect, only by the intercourse of civilised nations with those that are ignorant and barbarous.

But our work embraces another topic; the progress of commercial enterprise from the earliest period to the present time. That an extensive and interesting field is thus opened to us will be evident, when we contrast the state of the wants and habits of the people of Britain, as they are depicted by Cæsar, with the wants and habits even of our lowest and poorest classes. In Cæsar's time, a very few of the comforts of life,—scarcely one of its meanest luxuries,—derived from the neighbouring shore of Gaul, were occasionally enjoyed by British Princes: in our time, the daily meal of the pauper who obtains his precarious and scanty pittance by begging, is supplied by a navigation of some thousand miles, from countries in opposite parts of the globe; of whose existence Cæsar had not even the remotest idea. In the time of Cæsar, there was perhaps no country, the commerce of which was so confined:—in our time, the commerce of Britain lays the whole world under contribution, and surpasses in extent and magnitude the commerce of any other nation.

The progress of discovery and of commercial intercourse are intimately and almost necessarily connected; where commerce does not in the first instance prompt man to discover new countries, it is sure, if these countries are not totally worthless, to lead him thoroughly to explore them. The arrangement of this work, in carrying on, at the same time, a view of the progress of discovery, and of commercial enterprise, is, therefore, that very arrangement which the nature of the subject suggests. The most important and permanent effects of the progress of discovery and commerce, on the wealth, the power, the political relations, the manners and habits, and the general interests and character of nations, will either appear on the very surface of our work, or, where the facts themselves do not expose them to view, they will be distinctly noticed.

A larger proportion of the volume is devoted to the progress of discovery and enterprise among the ancients, than among the moderns; or,—to express ourselves more accurately,—the period that terminates with the discovery of America, and especially that which comprehends the commerce of the Phoeniceans, of the Egyptians under the Ptolemies, of the Greeks, and of the Romans, is illustrated with more ample and minute details, than the period which has elapsed since the new world was discovered. To most readers, the nations of antiquity are known by their wars alone; we wished to exhibit them in their commercial character and relations. Besides, the materials for the history of discovery within the modern period are neither so scattered, nor so difficult of access, as those which relate to the first period. After the discovery of America, the grand outline of the terraqueous part of the globe may be said to have been traced; subsequent discoveries only giving it more boldness or accuracy, or filling up the intervening parts. The same observation may in some degree be applied, to the corresponding periods of the history of commerce. Influenced by these considerations, we have therefore exhibited the infancy and youth of discovery and commerce, while they were struggling with their own ignorance and inexperience, in the strongest and fullest light.

At the conclusion of the work is given a select Catalogue of Voyages and Travels, which it is hoped will be found generally useful, not only in directing reading and inquiry, but also in the formation of a library.

This Historical Sketch has been drawn up with reference to, and in order to complete Kerr's Collection of Voyages and Travels, and was undertaken by the present Editor in consequence of the death of Mr. Kerr. But though drawn up with this object, it is strictly and entirely an independent and separate work.

Kerr's Collection contains a great variety of very curious and interesting early Voyages and Travels, of rare occurrence, or only to be found in expensive and voluminous Collections; and is, moreover, especially distinguished by a correct and full account of all Captain Cook's Voyages.

To the end of this volume is appended a Tabular View of the Contents of this Collection; and it is believed that this Tabular View, when examined and compared with the Catalogue, will enable those who wish to add to this Collection such Voyages and Travels as it does not embrace, especially those of very recent date, all that are deserving of purchase and perusal.

W. STEVENSON.
March 30, 1824.

TABLE OF CONTENTS

CHAPTER I

Historical Sketch Of The Progress Of Discovery And Of Commercial Enterprise From The Earliest Records To The Time Of Herodotus B.C. 450

The earliest traces of navigation and commerce are necessarily involved in much obscurity, and are, besides, few and faint. It is impossible to assign to them any clear and definite chronology; and they are, with a few exceptions, utterly uncircumstantial. Nevertheless, in a work like this, they ought not to be passed over without some notice; but the notice we shall bestow upon them will not be that either of the chronologist or antiquarian, but of a more popular, appropriate, and useful description.

The intercourse of one nation with another first took place in that part of the world to which a knowledge of the original habitation of mankind, and of the advantages for sea and land commerce which that habitation enjoyed, would naturally lead us to assign it. On the shores of the Mediterranean, or at no great distance from that sea, among the Israelites, the Phoenicians, and the Egyptians, we must look for the earliest traces of navigation and commerce; and, in the only authentic history of the remotest period of the world, as well as amidst the scanty and fabulous materials supplied by profane writers, these nations are uniformly represented as the most ancient navigators and traders.

The slightest inspection of the map of this portion of the globe will teach us that Palestine, Phoenicia, and Egypt were admirably situated for commerce both by sea and land. It is, indeed, true that the Phoenicians, by the conquests of Joshua, were expelled from the greatest part of their territory, and obliged to confine themselves to a narrow slip of ground between Mount Lebanon and the Mediterranean; but even this confined territory presented opportunities and advantages for commerce of no mean importance: they had a safe coast,—at least one good harbour; and the vicinity of Lebanon, and other mountains, enabled them to obtain, with little difficulty and expence, a large supply of excellent materials for shipbuilding. There are, moreover, circumstances which warrant the supposition, that, like Holland in modern times, they were rather the carriers of other nations, than extensively engaged in the commerce of their own productions or manufactures. On the north and east lay Syria, an extensive country, covered with a deep rich soil, producing an abundant variety of valuable articles. With this country, and much beyond it, to the east, the means and opportunities of communication and commerce were easy, by the employment of the camel; while, on the other hand, the caravans that carried on the commerce of Asia and Africa necessarily passed through Phoenicia, or the adjacent parts of Palestine.

Egypt, in some respects, was still more advantageously situated for commerce than Phoenicia: the trade of the west of Asia, and of the shores of the Mediterranean lay open to it by means of that sea, and by the Nile and the Red Sea a commercial intercourse with Arabia, Persia, and India seemed almost to be forced upon their notice and adoption. It is certain, however, that in the earliest periods of their history, the Egyptians were decidedly averse to the sea, and to maritime affairs, both warlike and commercial. It would be vain and unprofitable to explain the fabulous cause assigned for this aversion: we may, however, briefly and, incidentally remark that as Osiris particularly instructed his subjects in cultivating the ground; and as Typhon coincides exactly in orthography and meaning with a word still used in the East, to signify a sudden and violent storm, it is probable that by Typhon murdering his brother Osiris, the Egyptians meant the damage done to their cultivated lands by storms of wind causing inundations.

As the situation of Palestine for commerce was equally favourable with that of Phoenicia, it is unnecessary to dilate upon it. That the Jews did not engage more extensively in trade either by sea or land must be attributed to the peculiar nature of their government, laws, and religion.

Having thus briefly pointed out the advantages enjoyed by the Phoenicians, Egyptians, and Jews for commercial intercourse, we shall now proceed to notice the few particulars with which history supplies us regarding the navigation and commerce of each, during the earliest periods.

I. There is good reason to believe that most of the maritime adventures and enterprises which have rendered the Phoenicians so famous in antiquity, ought to be fixed between the death of Jacob, and the establishment of monarchy among the Israelites; that is, between the years 1700 and 1095 before Christ; but even before this, there are authentic notices of Phoenician commerce and navigation. In the days of Abraham they were considered as a very powerful people: and express mention is made of their maritime trade in the last words of Jacob to his children. Moses informs us that Tarshish (wherever it was situated) was visited by the Phoenicians. When this people were deprived of a great portion of their territory by the Israelites under Joshua, they still retained the city of Sidon; and from it their maritime expeditions proceeded. The order of time in which they took place, as well as their object and result, are very imperfectly known; it seems certain, however, that they either regularly traded with, or formed colonies or establishments for the purpose of trade at first in Cyprus and Rhodes, and subsequently in Greece, Sicily, Sardinia, Gaul, and the southern part of Spain. About 1250 years before Christ, the Phoenician ships ventured beyond the Straits, entered the Atlantic, and founded Cadiz. It is probable, also, that nearly about the same period they formed establishments on the western coast of Africa. We have the express authority of Homer, that at the Trojan war the Phoenicians furnished other nations with many articles that could contribute to luxury and magnificence; and Scripture informs us, that the ships of Hyram, king of Tyre, brought gold to Solomon from Ophir. That they traded to Britain for tin at so early a period as that which we are now considering, will appear very doubtful, if the metal mentioned by Moses, (Numbers, chap. xxxi. verse 22.) was really tin, and if Homer is accurate in his statement that this metal was used at the siege of Troy; for, certainly, at neither of these periods had the Phoenicians ventured so far from their own country.

Hitherto we have spoken of Sidon as the great mart of Phoenician commerce; at what period Tyre was built and superseded Sidon is not known. In the time of Homer, Tyre is not even mentioned: but very soon afterwards it is represented by Isaiah, Jeremiah, Ezekiel, and the other prophets, as a city of unrivalled trade and wealth. Ezekiel, who prophesied about the year 595 B.C. has given a most picturesque description of the wealth of Tyre, all of which must have proceeded from her commerce, and consequently points out and proves its great extent and importance. The fir-trees of Senir, the cedars of Lebanon, the oaks of Bashan, the ivory of the Indies, the fine linen of Egypt, and the hyacinth and purple of the isles of Elishah, are enumerated among the articles used for their ships. Silver, tin, lead, and vessels of brass; slaves, horses, and mules; carpets, ivory, and ebony; pearls and silk; wheat, balm, honey, oil and gums; wine, and wool, and iron, are enumerated as brought into the port of Tyre by sea, or to its fairs by land, from Syria, Damascus, Greece, Arabia, and other places, the exact site of which is not known.[1] Within the short period of fifteen or twenty years after this description was written, Tyre was besieged by Nebuchadnezzar; and after an obstinate and very protracted resistance, it was taken and destroyed. The inhabitants, however, were enabled to retire during the siege, with the greatest part of their property, to an island near the shore, where they built New Tyre, which soon surpassed the old city both in commerce and shipping.

A short time previous to the era generally assigned to the destruction of old Tyre, the Phoenicians are said to have performed a voyage, which, if authentic, may justly be regarded as the most important that the annals of this people record: we allude to the circumnavigation of Africa. As this voyage has given rise to much discussion, we may be excused for deviating from the cursory and condensed character of this part of our work, in order to investigate its probable authenticity. All that we know regarding it is delivered to us by Herodotus; according to this historian, soon after Nechos, king of Egypt, had finished the canal that united the Nile and the Arabian Gulf, he sent some Phoenicians from the borders of the Red Sea, with orders to keep always along the coast of Africa, and to return by the pillars of Hercules into the northern ocean. Accordingly the Phoenicians embarked on the Erythrean Sea, and navigated in the southern ocean. When autumn arrived, they landed on the part of Libya which they had reached, and sowed corn; here they remained till harvest, reaped the corn, and then re-embarked. In this manner they sailed for two years; in the third they passed the pillars of Hercules, and returned to Egypt. They related that in sailing round Libya, the sun was on their right hand. This relation, continues Herodotus, seems incredible to me, but perhaps it will not appear so to others. Before proceeding to an enquiry into the authenticity of this maritime enterprize, it may be proper to explain what is meant by the sun appearing on the right hand of the Phoenician navigators. The apparent motion of the heavens being from east to west, the west was regarded by the ancients as the foremost part of the world; the north, of course, was deemed the right, and the south the left of the world.

The principal circumstance attending this narrative, which is supposed to destroy or greatly weaken its credibility, is the short period of time in which this navigation was accomplished: it is maintained, that even at present, it would certainly require eighteen months to coast Africa from the Red Sea to the straits of Gibraltar; and "allowing nine months for each interval on shore, between the sowing and reaping, the Phoenicians could not have been more than eighteen months at sea."

To this objection it may be replied, in the first place, that between the tropics (within which space nearly the whole of the navigation was performed) nine months is much too long a time to allow for each interval on shore, between the sowing and the reaping: and, secondly, that though the period occupied by the whole voyage, and some of the circumstances attending it, may be inaccurately stated, the voyage itself ought not to be wholly discredited on these accounts.

The very circumstance which the historian rejects as incredible, is one of the strongest arguments possible in favour of the tradition; though this alone is not decisive, for the Phoenicians might have sailed far enough to the south to have observed the sun to the north, even if they had not accomplished the navigation of Africa. The strongest argument, however, in our opinion, in support of the actual accomplishment of this circumnavigation, has been unaccountably overlooked, in all the various discussion to which the subject has given rise. It is evident that in most voyages, false and exaggerated accounts may be given of the countries visited or seen, and of the circumstances attendant upon the voyage; whereas, with respect to this voyage, one most important and decisive particular lay within reach of the observation of those who witnessed the departure and arrival of the ships. If they sailed from the Red Sea, and returned by the Mediterranean, they must have circumnavigated Africa. It is obvious that if such a voyage was not performed, the story must have originated with Herodotus, with those from whom he received his information, or with those who were engaged in the expedition, supposing it actually to have been engaged in, but not to have accomplished the circumnavigation of Africa. The character of Herodotus secures him from the imputation; and by none is he charged with it:—Necho lived about six hundred and sixteen years before Christ; consequently little more than two hundred years before Herodotus; moreover, the communication and commerce of the Greeks with Egypt, was begun in the time of Psammeticus, the immediate predecessor of Necho, and was encouraged in a very particular manner by Amasis (who died in 525), who married a Greek, and was visited by Solon. From these circumstances, it is improbable that Herodotus, who was evidently not disposed to believe the account of the appearance of the sun, should not have had it in his power to obtain good evidence, whether a ship that had sailed from the Red Sea, had returned by the Mediterranean: if such evidence were acquired, it is obvious, as has been already remarked, that the third source of fabrication is utterly destroyed. Dr. Vincent is strongly opposed to the authenticity of this voyage, chiefly on the grounds that such ships as the ancients had, were by no means sufficiently strong, nor their seamen sufficiently skilful and experienced, to have successfully encountered a navigation, which the Portuguese did not accomplish without great danger and difficulty, and that the alleged circumnavigation produced no consequences.

It may be incidentally remarked that the incredulity of Herodotus with regard to the appearance of the sun to the north of the zenith, is not easily reconcileable with what we shall afterwards shew was the extent of his knowledge of the interior of Egypt. He certainly had visited, or had received communications from those who had visited Ethiopia as far south as eleven degrees north latitude. Under this parallel the sun appears for a considerable part of the year to the north. How, then, it may be asked, could Herodotus be incredulous of this phenomenon having been observed by the Phoenician circumnavigators. This difficulty can be solved by supposing either that if he himself had visited this part of Africa, it was at a season of the year when the sun was in that quarter of the heavens in which he was accustomed to see it; or, if he received his information from the inhabitants of this district, that they, not regarding the periodical appearance of the sun to the north of the zenith as extraordinary, did not think it necessary to mention it. It certainly cannot be supposed that if Herodotus had either seen himself, or heard from others, that the sun in Ethiopia sometimes appeared to the north of the zenith, he would have stated in such decided terms, when narrating the circumnavigation of the Phoenicians, that such a phenomenon appeared to him altogether incredible.

Before we return to the immediate subject of this part of our work, we may be allowed to deviate from strict chronological order, for the purpose of mentioning two striking and important facts, which naturally led to the belief of the practicability of circumnavigating Africa, long before that enterprise was actually accomplished by the Portuguese.

We are informed by Strabo, on the authority of Posidonius, that Eudoxus of Cyzicus, who lived about one hundred and fifty years before Christ, was induced to conceive the practicability of circumnavigating Africa, from the following circumstance. As Eudoxus was returning from India to the Red Sea, he was driven by adverse winds on the coast of Ethiopia: there he saw the figure of a horse sculptured on a piece of wood, which he knew to be a part of the prow of a ship. The natives informed him that it had belonged to a vessel, which had arrived among them from the west. Eudoxus brought it with him to Egypt, and subjected it to the inspection of several pilots: they pronounced it to be the prow of a small kind of vessel used by the inhabitants of Gadez, to fish on the coast of Mauritania, as far as the river Lixius: some of the pilots recognised it as belonging to a particular vessel, which, with several others, had attempted to advance beyond the Lixius, but had never afterwards been heard of. We are further informed on the same authority, that Eudoxus, hence conceiving it practicable to sail round Africa, made the attempt, and actually sailed from Gadez to a part of Ethiopia, the inhabitants of which spoke the same language as those among whom he had formerly been. From some cause not assigned, he proceeded no farther: subsequently, however, he made a second attempt, but how far he advanced, and what was the result, we are not informed.

The second fact to which we allude is related in the Commentary of Abu Sird, on the Travels of a Mahommedan in India and China, in the ninth century of the Christian era. The travels and commentary are already given in the first volume of this work; but the importance of the fact will, we trust, plead our excuse for repeating the passage which contains it.

"In our times, discovery has been made of a thing quite new: nobody imagined that the sea which extends from the Indies to China, had any communication with the sea of Syria, nor could any one take it into his head. Now behold what has come to pass in our days, according to what we have heard. In the Sea of Rum, or the Mediterranean, they found the wreck of an Arabian ship which had been shattered by tempest; for all her men perishing, and she being dashed to pieces by the waves, the remains of her were driven by wind and weather into the Sea of Chozars, and from thence to the canal of the Mediterranean sea, and at last were thrown on the Sea of Syria. This evinces that the sea surrounds all the country of China, and of Sila,—the uttermost parts of Turkestan, and the country of the Chozars, and then it enters at the strait, till it washes the shore of Syria. The proof of this is deduced from the built of the ship we are speaking of; for none but the ships of Sarif are so put together, that the planks are not nailed, or bolted, but joined together in an extraordinary manner, as if they were sewn; whereas the planking of all the ships of the Mediterranean Sea, and of the coast of Syria, is nailed and not joined together in the same way."

When we entered on this digression, we had brought the historical sketch of the discoveries and commerce of the Phoenicians down to the period of the destruction of Old Tyre, or about six hundred years before Christ. We shall now resume it, and add such particulars on these subjects as relate to the period that intervened between that event and the capture of New Tyre by Alexander the Great. These are few in number; for though New Tyre exceeded, according to all accounts, the old city in splendour, riches, and commercial prosperity, yet antient authors have not left us any precise accounts of their discoveries, such as can justly be fixed within the period to which we have alluded. They seem to have advanced farther than they had previously done along the west coast of Africa, and further along the north coast of Spain: the discovery of the Cassiterides also, and their trade to these islands for tin, (which we have shewn could hardly have taken place so early as is generally supposed,) must also have occurred, either immediately before, or soon after, the building of New Tyre. It is generally believed, that the Cassiterides were the Scilly Islands, off the coast of Cornwall. Strabo and Ptolemy indeed place them off the coast of Spain; but Diodorus Siculus and Pliny give them a situation, which, considering the vague and erroneous ideas the antients possessed of the geography of this part of the world, corresponds pretty nearly with the southern part of Britain. According to Strabo, the Phoenicians first brought tin from the Cassiterides, which they sold to the Greeks, but kept (as was usual with them) the trade entirely to themselves, and were utterly silent respecting the place from which they brought it. The Greeks gave these islands the name of Cassiterides, or the Tin Country; a plain proof of what we before advanced, that tin was known, and generally used, previous to the discovery of these islands by the Phoenicians.

There is scarcely any circumstance connected with the maritime history of the Phoenicians, more remarkable than their jealousy of foreigners interfering with their trade, to which we have just alluded. It seems to have been a regular plan, if not a fixed law with them, if at any time their ships observed that a strange ship kept them company, or endeavoured to trace their track, to outsail her if practicable; or, where this could not be done, to depart during the night from their proper course. The Carthaginians, a colony of the Phoenicians, adopted this, among other maritime regulations of the parent state, and even carried it to a greater extent. In proof of this, a striking fact may be mentioned: the master of a Carthaginian ship observing a Roman vessel following his course, purposely ran his vessel aground, and thus wrecked his own ship, as well as the one that followed him. This act was deemed by the Carthaginian government so patriotic, that he was amply rewarded for it, as well as recompensed for the loss of his vessel.

The circumstances attending the destruction of New Tyre by Alexander the Great are well known. The Tyrians united with the Persians against Alexander, for the purpose of preventing the invasion of Persia; this having incensed the conqueror, still further enraged by their refusal to admit him within their walls, he resolved upon the destruction of this commercial city. For seven months, the natural strength of the place, and the resources and bravery of the inhabitants, enabled them to hold out; but at length it was taken, burnt to the ground, and all the inhabitants, except such as had escaped by sea, were either put to death or sold as slaves.

Little is known respecting the structure and equipment of the ships which the Phoenicians employed in their commercial navigation. According to the apocryphal authority of Sanconiatho, Ousous, one of the most ancient of the Phoenician heroes, took a tree which was half burnt, cut off its branches, and was the first who ventured to expose himself on the waters. This tradition, however, probably owes its rise to the prevalent belief among the ancients, that to the Phoenicians was to be ascribed the invention of every thing that related to the rude navigation and commerce of the earliest ages of the world: under this idea, the art of casting accounts, keeping registers, and every thing, in short, that belongs to a factory, is attributed to their invention.[2] With respect to their vessels,— "Originally they had only rafts, or simple boats; they used oars to conduct these weak and light vessels. As navigation extended itself, and became more frequent, they perfected the construction of ships, and made them of a much larger capacity. They were not long in discovering the use that might be drawn from the wind, to hasten and facilitate the course of a ship, and they found out the art of aiding it by means of masts and sails." Such is the account given by Goguet; but it is evident that this is entirely conjectural history: and we may remark, by the bye, that a work otherwise highly distinguished by clear and philosophical views, and enriched by considerable learning and research, in many places descends to fanciful conjecture.

All that we certainly know respecting the ships of the Phoenicians, is, that they had two kinds; one for the purposes of commerce, and the other for naval expeditions; and in this respect they were imitated by all the other nations of antiquity. Their merchant-ships were called Gauloi. According to Festus's definition of this term, the gauloi were nearly round; but it is evident that this term must be taken with considerable restriction; a vessel round, or nearly so, could not possibly be navigated. It is most probable that this description refers entirely to the shape of the bottom or hold of the vessel; and that merchant ships were built in this manner, in order that they might carry more goods; whereas the ships for warfare were sharp in the bottom. Of other particulars respecting the construction and equipment of the ships of the Phoenicians, we are ignorant: they probably resembled in most things those of Greece and Rome; and these, of which antient historians speak more fully, will be described afterwards.

The Phoenicians naturally paid attention to astronomy, so far at least as might be serviceable to them in their navigation; and while other nations were applying it merely to the purposes of agriculture and chronology, by means of it they were guided through the "trackless ocean," in their maritime enterprises. The Great Bear seems to have been known and used as a guide by navigators, even before the Phoenicians were celebrated as a sea-faring people; but this constellation affords a very imperfect and uncertain rule for the direction of a ship's course: the extreme stars that compose it are more than forty degrees distant from the pole, and even its centre star is not sufficiently near it. The Phoenicians, experiencing the imperfection of this guide, seem first to have discovered, or at least to have applied to maritime purposes, the constellation of the Lesser Bear. But it is probable, that at the period when they first applied this constellation, which is supposed to be about 1250 years before Christ, they did not fix on the star at the extremity of the tail of Ursa Minor, which is what we call the Pole Star; for by a Memoir of the Academy of Sciences (1733. p. 440.) it is shewn, that it would at that period be too distant to serve the purpose of guiding their track.[3]

II. The gleanings in antient history respecting the maritime and commercial enterprises, and the discoveries and settlements of the Egyptians, during the very early ages, to which we are at present confining ourselves, are few and unimportant compared with those of the Phoenicians, and consequently will not detain us long.

We have already noticed the advantageous situation of Egypt for navigation and commerce: in some respects it was preferable to that of Phoenicia; for besides the immediate vicinity of the Mediterranean, a sea, the shores of which were so near to each other that they almost prevented the possibility of the ancients, rude and ignorant as they were of all that related to navigation and the management of ships, deviating long or far from their route; besides the advantages of a climate equally free from the clouded skies, long nights and tempestuous weather of more northern regions, and from the irresistible hurricanes of those within the tropics—besides these favourable circumstances, which, the Egyptians enjoyed in common with the Phoenicians, they had, running far into their territory, a river easily navigable, and at no great distance from this river, and bounding their country, a sea almost equally favourable for navigation and commerce as the Mediterranean. Their advantages for land journies were also numerous and great; though the vicinity of the deserts seemed at first sight to have raised an effectual bar to those countries which they divided from Egypt, yet Providence had wisely and benevolently removed the difficulty arising from this source, and had even rendered intercommunication, where deserts intervened, more expeditious, and not more difficult, than in those regions where they did not occur, by the creation of the camel, a most benevolent compensation to the Egyptians for their vicinity to the extensive deserts of Africa.

Notwithstanding the advantageous situation of the Egyptians for navigation, they were extremely averse, as we nave already remarked, during the earliest periods of their history, to engage in sea affairs, either for the purposes of war or commerce; nor did they indeed, at any time, enter with spirit, or on a large scale, into maritime enterprises.

The superstitious and fabulous reasons assigned for this antipathy of the Egyptians to the sea [has-]have] been noticed before; perhaps some other causes contributed to it, as well as the one alluded to. Egypt is nearly destitute of timber proper for ship-building: its sea-coasts are unhealthy, and do not appear to have been inhabited [near-]nearly] so early as the higher country: its harbours are few, of intricate navigation, and frequently changing their depth and direction; and lastly, the advantages which the Nile presents for intercourse and traffic precluded the necessity of applying to sea navigation and commerce.

Some authors are of opinion that the ancient Egyptians did not engage in navigation and commerce till the era of the Ptolemies; but this is undoubtedly a mistake, since traces of their commercial intercommunication with other nations may be found at a very early period of history. It is probable, however, that for a long time they themselves did not engage in commerce, but were merely visited by traders from foreign countries; for at this era it was a maxim with them, never to leave their own country. The low opinion they entertained of commerce may be gathered from Herodotus, who mentions, that the men disdained to meddle with it, but left it entirely to the women.

The earliest account we possess of traffic with Egypt, is to be found in the Old Testament, where we are informed, that the Midianites and Ismaelites traded thither as early as the time of Jacob.

Sesostris, who is generally supposed to have lived about 1650 years before Christ, is by most writers described as the king who first overcame the dislike of the Egyptians to the sea. That this monarch engaged in many enterprises both by sea and land, not only for conquest, but also for purposes of trade and colonization, there can be no doubt; though it is impossible either to trace his various routes, or to estimate the extent of his conquests or discoveries. The concurrent testimony of Diodorus and Herodotus assign to him a large fleet in the Red Sea; and according to other historians, he had also a fleet in the Mediterranean. In order the more effectually to banish the prejudices of the Egyptians against the sea, he is said to have instituted a marine class among his subjects. By these measures he seems to have acquired the sovereignty and the commerce of the greater part of the shores of the Red Sea; along which his ships continued their route, till, according to Herodotus, they were prevented from advancing by shoals and places difficult to navigate; a description which aptly applies to the navigation of this sea.

His expeditions and conquests in other parts of the globe do not fall within our object: one however must be noticed; we allude to the settlement of the Egyptians at Colchos. Herodotus is doubtful whether this was a colony planted by Sesostris, or whether part of his army remained behind on the banks of the Phasis, when he invaded this part of Asia. We allude to this colony, because with it were found, at the time of the Argonautic expedition, proofs of the attention which Sesostris had paid to geography, and of the benefits which that science derived from him. "Tradition," Gibbon observes, "has affirmed, with some colour of reason, that Egypt planted on the Phasis a learned and polite colony, which manufactured linen, built navies, and invented geographical maps." All the information we possess respecting these maps is derived from Apollonius Rhodius, and his scholiast: the substance of it is as follows: according to this poet,—Phineas, king of Colchos, predicted to the Argonauts the events which would accompany their return. Argus, one of the Argonauts, explained that prediction to his companions, and told them, that the route which they must keep was described on tables, or rather on columns, which an Egyptian conqueror had before left in the city of Oca, the capital of Colchis; on these columns, the whole extent of the roads, and the limits of the land and sea were marked out. An ingenious, and by no means an improbable inference, has been drawn from this circumstance: that if Sesostris left such columns in a part so remote from Egypt, it is to be supposed that they were more numerous in Egypt itself. In short, though on a point like this it is impossible to gain clear and undoubted testimony, we are, upon the whole, strongly disposed to coincide in opinion with Gibbon, that tradition has some colour of reason for affirming that the Egyptian colony at Phasis possessed geographical maps.

After the death of Sesostris, the Egyptians seem to have relapsed into their former dislike to the sea: they indeed sent colonies into Greece, and other parts; but these colonists kept up no relation with the mother country. Their commerce was carried on, as it had been before the time of Sesostris, by foreigners. The Old Testament informs us, that in the time of Solomon many horses were brought from Egypt: and, from the same authority, as well as from Herodotus and Homer, we learn that the Phoenicians carried on a regular and lucrative traffic with this country; and, indeed, for a long time, about this period, they were the only nation to whom the ports of Egypt were open. Of the navigation and commerce of the Red Sea they were equally negligent; so that while none of their ships were seen on it, it was covered with the fleets of the Syrians, Phoenicians, and other nations.

Bocchoris, who lived about seven hundred years before Christ, is represented by historians as having imitated the maxims of Sesostris, with respect to maritime affairs and commerce. Some of his laws on these subjects are still extant; and they display his knowledge of, and attention to, the improvement of his kingdom. By some of his immediate successors the ancient maxims of the Egyptians, which led them to avoid intercourse with strangers, were gradually done away; but it is to Psammeticus, historians ascribe the most decisive measures for rooting out this antipathy. In his reign the ports of Egypt were first opened to foreign ships generally. He seems particularly to have encouraged commercial intercourse with the Greeks; though afterwards, either from some particular cause of jealousy or dislike to this nation, or from the still operating antipathy of the Egyptians to foreigners, the Greeks were not permitted to enter any port except Naucratis, which they had been suffered to build for the residence of their merchants and convenience of their trade. This city lay on the Canopic branch of the Nile; and if a vessel entered any other mouth of this river, the master was obliged to return to the Canopic branch; or, if the wind did not permit this, to unlade his vessel, and send his merchandize to Naucratis by the country boats.

From the time of Psammeticus, when the Greeks were allowed to settle in Egypt, frequent intercourse and correspondence was kept up between them and their countrymen in Greece; and from this circumstance the Egyptian history may henceforth be more firmly depended upon. It has already been remarked, that as the alleged circumnavigation of Africa by the Phoenicians took place during the reign of Necho, the successor of Psammeticus, the grounds for its authenticity are much stronger than if it had occurred previously to the intercourse of the Greeks with Egypt.

The employment of Phoenician mariners by Necho, to circumnavigate Africa, bespeaks a monarch bent on maritime and commercial enterprise; and there are other transactions of his reign which confirm this character. It is said that Sesostris attempted to unite by a canal the Mediterranean and the Red Sea, but that he did not succeed in his attempt: Necho also made the attempt with as little success. He next turned his thoughts to the navigation and commerce of the Mediterranean and Red Sea, in each of which he had large fleets.

The superstitious antipathy of the Egyptians having been thus broken through, and the recurrence of this antipathy secured against, by the advantages they derived from navigation and commerce, the Egyptian monarchs seem, as long as Egypt continued free, to have directed their attention and resources, with considerable zeal and success, to maritime affairs. Their strength by sea, as well as their experience, may be estimated by an event during the reign of Apries, the grandson of Necho: this monarch was engaged in war with the Sidonians, Tyrians and Cypriots; he took the city of Sidon by storm, and defeated both the Phoenicians and Cypriots in a sea fight. In fact, during his reign the Egyptians had the command of the Mediterranean Sea. It is probable, that if they had continued long after this time an independent state, they would have been still more celebrated and successful in their maritime and commercial affairs; but in the year 525 before Christ, about seventy years after the reign of Apries, Egypt was conquered by the Persians.

Notwithstanding, therefore, this temporary dereliction of their antipathy to the sea, and intercourse with foreigners, the Egyptians can scarcely be regarded as a nation distinguished for their maritime and commercial enterprises; and they certainly by no means, either by sea or land, took advantages of those favourable circumstances by which their country seemed to be marked out for the attainment of an extensive and lucrative commerce. It is well remarked by Dr. Vincent, that "while Egypt was under the power of its native sovereigns Tyre, Sidon, Arabia, Cyprus, Greece, Sicily, and Carthage, were all enriched by the trade carried on in its ports, and the articles of commerce which could be obtained there, and there only; the Egyptians themselves were hardly known in the Mediterranean as the exporters of their own commodities; they were the Chinese of the ancient world, and the ships of all nations, except their own, laded in their harbours." As soon, however, as it passed from the power of its native sovereigns, and became subject successively to the Persians, Macedonians, and Romans, it furnished large fleets, and, as we shall afterwards notice, under the Greeks, Alexandria became one of the principal commercial cities in the world. The Greek inhabitants of Egypt were the carriers of the Mediterranean, as well as the agents, factors, and importers of oriental produce. The cities which had risen under the former system sank into insignificance; and so wise was the new policy, and so deeply had it taken root, that the Romans, upon the subjection of Egypt, found it more expedient to leave Alexandria in possession of its privileges, than to alter the course of trade, or to occupy it themselves.

We possess scarcely any notices respecting the construction and equipment of the Egyptian ships. According to Herodotus, they were made of thorns twisted together, and their sails of rush mats: they were built in a particular manner, quite different from those of other nations, and rigged also in a singular manner; so that they seem to have been the mockery of the other maritime states in the Mediterranean. But this description can hardly apply to the Egyptian ships, after they had become powerful at sea, though the expressions of Herodotus seem to have reference to the Egyptian ships of his age. There can be no doubt that the vessels that navigated the Nile, were very rude and singular in their construction; and most probably the description given by the historian ought to be regarded as exclusively confined to them. They were built of the Egyptian thorn, which seems to have been very extensively cultivated, especially in the vicinity of Acanthus: planks of small dimensions were cut from this tree, which were fastened together, or rather laid over one another, like tiles, with a great number of wooden pins: they used no ribs in the construction of their vessels: on the inside, papyrus was employed for the purpose of stopping up the crevices, or securing the joints. There was but one rudder; whereas the ships of the Greeks and Romans had generally two; this passed quite through the keel. The mast was made of Egyptian thorn, and the sail of papyrus. Indeed, these two plants appear to have been the entire materials used in the construction and rigging of their ships. They were towed up the Nile, as they were not fit to stem its stream, except when a strong favourable wind blew. Their mode of navigating these vessels down the river was singular; they fastened a hurdle of tamarisk with a rope to the prow of the vessel; which hurdle they strengthened with bands of reeds, and let it down into the water; they also hung a stone, pierced through the middle, and of a considerable weight, by another rope, to the poop. By this means, the stream bearing on the hurdle, carried down the boat with great expedition; the stone at the same time balancing and keeping it steady. Of these vessels they had great numbers on the river; some very large.

III. The Jews were still more averse than the Egyptians to intercourse with foreigners, and maritime and commercial enterprises; indeed, their country was comparatively ill-situated for maritime commerce. Josephus is not, however, quite correct, in stating that Judea was not situated on the sea, and that the people of that country did not carry on any trade, but that their whole thoughts were turned to agriculture. The words of Jacob, on his death-bed, are expressly against this opinion: in blessing his twelve sons, he says of Zebulon, "he shall dwell at the haven of the sea, and he shall be for an haven of ships;" and we know that the tribe of Zebulon was extended to the sea shore, and to the gates of Sidon.

It is not likely, that being in the immediate vicinity of this commercial city, the Jews would not be stimulated to follow its example, and endeavour to draw wealth from the same sources. Indeed, the Old Testament expressly speaks of Joppa as the port of Judea and Jerusalem, into which foreign articles, and especially many of the materials used by Solomon in the building of the temple, were imported.

On the conquest of the Amalekites and Edomites by King David, the Jews gained possession of some ports in the Red Sea; and during his reign, and that of Solomon, the Jews certainly employed the ships of their ally, Hiram king of Tyre, extensively in foreign commerce. Indeed, the commerce of the Phoenicians from the Red Sea, appears to have been carried on principally, if not entirely, from the harbours in that sea belonging to the Jews, though there is no ground for believing that the Jews themselves had any fleet on it, or were at all engaged in its commerce. These short notices are all that history supplies us with, on the subject of the navigation and commerce of the Jews. From the Old Testament we may, however, collect materials, by which we may estimate the progress they had made in geography. About 500 years before Christ, they do not appear to have extended their knowledge of the globe beyond Mount Caucasus to the north, the entrance of the Red Sea to the south, and the Mediterranean Archipelago to the west, besides Egypt, Asia Minor, Armenia, Syria, Arabia, and perhaps a small part of Abyssinia.

Having thus given a sketch of the progress of discovery, and of commercial enterprize by sea and land, among those nations who were the most early in directing their attention to these points, we shall next proceed to an account of the navigation and commercial enterprizes of the Greeks and Romans; and as in this part of our work we shall follow a more strictly chronological arrangement, the navigation and commercial enterprizes of the Carthaginians will be incidentally noticed in the order of time to which they belong. Before, however, we proceed to this subject, it may be proper to enter more particularly and fully than we have hitherto done, into a description of the construction and equipment of the ancient ships, since, so far as relates to the ships of the Greeks and Romans, we possess much more ample materials for such a description, than history supplies us with respecting the ships of the other nations of antiquity.

The traditionary story of the Phoenicians, that one of their heroes was the first man who had the courage to expose himself upon the waters, in a half burnt tree, stript of its branches, has already been noticed. It is probable, however, that the first vessels had not even so much resemblance to our present boats: indeed, conjecture, as well as history, warrant us in believing that rafts were the most ancient mode of conveyance on the water; and even in the time of Pliny they were extensively employed, especially in the navigation of rivers. Boats formed of slender rods or hurdles, and covered with skins, seem also to have preceded the canoe, or vessel mode of a single piece of timber. It is probable that a considerable time would elapse before the means of constructing boats of planks were discovered, since the bending of the planks for that purpose is not a very obvious art. The Greeks ascribe this invention to a native of Lydia; but at what period he lived, is not known. Among some nations, leather was almost the only material used in the construction of ships; and even in the time of Caesar, the Veneti, a people of Brittany, distinguished as a maritime and commercial tribe, made their sails of hides, and their tackle of thongs. In early ages, also, the Greeks used the common rushes of their country, and the Carthaginians, the spartum, or broom of Spain.

But it is to the ships of Greece and Rome, when they were constructed with more skill, and better adapted to navigation, that we are to pay attention; and of those, only to such as were used for commercial purposes. The latter were rounder and more capacious than ships used for war; they were principally impelled by sails; whereas the ships of war, though not wholly without sails, were chiefly rowed. Another difference between them was, that ships of war commonly had an helmet engraven on the top of their masts, and ships for trade had a basket suspended on the top of their mast as a sign. There seems to have been great variety in the construction of the latter, according to the particular trade in which they were to be engaged; and each ship of burden had its boat attached to it. The name of the ship, or rather of its tutelary deity, was inscribed on the stern: various forms of gods, animals, plants, &c. were also painted on other parts. The inhabitants of Phoeacia, or Corsica, are represented as the first who used pitch to fill up the seams, and preserve the timber; sometimes wax was used for this purpose, or rather it was mixed with the paint, to prevent its being defaced by the sun, winds, or water. The principal instruments used in navigation were the rudder, anchor, sounding line, cables, oars, sails, and masts.

It is evident from ancient authors, that the ships of the Phoenicians, Greeks, Romans, and other people of antiquity, had frequently more than one rudder; but it is not easy to perceive in what way more than one could be applied to the same end for which the rudder of modern ships is used. Small vessels had only one. Homer in his Odyssey mentions only one, which was fastened, and perhaps strengthened, so as to withstand the winds and waves on each side, with hurdles, made of sallow or osier; at the same period the ships of the Phoenicians had two rudders. When there were two, one was fixed at each end; this, however, seems to have been the case only where, as was not uncommon, the ships had two prows, so that either end could go foremost. With respect to vessels of four rudders, as two are described as being fixed to the sides, it is probable that these resembled in their construction and object the pieces of wood attached to the sides of small Dutch vessels and barges on the Thames, and generally all vessels that are flat-bottomed, for the purpose of preventing them from making much , when they are against the wind.

The first anchors were not made of iron, but of stone, or even of wood; these were loaded with lead. According to Diodorus, the Phoenicians, in their first voyages to Spain, having obtained more silver than their ships could safely hold, employed some of it, instead of lead, for their anchors. Very anciently the anchor had only one fluke. Anacharsis is said to have invented an anchor with two. Sometimes baskets full of stones, and sacks filled with sand, were employed as anchors. Every ship had two anchors, one of which was never used, except in cases of great danger: it was larger than the other, and was called the sacred anchor. At the period of the Argonautic expedition, it does not appear that anchors of any kind but stone were known; though the scholiast upon Apollonius Rhodius, quite at variance with the testimony of this author, mentions anchors of iron with two flukes. It has been supposed that anchors were not used by the Grecian fleet at the siege of Troy, because "the Greek word which is used to mean an anchor, properly so called, is not used in any of the poems of Homer." It is certain that iron anchors were not then known; but it is equally certain that large stones were used as anchors.

Homer is entirely silent respecting any implement that would serve the purpose of a sounding line; but it is expressly mention by Herodotus as common in his time: it was commonly made of lead or brass, and attached, not to a cord, but an iron, chain.

In very ancient times the cables were made of leather thongs, afterwards of rushes, the osier, the Egyptian byblus, and other materials. The Veneti used iron cables; hence we see that what is generally deemed an invention entirely modern, was known to a savage nation in Gaul, in the time of Caesar. This nation was so celebrated for the building and equipment of their vessels, which were, from all accounts, better able to withstand the fury of the ocean than the ships even of the Greeks and Romans, that Caesar gave orders for the building of vessels, on the Loire, similar to those of the Veneti, large, flat-bottomed, and high at the head and stern. Yet these vessels, built on such an excellent model, and supplied with chain-cables, had no sails but what were made of leather; and these sails were never furled, but only bound to the mast. Besides cables, the ancients had other ropes to fasten ships in the harbours: the usual mode was to erect stones for this purpose, which were bored through.

In the time of Homer, the ships of the ancients had only one bank of oars; afterwards two, three, four, five, and even nine and ten banks of oars are said not to have been uncommon: but it is not easy to understand in what manner so many oars could have been used: we shall not enter on this question, which is still unresolved. The Romans had seldom any vessels with more than five banks of oars. Such vessels as were intended for lightness, had only one bank of oars; this was particularly the case with the vessels of the Liburnians, a piratical tribe on the Adriatic.

The sails, in very ancient times, were made of leather; afterwards of rushes. In the days of Agricola, the Roman sails were made of flax: towards the end of the first century, hemp was in common use among them for sails, ropes, and new for hunting. At first there was only one sail in a ship, but afterwards there appear to have been several: they were usually white, as this colour was deemed fortunate; sometimes, however, they were coloured.

At the time of the Trojan war, the Greek ships had only one mast, which was lowered upon the deck when the ship was in harbour: near the top of the mast a ribband was fastened to point out the direction of the wind. In later times there seem to have been several masts, though this is denied by some authors.

It remains now to speak of the materials of which the ships were built, their size, and their crews.

The species of wood principally employed in the construction of the Grecian ships were alder, poplar, and fir: cedar, pine, and cypress, were also used. The Veneti, already mentioned as celebrated for their ships, built them of oak; but theirs are the only vessels of antiquity that seem to have been constructed of this kind of wood. The timber was so little seasoned, that a considerable number of ships are recorded as having been completely built and equipped in thirty days, after the timber was cut down in the forest. In the time of the Trojan war, no iron was used in the building of ships; the planks were fastened to the ribs with cords.

In the most ancient accounts of the Grecian ships, the only mode by which we can form a conjecture of their size, is from the number of men they were capable of holding. At the siege of Troy, Homer describes the ships of the Beotians as the largest; and they carried, he says, one hundred and twenty men. As Thucydides informs us that at this period soldiers served as rowers, the number mentioned by Homer must comprehend all the ship could conveniently accommodate. In general the Roman trading vessels were very small. Cicero represents those that could hold two thousand amphorae, or about sixty tons, as very large; there were, however, occasionally enormous ships built: one of the most remarkable for size was that of Ptolemy; it was four hundred and twenty feet long, and if it were broad and deep in proportion, its burden must have been upwards of seven thousand tons, more than three times the burden of one of our first rates; but it is probable that it was both flat bottomed and narrow. Of the general smallness of the Greek and Roman ships, we need no other proof, than that they were accustomed to draw them on land when in port, and during the winter; and that they were often conveyed for a considerable space over land. They were sometimes made in such a manner that they could easily and quickly be taken to pieces, and put together again. Thucydides asserts that the ships which carried the Greeks to Troy were not covered; but in this he is contradicted by Homer.

The principal officer in ships intended for trade was the pilot: he was expected to know the right management of the sails, rudder, &c. the wind, and celestial bodies, the harbours, rocks, quick-sands, and course to be steered. The Greeks were far behind the Phoenicians in many parts of nautical knowledge: we have seen that the latter at an early period changed the Greater for the Lesser Bear, for the direction of their course; whereas the Greeks steered by the Greater Bear. In very early periods it was the practice to steer all day by the course of the sun, and at night to anchor near the shore. Several stars were observed by the pilot for the purpose of foretelling the weather, the principal of which were Arcturus, the Dog Star, Orion, Castor and Pollux, &c. In the time of Homer, the Greeks knew only the four cardinal winds; they were a long time ignorant of the art of subdividing the intermediate parts of the horizon, and of determining a number of rhombs sufficient to serve the purposes of a navigation of small extent. Even so late as the date of the Periphes of the Erythræan Sea, which Dr. Vincent has fixed about the tenth year of Nero's reign, only eight points of the compass are mentioned; these are the same as are marked upon the temple of the winds at Athens. The utmost length to which the ancients arrived in subdividing the compass, was by adding two intermediate winds between each of the cardinal winds. We have noticed these particulars relative to the winds and the constellations, in order to illustrate the duty which the pilot had to perform, and the difficulty and responsibility of his office, at a period when navigators possessed such a small portion of experience and knowledge.

Besides the chief pilot, there was a subordinate one, whose duty it was to keep a look out at the prow, to manage and direct the sails and rowers, and to assist the principal pilot by his advice: the directions of the subordinate pilot were conveyed to the rowers by another officer, who seems to have answered to the boatswain of our men of war. The rowers were enabled to pull all at once, or to keep time, by a person who sung and played to them while they were employed. During the night, or in difficult navigations, the charge of the sounding lead, or of the long poles, which were used either for the same purpose, or to push the ship off, when she got a-ground, was committed to a particular officer. There were, besides, men whose duty it was to serve out the victuals, to keep the ship's accounts, &c.

The usual day's sail of a ship of the ancients was five hundred stadia, or fifty miles; and the course run over, when they sailed night and day, double that space.

We have confined ourselves, in this account of the ships of the ancients, principally to those particulars that are connected with the construction, equipment, &c. of those employed for commercial purposes, and shall now proceed to a historical sketch of the progress of discovery among the Greeks, from the earliest records to the era of Herodotus, the father of geographical knowledge.

The first maritime expedition of the Greeks, of which we have a particular narration, and certainly one of the most celebrated in ancient times, is the Argonautic expedition. As we purpose to go into some length on the subject of this expedition, it may be proper to defend ourselves from the charge of occupying too much space, and giving too much attention to an enterprize generally deemed fabulous, and so obscured by fable and uncertainty, as to be little capable of illustration, and little conducive to the improvement of geographical knowledge. This defence we shall borrow from a name deservedly high among those who have successfully illustrated ancient geography, for the happy and successful mutual adaptation of great learning and sound judgment, and not less worthy of respect and imitation for his candour and liberality: we allude to Dr. Vincent, the illustrator of the Voyage of Nearchus, and the Periplus of the Erythræan Sea.

"The reality of the Argonautic expedition, (he observes in the Preliminary Disquisition to the latter work), has been questioned; but if the primordial history of every nation but one is tinctured with the fabulous, and if from among the rest a choice is necessary to be made, it must be allowed that the traditions of Greece are less inconsistent than those of the more distant regions of the earth. Oriental learning is now employed in unravelling the mythology of India, and recommending it as containing the seeds of primæval history; but hitherto we have seen nothing that should induce us to relinquish the authority we have been used to respect, or to make us prefer the fables of the Hindoos or Guebres, to the fables of the Greeks. Whatever difficulties may occur in the return of the Argonauts, their voyage to Colchis is consistent: it contains more real geography than has yet been discovered in any record of the Bramins or the Zendevesta, and is truth itself, both geographical and historical, when compared with the portentous expedition of Rám to Ceylon."

In discussing the subject of the Argonautic expedition, we shall successively consider its probable era—its supposed object—the voyage to Colchis, and the various tracks by which the Argonauts are said to have returned.

I. Archbishop Usher fixes the era of this expedition at about 1280 years before Christ: Sir Isaac Newton, on the other hand, fixes it much later, about 937 years before Christ. His opinion is grounded principally on a supposition, that the Greek sphere was invented by two of the Argonauts, who delineated the expedition under the name of Argo, one of the constellations. And as the equinoctial colure passed through the middle of Aries, when that sphere was constructed, he infers, by calculations of their retrograde motion from their place then till the year A.D. 1690, that the expedition took place in 937 before Christ. To this, however, there seem to be insurmountable objections, which it is surprising did not occur to this great man. The chief star in Argo is only 37 degrees from the south pole; and the greatest part of the constellation is much nearer. The course of the Argonauts from Greece to Colchis, necessarily lay between 39 and 45 degrees of north latitude. It will be evident to any person acquainted with astronomy, that within these latitudes no star of the first magnitude, or such as would attract observation, especially in those times, could be visible. But, what is still more decisive against the whole of Sir Isaac

Newton's hypothesis, he takes for granted that the sphere was invented by the Argonauts: if this indeed could be proved, it would be easy to fix the era of the Argonautic expedition; but till such proof is given, all that can be fairly inferred from an inspection of this sphere is, that it was constructed 937 years before Christ. We have dwelt upon this point, because, thinking that the Argonautic expedition was not nearly so late as Newton supposes, we hence regard it as, proportionally to its antiquity, more creditable to the Greeks, and a stronger proof of their advancement in maritime skill and enterprize.

II. Its alleged object was the Golden Fleece: what that actually was can only be conjectured;—that no commercial advantages would tempt the people of that age is obvious, when we reflect on their habits and manners;—that the precious metals would be a powerful attraction, and would be regarded as cheaply acquired by the most hazardous enterprizes, is equally obvious. If Sir Walter Raleigh, sound as he was for his era in the science of political economy, was so far ignorant of the real wealth of nations, as to be disappointed when he did not find El Dorado in America, though that country contained much more certain and abundant sources of wealth,—can we be surprized if the Greeks, at the time of the Argonautic expedition, could be stimulated to such an enterprize, only by the hope of obtaining the precious metals? It may, indeed, be contended that plunder was their object; but it does not seem likely that they would have ventured to such a distance from Greece, or on a navigation which they knew to be difficult and dangerous, as well as long, for the sake of plunder, when there were means and opportunities for it so much nearer home. We must equally reject the opinion of Suidas, that the Golden Fleece was a parchment book, made of sheep-skin, which contained the whole secret of transmuting all metals into gold; and the opinion of Varro, that the Argonauts went to obtain skins and other rich furs, which Colchis furnished in abundance. And the remarks which we have made, also apply against the opinion of Eustathius, that the voyage of the Argonauts was at once a commercial and maritime expedition, to open the commerce of the Euxine Sea, and to establish forts on its shore.

Having rendered it probable, from general considerations, that the object was the obtaining of the precious metals, we shall next proceed to strengthen this opinion, by showing that they were the produce of the country near the Black Sea. The gold mines to the south of Trebizond, which are still worked with sufficient profit, were a subject of national dispute between Justinian and Chozroes; and, as Gibbon remarks, "it is not unreasonable to believe that a vein of precious metal may be equally diffused through the circle of the hills." On what account these mines were shadowed out under the appellation of a Golden Fleece, it is not easy to explain. Pliny, and some other writers, suppose that the rivers impregnated with particles of gold were carefully strained through sheeps-skins, or fleeces; but these are not the materials that would be used for such a purpose: it is more probable that, if fleeces were used, they were set across some of the narrow parts of the streams, in order to stop and collect the particles of gold.

III. It is said that there was an ancient law in Greece, which forbad any ship to be navigated with more than fifty men, and that Jason was the first who offended against this law. There can be little doubt, from all the accounts of the ancients, that Jason's ship was larger than the Greeks at that period were accustomed to. Diodorus and Pliny represent it as the first ship of war which went out of the ports of Greece; that it was comparatively large, well built and equipped, and well navigated in all respects, must be inferred from its having accomplished such a voyage at that era.

In their course to the Euxine Sea, they visited Lemnos, Samothrace, Troas, Cyzicum, Bithynia, and Thrace; these wanderings must have been the result of their ignorance of the navigation of those seas. From Thrace they directed their course, without further wanderings, to the Euxine Sea. At the distance of four or five leagues from the entrance to the sea, are the Cyanean rocks; the Argonauts passed between them not without difficulty and danger; before this expedition, the passage was deemed impracticable, and many fables were told regarding them: their true situation and form were first explored by the Argonauts. They now safely entered the Euxine Sea, where they seem to have been driven about for some time, till they discovered Mount Caucasus; this served as a land mark for their entrance into the Phasis, when they anchored near OEa, the capital of Colchis.

IV. The course of the Argonauts to Colchis is well ascertained; and the accessions to the geographical knowledge of that age, which we derive from the accounts given of that course, are considerable. But with respect to the route they followed on their return, there is much contradiction and fable. All authors agree that they did not return by the same route which they pursued in their outward voyage. According to Hesiod, they passed from the Euxine into the Eastern Ocean; but being prevented from returning by the same route, in consequence of the fleet of Colchis blockading the Bosphorus, they were obliged to sail round Ethiopia, and to cross Lybia by land, drawing their vessels after them. In this manner they arrived at the Gulph of Syrtis, in the Mediterranean. Other ancient writers conduct the Argonauts back by the Nile, which they supposed to communicate with the Eastern Ocean; while, by others, they are represented as having sailed up the Danube to the Po or the Rhine.

Amidst such obscure and evidently fictitious accounts, it may appear useless to offer any conjecture; but there is one route by which the Argonauts are supposed to have returned, in favour of which some probability may be urged. All writers agree in opinion that they did not return by the route they followed on going to the Euxine; if this be true, the least absurd and improbable mode of getting back into the Mediterranean is to be preferred: of those routes already mentioned, all are eminently absurd and impossible. Perhaps the one we are about to describe, may, in the opinion of some, be deemed equally so; but to us it appears to have some plausibility. The tradition to which we allude is, that the Argonauts sailed up some sea or river from the Euxine, till they reached the Baltic Sea, and that they returned by the Northern Ocean through the straits of Hercules, into the Mediterranean. The existence of an ocean from the east end of the Gulf of Finland to the Caspian or the Euxine Sea, was firmly believed by

Pliny, and the same opinion prevailed in the eleventh century; for Adam of Bremen says, people [could sail-]could formerly sail] from the Baltic down to Greece. Now the whole of that tract of country is flat and level, and from the sands near Koningsberg, through the calcareous loam of Poland and the Ukraine, evidently alluvial and of comparatively recent formation.

If the Trojan war happened, according to the Arundelian Marbles, 1209 years before Christ, this event must have been subsequent to the Argonautic expedition only about fifty years: yet, in this short space of time, the Greeks had made great advances in the art of ship building, and in navigation. The equipment of the Argonautic expedition was regarded, at the period it took place, as something almost miraculous; yet the ships sent against Troy seem to have excited little astonishment, though, considering the state of Greece at that period, they were very numerous.

It is foreign to our purpose to regard this expedition in any other light than as it is illustrative of the maritime skill and attainments of Greece at this era, and so far connected with our present subject. The number of ships employed, according to Homer, amounted to 1186: Thucydides states them at 1200; and Euripides, Virgil, and some other authors, reduce their number to 1000. The ships of the Boeotians were the largest; they carried 120 men each; those of the Philoctetæ were the smallest, each carrying only fifty men. Agamemnon had 160 ships; the Athenians fifty; Menelaus, king of Sparta, sixty; but some of his ships seem to have been furnished by his allies; whereas all the Athenian vessels belonged to Athens alone. We have already mentioned that Thucydides is contradicted by Homer, in his assertion that the Greek ships, at the siege of Troy, had no decks; perhaps, however, they were only half-decked, as it would appear, from the descriptions of them, that the fore-part was open to the keel: they had a mainsail, and were rowed by oars. Greece is so admirably situated for maritime and commercial enterprize, that it must have been very early sensible of its advantages in these respects. The inhabitants of the isle of Egina are represented as the first people in Greece who were distinguished for their intelligence and success in maritime traffic: soon after the return of the Heraclidæ they possessed considerable commerce, and for a long time they are said to have held the empire of the adjoining sea. Their naval power and commerce were not utterly annihilated till the time of Pericles.

The Corinthians, who are not mentioned by Homer as having engaged in the Trojan war, seem, however, not long afterwards, to have embarked with great spirit and success in maritime commerce; their situation was particularly favourable for it, and equally well situated to be the transit of the land trade of Greece. Corinth had two ports, one upon each sea. The Corinthians are said to have first built vessels with three banks of oars, instead of galleys.

Although the Athenians brought a considerable force against Troy, yet they did not engage in maritime commerce till long after the period of which we are at present treating.

Of the knowledge which the Greeks possessed at this time, on the subject of geography, we must draw our most accurate and fullest account from the writings of Homer and Hesiod. The former represents the shield of Achilles as depicting the countries of the globe; on it the earth was figured as a disk surrounded by the ocean; the centre of Greece was represented as the centre of the world; the disk included the Mediterranean Sea, much contracted on the west, and the Egean and part of the Euxine Seas. The Mediterranean was so much contracted on this side, that Ithaca, and the neighbouring continent, or at the farthest, the straits which separate Sicily from Italy, were its limits. Sicily itself was just known only as the land of wonders and fables, though the fable of the Cyclops, who lived in it, evidently must nave been derived from some obscure report of its volcano. The fables Homer relates respecting countries to the west of Sicily, cannot even be regarded as having any connection with, or resemblance to the truth. Beyond the Euxine also, in the other direction, all is fable. Colchis seems to have been known, though not so accurately as the recent Argonautic expedition might have led us to suppose it would have been. The west coast of Asia Minor, the scene of his great poem, is of course completely within his knowledge; the Phoenicians and Egyptians are particularly described, the former for their purple stuffs, gold and silver works, maritime science and commercial skill, and cunning; the latter for their river Egyptos, and their knowledge of medicine. To the west of Egypt he places Lybia, where he says the lambs are born with horns, and the sheep bring forth three times a year.

In the Odyssey he conducts Neptune into Ethiopia; and the account he gives seems to warrant the belief, that by the Ethiopians he meant not merely the Ethiopians of Africa, but the inhabitants of India: we know that the ancients, even so late as the time of Strabo and Ptolemy, considered all those nations as Ethiopians who lived upon the southern ocean from east to west; or, as Ptolemy expresses it, that under the zodiac, from east to west, inhabit the inhabitants black of colour. Homer represents these two nations as respectively the last of men, one of them on the east and the other on the west. From his description of the gardens of Alcinous, it may even be inferred that he had received some information respecting the climate of the tropical regions; for this description appears to us rather borrowed from report, than entirely the produce of imagination.

> Close to the gates a spacious garden lies,
> From storms defended and inclement skies.
> Four acres was th' allotted space of ground,
> Fenc'd with a green enclosure all around,
> Tall thriving trees confess'd the fruitful mould;
> The red'ning apple ripens here to gold.
> Here the blue fig with luscious juice o'erflows,
> With deeper red the full pomegranate glows,
> The branch here bends beneath the weighty pear,
> And verdant olives flourish round the year.
> The balmy spirit of the western gale
> Eternal breathes on fruits untaught to fail:

Each dropping pear a following pear supplies,
On apples apples, figs on figs arise:
The same mild season gives the blooms to blow,
The buds to harden, and the fruits to grow;
  Here order'd vines in equal ranks appear,
With all th' united labours of the year;
Some to unload the fertile branches run,
Some dry the black'ning clusters in the sun,
Others to tread the liquid harvest join,
The groaning presses foam with floods of wine.
Here are the vines in early flow'r descry'd,
Here grapes discolour'd on the sunny side,
And there in autumn's richest purple dy'd.
  Beds of all various herbs, for ever green,
In beauteous order terminate the scene.

  b. vii. v. 142.

This description perfectly applies to the luxuriant and uninterrupted vegetation of tropical climates.

From the time of Homer to that of Herodotus, the Greeks spread themselves over several parts of the countries lying on the Mediterranean sea. About 600 years before Christ, a colony of Phocean Greeks from Ionia, founded Massilia, the present Marseilles; and between the years 500 and 430, the Greeks had established themselves in Sicily, Sardinia, Corsica, and even in some of the southern provinces of Spain. They were invited or compelled to these emigrations by the prospect of commercial advantages, or by intestine wars; and they were enabled to accomplish their object by the geographical and nautical charts, which they are said to have obtained from the Phoenicians, and by means of the sphere constructed by Anaximander the Milesian. The eastern parts of the Mediterranean, however, seem still to have been unexplored. Homer tells us that none but pirates ventured at the risk of their lives to steer directly from Crete to Lybia; and when the Ionian deputies arrived at Egina, where the naval forces of Greece were assembled, with an earnest request that the fleet might sail to Ionia, to deliver their country from the dominion of Xerxes, who was at that time attempting to subdue Greece, the request was refused, because the Greeks were ignorant of the course from Delos to Ionia, and because they believed it to be as far from Egina to Samos, as from Egina to the Pillars of Hercules.

---

1 Dr. Vincent, in the 2nd vol. of his Periplus of the Erythrean Sea, has a very elaborate commentary on this chapter of Ezekiel, in which he satisfactorily makes out the nature of most of the articles mentioned in it, as well as the locality of the places from which they are said to have come.

2 One of the most celebrated gods of the Phoenicians was Melcartus. He is represented as a great navigator, and as the first that brought tin from the Cassiterides. His image was usually affixed to the stern of their vessels.

3 In the time of Solomon, about two hundred years after the period when it is supposed the Phoenicians began to direct their course by the Lesser Bear,— it was 17 1/2 degrees from the North Pole: in the time of Ptolemy, about one hundred and fifty years after Christ, its distance had decreased to 12 degrees.

CHAPTER II

Historical Sketch Of The Progress Of Discovery And Commercial
Enterprize, From The Age Of Herodotus To The Death Of
Alexander The Great, B.C. 324

From the scanty materials respecting the Phoenicians, with which we are supplied by ancient history, it is evident that they founded several colonies, either for the purpose of commerce, or, induced by other motives, in different parts of Africa. Of these colonies, the most celebrated was that of Carthage: a state which maintained an arduous contest with Rome, during the period when the martial ardour and enterprize of that city was most strenuously supported by the stern purity of republican virtue, which more than once drove it to the brink of ruin, and which ultimately fell, rather through the vice of its own constitution and government, and the jealousies and quarrels of its own citizens, and through the operation of extraneous circumstances, over which it could have no controul, than from the fair and unassisted power of its adversary.

The era of the foundation of Carthage is unknown. According to some writers, it was built so early as 1233 years before Christ; but the more general, as well as more probable opinion, assigns it a much later foundation—about 818 years before the Christian era. If this opinion be correct, Rome and Carthage were founded nearly about the same period. The circumstances which led to and accompanied the foundation of Carthage, though related with circumstantial fulness by the ancient poets, are by no means accurately know to authentic history.

The situation of Carthage was peculiarly favourable to commerce and maritime enterprize; in the centre of the Mediterranean; in reach of the east as well as of the west; the most fertile, and most highly cultivated and civilized part of Africa in her immediate vicinity. Carthage itself was built at the bottom of a gulph, on a peninsula, which was about forty-five miles in circumference; and its strength and security were further aided by the isthmus which connected this peninsula to the main land, as it was little more than three miles broad; by a projection of land on the west side, which was only half a stadium in breadth; and by a lake or morass which lay on the opposite side: this projection, which ran out considerably into the sea, was naturally strong by the rocks with which it was covered, and was rendered still stronger by art. In one point only had this projection been neglected; this was an angle, which from the foundation of the city had been overlooked, advancing into the sea towards the western continent, as far as the harbours, which lay on the same side of the city. There were two harbours, so placed and constructed as to communicate with each other. They had one entrance, seventy feet in breadth, which was shut up and secured by strong chains stretched across it. One of these harbours was exclusively set apart for merchant ships; and in its vicinity were to be found every thing necessary for the accommodation of the seamen. In the middle of the other harbour was an island called Cothon; though, according to some writers, this was the name of the harbour itself. The word Cothon, we are informed by Festus, (and his etymology is confirmed by Bochart and Buxtorf,) signifies, in the oriental languages, a port not formed by nature, but the result of labour and art. The second harbour, as well as the island in it, seems to have been intended principally, if not exclusively, for ships of war; and it was so capacious, that of these it would contain 220. This harbour and island were lined with docks and sheds, which received the ships, when it was necessary to repair them, or protect them from the effects of the weather. On the key were built extensive ranges of wharfs, magazines, and storehouses, filled with all the requisite materials to fit out the ships of war. This harbour seems to have been decorated with some taste, and at some expence; so that both it and the island, viewed at a distance, appeared like two extensive and magnificent galleries. The admiral's palace, which commanded a view of the mouth of the harbour and of the sea, was also a building of considerable taste. Each harbour had its particular entrance into the city: a double wall separated them so effectually, that the merchant vessels, when they entered their own harbour, could not see the ships of war; and though the admiral, from his palace, could perceive whatever was doing at sea, it was impossible that from the sea any thing in the inward harbour could be perceived.

Nor were these advantages, though numerous and great, the only ones which Carthage enjoyed as a maritime city; for its situation was so admirably chosen, and that situation so skilfully rendered subservient to the grand object of the government and citizens, that even in case the accidents of war should destroy or dispossess them of one of their harbours, they had it in their power, in a great measure, to replace the loss. This was exemplified in a striking and effective manner at the time when Scipio blocked up the old port; for the Carthaginians, in a very short time, built a new one, the traces and remains of which were plainly visible so late as the period when Dr. Shaw visited this part of Africa.

Carthage, at a comparatively early period of its history, possessed a very large extent of sea coast, though in it there were but few harbours fitted for commerce. The boundaries of the Carthaginian dominions on the west were the Philænorum Aræ, so called from two brothers of this name, who were buried in the sand at this place, in consequence of a dispute between the Carthaginians and the Cyreneans, respecting the boundaries of their respective countries. On the other, or western side, the Carthaginian dominions extended as far as the Pillars of Hercules, a distance, according to Polybius, of 16,000 stadia, or 2000 miles; but, according to the more accurate observations of Dr. Shaw, only 1420 geographical miles.

Next to Carthage itself, the city of Utica was most celebrated as a place of commerce: it lay a short distance to the west of Carthage, and on the same bay. It had a large and convenient harbour; and after the destruction of Carthage, it became the metropolis of Africa Propria. Neapolis was also a place of considerable trade, especially with Sicily, from which the distance was so short, that the voyage could be performed in two days and a night. Hippo was a frontier town on the side of Numidia; though Strabo says, there were two of the same name in Africa Propria. The Carthaginian Hippo had a port, arsenal, storehouses, and citadel: it lay between a large lake and the sea. We have already noticed the etymological meaning of the word Cothon: that this meaning is accurate may be inferred from the word being applied to several artificial harbours in the Carthaginian dominion, besides that of Cartilage itself: it was applied to the port of Adrumetum, a large city built on a promontory,—and to the port of Thapsus, a maritime town, situated on a kind of isthmus, between the sea and a lake. The artificial nature, of this latter harbour is placed beyond all doubt, as there is still remaining a great part of it built on frames: the materials are composed of mortar and small pebbles, so strongly and closely cemented, that they have the appearance, as well as durability, of solid rock. It is singular, that in the dominions of Carthage, extending, as we have seen, upwards of 1400 miles along the shores of the Mediterranean, there should be no river of any magnitude or importance for commerce: the Bagrada and the Catada alone are noticed by ancient historians, and both of these were insignificant streams.

Having thus pointed out the natural advantages for commerce possessed by the Carthaginians, we shall next proceed to notice such of their laws, and such parts of their political institutions, and features of their character, as either indicated their bias for commerce, or tended to strengthen it. The monarchical government of Carthage was not of long continuance; it afterwards became republican, though the exact form of the republic is not certainly known. As late as the time of Aristotle, there seems to have been such a complete and practical counterpoise of the powers in which the supreme authority was vested, that, according to him, there had been no instance from the foundation of the city, of any popular commotions sufficient to disturb its tranquillity; nor, on the other hand, of any tyrant, who had been able to destroy its liberty. This sagacious philosopher foresaw the circumstance which would destroy the constitution of Carthage; for when there was a disagreement between the two branches of the legislature, the suffetes and the senate, the question in dispute was referred to the people, and their resolve became the law. Till the second and third wars between Rome and Carthage, no fatal effects resulted from this principle of the constitution; but during these, the people were frequently called upon to exercise their dangerous authority and privileges; the senate yielded to them; cabals and factions took place among those who were anxious to please, for the purpose of guiding the people; rash measures were adopted, the councils and the power of Carthage became distracted and weak, and its ruin was precipitated and completed.

But though to this defect in the constitution of Carthage its ruin may partly be ascribed, there can be little doubt that commerce flourished by means of the popular form of its government. Commerce was the pursuit of all ranks and classes, as well as the main concern and object of the government The most eminent persons in the state for power, talents, birth, and riches, applied themselves to it with as much ardour and perseverance as the meanest citizens; and this similarity and equality of pursuit, as it sprang in some measure from the republican equality of the constitution, so also it tended to preserve it.

The notices which we possess respecting the political institutions of the Carthaginians are very scanty, and are almost entirely derived from Aristotle: according to him they had a custom, which must at once have relieved the state from those whom it could not well support, and have tended to enlarge the sphere of their commercial enterprize. They sent, as occasion required, colonies to different parts, and these colonies, keeping up their connection with the mother country, not only drew off her superabundant trade, but also supplied her with many articles she could not otherwise have procured at so easy and cheap a rate.

The fertility and high state of cultivation of those parts of Africa which adjoined Carthage, has already been alluded to; and their exports consisted either of the produce of those parts, or of their own manufactures. Of the former there were all kinds of provisions; wax, oil, honey, skins, fruits, &c.; their principal manufactures were cables, especially those fit for large vessels, made of the shrub ; all other kinds of naval stores; dressed leather; the particular dye or colour, called from them punic, the preparation of which seems not to be known; toys, &c. &c. From Egypt they imported flax, papyrus, &c.; from the Red Sea, spices, drugs, perfumes, gold, pearls, &c.; from the countries on the Levant, silk stuffs, scarlet and purple dyes, &c.; and from the west of Europe their principal imports seem to have been iron, lead, tin, and the other useful metals.

Such was the commerce by sea, as far as the imperfect notices on this subject, by the ancient historians, instruct us: but they also carried on a considerable and lucrative commerce by land, especially with the Persians and Ethiopians. The caravans of these nations generally resorted to Carthage; the rarest and most esteemed articles which they brought were carbuncles, which, by means of this traffic, became so plenty in this city, that they were generally known by the appellation of Carthaginian gems. The mode of selling by auction seems to have been practised by this nation; at least there are passages in the ancient authors, particularly one in Polybius, which would naturally lead to the conclusion, that in the sale of their merchandize, the Carthaginians employed a person to name and describe their various kinds and qualities, and also a clerk to note down the price at which they were sold. Their mode of trafficking with rude nations, unaccustomed to commerce, as described by Herodotus, strongly resembles that which has been often adopted by our navigators, when they arrive on the coast of a savage people. According to this historian, the Carthaginians trafficked with the Lybians, who inhabited the western coast of Africa, in the following manner: having conducted their vessels into some harbour or creek, they landed the merchandize which they meant to exchange or dispose of, and placed it in such a manner and situation, as exposed it to the view of the inhabitants, and at the same time indicated the purpose for which it was thus exposed. They afterwards lighted a fire of such materials as caused a great smoke; this attracted the Lybians to the spot, who laid down such a quantity of gold as they deemed an adequate price for the merchandize, and then retired. The Carthaginians next approached and examined the gold: if they deemed it sufficient, they took it away, and left the merchandize; if they did not, they left both. In the latter event, the Lybians again returned, and added to the quantity of gold; and this, if necessary, was repeated, till the Carthaginians, by taking it away, shewed that in their judgment it was an adequate price for their goods. During the whole of this transaction, no intercourse or words passed, nor did the Carthaginians even touch the gold, nor the Lybians the merchandize, till the former took away the gold.

The earliest notice we possess of a commercial alliance formed by the Carthaginians, fixes it a very few years before the birth of Herodotus: it was concluded between them and the Romans about the year 503 before Christ. The Carthaginians were the first nation the Romans were connected with out of Italy. Polybius informs us, that in his time (about 140 years before Christ) this treaty, written in the old language of Rome, then nearly unintelligible, was extant on the base of a column, and he has given a translation of it: the terms of peace between the Carthaginians and their allies, and the Romans and their allies, were to the following purport. The latter agreed not to sail beyond the fair promontory, (which lay, according to our historian, a very short distance to the north of Carthage,) unless they were driven beyond it by stress of weather, or by an enemy's vessel. In case they were obliged to land, or were shipwrecked, they were not to take or purchase any thing, except what they might need, to repair their ships, or for the purpose of sacrifice. And in no case, or under no pretext, were they to remain on shore above five days. The Roman merchants were not to pay any higher, or other duty, than what was allowed by law to the common crier and his clerk, already noticed, who, it appears from this treaty, were bound to make a return to government of all the goods that were bought or sold in Africa and Sardinia. It was moreover provided, that if the Romans should visit any places in Sicily, subject to the Carthaginians, they should be civilly treated, and have justice done them in every respect. On the other hand, the Carthaginians bound themselves not to interfere with any of the Italian allies, or subjects of the Romans; nor build any fort in their territory. Such were the principal articles in this commercial treaty; from it, it appears, that so early as the year 503 before Christ, the first year after the expulsion of the Tarquins, and twenty-eight years before the invasion of Greece by Xerxes, the Carthaginians were in possession of Sardinia, and part of Sicily;—that they were also acquainted with, and had visited the coasts of Italy; and there are expressions in the treaty, which render it highly probable that the Carthaginians had, before this period, attempted to establish, either for commerce or conquest, colonies and forts in Italy: it is also evident that they were acquainted with the art of fortification.

Though it will carry us rather out of chronological order, it may be proper to notice in this place a second treaty of commerce between the Carthaginians and Romans, which was entered into about 333 years before Christ, during the consulship of Valerius Corvus, and Popilius Laenas. The Carthaginians came to Rome for the purpose of concluding this treaty: it differed in some particulars from the former, and was to the following effect. The Romans and their allies were to possess the friendship of the people of Carthage, the Tyrians, and the inhabitants of Utica, provided they carried on no hostilities against them, and did not trade beyond the fair promontory, Mastica and Tarseium. In case the Carthaginians should take any town in Italy, not under the jurisdiction of the Romans, they might plunder it, but after that they were to give it up to the Romans. Any captives taken in Italy, who in any Roman port should be challenged by the Romans as belonging to any state in amity with Rome, were to be immediately restored. The Romans, in case they put into the harbours of the Carthaginians, or their allies, to take in water or other necessaries, were not to be molested or injured; but they were not to carry on any commerce in Africa or Sardinia; nor even land on those coasts, except to purchase necessaries, and refit their ships: in such cases, only five days were allowed them, at the expiration of which they were to depart. But, in the towns of Sicily belonging to the Carthaginians, and even in the city of Carthage itself, the Romans were permitted to trade, enjoying the same rights and privileges as the Carthaginians; and, on the other hand, the Carthaginians were to be allowed to traffic in Rome on terms equally favourable.

It is not our intention, because it would be totally foreign to the object and nature of this work, to give a history of Carthage; but only to notice such events and transactions, supplied by its history, as are illustrative of the commercial enterprise of by far the most enterprising commercial nation of antiquity. In conformity to this plan, we shall briefly notice their first establishment in Spain, as it was from the mines of this country that they drew great wealth, and thus were enabled, not only to equip formidable fleets and armies, but also to extend their traffic very considerably.

The city of Cadiz, was founded by the Phoenicians, as well as Carthage; and as there was a close connection between most of the Phoenician colonies, it is probable that some time before the Carthaginians established themselves in Spain, they traded with the people of Cadiz: at any rate it is certain, that when the latter were hard pressed by the Spaniards, they applied to the Carthaginians for assistance: this was readily given, and being effectual, the Carthaginians embraced the opportunity, and the pretext thus afforded for establishing themselves in the part of Spain adjoining Cadiz. It is singular, however, that though the Carthaginians were in possession of Majorca and Minorca from so remote an antiquity, "that their first arrival there is prior to every thing related of them by any historian now extant," yet they do not seem to have established themselves on the main land of Spain till they assisted the people of Cadiz. With respect to the other foreign possessions of the Carthaginians, we have already seen that, at the period of their first treaty with the Romans, they occupied Sardinia and part of Sicily; and there are several passages in the ancient historians, particularly in Herodotus, which render it highly probable that they had establishments in Corsica about the same time. Malta and its dependent islands were first peopled by the Phoenicians, and seem afterwards to have fallen into the possession of the Carthaginians.

Of the particular voyages undertaken by the Carthaginians, for the purpose either of discovery or of commercial enterprise, we possess little information; as, however, these topics are most particularly within the scope of our work, it will be indispensable to detail all the information relating to them which can be collected. The voyages of Hamilcar or Himilco, as he is called by some historians, and of Hanno, are the most celebrated, or, rather, to speak more accurately, the only voyages of the Carthaginians of which we possess any details, either with regard to their object or consequences. Himilco, who was on officer in the navy of Carthage, was sent by the senate to explore the western coasts of Europe: a journal of his voyage, and an account of his discoveries, were, according to the custom of the nation, inscribed in the Carthaginian annals. But the only information respecting them which we now possess, is derived from the writings of the Latin poet Rufus Festus Avienus. This poet flourished under Theodosius, A.D. 450, translated the Phænomena of Aratus, and Dionysius's Description of the World, and also wrote an original poem, on the sea coasts. In the last he mentions Himilco, and intimates that he saw the original journal of his voyage in the Carthaginian annals. According to the account of Festus, the voyage of Himilco lasted four months, or rather he sailed for the space of four months, towards the north, and arrived at the isles Ostrymnides and the coast of Albion. In the extracts given by Avienus from the journal of Himilco, frequent mention is made of lead and tin, and of ships cased with leather (or, more probably, entirely made of that material, like the coracles still used by the Greenlanders, and even in Wales, for crossing small rivers). In these parts, he adds, the East Rymni lived, with whom the people of Tartessus and Carthage traded: we have given this appellation to the inhabitants of the isles Ostrymnides, because in the first part of the latter word, the Teutonic word, OEst, distinctly appears.

Hanno was sent by the senate to explore the western coast of Africa, and to establish Carthaginian colonies wherever he might deem it expedient or advantageous. He sailed from Carthage with a fleet of 60 vessels, each rowed with 50 oars, and had besides, a convoy containing 30,000 persons of both sexes. He wrote a relation of his voyage, a fragment of a Greek version of which is still remaining, and has lately been illustrated by the learning and ingenuity of Dr. Falconer of Bath: his voyage is also cited by Aristotle, Pomponius Mela, and Pliny. The era at which it was performed, and the extent of the voyage, have given rise to much discussion. Isaac Vossius fixes the date of it prior to the age of Homer: Vossius the father, subsequent to it: Wesseling doubts whether it was even prior to Herodotus. Campomanes fixes it about the 93d Olympiad: and Mr. Dodwell somewhere between the 92d and the 129th Olympiad. According to Pliny, Hanno and Himilco were contemporaries; the latter author mentions the commentaries of Hanno, but in such a manner as if he had not seen, and did not believe them.

With respect to the extent of his voyage along the western coast of Africa, some modern writers assert, without any authority, that he doubled the Cape of Good Hope: this assertion is made in direct unqualified terms by Mickle the translator of the Lusiad. Other writers limit the extent of his navigation to Cape

Nun; while, according to other geographers, he sailed as far as Cape Three Points, on the coast of Guinea. That there should be any doubt on the subject appears surprising; for, as Dr. Vincent very justly remarks, we have Hanno's own authority to prove that he never was within 40 degrees of the Cape.

That the Carthaginians, before the voyage of Hanno, had discovered the Canary Islands, is rendered highly probable, from the accounts of Diodorus Siculus, and Aristotle: the former mentions a large, beautiful, and fertile island, to which the Carthaginians, in the event of any overwhelming disorder, had determined to remove their government; and Aristotle relates that they were attracted to a beautiful island in such numbers, that the senate were obliged to forbid any further emigration to it on pain of death.

The voyages of the Carthaginians were, from the situation of their territory, and the imperfect state of geography and navigation at that period, usually confined to the Mediterranean and to the western shores of Africa and Europe; but several years antecedent to the date usually assigned to the voyages of Himilco and Hanno, a voyage of discovery is said to have been accomplished by the king of a nation little given to maritime affairs. We allude to the voyage of Scylax, undertaken at the command of Darius the son of Hystaspes, about 550 years before Christ. There are several circumstances respecting this voyage which deserve attention or examination; the person who performed it, is said by Herodotus, (from whom we derive all our information on the subject), to have been a native of Caryandria, or at least an inhabitant of Asia Minor: he was therefore most probably a Greek: he was a geographer and mathematician of some eminence, and by some writers is supposed to have first invented geographical tables. According to Herodotus, Darius, after his Scythian expedition, in order to facilitate his design of conquest in the direction of India, resolved, in the first place, to make a discovery of that part of the world. For this purpose he built and fitted out a fleet at Cespatyrus, a city on the Indus, towards the upper part of the navigable course of that river. The ships, of course, first sailed to the mouth of the Indus, and during their passage the country on each side was explored. The directions given to Scylax were, after he entered the ocean, to steer to the westward, and thus return to Persia. Accordingly, he is said to have coasted from the mouth of the Indus to the Straits of Babelmandel, where he entered the Red Sea; and on the 30th month from his first embarking he landed at Egypt, at the same place from which Necho, king of that country, had despatched the Phoenicians to circumnavigate Africa. From Egypt, Scylax returned to Susa, where he gave Darius a full account of his expedition.

The reality of this voyage, or at least the accuracy of some of the particulars it records, has been doubted. Scylax describes the course of the Indus to the east; whereas it runs to the south-west. It is also worthy of remark, that as Darius, before the voyage of Scylax, was master of the Attock, Peukeli, and Multan, he needed no information respecting the route to India, as every conqueror has followed this very obvious and easy route. Dr. Vincent also objects to the authority of this voyage, or rather to the track assigned to it: "I cannot believe," he observes, "from the state of navigation in that age, that

Scylax could perform a voyage round India, from which the bravest of Alexander's navigators shrunk, or that men who had explored the desert coast of Gadrosia, should be less daring than an experienced native of Caryandria. They returned with amazement from the sight of Mussenden and Ras-al-had, while Scylax succeeded without a difficulty upon record. But the obstacles to such a voyage are numerous; first, whether Pactzia be Peukeli, and Caspatyrus, Multan: secondly, if Darius were master of Multan, whether he could send a ship or a fleet down the sea, through tribes, where Alexander fought his way at every step: thirdly, whether Scylax had any knowledge of the Indian Ocean, the coast, or the monsoon: fourthly, if the coast of Gadrosia were friendly, which is doubtful, whether he could proceed along the coast of Arabia, which must be hostile from port to port: these and a variety of other difficulties which Nearchus experienced, from famine, from want of water, from the construction of his ships, and from the manners of the natives, must induce an incredulity in regard to the Persian account, whatever respect we may have to the fidelity of Herodotus."

Such are the objections urged by Dr. Vincent to the authority of this voyage. In some of the particular objections there may be considerable force; but with respect to the general ones, from the manners or hostility of the natives inhabiting the coasts along which the voyage was performed, they apply equally to the voyages of the Carthaginians along the western coasts of Africa and Europe, and indeed to all the voyages of discovery, or distant voyages of the ancients. It may be added, that according to Strabo, Posidonius disbelieved the whole history of Scylax. In the Geographi Minores of Hudson, a voyage ascribed to Scylax is published; but great doubts are justly entertained on the subject of its authenticity. Dodwell is decidedly against it. The Baron de Sainte Croix, in a dissertation read before the Academy of Inscriptions, defends the work which bears the name of Scylax as genuine. Dr. Vincent states one strong objection to its authenticity: mention is made in it of Dardanus, Rhetium, and Illium, in the Troad; whereas there is great doubt whether Rhetium was in existence in the time of the real Scylax: besides, it is remarkable that nothing is said respecting India in the treatise now extant. That the original and genuine work described India is, however, undoubted, on the authority of Aristotle, who mentions that there was such a person as Scylax, that he had been in India, and that his account of that country was extant in his (Aristotle's) time.

In fact, the work which we possess under the name of Scylax, is evidently a collection of the itineraries of ancient navigators: it may have been drawn up by the Scylax whom Darius employed, though, if that were the case, it is very extraordinary he should not have included the journal of his own voyage; or his name, as that of a celebrated geographer may have been put to it; or there may have been another geographer of that name. The collection is evidently imperfect; what is extant contains the coasts of the Palus Maeotis, the Euxine, the Archipelago, the Adriatic, and all the Mediterranean, with the west coast of Africa, as far as the isle of Cerne, which he asserts to be the limit of the Carthaginian navigation and commerce in that direction. The sea, according to him, is not navigable further to the south than this island, on account of the thick weeds with which it was covered. The mention of this impediment is adduced by D'Anville to prove the reality of the Carthaginian voyages to the south: it is not, indeed, true, that the sea is impassable on account of these weeds to modern navigators, but it is easy to conceive that the timidity and inexperience of the ancients, as well as the imperfect construction of their vessels, would prevent them from proceeding further south, when they met with such a singular obstacle. If a ship has not   through the water, these weeds will impede her course. It has been very justly remarked, that if the latitude where these weeds commence was accurately determined, it would fix exactly the extent of the voyages of the Carthaginians in this direction. The weed alluded to is probably the fucus natans, or gulf-weed.

Hitherto the knowledge that the ancients possessed of the habitable world, had not been collected by any writer, and is to be gathered entirely from short, vague, and evidently imperfect narrations, scattered throughout a great number of authors. Herodotus has been celebrated as the father of history; he may with equal justice be styled the father of geographical knowledge: he flourished about 474 years before Christ. In dwelling upon the advances to geographical knowledge which have been derived from him, it will be proper and satisfactory, before we explain the extent and nature of them, to give an account of the sources from which he derived his information; those were his own travels, and the narrations or journals of other travellers. A great portion of the vigour of his life seems to have been spent in travelling; the oppressive tyranny of Lygdamis over Halicarnassus, his native country, first induced or compelled him to travel; whether he had not also imbibed a portion of the commercial activity and enterprize which distinguished his countrymen, is not known, but is highly probable. We are not informed whether his fortune were such as to enable him, without entering into commercial speculations, to support the expences of his travels; it is evident, however, from the extent of his travels, as well as from the various, accurate, and, in many cases, most important information, which he acquired, that these expences must have been very considerable. From his work it is certain that he was endowed with that faculty of eliciting the truth from fabulous, imperfect, or contradictory evidence, at all times so necessary to a traveller, and indispensably so at the period when he travelled, and in most of the countries where his enquiries and his researches were carried on. His great and characteristic merit consists in freeing his mind from the opinions which must have previously occupied it;—in trusting entirely either to what e himself saw, or to what he learned from the best authority;—always, however, bringing the information acquired in this latter mode to the test of his own observation and good sense. It is from the united action and guidance of these two qualifications—individual observation and experience gained by most patient and diligent research and enquiry on the spot, and a high degree of perspicacity, strength of intellect, and good sense, separating the truth from the fable of all he learnt from the observation and experience of others, that Herodotus has justly acquired so high degree of reputation, and that in almost every instance modern travellers find themselves anticipated by him, even on points in which such a coincidence was the least likely.

His travels embraced a variety of countries. The Greek colonies in the Black Sea were visited by him: he measured the extent of that sea, from the Bosphorus to the mouth of the river Phasis, at the eastern extremity. All that track of country which lies between the Borysthenes and the Hypanis, and the shores of the Palus Maeotis, he diligently explored. With respect to the Caspian, his information affords a striking proof of his accuracy, even when gained, as it was in this instance, from the accounts of others. He describes it expressly as a sea by itself, unconnected with any other: its length, he adds, is as much as a vessel with oars can navigate in fifteen days: its greatest breadth as much as such a vessel can navigate in eight days. It may be added, as a curious proof and illustration of the decline of geographical knowledge, or, at least, of the want of confidence placed in the authority of Herodotus by subsequent ancient geographers, that Strabo, Pomponius Mela, and Pliny, represent the Caspian Sea as a bay, communicating with the great Northern Ocean; and that even Arrian, who, in respect to care and accuracy, bears no slight resemblance to Herodotus, and for some time resided as governor of Cappadocia, asserts that there was a communication between the Caspian Sea and the Eastern Ocean.

But to return from this digression to the geographical knowledge of Herodotus, as derived from his own travels, he visited Babylon and Susa, and while there, or perhaps in excursions from those places, made himself well acquainted with the Persian empire. The whole of Egypt was most diligently and thoroughly explored by him, as well as the Grecian colonies planted at Cyrene, in Lybia. He traced the course of the river Ister, from its mouth nearly as far as its source. The extent of his travels in Greece is not accurately known; but his description of the Straits of Thermopylae is evidently the result of his own observation. All these countries, together with a portion of the south of Italy, were visited by him. The information which his history conveys respecting other parts of the world was derived from others: in most cases, it would seem, from personal enquiries and conversation with them, so that he had an opportunity of rendering the information thus acquired much more complete, as well as satisfactory, than it would have been if it had been derived from their journals.

Herodotus trusted principally or entirely to the information he received, with respect to the interior of Africa and the north of Europe, and Asia to the east of Persia. While he was in Egypt he seems to have been particularly inquisitive and interested respecting the caravans which travelled into the interior of Africa; and regarding their equipment, route, destination, and object, he has collected a deal of curious and instructive information. On the authority of Etearchus, king of the Ammonians, he relates a journey into the interior of Africa, undertaken by five inhabitants of the country near the Gulf of Libya; and, in this journey, there is good reason to believe that the river Niger is accurately described, at least as far as regards the direction of its course.

It is evident from the introduction to his third book that the Greek merchants of his time were eminently distinguished for their courage, industry, and abilities; that in pursuit of commercial advantages they visited very remote and barbarous countries in the north-eastern parts of Europe, and the adjacent parts of Asia; and that the Scythians permitted the Greek merchants of the Euxine to penetrate farther to the east and north "than we can trace their progress by the light of modern information." To them Herodotus was much indebted for the geographical knowledge which he displays of those parts of the world; and it is by no means improbable that the spirit of commercial enterprize which invited the Greek merchants on the Euxine to penetrate among the barbarous nations of the north-east, also led them far to the east and south-east; and that from them, as well as from his personal enquiries, while at Babylon and Susa, Herodotus derived much of the information with which he has favoured us respecting the country on the Indus, and the borders of Cashmere and Arabia. Having thus pointed out the sources from which Herodotus derived his geographical knowledge, we shall now sketch the limits of that knowledge, as well as mention in what respects he yielded to the fabulous and absurd notions of his contemporaries.

He fails most in endeavouring to give a general and combined idea of the earth; even where his separate sketches are clear and accurate, when united they lose both their accuracy and clearness. He seems to doubt whether he should divide the world into three parts; and at last, having admitted such a division, he makes the rivers Phasis and Araxes, and the Caspian Sea, the boundaries between Europe and Asia; and to Europe he assigns an extent greater than Asia and Libya taken together. His knowledge of the west of Europe was very imperfect: in some part he fixes the Cassiterides, from which the Phoenicians derived their tin. The Phoenician colony of Gadez was known to him. His geography extended to the greater part of Poland and European Russia. Such appear to have been its limits with respect to Europe; and such the general notion he entertained of this quarter of the world. As to Asia, he believed that a fleet sent by Darius had circumnavigated it from the Indus to the confines of Egypt; but though his general idea of it was thus erroneous, he possessed accurate information respecting it from the confines of Europe to the Indus. Of the countries to the east of that river, as well as of the whole of the north and southern parts of it, he was completely ignorant. He particularly notices that the Eastern Ethiopians, or Indians, differ from those of Africa by their long hair, as opposed to the woolly head of the African. In his account of India he interweaves much that is fabulous; but in the same manner as modern discoveries in geography have confirmed many things in Herodotus which were deemed errors in his geography, so it has been ascertained that even his fables have, in most instances, a foundation in fact. With regard to Africa, his knowledge of Egypt, and of the country to the north of it, seems to have been very accurate, and more minute and satisfactory than his knowledge of any other part of the world. It is highly probable that he was acquainted with the course of the western branch of the Nile, as far as the 11th degree of latitude. He certainly knew the real course of the Niger. On the east coast of Africa he was well acquainted with the shores of the Arabian Gulph; but though he sometimes mentions Carthage, and describes the traffic carried on, without the intervention of language, between the Carthaginians and a nation beyond the Pillars of Hercules, which we nave already mentioned in treating of the commerce of the Carthaginians, yet he seems to have been unacquainted with any point between Carthage and the Pillars of Hercules.

In the history of Herodotus, there is an account of a map constructed by Aristagoras, tyrant of Miletus, when he proposed to Cleomenes, king of Sparta, to attack Darius, king of Persia, at Susa; from this account, the vague, imperfect, and erroneous ideas entertained in his time of the relative situations and distances of places, as well as of the extremely rude and feeble advances which had been made towards the construction of maps, may be inferred. Major Rennell, in his Illustrations of Herodotus, has endeavoured to ascertain from his history the parallel and meridian of Halicarnassus, the birth-place of the historian. According to him, they intersect at right angles over that town, cutting the 37th degree of north latitude, and the 45-1/2 of east longitude, from the Fortunate Islands.

For a considerable period after the time of Herodotus, the ancients seem to have been nearly stationary in their knowledge of the world. About 368 years before Christ, Eudoxus, of Cnidus, whose desire of studying astronomy induced him to visit Egypt, Asia, and Italy, who first attempted to explain the planetary motions, and who is said to have discovered the inclination of the moon's orbit, and the retrograde motion of her nodes, is celebrated as having first applied geographical observations to astronomy; but he does not appear to have directed his researches or his conjectures towards the figure or the circumference of the earth, or the distances or relative situations of any places on its surface.

Nearly about the same period that Eudoxus died Aristotle flourished. This great philosopher, collecting and combining into one system of geographical knowledge the discoveries and observations of all who had preceded him, stamped on them a dignity and value they had not before possessed, as well as rendered them less liable to be forgotten or misapplied: he inferred the sphericity of the earth from the observations of travellers, that the stars seen in Greece were not visible in Cyprus or Egypt; and thus established the fundamental principle of all geography. But though this science, in its most important branch, derived much benefit from his powerful mind, yet it was not advanced in its details. He supposed the coasts of Spain not very distant from those of India; and he even embraced a modified notion of Homer's Ocean River, which had been ridiculed and rejected by Herodotus; for he describes the habitable earth as a great oval island, surrounded by the ocean, terminated on the west by the river Tartessius, (supposed to be the Guadelquiver,) on the east by the Indus, and on the north by Albion and Ierne, of which islands his ideas were necessarily very vague and imperfect. In some other respects, however, his knowledge was more accurate: he coincides with Herodotus in his description of the Caspian Sea, and expressly states that it ought to be called a great lake, not a sea. A short period before Aristotle flourished, that branch of geography which relates to the temperature of different climates, and other circumstances affecting health, was investigated with considerable diligence, ingenuity, and success, by the celebrated physician Hippocrates. In the course of his journeys, with this object in view, he seems to have followed the plan and the route of Herodotus, and sometimes to have even penetrated farther than he did.

Pytheas, of Marseilles, lived a short time before Alexander the Great: he is celebrated for his knowledge in astronomy, mathematics, philosophy, and geography, and for the ardour and perseverance with which either a strong desire for information, or the characteristic commercial spirit of his townspeople, or both united, carried him forward in the path of maritime discovery. The additions, however, which he made to geography as a science, or to the sciences intimately connected with it, are more palpable and undisputed, than the extent and discoveries of his voyages.

He was the first who established a distinction of climate by the length of days and nights: and he is said to have discovered the dependence of the tides upon the position of the moon, affirming that the flood-tide depended on the increase of the moon, and the ebb on its decrease. By means of a gnomon he observed, at the summer solstice at Marseilles, that the length of the shadow was to the height of the gnomon as 120 to 41-1/5; or, in other words, that the obliquity of the ecliptic was 23:50. He relates, that in the country which he reached in his voyage to the north, the sun, at the time of the summer solstice, touched the northern part of the horizon: he pointed out three stars near the pole, with which the north star formed a square; and within this square, he fixed the true place of the pole. According to Strabo, he considered the island of Thule as the most western part of the then known world, and reckoned his longitude from thence.

With respect to the extent and discoveries of his voyage to the north, there is great difference of opinion. The veracity of Pytheas is utterly denied by Strabo and Polybius, and is strongly suspected by Dr. Vincent: on the other hand, it has found able supporters in D'Anville, Huet, Gessner, Murray of Goettingen, Gosselin, and Malte Brun; and in our opinion, though it may not be easy to ascertain what was really the country which be reached in his voyage, and though some of the particulars he mentions may be fabulous, or irreconcileable with one another, yet it seems carrying scepticism too far to reject, on these accounts, his voyage as altogether a fiction.

The account is, that Pytheas departed from Marseilles, coasted Spain, France, and the east or north-east side of Britain, as far as its northern extremity. Taking his departure from this, he continued his voyage, as he says, to the north, or perhaps to the north-east; and after six days' navigation, he arrived at a land called Thule, which he states to be 46,300 stadia from the equator. So far there is nothing improbable or inconsistent; but when he adds, that being there at the summer solstice, he saw the sun touching the northern point of the horizon, and at the same time asserts that the day and night were each of six months' continuance, there is a palpable contradiction: and when he adds, that millet was cultivated in the north of this country, and wheat in the south, and that honey abounded, he mentions productions utterly incompatible with his description of the climate and latitude.

As, however, this voyage forms an important epoch in the history of discovery, it may be proper to endeavour to ascertain what country the Thule of Pytheas really was. We have already observed, that the day's sail of an ancient vessel was 500 stadia, or 50 miles; supposing the largest stadia of 666-2/3 equal to one degree of the equator, if the vessel sailed during the night as well as day, the course run was, on an average, 1000 stadia, or 100 miles. Now, as the voyage from the extremity of Britain to Thule was of course not a coasting voyage, and as the nights in that latitude, at the season of the year when the voyage was made, were very short, (Pytheas says the night was reduced to two or three hours) we must suppose that he sailed night as well as day; and consequently, that in six days he had sailed 600 miles, either directly north or to east or west of the north, for his exact course cannot well be made out.

What country lies 600 miles to the north or the north-east of the extremity of Britain? None exactly in this direction: if, however, we suppose that Pytheas could not fix exactly the point of the compass which he steered, (a supposition by no means improbable, considering the ignorance of the ancients,) and that his course tended to the west of the north, 600 miles would bring him nearly to Greenland. There were, however, other stadia besides those by which we computed the day's sail of the ancients; and though the stadia we have taken are more generally alluded to by the ancients, yet it may be proper to ascertain what results will be produced if the other stadia are supposed to have been used in this instance. The stadia we have already founded our calculations upon will bring us to the latitude of 69° 27': the latitude of the southernmost point of Greenland is very nearly 70°. But the description given by Pytheas of the productions of the country by no means coincides with Greenland. At the same time, other parts of his description agree with this country; particularly when he says, that there the sea, the earth, and the air, seem to be confounded in one element. In the south of Greenland the longest day is two months which does not coincide with Pytheas' account; though this, as we have already pointed out, is contradictory with itself.

Let us now consider what will be the result if we suppose that a different stadia were employed: the next in point of extent to that on which we have already founded our conjectures, (there being 700 equal to one degree of the equator) will bring him to the latitude of 66° 8'; the latitude of the northernmost part of Iceland is 66° 30', coinciding with this result as nearly as possible. The description of the climate agrees with Pytheas' description; but not his account of the length of the day, nor of the productions of the country. Of the third kind of stadia, 833-1/3 were equal to one degree of the equator; calculating that 1000 of these were sailed during a day and night's voyage, Pytheas would arrive in the latitude of 55° 34', at the end of six days. This, however, is absolutely at variance with the fact, that he took his departure from the northernmost point of Britain, and would in fact bring him back from it to the entrance of the Frith of Forth. It is supposed, however, that this is the real latitude; but that the west coast of Jutland is the country at which he arrived. But this obliges us to believe that his course from the northern extremity of Britain, instead of being north or north-east, or indeed at all to the north, was in fact south-west; a supposition which cannot be admitted, unless we imagine that the ancients were totally ignorant of the course which they steered. On the other hand, Pytheas' description of the productions of Thule agrees with Jutland; the culture of millet in the north, and of wheat in the south, and the abundance of honey: there is also, about a degree to the north of the latitude of 55° 34', a part of the coast still denominated Thyland; and in the ancient language of Scandinavia, Thiuland. The account of Pytheas, that near Thule, the sea, air, and earth, seemed to be confounded in one element, is supposed by Malte Brun to allude to the sandy downs of Jutland, whose hills shift with the wind; the marshes, covered with a crust of sand, concealing from the traveller the gulf beneath, and the fogs of a peculiarly dense nature which frequently occur. We must confess, however, that the course having been north, or north-east, or north-west, for this latitude of course may be allowed in consideration of the ignorance or want of accuracy of the ancients, never can have brought Pytheas to a country lying to the south-west of the extremity of Britain.

We are not assisted in finding out the truth, if, instead of founding our calculations and conjectures on the distance sailed in the six days, we take for their basis the distance which Pytheas states Thule to be from the equator. This distance, we have already mentioned, was 46,300 stadia; which, according as the different kinds of stadia are calculated upon, will give respectively the latitude of the south of Greenland, of the north of Iceland, or of the west coast of Jutland; or, in other words, the limit of Pytheas' voyage will be determined to be in the same latitude, whether we ascertain it by the average length of the day and night's sail of the vessels of the ancients, or by the distance from the equator which he assigns to Thule. It may be proper to state, that there is a district on the coast of Norway, between the latitudes of 60° and 62°, called Thele, or Thelemarle. Ptolemy supposes this to have been the Thule of Pytheas, Pliny places it within three degrees of the pole, Eratosthenes under the polar circle. The Thule discovered by Agricola, and described by Tacitus, is evidently either the Orkney or the Shetland Islands.

It may appear presumptuous as well as useless, after this display of the difficulties attending the question, to offer any new conjecture; and many of our renders may deem it a point of very minor importance, and already discussed at too great length. It is obvious, from the detail into which we have entered, that no country exists in the latitude which must be assigned to it, whether we fix that latitude by Pytheas' statement of the distance of Thule from the equator, or by the space sailed over in six days, the productions of which at all agree with those mentioned by Pytheas. On the other hand, we cannot suppose that his course was south-west, and not at all to the north, which must have been the case, if the country at which he arrived in sailing from the northern extremity of Britain, was Jutland. The object must, therefore, be to find out a country the productions of which correspond with those mentioned by Pytheas; for, with regard to those, he could not be mistaken: and a country certainly not the least to the south of the northern part of Britain. As it is impossible that he could have reached the pole, what he states respecting the day and night being each six months long must be rejected; and his other account of the length of the day, deduced from his own observation of the sun, at the time of the summer solstice, touching the northern point of the horizon, must be received. If we suppose that this was the limit of the sun's course in that direction (which, from his statement, must be inferred), this will give us a length of day of about twenty hours, corresponding to about sixty-two degrees of north latitude. The next point to be ascertained is the latitude of his departure from the coast of Britain. There seems no good reason to believe, what all the hypothesis we have examined assume, that Pytheas sailed along the whole of the east coast of Britain: on the other hand, it seems more likely, that having passed over from the coast of France to the coast of Britain, he traced the latter to its most eastern point, that is, the coast of Norfolk near Yarmouth; from which place, the coast taking a sudden and great bend to the west, it is probable that Pytheas, whose object evidently was to sail as far north as he could, would leave the coast and stretch out into the open sea. Sailing on a north course, or rather with a little inclination to the east of the north, would bring him to the entrance of the Baltic. We have already conceived it probable that the country he describes lay in the latitude of about 62°, and six days' sail from the coast of Norfolk would bring him nearly into this latitude, supposing he entered the Baltic. The next point relates to the productions of the country: millet, wheat, and honey, are much more the characteristic productions of the countries lying on the Gulf of Finland, than they are of Jutland; and Pytheas' account of the climate also agrees better with the climate of this part of the Baltic, than with that of Jutland.

That Pythias visited the Baltic, though perhaps the Thule he mentions did not lie in this sea, is evident from the following extract from his journal, given by Pliny:—"On the shores of a certain bay called Mentonomon, live a people called Guttoni: and at the distance of a day's voyage from them, is the island Abalus (called by Timæus, Baltea). Upon this the waves threw the amber, which is a coagulated matter cast up by the sea: they use it for firing, instead of wood, and also sell it to the neighbouring Teutones." The inhabitants on the coast of the Baltic, near the Frish or Curish Sea (which is probably the bay Pytheas describes) are called in the Lithuanian language, Guddai: and so late as the period of the Crusades, the spot where amber is found was called Wittland, or Whiteland; in Lithuanian, Baltika. From these circumstances, as well as from the name given by Timaeus to the island mentioned by Pytheas, as the place where amber is cast up by the waves, there appears no doubt that Pytheas was in the Baltic Sea, though his island of Thule might not be there. As amber was in great repute, even so early as the time of Homer, who describes it as being used to adorn the golden collars, it is highly probable that Pytheas was induced to enter the Baltic for the purpose of obtaining it: in what manner, or through whose means, the Greeks obtained it in Homer's time, is not known.

After all, the question is involved in very great obscurity; and the circumstance not the most probable, or reconcileable with a country even not further north than Jutland is, that, in the age of Pytheas, the inhabitants should have been so far advanced in knowledge and civilization, as to have cultivated any species of grain.

Till the age of Herodotus the light of history is comparatively feeble and broken; and where it does shine with more steadiness and brilliancy, its rays are directed almost exclusively on the warlike operations of mankind. Occasionally, indeed, we incidentally learn some new particulars respecting the knowledge of the ancients in geography: but these particulars, as must be obvious from the preceding part of this volume, are ascertained only after considerable difficulty; and when ascertained, are for the most part meagre, if not obscure. In the history of Herodotus, we, for the first time, are able to trace the exact state and progress of geographical knowledge; and from his time, our means of tracing it become more accessible, as well as productive of more satisfactory results. Within one hundred years after this historian flourished, geography derived great advantages and improvement from a circumstance which, at first view, would have been deemed adverse to the extension of any branch of science: we allude to the conquests of Alexander the Great. This monarch seems to have been actuated by a desire to be honoured as the patron of science, nearly as strong as the desire to be known to posterity as the conquerer of the world: the facilities he afforded to Aristotle in drawing up his natural history, by sending him all the uncommon animals with which his travels and his conquests supplied him, is a striking proof of this. With respect to his endeavours to extend geographical knowledge,—this was so intimately connected with his plans of conquest, that it may appear to be ascribing to him a more honourable motive than influenced him, if we consider the improvement that geography received through his means as wholly unconnected with his character as a conquerer: that it was so, in some measure, however is certain; for along with him he took several geographers, who were directed and enabled to make observations both on the coasts and the interior of the countries through which they passed; and from their observations and discoveries, a new and improved geography of Asia was framed. Besides, the books that till his time were shut up in the archives of Babylon and Tyre were transferred to Alexandria; and thus the astronomical and hydrographical observations of the Phoenicians and Chaldeans, becoming accessible to the Greek philosophers, supplied them with the means of founding their geographical knowledge on the sure basis of mathematical science, of which it had hitherto been destitute.

The grand maxim of Alexander in his conquests was, to regard them as permanent, and as annexing to his empire provinces which were to form as essential parts of it as Macedonia itself. Influenced by this consideration and design, he did not lay waste the countries he conquered, as had been done in the invasions of Persia, by Cimon the Athenian and the Lacedemonians: on the contrary, the people, and their religion, manners, and laws were protected. The utmost order and regularity were observed; and it is a striking fact, "that his measures were taken with such prudence, that during eight years' absence at the extremity of the East, no revolt of consequence occurred; and his settlement of

Egypt was so judicious, as to serve as a model to the Romans in the administration of that province at the distance of three centuries."

The voyage of Nearchus from Nicea on the Hydaspes, till he arrived in the vicinity of Susa (which we shall afterwards more particularly describe); the projected voyage, the object of which was to attempt the circumnavigation of Arabia; the survey of the western side of the Gulf of Persia, by Archias, Androsthenes, and Hiero, of which unfortunately we do not possess the details; the projected establishment of a direct commercial intercourse between India and Alexandria; and the foundation of this city, which gave a new turn and a strong impulse to commerce, as will be more particularly shown afterwards;— are but a few of the benefits geography and commerce received from Alexander, or would have received, had not his plans been frustrated by his sudden and early death at the age of 33.

We have the direct testimony of Patrocles, that Alexander was not content with vague and general information, nor relied on the testimony of others where he could observe and judge for himself; and in all cases in which he derived his information from others, he was particularly careful to select those who knew the country best, and to make them commit their intelligence to writing. By these means, united to the reports of those whom he employed to survey his conquests, "all the native commodities which to this day form the staple of the East Indian commerce, were fully known to the Macedonians." The principal castes in India, the principles of the Bramins, the devotion of widows to the flames, the description of the banyan-tree, and a great variety of other particulars, sufficiently prove that the Macedonians were actuated by a thirst after knowledge, as well as a spirit of conquest; and illustrate as well as justify the observation made to Alexander by the Bramin mandarin, "You are the only man whom I ever found curious in the investigation of philosophy at the head of an army."

When Alexander invaded India, he found commerce flourishing greatly in many parts of it, particularly in what are supposed to be the present Multan, Attock, and the Panjob. He every where took advantage of this commerce, not by plundering and thus destroying it for the purpose of filling his coffers, but by nourishing and increasing it, and thus at once benefitting himself and the inhabitants who wore engaged in it. By means of the commerce in which the natives of the Panjob were engaged on the Indus, Alexander procured the fleet with which he sailed down that river. This fleet is supposed to have consisted of eight hundred vessels, only thirty of which were ships of war, the remainder being such as were usually employed in the commerce of the Indus. Even before he reached this river, he had built vessels which he had sent down the Kophenes to Taxila. By the completion of his campaign at the sources of the Indus, and by his march and voyage down the course of that river, he had traced and defined the eastern boundary of his conquests: the line of his march from the Hellespont till the final defeat of Darius, and his pursuit of that monarch, had put him in possession of tolerably accurate knowledge of the northern and western boundaries; the southern provinces alone remained to be explored: they had indeed submitted to his arms; but they were still, for all the purposes of government and commerce, unknown.

"To obtain the information necessary for the objects they had in view, he ordered Craterus, with the elephants and heavy baggage, to penetrate through the centre of the empire, while he personally undertook the more arduous task of penetrating the desert of Gadrosia, and providing for the preservation of the fleet. A glance over the map will show that the route of the army eastward, and the double route by which it returned, intersect the whole empire by three lines, almost from the Tigris to the Indus: Craterus joined the division under Alexander in the Karmania; and when Nearchus, after the completion of his voyage, came up the Posityris to Susa, the three routes through the different provinces, and the navigation along the coast, might be said to complete the survey of the empire."

The two divisions of his army were accompanied on their return to Susa by Beton and Diognetus, who seem to have united the character and duties of soldiers and men of science; or, perhaps, were like the quarter-masters- general of our armies. It appears from Strabo and Pliny, in whose time the surveys drawn by Beton and Diognetus were extant, that they reduced the provinces through which they passed, as well as the marches of the army, to actual measurement; and thus, the distances being accurately set down, and journals faithfully kept, the principles of geographical science, next in importance and utility to astronomical observations, were established. The journals of Beton and Diognetus, the voyage of Nearchus, and the works of Ptolemy, afterwards king of Egypt, and Aristobulus, who accompanied Alexander in his expedition and wrote his life, all prove that the authority or the example of the sovereign influenced the pursuits of his officers and attendants; and it is highly to the credit of their diligence and accuracy, that every increase of geographical knowledge tends to confirm what they relate respecting the general appearance and features of the countries they traversed, as well as the position of cities, rivers, and mountains.

Alexander appears to have projected or anticipated an intercourse between India and the western provinces of his dominions in Egypt, not only by land but by sea: for this latter purpose he founded two cities on the Hydaspes and one on the Axesimes, both navigable rivers, which fall into the Indus. And this also, most probably, was one reason for his careful survey of the navigation of the Indus itself. When he returned to Susa, he surveyed the course of the Tigris and Euphrates. The navigation near the mouths of those rivers was obstructed by cataracts, occasioned by walls built across them by the ancient monarchs of Persia, in order to prevent their subjects from defiling themselves by sailing on the ocean[4]: these obstructions he gave directions to be removed. Had he lived, therefore, the commodites of India would have been conveyed from the Persian Gulf into the interior provinces of his Asiatic dominions, and to Alexandria by the Arabian Gulf.

To conclude in the words of Dr. Vincent: "The Macedonians obtained a knowledge both of the Indus and the Ganges: they heard that the seat of empire was, where it always has been, on the Ganges or Indus: they acquired intelligence of all the grand and leading features of Indian manners, policy, and religion [and he might have added, accurate information respecting the geography of the western parts of that country]: they discovered all this by penetrating through countries, where, possibly, no Greek had previously set his foot; and they explored the passage by sea which first opened the commercial intercourse with India to the Greeks and Romans, through the medium of Egypt and the Red Sea, and finally to the Europeans, by the Cape of Good Hope." When we reflect on the character and state of the Macedonians, prior to the reign of Alexander, and the condition into which they sunk after his death, we shall, perhaps, not hesitate to acknowledge that Alexander infused his own soul into them; and that history, ancient or modern, does not exhibit any similiar instance of such powerful individual influence on the character and fate of a nation. Alexander himself has always been honoured by conquerors, and is known to mankind only, as the first of conquerors; but if military renown and achievements had not, unfortunately for mankind, been more prized than they deserved, and, on this account, the records of them been carefully preserved, while the records of peaceful transactions were neglected and lost, we should probably have received the full details of all that Alexander did for geographical science and commerce; and in that case his character would have been as highly prized by the philosopher and the friend of humanity, civilization, and knowledge, as it is by the powerful and ambitious.

Fortunately the details of one of the geographical and commercial expeditions undertaken by order of Alexander are still extant; we allude to the voyage of Nearchus. Of this voyage we are now to speak; and as it is curious and important, not merely on account of the geographical knowledge it conveys, but also from the insight it gives us into the commercial transactions of the countries which he visited, we shall give rather a full abstract of it, availing ourselves of the light which has been thrown upon it by the learned and judicious researches of Dr. Vincent.

It was on the banks of the Hyphasis, the modern Beyah, that Alexander's army mutinied, and refused to proceed any farther eastward. In consequence of this insurmountable obstacle to his plans, he resolved to return to the Hydaspes, and carry into execution his design of sailing down it into the Indus, and thence by the ocean to the Persian Gulf. He had previously given orders to his officers, when he had left the Hydaspes to collect, build, and equip a sufficient number of vessels for this enterprise; and they had been so diligent and successful, that on his return he found a numerous fleet assembled. Nearchus was appointed to command the fleet: but Alexander himself resolved to accompany it to the mouth of the river.

On the 23d of October, 327 years before Christ, the fleet sailed from Nicoea, on the Hydaspes, a city built by Alexander on the scite of the battle in which he defeated Porus. The importance which he attached to this expedition, as well as his anxiety respecting its skilful conduct and final issue, are strongly painted by Arrian, to whom we are indebted for the journal of Nearchus.

Alexander at first did not know whom to trust with the management of the expedition, or who would undertake it. when the length of the voyage, the difficulties and dangers of a barren and unknown coast, the want of harbours, and the obstacles in the way of obtaining provisions, were considered. In this state of anxiety, doubt, and expectation, Alexander ordered Nearchus to attend him, and consulted him on the choice of a commander. "One," said he, "excuses himself, because he thinks the danger insuperable; others are unfit for the service from timidity; others think of nothing but how to get home; and many I cannot approve for a variety of other reasons." "Upon hearing this," says Nearchus, "I offered myself for the command: and promised the king, that under the protection of God, I would conduct the fleet safe into the Gulf of Persia, if the sea were navigable, and the undertaking within the power of man to perform." The only objection that Alexander made arose from his regard for Nearchus, whom he was unwilling to expose to the dangers of such a voyage; but Nearchus persisting, and the king being convinced that the enterprise, if practicable, would be achieved by the skill, courage, and perseverance of Nearchus, at length yielded. The character of the commander, and the regard his sovereign entertained for him, removed in a great degree the apprehension that the proposed expedition was desperate: a selection of the best officers and most effective men was now soon made; and the fleet was not only supplied with every thing that was necessary, but equipped in a most splendid manner. Onesicritus was appointed pilot and master of Alexander's own ship; and Evagoras was secretary of the fleet. The officers, including these and Nearchus, amounted to 33; but nearly the whole of them, as well as the ships which they commanded, proceeded no farther than the mouth of the Indus. The seamen were natives of Greece, or the Grecian Islands, Phoenicians, Egyptians, Cyprians, Ionians, &c. The fleet consisted of 800 ships of war and transports, and about 1200 gallies. On board of these, one-third of the army, which consisted of 120,000 men, embarked; the remainder, marching in two divisions, one on the left, the other on the right of the river.

"The voyage down the river is described rather as a triumphal procession, than a military progress. The size of the vessels, the conveyance of horses aboard, the number, and splendour of the equipment, attracted the natives to be spectators of the pomp. The sound of instruments, the clang of arms, the commands of the officers, the measured song of the modulators, the responses of the mariners, the dashing of the oars, and these sounds frequently reverberated from overhanging shores, are all scenery presented to our imagination by the historians, and evidently bespeak the language of those who shared with pride in this scene of triumph and magnificence."

No danger occurred to alarm them or impede their passage, till they arrived at the junction of the Hydaspes with the Akesines. At this place, the channel of the river became contracted, though the bulk of water was of course greatly increased; and from this circumstance, and the rapidity with which the two rivers unite, there is a considerable current, as well as strong eddies; and the noise of the rushing and confined waters, is heard at some distance. This noise astonished or alarmed the seamen so much, that the rowers ceased to row, and the modulators to direct and encourage them by their chant, till the commanders inspired them with confidence; and they plied the oars with their utmost strength in order to stem the current, and keep the vessels as steady and free from danger as possible. The eddy, however, caught the gallies, which from their length were more exposed to it than the ships of war: two of them sank, many more were damaged, while Alexander's own ship was fortunate enough to find shelter near a projecting point of land. At the junction of the Akesines with the Indus, Alexander founded a city; of which, however, no traces at present remain.

On the arrival of Alexander at Pattala, near the head of the Delta of the Indus, he seems to have projected the formation of a commercial city; and for this purpose, ordered the adjoining country to be surveyed: his next object was to sail down the western branch of the river. With this view he left Pattala with all his gallies, some of his half-decked vessels, and his quickest sailing transports, ordering at the same time a small part of his army to attend his fleet. Considerable difficulties arose, and some loss was sustained from his not being able to procure a native pilot, and from the swell in the river, occasioned by a violent wind blowing contrary to the stream. He was at length compelled to seize some of the natives, and make them act as pilots. When they arrived near the confluence of the Indus with the sea, another storm arose; and as this also blew up the river, while they were sailing down with the current and the tide, there was considerable agitation in the water. The Macedonians were alarmed, and by the advice of their pilots ran into one of the creeks of the river for shelter: at low tide, the vessels being left aground, the sharp-built gallies were much injured.

The astonishment of the Macedonians was greatly excited when they saw the waters of the river and of the sea ebb and flow. It is well known, that in the Mediterranean the tides are scarcely perceptible. The flux and reflux of the Euripus, a narrow strait which separates the island of Euboea from the coast of Beotia, could give them no idea of the regularity of the tides; for this flux and reflux continued for eighteen or nineteen days, and was uncommonly unsettled the rest of the month. Besides, the tides at the mouth of the Indus, and on the adjacent coast, are very high, and flow in with very great force and rapidity; and are known in India, in the Bay of Fundy, and in most other places where this phenomenon occurs, by the name of the Bore; and at the mouth of the Severn, by the name of Hygre, or Eagre. Herodotus indeed, mentions, that in the Red Sea there was a regular ebb and flow of the sea every day; but as Dr. Robertson very justly observes, "among the ancients there occur instances of inattention to facts, related by respectable authors, which appear surprising in modern times." Even so late as the time of Caesar, a spring tide in Britain, which occasioned great damage to his fleet, created great surprize, and is mentioned as a phenomenon with which he and his soldiers were unacquainted.

Soon after Alexander had repaired the damage that his fleet had sustained, he surveyed two islands lying at the west mouth of the Indus; and afterwards leaving the river entirely, entered the ocean, either for the purpose of ascertaining himself whether it were actually navigable, or, as Arrian conjectures, in order to gratify his vanity by having it recorded, that he had navigated the Indian Ocean.

Having accomplished this object, he returned to Pattala, where he had directed a naval arsenal to be formed, intending to station a fleet at this place. The eastern branch of the Indus was yet unexplored. In order, that an accurate knowledge of it might be gained, Alexander resolved to explore it himself: accordingly, he sailed from Pattala till he arrived at a large bay or lake, which probably, however, was only a number of the smaller branches of the Indus, overflowing their banks. The passage from this place to the ocean, he ascertained to be more open and convenient than that by the western branch. He does not seem, however, to have advanced into the ocean by it; but having landed, and proceeded along the coast, in the direction of Guzerat and Malabar, three days' march, making observations on the country, and directing wells to be sunk, he re-embarked, and returned to the head of the bay. Here he again manifested his design of establishing a permanent station, by ordering a fort to be built, a naval yard and docks to be formed, and leaving a garrison and provisions for four months.

Before the final departure of Alexander with his convoy from Pattala, he directed Nearchus to assume the entire command of the fleet, and to sail as soon as the season would permit. Twelve months, within a few days, elapsed between the departure of the fleet from Nicaea, and the sailing of Nearchus from the Indus; the former having taken place, as we have already observed, on the 23d of October, in the year 327 before Christ, and the latter on the 2d of October, in the year 326 B.C. Only about nine months, however, had elapsed in the actual navigation of the Indus and its tributary streams; and even this period, which to us appears very long, was considerably extended by the operations of the army of Alexander, as well as by the slow sailing of such a large fleet as he conducted.

In consequence, it is supposed, of the prevalence of the north-east monsoon, Nearchus, after having reached the ocean (which, however, he could not effect till he had cut a passage for his fleet through a sand bank or bar at the mouth of the Indus), was obliged to lie in a harbour which he called Port Alexander, and near which he erected a fort on the 3d of November; about which time we know that the monsoon changes. Nearchus again set sail. About the 8th of this month he reached the river Arabis, having coasted along among rocks and islands, the passage between which was narrow and difficult. The distance between this river and the Indus is nearly eighty miles, and the fleet had occupied almost forty days in completing the navigation of this space. During the greater part of this time, they were very scantily supplied with provisions, and seem, indeed, to have depended principally on the shell-fish found on the coast. Soon after leaving the mouth of the Arabis, they were obliged, by the nature of the shore and the violence of the wind, to remain on board their ships for two nights; a very unusual as well as inconvenient and uncomfortable circumstance for the ancients. We have already described their ships as either having no deck, or only a kind of half-deck, below which the cables were coiled. Under this deck there might be accommodation for part of the crew; but in cases where all were obliged to remain on board at night, the confinement must have been extremely irksome, as well as prejudicial to their health. At the end of these two days, they were enabled to land and refresh themselves; and here they were joined by Leonatus, one of Alexander's generals, who had been despatched with some troops to watch and protect their movements, as far on their course as was practicable. He brought a supply of provisions, which had become very necessary. On leaving this place, their progress became much more rapid than it had been before, owing probably to the wind having become more regularly and permanently favourable.

As it is our intention, in giving this short abstract of the voyage of Nearchus, to select only such particulars as illustrate the mode of navigation practised among the ancients—the progress of discovery, or the state of commerce,—we shall pass over every topic or fact not connected with these. We cannot, however, refrain from giving an account of the transactions of the fleet at the river Tomerus, when it arrived on the 21st of November, fifty days after it left the Indus; as on reading it, our readers will be immediately struck with the truth of Dr. Vincent's observation, that it bears a very strong resemblance to the landing of a party from the Endeavour, in New Zealand, under protection of the ship's guns. We make use of Dr. Vincent's translation, or rather abstract:—

"At the Tomerus the inhabitants were found living on the low ground near the sea, in cabins which seemed calculated rather to suffocate their inhabitants than to protect them from the weather; and yet these wretched people were not without courage. Upon sight of the fleet approaching, they collected in arms on the shore, and drew up in order to attack the strangers on their landing. Their arms were spears, not headed with iron, but hardened in the fire, nine feet long; and their number about 600. Nearchus ordered his vessels to lay their heads towards the shore, within the distance of bow-shot; for the enemy had no missile weapons but their spears. He likewise brought his engines to bear upon them, (for such it appears he had on board,) and then directed his light-armed troops, with those who were the most active and the best swimmers, to be ready for commencing the attack. On a signal given, they were to plunge into the sea: the first man who touched ground was to be the point at which the line was to be formed, and was not to advance till joined by the others, and the file could be ranged three deep. These orders were exactly obeyed; the men threw themselves out of the ships, swam forward, and formed themselves in the water, under cover of the engines. As soon as they were in order, they advanced upon the enemy with a shout, which was repeated from the ships. Little opposition was experienced; for the natives, struck with the novelty of the attack, and the glittering of the armour, fled without resistance. Some escaped to the mountains, a few were killed, and a considerable number made prisoners. They were a savage race, shaggy on the body as well as the head, and with nails so long and of such strength, that they served them as instruments to divide their food, (which consisted, indeed, almost wholly of fish,) and to separate even wood of the softer kind. Whether this circumstance originated from design, or want of implements to pare their nails, did not appear; but if there was occasion, to divide harder substances, they substituted stones sharpened, instead of iron, for iron they had none. Their dress consisted of the skins of beasts, and some of the larger kinds of fish."

Along the coast of the Icthyophagi, extending from Malan to Cape Jaser, a distance, by the course of the fleet, of nearly 625 miles, Nearchus was so much favoured by the winds and by the straightness of the coast, that his progress was sometimes nearly 60 miles a day. In every other respect, however, this portion of the voyage was very unfortunate and calamitous. Alexander, aware that on this coast, which furnished nothing but fish, his fleet would be in distress for provisions, and that this distress would be greatly augmented by the scarcity of water which also prevailed here, had endeavoured to advance into this desolate tract, to survey the harbours, sink wells, and collect provisions. But the nature of the country rendered this impracticable; and his army became so straightened for corn themselves, that a supply of it, which he intended for the fleet, and on which he had affixed his own seal, was seized by the men whom he had ordered to protect and escort it to the coast. At last he was obliged to give up all attempts of relieving Nearchus; and after struggling 60 days with want of water,—during which period, if he himself had not, at the head of a few horse, pushed on to the coast, and there obtained a supply, by opening the sands, his whole army must have perished,—he with great difficulty reached the capital of this desert country. Nearchus, thus left to himself, was indebted to the natives for the means of discovering water, by opening the sands, as the king had done; but to the Greeks, who regarded the want of bread as famine, even when its place was supplied by meat, the fish the natives offered them was no relief.

We have already remarked, that the real character of Alexander will be much elevated in the opinion of men of humanity and philosophers, if the particulars we possess of his endeavours to improve the condition of those he conquered, and to advance the interests of science, scanty and imperfect as they are, were more attentively considered, and had not been neglected and overlooked in the glare of his military achievements. His march through the deserts of Gadrosia has been ascribed solely to vanity; but this imputation will be removed, and must give way to a more worthy impression of his motives on this occasion, when it is stated, that it was part of the great design which he had formed of opening a communication between his European dominions and India by sea; and that as the accomplishment of this design mainly depended on the success of the expedition committed to Nearchus, it was a paramount object with him to assist the fleet, which he thrice attempted, even in the midst of his own distress in the deserts.

On their arrival at the river Kalama, which is supposed to be the Churmut, 60 days after their departure from the Indus, they at length obtained from the natives some sheep; but the flesh of it, as well as the fowls which they obtained, had a very fishy taste—the sheep, fowls, and inhabitants, all feeding on fish, there being no herbage or trees of any kind, except a few palm-trees. On the next day, having doubled a cape, they anchored in a harbour called Mosarna, where they found a pilot, who undertook to conduct the fleet to the Gulf of Persia. It would appear from Arrian, that the intercourse between this place and the Gulf was frequent, the voyage less dangerous, and the harbours on the coast better known. Owing to these favourable circumstances, the skill of the pilot, and the breeze which blew from the land during the night, their course was more rapid; and they sailed by night as well as day. The coast, however, still continued barren, and the inhabitants unable to supply them with any thing but fish till they arrived at Barna on the 64th day: here the inhabitants were more civilized; they had gardens producing fruit-trees, flowers, myrtle, &c., with which the Greek sailors formed garlands to adorn their hair.

On the 69th day, December 9., they arrived at a small town, the name of which is not given; nor is it possible to fix its scite. What occurred here we shall give in the words of Dr. Vincent:—

"When the fleet reached this place, it was totally without bread or grain of any kind; and Nearchus, from the appearance of stubble in the neighbourhood, conceived hopes of a supply, if he could find means of obtaining it; but he perceived that he could not take the place by assault, and a siege the situation he was in rendered impracticable. He concerted matters, therefore, with Archias, and ordered him to make a feint of preparing the fleet to sail; while he himself, with a single vessel, pretending to be left behind, approached the town in a friendly manner, and was received hospitably by the inhabitants. They came out to receive him upon his landing, and presented him with baked fish, (the first instance of cookery he had yet seen on the coast,) accompanied with cakes and dates. These he accepted with proper acknowledgments, and informed them he wished for permission to see the town: this request was granted without suspicion; but no sooner had he entered, than he ordered two of his archers to take post at the gate, and then mounting the wall contiguous, with two more and his interpreter, he made the signal for Archias, who was now under weigh to advance. The natives instantly ran to their arms; but Nearchus having taken an advantageous position, made a momentary defence till Archias was close at the gate, ordering his interpreter to proclaim at the same time, that if they wished their city to be preserved from pillage, they must deliver up their corn, and all the provisions which the place afforded. These terms were not rejected, for the gate was open, and Archias ready to enter: he took charge of this post immediately with the force which attended him; and Nearchus sent proper officers to examine such stores as were in the place, promising the inhabitants that, if they acted ingenuously, they should suffer no other injury. Their stores were immediately produced, consisting of a kind of meal, or paste made of fish, in great plenty, with a small quantity of wheat and barley. This, however insufficient for his wants, Nearchus received: and abstaining from farther oppression, returned on board with his supply."

The provisions he obtained here, notwithstanding the consumption of them was protracted by occasionally landing and cutting off the tender shoots of the head of the wild palm-tree, were so completely exhausted in the course of a few days, that Nearchus was obliged to prevent his men from landing, under the apprehension, that though the coast was barren, their distress on board would have induced them not to return. At length, on the 14th of December, on the seventy-fourth day of their departure, they reached a more fertile and hospitable shore, and were enabled to procure a very small supply of provisions, consisting principally of corn, dried dates, and the flesh of seven camels. Nearchus mentions the latter evidently to point out the extreme distress to which they were reduced. As it is evident that this supply would be soon exhausted, we are not surprised that Nearchus, in order to reach a better cultivated district, should urge on his course as rapidly as possible; and accordingly we find, that he sailed at a greater rate in this part of his voyage than he ever had done before. Having sailed day and night without intermission, in which time he passed a distance of nearly sixty-nine miles, he at length doubled the cape, which formed the boundary of the barren coast of the Icthyophagi, and arrived in the district of Karmania. At Badis, the first town in this district, which they reached on the 17th of December, after a voyage of 77 days, they were supplied with corn, wine, and every kind of fruit, except olives, the inhabitants being not only able but willing to relieve their wants.

The length of the coast of the Icthyophagi is about 462 miles; and, as Nearchus was twenty-one days on this coast, the average rate of sailing must have been twenty-one miles a day. The whole distance, from the Indus to the cape which formed the boundary of Karmania, is about 625 miles: this distance Nearchus was above seventy days in sailing. It must be recollected, however, that when he first set out the monsoon was adverse, and that for twenty-four days he lay in harbour: making the proper deductions for these circumstances, he was not at sea more than forty days with a favourable wind; which gives rather more than fifteen miles a day. The Houghton East Indiaman made the same run in thirteen days; and, on her return, was only five days from Gomeroon to Scindy Bay.

The manners of the wretched inhabitants have occasionally been already noticed; but Nearchus dwells upon some further particulars, which, from their conformity with modern information, are worthy of remark. Their ordinary support is fish, as the name of Icthyophagi, or fish-eaters, implies; but why they are for this reason specified as a separate tribe from the Gadrosians, who live inland, does not appear. Ptolomy considers all this coast as Karmania, quite to Mosarna; and whether Gadrosia is a part of that province, or a province itself, is a matter of no importance; but the coast must have received the name Nearchus gives it from Nearchus himself; for it is Greek, and he is the first Greek who explored it. It may, perhaps, be a translation of a native name, and such translations the Greeks indulged in sometimes to the prejudice of geography. "But these people, though they live on fish, are few of them fishermen, for their barks are few, and those few very mean and unfit for the service. The fish they obtain they owe to the flux and reflux of the tide, for they extend a net upon the shore, supported by stakes of more than 200 yards in length, within which, at the tide of ebb, the fish are confined, and settle in the pits or in equalities of the sand, either made for this purpose or accidental. The greater quantity consists of small fish; but many large ones are also caught, which they search for in the pits, and extract with nets. Their nets are composed of the bark or fibres of the palm, which they twine into a cord, and form like the nets of other countries. The fish is generally eaten raw, just as it is taken out of the water, at least such as are small and penetrable; but the larger sort, and those of more solid texture, they expose to the sun, and pound them to a paste for store: this they use instead of meal or bread, or form them into a sort of cakes or frumenty. The very cattle live on dried fish, for there is neither grass nor pasture on the coast. Oysters, crabs, and shell-fish, are caught in plenty; and though this circumstance is specified twice only in the early part of the voyage, there is little doubt but these formed the principal support of the people during their navigation. Salt is here the production of nature, by which we are to understand, that the power of the sun in this latitude, is sufficient for exhalation and crystallization, without the additional aid of fire; and from this salt they formed an extract which they used as the Greeks use oil. The country, for the most part, is so desolate, that the natives have no addition to their fish but dates: in some few places a small quantity of grain is sown; and there bread is their viand of luxury, and fish stands in the rank of bread. The generality of the people live in cabins, small and stifling: the better sort only have houses constructed with the bones of whales, for whales are frequently thrown upon the coast; and, when the flesh is rotted off, they take the bones, making planks and doors of such as are flat, and beams or rafters of the ribs or jaw-bones; and many of these monsters are found fifty yards in length." Strabo confirms the report of Arrian, and adds, that "the vertebræ, or socket bones, of the back, are formed into mortars, in which they pound their fish, and mix it up into a paste, with the addition of a little meal."— (Vincent's Nearchus, p. 265.)

Dr. Vincent, in this passage, does not seem to be aware that no whale was ever found nearly so long as fifty yards, and that half that length is the more common size of the largest whales, even in seas more suitable to their nature and growth. That the animal which Nearchus himself saw was a whale, there can be little doubt: while he was off Kyiza, the seamen were extremely surprised, and not a little alarmed, at perceiving the sea agitated and thrown up, as Arrian expresses it, as if it were forcibly lifted up by a whirlwind. The pilot informed them that it was occasioned by the whales blowing; this information, however, does not seem to have quieted their fears: they ceased rowing, the oars dropped from their hands, and Nearchus found himself under the necessity of exerting all his presence of mind and authority to recall them to their duty. He gave directions to steer towards the place where the sea was lifted up: in their advance the crew shouted all together, dashed the water with their oars, and sounded their trumpets. The whales were intimidated, sunk on the near approach of the vessels, and, though they rose again astern, and renewed their blowing, they now excited no alarm.

The Gulf of Persia, which Nearchus was now about to enter, comprehends the coasts of Karmania, Persis, and Susiana. Nothing important occurred till the vessels arrived off Cape Mussenden in Karmania, where they anchored: at this place Nearchus and Onesicritus differed in opinion relative to the further prosecution of the voyage; the latter wished to explore this cape, and extend the voyage to the Gulf of Arabia. The reason he assigned was, that they knew more of this gulf, than of the Gulf of Persia; and that, as Alexander was master of Egypt, in the former gulf they would meet with more assistance than in the latter. Nearchus, on the contrary, insisted that Alexander's plan in directing, this voyage should be exactly pursued: this plan was, to obtain a knowledge of the coast, with such harbours, bays, and islands, as might occur in the course of the voyage; "to ascertain whether there were any towns bordering on the ocean, and whether the country was habitable or desert." The opinion of Nearchus prevailed, and the voyage was pursued according to its original course and purpose.

As Nearchus had reason to believe that the army of Alexander was at no great distance, he resolved to land, form a naval camp, and to advance himself into the interior, that he might ascertain this point. Accordingly, on the 20th of December, the 80th day after his departure, he formed a camp near the river Anamis; and having secured his ships, proceeded in search of Alexander. The first intelligence of their sovereign, however, seems to have been obtained accidentally. The crew of Nearchus were strolling up the country, when some of them met with a man whose dress and language instantly discovered that he was a Greek: the joy of meeting with a countryman was greatly heightened when he informed them that the army which he had lately left, was encamped at no great distance, and that the governor of the province was on the spot. As soon as Nearchus learnt the exact situation of the army, he hastened towards it; but the governor, eager to communicate to Alexander intelligence of his fleet, anticipated him. Alexander was exceedingly pleased; but when several days elapsed, and Nearchus did not arrive, he began to doubt the truth of what the governor had told him, and at last ordered him to be imprisoned.

[Illustration]

In the mean time Nearchus was prosecuting his journey along with Archias and five or six others, when he fortunately fell in with a party from the army, which had been sent out with horses and carriages for his accommodation. The admiral and his attendants, from their appearance, might have passed unnoticed. Their hair long and neglected, their garments decayed, their countenance pale and weather-worn, and their persons emaciated by famine and fatigue, scarcely raised the attention of the friends they had encountered. They were Greeks, however; and if Greeks, it was natural to inquire after the army, and where it was now encamped. An answer was given to their inquiry; but still they were neither recognized by the party, nor was any question asked in return. Just as they were separating from each other, "Assuredly," says Archias, "this must be a party sent out for our relief, for on what other account can they be wandering about the desert? There is nothing strange in their passing us without notice, for our very appearance is a disguise. Let us address them once more, and inform them who we are, and learn from them on what service they are at present employed."

Nearchus approved of this advice, and approaching them again, inquired which way they were directing their course. "We are in search of Nearchus and his people," replied the officer: "And I am Nearchus," said the admiral; "and this is Archias. Take us under your conduct, and we will ourselves report our history to the king." They were accordingly placed in the carriages, and conducted towards the army without delay. While they were upon their progress, some of the horsemen, impatient to carry the news of this happy event, set off to the camp to inform the king, that Nearchus and Archias were arrived with five or six of his people; but of the rest they had no intelligence. This suggested to Alexander that perhaps these only were preserved, and that the rest of the people had perished, either by famine or shipwreck; nor did he feel so much pleasure in the preservation of the few, as distress for the loss of the remainder. During this interval, Nearchus and his attendants arrived. It was not without difficulty that the king discovered who they were, under the disguise of their appearance; and this circumstance contributed to confirm him in his mistake, imagining that both their persons and their dress bespoke ship wreck, and the destruction of the fleet. He held out his hand, however, to Nearchus, and led him aside from his guards and attendants without being able to utter a word. As soon as they were alone, he burst into tears, and continued weeping for a considerable time; till, at length recovering in some degree his composure,—"Nearchus," says he, "I feel some satisfaction in finding that you and Archias have escaped; but tell me where and in what manner did my fleet and my people perish?" "Your fleet," replied Nearchus, "are all safe,—your people are safe; and we are come to bring you the account of their preservation." Tears, but from a different source, now fell much faster from his eyes. "Where then are my ships?" says he. "At the Anamis," replied Nearchus; "all safe on shore, and preparing for the completion of their voyage." "By the Lybian Ammon and Jupiter of Greece, I swear to you," rejoined the king, "I am more happy at receiving this intelligence, than in being conqueror of all Asia; for I should have considered the loss of my fleet and the failure of this expedition, as a counterbalance to all the glory I have acquired." Such was the reception of the admiral; while the governor, who was the first bearer of the glad tidings, was still in bonds: upon the sight of Nearchus, he fell at his feet, and implored his intercession. It may be well imagined that his pardon was as readily granted as it was asked.—(Vincent's Nearchus, p. 312.)

Sacrifices, games, and a festival ensued; and when these were ended, Alexander told Nearchus that he would expose him to no further hazard, but despatch another to carry the fleet to Susa. "I am bound to obey you," replied the admiral, "as my king, and I take a pleasure in my obedience; but if you, wish to gratify me in return, suffer me to retain my command, till I have completed the expedition. I shall feel it as an injustice, if, after having struggled through all the difficulties of the voyage, another shall finish the remainder almost without an effort, and yet reap the honour of completing what I have begun." Alexander yielded to this just request, and about the end of the year Nearchus rejoined his fleet.

By the 6th of January, B.C. 345, he reached the island of Kataia, which forms the boundary between Karmania and Persis. The length of the former coast is rather more than three hundred miles: the time occupied by Nearchus in this part of his voyage was about twelve days. He arrived at Badis, the first station in Karmania, on the 7th of December; at Anamis on the 10th; here he remained three days. His journey to the camp, stay there, return, and preparations for again sailing, may have occupied fifteen days. Three hundred miles in twelve days is at the rate of twenty-five miles a day.

Hitherto the voyage of Nearchus has afforded no information respecting the commerce of the ancients. The coasts along which he sailed were either barren and thinly inhabited by a miserable and ignorant people, or if more fertile and better cultivated, Nearchus' attention and interest were too keenly occupied about the safety of himself and his companions, to gather much information of a commercial nature. The remainder of his voyage, however, affords a few notices on this subject; and to these we shall attend.

In the island of Schitwar, on the eastern side of the Gulf of Persia, Nearchus found the inhabitants engaged in a pearl fishery: at present pearls are not taken on this side of the Gulf. At the Rohilla point a dead whale attracted their attention; it is represented as fifty cubits long, with a hide a cubit in thickness, beset with shell-fish, probably barnacles or limpets, and sea-weeds, and attended by dolphins, larger than Nearchus had been accustomed to see in the Mediterranean Sea. Their arrival at the Briganza river affords Dr. Vincent an opportunity of conjecturing the probable draught of a Grecian vessel of fifty oars. At ebb-tide, Arrian informs us, the vessels were left dry; whereas at high tide they were able to surmount the breakers and shoals. Modern travellers state that the flood-tide rises in the upper part of the Gulf of Persia, nine or ten feet: hence it may be conjectured that the largest vessel in the fleet drew from six to eight feet water. The next day's sail brought them from the Briganza to the river Arosis, the boundary river between Persis and Susiana, the largest of the rivers which Nearchus had met with in the Gulf of Persia. The province of Persis is described by Nearchus as naturally divided into three parts. "That division which lies along the side of the Gulf is sandy, parched, and sterile, bearing little else but palm-trees." To the north and north-east, across the range of mountains, the country improves considerably in soil and climate; the herbage is abundant and nutritious; the meadows well watered; and the vine and every kind of fruit, except the olive, flourishes. This part of the province is adorned by the parks and gardens of the kings and nobles; the rivers flow from lakes of pure water, abounding in water-fowl of all descriptions; horses and cattle feed on the rich pastures, while in the woods there is abundance of animals for the chace. To this the third division of Persis forms a striking contrast. This lies farther north, a mountainous district, wild and rugged, inhabited by barbarous tribes: the climate is so cold, that the tops of the mountains are constantly covered with snow.

The coast of Susiana, along which Nearchus was now about to sail, he represents as difficult and dangerous, from the number of shoals with which it was lined. As he was informed that it would not be easy to procure water while he was crossing the mouths of the streams which divide the Delta, he took in a supply for five days before he left the Arosis. On account of the shoals which stretch a considerable way out to sea, they could not approach the coast, and were consequently obliged to anchor at night, and sleep on board. In order to pass this dangerous coast with the least risk, they formed a line by single ships, each following in order, through a channel marked by stakes; in the same manner, Arrian remarks, as the passage between Leukas and Akarnania in Greece, except that at Leukas there is a firm sand, so that a ship takes no damage, if she runs ashore: whereas in this passage there was deep mud on both sides, in which a vessel grounding stuck fast; and if her crew endeavoured to get her off by going overboard, they sunk above the middle in the mud. The extent of this difficult passage was thirty-seven miles, at the end of which Nearchus came to an anchor at a distance from the coast. Their course next day was in deep water, which continued till they arrived, after sailing a day and a half, at a village at the mouth of the Euphrates: at this village there was a mart for the importation of the incenses of Arabia. Here Nearchus learnt that Alexander was marching to Susa; this intelligence determined him to return back, to sail up the Pasi-Tigris, and join him near that city. At Aginis he entered the Pasi-Tigris, but he proceeded only about nine miles to a village which he describes as populous and flourishing; here he determined to wait, till he received further information respecting the exact route of the army. He soon learnt that Alexander with his troops was at a bridge which he had constructed over the Pasi-Tigris, at the distance of about one hundred and twenty miles: at this place Nearchus joined him. Alexander embraced Nearchus with the warmth of a friend; and his reception from all ranks was equally gratifying and honourable. Whenever he appeared in the camp, he was saluted with acclamations: sacrifices, games, and every other kind of festivity celebrated the success of his enterprize. Nearly five months had been occupied in performing the voyage from the mouth of the Indus—a voyage which a modern vessel could perform in the course of three weeks.

Immediately after the junction of the fleet and army, Alexander crossed the Pasi-Tigris, and proceeded to Susa: here he distributed rewards and honours among his followers for their long, arduous, faithful, and triumphant services. Those officers who had served as guards of Alexander's person received crowns of gold; and the same present was made to Nearchus as admiral, and to Onesicritus as navigator of the fleet.

We have already mentioned that Alexander projected the circumnavigation of Arabia to the Red Sea, in order to complete the communication between India and Egypt, and through Egypt with Europe. Nearchus was selected for this enterprize; its execution, however, was prevented by the death of Alexander. That he was extremely anxious for its completion, is evident from the personal trouble he took in the preparations for it, and in the necessary preliminary measures. In order that he might himself take a view of the Gulf of Persia, he embarked on board a division of his fleet, and sailed down the same stream which Nearchus had sailed up. At the head of the Delta, the vessels which had suffered most in Nearchus' voyages were directed to proceed with the troops they had on board, through a canal which runs into the Tigris, Alexander himself proceeding with the lightest and best sailing vessels through the Delta to the sea.

Soon after his return to Opis, where the mutiny of his troops took place, Alexander gave another proof of his attention to maritime affairs; for he despatched Heraclides into Hyrcania, with orders to cut timber and prepare a fleet for the purpose of exploring the Caspian Sea—an attempt which, like that of the projected voyage of Nearchus up the Arabian Gulf, was prevented by Alexander's death. In the mean time Nearchus had been collecting the vessels that were destined for his expedition; they were assembled at Babylon: to this city also were brought from Phoenicia forty-seven vessels which had been taken to pieces, and so conveyed over land to Thapsacus. Two of these were of five banks, three of four, twelve of three, and thirty rowed with fifteen oars on a side. Others likewise were ordered to be built on the spot of cypress, the only wood which Babyloni afforded; while mariners were collected from Phoenicia, and a dock was directed to be cut capable of containing one thousand vessels, with buildings and arsenals in proportion to the establishment. To accomplish this extensive design, Alexander had sent one of his officers to Phoenicia with 500 talents (about 106,830 .) to buy slaves fit for the oar, and hire mariners. These preparations were so extensive, that it seems highly probable that Alexander meant to conquer Arabia, as well as explore the navigation of the Arabian Gulf; and indeed his plan and policy always were to unite conquest with discovery. As soon as he had put these preparations in a proper train, he again embarked, and sailed down the Euphrates as far as Pallacopas. The immediate object of this voyage is not exactly known. As the Euphrates flows over the adjacent country at certain seasons, the Persian monarchs had cut a canal at Pallacopas, which diverted its superfluous waters into a lake, where they were employed to flood the land. This and similar canals had been long neglected; but as Alexander seems to have fixed on Babylon as the future capital of his empire, it was necessary to restore the canals to their original utility, in order that the ground on both sides of the Euphrates might be drained or flooded at the proper season. This may have been the only object of Alexander's voyage, or it may have been connected with the projected voyage of Nearchus. It is certain, however, that by his directions the principal canal was much improved; indeed it was in reality cut in a more convenient and suitable place; for the soil where it had been originally cut was soft and spongy, so that much labour and time were required to restore the waters to their course, and secure its mouth in a safe and firm manner. A little lower down, the soil was much more suitable, being strong and rocky; here then Alexander ordered the opening of the canal to be made: he afterwards entered it with his fleet, and surveyed the whole extent of the lake with which it communicated. On the Arabian side of the Gulf, he ordered a city to be built: immediately afterwards he returned to Babylon, where he died.

In the mean time, and while Nearchus was at Babylon, three vessels were sent down the Arabian side of the Gulf, to collect such information as might be useful to him in his projected voyage. One was commanded by Archias, who proceeded as far as Tylos, or Bahrein, the centre of the modern pearl fishery. A short distance from the mouth of the Euphrates, Archias discovered two islands; on one of which a breed of goats and sheep was preserved, which were never killed, except for the purpose of sacrifice. The second vessel sailed a little way round the coast of Arabia. The third, which was commanded by Hiero of Soli, went much farther than either of the other two, for it doubled Cape Mussendoon, sailed down the coast below Moscat, and came in sight of Cape Ras-el-hed: this cape he was afraid to double. On his return he reported that Arabia was much more extensive than had been imagined. None of these vessels proceeded so far as to be of much service to Nearchus, or to carry into effect the grand object of Alexander: for his instructions to Hiero in particular were, to circumnavigate Arabia; to go up the Red Sea; and reach the Bay of Hieropolis, on the coast of Egypt. All these vessels were small, having only fifty oars, and therefore not well calculated for such a long and hazardous navigation.

At the time when Alexander was seized with the illness which occasioned his death, Nearchus was ready to sail, and he himself, with the army, was to accompany him as far as was practicable, in the same manner as he had done from the Indus to the Tigris: two days before the fever commenced, he gave a grand entertainment to Nearchus and his officers.

Only a very few circumstances regarding Nearchus are known after the death of Alexander: he was made governor of Lycia and Pamphylia, and seems to have attached himself to the fortunes of Antigonus. Along with him, he crossed the mountains of Loristan, when he marched out of Susiana, after his combat with Eumenes. In this retreat he commanded the light-armed troops, and was ordered in advance, to drive the Cosseams from their passes in the mountains. When Antigonus deemed it necessary to march into Lesser Asia, to oppose the progress of Cassander, he left his son Demetrius, with part of his army, in Syria; and as that prince was not above 22 years old, he appointed him several advisers, of whom Nearchus was one. It is by no means improbable that the instructions or the advice of Nearchus may have induced Demetrius to survey with great care the lake of Asphaltes, and to form a computation of the profit of the bitumen which it afforded, and of the balm which grew in the adjacent country, and may have contributed to his love for and skill in ship-building; for after he was declared king of Macedonia, he built a fleet of five hundred gallies, several of which had fourteen, fifteen, and sixteen benches of oars. We are informed that they were all built by the particular contrivance of Demetrius himself, and that the ablest artizans, without his directions, were unable to construct such vessels, which united the pomp and splendour of royal ships to the strength and conveniences of ordinary ships of war. The period and circumstances of the death of Nearchus are not known. Dr. Vincent supposes that he may have lost his life at the battle of Ipsus, where Antigonus fell: or, after the battle, by command of the four kings who obtained the victory. Previous to his grand expedition, it appears that he was a native of Crete, and enrolled a citizen of Amphipolis, it is supposed, at the time when Philip intended to form there a mart for his conquests in Thrace. He soon afterwards came to the court of Philip, by whom he and some others were banished, because he thought them too much attached to the interests of Alexander in the family dissensions which arose on the secession of Olympias, and some secret transactions of Alexander in regard to a marriage with a daughter of a satrap of Caria. On the death of Philip, Nearchus was recalled, and rewarded for his sufferings by the favour of his sovereign.

---

4 The object of these dykes is supposed by Niebuhr to have been very different: be observes that they were constructed for the purpose of keeping up the waters to inundate the contiguous level: he found these dykes both in the Euphrates and Tigris. And Tavernier mentions one, 120 feet high, in the fall between Mosul and the great Zab.

CHAPTER III

Historical Sketch Of The Progress Of Discovery, And Commercial Enterprize, From The Death Of Alexander The Great, To The Time Of Ptolemy The Geographer, A.D. 150.—With A Digression On The Inland Trade Between India And The Shores Of The Mediterranean, Through Arabia, From The Earliest Ages.

For several centuries after the death of Alexander, the impulse and direction of discovery and commercial enterprize continued towards the countries of the East. Of his successors, Seleucus Nicanor and some of the Ptolemies of Egypt prosecuted his plans of commerce with this part of the world with the most zeal and success. Seleucus, after the death of Alexander, obtained possession of those provinces of his empire which were comprized under the name of Upper Asia; he, therefore, naturally regarded the conquered districts of India as belonging to him. In order to secure these, and at the same time to derive from them all the political and commercial advantages which they were capable of bestowing, he marched into India; and it is supposed that he carried his arms into districts that had not been visited by Alexander. The route assigned to his march is obscurely given; but it seems to point out the country from the Hyphasis to the Hysudrus, from thence to Palibothra, at the junction of the Saone and the Ganges, or, perhaps, where Patna now stands. There is no good reason to believe, with some authors, that he reached the mouth of the Ganges. Seleucus was stopt in his progress by the intelligence that Antigonus was about to invade his dominions; but before he retraced his steps towards the Euphrates, he formed a treaty with the Indian king Sandracottus, who resided at Palibothra: and afterwards sent Megasthenes, who had some knowledge of the country, from having accompanied Alexander, as his ambassador to him. In this city, Megasthenes resided several years, and on his return he published an account of that part of India; fragments of this account are given by Diodorus Siculus, Strabo, and Arrian; and though it contains many false and fabulous stories, yet these are intermixed with much that is valuable and correct. He gives a faithful picture of the Indian character and manners; and his account of the geography and dimensions of India is curious and accurate. Some further insight into these countries was derived from the embassy of Daimachus, to the son and successor of Sandracottus; this terminated the connection of the Syrian monarchs with India which was probably wrested from them soon after the death of Seleucus. At the time when this monarch was assassinated, Pliny informs us, that he entertained a design of joining the Euxine and Caspian seas, by means of a canal; he was undoubtedly the most sagacious of the Syrian kings, and the only one who imitated Alexander in endeavouring to unite conquest with commerce.

But it is to the Egyptian successors of Alexander that we must look for the systematic extension of commerce; towards which they were in a manner impelled by the highly favourable situation of Alexandria. It has justly been observed by Harris, in his Collection of Voyages, that most of the cities founded by the Syrian kings existed little longer than their founders; and, perhaps, with the exception of Antioch, on the Orontes, and Seleucia, on the Tigris, none of them, from the situation in which they were built, and the countries by which they were surrounded, could under any circumstances be of long duration. With respect to the cities founded by Alexander it was quite otherwise. The Alexandria of Paropamisus may still be traced in Candahar; and the Alexandria on the Iaxartes, in Cogend: and the Alexandria of Egypt, after surviving the revolutions of empires for eighteen ages, perished at last, (as a commercial city,) only in consequence of a discovery which changed the whole system of commerce through the world.

On the destruction of Tyre, Alexander sought for a situation on which he might build a city that would rival it in the extent of its commerce; and he quickly perceived the advantages that would be derived from the seat of commerce being established near one of the branches of the Nile. By means of this river his projected city would command at once the commerce of the Red Sea and the Mediterranean. It was, however, necessary to select a spot near the mouths of the Nile, which would secure these advantages in the highest degree, and which would at the same time be of the highest importance in a military point of view, and afford a harbour constantly accessible. The site of Alexandria combined all these advantages: on three sides it has the sea, or the lake Mareotis, which, according to Strabo, was nearly 300 stadia long, and 150 broad; the country adjoining this lake was fertile, and by means of it, and natural or artificial channels, there was a communication with the Delta and Upper Egypt. Between this lake and the Canopic branch of the Nile, Alexander built his city: to less sagacious minds this site would have appeared improper and injudicious in some respects; for the sea-coast from Pelusium to Canopus is low land, not visible at a distance; the navigation along this coast, and the approach to it, is dangerous, and the entrance into the mouths of the Nile, at some seasons, is extremely hazardous. But these disadvantages the genius of Alexander turned to the benefit of his city, by the erection of the Pharos, and the plan of a double harbour, which was afterwards completed by the Ptolemies; for he thus united in a single spot the means of defence and facility of access.

Denocrates, a Macedonian architect, who proposed to Alexander to cut Mount Athos in the form of a statue holding a city in one hand, and in the other a bason, into which all the waters of the mountain should empty themselves, was employed by that monarch to build and beautify Alexandria. Its site was on a deep and secure bay, formed by the shore on the one side, and the island of Pharos on the other; in this bay numerous fleets might lie in perfect safety, protected from the winds and waves. The form in which the city was built was that of a Macedonian chlamys, or cloak; the two ports, one of which only was built by Alexander, though both (as has been already observed) were projected by him, were formed and divided from each other by a moat a mile long, which stretched from the isle of Pharos to the continent: that harbour which lay to the north was called the Great Harbour, and the other, to the west, was called Eunostus, or the Safe Return. In order to secure the vessels from the storms of the Mediterranean, even more effectually than they could be by the natural advantages of these harbours, the piers on each side were bent like a bar, so that only a small space was left for the entrance of vessels.

The successors of Alexander in the Egyptian empire followed his example, in nourishing commerce and improving Alexandria. Ptolemy, the son of Lagus, as soon as he took possession of Egypt, established the seat of government there, and succeeded, partly by harsh and despotic measures, and partly by offering great advantages, and by his just and humane character, to draw thither a great number of inhabitants. He began, and his son completed, the famous watch-tower in the island of Pharos; the causeway which united it to the main land, already mentioned, was built by Dexiphanes. Sostratus, the son of this architect, was employed to erect the watch-tower: the design of this tower was to direct the vessels which entered the harbour, and it was justly reckoned one of the wonders of the world. It was a large and square structure of white marble, on the top of which fires were constantly kept burning for the direction of sailors. The building of this tower cost 800 talents, which, if they were Attic talents, were equivalent to 165,000 . sterling, but if they were Alexandrian, to double that sum. This stupendous and most useful undertaking was completed in the fortieth year of the reign of Ptolemy, the son of Lagus, and in first year of the reign of Ptolemy Philadelphus; and at the same time that Sostratus finished it, his father, Dexiphanes, finished the mole, which united the island of Pharos to the continent. The inscription on the tower was, "King Ptolemy to the Gods, the saviours, for the benefit of sailors;" but Sostratus put this inscription on the mortar, while underneath he cut, in the solid marble, the following inscription, "Sostratus the Cnidian, son of Dexiphanes, to the Gods, the saviours, for the benefit of sailors." In process of time the mortar wore off, the first inscription disappeared along with it, and the second inscription became visible.

The erection of the tower of Pharos was by no means the only service the first Ptolemy did to commerce; throughout all his reign he manifested great attention to it and maritime affairs, as well as to those sciences by which they might be improved and advanced. As soon as he had made himself master of Palestine, Syria, and Phoenicia, he turned his thoughts to the conquest of Cyprus: this island abounded in wood, of which Egypt was almost destitute; and on this account, as well as on account of its situation, in the bosom, as it were, of the Levant, it was of the utmost importance to a maritime power. He succeeded in obtaining possession of this valuable island, and thus improved and enlarged the commercial advantages of Egypt. His next step, with this view, was to invite the sailors of Phoenicia to his new capital. His increasing power, especially at sea, roused the envy of Antigonus, who, by extraordinary exertions, in the course of twelve months built and equipped a fleet, which was able to cope with the naval power of Ptolemy. It is foreign to our purpose to notice the wars between them, except in so far as they are connected with the commercial history of Alexandria. This city was benefited by these wars, for Antigonus, in his progress, had driven many of the inhabitants of Syria, Palestine, and Phoenicia from their native lands: to these Ptolemy gave great encouragement, and extraordinary privileges and immunities, which induced them to settle in Alexandria, where they followed their mercantile or commercial pursuits. The report of these advantages granted to foreigners, led Jews, Greeks and Macedonians to flock to Egypt, by which means the population and wealth of that country, and particularly of its capital, were greatly augmented.

The foundation of the museum and library of Alexandria, both of which contributed so essentially to science and to the establishment of the Alexandrian school of philosophy, which, as we shall afterwards perceive, produced men that greatly advanced geographical knowledge, is another proof of the wise and comprehensive character of Ptolemy's mind.

But Ptolemy rather prepared the way for the advancement of commerce and maritime discovery, than contributed directly to them himself: fortunately, his son, Ptolemy Philadelphus, was a worthy successor, and emulous of treading in his father's steps. About the beginning of his reign, Tyre, the ancient station of the trade with India, again reared its head as a commercial city, and engaged extensively and successfully in this lucrative traffic. It became necessary, therefore, in order to draw it from Tyre and to secure its centering in Alexandria, to extend the facilities and advantages of this city for this traffic. With this view, Ptolemy sent travellers to penetrate into the interior of his dominions, bordering on the Red Sea, by land, while his fleet was exploring the coast: he began to make a canal, 100 cubits broad and 30 deep, between Arsinoe on the Red Sea, and the eastern branch of the Nile, in order to complete a water-communication between India and Alexandria. This canal, however, was never completed; probably on account of the tedious and difficult navigation towards the northern extremity of the Red Sea. He therefore altered his plan, and instead of Arsinoe fixed on Myos Hormos, as the port from which the navigation to India should commence. The same reason which induced him to form this port; led him afterwards to the establishment of Berenice; he was farther led to this, as Berenice was lower down in the Red Sea, and consequently ships sailing from it reached the ocean sooner and with less difficulty. It appears, however, that till the Romans conquered Egypt, the greatest portion of the trade between Alexandria and [Egypt-]India] was carried on through Myos Hormos. The route in the time of Ptolemy and his successors was as follows: vessels passed up the Canopic branch of the Nile to Memphis, and thence to Coptus; from Coptus the goods were transported in caravans to Myos Hormos: from this port the vessels sailed for Africa, or Arabia in the month of September, and for India in July. As the country over which the caravans travelled was the desart of Thebais, which is almost destitute of water, Ptolemy ordered springs to be searched for, wells to be dug, and caravanseras to be erected.

In order to protect his merchant ships in the Mediterranean and the Red Sea, he fitted out two great fleets, one of which he constantly kept in each sea. That in the Mediterranean was very numerous, and had several ships of an extraordinary size: two of them in particular had 30 oars on a side, one 20, four 14, two 12, fourteen 11, thirty 9, &c., besides a great number of vessels of four oars and three oars on a side. With these fleets he protected the commerce of his subjects, and kept in subjection most of the maritime provinces of Asia Minor; viz. Cilicia, Pamphylia, Lycia and Caria. The names of some of the most celebrated geographers who were patronized by this monarch, have been handed down to us: Pliny mentions Dalion, Bion, Boselis, and Aristocreon, as having visited Ethiopia, and contributed to the geographical knowledge of that country; and Simonides as having resided five years at Meroe. Timosthenes lived in this reign: he published a description of the known sea-ports, and a work on the measure of the earth. He sailed down the coast of Africa, probably as far as Madagascar, certainly lower down than the Egyptians traded under the Ptolemies, or even under the Romans.

The reign of Ptolemy Euergetes was equally distinguished, with, those of his predecessors, by attention to commerce, and a desire to extend it. As the navigation of the Red Sea had now become a source of great wealth to his subjects, he deemed it necessary to free it as much as possible from the pirates that infested it's coasts; for this purpose, as well as to preserve a communication between Egypt and the countries which extended to its mouth, he established governors from the isthmus of Suez, along the Arabian and African coasts, as far as the straits of Babelmandeb; and planted colonies of Greeks and Egyptians to carry on the commerce, and protect the interests of his subjects. But the most extraordinary instance of his enterprising spirit is to be found in his conquest (evidently for the purpose of facilitating and securing the commerce of the Red Sea) of part of Abyssinia. The proof of this, indeed, rests entirely on an inscription found at Aduli, which there can be no doubt is the harbour and bay of Masuah; the only proper entrance, according to Bruce, into Abyssinia. The inscription to which we have alluded was extant in the time of Cosmas (A.D. 545), by whom it was seen. From it, Ptolemy appears to have passed to the Tacazze, which he calls the Nile, and to have penetrated into Gojam, in which province the fountains of the Nile are found. He made roads, opened a communication between this country and Egypt, and during this expedition obliged the Arabians to pay tribute, and to maintain the roads free from robbers and the sea from pirates; subduing the whole coast from [Leucke-]Leuke] Come to Sabea. The inscription adds: "In the accomplishment of this business I had no example to follow, either of the ancient kings of Egypt, or of my own family; but was the first to conceive the design, and to carry it into execution. Thus, having reduced the whole world to peace under my own authority, I came down to Aduli, and sacrificed to Jupiter, to Mars, and to Neptune, imploring his protection for all who navigate these seas."

Ptolemy Euergetes was particularly attentive to the interests of the library at Alexandria. The first librarian appointed by Ptolemy the successor of Alexander, was Zenodotus; on his death, Ptolemy Euergetes invited from Athens Eratosthenes, a citizen of Cyrene, and entrusted to him the care of the library: it has been supposed that he was the second of that name, or of an inferior rank in learning and science, because he is sometimes called Beta; but by this appellation nothing else was meant, but that he was the second librarian of the royal library at Alexandria. He died at the age of 81, A.C. 194. He has been called a second

Plato, the cosmographer and the geometer of the world: he is rather an astronomer and mathematician than a geographer, though geography is indebted to him for some improvements in its details, and more especially for helping to raise it to the accuracy and dignity of a science. By means of instruments, which Ptolemy erected in the museum at Alexandria, he ascertained the obliquity of the ecliptic to be 23° 51' 20". He is, however, principally celebrated as the first astronomer who measured a degree of a great circle, and thus approximated towards the real diameter of the earth.

The importance of this discovery will justify us in entering on some details respecting the means which this philosopher employed, and the result which he obtained.

It is uncertain whether the well at Syene, in Upper Egypt, which he used for this purpose, was dug by his directions, or existed previously. Pliny seems to be of the former opinion; but there is reason to believe that it had a much higher antiquity. The following observations on its structure by Dr. Horsley, Bishop of Rochester, are ingenious and important. "The well, besides that it was sunk perpendicularly, with the greatest accuracy, was, I suppose, in shape an exact cylinder. Its breadth must have been moderate, so that a person, standing upon the brink, might safely stoop enough over it to bring his eye into the axis of the cylinder, where it would be perpendicularly over the centre of the circular surface of the water. The water must have stood at a moderate, height below the mouth of the well, far enough below the mouth to be sheltered from the action of the wind, that its surface might be perfectly smooth and motionless; and not so low, but that the whole of its circular surface might be distinctly seen by the observer on the brink. A well formed in this manner would afford, as I apprehend, the most certain observation of the sun's appulse to the zenith, that could be made with the naked eye; for when the sun's centre was upon the zenith, his disc would be seen by reflection on the water, in the very middle of the well,—that is, as a circle perfectly concentric with the circle of the water; and, I believe, there is nothing of which the naked eye can judge with so much precision as the concentricity of two circles, provided the circles be neither very nearly equal, nor the inner circle very small in proportion to the outer."

Eratosthenes observed, that at the time of the summer solstice this well was completely illuminated by the sun, and hence he inferred that the sun was, at that time, in the zenith of this place. His next object was to ascertain the altitude of the sun, at the same solstice, and on the very same day, at Alexandria. This he effected by a very simple contrivance: he employed a concave hemisphere, with a vertical style, equal to the radius of concavity; and by means of this he ascertained that the arch, intercepted between the bottom of the style and the extreme point of its shadow, was 7° 12'. This, of course, indicated the distance of the sun from the zenith of Alexandria. But 7° 12' is equal to the fiftieth part of a great circle; and this, therefore, was the measure of the celestial arc contained between the zeniths of Syene and Alexandria. The measured distance between these cities being 5000 stadia, it followed, that 5000 X 50 = 250,000, was, according to the observations of Eratosthenes, the extent of the whole circumference of the earth.

If we knew exactly the length of the stadium of the ancients, or, to speak more accurately, what stadium is referred to in the accounts which have been transmitted to us of the result of the operations of Eratosthenes, (for the ancients employed different stadia,) we should be able precisely to ascertain the circumference which this philosopher ascribed to the earth, and also, whether a nearer approximation to the truth was made by any subsequent or prior ancient philosopher. The circumference of the earth was conjectured, or ascertained, by Aristotle, Cleomedes, Posidonius, and Ptolemy respectively, to be 400, 300, 240, and 180 thousand stadia. It is immediately apparent that these various measures have some relation to each other, and probably express the same extent; measured in different stadia; and this probability is greatly increased by comparing the real distances of several places with the ancient itinerary distances.

The observation of Eratosthenes respecting the obliquity of the ecliptic (though undoubtedly not so immediately or essentially connected with our subject as his observation of the circumference of the earth) is too important to be passed over entirely without notice. He found the distance between the tropics less than 53° 6', and greater than 52° 96', which gives a mean of 23° 51' for the obliquity of the ecliptic. The observations of Hipparchus (who flourished at Alexandria about 140 years before Christ, and whom we shall have occasion to mention more particularly afterwards) coincided with those of Eratosthenes. Plutarch, however, who died A.D. 119, informs us, that, in his time, the gnomons at Syene were no longer shadowless on the day of the summer solstice. As the interval between Eratosthenes and Plutarch was only about 512 years, Bishop Morsley has very naturally expressed his doubts of the accuracy of Plutarch's assertion. He says, that the change in the obliquity of the ecliptic in this interval was only 2' 36". "A gnomon, therefore, at Syene, of the length of twelve inches, if it cast no shadow on the day of the solstice in the time of Eratosthenes, should have cast a shadow in the time of Plutarch of the length only of 9/1000th, or not quite 1/100th part of an inch. The shadow of a perpendicular column of the height of 100 feet would have been 9/10ths of an inch." As, however, the ancients do not appear to have constructed gnomons of such a size, and as gnomons of inferior size would have given a shadow scarcely perceptible, it is probable that Plutarch is mistaken in his assertion; or, at any rate, that the very small variation which did take place between his time and that of Eratosthenes (if it were observed at all) was ascertained by means of the well itself, which would point it out much more distinctly and accurately than any gnomon the ancients can be supposed to have used.

We are also indebted to Eratosthenes for the first regular parallel of latitude, and also for tracing a meridian. His parallel of latitude began at the Straits of Gibraltar, and passed eastward through Rhodes to the mountains of India; the intermediate places being carefully set down. His meridian line passed through Rhodes and Alexandria, as far as Syene and Meroe. Meroe, on this account, became an object of the greatest interest and importance to all the succeeding ancient geographers and astronomers, and they have taken the utmost labour and care to ascertain its latitude accurately. Strabo informs us, that Eratosthenes constructed a map of the world; but he does not give such particulars as will enable us to trace the extent of his geographical knowledge. At the extremity of the world to the east, bounded by the ocean, Thina was placed in the map of Eratosthenes, in the parallel of Rhodes; a parallel which passes through the empire of China, within the Great Wall. Eratosthenes, according to Strabo, (to whom we are indebted for nearly all we know respecting this philosopher,) asserts that Thina had been, previously to the construction of his map, incorrectly placed in the more ancient maps. His information respecting Meroe or Abyssinia, is most probably derived from Dalion, Aristocreon, and Bion, who had been sent by Ptolemy Philadelphus and his successors into that country, or from Timosthenes, who sailed down the coast of Africa as low as Cerne. His information on the subject of India (which, however, as far as regards oriental commerce, is very confused) must have been derived from the Macedonians. There is little doubt that the library of Alexandria afforded him access to all the knowledge which then existed respecting the various countries of the globe; but the turn of his mind led him rather to astronomical than geographical studies; or rather, perhaps, he directed his labours and his talents to the discovery of the figure and circumference of the earth, thinking, that till this was effected, the delineation of the habitable world, and the relative position of different countries, must be very inaccurate as well as incomplete. This opinion regarding Eratosthenes, that he was more of a geometrician than a geographer, seems to be confirmed by the testimony of Marcian of Heraclia, who informs us, that Eratosthenes took the whole work of Timosthenes, preface and all, as it stood, and in the very same words. If this account be accurate, it is probable that Eratosthenes' knowledge of Thina, and his being able to correct the erroneous position of this country in more ancient maps, was derived from Timosthenes, who had commanded the fleet of Ptolemy Philadelphus on the Indian Ocean.

If we reflect on the rude and imperfect state of science at this period, the paucity and inadequacy of the instruments by means of which it might be improved, and the superstitions and prejudices which opposed the removal of error or the establishment of truth, we shall not be disposed to question the justice of the panegyric pronounced by Pliny on Eratosthenes. This author, after detailing all that was then known on the subject of the circumference of the earth, and on the distances which had been ascertained by actual admeasurement, or approximated by analogy or probable conjecture, between the most remarkable places on its surface, adds, that Eratosthenes, whose acuteness and application had advanced him far in every branch of knowledge, but who had outstripped all his predecessors or contemporaries in that particular branch which was connected with the admeasurement of the earth, had fixed its circumference at 250,000 stadia; a bold and almost presumptuous enterprize, (,) but which had been conducted with so much judgment, and on such sound principles, that it commanded and deserved our credit. Hipparchus, who was distinguished for his correctness and diligence in every part of geometrical and astronomical science, and who had specially exerted those qualities in his endeavours to correct the errors of Eratosthenes, had been able to add only the comparatively small extent of 25,000 stadia to the computation of Eratosthenes.— lib. ii. c. 108.

Eratosthenes seems, from the nature of his studies, not to have availed himself so much as he might have done of the treasures contained in the Alexandrian library under his care, to correct or extend the geographical knowledge of his contemporaries. The same observation will not apply to Agatharcides, who was president of the library after Eratosthenes. The exact time at which he flourished is not known: according to Blair, he was contemporary with Eratosthenes, though younger than him, and flourished 177 A.C., Eratosthenes having died at the age of eighty-one, in the year 194 A.C. Dodwell, however, fixes him at a later period; viz. 104 A.C.; but this date must be erroneous, because Artemidorus of Ephesus, who evidently copies Agatharcides, undoubtedly lived 104 A.C. Agatharcide's was born at Cnidus in Caria: no particulars are known respecting him, except that he was president of the Alexandrian library, in the reign of Ptolemy Philometor, if he flourished 177 A.C.; and in the reign of Ptolemy Lathyrus, if, according to Dodwell, he did not flourish till 104 A.C.

The only work of his which is preserved, is a Treatise on the Erythraean Sea; and this we possess only in the Bibliotheca of Photius, and incorporated in the history of Diodorus Siculus. The authority of Agatharcides was very high among the ancients. Strabo, Pliny, and Diodorus, always mention him with the utmost respect, and place implicit confidence in his details. Diodorus expressly states that Agatharcides and Artemidorus (who, as we have already mentioned, was merely his copyist) are the only authors who have written truth concerning Egypt and Ethiopia; and Strabo follows him in all that relates to the latter country, the countries lying to the south of Egypt, and the western coast of Arabia. In fact, for nearly 200 years, the ancient historians and geographers drew all the information they possessed respecting the portions of the world embraced in the work of Agatharcides from that work. It has been well observed, "that when Pliny speaks of the discoveries on the coast of Malabar in his own age, and adds, that the names he mentions are new, and not to be found in previous writers, we ought to consider him as speaking of all those who had followed the authority of the Macedonians, or the school of Alexandria; of which, in this branch of science, Eratosthenes and Agatharcides were the leaders." From the circumstance that Strabo appeals very frequently to the authority of Eratosthenes, in conjunction with that of Agatharcides, it has been conjectured, that the work of the latter contains all that the former knew, with the addition of his own information; and this conjecture is highly probable, considering that Agatharcides had access to the sources whence Eratosthenes drew his information; to the works of Eratosthenes themselves, which of course would be deposited in the Alexandrian library; and to all the additional works which had enriched the library from the time of Eratosthenes, as well as the additional information which the extensive commerce of Alexandria would supply.

The work of Agatharcides, therefore, having been in such estimation by the ancient historians and geographers, and the only source from which, during 200 years, they drew their information, and having been compiled by a person, who, it is probable, had better and fuller means of rendering it accurate and complete than any of his contemporaries enjoyed; it will be proper to give a pretty full abstract of the most interesting and important part of its contents.

The veracity of this author was questioned by Plutarch, from his narrating a circumstance, which, to us of the present day, is a strong confirmation of the truth and accuracy of his information. Agatharcides takes notice of the worm which is formed in the legs, and which insinuates itself there in such a manner, that it is necessary to wind it out with the utmost caution. Plutarch ridicules and rejects this story, and says it never has happened, and never will. But that such a worm exists, and that when it insinuates itself into the leg it must be drawn out with the utmost caution, lest the smallest portion of it remain, and thus produce disease, is directly and fully attested by all the travellers, and particularly by Bruce, who carried with him to the grave the marks and effects of the attack of this species of worm.

But the most curious and important portion of the work of Agatharcides on the Red Sea, relates to Abyssinia; for in this work we meet with the first genuine characteristics of this nation. He specifies particularly the gold mines wrought by the kings of Egypt on the coast of the Red Sea;—the process which they followed to procure and separate this metal;—the sufferings which the miners underwent in their operations are painted in very strong language: "The multitude of bones still found in these excavations, he says, is incredible, of wretches crushed by the falling-in of the earth, as must naturally happen in a loose and crumbling soil." He adds a circumstance, to which there are many parallel in our own country, in those mines which are supposed to have been wrought by the Romans; viz. the tools of copper found in these gold mines, supposed to have been used by the native Egyptians, prior to the conquest of Egypt by the Persians. The next particular mentioned by Agatharcides, respecting the Abyssinian coast of the Red Sea, is very conclusive, with respect to his accuracy and credibility. In Meroe, or Abyssinia, he says, they hunt elephants and hamstring them, and afterwards cut the flesh out of the animal alive: he adds, that the inhabitants are so extremely fond of the flesh of the elephant, thus procured, that when Ptolemy would have paid any price to purchase these animals alive, as he wanted them for his army, the Abyssinian hunters refused his offer, declaring that not all the wealth of Egypt would tempt them to forego their favourite and delicious repast. It is a remarkable fact, that the credit of Bruce on this topic should thus be confirmed by a writer who lived nearly 2000 years before him, of whose writings we possess only a very short treatise, and of whose life we know scarcely a single particular. It may be added, that Strabo, in a passage, in which he is apparently copying Agatharcides, mentions [Greek: Kreophagoi] and as he would scarcely particularize the fact of a native eating the flesh of animals cooked, it is to be presumed, he means raw flesh. In the same place he mentions the .

Every reader of Brace's Travels in Abyssinia must remember the fly, called Tsalpsalza, an insect more formidable than the strongest or most savage wild beasts: "As soon as the buzzing of this insect is heard, the utmost alarm and trepidation prevails; the cattle forsake their food and run wildly about the plain, till at length they fall down, worn out with terror, hunger and fatigue; even the camel, elephant and rhinoceros, are not safe from the attacks of this formidable insect." This fly is described by Agatharcides in the same manner as by Bruce. The ensete tree of Bruce, the leaves of which resemble the banana, with fruit like figs, but not eatable, with a trunk esculent till it reaches its perfect growth and is full of leaves, resembles in some of its particulars a tree described by Agatharcides. This author also describes the locusts, as generally used for food; the troglodytes; the rhinoceros; the cameleopard; what he calls sphinxes, but which are represented as tame, and are supposed to be apes, distinguished from the common ape in the face being smooth and without hair. He also mentions an animal he calls crocetta, which is described as being between a wolf and a dog, and as imitating the human voice; these particulars seem to point it out as the hyena, though some suppose it to be the jackall. It deserves to be remarked, that the animals enumerated by Agatharcides as natives of Abyssinia, are all named in the same manner, as well as depicted on the celebrated Palestrine Mosaic.

In his description of the coast of the Red Sea he commences with Arsinoe, and goes down the western side as far as Ptolemais Theron; a place so called, because elephants were there hunted and taken, and are still, according to Bruce. Agatharcides adds, that the usual navigation was to this place for elephants. He notices Myos Hormos, but not Berenice; he has even mentioned the islands at the straits of Babelmandeb, and the prodigies which in his time, and much later, were supposed to lie beyond them. There is, however, one part of his work, in which he seems to indicate the curvature of the African coast to the east beyond the straits; but it is doubtful whether in this place he is speaking of the coast within or without the straits.

In his description of the coast between Myos Hormos and Ptolemais, he points out a bay, which, both from the identity of the name, and the circumstances respecting it which he narrates, undoubtedly is the Foul Bay of the moderns. Strabo, who, as we have already stated, borrows freely and frequently from Agatharcides, describes this bay as full of shoals and breakers, and exposed to violent winds; and he adds, that Berenice lies at the bottom of it. The accuracy of our author, even when he is opposed by the testimony of Bruce, is fully proved in what he relates of the coast below Foul Bay: after mentioning two mountains, which he calls the Bulls, he particularly adverts to the dangerous shoals which often proved fatal to the elephant ships on their passage to and from Ptolemais. Bruce says no such shoals exist; but, as is justly observed by Dr. Vincent; the correctness of the ancients respecting them, especially Eratosthenes, Agatharcides and Artemidorus, is fully borne out by the danger and loss to which many English ships have been exposed by reason of these very shoals.

The description of Agatharcides of this side of the coast of the Red Sea, reaches no lower down than Ptolemais; this circumstance is remarkable, since we have seen that, from the inscription found at Aduli there can be no doubt that Ptolemy Euergetes had conquered Abyssinia, and established a commerce considerably lower down than Ptolemais Theron. As, however, we have not the original, and perhaps not the entire work of Agatharcides, we cannot infer any thing, either respecting his ignorance or inattention, from this omission.

Agatharcides, having thus described this coast, returns from Ptolemais to Myos Hormos, and passing the Bay of Arsinoe, crosses to Phoenicum, in the Elanitic Gulf, and describes the coast of Arabia as far as Sabea. Almost the very first particular noticed by him in this part of his work, bears evidence to his accuracy as a geographer. He states that, at the entrance of the Elanitic Gulph there are three islands, one of which is dedicated to Isis: he describes them as, "covering several harbours on the Arabian shore. To these islands succeeds the rocky coast of Thamudeni, where, for more than 1000 stadia, there is no harbour, no roadsted in which a vessel could anchor, no bay into which she could run for shelter, no point of land which could protect her; so that those who sail alone this part of the coast are exposed to certain destruction, if they should be overtaken by a storm." Yet these islands lying in such a conspicuous situation, and of such importance to the mariner, and this coast so dangerous to him, do not appear to have been noticed in any European chart or description, till, after the lapse of twenty centuries, they were restored to geography by Mr. Irwin.

As one of our principal objects is to do justice to the accuracy of the ancient geographers, by pointing out instances of the extreme care which many of them took to obtain correct information we shall adduce one other proof of this accuracy and care in Agatharcides. This author particularly describes the sea as having a white appearance off the coast of Arabia; on this point he was well informed though the circumstance is treated as fabulous by the ancients, and even by some of the moderns; but more observant modern travellers confirm this phenomenon. It is well observed by Dr. Vincent, that we are every day lessening the bulk of the marvellous imputed to the ancients; and as our knowledge of the east increases, it is possible that the imputation will be altogether removed.

The account which Agatharcides gives of Sabæa is very curious and important; and, as we shall afterwards have occasion to make use of it, in endeavouring to prove that, in very early ages, the Arabians supplied the western world with the productions of the east, we shall extract here what he says of Sabæa from the translation of Dr. Vincent.

"Sabæa, (says Agatharcides,) abounds with every production to make life happy in the extreme: its very air is so perfumed with odours, that the natives are obliged to mitigate the fragrance by scents that have an opposite tendency, as if nature could not support even pleasure in the extreme. Myrrh, frankincense, balsam, cinnamon, and casia are here produced, from trees of extraordinary magnitude. The king, as he is, on the one hand, entitled to supreme honour, on the other, is obliged to submit to confinement in his palace; but the people are robust, warlike, and able mariners: they sail in very large vessels to the country where the odoriferous commodities are produced; they plant colonies there, and import from thence the larimna, an odour no where else to be found. In fact, there is no nation on the earth so wealthy as the Gerrheans and Sabeans, as being in the centre of all the commerce that passes between Asia and Europe. These are the nations which have enriched the kingdom of Ptolemy: these are the nations that furnish the most profitable agencies to the industry of the Phoenicians, and a variety of advantages which are incalculable. They possess themselves every profusion of luxury, in articles of plate and sculpture, in furniture of beds, tripods, and other household embellishments, far superior in degree to any thing that is seen in Europe: their expence of living rivals the magnificence of princes: their houses are decorated with pillars glistening with gold and silver: their doors are crowned with vases and beset with jewels: the interior of their houses corresponds with the beauty of their outward appearance, and all the riches of other countries are here exhibited in a variety of profusion. Such a nation, and so abounding in superfluity, owes its independence to its distance from Europe; for their luxurious manners would soon render them a prey to the European sovereigns, who have always troops on foot prepared for any conquest; and who, if they could find the means of invasion, would soon reduce the Sabeans to the condition of their agents and factors; whereas they are now obliged to deal with them as principals."

The importance and the bearing of these curious facts, first brought to our notice by Agatharcides, as well as the inferences which may be drawn from them regarding the mode in which the ancients obtained their commodities of India, will call our particular attention afterwards: at present we shall merely notice the characteristic and minute picture which Agatharcides has drawn of the Sabeans, and the just notions he had formed on the nature of a commerce, of which all the other writers of antiquity seemed to have been utterly ignorant.

Beyond Sabæa to the east, Agatharcides possessed no information, though, like all the ancients, he is desirous of supplying his want of it by indulging in the marvellous: it is, however, rather curious that, among other particulars, undoubtedly unfounded, such as placing the Fortunate islands off the coast beyond Sabæa, and his describing the flocks and herds as all white, and the females as polled;—he describes that whiteness of the sea, to which we have already alluded, as confirmed by modern travellers. From these unfounded particulars, our author soon emerges again into the truth; for he describes the appearance of the different constellations, and especially notices that to the south of Sabæa there is no twilight in the morning; but when he adds, that the sun, at rising, appears like a column—that it casts no shadow till it has been risen an hour, and that the evening twilight lasts three hours after it has set; it is obvious that the information of that age (of which we may justly suppose the library of Alexandria was the great depository) did not extend beyond Sabæa.

That Agatharcides had access to and made ample use of the journal of

Nearchus (of which we have given such a complete abstract), is evident from various parts of his work; but it is also evident, by comparing his description of those countries and their inhabitants, which had been visited and described by Nearchus, that he had access to other sources of intelligence, by means of which he added to the materials supplied by the latter.

It will be recollected that Nearchus describes in a particular manner, the Icthyophagi of Gadrosia: Agatharcides also describes Icthyophagi, though it is not clear whether he means to confine his description to those of Gadrosia, or to extend it to others on the coast of Arabia and Africa. The mode practised by the Icthyophagi, according to him, is exactly that which was practised by them in catching fish, according to Nearchus: he also coincides with that author in various other particulars respecting the use of the bones of whales, or other large fish, in the construction of their houses; their ignorance and barbarism, their dress and mode of life. All this he probably borrowed from Nearchus; but he adds one circumstance which indubitably proves, that the knowledge of the eastern part of the world had considerably advanced since the era of Alexander: he expressly states, that beyond the straits that separate Arabia from the opposite coast, there are an immense number of islands, scattered, very small, and scarcely raised above the surface of the ocean. If we may advert to the situation assigned to these islands, on the supposition that the straits which separate Arabia from the opposite coast, mean the entrance to the Gulph of Persia, we shall not be able to ascertain what these islands are; but if in addition to the circumstances of their being scattered, very small, and very low, we add what Agatharcides also notices, that the natives have no other means of supporting life but by the turtles which are found near them in immense numbers, and of a very large size, we shall be disposed, with Dr. Vincent, to consider these as the Maldive Islands. It may be objected to this supposition, that the Maldives are situated at a very great distance from the straits that separate Arabia from the opposite coast; but a cursory acquaintance with the geographical descriptions of the ancients will convince us, that their information respecting the situation of countries was frequently vague and erroneous, (as indeed it must have been, considering the imperfect means they possessed of measuring or even judging of distances, especially by sea) while, at the same time, their information respecting the nature of the country, the productions of its soil, and the manners, &c. of its inhabitants, was surprisingly full and accurate. In identifying places mentioned by the ancients, we should therefore be guided more by the descriptions they give, than by the locality they assign to them. Agatharcides, it is true, adds that these islands extend along the sea, which washes Gadrosia and India; but he probably had very confused notions of the extent and form of India; and, at any rate, giving the widest latitude to the term, the same sea may be said to wash Gadrosia and the Maldive Islands. If these are the islands actually meant by Agatharcides, it is the earliest notice of them extant.

Our concern with Agatharcides relates only to the geographical knowledge which his writings display; and even of that we can only select such parts as are most important, and at the same time point out and prove the advances of geographical knowledge, and of commercial enterprize; before, however, we leave him, we may add one fact, not immediately relating to our peculiar subject, which he records: after stating that the soil of Arabia was, as it were, impregnated with gold, and that lumps of pure gold were found there from the size of an olive to that of a nut, he adds, that iron was twice, and silver ten times, the value of gold. If he is accurate in the proportionate values which he respectively assigns to these metals, it proves the very great abundance of gold; since, in most of the nations of antiquity, the values of gold and silver were the reverse of what they were in Arabia, gold being ten times the value of silver. The comparative high value of iron to gold is still more extraordinary, and seems to indicate not only a great abundance of the latter metal, but also a great scarcity of the former, or a very great demand for it in consequence of the extended and improved state of those arts and manufactures in which iron is an essential requisite, and which indicate an advanced degree of knowledge and civilization. We are not aware of a similar fact, with respect to the proportionate value of iron and silver, being recorded of any other nation of antiquity. It is not to be supposed, however, that the cheapness of gold, measured by iron and silver, could long continue in Arabia, unless we believe that their intercourse with other nations was very limited; because a regular and extensive intercourse would soon assimilate, in a great degree at least, the value of gold measured by iron and silver, as it existed in Arabia, to its value, as measured by the same metals in those countries with which Arabia traded.

But to return from this slight digression;—Artemidorus has been already mentioned as a geographer subsequent to Agatharcides, who copied Agatharcides, and from whom Diodorus Siculus and Strabo in their turns copied. There were two ancient writers of this name born at Ephesus; the one to whom we have alluded, is supposed to have lived in the reign of Ptolemy Lathyrus, A.C. 169; by others he is brought down to A.C. 104. Little is known respecting him; nor does he seem to have added much to geographical science or knowledge: he is said by Pliny to have first applied the terms of length and breadth, or latitude and longitude. By comparing those parts of Diodorus Siculus and Strabo, which they avowedly copy from him, with the track of Agatharcides: in the Red Sea, we are enabled to discover only a few additions of importance to the geographical knowledge supplied by the former: Agatharcides, it will be remembered, brings his account of the African side of the Red Sea no lower down than Ptolemais: he does not even mention the expedition of Ptolemy Euergetes to Aduli; nor the passage of the straits, though Eratosthenes, as cited by Strabo, proves that it was open in his time. In the time of Artemidorus, however, the trade of Egypt on the coast of Africa had reached as low down as the Southern Horn; that this trade was still in its infancy, is apparent from a circumstance mentioned by Strabo, on the authority of Artemidorus; that at the straits the cargo was transferred from ships to boats; bastard cinnamon, perhaps casia lignea or hard cinnamon, is specified as one of the principal articles which the Egyptians obtained from the coast of Africa, when they passed the straits of Babelmandeb.

The next person belonging to the Alexandrian school, to whom the sciences on which geography rest, as well as geography itself, is greatly indebted, was Hipparchus. Scarcely any particulars are known respecting him: even the exact period in which he flourished, is not accurately fixed; some placing him 159 years, others 149, and others again bringing him down to 129 years before Christ. He was a native of Nice in Bithynia, but spent the greater part of his life at the court of one of the Ptolemies. It is supposed that he quitted his native place in consequence of some ill treatment which he had received from his fellow citizens: at least we are informed by Aurelius Victor, that the emperor Marcus Aurelius obliged the inhabitants of Nice to send yearly to Rome a certain quantity of corn, for having beaten one of their citizens, by name Hipparchus, a man of great learning and extraordinary accomplishments. They continued to pay this tribute to the time of Constantine, by whom it was remitted. As history does not inform us of any other person of note of this name, a native of Nice in Bithynia, it is highly probable that this was the Hipparchus, the astronomer and geographer. That it was not unusual for conquerors and sovereigns to reward or punish the descendants of those who had behaved well or ill to celebrated men who had flourished long previously, must be well known to those conversant with ancient history. The respect paid to the memory of Pindar, by the Spartans, and by Alexander the Great, when they conquered Thebes, is a striking instance of the truth of this observation.

Hipparchus possessed the true spirit of philosophy: having resolved to devote himself to the study of astronomy, his first general [principal-]principle] was to take nothing for granted; but setting aside all that had been taught by former astronomers, to begin anew, and examine and judge for himself: he determined not to admit any results but such as were grounded either in observations and experiments entirely new, made by himself or on a new examination of former observations, conducted with the utmost care and caution. In short, he may justly be regarded as one of the first philosophers of antiquity who had a slight glimpse of the grand maxim, which afterwards immortalized Bacon, and which has introduced modern philosophers to a knowledge of the most secret and most sublime operations of nature.

One of his first endeavours was, to verify the obliquity of the ecliptic, as settled by Eratosthenes: he next fixed, as accurately as possible, the latitude of Alexandria; but it would lead us far from the object of our work, if we were even briefly to mention his discoveries in the science of pure astronomy. We must confine ourselves to those parts of his discoveries which benefitted geography, either directly or indirectly. After having, as successfully as his means and the state of the science would permit him to do, fixed the position of the stars, he transferred the method which he had employed for this purpose to geography: he was the first who determined the situation of places on the earth, by their latitudes and longitudes, with any thing like accuracy. The latitude, indeed, of many places had been fixed before; and the means of doing it were sufficiently simple and obvious: but with respect to some general and safe mode of ascertaining the longitudes, the ancient philosophers before Hipparchus, were ignorant of it. He employed for this purpose the eclipses of the moon. After having ascertained the latitudes and longitudes of a great many places, he proposed to draw up a catalogue of terrestial latitudes and longitudes, but this he was not able to accomplish: he had set the example, however and it was followed by subsequent astronomers. He fixed on the Fortunate Islands, which are supposed to be the Canaries, for his first meridian. His principal works most probably were destroyed in the conflagration of the Alexandrian library. His catalogue of the stars is preserved in the Almagest of Ptolemy; and his commentary on Aratus and Eudoxus is still extant.

Such is a brief sketch of the advantages which geography, as founded on astronomy, derived from the labours of Hipparchus. We possess little information respecting his ideas of the form of the earth, or the relative position or extent of the different quarters and countries on the surface of the globe. He seems to have been the first who conceived the idea of a southern continent, uniting Africa and India: he had evidently some information, though very vague and erroneous, of India, beyond the Ganges. On the east coast of Africa, his knowledge did not extend beyond Cape Guardaferi. On the whole, geography is more indebted to him for his discoveries in astronomy, and, above all, for his setting the example of carefully ascertaining facts, and not indulging, so much as his predecessors had done, in conjectures and hypotheses, than for any actual discoveries or advances he made in it. The eulogium which Pliny has pronounced on him is very eloquent, and fully deserved. "Hipparchus can scarcely receive too high praise: he has proved, more satisfactorily than any other philosopher, that man is allied to heaven, and his soul derived from on high. In his time, more than one new star was discovered, or rather appeared for the first time; and this induced him to believe, that future ages might witness stars for the first time moving from the immense regions of space, within the limits of our observation. But the grandeur and boldness of Hipparchus's mind rested not here: he attempted, and in some measure succeeded in doing, what seems above human knowledge and power: he numbered the stars, laid down rules by which their rising and setting might be ascertained beforehand; and, finally, he constructed an apparatus on which the position of each star was accurately given, and a miniature picture of the heavens, with the motions of the celestial bodies, their rising and setting, increase and diminution. He thus may be said to have left the heavens as a legacy to that man, if any such were to be found, who could rival him and follow his steps."

From the time of Hipparchus to that of Ptolemy the geographer, the Alexandrian school, though rich in philosophers, who devoted their studies and labour to other branches of physical and metaphysical science, did not produce one, who improved geography, or the sciences on which it depends, with the exception of Posidonius. This philosopher, who belonged to the sect of the Stoics, was born at Apamea in Syria: he usually resided at Rhodes, and was the friend of Pompey and Cicero. The former, on his return from Syria, came thither to attend his lectures. Arriving at his house, he forbad his lictor to knock, as was usual, at the door; and paid homage to philosophy, by lowering the fasces at the abode of Posidonius. Pompey, being informed that he was at that time ill of the gout, visited him in his confinement, and expressed himself very much disappointed that he could not have the benefit of his lectures. Posidonius, thus honoured and flattered, in spite of his pain, delivered a lecture in the presence of his noble visitor; the subject of which was to prove, that nothing is good which is not honourable. Cicero informs us, that he also attended his lectures; and according to Suidas Marcellus, brought him to Rome in the year of the city 702; in this, however, Suidas is not supported by other and contemporary writers.

We are indebted to Cleomedes for most of what we know of his opinions and discoveries; with such as relate to morals or to pure astronomy, we have no concern. But he was of service also to geography. He measured an arc of the terrestrial meridian; but his operation, as far as we can judge by the details which have reached us, was far from exact, and of course his result could not be accurate; it would appear, however, that his object was rather to verify the ancient measures of the earth, particularly that of Eratosthenes, and that he found them to agree nearly with his own. He explained the ebbing and flowing of the sea, from the motion of the moon, and seems to have been the first who observed the law of this phenomenon. In order to represent the appearance of the heavens, Cicero informs us that he constructed a kind of planetarium, by means of which he exhibited the apparent motion of the sun, moon, and planets round the earth. It is on the authority of Posidonius, that Strabo relates the voyage of Eudoxus of Cyzicum from the Persian Gulf round Africa to Cadiz, which we have already mentioned.

Having thus exhibited a view of the discoveries in geography, the advances in the sciences connected with it, and the commercial enterprises of the Egyptians, while under the dominion of the Ptolemies, it will be proper, before beginning an account of the geographical knowledge and commercial enterprises of the Romans (who, by their conquest of Egypt, may be said to have absorbed all the geographical knowledge, as well as all the commerce of the world, at that period), to recapitulate the extent of the Egyptian geography and commerce, especially towards the east We shall direct our retrospect to this quarter, because the commodities of the east being most prized, it was the grand object of the sovereigns and merchants of Egypt, to extend and facilitate the intercourse with that quarter of the globe as much as possible. And we are induced to undertake the retrospect, because the exact limit of the geographical knowledge and commercial enterprise of the Ptolemies is differently fixed by different authors: some maintaining that the Egyptians had a regular and extensive trade directly with India, and of course, were well acquainted with the seas and coasts beyond the Red Sea; while other authors maintain, that they never passed the straits of Babelmandeb, and that even within the straits, their geographical knowledge and commercial enterprises were very limited.

It cannot be doubted that commerce and the spirit of discovery flourished with more vigour, and pushed themselves to a greater distance in the reigns of Ptolemy Philadelphus, and Ptolemy Euergetes, than in the reign of any of their successors. If, therefore, there are no proofs or traces of a direct and regular trade with India in their time, we may safely conclude it did not exist in Egypt, previously to the conquest of that country by the Romans.

We are well aware, that there are great authorities opposed to the opinion which we hold; but these authorities are modern; they are not, we think, supported by the ancient writers, and in opposition to them, we can place the authority of Dr. Vincent, a name of the very greatest weight in questions of this nature. The authorities we alluded to in support of the opinion, that there was a direct trade with India under the Ptolemies, are Huet, in his History of the Commerce and Navigation of the Ancients; Dr. Robertson, in his Disquisition on India, and Harris, or perhaps, more properly speaking, Dr. Campbell, in his edition of Harris's Collection of Voyages and Travels. Huet, as is justly remarked by Dr. Vincent, drops the prosecution of the question at the very point he ought to introduce it; and afterwards countenances, or seems to countenance, the opposite opinion. Dr. Robertson bestows much labour, ingenuity, and learning in support of the opinion, that under the Ptolemies, a direct trade was carried on with India; yet, after all, he concludes in this manner: "it is probable that their voyages were circumscribed within very narrow limits, and that under the Ptolemies no considerable progress was made in the discovery of India:" and when he comes to the discovery of the Monsoon by Hippalus and the consequent advantage taken of it to trade directly to India, by sailing from shore to shore, he acknowledges that all proofs of a more early existence of such a trade are wanting. Dr. Campbell virtually gives up his support of the opinion, that a direct trade was carried on under the Ptolemies, in the same manner.

We have already remarked, that the strongest spirit of enterprize that distinguished Egypt existed in the reign of Ptolemy Philadelphus and Ptolemy Euergetes; that these monarchs pushed their discoveries, and extended their commercial connections much farther than any of their predecessors; and that therefore, if a direct and regular communication between Egypt and India did not take place in their reigns, we may be assured it was unknown to the Egyptians at the period of the Roman conquest. To their reigns, then, we shall principally direct our enquiries.

That Ptolemy Philadelphus was extremely desirous to improve the navigation of the Red Sea, is evident from his having built Myos Hormos, or rather improved it, because it was more convenient than Arsinoe, on account of the difficulty of navigating the western extremity of that sea: he afterwards fixed on Berenice in preference to Myos Hormos, when the navigation and commerce on this sea was extended and improved, since Berenice being lower down, the navigation towards the straits was shorter, as well as attended with fewer difficulties and dangers. But there is no evidence that his fleets, which sailed from Berenice, were destined for India, or even passed the Straits of Babelmandeb. It is, however, not meant to be asserted that no vessels passed these straits in the time of this Ptolemy. On the contrary, we know that his admiral, Timosthenes, passed the straits as low as Cerne, which is generally supposed to be Madagascar; but commerce, which in our times, directed by much superior skill and knowledge, as well as stimulated by a stronger spirit of enterprize and rivalship, and a more absorbing love of gain, immediately follows in the track of discovery, was then comparatively slow, languid, and timid as well as ignorant; so that it is not surprizing that it did not follow the track of Timosthenes. Ptolemy Philadelphus also pushed his discoveries by land as far as Meroc: he opened the route between Coptus and Berenice, establishing ports and opening wells; and from these and other circumstances he seems to have been actuated by a stronger wish to extend commerce, and to have formed more plans for this purpose, than any of his successors.

Ptolemy Euergetes directed his thoughts more to conquest than to commerce, though he rendered the former, in some degree, useful and subservient to the latter. After having passed the Nile, and subdued the nations which lay on the confines of Egypt, he compelled them to open a road of communication between their country and Egypt. The frankincense country was the next object of his ambition: this he subdued; and having sent a fleet and army across the Red Sea into Arabia, he compelled the inhabitants of the district to maintain the roads free from robbers, and the sea from pirates—a proof that these people had made some advances in seafaring matters, and also of the attention paid by Euergetes to the navigation of the Red Sea, as well as to the protection of land commerce. Indeed the whole of his progress to Aduli, which we have more particularly mentioned in another place, was marked as much by attention to commerce as by the love of conquest; but though by this enterprize he rendered both the coasts of the Red Sea tributary, and thus better adapted to commerce, there is no proof that he passed the Straits of Babelmandeb. It is true, indeed, that he visited Mosullon, which lies beyond the straits, but not by sea, having marched by land to that place, through the interior of Abyssinia and Adel. From the whole of this enterprize of Euergetes we may justly infer, that though he facilitated the intercourse by land between Egypt and those parts of Africa which lay immediately beyond the straits, yet his ships did not pass the straits, and that in his reign the discoveries of Timosthenes had not been followed up or improved for the purpose of trading by sea with the coast of Africa. The navigation of the whole of the Red Sea, at least on the Arabian side, from Leuake Kome to Sabaea, was undoubtedly known and frequently used at this period; but this was its utmost limit.

In the reign of Ptolemy Philometor, when Agatharcides lived, the commercial enterprizes of the Egyptians had begun rather to languish; on the Arabian side of the Red Sea, they did indeed extend to Sabaea, as in the time of Euergetes; but there is evidence that on the opposite coast they did not go so low, as in the reign of the latter sovereign. Agatharcides makes no mention of Berenice; according to his account, Myos Hormos had again become the emporium, and the only trade from that part seems to have been for elephants to Ptolemais Theron. It may, indeed, be urged that Berenice was not, properly speaking, a harbour, but only an open bay, to which the ships did not come from Myos Hormos, till their cargoes were completely ready. But that Myos Hormos was the great point of communication with Coptus is evident from the account which Agatharcides gives of the caravan road between these two places. Even so late as the time of Strabo, this road was much more frequented than the road between Coptus and Berenice: of the latter he merely observes, that Philadelphus opened it with his army, established ports, and sunk Wells; whereas he particularly describes the former road, as being seven or eight days' journey, formerly performed on camels in the night, by observation of the stars, and carrying water with them. Latterly, he adds, deep wells had been sunk, and cisterns formed for holding water. Every detail of the road to Berenice is Roman, and relates to periods considerably posterior to the conquest of Egypt by the Romans—a proof that the plan of Philadelphus, of substituting Berenice for Myos Hormos, had not been regularly adopted by his successors, nor till the Romans had firmly and permanently fixed themselves in Egypt.

In the extract we have already given from Agatharcides respecting Arabia, he expressly mentions that the Gerrheans and Sabeans are the centre of all the commerce that passes between Asia and Europe, and that these are the nations which have enriched the Ptolemais: this statement, taken in conjunction with the fact that his description of the coast of the Red Sea reaches no farther than Sabaea on the one side, and Ptolemais Theron on the other, seems decisive of the truth of the opinion, that in the time of Philometor the Egyptians did not trade directly to India. It may be proper to add, that in the extracts from Agatharcides, given by Photius, it is expressly mentioned that ships from India were met with by the Egyptian ships in the ports of Sabaea. The particulars of this trade between India and Egypt, by means of the Arabians, will be afterwards detailed, and its great antiquity traced and proved; at present we have alluded to it merely to bear us out in our position, that Indian ships, laden with Indian commodities, frequenting the ports of Sabaea, and those ports being described by Agatharcides as the limits of his knowledge of this coast of the Red Sea, we are fully justified in concluding, that, in the reign of Philometor, there was not only no direct trade to India, but no inducement to such trade; and that 146 years after the death of Alexander, the Greek sovereigns of Egypt had done little to complete what that monarch had projected, and in part accomplished by the navigation of Nearchus—the communication by sea between Alexandria and India.

Under the successors of Philometor, the trade in the Red Sea languished rather than increased, and the full benefits of it were not reaped till some time after the Roman conquest. Even in the time of Strabo, the bulk of the trade still passed by Coptus to Myos Hormos. We are aware of a passage in this author, which, at first, sight seems to contradict the position we have laid down, and to prove, that at least in his time, there was a direct and not unfrequent navigation between the Red Sea and India. He expressly states, that in the course of six or seven years, 120 ships had sailed from Myos Hormos to India: but on this it may be observed, in the first place, that he begins his description of India, with requesting his readers to peruse what he relates concerning it with indulgence, as it was a country very remote, and few persons had visited it; and even with regard to Arabia Felix, he says, that the knowledge of the Romans commenced with the expedition of his friend Ælius Gallus into that country;—facts not very consistent with his statement that 120 ships had sailed in six or seven years to India: secondly, he expressly mentions, that formerly scarcely twenty ships dared to navigate the Red Sea, so far as to shew themselves beyond the straits; but we can hardly suppose that skill, enterprize, and knowledge, had increased so rapidly as to extend within a very few years navigation, not merely beyond the straits, but even to India; we say a few years, for certainly, at the time when the Romans conquered Egypt, the straits were not usually passed: lastly, the name India was used so vaguely by the ancients, even by Strabo occasionally, that it is not improbable he meant by it, merely the coast of Arabia, beyond the straits. It is well asked by Dr. Vincent, in reference to this account of Strabo, might not that geographer, from knowing the ships brought home Indian commodities, have supposed that they sailed to India, when in reality they went no farther than Hadramant, in Arabia, or Mosullon, on the coast of Africa, where they found the produce of India?

It is not, however, meant to be denied that a few vessels, in the time of Ptolemies, reached some part of India from the Red Sea, by coasting all the way. The author of the Periplus of the Red Sea, informs us that, before the discovery of the monsoon, by Hippalus, small vessels had made a coasting voyage from Cana, in Arabia, to the Indies. But these irregular and trifling voyages are deserving of little consideration, and do not militate against the position we have laid down and endeavoured to prove, that in the time of the Ptolemies the commerce of Egypt was confined within the limits of the Red Sea, partly from the want of skill and enterprize, and from the dangers that were supposed to exist beyond the straits, but principally because the commodities of India could be procured in the ports of Sabæa.

Many instances have already been given of the patronage which the Ptolemies bestowed on commerce, of the facilities and advantages they afforded, and of the benefits which the science of geography derived from the library and observatory of Alexandria: every instrument which could facilitate the study of astronomy was purchased by the Ptolemies and placed in that observatory, for they were fully aware of the dependency of a full and accurate knowledge of geography, as a science, on a full and accurate knowledge of astronomy. With respect to commerce, the advancement of which, may fairly be supposed to have had some weight in their patronage of these sciences, they encouraged it as much as possible to centre in Alexandria, and with citizens of Egypt, by making it a standing law of the country, that no goods should pass through the capital, either to India or Europe, without the intervention of an Alexandrian factor, and that even when foreign merchants resided there, they should employ the same agency. The roads and canals they formed, and the care they took to keep the Red Sea free from pirates, are further proofs of their regard for commerce.

And justly was it held by the Ptolemies in high estimation, for from it they derived their immense wealth. We are informed by Strabo, that the revenue of Alexandria, in the worst of times, was 12,500 talents, equivalent to nearly two millions and a half sterling; and if this was the revenue under the last and most indolent of the Ptolemies, what must it have been under Ptolemy Philadelphus, or Ptolemy Euergetes? But the account given by Appian of the treasure of the Ptolemies is still more extraordinary: the sum he mentions is 740,000 talents, or £191,166,666, according to Dr. Arbuthnot's computation; we should be disposed to doubt the accuracy of this statement, did we not know that Appian was a native of Alexandria, and did he not moreover inform us, that he had extracted his account from the public records of that city. When we consider that this immense sum was accumulated by only two of the Ptolemies, Ptolemy Soter and Ptolemy Philadelphus, and that the latter maintained two great fleets, one in the Mediterranean, and the other in the Red Sea, besides an army of 200,000 foot, and 40,000 horse; and that he had 300 elephants, 2000 armed chariots, and an armoury at Alexandria, stocked with 300,000 complete suits of armour, and all other necessary weapons and implements of war,—we shall form some idea of the extent and fruitfulness of Egyptian commerce, from which the whole, or nearly the whole, of this immense wealth must have been derived.

Having thus brought our historical sketch of the progress of discovery and commercial enterprize among the Egyptians down to the period of the conquest of Egypt by the Romans, we shall, in the next place, revert to the Romans themselves, in whom, at the date of their conquest of this country, the geographical knowledge and the commerce of the whole world may justly be said to have centered. As, however, we have hitherto only adverted to the Romans, in our account of the discoveries and commerce of the Carthaginians, it will be proper to notice them in a much more detailed and particular manner. We shall, therefore, trace, their geographical knowledge, their discoveries and their commerce, from the foundation of Rome, to the period of their conquest of Egypt; and in the course of this investigation, we shall give a sketch of the commerce of those countries which successively fell under their dominion—omitting such as we have already noticed: by this plan, we shall be enabled to trace the commerce of all the known world at that time, down to the period when Rome absorbed the whole.

The account which Polybius gives, that before the first Carthaginian war the Romans were entirely ignorant of, and inattentive to sea affairs—if by this statement he means to assert that they were unacquainted with maritime commerce, as well as maritime warfare, is expressly contradicted by the treaties between Rome and Carthage, which we have already given in our account of the commerce of Carthage. The first of those treaties was made 250 years before the first Punic war; and the second, about fifty years before it. Besides, it is not probable that the Romans should have been entirely ignorant of, and inattentive to maritime commerce for so long a period; since several nations of Italy, with which they were at first connected, and which they afterwards conquered, were very conversant in this commerce, and derived great consideration, power, and wealth from it.

The Romans had conquered Etruria, and made themselves masters of the Tuscan powers both by sea and land, before the commencement of the first

Punic war; and though at this period, the Tuscans were not so celebrated for their commerce as they had been, yet the shipping and commerce they did possess, must have fallen into the power of the Romans; and we can scarcely suppose that these, together with the facilities which the Tuscans enjoyed for commerce, by means of their ports, and their skill and commercial habits and connections, would be entirely neglected by their conquerors. Besides, there are several old Roman coins, by some supposed to have been as old as the time of the kings, and certainly prior to the first Punic war, on the reverses of which different parts of ships are visible. Now, as the Roman historians are diffuse in the accounts they give of the wars of the Romans, but take no notice of their commercial transactions, we may safely conclude, from their not mentioning any maritime wars, or expeditions of a date so early as these coins, that the ships at that period preserved by the Romans, and deemed of such consequence as to be struck on their coins, were employed for the purposes of commerce.

The Tuscans and the Grecian colonies in the south of Italy, certainly had made great progress in commerce at an early period; and as,—if their example did not stimulate the Romans to enterprises of the same kind,—the Romans, at least when they conquered them, became possessed of the commerce which they then enjoyed, it will be proper to take a brief view of it.

If we may credit the ancient historians, the Etrurians or Tyrrhenians, even before the reign of Minos, had been for a long time masters of the greatest part of the Mediterranean Sea, and had given their name to the Tyrrhenian Sea, upon which they were situate. Piracy, as well as commerce, was followed by them; and they became at last so expert, successful, and dangerous, for their piracies, that they were attacked, and their maritime power greatly abridged, by the Carthaginians and the Sicilians. Their most famous port was Luna, which was situated on the Macra, a river which, flowing from the Apennines, divided Liguria from Etruria, and fell into the Tyrrhenian Sea. There seems good reason to believe that Luna was a place of great trade before the Trojan war; it was extremely capacious, and in every respect worthy of the commercial enterprise and wealth of the Tuscans. Populonium, a city which was situate on a high promontory of the same name, that ran a considerable way into the sea, also possessed a very commodious harbour, capable of receiving a great number of ships. It had an arsenal well supplied with all kinds of naval stores, and a quay for shipping or landing merchandize. One of the principal articles of export consisted in copper vessels, and in arms, machines, utensils, &c. of iron: these metals were at first supplied to the inhabitants from the island of Æthalia (now Elba); but the copper-mines there failing, iron alone, from the same island, was imported for the purpose of their various manufactures; the trade in these flourished in very remote times, and continued in the days of Aristotle and Strabo.

But the most direct and unequivocal testimony to the power of the Tuscans, and that that power was principally, if not entirely, derived from their maritime skill and commerce, is to be found in Livy. This historian informs us, "that before the Roman empire, the Tuscan dominions extended very far both by sea and land, even to the upper and lower sea, by which Italy is surrounded, in form of an island. Their very names are an argument for the vast power of this people; for the Italian natives call the one the Tuscan Sea, and the other the Adriatic, from Adria, a Tuscan colony. The Greeks call them the Tyrrhenian and Adriatic Seas. This people, in twelve cities, inhabited the country extending to both seas; and by sending out colonies equal in number to the mother cities, first on this side of the Apennines towards the lower sea, and afterwards as many on the other side, possessed all the country beyond the Po, even to the Alps, except the corner belonging to the Venetians, who dwelt round a bay of the sea." Homer, Heraclides, Aristides, and Diodorus Siculus, all concur in their representations of the maritime power and commercial opulence of the Tuscans at a very early period. Diodorus Siculus expressly says, that they were masters of the sea; and Aristides, that the Indians were the most powerful nation in the east, and the Tuscans in the west.

Of the Grecian colonies in the south of Italy, that of Tarentum was the most celebrated for its commerce. Polybius expressly informs us, that Tarentum, their principal city, was very prosperous and rich, long before Rome made any figure, and that its prosperity and riches were entirely the fruit of the extensive and lucrative trade they carried on, particularly with Greece. The city of Tarentum stood on a peninsula, and the citadel, which was very strong, was built on the narrowest and extremest part of it; on the east was a small bay, on the west the main sea; the harbour is represented by ancient historians as extremely large, beautiful and commodious. Its vicinity to Greece, Sicily, and Africa, afforded it great opportunities and facilities for commerce. The inhabitants are represented by some authors as having been the inventors of a particular kind of ship, which retained in some degree the form of a raft or float. Their government, which at first was aristocratical, was afterwards changed to a democracy; and it is to this popular form of government that their prosperity and wealth are ascribed. The number of people in the whole state amounted to 300,000; Tarentum had twelve other cities under its dominion. Besides a considerable fleet in the Mediterranean Sea, they had constantly on foot a very large army, principally of mercenaries. Eighteen years before the first Punic war, the Romans had entered into a maritime treaty with the Tarentines; according to this treaty, neither party were to navigate beyond the Cape of Lacinia. Soon afterwards, however, the Roman fleet accidentally appearing near Tarentum, the inhabitants took the alarm, sunk four of the ships, killed or took prisoners the commander and some other officers, sold the seamen for slaves, and behaved with great insolence to the ambassador whom the Romans sent to remonstrate and demand satisfaction. They were soon, however, obliged to submit to the superior power of the Romans. In the second Punic war, it was finally subdued, and a Roman colony planted there.

The Spinetes, Liburnians, and Locrians, were also celebrated for their skill in naval affairs, and for their commerce, before Rome manifested the slightest wish to distinguish herself in this manner. Indeed, the situation of Italy naturally turned the attention of its inhabitants (especially of those who were early civilized, as the Tuscans, or those who had emigrated from a civilized country, as the nations in the south of Italy,) to naval affairs and maritime commerce. Washed by three seas, the Adriatic on the north-east, the Tyrrhenian on the west, and the Ionian on the south, Italy enjoyed advantages possessed by few nations of antiquity. Of the first of these seas, the Spinetes became masters, of the second the Tuscans, and of the third the Tarentines. The Spinetes, were originally Pelasgi, who had emigrated and settled by chance rather than design, on the south banks of the Po. Spina, their capital, was situated on the north side of the southernmost mouth of that river. We do not possess any particular account of their commerce, but that it rendered them powerful and rich we are assured; and their dominion over the Adriatic is a decisive proof of the former, while their magnificent offerings to Delphos may as justly be deemed a proof of the latter. Spina was strong both by nature and art, on the sea side, but the reverse on the land side; so that at last it was abandoned by its inhabitants not being able to withstand the attacks of their neighbours, who were either jealous of their prosperity, or attracted to the assault by the love of plunder. In the reign of Augustus it was reduced to a small village; and the branch of the Po, on which it was situated, had changed its course so much, that it was then upwards of fifteen miles distant from the sea, on the shore of which it had been built. The gradual alteration in the course of the river, it is probable, contributed with the other cause already mentioned to reduce it to comparative insignificance.

Opposite to the Spinetes across the Adriatic, on the coast of Dalmatia, the Liburnians dwelt. In some respects their coast was preferable to that of Italy for maritime affairs, as it is studded with islands, which afforded shelter to ships, and likewise possessed many excellent harbours; but the Liburnians, as well as most of the inhabitants of Illyria, were more eager after piracy than commerce; and, as we shall afterwards see, carried their piracies to such a daring and destructive extent, that the Romans were compelled to attack them. Their devotedness to piracy explains what to Mons. Huet appears unaccountable. He observes, that it is remarkable that neither the Dalmatians, who were powerful at sea by means of their port Salona, which was their capital, nor the Liburnians themselves, according to all appearance, had the use of money among them. Commerce cannot be carried on to great extent, or in a regular and expeditious manner, by natives ignorant of the use of money; but money seems to be not at all requisite to the purposes of piracy. The Liburnian ships, or more properly speaking, those ships which were denominated Liburnian, from having been invented and first employed by this people, were of two kinds; one large, fit for war and long voyages, but at the same time built light and for quick sailing. After the victory of Actium, which Augustus gained in a great measure by means of these ships, few were built by the Romans of any other construction. The other Liburnian vessels were small, for fishing and short voyages; some of these were made with osiers and covered with hides. But strength and lightness, and quick sailing, were the qualities by which the Liburnian ships were chiefly distinguished and characterised.

At what precise period the Romans directed their attention to maritime affairs we are not accurately informed: that the opinion of Polybius on this subject is not well founded, is evident from several circumstances. He says, that before the first Punic war the Romans had no thought of the sea; that Sicily was the first country, out of Italy, in which they ever landed; and that, when they went to that island to assist the Mamertines, the vessels which they employed in that expedition were hired, or borrowed from the Tarentines, the Locrians, &c. He is correct in his statement that Sicily was the first country in which the Romans had any footing; but that he is inaccurate with respect to the period when the Romans first applied themselves to maritime affairs, will appear from the following facts.

In the first place, the Romans (as we have already shown in our account of the Carthaginian commerce,) had several treaties with the Carthaginians, which may properly be called commercial treaties, before the first Punic war. The earliest treaty, according to Polybius himself, was dated about 250 years before the war; and in this treaty the voyages undertaken by the Romans on account of trade to Africa, Sardinia, and that part of Sicily at that time possessed by the Carthaginians, are expressly mentioned and regulated. The second treaty, about 100 years before the first Punic war, is not so specific respecting commerce. The third treaty, occasioned by the invasion of Italy by Pyrrhus, points out a decline in the naval power of the Romans; for it stipulates, that the Carthaginians should furnish them with ships, if required, either for trade or war. Secondly, seventy-four years before the first Punic war, the Romans having subdued the Antiates, and thus become masters of their fleet, among which were six armed with beaks, the tribune was ornamented with these beaks, the ships to which they belonged were burnt, and the others were brought to Rome and laid upon the place allotted to the building and preservation of ships. Lastly, the circumstances which gave rise to the war between the Romans and Tarentines, to which we have already adverted, plainly prove that Polybius is wrong in his assertion. Valerius, who commanded the Roman fleet, which was attacked by the Tarentines, according to Livy, was one of the , officers who had been already appointed nearly thirty years (that is, nearly fifty years before the first Punic war), on the motion of Decius Mus, expressly for the purpose of equipping, repairing, and maintaining the fleets.

From these circumstances, it appears that the Romans possessed ships both for war and commerce, previous to the commencement of their wars with the Carthaginians, though it is extremely probable that their commerce was very limited, and for the most part carried on in vessels belonging to the other maritime nations of Italy, and that their ships of war were very small and rude in their construction and equipment.

It is foreign to the object of this work to enter into a detail of the wars between the Romans and the Carthaginians: but as the great efforts of the Romans to become powerful at sea were made during these wars; as these efforts, being successful, laid the foundation of the future commerce of Rome; and as by the destruction of Carthage, in some measure caused by the naval victories gained by the Romans, the most commercial nation of antiquity was utterly ruined, and their commerce transferred to Rome, it will be proper briefly to notice the naval contests between these rival powers during the three wars in which they were engaged.

The first Punic war was occasioned by a desire on the part of the Carthaginians to enlarge and secure their acquisitions in Sicily, and to preserve their dominion of the sea, and by a determination on the part of the Romans to check the progress of the Carthaginians in that island, so immediately adjoining the continent of Italy. An opportunity soon occurred, which seemed to promise to each the accomplishment of their respective objects: the Mamertines, being hard pursued by Hiero king of Syracuse, and shut up in Messina, the only city which remained to them, were divided in opinion; some were for accepting the protection offered them by Hannibal, who at that time commanded the Carthaginian army in Sicily; others were for calling in the aid of the Romans. Both these powers gladly accepted the proffered opportunity of extending their conquests, and checking their rival.

The consul Appius Claudius, was ordered by the senate to proceed to Sicily: previously to his departure, he despatched Caius Claudius, a legionary tribune, with a few vessels to Rhegium, principally, it would seem, to reconnoitre the naval force of the Carthaginians. The consul himself soon followed with a small fleet, hired principally from the Tarentines, Locrians, and Neapolitans. This fleet being attacked by the Carthaginian fleet, which was not only much more numerous, but better equipped and manned, and a violent storm rising during the engagement, which dashed many of the Roman vessels in pieces among the rocks, was completely worsted. The Carthaginians, however, restored most of the vessels they captured, only expostulating with the Romans on the infraction of the treaty at that time subsisting between the two republics. This loss was in some measure counterbalanced by Claudius capturing, on his voyage back to Rhegium, a Carthaginian quinquireme, the first which fell into the possession of the Romans, and which served them for a model. According to other historians, however, a Carthaginian galley, venturing too near the shore, was stranded, and taken by the Romans; and after the model of this galley, the Romans built many of their vessels.

Claudius was not in the least discouraged by his defeat, observing that he could not expect to learn the art of navigation without paying dear for it; but having repaired his fleet, he sailed again for Sicily, and eluding the vigilance of the Carthaginian admiral, arrived safe in the port of Messina.

After the alliance formed between the Romans and Hiero king of Syracuse, and the capture of Agrigentium, they resolved to use all their efforts for the entire subjugation of Sicily. As, however, the Carthaginians were extremely powerful by sea, they could not hope to accomplish this object, unless they were able to cope with them on that element. They resolved, therefore, no longer to trust in any degree to hired vessels, but to build and equip a formidable fleet of their own. Powerfully actuated by this resolution, they began the arduous undertaking with that ardour and spirit of perseverance, which so eminently distinguished them; they deemed it absolutely necessary to have 120 ships. Trees were immediately cut down in the forests, and the timber brought to the sea shore: and the whole fleet, according to Polybius, was not only built, but perfectly equipped and ready for sea, in two months from the time the trees were felled. Of the 120 vessels of which it was composed, 100 had five benches of rowers, and 20 of them had three benches.

There was, however, another difficulty to be overcome. It was absolutely necessary that the men, who were to navigate and fight these ships, should possess some knowledge of their art; but it was in vain to expect that with the Carthaginians, so powerful and watchful at sea, the Roman ships would be permitted to cruise safely long enough to make them practised sailors and fighters. To obviate this difficulty, they had recourse, according to Polybius, to a singular but tolerably effectual mode. "While some men were employed in building the galleys, others, assembling those who were to serve in the fleet, instructed them in the use of the oar after the following manner: they contrived benches on the shore in the same fashion and order as they were to be in the galleys, and placing their seamen, with their oars, in like manner on the benches, an officer, by signs with his hand, instructed them how to dip their oars all at the same time, and how to recover them out of the water. By this means they became acquainted with the management of the oar; and as soon as the vessels were built and equipped, they spent some time in practising on the water, what they had learnt ashore."

The necessity of possessing a fleet adequate to cope with that of the Carthaginians became more and more apparent; for though the Romans had obtained possession of all the inland cities in Sicily, the Carthaginians compensated for this by having the ascendancy by sea, and in the cities on the coast. The Roman fleet was commanded by Cornelius Scipio, who put to sea with seventeen ships, in order to secure at Messina reception and security for the whole fleet; but his enterprise was unfortunate; for, being deceived by false information, he entered the port of Lipara, where he was blockaded by the enemy, and obliged to surrender. This partial loss, however, was soon counterbalanced by a naval victory; for the remainder of the Roman fleet, amounting to 103 sail, being encountered by a Carthaginian fleet under Hannibal, who despising the Romans, had advanced to the contest with only fifty galleys, succeeded in capturing or destroying the whole of them.

In the mean time, the senate had appointed Duilius commander of the fleet; and his first object was to survey it accurately, and, if possible, to improve the construction or equipment of the vessels, if they appeared defective, either for the purpose of sailing or fighting. It seemed to him, on examining them, that they could not be easily and quickly worked during an engagement, being much heavier and more unwieldy than those of the Carthaginians. As this defect could not be removed, he tried whether it could not be compensated; and an engineer in the fleet succeeded in this important object, by inventing that machine which was afterwards called .

The immediate purpose which this machine was to serve is clearly explained by all the ancient authors who mention it: its use was to stop the enemy's ships as soon as the Roman vessels came up with them, and thus to give them an opportunity of boarding them; but the construction and mode of operation of these machines it is not easy to ascertain from the descriptions of ancient authors. Polybius gives the following description of them: "They erected on the prow of their vessels a round piece of timber, about one foot and a half in diameter, and about twelve feet long, on the top of which a block or pully was fastened. Round this piece of timber a stage or platform was constructed, four feet broad, and about eighteen feet long, which was strongly fastened with iron. The entrance was lengthways, and it could be moved about the piece of timber, first described, as on a spindle, and could be hoisted within six feet of the top. Round this there was a parapet, knee high, which was defended with upright bars of iron, sharpened at the end. Towards the top there was a ring, through which a rope was fastened, by means of which they could raise and lower the engine at pleasure. With this machine they attacked the enemy's vessels, sometimes on their bow, and sometimes on their broadside. When they had grappled the enemy with these iron spikes, if the ships happened to swing broadside to broadside, then the Romans boarded them from all parts; but when they were obliged to grapple them on the bow, they entered two and two, by the help of this engine, the foremost defending the forepart, and those who followed the flanks, keeping the boss of their bucklers level with the top of the parapet."

From this description of the corvus, it is evident that it had two distinct uses to serve: in the first place, to lay hold of and entangle the enemy's ships; and, secondly, after it had accomplished this object, it served as a means of entering the enemy's vessels, and also as a protection while the boarding was taking place. With respect to the question, whether the   or manus ferræ; were the same with the , it appears to us that the former were of much older invention, as they certainly were much more simple in their construction; and that, probably, the engineer who invented the corvi, borrowed his idea of them from the harpagones, and in fact incorporated the two machines in one engine. The harpagones were undoubtedly grappling irons, but of such light construction that they could be thrown by manual force; but they were of no other service; whereas the corvi were worked by machinery, and served, as we have shown, not only to grapple, but to assist and protect the boarders. We have been thus particular in our account of the corvus, because it may fairly be regarded as having essentially contributed to the establishment of the Roman naval power over that of the Carthaginians.

After Duilius had made a trial of the efficacy of this machine, he sailed in quest of the enemy. The Carthaginians, despising the Romans as totally inexperienced in naval affairs, did not even take the trouble or precaution to draw up their ships in line of battle, but trusting entirely to their own superior skill, and to the greater lightness of their ships, they bore down on the Romans in disorder. They, however, were induced, for a short time, to slacken their advance at the sight of the corvi; but not giving the Romans credit for any invention which could counterbalance their want of skill, experience, and self-confidence, they again pushed forward and attacked the Romans. They soon suffered, however, the consequences of their rashness: the Romans, by means of their corvi, grappled their ships so closely and steadily, that the fight resembled much more a land than a sea battle; and thus feeling themselves, as it were, on their own element, while their enemies seemed to themselves no longer to be fighting in ships, the confidence of the former rose, while that of the latter fell, from the same cause, and nearly in the same proportion. The result was, that the Romans gained a complete victory. The loss of the Carthaginians is variously related by the Roman writers: this is extraordinary, since they must have had access to the best possible authority; the inscription of the Columna Rostrata of Duilius, which is still preserved at Rome. According to this inscription, Duilius fitted out a fleet in sixty days, defeated the Carthaginians, commanded by Hannibal, at sea, took from them thirty ships, with all their rigging, and the septireme which carried the admiral himself; sunk thirty, and took several prisoners of distinction. When Hannibal saw the Romans about to enter his septireme, he leaped into a small boat and escaped.

A circumstance occurred during this engagement which clearly manifested the ardour and perseverance, by means of which the Romans had already become expert, not only in the management of their ships, but also in the use of their corvi. It has already been noticed that the Carthaginians bore down on them in disorder, each ship endeavouring to reach them as soon as possible, without waiting for the rest: among the foremost was Hannibal. After the defeat of this part of the fleet, the rest, amounting to 120, having come up, endeavoured to avoid the fate of their companions by rowing as quickly as possible round the Roman ships, so as not to allow them to make use of the corvi. But the Romans proved themselves to be even more expert seamen than their enemies; for, though their vessels were much heavier, they worked them with so much ease, celerity, and skill, that they presented the machines to the enemy on whatever side they approached them.

The vanquished Hannibal was disgraced by his country; whereas the victorious Roman was honoured and rewarded by the senate, who were fully sensible of all the advantages derived by a naval victory over the Carthaginians. The high and distinguished honour of being attended, when he returned from supper, with music and torches, which was granted for once only to those who triumphed, was continued to Duilius during life. To perpetuate the memory of this victory, medals were struck, and the pillar, to which we have already alluded, was erected in the forum. This pillar, called Columna Rostrata, from the beaks of the ships which were fastened to it, was discovered in the year 1560, and placed in the capital.

In the year after this splendid victory the Romans resolved to attempt the reduction of Corsica and Sardinia; for this purpose L. Cornelius Scipio sailed with a squadron under his command. He easily succeeded in reducing Corsica; but it appears, from an inscription on a stone which was dug up in the year 1615, in Rome, that he encountered a violent storm off the coast of that island, in which his fleet was exposed to imminent danger. The words of the inscription are, "He took the city of Aleria and conquered Corsica, and built a temple to the tempests, with very good reason." This storm is not mentioned in any of the ancient authors. Scipio was obliged to be more cautious in his attempts on Sardinia, but afterwards the Romans succeeded in gaining possession of this island.

The Romans having thus acquired Corsica and Sardinia, and all the maritime towns of Sicily, determined to invade, or at least to alarm, the African dominions of Carthage. Accordingly Sulpicius, who commanded their fleet, circulated a report that he intended to sail for the coasts of Africa: this induced the Carthaginians to put to sea; but after the hostile fleets had approached each other, and were about to engage, a storm arose and separated them, and obliged them both to take shelter in the ports of Sardinia. As soon as it abated, Sulpicius put to sea again, surprised the Carthaginians, and captured or destroyed most of their ships.

Five years after the victory of Duilius, the Romans were able to put to sea a fleet of 330 covered gallies. Ten of these were sent to reconnoitre the enemy, but approaching too near, they were attacked and destroyed. This unfortunate event did not discourage the consul Attilius Regulus, who commanded: on the contrary, he resolved to wipe off this disgrace by signalizing his consulship in a remarkable manner. He was ordered by the senate to cross the Mediterranean, and invade Carthage. The Roman fleet, which consisted of 330 galleys, on board of each of which were 120 soldiers and 300 rowers, was stationed at Messina: from this port they took their departure, stretching along the coast of Sicily, till they doubled Cape Pachynum, after which they sailed directly to Ecnomos. The Carthaginian fleet consisted of 360 sail, and the seamen were more numerous, as well as more skilful and experienced, than those of the Romans: it rendezvoused at Heraclea, not far from Ecnomos. Between these two places the hostile fleets met, and one of the most obstinate and decisive battles ensued that are recorded in ancient history. As Polybius has given a very particular account of the manner in which the respective fleets were drawn up, and of all the incidents of the battle, we shall transcribe it from him, because the issue of it may justly be regarded as having proved the Roman superiority at sea, and because the details of this accurate historian will afford us a clear insight into the naval engagements of the ancients.

As there were 330 ships, and each ship had on board 300 rowers, and 120 soldiers, the total number of men in the fleet amounted 140,000. The whole fleet was formed into four divisions: the first was called the first legion; the second, the second; and the third, the third legion. The fourth division had a different name; they were called triarians: the triarii who were on board this division, being old soldiers of approved valour, who, in land battles, formed the third line of the legion, and hence obtained their appellation. The first division was drawn up on the right, the second on the left, and the third in the rear of the other two, in such a manner that these three divisions formed a triangle, the point of which was the two gallies, in which were the consuls, in front of their respective squadrons, parallel to the third legion, which formed the base of the triangle, and in the rear of the whole fleet; the triarian division was drawn up, but extended in such a manner as to out-flank the extremes of the base. Between the triarian division and the other part of the squadron, the transports were drawn up, in order that they might be protected from the enemy, and their escape accelerated and covered in case of a defeat; on board of the transports were the horses, and baggage of the army.

According to Polybius, the seamen and troops on board the Carthaginian fleet amounted to 150,000 men. Their admiral waited to see the disposition of the Roman fleet before he formed his own in order of battle; he divided it into four squadrons, drawn up in one line; one of these was drawn up very near the shore, the others stretched far out to sea, apparently for the purpose of out-flanking the Romans. The light vessels were on the right, under the command of Hanno; the squadron on the left, which was formed of heavier vessels, was under the command of Hamilcar.

It is evident from this description of the order of battle of the Carthaginians, that their line, being so much extended, could easily be broken; the Romans perceiving this, bore down on the middle with their first and second divisions. The Carthaginians did not wait the attack, but retired immediately with the intention of drawing the Romans after them, and thus by separating, weakening their fleet. The Romans, thinking the victory was their own, pushed after the flying enemy, thus weakening their third division, and at the same time exposing themselves to an attack while they were scattered. The Carthaginians, perceiving that their manoeuvre had so far succeeded, tacked about, and engaged with their pursuers. But the Romans, by means of their corvi, which they were now very skilful in using, grappled with the enemy, and as soon as they had thus rendered the engagement similar to a land battle, they overcame them.

While these things were going on between Hamilcar with the left wing of the Carthaginian fleet, and the first and second divisions of the Romans, Hanno, with his light vessels, which formed the right wing, attacked the triarians, and the ships which were drawn up near the shore, attacked the third legion and the transports. These two attacks were conducted with so much spirit and courage, that many of the triarians, transports, and third legion were driven on shore, and their defeat would probably have been decisive, had not the Roman first and second divisions, which had defeated and chased to a considerable distance the Carthaginians opposed to them, returned most opportunely from the chace, and supported them. The Carthaginians were no longer able to withstand their enemies, but sustained a signal defeat; thirty of their vessels having been sunk, and sixty-three taken. The immediate result of this victory was, that the Romans landed in Africa without opposition.

The next victory obtained by the Romans over the Carthaginians was achieved soon after the defeat and captivity of Regulus, and was justly regarded by them as an ample compensation for that disaster. It was a wise and politic maxim of the Roman republic never to appear cast down by defeat, but, on the contrary, to act in such a case with more than their usual confidence and ardour. Acting on this maxim they equipped a fleet and sent it towards Africa, immediately after they learnt the defeat of Regulus. The Carthaginians, who were endeavouring to take all possible advantage of their victory, by expelling the Romans from Africa, as soon as the news arrived of the sailing of this fleet, abandoned the seige of Utica, before which they had sat down,—refitted their old ships, built several new ones, and put to sea. The hostile fleets met near Cape Herme, the most northern point of Africa, a little to the north-east of Carthage. They were again unsuccessful on what they had formerly justly regarded as their own element. One hundred and four of their ships were captured, and 15,000 men, soldiers, and rowers, were killed in the action.

This victory, however, proved of little benefit to the Romans in their grand enterprise of establishing a firm and permanent footing, in Africa; for, in consequence of their inability to obtain a regular supply of provisions for their army, they were obliged soon afterwards to evacuate Clupea and Utica, the principal places they held there, and to re-embark their troops for Italy.

In order to make up for this hard necessity, they resolved to land in Sicily on their return, and, if possible, reduce some cities which the Carthaginians still retained in that island. Such was the plan of the consuls, but it was vehemently opposed by the pilots of the fleet, who represented to them, that as the season was far advanced, the most prudent measure would be to sail directly for Italy, and not go round the northern coast of Sicily, as the consuls wished. The latter, however, persisted in their resolution; the consequences were extremely fatal; a most violent storm arose, during which the greater part of the fleet was destroyed or rendered completely useless, either foundering, or being driven on shore. All the sea coast from Camarina to Pachynum, was covered with dead bodies of men and horses, as well as with the wrecks of the ships. The exact number of ships that were lost is differently represented by different authors, but according to the most accurate account, out of 370 which composed the fleet, only eighty escaped. Besides the destruction of these vessels, a numerous army was lost, with all the riches of Africa, which had been amassed and deposited in Clupea, by Regulus, and which was in the act of being conveyed to Rome.

The Carthaginians, animated by the news of this event, resolved to attempt the subjugation of Sicily, Africa being now liberated from the enemy. But the Romans, by incredible efforts, fitted out a new fleet in the short space of three months, consisting of 120 ships; which, with the old vessels which had escaped, made up a fleet of 250 sail. With these, they passed over to Sicily, where they were successful in reducing the Carthaginian capital in that island.

The next year they sent to sea a fleet of 260 ships to attempt the reduction of Lilibæum, but this place being found too strong, the consuls directed their course to the eastern coast of Africa, on which they carried on a predatory warfare. Having filled their ships with the spoils, they were returning to Italy, when they narrowly escaped shipwreck. On the coast of Africa, there were two sand-banks, called the Greater and Lesser Syrtes, which were very much dreaded by the ancients, on account of their frequently changing places; sometimes being easily visible, and at other times considerably below the water. On the Lesser

Syrtes the Roman fleet grounded; fortunately it was low water, and moderate weather at the time, so that on the return of flood tide, the vessels floated off, with little or no damage, but the consuls were dreadfully alarmed.

This, however, was only a prelude to real disaster: the fleet arrived safe at Panormus, where they remained a short time. On their departure for Italy, the wind and weather were favourable till they reached Cape Palinurus; here a dreadful storm arose, in which 160 galleys, and a considerable number of transports, were lost. This second storm seems to have so dispirited the Roman senate, that they resolved to confine their efforts to land, and accordingly a decree was issued, that, as it seemed the will of the gods that the Romans should not succeed against their enemy by sea, no more than fifty vessels should in future be equipped; and that these should be employed exclusively in protecting the coasts of Italy, and in transporting troops to Sicily.

This decree, however, was not long acted upon; for the Carthaginians, perceiving that the Romans no longer dared to meet them at sea, made such formidable preparations for invading Sicily, by equipping a fleet of 200 sail, and raising an army of 30,000 men, besides 140 elephants, that the Romans, being reduced to the alternative of either losing that valuable island, or of again encountering their enemy at sea, resolved on the latter measure. Accordingly a new fleet was built, consisting of 240 galleys, and sixty smaller vessels, and Lilibæum was besieged by sea and land. This city was deemed impregnable, and as it was the only place of retreat for the Carthaginian armies in Sicily, it was defended with the utmost obstinacy.

During this siege, two bold and successful enterprises were undertaken for the purpose of supplying the garrison with provisions. The Romans had shut up the port so closely, that the governor could have no communication with Carthage: nevertheless, Hannibal, the son of Hamilcar, resolved to enter it with a supply of provisions. With this intention, he anchored with a few vessels under an island near the coast, and as soon as a strong south wind arose, he set all sail, and plied his oars with so much vigour and alacrity, that he passed safely through the midst of the Roman fleet, and landed 10,000 men and a considerable quantity of provisions. Having succeeded thus far, and being convinced that the Romans would be on the alert to prevent his sudden escape, he resolved to intimidate them, if possible, by the open boldness of the attempt; and in this also he succeeded.

Shortly afterwards the harbour was again so closely blockaded, that the senate of Carthage were quite uninformed of the state and resources of the garrison. In this emergency, a Rhodian, of the name of Hannibal, undertook to enter the harbour, and to come back to Carthage with the requisite and desired intelligence. The Roman fleet lay at anchor, stretched across the mouth of the harbour. Hannibal, following the example of his namesake, with a very light galley of his own, concealed himself near one of the islands which lie opposite to Lilibæum. Very early in the morning, before it was light, with a favourable wind blowing rather strong, he succeeded in getting through the Roman fleet, and entered the port. The consul, mortified at this second enterprise, ordered ten of his lightest vessels to lie as close as possible to each other, across the mouth of the harbour; and that they might not be taken by surprise and unprepared, he further directed that the men should constantly have their oars in their hands, stretched out, so as to be ready to plunge them into the water at a moment's warning. The skill and experience of the Rhodian, however, and the extreme lightness and celerity of his vessel, rendered all these precautions unavailing; for, not content with securing his escape, he mocked the Romans, by often lying to till they came near him, and then rowing round them. The Carthaginian senate were now able to have frequent communication with the garrison by means of this Rhodian: his success, and the recompence which rewarded it, induced several Carthaginians to make the same attempt. They were all successful except one, who, not knowing the force and direction of the currents, was carried by them ashore, and fell into the power of the Romans. The Rhodian still continued to pass between the besieged and Carthage; but his good fortune was near an end. The Romans had fitted out the Carthaginian galley which they had captured, and "waited with impatience for a fresh insult from the Rhodian: it was not long before he entered the port in the night time, according to custom, and was preparing to sail out in broad day, not knowing that the Romans were now masters of a galley which was as good a sailer as his own. He weighed anchor with great confidence, and sailed out of the port in sight of the enemy's fleet, but was greatly surprized to see the Romans pursue him close, and at length come up with him, notwithstanding the lightness of his vessel. He had now no way left but to engage them, which he did with an undaunted bravery; but the Romans, who were all chosen men, soon put an end to the dispute. The Rhodian vessel was boarded and taken with all her crew. The Romans being now in possession of two light galleys, shut up the port so effectually, that no Carthaginian ever after attempted to enter it."

The following year the Romans were obliged to convert the siege into a blockade, in consequence of the Carthaginians having succeeded in destroying all their works. One of the consuls was P. Claudius Pulcher, an obstinate and ambitious man, who, contrary to the advice of those who were better skilled in maritime affairs, and better acquainted with the Carthaginians than he was, determined to surprize Drepanon, where the Carthaginian admiral was posted. Claudius had under his command a fine and formidable fleet of 120 galleys; with these he sailed from before Lilibæum in the night time, having taken on board a great number of the best troops employed in the blockade of that place. At break of day, Asdrubal, the Carthaginian admiral, was surprized to perceive the hostile fleet approaching Drepanon: he formed his plan immediately, preferring an immediate engagement to the certainty of being shut up in the harbour. Accordingly, with ninety ships, he sailed out, and drew them up behind some rocks which lay near the harbour. As the Romans had not perceived him come out, they continued to sail on without forming themselves into line of battle, when as they were about to enter the harbour, the Carthaginians attacked them, with such celerity and vigour, that, being taken quite unprepared, they were thrown into confusion. Claudius might still have saved his fleet by immediate flight, but this he absolutely refused to do, notwithstanding the strong and urgent remonstrances of his officers. By great exertions the Roman fleet was formed into line of battle, on a lee shore, and close to rocks and shoals. It was on this occasion, that the Romans' veneration for auguries was so dreadfully shocked, by Claudius exclaiming, when the sacred chickens refused to feed, "If they will not feed, let them drink," at the same time ordering them to be thrown into the sea. The bad omen, and the sacrilegious insult, added to the situation in which they were placed, and their want of confidence in Claudius, seemed to have paralysed the efforts of the Romans: they fought feebly: the enemy boarded their ships without difficulty or resistance; so that ninety vessels were either taken or driven ashore, 8,000 of their seamen and soldiers were killed, and 20,000 taken prisoners. As soon as Claudius perceived the probable result of the battle, he fled precipitately with thirty vessels. The Carthaginians did not lose a single ship or man on this occasion. This was the most signal and disastrous defeat which the Romans had suffered at sea since the commencement of the war. According to Polybius, Claudius was tried, condemned, and very severely punished.

The other consul, Lucius Pullus, was not more successful, though his want of success did not, as in the case of Claudius, arise from ignorance and obstinacy. He was ordered to sail from Syracuse with a fleet of 120 galleys, and 800 transports, the latter laden with provisions and stores for the army before Lilibaeum. As the army was much pressed for necessaries, and the consul himself was not ready to put to sea directly, he sent the quaestors before him with a small squadron. The Carthaginians, who were very watchful, and had the best intelligence of all the Romans were doing, having learnt that the consul was at sea with a large fleet, sent 100 galleys to cruize off Heraclea. As soon as the squadron under the quaestors came in sight, the Carthaginian admiral, though he mistook it for the consular fleet, yet resolved to engage it: but the quaestors, having received orders not to hazard a battle if they could possibly avoid, took refuge behind some rocks, where they were attacked by the enemy. The Romans defended themselves so well with balistae and other engines, which they had erected on the rocks, that the Carthaginian admiral, after having captured a few transports, was obliged to draw off his fleet.

In the mean time, the light vessels, employed on the lookout, informed him that the whole consular fleet were directing their course for Lilibaeum: his obvious plan was to engage this fleet before it could join that of the quæstors; he therefore steered his course to meet them. But the consul was equally averse with the quaestors to hazard the supply of the army by a battle, and he, therefore, also took shelter near some rocks. The Carthaginian admiral was afraid to attack him in this position, but resolved to watch him: while thus employed his pilots observed certain indications of an approaching storm, which induced him to take shelter on the other side of Cape Pachynum. He had scarcely doubled the cape, when the storm arose with such violence that the whole Roman fleet was destroyed. According to Polybius, not one vessel, not even a plank, was saved out of a fleet which consisted of 120 galleys and 800 transports.

Two such losses occurring during the same consulate, induced the Romans again to resolve to desist from all naval enterprizes and preparations, so that for some time no public fleet was equipped. This resolution, however, yielded to the conviction that they could not hope even to retain their possessions in Sicily, or even to secure their commerce on the coasts of Italy, if they did not endeavour to cope with the Carthaginians by sea. But as the senate thought it would appear derogatory to their dignity and consistency to equip a public fleet, after they had a second time resolved solemnly and officially not to do so, they passed a decree, by which all the Roman citizens who were able and so disposed, were permitted to build, equip, and arm vessels at their own expence; with these ships they were directed to land on the coast of Africa, for the purpose of pillage, the fruit of which was to be their own private gain. The senate even went further to evade, by a pitiful subterfuge their own decree, for they lent the few ships which still remained to the republic, to private citizens, on condition that they should keep them in repair, and make them good if they were lost. By these measures a very considerable fleet was equipped, which committed great depredations on the coast of Africa. Emboldened by their predatory warfare, they resolved to attempt a more arduous enterprize. One of the most celebrated of the Carthaginian harbours was that of Hippo; besides the port there was a citadel, and large arsenals for naval stores, &c. As the inhabitants were much engaged in commerce, there were in the town always a considerable quantity of merchandize. This port the privateer squadron determined to enter. The inhabitants, aware of their design, stretched a very strong chain across the harbour mouth; but it did not avail; for the Roman ships broke through it, took possession of the town and ships, burnt most of them, and returned safe with an immense booty. This success was quickly followed by another, for as they were re-entering Panormus, they fell in with a Carthaginian fleet loaded with provisions for Hamilcar, who commanded in Sicily, and captured several of the transports. These advantages began to inspire the Romans with renewed confidence and hopes that their naval disasters were at an end, and that the gods had at length permitted them to become masters of the sea, when the privateer fleet, after having gained a considerable victory over a Carthaginian squadron, near the coast of Africa, was almost totally destroyed in a storm.

For a few years afterwards, the Romans seem to have desisted entirely from maritime enterprizes; but in the year of the city 516, they changed their plan, as it was indeed evident that unless they were masters at sea, they must be content to lose the island of Sicily. In order, however, that the Roman armies might not suffer by their losses at sea, it was decreed that the new fleet should be manned with hired troops. There was still another difficulty to overcome; the protracted war with Carthage, and the heavy and repeated losses which they had suffered during it, had nearly exhausted the Roman treasury; from it therefore could not possibly be drawn the sums requisite for the proper and effective equipment of such a fleet as would be adequate to meet that of the enemy. This difficulty was removed by the patriotism of all ranks and classes of the citizens. The senators set the example; the most wealthy of whom built, each at his own cost, a quinquereme: those who were not so wealthy joined together, three or four of them fitting out a single galley. By these means a fleet of 200 large vessels was made ready for any expedition, the state having bound themselves to repay the individuals whenever her finances were adequate to such an expence. This fleet was not only very numerous and well equipped, but most of the vessels which composed it were built on an entirely new model, which combined an extraordinary degree of celerity with strength. The model was taken from that light Rhodian galley, which we have already mentioned, as having been employed by its owner, Hannibal, in conveying intelligence between Carthage and Lilibæum, and which was afterwards captured by the Romans. The command of this fleet was given to the consul Lutatius: and the great object to be accomplished was the reduction of Lilibæum, which still held out. The first step of the consul was to occupy all the sea-ports near this place: the town of Drepanon, however, resisting his efforts, he resolved rather to decide its fate, and that of Sicily in general, by a sea battle, than to undertake a regular siege.

The Carthaginians soon gave him an opportunity of acting in this manner, for they sent to sea a fleet of 400 vessels, under the command of Hanno. In the building and equipment of this fleet, the senate of Carthage had nearly exhausted all their means; but though their fleet was numerically much greater than that of Rome, in some essential respects it was inferior to it. Most of the seamen and troops on board it were inexperienced and undisciplined; and the ships themselves were not to be compared, with regard to the union of lightness and strength, with the Roman vessels, as they were now built. Besides, the Romans trusted entirely to themselves— the Carthaginians, in some measure, to their allies or to hired seamen. The Romans, though firm and determined, were not rashly confident; whereas the Carthaginians even yet regarded their adversaries with feelings of contempt.

The hostile fleets met off Hiera, one of the Aeolian islands. The Carthaginian admiral's first object was to reach Eryx, a city which had lately been taken by Hamilcar, there to unload his vessels, and after having taken on board Hamilcar and the best of his troops, to sail again in quest of the Roman fleet. But the consul prevented this design from being carried into execution, by coming up with the Carthaginians, as we have just stated, off Hiera, while they were steering for Eryx. As the wind was favourable for the Romans, they were extremely anxious to commence the engagement immediately; but before they had formed into order of battle, it changed, blew hard, and a heavy sea arose. The determination of the consul to engage was for a short time shaken by this circumstance, but he reflected that though the sea was rough, the enemy's ships were heavily laden, and therefore would suffer more from it than his ships would; while if, on the other hand, he delayed the engagement till the Carthaginians reached Eryx, they would then have lighter vessels, as well as a greater number of experienced seamen and soldiers on board of them. These considerations determined him to fight immediately, and accordingly he gave orders for the line of battle to be formed. The battle was of very short duration, and terminated decidedly in favour of the Romans. The loss of the Carthaginians is variously stated, but, according to Polybius, who is the best authority for every thing relating to the Punic wars, the Romans sunk fifty of their vessels, and captured seventy, with all their crews. The remainder would probably have been either captured or destroyed, had not the wind again changed, and enabled them to save themselves by flight.

The consequences of this defeat, in the capitulation of Hamilcar, which, in a manner, determined the fate of Sicily, were so disheartening to the Carthaginians, that they were obliged to submit to a disadvantageous and dishonorable peace. Among other terms, it was stipulated that they should evacuate all the places they held in Sicily, and entirely quit that island; that they should also abandon all the small islands that lie between Italy and Sicily; and that they should not approach with their ships of war, either the coasts of Italy or any of the territories belonging to the Romans or their allies.

Soon after the conclusion of the first Punic war, a circumstance occurred which nearly renewed the hostilities. The Carthaginians were engaged in a bloody and arduous contest with their Mercenaries, and the Roman merchants supplied the latter with military stores and provisions. While engaged in this unlawful enterprize, several of them were captured by the Carthaginians, and their crews detained as prisoners of war. The senate of Carthage, however, were not then in a condition to offend the Romans; they therefore restored both the ships and their crews. During this war between the Carthaginians and the Mercenaries, the latter having obtained possession of Sardinia, (which though formerly conquered by the Romans, had been restored to the Carthaginians,) offered to put the Romans in possession of it. At first the senate refused to occupy it; but they soon changed their mind, and accepted the offer, and moreover obliged the Carthaginians to pay the expence of the armament by which it was occupied, and the further sum of 1200 talents.

Sicily, which immediately after the conclusion of the Punic war, was made a Roman province, and Sardinia, were the first territories which the Romans possessed out of Italy. In conformity with our plan, we shall enquire into the advantages they brought to the commerce of the Romans, before we proceed to the naval occurrences of the second Punic war.

Sicily was anciently called Sicania, Trinâcria, and Triquetra; its three promontories are particularly celebrated in the classic authors; viz. Lilibæum on the side of Africa; Pachynum on the side of Greece, and Pelorum towards Italy. Its vicinity to the continent of Italy, and the resemblance of their opposite shores, gave rise to an opinion among the ancients that it was originally joined to Italy. Pliny particularly mentions their separation, as a circumstance beyond all doubt. The dangers which were supposed to beset mariners in their passage through the narrow strait which divides it from Italy, on one side of which was Sylla, and on the other Charybdis, sufficiently point out the ignorance and inexperience of the ancients in the construction and management of their ships.

The principal town on the eastern coast of Sicily, opposite Greece, was Messana, now called Messina: it was the first which the Romans possessed in the island: it was one of the most wealthy and powerful cities in ancient Sicily. Taurominium stood near Mount Taurus, on the river Taurominius; the coast in its vicinity was anciently called Coproea, because the sea was supposed to throw up there the wrecks of such vessels as were swallowed up by Charybdis. The hills near this city were famous for the excellent grapes they produced. On a gulph in the Ionian Sea, called Catana, stood a city of the same name; it was one of the richest and most powerful cities in the island.

But by far the most celebrated city in this island for its advantageous situation, the magnificence of its buildings, its commerce, and the wealth of its inhabitants, was Syracuse. According to Thucydides, in his time it might justly be compared to Athens, even when that city was at the height of its glory; and Cicero describes it as the greatest and most wealthy of all the cities possessed by the Greeks. Its walls were eighteen miles in circumference, and within them were in fact four cities united into one. It seems also to have possessed three harbours: the great harbour was nearly five thousand yards in circumference, and the entrance to it five hundred yards across; it was formed on one side by a point of the island Ortygia, and on the other by another small island, on each of which were forts. The second harbour was divided from the greater by an island of inconsiderable extent; both these were surrounded with warehouses, arsenals, and other buildings of great magnificence. The river Anapis emptied itself into the great harbour; at the mouth of this river was the castle of Olympia. The third harbour stood a little above the division of the city called Acradina. The island of Ortygia, which formed one of the divisions, was joined to the others by a bridge.

The other maritime towns of consequence were Agrigentum, Lilibaeum, and Drepanum; though the first stood at a short distance from the sea, yet being situated between and near two rivers, it conveniently imported all sorts of provisions and merchandize. Lilibaeum was famous for its port, which was deemed a safe retreat for ships, either in case of a storm, or to escape from an enemy. During the wars between the Romans and Carthaginians, the former repeatedly attempted to render it inaccessible and useless by throwing large stones into it, but they were always washed away by the violence of the sea, and the rapidity of the current. Drepanum, which had an excellent harbour, was much resorted to by foreign ships, and possessed a very considerable commerce.

The Greeks were the first who colonized Sicily; and they founded Syracuse and other towns. About the same period the Phoenicians settled on the coast for the purposes of commerce; but they seem to have retired soon after the Greek colonies began to flourish and extend themselves. The Carthaginians, who generally pushed their commerce into all the countries with which their parent state had traded, seem to have visited Italy as merchants or conquerors at a very early period; but when their first visit took place in either character is not known. The treaty between them and the Romans, (to which we have had occasion to refer more than once,) which was formed in the year after the expulsion of the Tarquins, expressly stipulated that the Romans, who should touch at Sardinia, or that part of Sicily which belonged to the Carthaginians, should be received there in the same manner as the Carthaginians themselves. They must, however, soon afterwards have been driven out of the island; for at the time of the invasion of Greece by Xerxes, (which happened about thirty years after the expulsion of the Tarquins,) Gelon, the king of Syracuse, expressly states that they no longer possessed any territory there, in a speech which he made to the ambassadors of Athens and Sparta, the Cathaginians having united with Xerxes, and he having offered to ally himself with the Greeks. The circumstances and even the very nature of the victory which Gelon gained over the Carthaginians, which ended in their expulsion from Sicily, cannot accurately be ascertained: but from a comparison of the principal authorities on this point, it would, appear that it was a naval victory; or at least that the Carthaginian fleet was defeated as well as their army. Their loss by sea was enormous, amounting to nearly the whole of their ships of war and transports, the former consisting of 2000 and the latter of 3000.

Such is a short sketch of the island of Sicily, so far as its commercial facilities and its history are concerned previously to its conquest by the Romans. It was peculiarly valuable to them on account of its extreme fertility in corn; and by this circumstance it seems to have been distinguished in very early times; for there can be no doubt that by its being represented by the poets as the favourite residence of the goddess Ceres, the fertility of the island in corn, as well as its knowledge of agriculture, were intended to be represented. When Gelon offered to unite with the Greeks in their war with Xerxes, one of his proposals was that he would furnish the whole Greek army with corn, during all the time of hostilities, if they would appoint him commander of their forces. In the latter period of the Roman republic, it became their principal dependence for a regular supply of corn.

Sardinia seems to have been as little explored by and known to the ancients, as it is to the moderns. The treaty between the Carthaginians and Romans, the year after the expulsion of the Tarquins, proves that the former nation possessed it at that time. Calaris, the present Cagliari, was the principal town in it. From the epithet applied to it by Horace, in one of his odes, , it must have been much more fertile in former times than it is at present; and Varro expressly calls it one of the granaries of Rome. Its air, then, as at present, was in most parts very unwholsome; and it is a remarkable circumstance that the character of the Sardi, who, after the complete reduction of the island by Tiberius Sempronius Gracchus, were brought to Rome in great numbers, and sold as slaves, and who were proverbial for their worthlessness, is still to be traced in the present inhabitants; for they are represented as extremely barbarous, and so treacherous, and inhospitable, that they have been called the Malays of the Mediterranean. The island of Corsica, which, indeed, generally followed the fate of Sardinia, was another of the fruits of the first Punic war which the Romans reaped, in some degree favourable to their commerce. It possessed a large and convenient harbour, called Syracusium. The Carthaginians must have reduced it at an early period, since, according to Herodotus, the Cyrnians (the ancient name for the inhabitants), were one of the nations that composed the vast army, with which they invaded Sicily in the time of Gelon.

During the interval between the first and second Punic wars, the Roman commerce seems to have been gradually, but slowly extending itself, particularly in the Adriatic: we do not possess, however, any details on the subject, except a decisive proof of the attention and protection which the republic bestowed upon it, in repressing and punishing the piracies of the Illyrians and Istrians. These people, who were very expert and undaunted seamen, enriched themselves and their country by seizing and plundering the merchant vessels which frequented the Adriatic and adjacent Mediterranean sea; and their piracies were encouraged, rather than restrained by their sovereigns. At the period to which we allude, they were governed by a queen, named Teuta, who was a woman of a bold and enterprising spirit: the Roman merchants, who traded, in the Adriatic, had frequently been plundered and cruelly treated by her subjects; upon this, the Roman senate sent two ambassadors to her, to insist that she should put a stop to these measures. The Romans had also other grounds of complaint against her and her subjects; for the latter extended their piracies to the allies of Rome, as well as to the Romans themselves, and the former was at that time besieging the island of Issa, in the Adriatic, which was under the protection of the republic. The inhabitants of this island seem to have been rather extensively engaged in commerce, and were celebrated for building a kind of light ships, thence called .

Teuta received and treated the Roman ambassadors with great scorn and haughtiness; she promised, indeed, that she would no longer authorise the piracies of her subjects; but, with regard to restraining them, she would not do it, as they enjoyed a perfect and full right to benefit themselves as much as possible, and in every way they could, by their skill and superiority in maritime affairs. On the ambassadors' replying in rather threatening language, she ordered one of them to be put to death.

For a short time Teuta was alarmed at the probable consequences of her conduct, and endeavoured to avert them by submission; but, the Romans being otherwise engaged, and she having experienced some successes over the Acheans, her haughtiness and confidence revived, and she sent a fleet to assist in the reduction of Issa. Upon this, the Romans resolved to act with immediate vigour; and they had little difficulty in compelling Teuta to sue for peace. It was granted to her, on condition that not more than three ships of war should at any one time sail beyond Lyssus, on the frontier of Macedonia, and that the islands of Corcyra, Issa, and Pharos, together with Dyrrhachium should be given up to the Romans.

It was not, however, to be supposed that the Illyrians and Istrians, who had been so long accustomed to piracy, and who in fact derived nearly all their wealth from this source, would totally abstain from it. A few years after this treaty of peace, they resumed their depredations, which they carried on with so much audacity and disregard to the power of Rome, that they even seized the ships that were laden with corn for Rome. As this commerce was one of the greatest consequence to the Romans, in which the Roman government, as well as individuals, principally embarked, and on the regularity and safety of which the subsistence and tranquillity of the city itself depended, the senate resolved to punish them more effectually; and this resolution was strengthened by the Illyrians having broken the terms of the peace by sending no fewer than 50 vessels of war beyond the prescribed limits, as far as the Cyclades. The consequence of the new war which the Romans waged against them, was the reduction of Istria and of Illyricum Proper.

The destruction of Saguntum by the Carthaginians was the cause of the second Punic war. At what period the Carthaginians first established themselves in Spain, is not known. Their principal object in colonizing and retaining it, undoubtedly may be found in the richness of its mines, and the fertility of its soil. According to Diodorus Siculus, they were principally enabled to equip and support their numerous, and frequently renewed fleets, by the silver which they drew from these mines. And Strabo expressly informs us, that when the Carthaginians first colonized Spain, silver was in such abundance, and so easily obtained, that their most common utensils, and even the mangers for their horses, were made of it. One mine of extreme richness is particularly described by Pliny: according to him, it yielded 300 pounds of silver in a day. There are other circumstances which point out the extreme value of Spain to whoever possessed it, and lead us to the motives which induced the Romans to use all their efforts to wrest it from the Carthaginians. It cannot be doubted that the Carthaginians drew from it all the wealth, in various shapes, which it could possibly supply; and yet we know that in the short space of nine years, 111,542 pounds weight of silver, 4095 of gold, besides coin, were brought out of it by the Roman praetors, who governed it. Scipio, when he returned to Rome, brought from Spain 14,342 pounds weight of silver, besides coin, arms, and corn, &c. to an immense amount. And Lentulus returned from this country with 44,000 pounds of silver, and 2550 of gold, besides the coin, &c., which was divided among his soldiers. Manlius brought with him 1200 pounds of silver, and about 30 of gold. Cornelius Lentulus, who was praetor of Hither Spain for two years, brought with him 1515 pounds of gold, and 2000 of silver, besides a large amount of coin, while the praetor of Farther Spain returned with 50,000 pounds of silver. And these immense sums, as we have already stated, were brought away in the space of nine years.

Cornelius Scipio was sent into Spain at the commencement of the second Punic war. Of the events of this war, however, we shall confine ourselves exclusively to such as were maritime, and which trace the steps of the Roman superiority at sea, and, consequently, of the advancement and extension of their commerce. The exertions of the rival nations to contest the empire of the sea were very great: the Romans equipped 220 quinqueremes, and twenty other light vessels, beside 160 galleys, and twenty light vessels, which were employed to transport troops to Africa. Their allies, the Syracusans, also, were active and alert in the equipment of a fleet to assist their allies, the Romans; and Hiero, their king, had the good fortune to give an auspicious commencement to the war, by capturing some Carthaginian ships, part of a fleet, whose object was to plunder the coasts of Italy, but which had been dispersed by a storm. The Carthaginians were equally unfortunate in their second maritime enterprise against Lilibaeum, for the Syracusans and Romans, having learnt their intention, anchored before the mouth of the harbour. The Carthaginians, finding that they could not, as they expected, surprise the place, drew up their fleet in line of battle, a little way out at sea: the allies immediately got under weigh; a battle ensued, in which the Carthaginians were defeated, with the loss of seven ships. These successes, however, were dreadfully counterbalanced by the advance of Hannibal into Italy, and the decisive victories which he obtained in the very heart of the Roman territories. Under these circumstances, maritime affairs were naturally disregarded.

Of the actual state of the Roman commerce about this time we know very little, but that it was lucrative, may fairly be inferred from the following circumstance:—A little before the commencement of the second Punic war, Caius Flaminnus was extremely desirous to obtain the support and good will of the populace; with this object in view, he joined the tribunes of the people in passing a law, which is called the Flaminian, or Claudian law. By it, the senators, who had been accustomed to acquire considerable wealth by fitting out ships and trading, were expressly forbidden to possess or hire any vessel above the burden of 300 amphorae or eight tons, and not more than one vessel even of that small tonnage. This vessel was allowed them, and was deemed sufficient to bring the produce of their farms to Rome. By the same law, the scribes, and the clerks, and attendants of the quæstors, were prohibited from trading; and thus the liberty of commerce was exclusively confined to the plebeians.

Whilst Hannibal threatened the Romans in the vicinity of Rome itself, they had neither leisure, inclination, or means, to cope with the Carthaginians by sea; at length, however, Marcellus, having checked the enemy in Italy, maritime affairs were again attended to. Scipio, who had been successful in Spain, resolved to attempt the reduction of New Carthage: this place was situated, like Old Carthage, on a peninsula betwixt a port and a lake: its harbour was extremely commodious, and large enough to receive and shelter any fleet. As it was the capital of the Carthaginian dominions in Spain, here were deposited all their naval stores, machines used in war, besides immense treasures. It was on this account extremely well fortified, and to attempt to take it by a regular siege seemed to Scipio impracticable: he, therefore, formed a plan to take it by surprise, and this plan he communicated to C. Lælius, the commander of the fleet, who was his intimate friend. The Roman fleet was to block up the port by sea, while Scipio was to blockade it by land. The ignorance of the Romans with regard to one of the most common and natural phenomena of the sea, is strongly marked in the course of this enterprise. Scipio knew that when the tide ebbed, the port of New Carthage would become dry and accessible by land; but his soldiers, and even his officers, were ignorant of the nature of the tides, and they firmly believed that Neptune had wrought a miracle in their favour, when, according to Scipio's prediction, the tide retired, and the army was thus enabled to capture the town, the walls of which on that side were extremely low, the

Carthaginians having directed all their attention and efforts to the opposite side. The capture of New Carthage depressed, in a great degree, the spirits, as well as weakened the strength of the Carthaginians in Spain: eighteen galleys were captured in the port, besides 113 vessels laden with naval stares; 40,000 bushels of wheat, 260,000 bushels of barley, a large number of warlike machines of all descriptions, 260 cups of gold, most of which weighed a pound, 18,300 pounds weight of silver, principally coin, besides brass money, were among the spoils.

About the year of Rome 556, Scipio had succeeded in reducing all Spain. It does not appear, however, that the Romans were thus enabled greatly to extend their commerce; indeed, at this period, we have no evidence that any other town in Spain, except Gades, possessed any considerable trade. This island and city were situated in a gulph of the same name, between the straits of Gibraltar and the river Boetis; and, from the remotest period of which we possess any records, was resorted to by foreigners for the purposes of commerce. Gradually, however, the inhabitants of Spain, under the Roman government, enriched themselves and their conquerors by their industry: large quantities of corn, wine, and oil were exported, besides wax, honey, pitch, vermilion, and wool. The oil and wool were deemed equal, if not superior, to those of any other part of the world: the excellent quality of the wool is a strong fact, against an opinion entertained by many, that the fineness of the Spanish was originally derived from the exportation of some English sheep to Spain, since it appears to have been celebrated even in the time of the Romans: how important and lucrative an object it was considered, may be collected from the attention that was paid to the breed of sheep; a ram, according to Strabo, having been sold for a talent, or nearly 200 . Horace incidentally gives evidence of the commercial wealth of Spain in his time, when he considers the master of a Spanish trading vessel and a person of great wealth as synonimous terms.

As Hannibal still continued in Italy, the senate of Rome resolved to send Scipio into Italy, with a discretionary power to invade Africa from that island. He lost no time in equipping a fleet for these purposes, and his efforts were so well seconded by the zeal and activity of the provinces and cities, many of which taxed themselves to supply iron, timber, cloth for sails, corn, &c. that, in forty days after the timber was felled, Scipio had a fleet of thirty new galleys.

Soon after he landed in Sicily, he resolved to invade Africa: for this purpose his fleet was collected in the port of Lilibæum. Never was embarkation made with more order and solemnity: the concourse of people who came from all parts to see him set sail, and wish him a prosperous voyage, was prodigious. Just before he weighed anchor, he appeared on the poop of his galley, and, after an herald had proclaimed silence, addressed a solemn prayer to the gods. It is foreign to our purpose to give any account of the campaign in Africa, which, it is well known, terminated in the utter defeat of the Carthaginians, who were obliged to sue for peace. This was granted them on very severe terms: all the cities and provinces which they possessed in Africa previously to the war, they were indeed permitted to retain, but they were stripped of Spain, and of all the islands in the Mediterranean; all their ships of war, except ten galleys, were to be delivered up to the Romans; and, for the future, they were not to maintain above that number at one time: even the size of their fishing boats and of their trading vessels was regulated. In the course of fifty years ten thousand talents were to be paid to the Romans. During a short truce which preceded the peace, the Carthaginians had seized and plundered a Roman squadron, which had been dispersed by a storm, and driven near Carthage; as a satisfaction for this, they were obliged to pay the Romans 25,000 pounds weight of silver. The successful termination of the second Punic war gave to the Romans complete dominion of the sea, on which they maintained generally 100 galleys. Commerce flourished, particularly that most important branch, the trade in corn, with which Rome, at this period, is said to have been so plentifully furnished, that the merchants paid their seamen with it.

The power of the Romans at sea was now so well established, that no foreign power could hope to attack, or resist them, unless they were expert navigators, as well as furnished with a numerous fleet. Under this impression, Philip king of Macedon, who had long been jealous and afraid of them, applied himself sedulously to maritime affairs. As it was about this period that the Romans began to turn their thoughts to the conquest of Greece, it may be proper to take a retrospective view of the maritime affairs and commerce of that country. An inspection of the map of Greece will point out the advantages which it possessed for navigation and commerce. Lying nearly in the middle of the Mediterranean, with the sea washing three of its sides; possessed of almost innumerable inlets and bays, it was admirably adapted to ancient commerce. Its want of large and navigable rivers, which will always limit its commerce in modern times, presented no obstacle to the small vessels in which the ancients carried on their trade; as they never navigated them during the winter, and from their smallness and lightness, they could easily drag them on shore.

Athens, the most celebrated state in Greece for philosophy, literature, and arms, was also the most celebrated for commerce. The whole of the southern angle of Attica consisted of a district called Parali, or the division adjacent to the sea. In the other districts of Attica, the soldiers of the republic were found: this furnished the sailors; fishing and navigation were the chief employments of its inhabitants. About 46 miles distant from the Piraeus, stood Sunium, the most considerable town in this district: it possessed a double harbour in the Mediterranean.

The principal commerce of Attica, however, was carried on at Athens: this city had three harbours: the most ancient was that of Phalerum, distant from the city, according to some authors, 35 stadia; according to others only 20 stadia. It was nearer Athens than the other two, but smaller, and less commodious. Munichea was the name of the second harbour: it was formed in a promontory not far distant from the Pirasus, a little to the east of Athens, and naturally a place of great strength; it was afterwards, at the instance of Thrasybulus, rendered still stronger by art. But by far the most celebrated harbour of Athens was the Piraeus. The republic of Athens, in order to concentrate its military and mercantile fleets in this harbour, abandoned that of Phalerum, and bent all their efforts to render the Piraeus as strong and commodious as possible. This occurred in the time of Themistocles; by whose advice both the town and the harbour were inclosed with a wall, about seven miles and a half long, and sixty feet high. Themistocles' intention was to have made it eighty cubits high, but in this he was opposed. Before this connecting wall was built, the Piraeus was about three miles distant from the city. As the strength of the wall was of the utmost importance, it was built of immense square stones, which were fastened together with iron or leaden cramps. It was so broad that two waggons could have been driven along it. The Pireus contained three docks; the first called Cantharus, the second Aphrodisium, and the third Zea. There were likewise five porticos, and two forums. The Piraeus was so celebrated for its commerce, that it became a proverbial saying in Greece, "Famine does not come from the Piræus." The extent and convenience of the Piræus may be judged of from this circumstance, that under the demagogue Lycurgus, the whole naval force of the nation, amounting to 400 triremes, were safely and easily laid up in its three harbours.

Before the time of Themistocles, Athens does not appear to have devoted her attention or resources to maritime affairs: but this celebrated general not only rendered the Piræus stronger and more commodious, but also procured a decree, which enabled him to add twenty ships to the fleet annually. The sums arising from the sale of the privileges of working the mines, or the eventual profits of the mines, which had formerly been distributed among the people, were, through his influence, set apart for the building of ships. Afterwards a law was passed, which taxed all the citizens who possessed land, manufactories, or money in trade or with their bankers; these classes of the citizens were also obliged to keep up, and increase, if occasion required it, the naval force of the republic. When it was necessary to fit out an armament, as many talents as there were galleys to be built and equipped, were raised in each of the ten tribes of Athens. The money thus collected was given to the captains of the galleys, to be expended in the maintenance of the crew. The republic furnished the rigging and sailors: two captains were appointed to each galley, who served six months each.

Although the vessels employed by the Athenians both for war and commerce were small compared with those of modern days, and their merchant ships even much smaller than those of the Phoenicians, if we may judge by the description given by Xenophon of a Phoenician merchant vessel in the Piræus, yet the expence attending their equipment was very great. We learn from Demosthenes, that the light vessels could not be kept in commission, even if the utmost attention was paid to economy, and no extraordinary damage befel them, for a smaller sum than about 8000 . annually; of course, such vessels as from their size, strength, and manning, were capable of standing the brunt of an engagement, must have cost more than double that sum.

In the time of Demosthenes, the trade of Athens seems to have been carried on with considerable spirit and activity; the greater part of the money of the Athenians having been employed in it. From one of his orations we learn, that in the contract executed when money was lent for this purpose, the period when the vessel was to sail, the nature and value of the goods with which she was loaded, the port to which she was to carry them, the manner in which they were to be sold there, and the goods with which she was to return to Athens, were all specifically and formally noticed. In other particulars the contracts varied: the money, lent was either not to be repaid till the return of the vessel, or it was to be repaid as soon as the outward goods were sold at the place to which she was bound, either to the agent of the lender, or to himself, he going there for that express purpose. The interest of money so lent varied: sometimes it rose as high as 30 per cent: it seems to have depended principally on the risks of the voyage.

In another oration of Demosthenes we discover glimpses of what by many has been deemed maritime insurance, or rather of the fraud at present called barratry, which is practised to defraud the insurer: but, as Park in his learned Treatise on Marine Insurance has satisfactorily proved, the ancients were certainly ignorant of maritime insurance; though there can be no doubt frauds similar to those practised at present were practised. According to Demosthenes, masters of vessels were in the habit of borrowing considerable sums, which they professed to invest in a cargo of value, but instead of such a cargo, they took on board sand and stones, and when out at sea, sunk the vessel. As the money was lent on the security either of the cargo or ship, or both, of course the creditors were defrauded: but it does not appear how they could, without detection, substitute sand or stones for the cargo.

The Athenians passed a number of laws respecting commerce, mostly of a prohibitory nature. Money could not be advanced or lent on any vessel, or the cargo of any vessel, that did not return to Athens, and discharge its cargo there. The exportation of various articles, which were deemed of the first necessity, was expressly forbidden: such as timber for building, fir, cypress, plane, and other trees, which grew in the neighbourhood of the city; the rosin collected on Mount Parnes, the wax of Mount Hymettus—which two articles, incorporated together, or perhaps singly, were used for daubing over, or caulking their ships. The exportation of corn, of which Attica produced very little, was also forbidden; and what was brought from abroad was not permitted to be sold any where except in Athens. By the laws of Solon, they were allowed to exchange oil for foreign commodities. There were besides a great number of laws respecting captains of ships, merchants, duties, interest of money, and different kinds of contracts. One law was specially favourable to merchants and all engaged in trade; by it a heavy fine, or, in some cases, imprisonment, was inflicted on whoever accused a merchant or trader of any crime he could not substantiate. In order still farther to protect commerce, and to prevent it from suffering by litigation, all causes which respected it could be heard only during the period when vessels were in port. This period extended generally to six months—from April to September inclusive—no ships being at sea during the other portion of the year.

The taxes of the Athenians, so far as they affected commerce, consisted of a fifth, levied on the corn and other merchandize imported, and also on several articles which were exported from Athens. These duties were generally farmed. In an oration of Andocides, we learn that he had farmed the duty on foreign goods imported for a term of three years, at twelve talents annually. In consequence of these duties, smuggling was not uncommon. The inhabitants of the district called Corydale were celebrated for illicit traffic: there was a small bay in this district, a little to the north of Piræus, called. Thieves' Harbour, in which an extensive and lucrative and contraband trade was carried on; ships of different nations were engaged in it. Demosthenes informs us, that though this place was within the boundaries of Attica, yet the Athenians had not the legal power to put a stop to traffic by which they were greatly injured, as the inhabitants of Corydale, as well as the inhabitants of every other state, however small, were sovereigns within their own territory.

In an oration of Isocrates an operation is described which bears some resemblance to that performed by modern bills of exchange. A stranger who brought grain to Athens, and who, we may suppose, wished to purchase goods to a greater amount than the sale of his grain would produce, drew on a person living in some town on the Euxine, to which the Athenians were in the habit of trading. The Athenian merchant took this draft; but not till a banker in Athens had become responsible for its due payment.

The Athenian merchants were obliged, from the nature of trade in those ancient times, to be constantly travelling from one spot to another; either to visit celebrated fairs, or places where they hoped to carry on an advantageous speculation. We shall afterwards notice more particularly the Macedonian merchant mentioned by Ptolemy the Geographer, who sent his clerks to the very borders of China; and from other authorities we learn that the Greek merchants were accurately informed respecting the interior parts of Germany, and the course of most of the principal rivers in that country. The trade in aromatics, paints, cosmetics, &c., was chiefly possessed by the Athenians, who had large and numerous markets in Athens for the sale of these articles. Even in the time of Hippocrates, some of the spices of India were common in the Peloponnesus and Attica; and there is every reason to believe that most of these articles were introduced into Greece in consequence of the journeys of their merchants to some places of depôt, to which they were brought from the East.

We have already mentioned that the importation of corn into a country so unfertile as Attica, was a subject of the greatest moment, and to which the care and laws of the republic were most particularly directed. There were magistrates, whose sole business and duty it was to lay in corn for the use of the city; and other magistrates who regulated its price, and fixed also the assize of bread. In the Piræus there were officers, the chief part of whose duty it was to take care that two parts at least of all the corn brought into the port should be carried to the city. Lysias, in his oration against the corn merchants, gives a curious account of the means employed, by them to raise its price, very similar to the rumours by which the same effect is often produced at present: an embargo, or prohibition of exporting it, by foreigners, an approaching war, or the capture or loss of the vessels laden with it, seem to have been the most prevalent rumours.

Sicily, Egypt, and the Crimea were the countries which principally supplied Attica with this necessary article. As the voyage from Sicily was the shortest, as well as exposed to the least danger, the arrival of vessels with corn from this island always reduced the price; but there does not appear to have been nearly such quantities brought either from it or Egypt, as from the Crimea. The Athenians, therefore, encouraged by every possible means their commerce with the Cimmerian Bosphorus. One of the kings of that country, Leucon II., who reigned about the time of Demosthenes, favoured them very much. As the harbours were unsafe and inconvenient, he formed a new one, called Theodosia, or, in the language of the country, Ardauda: he likewise exempted their vessels from paying the duty on corn, to which all other vessels were subject on exporting it—this duty amounted to a thirtieth part,—and allowed their merchants a free trade to all parts of his kingdom. In return, the Athenians made him and his children citizens of Athens, and granted to such of his subjects as traded in Attica the same privileges and exemptions which their citizens enjoyed in Bosphorus. It was one of the charges against Demosthenes, by his rival, the orator Dinarchus, that the sons and successors of Leucon sent yearly to him a thousand bushels of wheat. Besides the new port of Theodosia, the Athenians traded also to Panticapæum for corn: the quantity they exported is stated by Demosthenes to have amounted to 400,000 mediniri, or bushels, yearly, as appeared from the custom books; and this was by far the greatest quantity of corn they received from foreign countries. Lucian, indeed, informs us that a ship, which, from his description, must have been about the size of our third-rates, contained as much corn as maintained all Attica for a twelvemonth; but, in the time of this author, Athens was not nearly so populous as it had been: and besides, as is justly remarked by Hume, it is not safe to trust to such loose rhetorical illustrations.

From a passage in Thucydides we may learn that the Athenians derived part of their supply of corn from Euboea; this passage is also curious as exhibiting a surprising instance of the imperfection of ancient navigation. Among the inconveniences experienced by the Athenians, from the fortifying of Dacelia by the Lacedemonians, this historian particularly mentions, as one of the most considerable, that they could not bring over their corn from Euboea by land, passing by Oropus, but were under the necessity of embarking it, and sailing round Cape Sunium; and yet the water carriage could not be more than double the land carriage.

The articles imported by the Athenians from the Euxine Sea, besides corn, were timber for building, slaves, salt, honey, wax, wool, leather, and goat-skins; from Byzantium and other ports of Thrace and Macedonia, salt fish and timber; from Phrygia and Miletus, carpets, coverlets for beds, and the fine wool, of which their cloths were made; from the islands of Egean Sea, wine and different fruits; and from Thrace, Thessaly, Phrygia, &c., a great number of slaves.

The traffic in slaves was, next to that in corn, of the greatest consequence to the Athenians, for the citizens were not in sufficient numbers, and, if they had been, were not by any means disposed, to cultivate the land, work the mines, and carry on the various trades and manufactures. The number of slaves in Attica, during the most flourishing period of the republic, was estimated at 400,000: of these the greater part had been imported; the rest were natives of Greece, whom the fate of arms had thrown into the hands of a conqueror irritated by too obstinate a resistance. The slaves most esteemed, and which brought the highest price, were imported from Syria and Thrace, the male slaves of the former country, and the females of the latter: the slaves from Macedonia were the least valued. The price of a slave seems to have been extremely low, as Xenophon mentions that some were sold at Athens for half an Attic mina, or rather more than thirty shillings: those, however, who had acquired a trade, or were otherwise particularly useful, were valued at five minæ, or about fifteen pounds.

Our idea of the commerce of Athens, and of Greece in general, would be very imperfect and inadequate if we neglected to notice their fairs. It has been ingeniously supposed, that at the celebrated games of Greece, such as those of Olympia, &c., trade was no subordinate object; and this idea is certainly confirmed by various passages in ancient authors. Cicero expressly informs us, that even so early as the age of Pythagoras, a great number of people attended the religious games for the express purpose of trading. At Delphi, Nemæa, Delos, or the Isthmus of Corinth, a fair was held almost every year. The amphyctionic fairs were held twice a year. In the time of Chrysostom, these fairs were infamously distinguished for a traffic in slaves, destined for public incontinence. The amphyctionic spring fair was held at Delphi, and at Thermopylæ in the autumn; in fact, at the same times that the deputies from the states of Greece formed the amphyctionic council;—another proof that wherever large assemblies of people took place in Greece, for religious or political purposes, advantage was taken of them to carry on traffic. At the fairs of Thermopylæ medicinal herbs and roots, especially hellebore, were sold in large quantities. One principal reason why the religious games or political assemblies of the states were fixed upon to hold fairs was, that during them all hostilities were suspended; and every person might go with his merchandize in safety to them, even through an enemy's country. The priests, so far from regarding these fairs as a profanation of the religions ceremonies, encouraged them; and the priests of Jupiter, in particular, advanced large sums on interest to such merchants as had good credit, but had not sufficient money with them.

The island of Delos calls for our particular attention, as the grand mart of the Athenians, as well as of the rest of Greece, and of the other countries in the Mediterranean, which at this period were engaged in commerce. The peace of this island always remained undisturbed, from an opinion that it was under the special protection of Apollo and Diana; and when the fleets of enemies met there, out of respect to the sacredness of the place, they forbore all manner of hostilities. There were also other circumstances which contributed to render it a place of great importance to commerce: its commodious situation for the navigation from Europe into Asia; its festivals, which brought immense crowds to it (and as we have just observed, wherever a multitude of Greeks were collected, by superstitious rites or amusements, commerce was mingled with their duties and pursuits); and the bias which its original, or at least its very early inhabitants, had to commerce: all these combined to render it a place of great importance to commerce. Its trade consisted chiefly in slaves: according to Strabo, in the time of Perseus, king of Macedonia, above 10,000 slaves came in and went out daily. The corn, wine, and other commodities of the neighbouring islands; the scarlet linen tunics, manufactured in the island of Amorgos; the rich purple stuffs of Cos; the highly esteemed alum of Melos, and the valuable copper, which the mines, of Delos itself (that had been long worked,) and the elegant vases, manufactured from this copper,—were the principal commodities exported from Delos. In return and exchange, foreign merchants brought the produce and manufactures of their respective countries; so that the island became, as it were, the storehouse of the treasures of nations; and the scene, during this mixture of religious festivals and commercial enterprise, was peculiarly gay and animated. The inhabitants were, by an express law, which is noticed by Athenæus, obliged to furnish water to all the strangers who resorted thither; to which, it would appear, they added, either gratuitously, or for a small remuneration, cakes and other trifling eatables.

The Athenians were so anxious to protect and extend the commerce carried on in Delos, that they gave encouragement to such strangers to settle there as were conversant in commerce, as well as strictly guarded its neutrality and privileges. On the destruction of Tyre, and afterwards of Carthage, events which gave a new direction to the commerce of the Mediterranean, a great number of merchants from these cities fled to Delos, where they were taken under the protection of the Athenians; and it appears by an inscription found in the 17th century, that the Tyrians formed a company of merchants and navigators there. The Romans traded to it, even before their war with Philip, king of Macedon. After the restoration of Corinth, the Athenians used all their efforts to keep up the commerce of Delos; but the wars of Mithridates put an end to it; and in a very short period afterwards, it seems to have been entirely abandoned by the merchants of all nations, and, as a commercial place, to have fallen into utter neglect and decay.

Corinth, next to Athens, demands our notice, as one of the most commercial cities of Greece. The Corinthian dominions were extremely small, their extent from east to west being about half a degree, and from north to south about half that space: according to the geographer Scylax, a vessel might sail from one extremity to the other in a day. It had no rivers of any note, and few rich plains, being in general uneven, and but moderately fertile. The situation of Corinth itself, however, amply compensated for all these disadvantages: it was built on the middle of the isthmus of the same name, at the distance of about 60 stadia on either side from the sea; on one side was the Saronic Gulf, on the other the sea of Crissa. On the former was the port of Lechæum, which was joined to the city by a double wall, 12 stadia in length; on the latter sea, was the port of Cinchræa, distant from Corinth 70 stadia. There was, besides, the port and castle of Cromyon, about 120 stadia distant from the capital. Hence, it will appear that Corinth commanded the trade of all the eastern part of the Mediterranean by the port of Cinchræa; and of the Ionian sea, by that of Lechæum. But the Corinthians possessed other advantages; for their citadel was almost impregnable, commanded from its situation both these seas, and stood exactly in the way of communication by land between one part of Greece and the other. The other states, however, would not permit the Corinthians to interdict them the passage of the Isthmus; but they could not prevent them from taking advantage of their situation, by carrying on an extensive and lucrative commerce. The Isthmian games, which were celebrated at Corinth, also contributed very much to its splendour and opulence, and drew additional crowds to it, who, as usual, mingled commerce with religion. According to Thucydides, Corinth had been a city of great traffic, even when the Greeks confined their trade to land: at this period, the Corinthians imposed a transit duty on all commodities, which entered or left the Peloponnessus by the Isthmus. But the extended knowledge and enterprise of the Greeks, and, above all, the destruction of the pirates which infested the narrow seas, led them to prefer sea carriage part of the way. The reason why they did not transport their goods the whole passage by sea, may be found in their ignorance and fears: their inexperienced mariners and frail ships could not succeed in doubling Cape Malea in Laconia; off which, and between it and Crete, the sea was frequently very boisterous. Hence, the merchants were under the necessity of transporting, by land carriage, their goods to the seas which formed the Isthmus. Such as came from Italy, Sicily, and the countries to the west, were landed at Lechæum; while the merchandize from Asia Minor, Phœnicia, and the islands in the Egean Sea, were landed at the port of Cinchræa. The breadth of the Isthmus was so small that the goods were easily and quickly conveyed from one harbour to the other; and afterwards the Corinthians succeeded in transporting the ships themselves.

At first it would appear that the Corinthians contented themselves with the wealth derived from their city being the great mart of commerce, and from the duties which they imposed: but they soon began to engage very extensively and with great spirit in trade themselves. Several kinds of manufactures were encouraged, which were highly valued by foreign nations, especially coverlets for beds, and brass and earthen-ware vessels. But their most valuable manufacture consisted in a metal compounded of copper and a small quantity of gold and silver, which was extremely brilliant, and scarcely liable to rust or decay. From this metal they made helmets, &c., little figures, cups, vessels, &c., which were highly esteemed, not only on account of the metal of which they were formed, but still more on account of the tasteful foliage and other ornaments with which they were covered. Their earthen-ware was ornamented in the same beautiful and tasteful manner.

All these were exported by the Corinthians in great quantities, and formed very lucrative articles of trade. Paper and sailcloth from Egypt; ivory from Lybia; leather from Cyrene; incense from Syria; dates from Phœnicia; carpets from Carthage; corn and cheese from Sicily; apples and pears from Euboea;—filled the warehouses of Corinth.

As soon as Corinth resolved to participate in maritime commerce, she applied herself to this object with great industry and success: she built ships of a novel form, and first produced galleys with three benches of oars; and history assures us that the Greeks obtained their first maritime experience during the naval war between the Corinthians and the inhabitants of Corfu; and by their instruction the Samians put to sea those powerful fleets for which they were distinguished.

Besides Athens and Corinth, there were no states in ancient Greece, the consideration of whose maritime and commercial affairs will detain us long. Lacedæmonia was favourably situated in these respects; but either her laws, or the disposition and pursuits of her inhabitants, prevented her from taking advantage of her situation. All the south part of Laconia was encompassed by the sea, and on the east and north-east was the Argelic Bay: on its coasts were a great number of capes, the most celebrated of which were those of Malea and Tanara; they were also furnished with a great number of sea-port towns and commodious harbours. In consequence of the capes extending far into the sea, and the deepness of some of the bays, the ancients took three days to navigate the length of the coast in vessels wrought by oars, following, as they generally did, all the windings of the land. The little river Pameros, which divided Beotia from Laconia, formed one extremity, and the port of Prais, on the Gulf of Argelis, formed the other. The most difficult and dangerous part of this navigation consisted in doubling Cape Malea.

The most convenient and frequented sea-ports in Laconia were Trinassus and Acria, situated on each side the mouth of the Eurotas; and Gythium, not far from Trinassus, at the mouth of a small river on the Laconic Gulf. The mouth of this river, which was navigable up to Sparta, was defended by a citadel, the ruins of which were remaining in the time of Pausanias. As the Lacedæmonians regarded this town as their principal port, in which their naval forces, as well as the greater part of their merchant ships assembled, they employed considerable labour and expence in rendering it commodious and safe; for this purpose they dug a very spacious basin which, on one side was defended by motes, and on the other by numerous fortifications: the strength of these may be judged of from the circumstance, that even after the armies of Sparta had been utterly defeated by Epaminondas, and Philip, the son of Demetrius, neither of these conquerors could capture this sea-port. In it were deposited all the requisites for their naval force, and from it sailed their merchant ships with cargoes to Crete, Africa, and Egypt; to all of which countries, according to Thucydides, the Lacedæmonians carried on a lucrative and regular traffic. Another of their sea-ports was Epidaurus, situated on the Gulf of Argos, in the eastern part of Laconia. The country round it contained many vineyards, the wine of which was exported in considerable quantities, and supplied other parts of Greece. This district is still celebrated for its wine, called Malvasia, (or Malmsey,) a corruption from Maleates, the ancient name of this part of Laconia.

We have already alluded to the supposed aversion of the Spartans to maritime affairs, which, according to some authors, arose from Lycurgus having prohibited them from building vessels, or employing sailors; but this idea is unfounded, and seems to have arisen from the fact, that their kings were prevented, by a positive law, from commanding the fleets. That the Spartans engaged in commerce, we have, as has been just stated, the express testimony of Thucydides; and there is abundant evidence that they had always armed vessels during their wars; and even so early as the time of Croesus, they sent some troops to Satnos, and plundered that island: and in later times, they used such efforts to equip vessels, in order to gain the mastery of the seas, that, according to Xenophon, they entirely neglected their cavalry. They were stimulated to this line of conduct by Alcibiades, who advised the kings, ephori, and the nation at large, to augment their marine, to compel the ships of all other nations to lower their flag to theirs, and to proclaim themselves exclusive masters of the Grecian seas. Isocrates informs us, that, before Alcibiades came to Lacedaemon, the Spartans, though they had a navy, expended little on it; but afterwards they increased it almost daily. The signal defeat they sustained at the battle of Cnidus, where Conon destroyed their whole fleet, not only blasted their hopes of becoming masters of the seas, but, according to Isocrates, led to their defeat at the battle of Leuctra.

Off the coast of Laconia, and about forty stadia from Cape Malea, lies the island of Cythera; the strait between it and the mainland was deemed by the ancients extremely dangerous in stormy weather; and indeed its narrowness, and the rocks that lay off Cape Malea must, to such inexperianced navigators, have been very alarming. The Phoenicians are supposed to have had a settlement in this island: afterwards it became an object of great consequence to the Lacedaemonians, who fortified, at great expence, and with much labour and skill, its two harbours, Cythera and Scandea. The convenience of these harbours to the Lacedaemonians compensated for the sterility of the island, which was so great that when the Athenians conquered it, they could raise from it only four Attic talents annually. The chief employment and source of wealth to the inhabitants consisted in collecting a species of shell-fish, from which an inferior kind of Tyrian dye was extracted. There were several fisheries on the mainland of Laconia for the same purpose.

Some of the other Greek islands require a short and general notice, on account of the attention they paid to maritime affairs. Corcyra was inhabited by skilful mariners, who, in the time of Herodotus, possessed a greater number of ships than any other people in Greece, with the exception of the Athenians; and, according to Thucydides, at one period they were masters of the Mediterranean Sea. On the invasion of Greece by Xerxes, they fitted out a fleet of sixty ships, with which they promised to assist their countrymen; but, instead of this, their ships anchored in a place where they could see the result of the battle of Salamis, and when they ascertained that the Greeks were victorious, they pretended that they had been prevented from affording the promised succours by contrary winds, so that they could not double Cape Malea. Of the commerce of this island we have no particulars detailed by ancient writers.

Egina, in the Saronic Gulf, acquired great wealth from the cultivation of commerce: in the time of the Persian war, they equipped a very powerful and well-manned fleet for the defence of Greece; and at the battle of Salamis they were adjudged to have deserved the prize of valour. According to Elian, they were the first people who coined money.

The island of Euboea possessed excellent harbours, from which, as it was very fertile, the Athenians exported large quantities of corn. This island is divided from the mainland of Greece by the Euripus, which the ancients represented to be so extremely narrow, that a galley could scarcely pass through it: its frequent and irregular tides were, also the subject of their wonder, and the cause of them, of their fruitless researches and conjectures. It hits several promontories, the doubling of one of which, Cape Catharius, was reckoned by the ancients very dangerous, on account of the many rocks and whirlpools on the const. Of all the cities of Euboea, Chalcis was the most famous: its inhabitants applied themselves, at a very early period, to navigation, and sent numerous colonies to Thrace, Macedon, Italy, &c. In the vicinity of another of its towns, Carystus, there were quarries of very fine marble, the exportation of which seems to have been a lucrative trade: in the same part of the island also was found the asbestos. Euboea possessed several rich copper and iron mines; and as the inhabitants were very skilful in working these metals, the exportation of armour, and various vessels made from them, was also one important branch of their commerce.

Of the numerous colonies sent out by the Greeks, we shall notice only those which were established for the purposes of commerce, or which, though not established for this express purpose, became afterwards celebrated for it. None of the Athenian colonies, which they established expressly for the purpose of trading with the capital, was of such importance as Amphipolis. This place was situated at the mouth of the river Strymon, on the borders of Macedonia. The country in its vicinity was very fertile in wood, and from it, for a considerable length of time, the Athenians principally derived timber for building their fleets: they also levied on its inhabitants a heavy tribute in silver coin. As this city was well situated for commerce, and the Athenians, wherever they went, or were settled, were eager in pursuit of gain, their colonists in Amphipolis extended their trade, on one side into Thrace, and on the other into Macedonia. They were enabled, in a great measure, to monopolize the commerce of both these countries, at least those parts of them which were contiguous, from the situation of their city on the Strymon; of which river they held, as it were, the key, so that nothing could depart from it without their consent. The ancients represent this river as frequently exhibiting immense logs of wood floating down it, which had been felled either on Mount Rhodope, or in the forests of Mount Hemus. The Athenians retained this important and valuable colony till the time of Philip, the father of Alexander, by whom it was taken from them.

The island of Samos may justly be regarded as a Grecian colony; having been chiefly inhabited by the Iones, to whose confederacy it belonged. Its situation between the mainland of Asia and the island of Icaria, from both of which it is separated by very narrow straits, which were the usual course for the ancient vessels in their voyage from the Black Sea to Syria and Egypt, rendered it the resort of pirates, as well as celebrated for its ships and commerce. The city of Samos, as described by the ancients, seems to have been a place of great consequence. Herodotus mentions three things for which it was remarkable in his time; one of which was a mole or pier, 120 feet long, which formed the harbour, and was carried two furlongs into the sea. The principal design of this mole was to protect ships from the south wind, to which they would otherwise have been much exposed. Hence it would appear, that even at this early period, they had made great advances in commerce, otherwise they would neither have had the disposition or ability to build such a mole. But we have the express testimony of Thucydides, that even at a much earlier period,—nearly 300 years before the Peloponnesian war,—the Samians gave great encouragement to shipbuilding, and employed Aminodes, the Corinthian, who was esteemed the most skilful ship-builder of his time; and Herodotus speaks of them as trading to Egypt, Spain, &c., before any of the other Greeks, except Sostrates, of Egina, were acquainted with those countries. The same author informs us, that the Samians had a settlement in Upper Egypt, and that one of their merchant ships, on its passage thither, was driven by contrary winds, beyond the Pillars of Hercules, to the island of Tartessus, which till then was unknown to the Greeks. This island abounded in gold; of the value of which, the inhabitants were so utterly ignorant, that they readily allowed the Samians to carry home with them sixty talents, or about 13,500 . According to Pliny, they first built vessels fit to transport cavalry. We are not informed of what articles their exports and imports consisted, except that their earthen-ware was in great repute among the ancients, in their most splendid entertainments, and was exported in great quantities for this purpose. The Samian earth, from which these vessels were made, was itself also exported, on account of its medicinal properties. It is well known that the victory obtained by the Greeks over the Persians, at the sea-fight of Mycale, was chiefly owing to the Samians.

The commerce of the Black Sea was of so much importance and value to the Greeks, that we cannot be surprised that they founded several colonies on its shores, and in the adjacent countries. Heraclea, in this sea, is said to have been founded by the Beotians: the inhabitants availed themselves of their situation to engage very extensively in maritime affairs and in commerce, so that in a short time they were not inferior in wealth or power to any of the Greek states in Asia. When Xenophon was obliged to retreat after his expedition into Asia Minor, the Heracleans supplied him with ships, to transport his army into Greece. Their maritime strength and skill, or their commercial pursuits, involved them in almost every maritime war, their friendship and support being sought after by all the Asiatic princes. When the war broke out between Ptolemy and Antigonus, they sent to the assistance of the former a numerous fleet, all of which were well equipped and manned. Some were of an extraordinary size, especially one, which had on each side 800 oars, besides 1200 fighting men.

Trapezus was a Greek city, in Pontus, situated on a peninsula, in the Black

Sea, where it begins to turn to the east: it had a large and convenient port, and carried on a considerable trade. But the most celebrated of the Grecian colonies in this part of the world, was Byzantium: it was anciently founded by the Megareans, and successively rebuilt by the Milesians and other nations of Greece. Its harbour, which was in fact an arm of the Bosphorus, obtained, at a very remote period, the appellation of the Golden Horn; most of the recesses, which were compared to the horn of a stag, are now filled up. The epithet "golden" was given to it as expressive of the riches, which (to use the language of Gibbon) every wind wafted from the most distant countries into its secure and capacious port. Never was there a happier or more majestic situation. The river Lycus, which was formed by the junction of two small streams, pouring into the harbour, every tide, a regular supply of fresh water, cleansed the bottom; while the tides in those seas being very trifling, the constant depth of the harbour allowed goods to be landed on the quay without the assistance of boats: and in some parts, the depth near the shore was so considerable, that the prows of the vessels touched the houses, while they were fully afloat. The distance from the mouth of the river to that of the harbour, or the length of this arm of the Bosphorus is seven miles; the entrance, about 500 yards broad, was defended, when necessary, by a strong chain drawn across it. The city of Byzantium was situated on a promontory, nearly of a triangular form; on the point of the promontory stood the citadel. The walls of the city itself were very strong, but not so lofty towards the sea as towards the land, being on the former side defended by the waves, and in some places by the rocks on which they were built, and which projected into the sea.

Thus favoured by nature, and strengthened by art, and situated in a territory abounding in grain and fruits, Byzantium was crowded with merchants, and supported and enriched by an active and flourishing commerce: its harbour, which was sheltered on every side from tempests, besides being easy of access and capacious, attracted to it ships from all the states of Greece, while its situation at the head of the strait enabled, and seemed to authorize it to stop and subject to heavy duties, the foreign merchants who traded to the Euxine, or to reduce the nations who depended on the countries bordering on this sea for their supplies of corn to great difficulties, and in some cases, even to famine. On these accounts the Athenians and Lacedaemonians were generally rivals for its alliance and friendship. Besides the necessary article of grain and abundance of rich and valuable fruit, the Byzantines derived great wealth from their fisheries: these were carried on with great spirit, enterprize, and success. A surprising quantity of fish was caught in the harbour itself, in autumn, when they left the Euxine for the Archipelago; and in the spring, on their return to Pontus. A great many people were employed both in this fishery, and in the curing of the fish: great sums were derived from this source, as well as from the sale of salt provisions; for the quality of which, Byzantium was in greater renown than even Panticapeum. The only disadvantage under which the Byzantines laboured, to counterbalance the excellence of their harbour, the fertility of their soil, the productiveness of their fisheries, and the extent of their commerce, arose from the frequent excursions of the Thracians, who inhabited the neighbouring villages.

There were many other Grecian colonies on the Bosphorus and the adjacent seas. Panticapeum, built by the Milesians, according to Strabo, the capital of the European Bosphorus, with which, as has been already mentioned, the Athenians carried on a considerable trade. Theodosia, also mentioned before, was likewise formed and colonized by the Milesians: its port could contain 100 ships. Tanais, on the Cimmerian Bosphorus; Olbia and Borysthenes, both situated near the mouth of the river from which the latter took its name; Panagorea and Hermonassa on the Bosphorus, and several others. Besides these colonies in this part of the world, the Greeks founded others, for the express purposes of commerce; as Syracuse, in Sicily; Marseilles, in Gaul, the mother of several colonies established on the neighbouring coasts, and, as we shall afterwards notice, a place of very considerable wealth, consequence, and strength, derived entirely from commerce, as well as the seat of the arts and sciences; Cyrene, an opulent city in Africa, and Naucratis, situated on one of the mouths of the Nile. They likewise formed settlements in Rhodes and Crete, in the islands of the Egean Sea, on the opposite coasts of Asia, &c.; most of which were of importance to the mother country, from the facilities they offered to the extension of its commerce.

The war between the Romans, and Philip king of Macedon, which intervened between the second and third Punic war, first afforded the former an opportunity and an excuse for interfering in the affairs of Greece. Till the time of Philip, the father of Alexander, Macedonia does not appear to have had any connexion with the rest of this celebrated portion of the ancient world; the Greeks, indeed, regarded its inhabitants as savages; but from that period, Macedonia became the most important and influential state in Greece. Its boundaries varied at different periods of its history: it seems originally to have been bounded on the east by the Egean Sea; on the south by Thessaly and Epirus; on the west by the Ionian Sea; and on the north by the river Strymon, at the mouth of which, as has been already mentioned, the Athenians founded one of their most flourishing and useful colonies. The princes of Macedonia viewed with jealousy, but for a long time were unable to prevent the states of Greece from forming colonies in the immediate vicinity of their dominions: their union, however, with the king of Persia, when he first fixed his ambition on Greece, was rewarded by a great accession of territory, which enabled them to contest the possession of the sea-coasts with the most powerful of the Greek republics. They then extended their territories to the Eastern Sea, but there were till the reign of Philip, the father of Alexander, several nations between them and the Adriatic, all of which were subdued by him; and thus this sea became their western boundary.

Some of the most celebrated cities of Macedonia were founded by foreign nations. Epidamnus, which was seated at the entrance of the Ionian Gulf, was a colony of the Corcyrians: it was the occasion of a fierce naval war between them and the Corinthians, generally called the Corinthian war. Apollonia, distant seven miles from the sea, on the river Laus, was a Corinthian colony: it was renowned for its excellent laws. On another part of the coast of the Adriatic were the sea-ports of Elyma and Bullis. The district of Paraxis, which was full of gulfs and inlets formed by the Egean Sea, had several ports, but none of any repute. From this description of Macedonia and its principal sea coasts and ports, it is evident that it possessed many advantages for commerce and naval affairs, which, however, were never embraced till the period when the Romans first turned their thoughts to Greece. Had its sovereigns been disposed to engage in commerce, the Adriatic, with its extensive and safe haven of Epidamnus, in which there were several ports, would have opened the trade to Italy; the Egean Sea, still more advantageous, would have secured the trade of Greece and Asia, by means of its spacious bays, one of which, the Sinus Thermæus, was at least sixty miles long.

The produce of Macedonia also would have favoured its commerce; the soil was every where fruitful, and, especially near the sea, abounding in corn, wine, and oil: its principal riches, however, consisted in its mines of almost all kinds of metals, but particularly of gold. In the district of Pieria, it is said, there were found large quantities of this metal in the sand, sometimes in lumps of considerable size: but by far the most productive and valuable mines of gold were in the mountain Pangæus, in a district which Philip, the father of Alexander, added to Macedonia. The people who inhabited the country near the river Strymon derived great wealth from these mines, and it was the knowledge of this, as much as the facility of obtaining timber, which induced the Athenians to found their colony near this river. The Thracians drove the Athenians from this part of Macedonia, and Philip expelled them: he paid great attention to the working of the mines; and by employing persons well skilled in this and in refining the ore, he rendered them so extremely valuable, that, according to ancient authors, he obtained the empire of Greece principally by means of the immense sums he drew from them, amounting annually, according to Diodorus, to 1000 talents of gold. When the Romans reduced Macedonia, they expressly forbade the inhabitants from working the mines of gold or silver, or refining either of those metals; permitting them, however, to manufacture any other metal.

The princes of Macedonia previous to Philip, the father of Alexander, notwithstanding the great advantage for maritime affairs and commerce afforded by the sea-coasts, bays, harbours, &c., neither practised nor understood them: this arose in a great measure from their being continually engaged in wars, or having their ports occupied or blocked up by the maritime states of Greece. Philip was the first who freed his country from these evils and inconveniences; but his thoughts were too intently and constantly fixed on other objects to allow him to turn his attention to maritime affairs or commerce. Alexander, as we have already seen, bestowed much care on his fleet, while engaged in the conquest of Asia; and when he died at Babylon, had formed the design of placing his fleets, in every port of his dominions, on a regular and extensive scale. But the advantages of Macedonia for commerce were neglected in the midst of his vast plans elsewhere, and the Macedonians, at the period of his death, were still inattentive to maritime affairs.

Philip, the antagonist of the Romans, of whose power and success he was not only jealous but apprehensive, as soon as he resolved to engage in hostilities with them, applied himself to maritime affairs. His determination seems to have been fixed when he learnt that the Romans had been defeated at the Lake of Thrasymenus: he instantly formed the plan of invading Illyrium, and then crossing over to Italy. But the latter step could not be taken, nor, indeed, could he expect to cope with the Romans, till he had formed a fleet, and trained his subjects to the management of it. At this period the Macedonians seem to have had some merchant ships; for we are informed that a petty king of Illyria seized some of them in the port of Leucas, and also all that his squadron met with on the coast of Greece, as far as Malea. This insult and attack afforded Philip an excellent reason for declaring war against Illyricum: he began by exercising the Macedonians in the art of navigation; he built ships after the Illyrian manner, and he was the first king of Macedonia that put to sea 100 small vessels at one time.

He was urged still more strongly to go on with his plan of invading Italy, when he learnt the result of the battle of Cannæ; he immediately formed an alliance with Hannibal, and engaged to invade Italy with 200 sail of ships, and plunder its eastern coasts: in return for this service he was to retain all the islands in the Adriatic, lying near the coast of Macedonia, that he might subdue.

His first naval enterprize was the siege of Oricum on the coast of Epirus, and of Apollonia on the coast of Macedonia, both of which he carried on at the same time, with 120 ships of two banks of oars. He was, however, successfully opposed by the Roman consul Laevinus, who obliged him to burn great part of his fleet, and raise the siege of Doth the places.

About twelve years afterwards, or about 200 years before Christ, Philip engaged in a maritime war with Attalus, king of Pergamus, and the Rhodians, near the isle of Chio: the fleet of Philip consisted of fifty-three decked vessels and 150 gallies; besides these he had several ships called pristis, from the figure of a large fish which was affixed to, or engraved on their bows, either to distinguish them, or as a mark of their swift sailing. The fleet of his opponents consisted of sixty-five covered ships, besides those of their allies, the people of Byzantium.

Notwithstanding, however, the exertions he made to acquire a naval force equal to that of the Romans, and the experience which his subjects gradually obtained in maritime affairs, he was not able to sustain their attacks, either by land or sea, but was compelled in a very few years to sue for peace. This he obtained, on the condition, that he should deliver up to the Romans all his covered gallies, and reserve to himself only a few smaller vessels: he was permitted, however, to retain one galley of sixteen banks of oars, a vessel rather for shew than use.

The success of the Romans, the extent of their conquests, and the ambitious views, which seemed wider and wider in proportion to their successes, alarmed

Antiochus, king of Syria, who, not intimidated by the fate of Philip, resolved to declare war against them. They were never averse to engage in hostilities. The fleet of Antiochus consisted of 100 ships; that of the Romans was nearly equal in number; the ships of Antiochus, however, were inferior to those of his opponents in respect to strength and size, though surpassing them in swiftness. The hostile fleets met and engaged on the coast of Ionia; that of Antiochus was defeated, and would have been utterly captured or destroyed, had it not been for the swiftness of the vessels. In order to repair his loss, Antiochus sent for additional vessels from Sicily and Phoenicia; but these were taken on their passage by the Rhodians, who were at this time in alliance with the Romans. The Rhodians, however, in their turn were attacked and defeated by the fleet of Antiochus, near Samos, whither they had gone to join a Roman squadron.

In the meantime the Romans had collected a fleet of eighty ships, and with these they fought one hundred ships of their opponent off the coast of Ionia; the victory of the former was decisive, all the ships of Antiochus being captured or destroyed. This disaster, in connection with a signal defeat he sustained by land, compelled him to submit; and the Romans, always attentive to their maritime interests, which however they had not hitherto pushed nearly to the extent which they might have done, refused to grant him peace, except on the conditions, that he should cede all that part of Asia which lies between the sea and Mount Taurus; that he should give up all his vessels except ten; and that these should not, on any account, sail beyond the promontories of Cilicia. The Romans, extremely strict, and even severe, in enforcing the conditions of peace, not only destroyed fifty covered galleys, but, the successor of Antiochus having built additional vessels to the ten he was by treaty allowed to keep, they compelled him to burn them.

The temporary success of the Carthaginians against the Romans induced Philip, king of Macedon, to engage in that war which proved his ruin. The advice of Hannibal, when an exile at the court of Antiochus, likewise led to the disastrous war of that monarch with the same people; and by the advice of Hannibal also, Prusias, king of Bythinia, was engaged in hostilities with them. This king seems to have paid considerable attention to naval and commercial affairs, for both of which, indeed, his territories were admirably suited. In conjunction with the Rhodians, he made war against the inhabitants of Byzantium, and obliged them to remit the tax which they had been accustomed to levy on all vessels that sailed to or from the Euxine Sea, The maritime war between this sovereign and the Romans, who were at this time in alliance with Eumenes, king of Pergamus, offers nothing deserving our notice, except a stratagem executed by Hannibal. In order to compensate for the inferiority of Prusias' fleet, Hannibal ordered a great many serpents to be collected; these were put into pots, which, during the engagement, were thrown into the enemy's ships. The alarm and consternation occasioned by this novel and unexpected mode of warfare, threw his opponents into disorder, and compelled them to save themselves by flight.

The conquest of all the islands on the coast of Greece, from Epirus to Cape

Malea, by the Romans, was the result of a naval war, in which they engaged with the Etolians, a people who, at this time, were so powerful at sea, and so much addicted to piracy, as to have drawn upon themselves the jealousy and the vengeance of the Romans. This extension of their dominions was followed by a successful war with the Istrians, which made them masters of all the western parts of the Mediterranean Sea; and by an equally successful war with Nabis, the tyrant of Sparta, who was compelled to deliver up his fleet to them, as well as all the sea-ports of consequence on the coast of Sparta.

The Rhodians hitherto had been generally in alliance with the Romans; but differences arose between them during the war between the latter and Perseus, king of Macedon.

The island of Rhodes was remarkably well situated for maritime commerce; and its inhabitants did not fail to reap all the advantages in this respect which nature had so kindly bestowed on them. It appears from Homer, that in his time there were three cities in the island; but during the Peloponnesian war, the greater part of the inhabitants, having formed the resolution to settle in one place, built the city of Rhodes, after the designs of the same Athenian architect, who built the Piræus. This city was situated on the east coast of the island, at the foot of a hill, in the form of an amphitheatre: it possessed a very convenient and safe harbour, at the entrance of which there were two rocks; and on these, which were fifty feet asunder, the famous Colossus was placed. The arsenals of Rhodes were filled with every thing requisite for the defence of the city, or the equipment of a large fleet: its walls, which were extremely high, were defended by towers: its houses were built of stone: in short, the whole city presented a striking picture of wealth, magnificence, and beauty, for which it was not less indebted to art and commerce than to nature.

Before the era of the Olympiads, the Rhodians applied themselves to maritime affairs: for many years they seem to have been masters of the Mediterranean Sea; and their code of maritime laws became the standard with all the maritime nations of antiquity, by which all controversies regarding maritime affairs were regulated. There is great doubt among the learned, whether what still exist as the fragments of these laws are genuine: we know, however, that the Romans had a law which they called Lex Rhodia; according to some, this contained the regulations of the Rhodians concerning naval affairs; according to others, however, only one clause of the law, , about throwing goods overboard in a storm, was borrowed from the Rhodians.

Besides the commerce in which they themselves were engaged, the constant arrival of ships from Egypt to Greece, and from Greece to Egypt, the island being situated exactly in the passage between these countries, contributed much to their wealth. As this encreased, they formed settlements and colonies in many places; at Parthenope and Salapia, in Italy; Agrigentum and Geta, in Sicily; Rhodes, on the coast of Spain, near the foot of the Pyrenees, &c. They were particularly celebrated for and attentive to the construction of their vessels; aiming principally at lightness and speed, the discipline observed on board of them, and the skill and ability of their captains and pilots. All these things were under the direct management and controul of magistrates, appointed for the express purpose, who were excessively attentive and even rigid in the execution of their duty. Whoever entered certain places in the arsenals without permission, was punished with death.

A few of the most remarkable events in the maritime history of Rhodes, prior to their dispute with the Romans, call for some general and cursory notice. Till the foundation of the city of Rhodes, which, as we have already stated, took place during the Peleponnesian war, there is scarcely any thing to attract our attention: a short time before this, the republican form of government was established, and the trade and navigation of the Rhodians seem to have acquired a fresh impulse and spirit. But their enterprizes were soon checked by Artemisia, queen of Caria, gaining possession of their city: this she effected by a stratagem. The Rhodians invaded Caria with a design of gaining possession of Halicarnassus: by the direction of the queen, the inhabitants made a signal that they surrendered; the Rhodians suspecting no treachery, and delighted with their apparent success, left their fleet to take possession of the town; in the meantime, the queen brought her fleet from an adjoining creek, by means of some canal or other inland communication, to the port where the Rhodian vessels lay, and quietly took them. This disaster was the cause of another, still more calamitous to the Rhodians; for Artemisia sailed with the Rhodian ships to Rhodes, and the inhabitants, under the belief that their fleet was returning victorious, permitted the enemy to land and to seize the city. To what cause the Rhodions were indebted for the restoration of their liberty and independence we are not informed; but it was owing, either to the interference of the Athenians, or the death of Artemisia.

From the period of these events, which occurred about 350 years before Christ, till the reign of Alexander the Great, the Rhodians enjoyed profound and uninterrupted tranquillity; their commerce extended, and their wealth encreased. To this conqueror they offered no resistance, but of their own accord surrendered their cities and harbours; as soon, however, as they learnt that he was dead, they resumed their independence. About this time the greater part of their city was destroyed by a dreadful inundation, which would have swept the whole of it away, if the wall between it and the sea had not been broken down by the force of the waters, and thus given them free passage. This misfortune seems only to have encouraged the inhabitants to attend still more closely and diligently to commerce, which they carried on with so much industry and skill, and in such a profitable manner, that they soon rebuilt their city, and repaired all the losses they had sustained. Their alliance was courted by all their neighbours; but they resolved to adhere to a strict neutrality, and thus, while war raged among other nations, they were enabled to profit by that very circumstance, and thus became one of the most opulent states of all Asia. Their commerce, as well as that of all the states on the Mediterranean, being much molested and injured by the pirates, they undertook, of their own accord, and at their own expence, to root them out; and in this they completely succeeded.

But that commerce, on account of which they were so very anxious to keep at peace, involved them in war. Their most lucrative trade was with Egypt. When hostilities began between Ptolemy and Antigonus, the latter insisted that they should join him; this they refused to do; upon which his fleet blockaded Rhodes, to prevent their commerce with Egypt. The Rhodians were thus compelled to act against him in their own defence, in order to free their harbour. The raising of the blockade, and the defeat of his fleet, incensed Antiochus; and to the remonstrances and entreaties of the Rhodians to be permitted to remain at peace, he replied, "that they must declare war against Ptolemy, admit his fleet into their harbour, and give hostages for the performance of these articles." War now was inevitable, and great preparations for it were made on both sides: the attack on the city was committed by Antigonus to his son Demetrius; for this purpose he collected a fleet of 200 ships of war, 170 transports with 40,000 men on board, and 1000 vessels laden with provisions, stores, warlike engines, etc. This immense armament was composed partly of pirates and mercenaries, who were induced to join Demetrius, by the hope of partaking in the plunder of Rhodes. It is foreign to our purpose to enter on the details of this memorable siege: the Rhodians trusted principally to their own valour and resources; from Ptolemy, however, they received most ample and seasonable supplies of provisions: at one time he sent them 300,000 measures of corn; a few days afterwards Cassandra sent them 100,000 bushels of barley, and Lysimachus 400,000 bushels of corn, and as many of barley: these supplies, the valour of the inhabitants, and the ill success of some new and immense engines, on which Demetrius had mainly depended, at length induced him to raise the siege and make peace with the Rhodians.

The Rhodians endeavoured to make up for the time they had lost, and the money they had expended, during their war with Antiochus, by applying themselves entirely to navigation and commerce; so that, according to Polybius, they became masters of the sea, and the most opulent and flourishing state of those times. The next war in which they were engaged was occasioned entirely by their attention and regard to their commercial interests. We have already slightly noticed this war; but in this place it will be proper to go more into detail respecting it. The people of Byzantium determined to lay a toll on all ships that traded to the Euxine, in order to defray an annual tribute which they were obliged to pay to the Greeks. As one of the most important and lucrative branches of the commerce of Rhodes was to the countries lying on this sea, they were much aggrieved by this toll, and endeavoured to persuade the Byzantines to take it off, but in vain. Under these circumstances, they, in conjunction with Prusias, king of Bythinia, declared war against the Byzantines; and while their ally took Hieron, which seems to have been a great mart of the Byzantines, and the resort of most of the merchants trading to these parts, the Rhodians, with a powerful fleet, ravaged their coasts, and seized all their ships trading to the Euxine. The war was at length terminated under the mediation of the king of the Thracian Gauls; the Byzantines agreeing to take off the toll.

Their success in this war was counterbalanced by a dreadful earthquake, which threw down the Colossus, destroyed the arsenal, and damaged part of the walls and city. As the Rhodians, however, were much esteemed by most of their neighbours, who found their prosperity intimately connected with the prosperity of Rhodes, they soon recovered from these calamities and losses. Hiero, king of Syracuse, gave them 100 talents, and exempted them from all duties and taxes. Ptolemy gave them also the like sum, besides one million measures of wheat, and timber, etc. requisite for building fifty ships. Antiochus exempted all their vessels, which traded to his ports, from every kind of tax and duty. They received from other princes presents or privileges of equal importance and value; so that, in a very short time, they recovered their former opulence and trade, and rebuilt their walls, etc.

Their alliance with Attalus, king of Pergamus, involved them in a war with Philip king of Macedonia, and was the cause of their forming an alliance with the Romans. In this war the Rhodian fleet, in conjunction with the fleets of their allies, gained several victories over the fleet of Philip. The latter was at length obliged to sue to the Romans for peace, and they, in fixing the terms, included the Rhodians, to whom were ceded Stratonice, and the greater part of Caria. In the meantime Antiochus and the Romans had commenced hostilities, and the Rhodians were again involved in them: almost at their very commencement, their fleet was surprized by a stratagem of Antiochus's admiral, and of thirty ships of war of which it consisted, only seven escaped.

They soon, however, repaired their losses, and fitted out another fleet, with which they put to sea, for the purpose of preventing the junction of Hannibal with Antiochus's ships: the former had thirty-seven large ships; the Rhodian fleet was nearly equal in numbers, but inferior in size. The hostile fleets met off the coast of Pamphilia. The battle was obstinate: at first, by an oversight of the Rhodian admiral, some disorder occurred in part of his fleet; but this was soon repaired, and a decisive victory obtained. Part of Hannibal's fleet was captured, and the rest blocked up in the harbours of Pamphilia. The defeat of Antiochus, both at sea and land, by the Romans, to which we have already adverted, obliged this monarch to sue for peace, in which the Rhodians were included.

We have now arrived at that period of the history of Rhodes when the first difference arose between that city and the Romans: the latter suspected that the Rhodians favoured Perseus king of Macedon, with whom they were at war, and were moreover displeased at their presuming to interfere with them in his favour. In order to watch their inclinations and motions, the senate sent three commissioners to Rhodes: these found a fleet of forty galleys, which there was reason to believe had been intended to act against the Romans; but which, by the advice of the chief magistrate, were, on the arrival of the commissioners, ordered to sea, to act in union with them. Scarce, however, were the commissioners departed, when the Rhodians became lukewarm in the cause of the Romans; and although they sent a few of their galleys to join the Roman admiral, they kept the greatest number in port, waiting the issue of the war between them and the king of Macedonia. As soon as they heard of the defeat of the former in Thessaly, they entered into negotiations with Perseus, and at the same time sent ambassadors to Rome, who complained, that in consequence of the war between Perseus and the Romans, the navigation and commerce of Rhodes was greatly injured, their island deprived of provisions and other necessaries, and the customs and duties which their maritime situation formerly afforded them kept back, from their no longer being able to sail with safety along the coasts of Asia, where they used to levy the most important and productive of them.

After the defeat of Perseus, they ceased to remonstrate, and became submissive to the Romans. It is probable, however, that the Romans would have seized this opportunity of attacking them, had not Cato spoken very strongly in their favour: in consequence of his arguments and influence, and by the cession of Lycia and Caria, they were again admitted to an alliance with the Romans.

The advantages they derived from this alliance were so great, that they resisted the promises and the threats of Mithridates, when he engaged in hostilities with the Romans. This monarch, therefore, resolved to employ his whole force by sea and land against them: they were not however dismayed, but placed a firm reliance on their skill in maritime affairs. They divided their fleet into three squadrons: one drawn up in a line protected the entrance of the harbour; and the other two, at a greater distance from the shore, were stationed to watch the approach of the enemy. Mithridates also divided his fleet, which was more numerous than that of the Rhodians, into three squadrons; one of these he himself commanded, on board of a quinquereme, and directed to attack the squadron which was protecting the port. The Rhodians gradually retired before the enemy, till they came close to the mouth of the harbour: Mithridates in vain endeavoured to break their line, and force an entrance; in all his attempts he was defeated with considerable loss; and his land forces, which he had embarked in transports, being dispersed in a storm, he was obliged to retire from before the city.

The Romans acknowledged the benefits they derived from the valour of the Rhodians on this occasion; and they again experienced it, in the war which Pompey carried on against the Cilician pirates, though that commander took all the merit to himself. In the civil war between him and Caesar, they assisted the former with a numerous fleet, under the command of one of their best seamen, who distinguished himself above all Pompey's captains, and gained very considerable advantages over Caesar's fleet. On the death of Pompey they joined Cæsar: this exposed them to the hostility of Cassius; they endeavoured to pacify him by promising to recal the ships they had sent to the assistance of Caesar, but he demanded the delivery of their whole fleet, and that he should be put in possession of their harbour and city. To these terms they would not accede, but prepared for war, by equipping a fleet of thirty-three ships, and placing it under the command of one of their best officers. A battle ensued which was fought on both sides with great skill and bravery; but the Rhodians were obliged to yield to the superior number of the Roman fleet, and to return to the harbour, having lost two of their ships, and the rest being very much damaged. It is remarked by the ancient historians who relate this battle, that it was the first time the Rhodians were fairly overcome in a sea-fight.

Cassius followed up his success by bringing against Rhodes a fleet of eighty ships of war, and 200 transports. Against this formidable armament the Rhodians again put to sea, and a second battle ensued, which was more obstinately contested than the first: the Romans however were again victorious, and the city of Rhodes was blocked up by sea and land. Its fate was soon determined; for some of the inhabitants, dreading a famine, opened the gates to the Romans. Cassius, besides other severe terms, obliged the Rhodians to deliver up all their ships, and all their public treasures; the temples were plundered, and 8000 talents extorted from private individuals, besides a fine of 500 levied on the city.

From this time till the reign of Vespasian, when the island became a Roman province, it was sometimes oppressed, and sometimes favoured by the Romans; according, as Tacitus remarks, as they obliged them with their assistance in foreign wars, or provoked them with their seditions at home.

In order to complete the maritime history of Rhodes, we have rather advanced beyond the period to which we had brought down our notices of the Roman navigation and commerce: these therefore we shall now resume at the war between Perseus king of Macedonia and the Romans. Perseus harassed the coasts of Italy, plundered and sunk all their ships, while they found it difficult to oppose him by sea, or protect their coasts, for want of a fleet. This induced them to prepare for service fifty vessels; but though their allies augmented this number, the Romans do not seem to have performed any thing of consequence by sea. This is attributed principally to the circumstance, that the fleet, on examination, was discovered to be in bad condition, neither equipped sufficiently in stores or provisions, and the seamen who were to have navigated it were either dead or absent, while those who did appear were ill paid and worse clothed; these facts sufficiently demonstrate the little care which the Romans, even at this period, bestowed on maritime affairs. The defeat of Perseus at Pidna, and his subsequent capture by the Romans in the island of Samothrace, rendered it unnecessary for them to supply the deficiences of their fleet. The immense ship, which, as we have already mentioned, Philip, Perseus's father, employed in his war against the Romans, was taken on this occasion; and Paulus Emilius, the consul, sailed up the Tiber in it: it had 16 banks of oars. Many other ships of large size were also captured; these were brought to Rome, and drawn into the Campus Martius.

One of the allies of the unfortunate Perseus was the king of Illyria, who was powerful at sea, and ravaged the coasts of Italy opposite to his dominions. While the consul was sent against Perseus, the management of the naval war against the Illyrians was committed to the praetor: as he was well aware of the maritime force of his opponent, he acted with great caution; his first success, in capturing some of their snips, induced him to land all his forces in Illyria, where, after an obstinate battle, he compelled the king to surrender at discretion. Macedonia and Illyria were thus reduced to the state of Roman provinces; but the Romans regarded these victories as of importance, more on account of the accession they made to their territories, than on account of the advantages which they might thence derive to their commerce or their naval power: so little, indeed, did they regard them in the latter point of view, that they gave the 220 ships which were surrendered to them by the king of Illyria, to the inhabitants of Cephalonia, of Apollonia, and Dyrrhachium, who at the time were much celebrated for their trade and navigation. Although their seacoasts had been repeatedly ravaged, we are informed by Polybius, that, from the time of Philip, king of Macedonia, till long after the defeat of Perseus, they entirely neglected the coasts of Illyria, from which, till this country was subdued by them, their own coasts were generally invaded, and by means of the ports and produce of which, after it became a Roman province, they might greatly have augmented their navy and commerce.

The Carthaginians had been gradually recovering from the losses which they had sustained during the second Punic war, and witnessed with satisfaction their enemies involved in constant hostilities, in the hope that the issue of these would prove fatal to them, or, at least, so far weaken them, as to enable them to oppose Rome with more success than they had hitherto done. While the war was carried on between the Romans and the Macedonians, they made great, but secret, preparations to regain their former power; but the Romans, who always kept a watchful and jealous eye on the operations of all their rivals, were particularly nearsighted with regard to whatever was doing by the Carthaginians. They received information that at Carthage there was deposited a large quantity of timber, and of other naval stores: on learning this, Cato, their inveterate enemy, who had been sent into Africa, to mediate between them and Masinissa, with whom they were at war, went to Carthage himself, where he examined every thing with a malicious eye. On his return to Rome, he reported that Carthage was again become excessively rich,—that her magazines were filled with all kinds of warlike stores,—that her ports were crowded with ships, and that by her war with Masinissa, she was only preparing to renew the war against Rome. His exhortations to his countrymen to anticipate the Carthaginians, by immediately commencing hostilities, had no effect at first; but being frequently repeated, and intelligence being received, that preparations were making at Carthage for an open declaration of war, and that the Carthaginians were fitting out a fleet, contrary to the terms of their treaty with the Romans; and this information being confirmed by the report of deputies sent to Carthage; war was declared against Carthage in the year of Rome 605. The Carthaginians endeavoured to pacify the Romans by surrendering to them their cities, lands, rivers, &c., in short, by a complete surrender of whatever they possessed, as well as of themselves. At first the Romans appeared disposed to abstain from war on these conditions; and the Carthaginians actually delivered up all their arms and warlike engines, and witnessed the burning of their fleet; but the Romans, having thus degraded them, and stript them in a great measure of the means of defence, now insisted that Carthage itself should be destroyed, and that the inhabitants should build a city at the distance of five leagues from, the sea. Indignant at these demands, they resolved to sustain a siege; and, in a very short time, they made immense preparations for defending their city. At first they gained some success over the Romans; for their fleet having come very near the shore, to transport the troops, who were suffering from the vicinity of the marshes, to a healthier spot, the Carthaginians fitted out a great number of fire ships, filled with tar, sulphur, bitumen, &c., and taking advantage of a favourable wind, they sent them among the Roman fleet, great part of which was thus destroyed.

But these and other successes did not ultimately avail them: Scipio who had been chosen consul, arrived in Africa, and Carthage was immediately strictly blocked up by sea and land. His exertions were indeed astonishing; as the new port of Carthage was effectually shut up by the Roman fleet, so that no assistance or provisions could enter by it; and as lines of circumvallation were formed on land, the consul's great object was to block up the old port. The Romans were masters of the western neck of land, which formed one side of its entrance; from this to the other side they built a mole, ninety feet broad at bottom, and eighty at top; when this was completed, the old port was rendered quite inaccessible and useless.

The Carthaginians on their part, imagined and executed works as surprising as those of the Romans: deprived of both their ports, they dug, in a very short time, a new harbour, from which they cut a passage to the sea; and they built and equipped a fleet of fifty ships, which put to sea through this new harbour. The Romans were astonished when they beheld a fleet, of the existence or possibility of which they had no conception, advancing out of a harbour, the formation of which equally astonished them, and this fleet daring to hazard an engagement. The battle continued during the whole day, with little advantage on either side; but, notwithstanding all their efforts, and some partial and temporary successes, Carthage was at length compelled to submit to Scipio, and was at first plundered, and afterwards destroyed. The Romans burnt the new fleet which the Carthaginians had built: indeed, in general, instead of augmenting their own naval force, when they subdued any of their maritime enemies, they either destroyed their ships or bestowed them on some of their allies; a certain proof, as Huet remarks, of the very little regard they paid to sea affairs.

We are expressly informed, in the Life of Terence, generally ascribed to Suetonius, that before the destruction of Carthage, the Romans did not trade to Africa: but though his words are express, they must not be taken literally; for we have already proved, that in the treaties between Rome and Carthage at a very early period, the voyages undertaken by the Romans, on account of trade, to Sicily, Sardinia, and parts of Africa are expressly mentioned in diem, and the people of Utica are particularized as the allies of the Romans, and a people with whom they traded. It is certain, however, that the author of the Life of Terence is correct, if he merely meant, that till after the destruction of Carthage the Romans had no regular commerce with Africa. From the date of this event, it became of great importance, though confined chiefly to slaves, most of whom were brought from Africa, to the island of Delos: this, as has been already stated, was a great depôt for them, as well as other kinds of merchandize. The capture of Carthage and of Corinth, which took place nearly at the same time, increased considerably the number of slaves for sale.

Still, however, though the Romans now began to be sensible of the value of commence, they did little to protect it; for soon after the termination of the third Punic war, the Mediterranean swarmed with pirates, who plundered the merchant ships of all nations. These pirates belonged principally to the Balearic islands, to Cilicia and to Crete. In one of the Balearic islands, called Minor by the ancients, the present Minorca, there were two cities built near the mouths of convenient harbours; the inhabitants of these carried on a considerable commerce, and at the same time engaged in piracy. They were uncommonly active and daring in this pursuit, attacking and robbing every ship they met with; they even had the courage, or the rashness, to oppose the Roman fleet, under the command of the consul Metellus; but they were beaten, and for a time obliged to abstain from their piratical proceedings.

They were soon again, however, emboldened to resume them, by the assistance and example of the inhabitants of Crete and Cilicia. This latter country, situated in Asia Minor, and possessing a sea-coast which extended along the Mediterranean, from east to west, nearly 250 miles, was fertile beyond most parts of Asia Minor; though on the coast, it was reckoned unhealthy. The principal commercial town was Alexandria, built by Alexander the Great, between Issus and the straits that lead from Cilicia into Syria; its situation being very favourable for carrying on trade to all the western parts of the Mediterranean, as well as to Egypt, the Euxine, &c. it soon became one of the most flourishing cities in the world. But the Cilicians were not content with lawful and regular trade: in the time of the Mithridatic war, and even before it, they began to plunder the neighbouring coasts; and being successful in these predatory expeditions, they extended them as far as the coasts of Greece and Italy, on which they landed, and carried off a great number of the inhabitants, whom they sold as slaves. The Romans at length deemed it absolutely necessary to act with vigour against them. Publius Servilius, who was employed on this occasion, defeated them in a sea-battle, and took most of their strong-holds. For a short time afterwards, they abstained from their predatory excursions; but, as we shall soon have occasion to notice, they resumed them whenever they had repaired their losses, and thought the Romans otherwise employed.

The island of Crete was regarded by the ancients as difficult of access; most of its harbours were exposed to the wind; but as it was easy for ships to sail out of them, when the wind was moderate and favourable, they were convenient for commerce to almost any part of the then commercial world. The ancients, according to Strabo, reckoned that ships which sailed from the eastern part of Crete would arrive in Egypt in three or four days; and, according to Diodorus Siculus, in ten days they would arrive at the Pulus Mæotis. The principal seaports were Bithynia, which had a very convenient haven; and Heracles, the seaport of the Gnossians. To these, merchants from all parts of the world resorted. There were, besides, a great many creeks and bays. This island would have been much more commercial and flourishing than it actually was, considering its favourable situation, &c., had it not been divided into a great number of independent states, who were jealous of each other's prosperity, and almost constantly at war amongst themselves. In very early times, when the whole island was subject to one sovereign, the Cretans were powerful at sea; they had subjected even before the Trojan war, some of the islands in the Egean Sea, and formed colonies and commercial establishments on the coasts of Asia Minor and Europe. At the breaking out of the Trojan war, they sent eighty ships to the assistance of the Greeks. But as soon as the island was divided into independent republics, their navigation and commerce seem to have declined. Their piratical expeditions were conducted with so much boldness and success, especially at the time when the Romans were engaged in hostilities with Mithridates, that they determined to curb them. Anthony, the father of Marc Anthony, was appointed to execute their vengeance; but, too confident of success, he was beaten by the Cretans in a sea-battle. This naturally encouraged them to carry on their piracies on a greater scale, and with more boldness; but their triumph was of short duration, for Metellus, the proconsul, having defeated their forces, united with those of the Cilician pirates, landed on the island, and subdued the whole of it.

In the meantime, Mithridates, who had been very instrumental in encouraging the pirates to commit depredations on the Roman vessels and coasts, was vigorously preparing for war with the republic. His naval force, formed partly of his own ships, and partly from those of most of the maritime states, all of whom were jealous and afraid of the Romans, and regarded Mithridates as their protector and deliverer, insulted even the coasts of Italy. We have already noticed his unsuccessful sea-fight with the Rhodians, almost the only people who continued faithful to the Romans. The latter, at length, were fully sensible of the absolute necessity of forming such a fleet as would enable them successfully to oppose Mithridates, who was master, not only of Asia, but of all Greece, and the adjacent islands, except Rhodes. Sylla was employed against him; but as he had very few ships, he sent Lucullus to Syria, Egypt, Lybia, and Cyprus, to collect a fleet. From Ptolemy, who was afraid of the power of Mithridates, and, perhaps, jealous of the Romans, he received no vessels; but from the other quarters he received considerable supplies of ships and experienced mariners. It is probable, however, that by sea the Romans would not have been able to cope with Mithridates, had not that monarch been beaten by land, and had not his admiral, Archelaus, delivered up the fleet under his command to Sylla. In the meantime, Mithridates was blocked up in Pitane, a city near Troy, from which he could not have escaped, if Lucullus had brought his fleet against it; this, however, out of jealousy to the Roman general Fimbria, he refused to do, contenting himself with naval operations. In these he was successful, gaining two victories over Mithridates's fleet, near the coast of Troy. These defeats, and the treachery of Archelaus, nearly annihilated the maritime force of Mithridates. But this monarch was not easily dispirited; in a short time he collected another fleet, and invaded Bithynia. It was therefore necessary for the Romans to send a fleet thither, which they did, under the command of Cotta. This fleet, however, was far inferior to that of the king, which consisted of 400 ships of thirty oars, besides a great many smaller vessels. On learning this, Lucullus, who had the chief command, ordered Cotta to remain in the harbour of Chalcedon; but Mithridates, relying on his strength, sailed into the very harbour, and burnt the Roman fleet. The loss of the Romans consisted of sixty ships, and 8000 of their mariners slain, besides 4500 taken prisoners. As this success of Mithridates encouraged the cities of Asia to revolt, Lucullus resolved, if possible, to counterbalance it with still more decisive success on his part by land; he accordingly besieged him in his camp. Being reduced to great straits, Mithridates was forced to escape by sea towards Byzantium; but on his voyage he was overtaken by a violent storm, in which sixty of his ships were sunk; he himself must have perished, if he had not been rescued by a pirate, who landed him safe in Pontus. Mithridates still had a small float of fifty ships, on board of which were 10,000 land forces. These were at sea; but with what object does not appear: they were met, however, near Lemnos, by a Roman squadron, and entirely defeated; thirty-two of them being captured, and the rest sunk. On receiving information of this victory, the Roman senate ordered Lucullus to be paid 3000 talents to repair and augment his fleet; but he refused them, answering, "that with the succours he could get from their allies, he should be able to gain the dominion of the sea, and conquer Mithridates:" at the same time he sent to Rome 110 galleys, armed with beaks. Mithridates, however, was still formidable at sea, and continued so, till the Romans gained another victory over him, near the island of Tenedos, in which they took and sunk sixty ships: after this, he was not able to fit out another fleet. As the remainder of the war between him and the Romans was entirely confined to land operations, we shall pass it by, and proceed to the other naval enterprizes of the Romans about this period.

The war with Mithridates employed the attention and the resources of the Romans so completely, that the pirates again infested the Mediterranean seas without control. Their numbers and force were greatly augmented by the destruction of Carthage and Corinth; for the inhabitants of these cities, having neither a place of retreat, nor the means of subsistence, naturally turned their thoughts to piracy, having been accustomed to sea affairs, and to commerce. In this they were encouraged by Mithridates, and assisted by some persons of considerable rank and wealth. The inability of the Romans to attend to them, and the success and encouragement they obtained, induced them to conduct their piracies on a regular, systematic, and extensive plan. Their ships were constantly at sea: all commerce was interrupted; with their 1000 galleys—for so numerous were they—they exercised a complete sovereignty over all the coasts of the Mediterranean. They formed themselves into a kind of commonwealth, selected magistrates and officers, who appointed each fleet its respective station and object, and built watch-towers, arsenals, and magazines. They depended chiefly on Cilicia for the necessary supplies for their fleets. Emboldened by their success, and by the occupation afforded to the Romans by Mithridates, they ravaged the whole line of the Italian coast; sacked the towns and temples, from which they expected a considerable booty; plundered the country seats on the sea-shore; carried off the inhabitants for slaves; blocked up all the ports of the republic; ventured as far as the entrance of the Tiber; sunk part of the Roman fleet at Ostia, and even threatened Rome itself, which they more than once deprived of its ordinary and necessary subsistence. The scarcity of provisions was, indeed, not confined to Rome; but no vessel venturing to sea in the Mediterranean without being captured, it extended to those parts of Asia and Africa which lie on that sea. Their inveteracy, however, was principally directed against the Roman commerce, and the Romans themselves. If any of their captives declared himself to be a Roman, they threw themselves in derision at his feet, begging his pardon, and imploring his protection; but after they had insolently sported with their prisoner, they often dressed him in a toga, and then, casting out a ship's ladder, desired him to return home, and wished him a good journey. If he refused to leap into the sea, they threw him overboard, saying, "that they would not by any means keep a free-born Roman in captivity!"

In order to root out this dreadful evil, Gabinius, the tribune of the people, proposed a law, to form, what he called, the proconsulate of the seas. This law, though vigorously opposed at first, eventually was carried. The person to whom this new office was to be entrusted, was to have maritime power, without control or restriction, over all the seas, from the Pillars of Hercules to the Thracian Bosphorus, and the countries lying on these seas, for fifty miles inland: he was to be empowered to raise as many seamen and troops as he deemed necessary, and to take, out of the public treasury, money sufficient to pay the expence of paying them, equipping the ships, and executing the objects of the law. The proconsulate of the seas was to be vested in the same person for three years.

As Gabinius was the known friend of Pompey, all Pompey's enemies strenuously opposed this law, as evidently intended to confer authority on him; but the people not only passed it, but granted Pompey, who was chosen to fill the office, even more than Gabinius had desired, for they allowed him to equip 500 ships, to raise 120,000 foot, and to select out of the senate twenty senators to act as his lieutenants.

As soon as Pompey was vested with the authority conferred by this law, he put to sea; and, by his prudent and wise measures, not less than by his activity and vigour, within four months (instead of the three years which were allowed him) he freed the seas from pirates, having beaten their fleet in an engagement near the coast of Cilicia, and taken or sunk nearly 1000 vessels, and made himself master of 120 places on the coast, which they had fortified: in the whole of this expedition he did not lose a single ship. In order effectually to prevent the pirates from resuming their depredations, he sent them to people some deserted cities of Cilicia.

It might have been supposed that as the Romans had suffered so much from the pirates, and as Rome itself was dependent for subsistence on foreign supplies of corn, which could not be regularly obtained, while the pirates were masters of the seas, they would have directed their attention more than they did to maritime affairs and commerce, especially after the experience they had had of the public calamities which might thus be averted. This, however, was not the case, even after the war against the pirates, which was so successfully terminated by Pompey; for Pompey's son, who opposed the triumvirate, by leaguing with the pirates, (of what nation we are not informed,) repeatedly, during his warfare, reduced the city of Rome to great straits for want of corn.

As the operations by sea which he carried on, in conjunction with the pirates, are the last recorded in history, by means of which Rome was reduced to such straits, and as this repeated proof of the absolute necessity of rendering her independent of any maritime power for supplies of corn, seems to have been the chief inducement with Augustus to establish regular and powerful corn fleets, we shall notice them in this place, though rather posterior to the period of Roman history at which we have arrived.

The younger Pompey, it would appear, was sensible that his father's fame and fortune had been first established by his success at sea: this induced him to apply himself to maritime affairs, and, when he resolved to oppose the triumvirate, to trust principally to his experience and force by sea, to oblige them to comply with his terms. Accordingly, he built several ships, some of which are said to have been covered with leather: he associated himself with all the pirates he could meet with; and, when sufficiently powerful, he took possession of Sardinia, Sicily, and Corcyra, made himself master of the whole Mediterranean sea, and intercepted all the convoys which were carrying provisions and other necessaries to Rome. The occupation of Sicily enabled him to prevent any corn from being shipped from that island, and to intercept all that came from the eastern ports of the Mediterranean. His possession of Sardinia and Corcyra enabled him to intercept all that came from the west, while he captured all that came from Africa by his squadrons, which were constantly cruising in that direction.

It may easily be imagined, that when Rome was deprived of her supplies of corn from Sicily, Africa, and the Euxine, she could not long subsist, without being threatened with famine: this was actually the case, the inhabitants were near starving, and it became necessary for the triumvirate to relieve them, either by conquering Pompey, or coming to terms with him. But Rome alone did not suffer: the rest of Italy was also deprived, in a great measure, of provisions, and its coasts insulted and plundered. Octavianus, one of the triumvirate, at first resolved, with the advice of Anthony, to raise a naval force, and oppose Pompey; but when he attempted to lay a tax on the inhabitants of Rome and the rest of Italy, though it was to prevent them from starving, they resisted it with so much violence and determination, that he was obliged to abandon the measure.

As, however, the famine still continued, the triumvirate agreed to come to an accommodation with Pompey: the principal terms were, that the latter should retain possession of Sicily, Sardinia,. &c.; and that he should moreover receive Peloponnesus; that he might endeavour to obtain the consulate; that the dignity of Pontifex Maximus should be granted him; that he should be paid 70,000 great sesterces out of his father's confiscated estate; and that such of his companions as chose should be allowed to return. On his part, he promised, that he would no longer interrupt the Roman trade and navigation; that he would no longer build ships, nor make descents on the coasts of Italy, nor receive the slaves who fled to him; and that he would immediately send to Rome the corn he had detained, oblige the Sicilians to pay annually the tribute of corn due to Rome by that island, and clear the seas of all the pirates.

From these terms it may be seen how dependent Rome, even at this period, was on foreign supplies of corn, and how weak she was at sea. Pompey and the triumvirate seem neither to have been sincere in this treaty: the former, who still retained the title of governor of the maritime coasts, had derived too great advantage from his superiority at sea, and his connection with the pirates, easily to relinquish either; while, on the other hand, the triumvirate could not regard themselves as masters of the republic, so long as Pompey had it in his power to starve the city of Rome. They, therefore, soon quarrelled; upon which Pompey caused his old ships to be refitted, and new ones to be built; and, when he had got a sufficient force, he again blocked up the ports of Italy, and reduced the inhabitants of the capital to the utmost distress for want of provisions. Octavianus, (Augustus Cæsar,) to whom the protection of Italy was assigned, had neither the courage nor the means to oppose Pompey, who, probably, would speedily have forced the triumvirate, to grant him conditions still more favourable than the former ones, had it not been for the defection of one of his admirals. As he was an officer of great valour and experience in maritime affairs, and carried over with him the numerous fleet which he commanded, Augustus was emboldened and rendered better able to cope with Pompey by sea. The latter, rather enraged than intimidated by this defection, sent another of his admirals, who had always been jealous of the one who had gone over to Augustus, with a numerous fleet, to ravage the coasts of Italy. On his return, he fell in with a fleet of Augustus, on board of which was his rival. An obstinate battle ensued: at first Pompey's fleet was worsted; but in the issue it was victorious, and the greater number of Augustus' ships were sunk, captured, or driven on shore. As soon as Augustus learnt the issue of this battle, he resolved to sail from Tarentum, where he then was, pass the straits of Messina, and reinforce the shattered remains of his squadron; but, while he was in the straits, his ships were attacked by Pompey himself, and most of them sunk or dashed to pieces: with great difficulty he escaped. He was now in a dreadful situation; without ships or money; while the inhabitants of Rome were on the point of rising against his authority, for want of corn. In this extremity he applied to Anthony, who immediately came to his aid with 300 sail of ships. As Anthony needed land-forces, which, under the present circumstances, were of no use to Augustus, they agreed to an interchange: Augustus gave Anthony two legions; and Anthony, on his part, left with Augustus 100 armed galleys. In addition to these, Octavia obtained from her husband twenty small ships, as a reinforcement to her brother.

Augustus, though now superior in naval force to Pompey, (for his ships were more numerous, as well as larger and stronger, though not so light and expeditious, nor so well manned,) was not willing to expose himself any more to the hazards of a sea-fight: he therefore appointed Agrippa commander-in-chief of his navy, with directions to cruise off Mylæ, a city on the northern coast of Sicily, where Pompey had assembled all his naval forces. As the possession of this important island was absolutely necessary to the reduction of Pompey's power, and the relief and supply of the city of Rome, Augustus, Lepidus, and another general were to invade it in three different places, while Agrippa was watching Pompey's fleet. The whole of Augustus's expeditions sailed from different ports of Italy at the same time; but they had scarcely put to sea, when a violent storm arose, in which a great number of his ships perished. On this occasion Augustus behaved with great presence of mind and judgment: his first object and care was to send Mæcenas to Rome, to prevent the disturbances which the intelligence of this disaster might occasion there: Mæcenas succeeded in his mission completely. In the meantime Augustus went in person to the several ports, into which his ships had escaped from the storm, encouraged and rewarded the workmen, and soon got his fleet refitted and ready for sea. In his second attempt to invade Sicily, which he put in execution as soon as his fleet was repaired, he was more successful than in his first; and Agrippa considerably weakened Pompey's naval forces, by defeating one of his admirals, from whom he captured thirty galleys. Pompey was still so formidable at sea, at least to the fears of Augustus, that, when he appeared unexpectedly on the coast of Sicily with his fleet, the latter was completely intimidated: apprehending that Pompey would land and attack his camp, he deserted it and went on board his fleet. Pompey, however, who always preferred naval enterprizes, attacked the fleet, put it to flight at the first onset, captured most of the ships, and burnt and sunk the remainder. Augustus with difficulty escaped in a boat; but, instead of returning to his camp, in Sicily, he fled to Italy, attended only by one domestic.

As soon as he recovered from his alarm, he, in conjunction with Lepidus, determined to attack Messina, in which place Pompey had deposited all his stores, provisions, and treasure. The city accordingly was closely invested, both by sea and land. Pompey, in this emergency, challenged Augustus to decide the war by a sea-fight, with 300 ships on each side. Augustus acceding to this proposal, both fleets were drawn up in line of battle, between Mylæ and Naulocus; the land forces having agreed to suspend hostilities, and wait the event of the engagement. Agrippa, who commanded Augustus's fleet, fought with great bravery, and was as bravely opposed by Pompey; their respective officers and men emulated their example. For a considerable time, the event was doubtful; but, at last, Pompey's fleet was defeated: only seventeen of his vessels escaped, the rest were taken or burnt. This victory Agrippa obtained at an easy rate, not more than three of his ships being sunk or destroyed. Augustus, who, according to all accounts, behaved in a most cowardly manner during the battle, was so fully sensible of the obligations he was under to Agrippa, that he immediately honoured him with a blue standard and a rostral crown, that is, a crown, the flower-work of which represented the beaks of galleys, and afterwards, when he became emperor, he raised him, by rank and honours, above all his other subjects. According to Livy, and some other authors, the rostral crown had never been given in any preceding wars, nor was it afterwards bestowed; but Pliny is of a different opinion, he says that it was given to M. Varro, in the war against the pirates, by Pompey.

After this signal and decisive defeat of his fleet, Pompey fled from Sicily to Asia, where he attempted to raise disturbances; but he was defeated, taken prisoner, and put to death.

We must now look back to the naval and commercial history of Rome, immediately after the defeat of the pirates by Pompey the Great. The immediate consequence of his success against them was the revival of trade among the people who inhabited the coasts of the Mediterranean; but the Romans, intent on their plans of conquest, or engaged in civil wars, had little share in it The very nature and extent, however, of their conquests, by making them masters of countries which were either commercial, or which afforded articles of luxury, gradually led them to become more commercial. Hitherto, their conquests and their alliances had been confined almost entirely to the nations on the Mediterranean, or within a short distance of that sea: but Julius Cæsar directed his ambition to another district of the world; and Gaul was added to the Roman dominions.

Transalpine Gaul comprehended Flanders, Holland, Switzerland, and part of Germany, as well as France, Its situation, having the ocean to the north and west, and the Mediterranean Sea to the south, was particularly favourable to commerce; and though, when Caesar conquered it, its inhabitants in general were very ignorant and uncivilized, yet we have his express authority, that the knowledge they possessed of foreign countries, and commodities from abroad, made them abound in all sorts of provisions. About 100 years before the Christian era, the Romans, under pretence of assisting the people of Marseilles, carried their arms into Gaul, and conquered the district to the south of the Rhine.

This part of Gaul, long before the Romans invaded it, was celebrated for its commerce, which was carried on very extensively at the port of Marseilles. We have already mentioned, that this city was founded, or, at least, greatly increased by the Greeks. As the colonists could not, from the narrow boundaries of their territory, and the barrenness of the soil, support themselves by their own industry on land, they applied themselves to the sea: at first, as fishermen; then, as pirates; and afterwards, as merchants. For forty years they are said to have been the most warlike, as well as the most commercial people who frequented the Mediterranean, and were celebrated for the excellent construction and equipment, both of their merchant ships, and their ships of war. Their maritime laws and institutions were nearly as much celebrated and respected as those of the Rhodians. The wealth which the inhabitants of Marseilles had acquired by commerce, and which was contained or displayed in their fleets, arsenals, and magazines, and in their public buildings, drew upon them the envy of their more savage and poorer neighbours; and it is probable they would have fallen a prey to their more warlike habits, had they not formed an alliance with the Romans, who sent an army to their assistance. The commander of this army, after defeating their enemies, granted them all the harbours, and the whole sea-coast, between their city and the confines of Italy; and thus at once secured their safety and extended their territory. A short time afterwards, Marius conferred on them another benefit, not inferior in importance and utility. While he was waiting for the Cimbri in Transalpine Gaul, he was under great difficulty to procure provisions up the Rhone, in consequence of the mouth of the river being obstructed with sand-banks. To remedy this inconvenience, he undertook a great and laborious work, which, from him, was called Fossa Marina: this was a large canal, beginning at his camp, near Arles, and carried on to the sea, which was fed with water from the Rhone; through this canal, the largest transports could pass. After his victory over the Cimbrians, Marius gave this canal to the people of Marseilles, in return for the support and supplies they had afforded him in his war against them. As there was no passage into the interior of this part of Gaul, except either through the Rhone or this canal, the Marseillians, who were now masters of both, enriched themselves considerably, partly by the traffic they carried on, and partly by the duties they levied on all goods which were sent up the canal and the river. In the civil war between Pompey and Cæsar, they took part with the former, who, in return, gave them all the territory on the western bank of the Rhone. Cæsar, exasperated at their hostility towards him, and at their ingratitude (for he, on the conquest of Gaul, had enlarged their territories, and augmented their revenues), blocked up their port by sea and land, and soon obliged them to surrender. He stripped their arsenals of arms, and obliged them to deliver up all their ships, as well as deprived them of the colonies and towns that were under their dominion.

The Marseillians, in the pursuit of commerce, made several voyages to distant, and, till then, unknown parts of the world: of these, the voyage of Pytheas, the extent, direction, and discoveries of which we have already investigated, was the most remarkable and celebrated. Euthymenes, another Marseillian navigator, is said to have advanced to the south, beyond the line; but little credit seems due to the very imperfect accounts which we possess of his voyage. The Marseillians also planted several colonies on the coasts of Gaul, Italy, and Spain, viz. Nicæa, Antipolis (Antibes,) Telo Martius (Toulon,) &c.

Arelas (Arles) was also a place of some trade, and celebrated for its manufactures, especially its embroidery, and its curious and rich works in gold and silver. It was at this place that Cæsar built, in the short period of thirty days, the twelve galleys which he used in blocking up the port of Marseilles; and he manned them with its inhabitants;—a proof, as Huet observes, that they were well versed in maritime affairs at this time.

Narbo Marcius (Narbonne) was founded by Marius: it soon became, according to Strabo and Diodorus Siculus, a place of very great trade. The British tin, besides other articles, was brought by land-carriage through the centre of Gaul, and exported, either from it or Marseilles, to the different countries on the Mediterranean. It derived great importance and wealth, from its being a convenient place of rest and refreshment for the Roman troops, as they passed from the Pyrennees to the Alps, or from the Alps to the Pyrennees. Its harbour was crowded with ships from Africa, Spain, Italy, &c.; but, in the latter ages of the Roman Empire, it fell into decay, principally in consequence of the course of the river being changed, so that it no longer ran through it. The

Romans endeavoured to supply this misfortune, by cutting a canal to the sea, the traces and remains of which are still visible.

Lugdunum (Lyons), at the confluence of the Rhone and Arar, was founded by Manucius Plancus, after the death of Julius Caesar. In the time of Augustus, according to Strabo, it had increased so much, by means of its commerce, that it was not inferior to any city in Gaul, except Narbonne. Indeed, not long after the entire conquest of Gaul by the Romans, the advantages which that country might derive, with respect to foreign commerce, and internal trade, by its rivers, seem to have been fully and clearly understood. The head of the Saone being near to that of the Moselle and the Seine, merchandize was easily conveyed by land from one of these rivers to the other. The Rhone also received many goods by means of the rivers which joined it, which were conveyed, not only to the Saone, but also to the Loire, in carriages. The Seine brought up goods almost as far as the Moselle, from which they were conveyed to the Rhine. In the fourth year of Nero's reign, the commander of the Roman army in Gaul joined the Saone and the Moselle by a canal; and, though these canals were generally made by the Romans, for purposes connected with the army, yet they were soon applied to commerce. The merchandize of the Saone was brought by land carriage to the Seine, and by it conveyed to the ocean, and thence to Britain. There seems to have been regular and established companies of watermen on these rivers, whose business it was to convey goods on them: an ancient inscription at Lyons mentions Tauricius of Vannes, as the general overseer of the Gallic trade, the patron or head of the watermen on the Seine and Loire, and the regulator of weights, measures, and carriages; and other ancient inscriptions state, that the government of the watermen who navigated the Rhone and the Saone, was often bestowed on Roman knights.

Besides the ports on the Mediterranean, or on the rivers which flow into that sea, the Gauls in Cæsar's time, or shortly afterwards, seem to have had several, ports on the ocean. Cæsar reckons the present Nantz, though at some distance from the sea, as inhabited by people who were skilled in maritime affairs; and he expressly informs us, that he built his ships at a port at the mouth of the Seine, when he was preparing to invade Britain. In his wars against the Vanni he brought ships from the present provinces of Saintoinge and Poitou, which we may thence conclude were inhabited by people skilled in maritime affairs. In later times, there was a marsh filled with sea-water, not far from Bourdeaux, which made that city a convenient port, and a place of considerable commerce. Strabo mentions a town of some commerce, situated on the Loire, which he represents as equal in size to Narbonne and Marseilles; but what town that was has not been ascertained.

The most powerful and commercial, however, of all the tribes of Gaul, that inhabited the coasts near the ocean, in the time of Cæsar, were the Vanni. These people carried on an extensive and lucrative trade with Britain, which was interrupted by the success of Cæsar, (who obliged them, as well as the other tribes of Gaul, to give him hostages,) and which they apprehended was likely to be still further injured by his threatened invasion of Britain; in order to prevent this, as well as to liberate themselves, they revolted against the Romans. As Cæsar was sensible that it would be imprudent and unsafe to attempt the invasion of Britain, so long as the Vanni were unsubdued and powerful at sea, he directed his thoughts and his endeavours to build and equip such a fleet as would enable him successfully to cope with them on their own element. In building his ships, he followed the model of those of his enemies, which were large, flat-bottomed, and high in the head and stern: they were strong-built, and had leathern sails, and anchors with iron chains. They had a numerous squadron of such vessels, which they employed chiefly in their trade with Britain: they seem also to have derived considerable revenue from the tribute which they levied on all who navigated the adjacent seas, and to have possessed many ports on the coast. Besides their own fleet, the Britons, who were their allies, sent ships to their assistance; so that their united force amounted to 220 sail, well equipped, and manned by bold and expert seamen.

To oppose this formidable fleet, Caesar ordered ships to be built on the Loire, and the rivers running into it, exactly, as we have just stated, after the model of the ships of the Vanni; for he was informed, or learnt by experience, that the vessels which were used in the Mediterranean were not fit for navigating and fighting on the ocean, but that such as were employed on the latter must be built, not only stronger, but flat-bottomed, and high at the head and stern, in order to withstand the fury of the waves and winds, which was greater in the ocean than in the Mediterranean, and at the same time to sail up the rivers, or in very shallow water, and to take the ground, without injury or danger. Not being able, however, to build in time a sufficient number of ships in Gaul, after the model of those of the Vanni, he was under the necessity of bringing some from the south coast of Gaul, and other parts of the Mediterranean Sea; he also collected all the experienced pilots he could meet with, who were acquainted with the coasts, and with the management of such ships, and exercised a sufficient number of men at the oar, to navigate them.

These preparations were all indispensably requisite; for in the battle which ensued, the Vanni and their allies fought their ships with a skill and a valour of which the Romans had not had any previous example; and they would certainly have been beaten, if they had not, by means of sharp engines, cut the ropes and sails of the hostile fleet, and thus rendered their ships unmanageable: in this state they were easily and speedily captured. As the Vanni had on this occasion mustered all their forces, their defeat put an end to their resistance, and removed Cæsar's principal obstacle to the invasion of Britain.

The motives which induced Caesar to invade Britain can only be conjectured, if, indeed, any other motive operated on his mind besides ambition, and the love of conquest and glory; stimulated by the hope of subduing a country, which seemed the limit of the world to the west, and which was in a great measure unknown. He was, probably, also incited by his desire to punish the Britons for having assisted the Vanni; and Suetonius adds, that he was desirous of enriching himself with British pearls, which were at that time in high repute.

Before he undertook this expedition, which, even to Caesar, appeared formidable, he resolved to learn all he could respecting Britain. For this purpose, he collected the merchants who traded thither from all parts of Gaul; but they could afford him no satisfactory information. They had visited only the opposite coast of Britain; of the other parts of the country, of its extent, its inhabitants, &c., they were utterly ignorant. Under these circumstances, therefore, he sent one of his officers in a galley, who, after being absent five days, during which however he had not ventured to land, returned to Caesar, and acquainted him with the little he had observed.

Caesar resolved to invade Britain immediately: for this purpose, he ordered eighty transports to take on board two legions; and the cavalry to be embarked in eighteen more, at a port a few miles off. The enterprize was attended with considerable difficulty, from the opposition of the Britons, and the large ships of the Romans not being able to approach very near the land. It was however successful, and the Britons sued for and obtained peace.

This they were soon induced to break, in consequence of Caesar's fleet being greatly injured by a storm; and the violence of the wind raising the tide very high, the Roman sailors, unaccustomed to any tides except the very trifling ones of the Mediterranean, were still more alarmed and dispirited. The Britons, after attacking one of the legions, ventured on a still bolder enterprize, for they endeavoured to force the Roman camp: in this attempt they were defeated, and again obliged to sue for peace. This was granted, and Caesar returned to Gaul. But the Britons not fulfilling the conditions of the peace, Caesar again invaded their country with 600 ships and twenty-eight galleys; he landed without opposition, and defeated the Britons. His fleet again encountered a storm, in which forty ships were lost, and the rest greatly damaged. In order to prevent a similar accident, he drew all his ships ashore, and enclosed them within the fortifications of the camp. After this, he had no further naval operations with the Britons.

It will now be proper to consider the state of Britain at the period of its invasion by the Romans, with respect to its navigation and commerce. It is the generally received opinion, that the Britons, at the time of the invasion of their island by Caesar, had no ships except those which he and other ancient authors, particularly Solinus and Lucan, describe. These were made of light and pliant wood, their ribs seem to have been formed of hurdles, and they were lined as well as covered (so far as they were at all decked) with leather. They had, indeed, masts and sails; the latter and the ropes were also made of leather; the sails could not be furled, but, when necessary, were bound to the mast. They were generally, however, worked with oars, the rowers singing to the stroke of their oars, sometimes accompanied by musical instruments. These rude vessels seem not to have been the only ones the Britons possessed, but were employed solely for the purpose of sailing to the opposite coasts of Gaul and of Ireland. They were, indeed, better able to withstand the violence of the winds and waves than might be supposed from the materials of which they were built. Pliny expressly states that they made voyages of six days in them; and in the life of St Columba, (in whose time they were still used, the sixth century,) we are informed of a vessel lined with leather, which went with oars and sails, sailing for fourteen days in a violent storm in safety, and gaining her port. The passage therefore in these boats across the Irish Channel, could not be so very dangerous as it is represented by Solinus.

But notwithstanding the authority of Caesar, Pliny, Solinus, and Lucan, who mention only these leathern vessels, and that the poet Avienus, who lived in the fourth century, expressly states, that even in his time the Britons had no ships made of timber, but only boats covered with leather or hides; there are circumstances which must convince us that they did possess larger, stronger, and more powerful ships. Caesar informs us, that the Britons often assisted the Gauls, both by land and sea; and we have seen that they sent assistance to the Vanni, in their sea-fight against Caesar; but it is not to be supposed that their leathern boats, small and weak as they were, could have been of any material advantage in an engagement with the Roman ships. Besides, the Britons, who inhabited the coast opposite to Gaul, carried on, as we have remarked, a considerable and regular trade with the Vanni; it is, therefore, reasonable to presume, that they would learn from this tribe, the art of building ships like theirs, which were so well fitted for these seas, as well as for war, that Caesar built vessels after their model, when he formed the determination of opposing them by sea.

The Britons, however, certainly did not themselves engage much in the traffic with Gaul, and therefore could not require many vessels of either description for this purpose. From the earliest period, of which we have any record, till long after the invasion by Caesar, the commodities of Britain seem to have been exported by foreign ships, and the commodities given in exchange brought by these.

In our account of the commerce of the Phoenicians, their trade to Britain for tin has been described. Pliny, in his chapter on inventions and discoveries, states that this metal was first brought from the Cassiterides by Midacritus, but at what period, or of what nation he was, he does not inform us. This trade was so lucrative, that a participation in it was eagerly sought by all the commercial nations of the Mediterranean, and even by the Romans, who, as we have seen, were not at this period, much given to commerce. This is evident, by the well known fact, of one of their vessels endeavouring to follow the course of a Phoenician or Carthaginian vessel, in her voyage to Britain. The Greeks of Marseilles, according to Polybius, first followed, successfully, the course of the Phoenicians, and, about 200 years before Christ, began to share with them in the tin trade. Whether, at this period, they procured it exclusively by direct trade with Britain, is not known; but afterwards, as we have already mentioned, Marseilles became one of the principal depots for this metal, which was conveyed to it through Gaul, and exported thence by sea.

If we may believe Strabo, the Romans had visited Britain before it was invaded by Caesar, as he expressly mentions that Publius Crassus made a voyage thither: if he means P. Crassus the younger, he was one of Caesar's lieutenants in

Gaul; and, as he was stationed in the district of the Vanni, it is not improbable that he passed from thence into Britain; or he may have been sent by Caesar, at the same time that Volusenus was sent, and for the same purpose.

However this may be, there was no regular intercourse between Britain and Rome till some time after Caesar's invasion; in the time of Tiberius, however, and probably earlier, the commerce of Britain was considerable. Strabo, who died at the beginning of that emperor's reign, informs us, that corn, cattle, gold, silver, tin, lead, hides, and dogs, were the commodities furnished by the Britons. The tin and lead, he adds, came from the Cassiterides. According to Camden, 800 vessels, laden with corn, were freighted annually to the continent; but this assertion rests on very doubtful authority, and cannot be credited if it applies to Britain, even very long after the Roman conquest. Though Strabo expressly mentions gold and silver among the exports, yet Caesar takes notice of neither; and Cicero, in his epistles, writing to his friend, respecting Britain, states, on the authority of his brother, who was there, that there were neither of these metals in the island. The dogs of Britain formed a very considerable and valuable article of export; they seem to have been known at Rome even before Caesar's expedition: the Romans employed them in hunting, and the Gauls in hunting and in their wars: they were of different species. Bears were also exported for the amphitheatres; but their exportation was not frequent till after the age of Augustus. Bridle ornaments, chains, amber, and glass ware, are enumerated by Strabo among the exports from Britain; but, according to other authors, they were imported into it. Baskets, toys made of bone, and oysters, were certainly among the exports; and, according to Solinus, gagates, or jet, of which Britain supplied a great deal of the best kind. Chalk was also, according to Martial, an article of export: there seems to have been British merchants whose sole employment was the exportation of this commodity, as appears by an ancient inscription found in Zealand, and quoted by Whitaker, in his history of Manchester. This article was employed as a manure on the marshy land bordering on the Rhine. Pliny remarks that its effect on the land continued eighty years. The principal articles imported into Britain were copper and brass, and utensils made of these metals, earthen ware, salt, &c. The traffic was carried on partly by means of barter, and partly by pieces of brass and iron, unshaped, unstamped, and rated by weight. The duties paid in Gaul, on the imports and exports of Britain, formed, according to Strabo, the only tribute exacted from the latter country by the Romans in his time.

Of that part of Europe which lies to the north of Gaul, the Romans, at the period of which we are treating, knew little or nothing, though some indirect traffic was carried on with Germany. The feathers of the German geese were preferred to all others at Rome; and amber formed a most important article of traffic. This was found in great abundance on the Baltic shore of Germany: at first, it seems to have been carried the whole length of the continent, to the Veneti, who forwarded it to Rome. Afterwards, in consequence of the great demand for it there, and its high price, the Romans sent people expressly to purchase it in the north of Germany: and their land journies, in search of this article, first made them acquainted with the naval powers of the Baltic. The Estii, a German tribe, who inhabited the amber country, gathered and sold it to the Roman traders, and were astonished at the price they received for it. In Nero's time it was in such high request, that that emperor resolved to send Julianus, a knight, to procure it for him in large quantities: accordingly, a kind of embassy was formed, at the head of which he was placed. He set out from Carnuntum, a fortress on the banks of the Danube, and after travelling, according to Pliny, 600 miles, arrived at the amber coast. There he bought, or received as a present, for the emperor, 13,000 pounds weight, among which was one piece that weighed thirteen pounds. The whole of this immense quantity served for the decoration of one day, on which Nero gave an entertainment of gladiators. In the time of Theodoric, king of the Goths, the Estii sent that monarch a large quantity of amber, as the most likely present by means of which they could obtain his alliance. They informed the ambassadors, whom he sent with a letter acknowledging this present, that they were ignorant whence the amber came, but that it was thrown upon their coast by the sea, a fact which exactly agrees with what occurs at present.

Whether the Estii, with whom the Romans carried on this traffic, were a maritime nation, we are not informed; but there was another nation or tribe of Germans on the Baltic, of whose maritime character some notices are given. These were the Sitones, who, according to Tacitus, had powerful fleets; their ships were built with two prows, so as to steer at both ends, and prevent the necessity of putting about; their oars were not fixed, like those of the Mediterranean vessels, but loose, so that they could easily and quickly be shifted: they used no sails. The people of Taprobane (Ceylon)—the Byzantines, and, on some occasions, the Romans also, employed vessels, like those of the Sitones, which could be steered at both ends.

One of the most considerable revolutions in the maritime and commercial affairs of Rome, was brought about by the battle of Actium. The fleet of Anthony was composed chiefly of ships belonging to the Egyptians, Tyrians, and other nations of the east, and amounted, according to some accounts, to 200 sail, whereas the fleet of Augustus consisted of 400 sail. Other authors estimate them differently; but all agree that the ships of Anthony were much larger, stronger, and loftier, than those of Caesar: they were consequently more unwieldy. We have the express testimony of Plutarch, that it was principally this victory which convinced Caesar of the advantages and extraordinary use of the Liburnian ships; for though they had been employed before this time in the Roman fleet, yet they had never been so serviceable in any previous battle. Augustas, therefore, as well as most of the succeeding emperors of Rome, scarcely built any other ships but those according to the Liburnian model.

One of the first objects of Augustus, after he had obtained the empire, was to secure the command of the sea: he made use of the ships which he had captured from Anthony to keep the people of Gaul in subjection; and he cleared the Mediterranean of the pirates which infested it and obstructed commerce. He formed two fleets, one at Ravenna, and the other at Misenum; the former to command the eastern, the latter the western division of the Mediterranean: each of these had its own proper commanders, and to each was attached a body of several thousand mariners. Ravenna, situated on the Adriatic, about ten or twelve miles from the most southern of the seven mouths of the Po, was not a place of much consequence till the age of Augustus: that emperor, observing its advantages, formed at the distance of about three miles from the old town and nearer the sea, a capacious harbour, capable of containing 250 ships of war. The establishment was on a large and complete scale, consisting of arsenals, magazines, barracks, and houses for the ship-carpenters, &c.: the principal canal, which was also formed by Augustus, and took its name from him, carried the waters of the river through the middle of Ravenna to the entrance of the harbour. The city was rendered still stronger by art than nature had formed it. As early as the fifth or sixth centuries of the Christian era the port was converted, by the retreat of the sea, into dry ground, and a grove of pines grew where the Roman fleet had anchored.

Besides the principal ports of Ravenna and Misenum, Augustus stationed a very considerable force at Frejus, on the coast of Provence, forty ships in the Euxine, with 3000 soldiers; a fleet to preserve the communication between Gaul and Britain, another near Alexandria, and a great number of smaller vessels on the Rhine and the Danube. As soon as the Romans had constant and regular fleets, instead of the legionary soldiers, who used to fight at sea as well as at land, a separate band of soldiers were raised for the sea service, who were called Classiarii; but this service was reckoned less honourable than that of the legionary soldiers.

The period at which we are arrived seems a proper one to take a general view of the commerce of the Roman empire; though, in order to render this view more complete, it will be necessary in many instances to anticipate the transactions posterior to the reign of Augustus. We shall, therefore, in the first place, give a statement of the extent of the Roman empire when it had reached its utmost limits; secondly, an account of its roads and communications by land; and, lastly, an abstract of the principal imports into it, and the laws and finances, so far as they respect its commerce.

1. The empire, at the death of Augustus, was bounded on the west by the Atlantic ocean, on the north by the Rhine and the Danube, on the east by the Euphrates, and on the south by the deserts of Arabia and Africa. The only addition which it received during the first century was the province of Britain: with this addition it remained till the reign of Trajan. That emperor conquered Dacea, and added it to the empire: he also achieved several conquests in the east; but these were resigned by his successor Adrian. At this period, therefore, the Roman empire may be considered as having attained its utmost limits. It is impossible to ascertain the number of people that were contained within these limits. In the time of Claudius the Roman citizens were numbered; they amounted to 6,945,000: if to these be added the usual proportion of women and children, the number will be encreased to about 20,000,000. If, therefore, we calculate, as we may fairly do, that there were twice as many provincials as there

were citizens with their wives and children, and that the slaves were at least equal in number to the provincials, the total population of the Roman empire will amount to 120,000,000.

Our ideas of the vastness and wealth of the empire will be still farther encreased, if we regard the cities which it contained, though it is impossible to decide in most instances the extent and population of many places which were honoured with the appellation of cities. Ancient Italy is said to have contained 1197, Gaul 1200, of which many, such as Marseilles, Narbonne, Lyons, &c. were large and flourishing; Spain 300, Africa 300, and Asia Proper 500, of which many were very populous.

2. All these cities were connected with one another and with Rome itself by means of the public highways: these issuing from the forum, traversed Italy, pervaded the provinces, and were terminated only by the frontiers of the empire. The great chain of communication formed by means of them from the extreme north-west limit of the empire, through Rome to the south-east limit, was in length nearly 4000 miles. These roads were formed in the most substantial manner, and with astonishing labour and expence; they were raised so as to command a prospect of the adjacent country; on each side was a row of large stones for foot passengers. The miles were reckoned from the gates of the city and marked on stones: at shorter distances there were stones for travellers to rest on, or to assist those who wished to mount their horses: there were cross roads from the principal roads. The care and management of all the roads were entrusted only to men of the highest rank. Augustus himself took charge of those near Rome, and appointed two men of prætorian rank to pave the roads: at the distance of five or six miles houses were built, each of which was constantly provided with forty horses; but these could only be used in the public service, except by particular and express authority. By means of the relays thus furnished, the Romans could travel along their excellent roads 100 miles a day: they had no public posts. Augustus first introduced public couriers among the Romans; but they were employed only to forward the public despatches, or to convey public intelligence of great and urgent importance.

Such was the facililty of communication by land from all parts of the empire to Rome, and from each part to all the other parts: nor was the communication of the empire less free and open by sea than it was by land. "The provinces surrounded and enclosed the Mediterranean; and Italy, in the shape of an immense promontory, advanced into the midst of that great lake." From Ostia, situated at the mouth of the Tiber, only sixteen miles from the capital, a favourable wind frequently carried vessels in seven days to the straits of Gibraltar, and in nine or ten to Alexandria, in Egypt.

3. In enumerating the principal articles imported into Rome, for the use of its immense and luxurious population, we shall, necessarily, recapitulate, in some degree, what has already been stated in giving an account of the commerce of the different countries which were conquered by the Romans. But this objection, we conceive, will be abundantly counterbalanced by the connected and complete view which we shall thus be enabled to give of the commerce of

the Roman empire.

Before, however, we enter on this subject, we shall briefly consider the ideas entertained by the Romans on the subject of commerce. We have already had occasion incidentally to remark that the Romans thought meanly of it, and that their grand object in all their conquests was the extension of their territory; and that they even neglected the commercial facilities and advantages, which they might have secured by their conquests. This was most decidedly the case during the time of the republic. The statue of Victory, which was erected in the port of Ostia, and the medals of the year of Rome 630, marked on the reverse with two ships and a victory, prove that at this period the Roman fleets that sailed from this port were chiefly designed for war. The prefects of the fleet were not employed, nor did they consider it as their duty to attend to commerce, or to the merchant ships, except so far as to protect them against the pirates. Of the low opinion entertained by the Romans respecting commerce we have the direct testimony of Cicero: writing to his son on the subject of professions, he reprobates and condemns all retail trade as mean and sordid, which can be carried on successfully only by means of lying. Even the merchant, unless he deals very extensively, he views with contempt; if, however, he imports from every quarter articles of great value and in great abundance, and sells them in a fair and equitable manner, his profession is not much to be contemned; especially if, after having made a fortune, he retires from business, and spends the rest of his life in agricultural pursuits: in this case, he deserves even positive praise. There is another passage of Cicero, quoted by Dr. Vincent, in his Periplus, in which the same sentiments are expressed: he says, "Is such a man, who was a merchant and neighbour of Scipio, greater than Scipio because he is richer?" Pliny, also, though in his natural history he expatiates in praise of agriculture and gardening, medicine, painting and statuary, passes over merchandize with the simple observation that it was invented by the Phoenicians. In the periplus of the Erythrean sea, and in the works of Ptolemy, &c. the names of many merchants and navigators occur; but they are all Greeks. Even after the conquest of Egypt, which gave a more commercial character to the Roman manners, habits and mode of thinking than they previously possessed, no Roman was permitted to engage in the trade of that country.

Although, however, mercantile pursuits were thus underrated and despised by the warlike portion of the nation, as well as by the philosophers, yet they were followed by those who regarded gain as the principal object of life. The wealth of merchants became proverbial: immense numbers of them followed the armies, and fixed in the provinces subdued or allied,—the , who were agents, traders, and monopolizers, such as Jugurtha took in Zama, or the 100,000 Mithridates slaughtered in Asia Minor, or the merchants killed at Genabum (Orleans).

In the passage quoted from Cicero de Officiis, he expressly mentions the merchant who ; but he does not once allude to exportation. Indeed, the commerce of the Romans, in the most luxurious period of the empire, was entirely confined to importation, and may, with few exceptions, be designated as consisting in the expenditure of the immense revenue they derived from their conquests, and the immense fortunes of individuals, in the necessaries, comforts, and, above all, the luxuries of the countries which they had conquered.

By far the most extensive and important trade which the Romans carried on at all periods of their history, was the conveyance of corn and other provisions to the capital. The contiguous territory at no time was sufficient to supply Rome with corn; and, long before the republic was destroyed, even Italy was inadequate to this purpose. As the population encreased, and the former corn fields were converted into pleasure-grounds or pasture, the demand for corn was proportionally encreased, and the supply from the neighbourhood proportionally diminished. But there was another circumstance which rendered a regular and full supply of corn an object of prime importance: the influence of the patron depended on his largesses of corn to his clients; and the popularity, and even the reign of an emperor, was not secure, unless he could insure to the inhabitants this indispensable necessary of life. There were several laws respecting the distribution of corn: by one passed in the year of Rome 680, five bushels were to be given monthly to each of the poorer citizens, and money was to be advanced annually from the treasury, sufficient to purchase 800,000 bushels of wheat, of three different qualities and prices. By the Sempronian law, this corn was to be sold to the poor inhabitants at a very low price; but by the Clodian law it was to be distributed : the granaries in which this corn was kept were called Horrea Sempronia. The number of citizens who received corn by public distribution, in the time of Augustus, amounted to 200,000. Julius Caesar had reduced the number from 320,000 to 150,000. It is doubtful whether five bushels were the allowance of each individual or of each family; but if Dr. Arbuthnot be correct in estimating the   at fourteen pounds, the allowance must have been for each family, amounting to one quarter seven bushels, and one peck per annum.

We have dwelt on these particulars for the purpose of pointing out the extreme importance of a regular and full supply of corn to Rome; and this importance is still further proved by the special appointment of magistrates to superintend this article. The prefect, or governor of the market, was an ancient establishment in the Roman republic; his duty was to procure corn: on extraordinary occasions, this magistrate was created for this express purpose, and the powers granted him seem to have been increased in the latter periods of the republic, and still more, after the republic was destroyed. Pompey, who held this office, possessed greater power and privileges than his immediate predecessor, and in a time of great scarcity. Augustus, himself, undertook the charge of providing the corn: it was at the same time determined, that for the future, two men of the rank of praetors should be annually elected for this purpose; four were afterwards appointed. It would seem, however, that even their appointment became an ordinary and regular thing: the emperors themselves superintended the procuring of corn, for one of their titles was that of commissary-general of corn.

Besides this magistrate, whose business was confined to the buying and importing of corn, there were two aediles, first appointed by Julius Caesar, whose duty it was to inspect the public stores of corn and other provisions.

Till the time of Julius Caesar, the foreign corn for the supply of Rome was imported into Puteoli, a town of Campania, between Baiae and Naples, about seventy miles from the capital. As this was very inconvenient, Caesar formed the plan of making an artificial harbour at the mouth of the Tiber, at Ostia. This plan, however, was not at this time carried into execution: Claudius, however, in consequence of a dreadful famine which raged at Rome, A.D. 42, resolved to accomplish it. He accordingly dug a spacious basin in the main land; the entrance to which was formed and protected by artificial moles, which advanced far into the sea; there was likewise a little island before the mouth of the harbour, on which a light-house was built, after the model of the Pharos of Alexandria. By the formation of this harbour, the largest vessel could securely ride at anchor, within three deep and capacious basins, which received the northern branch of the Tiber, about two miles from the ancient colony of Ostïa.

Into this port corn arrived for the supply of Rome from various countries; immense quantities of wheat were furnished by the island of Sicily. Egypt was another of the granaries of the capital of the world; according to Josephus, it supplied Rome with corn sufficient for one-third of its whole consumption: and Augustus established regular corn voyages from Alexandria to the capital. Great quantities were also imported from Thrace, and from Africa Proper. The ships employed in the corn trade, especially between Egypt and Rome, were the largest of any in the Mediterranean: this probably arose from the encouragement given to this trade by Tiberius, and afterwards increased by Claudius. The former emperor gave a bounty of about fourpence on every peck of corn imported: and Claudius, during the time of the famine, made the bounty so great as, at all events, and in every instance, to secure the importers a certain rate of profit. He also used all his efforts to persuade the merchants to import it even in winter, taking upon himself all the losses, &c. which might arise from risking their ships and cargoes, at a time of the year when it was the invariable practice of the ancients to lay the former up. Whenever an emperor had distinguished himself by a large importation of corn, especially, if by this means a famine was avoided or removed, medals seem to have been struck commemorative of the circumstance; thus, on several medals there is a figure of a ship, and the words . or . Many of these were struck under Nero, and Antoninus Pius. During the time of the republic, also, similar medals were struck, with the figure of a prow of a ship, and an inscription shewing the object for which the fleets had been sent.

Having been thus particular in describing the importation of corn, we shall notice the imports of other articles in a more cursory manner. The northern parts of Italy furnished salt pork, almost sufficient for the whole consumption of Rome, tapestry, and woollen cloths, wool, and marble; to convey the latter, there were ships of a peculiar form and construction; steel, crystal, ice, and cheese.

From Liguria, Rome received wood for building, of a very large size, ship timber, fine and beautiful wood for tables, cattle, hides, honey, and coarse wool. Etruria, also, supplied timber, cheese, wine, and stone; the last was shipped at the ports of Pisa and Luna. Pitch and tar were sent from Brutium; oil and wine from the country of the Sabines. Such were the principal imports from the different parts of Italy.

From Corsica, timber for ship building; from Sardinia, a little corn and cattle; from Sicily, besides corn,—wine, honey, salt, saffron, cheese, cattle, pigeons, corals, and a species of emerald. Cloth, but whether linen or cotton is uncertain, was imported from Malta; honey, from Attica. Lacedemon supplied green marble, and the dye of the purple shell-fish. From the Grecian islands, there were imported Parian marble, the earthenware of Samos, the vermilion of Lemnos, and other articles, principally of luxury. Thrace supplied salted tunnies, the produce of the Euxine Sea, besides corn. The finest wool was imported from Colchis, and also hemp, flax, pitch, and fine linens: these goods, as well as articles brought overland from India, were shipped from the port of Phasis. The best cheese used at Rome, was imported from Bithynia. Phrygia supplied a stone like alabaster, and the country near Laodicea, wool of excellent quality, some of which was of a deep black colour. The wine drank at Rome, was principally the produce of Italy; the best foreign wine, was imported from Ionia. Woollen goods, dyed with Tyrian purple, were imported from Miletus, in Caria. An inferior species of diamond, copper, resin, and sweet oil were imported from Cyprus. Cedar, gums, balsam, and alabaster, were supplied by Syria, Phoenicia, and Palestine. Glass was imported from Sidon, as well as embroidery and purple dye, and several kinds of fish, from Tyre. The goods that were brought from India, by the route of Palmyra, were shipped for Rome, from the ports of Syria. Egypt, besides corn, supplied flax, fine linen, ointments, marble, alabaster, salt, alum, gums, paper, cotton goods, some of which, as well as of their linens, seem to have been coloured or printed, glass ware, &c. The honey lotus, the lotus, or nymphæa of Egypt, the stalk of which contained a sweet substance, which was considered as a luxury by the Egyptians, and used as bread, was sometimes carried to Rome; it was also used as provision for mariners. Alexandria was the port from which all the produce and manufactories of Egypt, as well as all the ports which passed through this country from India, were shipped. In consequence of its becoming the seat of the Roman government in Egypt, of the protection which it thus received, and of its commerce being greatly extended by the increased wealth and luxury of Rome, its extent and population were greatly augmented; according to Diodorus Siculus, in the time of Augustus, from whose reign it became the greatest emporium of the world, it contained 300,000 free people.

That part of Africa which was formerly possessed by the Carthaginians, besides corn, sent to Rome, honey, drugs, marble, the eggs and feathers of the ostrich, ostriches, elephants, and lions; the last for the amphitheatre. From Mauritania, there were exported to the capital, timber of a fine grain and excellent quality, the exact nature of which is not known; this was sold at an enormous rate, and used principally for making very large tables.

Spain supplied Rome with a very great number and variety of articles; from the southern parts of it were exported corn, wine, oil, honey, wax, pitch, scarlet dye, vermilion, salt, salted provisions, wool, &c. From the eastern part of the north of Spain were exported salted provisions, cordage made of the , silver, earthenware, linen, steel, &c. The Balearic islands exported some wine. The trade of Spain to Rome employed a great number of vessels, almost as many as those which were employed in the whole of the African trade; this was especially the case in the reigns of Augustus and Tiberius. Even in the time of Julius Caesar, Spain had acquired great wealth, principally by her exports to Rome. The ports from which the greatest part of these commodities were shipped, were Cadiz, New Carthage, and a port at the mouth of the Boetis, where, for the security of the shipping, a light-house had been built. Cadiz was deemed the rival of Alexandria in importance, shipping, and commerce; and so great was the resort of merchants, &c. to it, that many of them, not being able to build houses for want of room on the land, lived entirely upon the water.

From Gaul, Rome received gold, silver, iron, &c. which were sent as part of the tribute; also linens, corn, cheese, and salted pork. Immense flocks of geese travelled by land to Rome. The chief ports which sent goods to Rome were Marseilles, Arles, and Narbonne, on the Mediterranean; and on the Ocean, Bourdeau, and the port of the Veneti. It appears that there were a considerable number of Italian or Roman merchants resident in Gaul, whose principal trade it was to carry the wine made in the south of this province, up the Rhine, and there barter it for slaves.

From Britain, Rome was supplied with tin, lead, cattle, hides, ornaments of bone, vessels made of amber and glass, pearls, slaves, dogs, bears, &c. The tin was either shipped from the island of Ictis (Isle of Wight), or sent into Gaul: most of the other articles reached Rome through Gaul. The principal article brought to Rome was amber.

We now come to the consideration of the articles with which Asia supplied Rome; these, as may be easily imagined, were principally articles of luxury. The murrhine cups, of the nature of which there has been much unsatisfactory discussion, according to Pliny, came from Karmania in Parthia; from Parthia they came to Egypt, and thence to Rome. It is probable, however, that they came, in the first instance, from India, as they are expressly mentioned by the author of the Periplus of the Erythrean Sea, as brought down from the capital of Guzerat, to the port of Baragyza. These cups were first seen at Rome, in the triumphal procession of Pompey, when he returned from the shores of the Caspian Sea. They sold at enormous prices; and were employed at the tables only of the great and wealthy, as cups for drinking; they were in general of a small size. One, which held three pints, sold for nearly 14,000 .; and Nero gave nearly 59,000 . for another. So highly were they prized, that, in the conquest of Egypt, Augustus was content to select, for his own share, out of all the spoils of Alexandria, a single murrhine cup.[5] Precious stones and pearls were imported from Persia and Babylonia; the latter country also furnished the wealthy Romans with , which was furniture of some description, but whether quilts, carpets, or curtains is not ascertained. Persia supplied also incense of a very superior quality. The various and valuable commodities with which Arabia supplied the profusion and luxury of Rome, reached that capital from the port of Alexandria in Egypt. We cannot enumerate the whole of them, but must confine ourselves to a selection of the most important and valuable. Great demand, and a high rate of profits necessarily draw to any particular trade a great number of merchants; it is not surprising, therefore, that the trade in the luxuries of the east was so eagerly followed at Rome. Pliny informs us, that the Roman world was exhausted by a drain of 400,000 . a year, for the purchase of luxuries, equally expensive and superfluous; and in another place, he estimates the rate of profit made at Rome, by the importation and sale of oriental luxuries at 100 per cent.

Arabia furnished diamonds, but these were chiefly of a small size, and other gems and pearls. At Rome the diamond possessed the highest value; the pearl, the second; and the emerald, the third. Nero used an emerald as an eye-glass for short sight. But though large and very splendid diamonds brought a higher price at Rome than pearls, yet the latter, in general, were in much greater repute; they were worn in almost every part of the dress, by persons of almost every rank. The famous pearl ear-rings of Cleopatra were valued at 161,458 ., and Julius Caesar presented the mother of Brutus with a pearl, for which he paid 48,457 . Frankincense, myrrh, and other precious drugs, were also brought to Rome from Arabia, through the port of Alexandria. There was a great demand at Rome for spices and aromatics, from the custom of the Romans to burn their dead, and also from the consumption of frankincense, &c. in their temples. At the funeral of Sylla 210 bundles of spices were used. Nero burnt, at the funeral of Poppaea, more cinnamon and cassia than the countries from which they were imported produced in one year. In the reign of Augustus, according to Horace, one whole street was occupied by those who dealt in frankincense, pepper, and other aromatics. Frankincense was also imported into Rome from Gaza, on the coast of Palestine; according to Pliny, it was brought to this place by a caravan, that was sixty-two days on its journey: the length of the journey, frauds, impositions, duties; &c. brought every camel's load to upward of 22*l.*; and a pound of the best sort sold at Rome for ten shillings. Alexandria, however, was the great emporium for this, as well as all the other produce of India and Arabia. Pliny is express and particular on this point, and takes notice of the precautions employed by the merchants there, in order to guard against adulteration and fraud. Cinnamon, another of the exports of Arabia to Rome, though not a production of that country, was also in high repute, and brought an extravagant price. Vespasian was the first who dedicated crowns of cinnamon, inclosed in gold filagree, in the Capitol and the Temple of Peace; and Livia dedicated the root in the Palatine Temple of Augustus. The plant itself was brought to the emperor Marcus Aurelius in a case seven feet long, and was exhibited at Rome, as a very great rarity. This, however, we are expressly informed came from Barbarike in India. It seems to have been highly valued by other nations as well as by the Romans: Antiochus Epiphanes carried a few boxes of it in a triumphal procession: and Seleucus Callinicus presented two minae of it and two of cassia, as a gift to the king of the Milesians. In the enumeration of the gifts made by this monarch, we may, perhaps, trace the comparative rarity and value of the different spices of aromatics among the ancients: of frankincense he presented ten talents, of myrrh one talent, of cassia two pounds, of cinnamon two pounds, and of costus one pound. Frankincense and myrrh were the productions of Arabia; the other articles of India; of course the former could be procured with much less difficulty and expence than the latter. Spikenard, another Indian commodity, also reached Rome, through Arabia, by means of the port of Alexandria. Pliny mentions, that both the leaves and the spices were of great value, and that the odour was the most esteemed in the composition of all unguents. The price at Rome was 100 denarii a pound. The markets at which the Arabian and other merchants bought it were Patala on the Indus, Ozeni, and a mart on or near the Ganges.

Sugar, also, but of a quality inferior to that of India, was imported from Arabia, through Alexandria, into Rome. The Indian sugar, which is expressly mentioned by Pliny, as better and higher priced, was brought to Rome, but by what route is not exactly known, probably by means of the merchants who traded to the east coast of Africa; where the Arabians either found it, or imported it from India. In the Periplus of the Erythrean Sea, and likewise in the rescript of the Roman emperors, relative to the articles imported into Egypt from the East, which was promulgated by Marcus Aurelius and his son Commodus, about the year A.D. 176, it is denominated cane-honey, otherwise called sugar (sacchar). So early, therefore, as the Periplus (about the year A.D. 73,) the name of sacchar was known to the Romans, and applied by them to sugar. This word does not occur in any earlier author, unless Dioscorides lived before that period, which is uncertain. It may be remarked, that the nature, as well as the proper appellation of sugar, must have been but imperfectly, and not generally known, even at the time of the rescript, otherwise the explanatory phrase, honey made from cane, would not have been employed.

The first information respecting sugar was brought to Europe by Nearchus, the admiral of Alexander. In a passage quoted from his journal by Strabo, it is described as honey made from reeds, there being no bees in that part of India. In a fragment of Theophrastus, preserved by Photius, he mentions, among other kinds of honey, one that is found in reeds. The first mention of any preparation, by which the juice of the reed was thickened, occurs in Eratosthenes, as quoted by Strabo, where he describes roots of large reeds found in India, which were sweet to the taste, both when raw and boiled. Dioscorides and Pliny describe it as used chiefly, if not entirely, for medical purposes. In the time of Galen, A.D. 131, it would appear to have become more common and cheaper at Rome; for he classes it with medicines that may be easily procured. It seems probable, that though the Arabians undoubtedly cultivated the sugar-cane, and supplied Rome with sugar from it, yet they derived their knowledge of it from India; for the Arabic name, shuker, which was adopted by the Greeks and Romans, is formed from the two middle syllables of the Sanskrit word, ich-shu-casa.

But to return from this digression to the view of the imports into Rome:

Ethiopia supplied the capital with cinnamon of an inferior quality; marble, gems, ivory; the horns of the rhinoceros and tortoiseshell. The last article was in great demand, and brought a high price: it was used for ornament, for furniture; as beds, tables, doors, &c.; not only in Italy, but in Greece and Egypt: the finest sort was sold for its weight of silver. It was imported not only from Ethiopia but also from the east coast of Africa, and reached Rome even from Malabar and Malacca. The opsian stone mentioned in the Periplus, and the opsidian stone described by Pliny, are stated in both these authors to have come from Ethiopia; but whether they were the same, and their exact nature, are not known. The opsian is described as capable of receiving a high polish, and on that account as having been used by the Emperor Domitian to face a portico. Pliny describes it as employed to line rooms in the same manner as mirrors; he distinguishes it from a spurious kind, which was red, but not transparent. The dye extracted from the purple shell fish was imported into Rome from Getulia, a country on the south side of Mauritania.

Rome was supplied with the commodities of India chiefly from Egypt; but there were other routes by which also they reached the capital: of these it will be proper to take some notice.

The most ancient communication between India and the countries on the Mediterranean was by the Persian Gulf, through Mesopotamia, to the coasts of Syria and Palestine. To facilitate the commerce which was carried on by this route, Solomon is supposed to have built Tadmor in the wilderness, or Palmyra: the situation of this place, which, though in the midst of barren sands, is plentifully supplied with water, and has immediately round it a fertile soil, was peculiarly favorable; as it was only 85 miles from the Euphrates, and about 117 from the nearest part of the Mediterranean. By this route the most valuable commodities of India, most of which were of such small bulk as to beat the expence of a long land carriage, were conveyed. From the age of Nebuchadnezzar to the Macedonian conquest, Tiredon on the Euphrates was the city at which this commercial route began, and which the Babylonians made use of, as the channel of their oriental trade. After the destruction of Tyre by that monarch, a great part of the traffic which had passed by Arabia, or the Red Sea, through Idumea and Egypt, and that city, was diverted to the Persian Gulf, and through his territories in Mesopotamia it passed by Palmyra and Damascus, through Syria to the west. After the reduction of Babylon by Cyrus, the Persians, who paid no attention to commerce, suffered Babylon and Ninevah to sink into ruin; but Palmyra still remained, and flourished as a commercial city. Under the Seleucidæ it seems to have reached its highest degree of importance, splendour, and wealth; principally by supplying the Syrians with Indian commodities. For upwards of two centuries after the conquest of Syria by the Romans it remained free, and its friendship and alliance were courted both by them and the Parthians. During this period we have the express testimony of Appian, that it traded with both these nations, and that Rome and the other parts of the empire received the commodities of India from it. In the year A.D. 273, it was reduced and destroyed by Aurelian, who found in it an immense treasure of gold, silver, silk, and precious stones. From this period, it never revived, or became a place of the least importance or trade.

On the conquest of Babylon by Cyrus, the commercial communication between India and Europe returned to Arabia in the south, and to the Caspian and the Euxine in the north: there seem to have been two routes by these seas, both of great antiquity. In describing one of them, the ancient writers are supposed to have confounded the river Ochus, which falls into the Caspian, with the Oxus, which falls into the lake of Aral. On this supposition, the route may be traced in the following manner: the produce and manufactuers of India were collected at Patala, a town near the mouth of the Indus; they were carried in vessels up this river as far as it was navigable, where they were landed, and conveyed by caravans to the Oxus: being again shipped, they descended this river to the point where it approached nearest to the Ochus, to which they were conveyed by caravans. By the Ochus they were conveyed to the Caspian, and across it to the mouth of the river Cyrus, which was ascended to where it approached nearest the Phasis: caravans were employed again, till the merchandize were embarked at Serapana on the Phasis, and thus brought to the Black Sea. According to Pliny, Pompey took great pains to inform himself of this route; and he ascertained, that by going up the Cyrus the goods would be brought within five day's journey of the Phasis. There seems to have been some plan formed at different times, and thought of by the Emperor Claudius, to join Asia to Europe and the Caspian Sea, by a canal from the Cimmerian Bosphorus to the Caspian Sea.

The route which we have thus particularly described was sometimes deviated from by the merchants: they carried their goods up the Oxus till it fell into lake Aral; crossing this, they transported them in caravans to the Caspian, and ascending the Wolga to its nearest approach to the Tanais, they crossed to the latter by land, and descended it to the sea of Azoph.

Strabo describes another route: viz. across the Caucasus, from the Caspian to the Black Sea; this writer, however, must be under some mistake, for camels, which he expressly says were employed, would be of no use in crossing the mountains; it is probable, therefore, that this land communication was round by the mouth of the Caspian,—a route which was frequented by the merchants of the middle ages.

As the Euxine Sea was the grand point to which all these routes tended, the towns on it became the resort of an immense number of merchants, even at very early ages; and the kingdoms of Prusias, Attalus, and Mithridates were enriched by their commerce. Herodotus mentions, that the trade of the Euxine was conducted by interpreters of seven different languages. In the time of Mithridates, 300 different nations, or tribes, met for commercial purposes at Dioscurias in Colchis; and soon after the Romans conquered the countries lying on the Euxine, there were 130 interpreters of languages employed in this and the other trading towns. The Romans, however, as soon as they became jealous, or afraid, of the power of the Parthians, would not suffer them, or any other of the northern nations, to traffic by the Euxine; but endeavoured, as far as they could, to confine the commerce of the East to Alexandria: the consequence was, that even so early as the age of Pliny, Dioscurias was deserted.

The only article of import into Rome that remains to be considered is silk: the history of the knowledge and importation of this article among the ancients, and the route by which it was obtained, will comprise all that it will be necessary to say on this subject.

The knowledge of silk was first brought into Europe through the conquests of Alexander the Great. Strabo quotes a passage from Nearchus, in which it is mentioned, but apparently confounded, with cotton. It is well known that Aristotle obtained a full and accurate account of all the discoveries in natural history which were made during the conquests of Alexander, and he gives a particular description of the silk worm; so particular, indeed, that it is surprising how the ancients could, for nearly 600 years after his death, be ignorant of the nature and origin of silk. He describes the silk worm as a horned worm, which he calls bombyx, which passes through several transformations, and produces bombytria. It does not appear, however, that he was acquainted either with the native country of this [work-]worm], or with such a people as the Seres; and this is the only reason for believing that he may allude entirely to a kind of silk made at Cos, especially as he adds, that some women in this island decomposed the bombytria, and re-wove and re-spun it. Pliny also mentions the bombyx, and describes it as a natiye of Assyria; he adds, that the Assyrians made bombytria from it, and that the inhabitants of Cos learnt the manufacture from them. The most propable supposition is, that silk was spun and wove in Assyria and Cos, but the raw material imported into these countries from the Seres; for the silk worm was deemed by the Greeks and Romans so exclusively and pre-eminently the attribute of the Sinae, that from this very circumstance, they were denominated seres, or silk worms, by the ancients.

The next authors who mention silk are Virgil, and Dionysius the geographer; Virgil supposed the Seres to card their silk from leaves,—*Velleraque ut foliis depectunt tentuia Seres.*—Dionysius, who was sent by Augustus to draw up an account of the Oriental regions, says, that rich and valuable garments were manufactured by the Seres from threads, finer than those of the spider, which they combed from flowers.

It is not exactly known at what period silk garments were first worn at Rome: Lipsius, in his notes on Tacitius, says, in the reign of Julius Csesar. In the beginning of the reign of Tiberius, a law was made, that no man should dishonor himself by wearing a silken garment. We have already stated the opinion entertained by Pliny respecting the native country of the silk worm; this author condemns in forcible, though affected language, the thirst of gain, which explored the remotest parts of the earth for the purpose of exposing to the public eye naked draperies and transparent matrons. In his time, slight silks, flowered, seem to have been introduced into religious ceremonies, as he describes crowns, in honour of the deities, of various colours, and highly perfumed, made of silk. The next author who mentions silk is Pausanias; he says, the thread from which the Seres form their web is not from any kind of bark, but is obtained in a different way; they have in their country a spinning insect, which the Greeks call seer. He supposes that the insect lived five years, and fed on green haulm: by the last particular, it is not improbable he meant the leaves of the mulberry tree. For 200 years after the age of Pliny, the use of silk was confined to the female sex, till the richer citizens, both of the capital and the provinces, followed the example of Heliogabalus, the first man, who, according to Lampridius, wore *holosericum* that is, a garment which was all of silk. From this expression, however, it is evident, that previous to this period the male inhabitants of Rome had been in the habit of wearing garments made of silk mixed with linen or woollen.

Hitherto there is no intimation in ancient authors of the price of silk at Rome; in the time of Aurelian, however, that is towards the end of the third century, we learn the high price at which it was rated, in an indirect manner. For when the wife of that Emperor begged of him to permit her to have but one single garment of purple silk; he refused it, saying, that one pound of silk sold at Rome for 12 ounces, or its weight of gold. This agrees with what is laid down in the Rhodian maritime laws, as they appear in the eleventh book of the Digests, according to which unmixed silk goods paid a salvage, if they were saved without being damaged by the sea water, of ten per cent., as being equal in value to gold.

In about 100 years after the reign of Aurelian, however, the importation of silk into Rome must have increased very greatly; for Ammianus Marcellinus, who flourished A.D. 380, expressly states that silk, which had formerly been confined to the great and rich, was, in his time, within the purchase of the common people. Constantinople was founded about forty years before he wrote; and it naturally found its way there in greater abundance than it had done, when Rome was the capital of the empire.

From this time, till the middle of the sixth century, we have no particular information respecting the silk trade of the Roman empire. At this period, during the reign of Justinian, silk had become an article of very general and indispensible use: but the Persians had occupied by land and sea the monopoly of this article, so that the inhabitants of Tyre and Berytus, who had all along manufactured it for the Roman market, were no longer able to procure a sufficient supply, even at an extravagant price. Besides, when the manufactured goods were brought within the Roman territories, they were subject to a duty of ten per cent. Justinian, under these circumstances, very impolitically ordered that silk should be sold at the rate of eight pieces of gold for the pound, or about 3*l.* 4s. The consequence was such as might have been expected: silk goods were no longer imported; and to add to the injustice and the evil, Theodora, the emperor's wife, seized all the silk, and fined the merchants very heavily. It was therefore necessary, that Justinian should have recourse to other measures to obtain silk goods; instead, however, of restoring the trade of Egypt, which at this period had fallen into utter decay, and sending vessels directly from the Red Sea to the Indian markets, where the raw material might have been procured, he had recourse to Arabia and Abyssinia. According to Suidas, he wished the former to import the silk in a raw state, intending to manufacture it in his own dominions. But the king of Abyssinia declined the offer; as the vicinity of the Persians to the Indian markets for silk enabled them to purchase it at a cheaper rate than the Abyssinians could procure it. The same obstacle prevented the Arabians from complying with the request of Justinian.

The wealthy and luxurious Romans, therefore, must have been deprived of this elegant material for their dresses, had not their wishes been gratified by an unexpected event. Two Persian monks travelled to Serindi, where they had lived long enough to become acquainted with the various processes for spinning and manufacturing silk. When they returned, they communicated their information to Justinian; and were induced, by his promises, to undertake the transportation of the eggs of the silk-worm, from China to Constantinople. Accordingly, they went back to Serindi, and brought away a quantity of the eggs in a hollow cane, and conveyed them safely to Constantinople. They superintended and directed the hatching of the eggs, by the heat of a dunghill: the worms were fed on mulberry leaves: a sufficient number of butterflies were saved to keep up the stock; and to add to the benefits already conferred, the Persian monks taught the Romans the whole of the manufacture. From Constantinople, the silk-worms were conveyed to Greece, Sicily, and Italy. In the succeeding reign, the Romans had improved so much in the management of the silk-worms, and in the manufacture of silk, that the Serindi ambassadors, on their arrival in Constantinople, acknowledged that the Romans were not inferior to the natives of China, in either of these respects. It may be mentioned, in further proof of the opinion already given, that the silk manufactures of Cos were not supplied from silk-worms in that island, that we have the express authority of Theophanes and Zonaras, that, before silk-worms were brought to Constantinople, in the reign of Justinian, no person in that city knew that silk was produced by a worm. This, certainly, would not have been the case, if there had been silk-worms so near Constantinople as the island of Cos is. All the authors whom we have quoted, (with the exception of Aristotle, Pliny, and Pausanias,) including a period of six centuries, supposed that silk was made from fleeces growing upon trees, from the bark of trees, or from flowers. These mistakes, may, indeed, have arisen from the Romans having heard of the silk being taken from the mulberry and other trees, on which the worms feed; but, however they originated, they plainly prove that the native country of the silk-worm was at a very great distance from Rome, and one of which they had very little knowledge.

Having thus brought the history of this most valuable import into Rome, down to the period, when, in consequence of the Romans having acquired the silk-worm, there existed no longer any necessity to import the raw materials; we shall next proceed to investigate the routes by which it was brought from the Seres to the western parts of Asia, and thence to Rome. It is well ascertained, that the silk manufacture was established at Tyre and Berytus, from a very early period; and these places seem to have supplied Rome with silk stuffs. But, by what route did silk arrive thither, and to the other countries, so as to be within the immediate reach of the Romans?—There were two routes, by which it was introduced to Europe, and the contiguous parts of Asia: by land and sea.

The route by sea is pointed out in a clear and satisfactory manner, by some of the ancient authors, particularly the author of the Periplus of the Erythrean Sea. In enumerating the exports from Nelkundah, he particularly mentions silk stuffs, and adds, that they were brought to this place from countries further to the east. Nelkundah was a town in Malabar, about twelve miles up a small river, at the mouth of which was the port of Barake; at this port, the vessels of the ancients rode till their lading was brought down from Nelkundah. This place seems to have been the centrical mart between the countries that lie to the east and west of Cape Comorin, or the hither and further peninsula of India; fleets sailed from it to Khruse, which there is every reason to believe was part of the peninsula of Malacca; and we have the authority of Ptolemy, that there was a commercial communication between it and the northern provinces of China. But at a later period than the age of the Periplus, silk was brought by sea from China to Ceylon, and thence conveyed to Africa and Europe. Cosmos, who lived in the sixth century, informs us, that the Tzenistæ or Chinese, brought to Ceylon, silks, aloes, cloves, and sandal wood. That his Tzenistæ, are the Chinese, there can be no doubt; for he mentions them as inhabiting a country producing silk, beyond which there is no country, for the ocean encircles it oh the east. From this it is evident that the Tzenistæ of this author, and the Seres of the ancients, are the same; and in specifying the imports into Ceylon, he mentions silk thread, as coming from countries farther to the east, particularly from the Chinese. We thus see by what sea route silk was brought from China to those places with which the western nations had a communication; it was imported either into the peninsula of Malacca by sea, and thence by sea to Nelkundah, whence it was brought by a third voyage to the Red Sea; or it was brought directly from China to Ceylon, from which place there was a regular sea communication also with the Red Sea.

The author of the Periplus informs us, that raw as well as manufactured silk were conveyed by land through Bactria, to Baraguza or Guzerat, and by the Ganges to Limurike; according to this first route, the silks of China must have come the whole length of Tartary, from the great wall, into Bactria; from Bactria, they passed the mountains to the sources of the Indus, and by that river they were brought down to Patala, or Barbarike, in Scindi, and thence to Guzerat: the line must have been nearly the same when silk was brought to the sources of the Ganges; at the mouth of this river, it was embarked for Limurike in Canara. All the silk, therefore, that went by land to Bactria, passed down the Indus to Guzerat; all that deviated more to the east, and came by Thibet, passed down the Ganges to Bengal.

A third land route by which silk was brought to the Persian merchants, and by them sold to the Romans, was from Samarcand and Bochara, through the northern provinces of China, to the metropolis of the latter country: this, however, was a long, difficult, and dangerous route. From Samarcand to the first town of the Chinese, was a journey of from 60 to 100 days; as soon as the caravans passed the Jaxartes, they entered the desert, in which they were necessarily exposed to great privations, as well as to great risk from the wandering tribes. The merchants of Samarcand and Bochara, on their return from China, transported the raw or manufactured silk into Persia; and the Persian merchants sold it to the Romans at the fairs of Armenia and Nisibis.

Another land route is particularly described by Ptolemy: according to his detail, this immense inland communication began from the bay of Issus, in Cilicia; it then crossed Mesopotamia, from the Euphrates to the Tigris, near Hieropolis: it then passed through part of Assyria and Media, to Ecbatana and the Caspian Pass; after this, through Parthia to Hecatompylos: from this place to Hyrcania; then to Antioch, in Margiana; and hence into Bactria. From Bactria, a mountainous country was to be crossed, and the country of the Sacæ, to Tachkend, or the Stone Tower. Near this place was the station of those merchants who traded directly with the Seres. The defile of Conghez was next passed, and the region of Cosia or Cashgar through the country of the Itaguri, to the capital of China. Seven months were employed on this journey, and the distance in a right line amounted to 2800 miles. That the whole of this journey was sometimes performed by individuals for the purchase of silk and other Chinese commodities, we have the express testimony of Ptolemy; for he informs us, that Maes, a Macedonian merchant, sent his agent through the entire route which we have just described. It is not surprising, therefore, that silk should have borne such an exorbitant price at Rome; but it is astonishing that any commodity, however precious, could bear the expence of such a land carriage.

The only other routes by land, by which silk was brought from China into Europe, seem to have corresponded, in the latter part of their direction, with the land routes from India, already described. Indeed, it may naturally be supposed, that the Indian merchants, as soon as they learned the high prices of silk at Rome, would purchase it, and send it along with the produce and manufactures of their own country, by the caravans to Palmyra, and by river navigation to the Euxine: and we have seen, that on the capture of Palmyra, by Aurelian, silk was one of the articles of plunder.

We are now to take notice of the laws which were passed by the Romans for the improvement of navigation and commerce; and in this part of our subject we shall follow the same plan and arrangement which we have adopted in treating of the commerce itself; that is, we shall give a connected view of these laws, or at least the most important of them, from the period when the Romans began to interest themselves in commerce, till the decline of the empire.

These laws may be divided into three heads: first, laws relating to the protection and privileges allowed to mariners by the Roman emperors; secondly, laws relating to particular fleets; and lastly, laws relating to particular branches of trade.

1. The fifth title of the thirteenth book of the Theodosian code of laws entirely relates to the privileges of mariners. It appears, from this, that by a law made by the Emperor Constans, and confirmed by Julian, protection was granted to them from all personal injuries; and it was expressly ordered, that

they should enjoy perfect security, and be defended from all sort of violence and injustice. The emperor Justinian considered this law so indispensably necessary to secure the object which it had in view, that he not only adopted it into his famous code, but decreed that whoever should seize and apply the ships of mariners, against their wishes, to any other purpose than that for which they were designed, should be punished with death. In the same part of his code, he repeats and confirms a law of the emperors Valentinian, Valens, and Gratian, inflicting death on any one who should insult seafaring men. In another law, adopted into the same code from the statutes of former emperors, judges and magistrates are forbidden, on pain of death, to give them any manner of trouble. They were also exempted from paying tribute, though the same law which exempts them, taxes merchants. No person who had exercised any mean or dishonourable employment was allowed to become a mariner; and the emperors Constantine and Julian raised them to the dignity of knights, and, shortly afterwards, they were declared capable of being admitted into the senate.

As a counterbalance to those privileges and honours, it appears, that mariners, at least such of them as might be required for the protection of the state, were obliged to conform themselves to certain rules and conditions, otherwise the laws already quoted did not benefit them. They were obliged to possess certain lands; and, indeed, it would seem that the profession and privileges of a mariner depended on his retaining these lands. When these lands were sold, the purchaser was obliged to perform towards the state all those services which were required of a mariner, and in return he obtained all the privileges, dignities, and exemptions granted to that class of men. This, however, was productive of great inconvenience to the state; since, if the lands were purchased by persons ignorant of maritime affairs, they could not be so effective as persons accustomed to the sea. From this consideration a law was passed, that when such lands as were held on condition of sea-service passed into the possession of those who were unaccustomed to the sea, they should revert to their original owners. It was also ordered, that such privileged mariners should punctually perform all services required of them by the state; that they should not object to carry any particular merchandize; that they should not take into their vessels above a certain quantity of goods, in order that they might not, by being over laden, be rendered unfit for the service of the state; and that they should not change their employment for any other, even though it were more honourable or lucrative. The whole shipping, and all the seamen, seem thus to have been entirely under the management and controul of the state; there were, however, a few exceptions. Individuals, who possessed influence sufficient, or from other causes, were permitted to possess ships of their own, but only on the express condition that the state might command them and the services of their crews, whenever it was necessary. The legal rate of interest was fixed by Justinian at six per cent.; but for the convenience and encouragement of trade, eight was allowed on money lent to merchants and manufacturers; and twelve on the risk of bottomry.

2. There are several laws in the Theodosian code which relate to the

different fleets of the empire: the Eastern fleet, the principal port of which was Seleucia, a city of Syria, on the Orontes, by which were conveyed to Rome and Constantinople, all the oriental merchandize that came by the land route we have described to Syria, was particularly noticed, as well as some smaller fleets depending on it, as the fleet of the island of Carpathus. The privileges granted to the African fleet are expressly given to the Eastern fleet.

In another part of the code of Justinian, the trade between the Romans and Persians is regulated: the places were the fairs and markets are to be kept are fixed and named; these were near the confines of the two kingdoms; and these confines neither party was allowed to pass.

From a law of the emperor Constans, inserted in the Theodosian code, it appears that some of the ships which came from Spain to Rome were freighted for the service of the state; and these are particularly regulated and privileged in this law.

There were several laws made also respecting the fleet which the emperors employed for the purpose of collecting the tribute and revenue, and conveying it to Home and Constantinople. The law of the emperors Leo and Zeno, which is inserted in the Justinian code, mentions the fleet which was kept to guard the treasures: and by another law, taken from the Theodosian code, we learn, that the guards of the treasures, who went in this fleet, were officers under the superintendent of the imperial revenue.

3. We have already mentioned the dependence of Rome on foreign nations for corn, and the encouragement given, during the republic and in the early times of the empire, to the importation of this necessary article. In the Theodosian and Justinian code, encouragement to the importation of it seems still to have been a paramount object, especially from Egypt; for though from an edict of Justinian it would appear that the cargoes from this country, of whatever they consisted, were guarded and encouraged by law, yet we know that the principal freight of the ships which traded between Alexandria and Rome and Constantinople was corn, and that other merchandize was taken on board the corn fleets only on particular occasions, or, where it was necessary, to complete the cargoes. Among the other edicts of Justinian, regulating the trade of Egypt, there is one which seems to have been passed in consequence of the abuses that had crept into the trade of corn and other commodities, which were shipped from Alexandria for Constantinople. These abuses arose from the management of this trade being in the hands of a very few persons: the emperor therefore passed a law, dividing the management into different branches, each to be held by separate individuals. From the code of Justinian we also learn, that corn was embarked from other ports of Egypt besides Alexandria, by private merchants; but these were not permitted to export it without permission of the emperor, and even then not till after the imperial fleet was fairly at sea. The importance of the corn trade of Egypt fully justified these laws; for at this period Constantinople was annually supplied with 260,000 quarters of wheat from this country.

The resources of the Romans were principally derived from the tribute levied on the conquered countries; but in part also from duties on merchandize: in the latter point of view, alone, they fall under our notice. No custom duties seem to have been imposed till the time of Augustus; but in his reign, and that of his immediate successors, duties were imposed on every kind of merchandize which was imported into Rome; the rate varied from the eighth to the fortieth part of the value of the article. The most full and minute list of articles of luxury on which custom duties were levied, is to be found in the rescript of the emperors Marcus and Commodus, relating to the goods imported into Egypt from the East. In the preamble to this rescript it is expressly declared, that no blame shall attach to the collectors of the customs, for not informing the merchant of the amount of the custom duties while the goods are in transit; but if the merchant wishes to enter them, the officer is not to lead him into error. The chief and most valuable articles on which, by this rescript, duties were to be levied, were cinnamon, myrrh, pepper, ginger, and aromatics; precious stones; Parthian and Babylonian leather; cottons; silks, raw and manufactured: ebony, ivory, and eunuchs.

Till the reign of Justinian, the straits of the Bosphorus and Hellespont were open to the freedom of trade, nothing being prohibited but the exportation of arms for the service of the barbarians: but the avarice, or the profusion of that emperor, stationed at each of the gates of Constantinople a praetor, whose duty it was to levy a duty on all goods brought into the city, while, on the other hand, heavy custom duties were exacted on all vessels and merchandize that entered the harbour. This emperor also exacted in a most rigorous manner, a duty in kind: which, however, had existed long before his time: we allude to the annona, or supply of corn for use of the army and capital. This was a grievous and arbitrary exaction: rendered still more so "by the partial injustice of weights and measures, and the expence and labour of distant carriage." In a time of scarcity, Justinian ordered an extraordinary requisition of corn to be levied on Thrace, Bithynia, and Phrygia; for which the proprietors, (as Gibbon observes,) "after a wearisome journey, and a perilous navigation received so inadequate a compensation, that they would have chosen the alternative of delivering both the corn and price at the doors of their granaries."

Having thus given a connected and general view of the Roman commerce, we shall next proceed to investigate the progress of geographical knowledge among them. In our chronological arrangement of this progress, incidental and detached notices respecting their commerce will occur, which, though they could not well be introduced in the general view, yet will serve to render the picture of it more complete.

It is evident that the principal accessions to geographical knowledge among the Romans, at least till their ambition was satinted, or nearly so, by conquest, must have been derived from their military expeditions. It is only towards the time of Augustus that we find men, whose sole object in visiting foreign countries was to become acquainted with their state, manners, &c.

Polybius is one of the earliest authors who give us a glimpse of the state of geographical knowledge among the Romans, about the middle of the second century before Christ, the period when he flourished. lie was the great friend of Scipio, whom he accompanied in his expedition against Carthage. From his enquiries while in Africa, he informed himself of the geography of the northern parts of that quarter of the world; and he actually visited the coast as far as Mount Atlas, or Cape Nun, beyond which, however, he does not seem to have proceeded. He wrote a Periplus, or account of his voyage, which is not in existence, but is referred to and quoted by Pliny. He possessed also more accurate information of the western coasts of Europe than was had before; derived, it would appear, from the voyages of some Romans. Yet, with all this knowledge of what we may deem distant parts, Polybius was ignorant of the real shape of Italy, which he describes as stretching from east to west; a mistake which seems to have originated with him, and was copied by Strabo.

Varro, who was Pompey's lieutenant during the war against the pirates, and obtained a naval crown on that occasion, among the almost infinite variety of topics on which he wrote, was the author of a work on navigation; unfortunately, however, only the title of it is extant: had it yet remained, it would have thrown much light on the state of navigation, geography, and commerce among the Romans in his time.

Julius Caesar's attention to science in the midst of his wars and perils is well known. He first formed the idea of a general survey of the whole empire; and for this purpose obtained a decree of the senate. The survey was finished by Augustus: the execution of it was committed to three Greek geographers. The survey of the eastern portion of the empire was committed to Zenodoxus, who completed it, in fourteen years, five months, and nine days. The northern division was finished by Theodoras in twenty years, eight months, and ten days: and the southern division was finished in twenty-five years, one month, and ten days. This survey, with the supplementary surveys of the new provinces, as they were conquered and added to the empire, formed the basis of the geography of Ptolemy. It appears from Vegetius, that every governor of a province was furnished with a description of it, in which were given the distance of places, the nature of the roads, the face of the country, the direction of the rivers, &c.: he adds, that all these were delineated on a map as well as described in writing. Of this excellent plan for the itineraries and surveys of the Roman empire, from which the ancient geographers obtained their fullest and most accurate information, Julius Cæsar was the author.

Julius Cæsar certainly added much to geographical knowledge by his conquests of Gaul and Britain: his information respecting the latter, however, as might be expected, is very erroneous. Yet, that even its very northern parts were known by name to the Romans soon after his death, is apparent, from this circumstance, that Diodorus Siculus, who died towards the middle of the reign of Augustus, mentions Orkas; which, he says, forms the northern extremity of the island of Britain. This is the very first mention of any place in Scotland by any writer.

One of the first objects of Augustus, after he had reduced Egypt, was to explore the interior of Africa, either for the purpose of conquest, or to obtain the precious commodities, especially frankincense and aromatics, which he had learned were the produce of those countries. Ælius Gallus was selected by the emperor for this expedition, and he was accompanied by the geographer Strabo; who, however, has not given such accurate information of the route which was pursued as might have been expected. This is the more to be lamented, as Pliny informs us that the places which were visited during this expedition are not to be found in authors previous to his time.

Gallus was directed by the emperor to explore Ethiopia, the country of the Troglodytæ and Arabia. The expedition against Ethiopia, which Gallus entrusted to Petronius, we shall afterwards examine, confining ourselves at present to the proceedings and progress of Gallus himself. His own force consisted of 10,000 men, to which were added 500, supplied by Herod, king of the Jews; and 1000 Nabathians from Petra; besides a fleet of eighty ships of war and 130 transports. Syllæus, the minister of the king of the Nabathians, undertook to conduct the expedition; but as it was not for the interest either of his king or country that it should succeed, he betrayed his trust, and, according to Strabo, was executed at Rome for his treachery on this occasion. His object was to delay the expedition as much as possible: this he effected by persuading Gallus to prepare a fleet, which was unnecessary, as the army might have followed the route of the caravans, through a friendly country, from Cleopatris, where the expedition commenced, to the head of the Elanitic Gulf. The troops, however, were embarked, and, as the navigation of the Sea of Suez was intricate, the fleet was fifteen days in arriving at Leuke Kome: here, in consequence of the soldiers having become, during their voyage, afflicted with various disorders, and the year being far advanced, Gallus was obliged to remain till the spring. Another delay was contrived by Syllæus on their leaving Leuke Kome. After this, they seem to have proceeded with more celerity, and with very little opposition from the natives, till they came to a city of some strength: this they were obliged to besiege in regular form; but, after lying before it for six days, Gallus was forced, for want of water, to raise the siege, and to terminate the expedition. He was told that at this time he was within two days' journey of the land of aromatics and frankincense, the great object which Augustus had in view. On his retreat, he no longer trusted to Syllæus, but changed the route of the army, directing it from the interior to the coast. At Nera, in Petræa, the army embarked, and was eleven days in crossing the gulf to Myos Hormos: from this place it traversed the country of the Troglodytes to Coptus, on the Nile. Two years were spent in this unfortunate expedition. It is extremely difficult to fix on the limit of this expedition, but it is probable that the town which Gallus besieged, and beyond which he did not penetrate, was the capital of the Mineans. From the time of this expedition, the Romans always maintained a footing on the coast of the Red Sea; and either during the residence of Gallus at Leuke Kome, or soon afterwards, they placed a garrison in this place, where they collected the customs, gradually extending their conquests and their geographical knowledge down the Gulf, till they reached the ocean. This seems to have been the only beneficial consequence resulting from the expedition of Gallus.

We must now attend to the expedition of Petronius against the Ethiopians. This was completely successful, and Candakè, their queen, was obliged, as a token of her submission, to send ambassadors to Augustus, who was at that time in the island of Samos. About this period the commerce of the Egyptians,—which, in fact, was the commerce of the Romans,—was extended to the Troglodytes,—with whom previously they had carried on little or no trade.

The first account of the island of Ceylon, under the name of Taprobane, was brought to Europe by the Macedonians, who had accompanied Alexander into the east. It is mentioned, and a short description given of it, by Onesicritus and Eratosthenes. Iambulus, however, who lived in the time of Augustus, is the first author who enters into any details regarding it; and though much of what he states is undoubtedly fabulous, yet there are particulars surprizingly correct, and such as confirm his own account, that he actually, visited the island. According to Diodorus Siculus, he was the son of a merchant, and a merchant himself; and while trading in Arabia for spices, he was taken prisoner and carried into Arabia, whence he was carried off by the Ethiopians, and put into a ship, which was driven by the monsoon to Ceylon. The details he mentions, that are most curious and most conformable to truth, are the stature of the natives and the flexibility of their joints; the length of their ears, bored and pendant; the perpetual verdure of the trees; the attachment of the natives to astronomy; their worship of the elements, and particularly of the sun and moon; their cotton garments; the men having one wife in common; the days and nights being equal in length; and the Calamus, or Maiz. It is extraordinary, howeve'r, that Iambulus never mentions cinnamon, which, as he was a dealer in spices, it might have been supposed would have attracted his particular attention.

One of the most celebrated geographers among the ancients, flourished during the reign of Augustus;—we allude to Strabo: his fundamental principles are, the globosity of the earth, and its centripetal force; he also lays down rules for constructing globes, but he seems ignorant of the mode of fixing the position of places by their latitude or longitude, or, at least, he neglects it. In order to render his geographical knowledge more accurate and complete, he travelled over most of the countries between Armenia on the east and Etruria on the west, and from his native country, on the borders of the Euxine sea, to the borders of Ethiopia. The portion of the globe which he describes, is bounded on the north by the Baltic, on the east by the Ganges, on the south by the mouth of the river Senegal, and on the west by Spain. In describing the countries which he himself had visited, he is generally very accurate, but his accounts of those he had not visited, are frequently erroneous or very incomplete. His information respecting Ceylon and the countries of the Ganges, seems to have been derived entirely from the statements brought to Europe by the generals of Alexander.

In the reign of Claudius, the knowledge of the Romans respecting the interior of Africa, was slightly extended by the expedition of Suetonius Paulinus; he was the first Roman who crossed Mount Atlas, and during the winter penetrated through the deserts, which are described as formed of black dust, till he reached a river called the Niger. Paulinus wrote an account of this expedition, which, however, is not extant: Pliny quotes it. In the reign of Claudius, also, the island of Ceylon became better known, in consequence of an accident which happened to the freedman of a Roman, who farmed the customs in the Red Sea. This man, in the execution of his duty, was blown off the coast of Arabia, across the ocean to Taprobane, or Ceylon; here he was hospitably received by the king, and after a residence of six months was sent back, along with ambassadors, to Claudius. They informed the emperor that their country was very extensive, populous, and opulent, abounding in gold, silver, and pearls. It seems probable that the circumstance of the freedman having been carried to Ceylon by a steady and regular wind, and this man and the ambassadors having returned by a wind directly opposite, but as steady and regular, had some influence in the discovery of the monsoon. As this discovery led necessarily to a direct communication between Africa and India, and grea'ly enlarged the knowledge of the Romans respecting the latter country, as well as their commercial connections with it, it will be proper to notice it in a particular manner.

This important discovery is supposed to have been made in the seventh year of the reign of Claudius, answering to the forty-seventh of the Christian era. The following is the account given of it by the author of the Periplus of the Erythrean Sea, as translated by Dr. Vincent:

"The whole navigation, such as it has been described from Adan in Arabia Felix and Kanè to the ports of India, was performed formerly in small vessels, by adhering to the shore and following the indention of the coast; but Hippalus was the pilot who first discovered the direct course across the ocean, by observing the position of the ports and the general appearance of the sea; for, at the season when the annual winds peculiar to our climate settle in the north, and blow for a continuance upon our coast from the Mediterranean, in the Indian ocean the wind is constantly to the south west; and this wind has in those seas obtained the name of Hippalus, from the pilot who first attempted the passage by means of it to the east.

"From the period of that discovery to the present time, vessels bound to India take their departure either from Kanè on the Arabian, or from Cape Arometa on the African side. From these points they stretch out to the open sea at once, leaving all the windings of the gulfs and bays at a distance, and make directly for their several destinations on the coast of India. Those that are intended for Limurike waiting some time before they sail, but those that are destined for Barugaza, or Scindi, seldom more than three days."

If we may credit Pliny, the Greek merchants of Egypt for some years after the discovery of the monsoon, did not venture further out to sea than was absolutely necessary, by crossing the widest part of the entry of the Persian Gulf, to reach Patala at the mouth of the Indus; but they afterwards found shorter routes, or rather stretched more to the south, so as to reach lower down on the coast of India: they also enlarged their vessels, carried cargoes of greater value, and in order to beat off the pirates, which then as at present infested this part of the Indian coast, they put on board their vessels a band of archers. Myos Hormos, or Berenice, was the port on the Red Sea from which they sailed; in forty days they arrived at Musiris, on the west coast of India. The homeward passage was begun in December or January, when the north east monsoon commenced; this carried them to the entrance of the Red Sea, up which to their port they were generally favored by southerly winds.

As there is no good reason to believe that the ancients made regular voyages to India, previously to the discovery of the monsoons; yet, as it is an undoubted fact that some of the exclusive productions of that country, particularly cinnamon, were obtained by them, through their voyages on the Red Sea; it becomes an important and interesting enquiry, by what means these productions were brought to those places on this sea, from which the Romans obtained them. In our opinion, the Arabians were the first who introduced Indian productions into the west from the earliest period to which history goes back, and they continued to supply the merchants who traded on the Red Sea with them, till, by the discovery of the monsoon, a direct communication was opened between that sea and India.

At least seventeen centuries before the Christian era, we have undoubted evidence of the traffic of the Arabians in the spices, &c. of India; for in the 27th chapter of Genesis we learn, that the Ishmaelites from Gilead conducted a caravan of camels laden with the spices of India, and the balsam and myrrh of Hadraumaut, in the regular course of traffic to Egypt for sale. In the 30th chapter of Exodus, cinnamon, cassia, myrrh, frankincense, &c. are mentioned, some of which are the exclusive produce of India; these were used for religious purposes, but at the same time the quantities of them specified are so great, that it is evident they must have been easily obtained. Spices are mentioned, along with balm and other productions of Canaan, in the present destined by Jacob for Joseph. These testimonies from holy writ are perfectly in unison with what we learn from Herodotus; this author enumerates oriental spices as regularly used in Egypt for embalming the dead.

It is sufficiently evident, therefore, that, at a very early period, the productions of India were imported into Egypt. That the Arabians were the merchants who imported them, is rendered highly probable from several circumstances. The Ishmaelites, mentioned in the 37th chapter of Genesis, are undoubtedly the Nabathians, whose country is represented by all the geographers, historians, and poets, as the source of all the precious commodities of the east; the ancients, erroneously supposing that cinnamon, which we know to be an exclusive production of India, was the produce of Arabia, because they were supplied with it, along with other aromatics, from that country. The proof that the Nabathians and the Ishmaelites are the same, is to be found in the evident derivation of the former name, from Nebaioth, the son of Ishmael. The traditions of the Arabians coincide with the genealogy of the Scriptures, in regarding Joktan, the fourth son of Shem, as the origin of those tribes which occupied Sabæa and Hadraumaut, or the incense country; Ishmael as the father of the families which settled in Arabia Deserta; and Edom as the ancestor of the

Idumeans, who settled in Arabia Petræa.

Eight hundred years before the Christian era, the merchandize of the Sabeans is particularly noticed by the prophet Isaiah; and even long before his time, we are informed, that there were no such spices as the Queen of Sheba gave to Solomon. That Sheba is Sabæa, or Arabia Felix, we learn from Ezekiel:—"The merchants of Sheba and Ramah, they were thy merchants: they occupied in thy fairs with chief of all spices, and with all precious stones and gold." Six hundred and fifty years after Isaiah bore his testimony to the commerce of Sabæa, we have the authority of Agatharcides, that the merchants of this country traded to India; that the great wealth and luxury of Sabæa were principally derived from this trade; and that, at the time when Egypt possessed the monopoly of the Indian trade, with respect to Europe, the Sabeans enjoyed a similar advantage with regard to Egypt.

Having thus established the fact, that, from the earliest period of which we have any record, the Arabians were the merchants who brought the cinnamon, &c. of India into the west, we must, in the next place, endeavour to ascertain by what means and route this commerce was carried on; and we think we can prove that the communication between Arabia and India, at a very early period, was both by sea and land.

There were many circumstances connected with Arabia and the Arabians, which would necessarily turn their thoughts to maritime affairs, and when they had once embarked in maritime commerce, would particularly direct it to India. The sea washed three sides of the peninsula of Arabia: the Arabians were not, like the Egyptians, prejudiced, either by their habits or their religion, against the sea. The monsoons must have been perceived by them, from part of the sea-coast lying within their influence; and it can hardly be supposed that a sea-faring people would not take advantage of them, to embark in such a lucrative trade as that of India. "There is no history which treats of them which does not notice them as pirates, or merchants, by sea, as robbers, or traders, by land. We scarcely touch upon them, accidentally, in any author, without finding that they were the carriers of the Indian Ocean." From the earliest period that history begins to notice them, Sabæa, Hadraumaut, and Oman, are described as the residences of navigators; and as these places are, in the earliest historians, celebrated for their maritime commerce, it is reasonable to suppose that they were equally so before the ancient historians acquired any knowledge of them.

We cannot go farther back, with respect to the fact of the Arabians being in India, than the voyage of Nearchus; but in the journal of this navigator, we find manifest traces of Arabian navigators on the coast of Mekran, previous to his expedition: he also found proofs of their commerce on the coast of Gadrosia, and Arabic names of places—a pilot to direct him, and vessels of the country in the Gulf of Persia. Large ships from the Indus, Patala, Persis, and Karmania came to Arabia, as early as the time of Agatharcides; and it is probable that these ships were navigated by Arabians, as the inhabitants of India were not, at this time, and, indeed, never have been celebrated for their maritime enterprize and skill. The same author mentions a town, a little without the Red Sea, from whence, he says, the Sabeans sent out colonies or factories into India, and to which the large ships he describes came with their cargoes from India. This is the first historical evidence to prove the establishment of Arabian factories and merchants in the ports of India. In the time of Pliny, the Arabians were in such numbers on the coast of Malabar, and at Ceylon, that, according to that author, the inhabitants of the former had embraced their religion, and the ports of the latter were entirely in their power. Their settlements and commerce in India are repeatedly mentioned in the Periplus of the Erythrean Sea, and likewise their settlements down the coast of Africa to Rhaptum, before it was visited by the Greeks from Egypt. For, besides their voyages from India to their own country, they frequently brought Indian commodities direct to the coast of Africa. At Sabaea, the great mart of the Arabian commerce with India, the Greeks, as late as the reign of Philometor, purchased the spices and other productions of the east. As there was a complete monopoly of them at this place, in the hands of the Arabians, the Greek navigators and merchants were induced, in the hopes of obtaining them cheaper, to pass the Straits of Babelmandeb, and on the coast of Africa they found cinnamon and other produce of India, which had been brought hither by the Arabian traders.

The evidence of the land trade between Arabia and India, from a very early period, is equally clear and decisive: Petra, the capital of Arabia Petrea, was the centre of this trade. To it the caravans, in all ages, came from Minea, in the interior of Arabia, and from Gherra, in the Gulf of Persia,—from Hadraumaut, on the Ocean, and some even from Sabaea. From Petra, the trade again spread in every direction—to Egypt, Palestine, and Syria, through Arsinoe, Gaza, Tyre, Jerusalem, Damascus, and other places of less consequence, all lying on routes terminating in the Mediterranean.

The Gherrheans, who were a Babylonian colony settled in that part of Arabia, which extends along the south coast of the Persian Gulf, are the earliest conductors of caravans upon record. They are first mentioned by Agatharcides, who compares their wealth with that of the Sabeans, and describes them as the agents for all the precious commodities of Asia and Europe: he adds that they brought much wealth into Syria, and furnished a variety of articles, which were afterwards manufactured or resold by the Phoenicians. But the only route by which Syria and Phoenicia could have been supplied by them, was through Petra. The particular articles with which their caravans were loaded, according to Strabo, were the produce of Arabia, and the spices of India. Besides the route of their caravans, across the whole peninsula to Petra, it appears that they sometimes carried their merchandize in boats up the Euphrates to Babylon, or even 240 miles higher up, to Thapsacus, and thence dispersed it in all directions by land.

The exact site of the country of the Mineans cannot be certainly fixed; but it is probable that it was to the south of Hedjaz, to the north of Hadraumaut, and to the eastward of Sabaea. According to Strabo, their caravans passed in seventy days from Hadraumaut to Aisla, which was within ten miles of Petra. They were laden with aloes, gold, myrrh, frankincense, and other aromatics.

We can but faintly and obscurely trace the fluctuations in the trade of Petra, in the remote periods of history. We know that Solomon was in possession of Idumea, but whether it was subdued by Nebuchadnezzar is doubtful. This sovereign, however, seems to have formed some plan of depriving the Gherrheans of the commerce of the Gulf of Persia. He raised a mound to confine the waters of the Tigris: he built a city to stop the incursions of the Arabs, and opened a communication between the rivers Tigris and Euphrates. After this there is no account of Idumea till some years subsequent to the death of Alexander the Great: at this period two expeditions were sent into it against its capital, Petra, by Antigonus, both of which were unsuccessful. These expeditions were undertaken about the years 308 and 309 before Christ. The history of Idumea, from this period, is better ascertained: harassed by the powerful kingdoms of Syria and Egypt,—contiguous to both of which it lay,—it seems to have been governed by princes of its own, who were partly independent, and partly under the influence of the monarchs of Syria and Egypt. About sixty-three years before Christ, Pompey took Petra; and, from that period, the sovereigns of Idumea were tributary to the Romans. This city, however, still retained its commerce, and was in a flourishing condition, as we are informed by Strabo, on the authority of his friend Athenedorus, who visited it about thirty-six years after it. He describes it as built on a rock, distinguished, however, from all the rocks in that part of Arabia, from being supplied with an abundant spring of water. Its natural position, as well as art, rendered it a fortress of importance in the desert. He represents the people as rich, civilized, and peaceable; the government as regal, but the chief power as lodged in a minister selected by the king, who had the title of the king's brother. Syllaeus, who betrayed Elius Gallus, appears to have been a minister of this description.

The next mention that occurs of the trade of Petra is in the Periplus of the Erythrean Sea, the date of which, though uncertain, there is good reason to fix in Nero's reign. According to this work, Leuke Kome, at the mouth of the Elanitic Gulf, was the point of communication with Petra, the capital of the country, the residence of Malachus, the king of the Nabathians. "Leuke Kome, itself, had the rank of a mart in respect to the small vessels which obtained their cargoes in Arabia, for which reason there was a garrison placed in it, under the command of a centurion, both for the purpose of protection, and in order to collect a duty of twenty-five in the hundred." In the reign of Trajan, Idumea was reduced into the form of a Roman province, by one of his generals; after this time it not does fall within our plan to notice it, except merely to state, that its subjection does not seem to have been complete or permanent, for during the latter empire, there were certainly sovereigns of this part of Arabia, in some degree independent, whose influence and alliance were courted by the Romans and Persians, whenever a war was about to commence between these two powers.

From this sketch of the trade of the Arabians from the earliest period, we may conclude, in the first place, that when navigation was in its infancy, it was confined, or almost entirely so, to a land trade carried on by caravans; and that

Petra was the centre to which these caravans tended from the east and the south, bringing with them from the former the commodities of India, and from the latter the commodities of the more fertile part of Arabia. From Petra, all these goods were again transported by land to the shores of the Mediterranean and to Egypt. In the second place, when navigation became more commonly known and practised, (and there is good reason to believe that it was known and practised among the Arabians, especially those near the Persian Gulf, at a very early period,) a portion of the Indian commodities, which before had been carried by land to Petra were brought by sea to Sabaea. It appears that in the age of Agatharcides, the monopoly of the trade between India and Europe by this route was wholly possessed by the Sabeans; that, in order to evade the effects of this monopoly, the Greeks of Egypt found their way to Aden and Hadraumaut, in Arabia, and to Mosullon on the coast of Africa. Here they met with other Arabians, who at this time also traded to India, and sold them Indian goods at a cheaper rate. And, lastly, we have seen that these ports on the southern coast of Arabia, and on the coast of Africa, were frequented by the merchants of Egypt, till, by the discovery of the monsoon, their ships were enabled to sail directly to India. It is undoubtedly true that before this discovery, single ships occasionally reached India by adhering to the coast all the way, but the direct communication was very rare. After the nature of the monsoon was thoroughly understood, and it was ascertained that complete dependence could be placed on its steadiness and regularity, and that by its change, the ships could be brought as safely and quickly back from India, as they had reached it, the ancients, who at first only ventured to the mouth of the Indus, gradually made their way down the western coast of the Indian peninsula.

The Periplus of the Erythrean Sea, a work which has been frequently referred to, is rich in materials to illustrate the geographical knowledge and the commercial enterprize of the ancients in the part of the world to which it relates. We have already assigned its date to the age of Nero. Our limits will prevent us from giving a full account of this work; we shall therefore, in the first place, give a short abstract of the geographical knowledge which it displays, and in the next place, illustrate from it, the nature of the commerce carried on, on the Red Sea, the adjacent coasts of Africa and Arabia, and the ports of India, which are noticed in it.

At the time of Strabo, the geography of the ancients did not extend, on the eastern coast of Africa, further to the south than a promontory called Noti Cornu, (the Southern Horn,) which seems to have been in about 12-1/2 degrees north latitude. Beyond this an arid coast, without ports or fresh water, arrested the progress of navigation; but it appears by the Periplus, that this promontory was now passed, and commerce had extended to the port of Rhapta and the isle of Menutias, which are supposed to correspond with Babel Velho and the island of Magadoxa. The author of the Periplus, who seems to have been a merchant personally acquainted with most of the places he describes, had heard of, but not visited the promontory Prasum: he represents the ocean beyond Rhapta as entirely unknown, but as believed to continue its western direction, and after having washed the south coast of Ethiopia, to join the Western Ocean. The whole of the west coast of India, from the Indus to Trapobane, is minutely described in the Periplus. Some of the particulars of the manners and customs of the inhabitants coincide in a striking manner with those of the present day; this observation applies, among other points, to the pirates between Bombay and Goa.

Dr. Vincent, in his learned commentary on the Periplus, gives it as his opinion, that the author of the Periplus never went further than Nelkundah himself, that is, to the boundary between the provinces of Canara and Malabar. The east coast of the Indian peninsula is not traced so minutely nor so accurately as the west coast, though there are names and descriptions in the Periplus, from which it may fairly be inferred, that the author alludes to Cavary, Masulapatam, Calingapatam, Coromandel, and other places and districts of this part of India. The countries beyond the Ganges, the Golden Chersonese, and the countries towards China, are very obscurely noticed in the Periplus, though the information he gives respecting the trade carried on in these parts is much more minute and accurate. His description of the direction of the coast of India, is on the whole, surprisingly consonant to truth: according to him, it tends from north to south, as far as Colchos (Travancore); at this place it bends to the east, and afterwards to the north; and then again a little to the east, as far as the Ganges. He is the first author in whom can clearly be traced the name of the great southern division of India: his term is Dachanabades,—Dachan signifying south, and abad a city; and Decan is still the general name of all the country to the south of Baroche, the boundary assigned by the author. The particulars he mentions of the bay of Cutch, of Cambay, of Baroche, and of the Ghauts, may also be mentioned as proofs of his accuracy with respect to those parts of India, which he visited in person.

Having thus given a sketch of the geographical knowledge contained the Periplus, we shall next attend to the commercial information which it conveys. As this work is divided into two distinct parts, the first comprising the coast of the Red Sea, and of Africa, from Myos Hormos on the former, to Rhapta in the latter: and the second part, beginning at the same place, and including the whole coast of Arabia, both that which lies on the Red Sea, and that which lies on the Ocean, and then stretching from the Gulf of Persia to Guzerat, describing the coast of Malabar, as far as Ceylon, we shall, in our abstract of the commercial intelligence it contains, enumerate the principal imports and exports of the most frequented marts in Africa, (including the Red Sea,) Arabia, and India.

I. The Red Sea and Africa. Myos Hormos is described as the first port of Egypt on the Red Sea; as it lies in twenty-seven degrees north latitude, and Rhapta, the boundary of the Periplus to the south, in nearly ten degrees south latitude, the distance between them will be about 2,500 miles. It is to be supposed, that every thing relating to the geography, navigation, and commerce of the Red Sea, from Myos Hormos to Aduli, on the western side, and Moosa, on the eastern side of it, was well known to the merchants of Egypt, as the author of the Periplus gives no circumstantial account of any port, till he arrives at these places. It appears, also, that till the ships arrived at these places, they kept the mid-channel of the Red Sea, and, consequently, there was no occasion, or indeed, opportunity of describing the intermediate ports. We have already mentioned, that Myos Hormos was fixed on by Ptolemy Philadelphus, in preference to Arsinoe, because the navigation of the western part of the Red Sea, on which the latter was placed, was intricate and tedious. Berenice was afterwards selected, as being still lower down: but it is worthy of remark, that neither Berenice, nor Ptolemais Theron, another port of the Ptolemies, were harbours, but merely roadsteads, though from our author's description, there were an almost infinite number of safe harbours, creeks, bays, &c. in every part of the Red Sea.

Aduli, the first port on the west side of the Red Sea, and the port of communication with Axuma, was, in the age of the Periplus, subject to the same prince, who possessed the whole coast, from Berenice. The exports from this place were confined to ivory, brought from the interior on both sides of the Nile; the horns of the rhinoceros, and tortoise-shell. The imports were very numerous, forming an assortment, as Dr. Vincent justly observes, as specific as a modern invoice: the principal articles were, cloth, manufactured in Egypt, unmilled, for the Barbarian market. The term, Barbarii, was applied to the Egyptians, to the whole western coast of the Red Sea, and was derived from Barbar, the native name of the country inhabited by the Troglodytes, Icthyophagi, and shepherds: as these were much hated and dreaded by the Egyptians, Barbarii became a term of reproach and dread, and in this sense it was adopted by the Greeks and Romans, and has passed into the modern European languages. But to return from this digression,—the other imports were robes, manufactured at Arsinoe; cloths dyed, so as to imitate the Tyrian purple; linens, fringed mantles, glass or crystal, murrhine cups, orichalchum, or mixed metal for trinkets and coin; brass vessels for cooking, the pieces of which, when they happened to be broken, were worn by the women as ornaments; iron, for weapons and other purposes; knives, daggers, hatchets, &c.; brass bowls, wine, oil, gold and silver plate, camp cloaks, and cover-lids: these formed the principal articles of import from Myos Hormos, and as they are very numerous, compared with the exports, it seems surprising that coin should also have been imported, but that this was the case, we are expressly told by the author of the Periplus, who particularizes Roman currency, under the name of Denarii. The following articles imported into Aduli, must have come through Arabia, from India: Indian iron; Indian cottons; coverlids, and sashes made of cotton; cotton cloth, dyed the colour of the mallow-flower, and a few muslins.

The Periplus next passes without the Straits of Babelmandeb: on the African side, four principal marts are mentioned, to all of which the epithet of Tapera, is applied, signifying their position beyond the straits. The first of these marts is Abalitis: as this place had no port, goods were conveyed to the ships in boats and rafts; they were also employed by the natives, in carrying on a trade with the opposite ports of Arabia: what they imported from Arabia, is not specified; but they exported thither gums, a small quantity of ivory, tortoise-shell, and myrrh of the finest quality. This last article being purchased by the Greek merchants, in Sabæa, was regarded by them as a native production of that part of Arabia, when, in reality, as we learn from the Periplus, it was the produce of Africa. There were imported into Abalitis, from Egypt, flint glass, and glass vessels unsorted; unripe grapes from Diospolis, which were used to make the rob of grapes; unmilled cloths, for the Barbaric market; corn, wine, and tin; the last article must have come from Britain.

The next mart is Malao, likewise a roadstead; the imports were the same as those of Abalitis, with the addition of tunics; cloaks manufactured at Arsinoe, milled and dyed; iron, and a small quantity of specie: the exports were, myrrh, frankincense, cassia, inferior cinnamon, substituted for the oriental; gum, and a few slaves. The only article of export peculiar to the third mart, Mundus, was a fragrant gum, which seems to have grown only in its vicinity.

The fourth and last mart mentioned as lying on the African side of the channel, which opens from the Straits of Babelmandeb, is Mosullon; this was the most important mart on the whole coast, and that which gave a specific name to the trade of the ancients: the imports were numerous, comprising, besides those already mentioned, some that were peculiar to this place, such as vessels of silver, a small quantity of iron, and flint glass: the exports were, cinnamon, of an inferior quality; the quantity of this article is noticed as so great, that larger vessels were employed in the trade of this port, expressly for conveying it, than were seen in the other ports of Africa. We are informed by Pliny, that Mosullon was a great market for cinnamon,—and it would seem, from its being conveyed in large vessels by sea, that it came from Arabia. The cinnamon mentioned in the Periplus, is, indeed, particularized as of an inferior quality, which is directly at variance with the authority of Dioscorides, who expressly states that the Mosulletic species is one of prime quality; if this were the case, it must have been Indian. The other exports were gums, drugs, tortoise-shell, incense, frankincense, brought from distant places; ivory, and a small quantity of myrrh. The abundance of aromatic articles, which the Greeks procured on this part of the coast, induced them to give the name of Aromatic to the whole country, and particularly to the town and promontory at the eastern extremity of it. Cape Aromata, the Gardefan of the moderns, is not only the extreme point east of the continent of Africa, but also forms the southern point of entrance on the approach to the Red Sea, and is the boundary of the monsoon. At the marts between Mosullon and this Cape, no articles of commerce are specified, except frankincense, in great abundance and of the best quality, at Alkannai. At the Cape itself, there was a mart, with an exposed roadsted; and to the south of it, was another mart; from both these, the principal exports consisted of various kinds of aromatics.

At Aromata, the Barbaria of the ancients, or the Adel of the moderns, terminates; and the coast of Azania, or Agan, begins. The first mart on this coast is Opone, from which there were exported, besides the usual aromatics and other articles, slaves of a superior description, chiefly for the Egyptian market, and tortoise-shell, also of a superior sort, and in great abundance. There was nothing peculiar in the imports. In this part of his work, the author of the Periplus, mentions and describes the annual voyage between the coast of Africa and India: after enumerating the articles imported from the latter country, which consisted chiefly of corn, rice, butter; oil of Sesanum; cotton, raw and manufactured sashes; and honey from the cane, called sugar; he adds, that "many vessels are employed in this commerce, expressly for the importation of these articles, and others, which have a more distant destination, sell part of their cargoes on this coast, and take in the produce in return." This seems to be the first historical evidence of a commercial intercourse between India and Africa, independent of the voyages of the Arabians; and as the parts from which the ships sailed to India, lay within the limits of the monsoon, it most probably was accomplished by means of it, and directly from land to land, without coasting round by the Gulf of Persia. The ports on the west coast of India, to which the trade was carried on, were Ariake and Barugaza, in Guzerat and Concan.

No mart is mentioned after Opone, till we arrive at Rhapta. This place was so named by the Greeks, because the ships employed by the inhabitants were raised from a bottom composed of a single piece of wood, and the sides were sewed to it, instead of being nailed. In order to preserve the sewing, the whole outside was covered over with some of the gums of the country. It is a circumstance worthy of notice, that when the Portuguese first visited this coast, they found ships of exactly the same materials and construction. At Rhapta, the customs were farmed by the merchants of Moosa, though it was subject to one of the princes of Yeman. Arabian commanders and supercargoes were always employed in their ships, from their experience in the navigation: the imports of Rhapta were, lances, principally manufactured at Moosa; axes, knives, awls, and various kinds of glass: the exports were, ivory, inferior to the Aduli ivory, but cheap, and in great abundance; the horns of the rhinoceros, tortoise shell, superior to any of this coast, but not equal to the Indian; and an article called Nauplius, the nature of which is not known.

At the period when the Periplus was written, the coast was unknown beyond Rhapta; at this place, therefore, the journal of this voyage terminates; but this place, there is every reason to believe that the author visited in person.

The commencement of the second voyage is from Berenice: from this port he conducts us to Myos Hormos, and there across the Red Sea to Leuke Kome in Arabia. This port we have already noticed as in the possession of the Romans, and forming the point of communication with Petra. We have also stated from our author, that at Leuke Kome the Romans kept a garrison, and collected a duty of twenty-five per cent. on the goods imported and exported. From it to the coast below Burnt Island, there was no trade carried on, in consequence of the dangers of the navigation from rocks, the want of harbours, the poverty and barbarism of the natives, who seem to have been pirates, and the want of produce and manufactures.

In the farthest bay of the east or Arabian coast of the Red Sea, about thirty miles from the straits, was Moosa, the regular mart of the country, established, protected, and privileged as such by the government. It was not a harbour, but a road with good anchorage on a sandy bottom. The inhabitants were Arabians, and it was much resorted to by merchants, both on account of the produce and manufactures of the adjacent country, and on account of its trade to India. The imports into Moosa were principally purple cloth of different qualities and prices; garments made in the Arabian manner, with sleeves, plain and mixed; saffron; an aromatic rush used in medicine; muslins, cloaks, quilts, but only a few plain, and made according to the fashion of the country; sashes of various colours; some corn and wine, and coin to pay for the balance of trade. In order to ingratiate the sovereigns of the country, horses, mules, gold plate, silver plate richly embossed, splendid robes, and brass goods were also imported, expressly as presents to them. One of these sovereigns was styled the friend of the Roman emperors. Embassies were frequently sent to him from Rome, and it is probable that for him the presents were chiefly designed. The exports from Moosa were myrrh of the best quality, gum, and very pure and white alabaster, of which boxes were made; there was likewise exported a variety of articles, the produce and manufacture of Aduli, which were brought from that place to Moosa.

We are next directed to the ports beyond the Straits of Babelmandeb. The wind in passing them is described as violent, coming on in sudden and dangerous squalls, in consequence of its confinement between the two capes which formed the entrance to the straits. The first place beyond them, about 120 miles to the east, described in the Periplus, is a village called Arabia Felix: this, there is every reason to believe, is Aden. It is represented in the Periplus as having been a place of great importance before the fleets sailed directly from India to Egypt, or from Egypt to the east. Till this occurred, the fleets from the east met in this harbour the fleets from Egypt. This description and account of it exactly corresponds with what Agatharcides relates: he says it received its name of Eudaimon, (*fortunate,*) on account of the ships from India and Egypt meeting there, before the merchants of Egypt had the courage to venture further towards the eastern marts. Its importance seems to have continued in some degree till it was destroyed by the Romans, probably in the time of Claudius: the object and reason of this act was to prevent the trade, which in his time had begun to direct its course to India, from reverting to this place.

About 200 miles to the east of Aden was the port of Kane. The country in its vicinity is represented as producing a great quantity of excellent frankincense, which was conveyed to Kane by land in caravans, and by sea in vessels, or in rafts which were floated by means of inflated skins. This was a port of considerable trade; the merchants trading to Baragyza, Scindi, Oman, and Persis, as well as to the ports in Africa, beyond the straits. The goods imported were principally from Egypt, and consisted of a small quantity of wheat, wine, cloaths for the Arabian market, common, plain, and mixed; brass, tin, Mediterranean coral, which was in great repute in India, so that the great demand for it prevented the Gauls in the south of France, according to Pliny, from adorning their swords, &c. with it, as they were wont to do; storax, plate, money, horses, statues or images, and cloth. The exports were confined to the produce of the country, especially frankincense and aloes. At Syagros, which is described as a promontory fronting the east, and the largest in the world, there was a garrison for the protection of the place, which was the repository of all the incense collected in these parts.

The island of Dioscorides (Socotra) is next described. It was inhabited on its northern side, (the only part of it that was then inhabited,) by a few Arabians, Indians, and Greeks, who seem to have fixed a permanent or temporary abode here, for the purpose of obtaining tortoise-shell: this was much prized, being of a yellow colour, very hard and durable, and used to make cases, boxes, and writing tables; this and dragon's blood were its chief productions. In exchange for them, there were imported rice, corn, Indian cotton goods, and women slaves.

The first mart beyond Cape Syagros is Moscha, which is represented as much resorted to on account of the sacchalitic incense which is imported there. This was so extremely abundant that it lay in heaps, with no other protection than that which was derived from the gods, for whose sacrifices it was intended. It is added that it was not possible for any person to procure a cargo of it without the permission of the king; and that the vessels were observed and searched so thoroughly, that not a single grain of it could be clandestinely exported. The intercourse between this port and Kane was regular; and besides this, it was frequented by such ships as arrived from India too late in the season: here they continued during the unfavourable monsoon, exchanging muslins, corn, and oil, for frankincense. A small island, which is supposed to be the modern Mazeira, was visited by vessels from Kane to collect or purchase tortoise-shell: the priests in the island are represented in the Periplus as wearing aprons made of the fibres of the cocoa tree: this is the earliest mention of this tree.

Moçandon, the extreme point south of the Gulf of Persia, was the land from which the Arabians, (to use a maritime phrase) took their departure, with various superstitious observances, imploring a blessing on their intended voyage, and setting adrift a small toy, rigged like a ship, which, if dashed to pieces, was supposed to be accepted by the god of the ocean, instead of their ship.

It is impossible to determine from the Periplus, whether the author was personally acquainted with the navigation, ports, and trade of the Gulf of Persia: the probability is that he was not, as he mentions only two particulars connected with it; the pearl fishery, and the town of Apologus, a celebrated mart at the mouth of the Euphrates; the pearl fishery he describes as extending from Moçandon to Bahrain. Apologus is the present Oboleh, on the canal that leads from the Euphrates to Basra.

If the author of the Periplus did not enter the Gulf of Persia, he certainly stretched over, with the monsoon, either to Karmania, or directly to Scindi, or to the Gulf of Cambay; for at these places the minuteness of information which distinguishes the journal again appears.

Omana in Persia is the first mart described; it lay in the province of Gadrosia, but as it is not mentioned by Nearchus, who found Arabs in most other parts of the province, we may conclude that it was founded after his time.

The trade between this place and Baragaza in India, was regular and direct, and the goods brought from the latter to the former, seems afterwards to have been sent to Oboleh at the head of the Gulf; the imports were brass, sandal-wood; timber, of what kind is not specified; horn, ebony; this is the first port the trade of which included ebony and sandal-wood: frankincense was imported from Kane. The exports to Arabia and Baragaza were purple cloth for the natives; wine, a large quantity of dates, gold, slaves, and pearls of an inferior quality.

The first place in India to which the merchants of Egypt, while they followed the ancient course of navigation by coasting, were accustomed to trade, was Patala on the Indus; for we have admitted that single vessels occasionally ventured beyond the Straits of Babelmandeb, before the discovery of the monsoon, though the trade from Egypt to India, previously to that discovery, was by no means frequent or regular. The goods imported into Patala were woollen cloth of a slight fabric, linen, woven in checquer work, some precious stones, and some kind of aromatics unknown in India, probably the produce of Africa or Arabia; coral, storax, glass vessels of various descriptions, some plate, money, and wine. From Patala, the Egyptian merchants brought spices, gems of different kinds, particularly sapphires, silk stuffs, silk thread, cotton cloths, and pepper. As Patala is not mentioned in the Periplus, it is probable it was abandoned for Baragaza, a far more considerable mart on the same coast, and most probably Baroche on the Nerbuddah.

Before describing Baragaza, however, the author of the Periplus mentions two places on the Indus, which were frequented for the purposes of commerce: the first near the mouth of the river, called Barbarike; and the other higher up, called Minagara: the latter was the capital of a kingdom which extended as far as Barogaza. As the king of this country was possessed of a place of such consequence to the merchants as Baragaza, and as from his provinces, or through them, the most valuable cargoes were obtained, it was of the utmost moment that his good will and protection should be obtained and preserved. For this purpose there were imported, as presents for him, the following articles, all expensive, and the very best of their kind: plate of very great value; musical instruments; handsome virgins for the haram; wine of the very best quality; plain cloth, but of the finest sort; and perfumes. Besides these presents, there were likewise imported a great quantity of plain garments, and some mixed or inferior cloth; topazes, coral, storax, frankincense, glass vessels, plate, specie, and wine. The exports were costus, a kind of spice; bdellium, a gum; a yellow dye, spikenard, emeralds, sapphires, cottons, silk thread, indigo, or perhaps the indicum of Pliny, which was probably Indian ink: skins are likewise enumerated, with the epithet *serica* prefixed to them, but of what kind they were cannot be determined: wine is specified as an article of import into this and other places; three kinds of it are particularized: wine from Laodicea in Syria, which is still celebrated for its wine; Italian wine, and Arabian wine. Some suppose that the last was palm or toddy wine, which seems to have been a great article of trade.

We come now to Baragaza: the author first mentions the produce of the district; it consisted of corn, rice, oil of Sesamum, ghee or butter, and cotton: he then, in a most minute and accurate manner, describes the approach to the harbour; the extraordinarily high tides, the rapidity with which they roll in and again recede, especially at the new moon, the difficult pilotage of the river, are all noticed. On account of these dangers and difficulties, he adds, that pilots were appointed by the government, with large boats, well manned, who put to sea to wait the approach of ships. These pilots, as soon as they come on board, bring the ship's head round, and keep her clear of the shoals at the mouth of the river; if necessary, they tow the ship from station to station, where there is good anchorage; these stations were called Basons, and seem to have been pools retaining the water, after the tide had receded from other parts. The navigation of the river was performed only as long as the tide was favorable; as soon as it turned, the ships anchored in these stations.

The sovereign to whom Baragaza belonged is represented as so very anxious to render it the only mart, that he would not permit ships to enter any of his other harbours; if they attempted it, they were boarded and conducted to Baragaza; at this place were collected all the produce and manufactures of this part of India: some of which were brought down the river Nerbuddah; others were conveyed across the mountains by caravans. The merchandize of Bengal, and even of the Seres, was collected here, besides the produce of Africa, and of the countries further to the south in India. The whole arrangement of this place was correspondent to this extensive commerce, for the author informs us, that such was the despatch in transacting business, that a cargo could be entirely landed and sold, and a new cargo obtained and put on board in the space of three days.

From Ozeni to the east of Baragaza, formerly the capital of the country, there was brought to the latter place for exportation, chiefly the following articles: onyx stones, porcelaine, fine muslins, muslins dyed of the colour of the melon, and common cotton in great quantities: from the Panjab there were brought for exportation, spikenard of different kinds, costus, bdellium, ivory, murrhine cups, myrrh, pepper, &c. The imports were wine, of all the three sorts already mentioned, brass, tin, lead, coral, topazes, cloth of different kinds, sashes, storax, sweet lotus, white glass, stibium, cinnabar, and a small quantity of perfumes: a considerable quantity of corn was also imported; the denarius, both gold and silver, exchanging with profit against the coin of the country, on account of its greater purity.

From Baragaza the author proceeds to a description of the coast of the Decan, which, as we have already mentioned, is remarkable for its accuracy, as well as for its first mentioning the appellation Decan. At the distance of twenty days' journey to the south lies Plithana, and ten days' journey to the east of this is Tagara, both marts of great consequence, and the latter the capital of the country. From these are brought down, through difficult roads, several articles to Baragaza, particularly onyx stones from Plithana, and cottons and muslin from Tagara "If we should now describe, (observed Dr. Vincent) the arc of a circle from Minnagar, on the Indus, through Ougein to Dowlatabad on the Godavery, of which Baroche should be the centre, we might comprehend the extent of the intelligence acquired by the merchant of the Periplus. But allowing that this was the knowledge of the age, and not of the individual only, where is this knowledge preserved, except in this brief narrative? which, with all the corruption of its text, is still an inestimable treasure to all those who wish to compare the first dawning of our knowledge in the east with the meridian light which we now enjoy by the intercourse and conquests of the Europeans. An arc of this sort comprehends near three degrees of a great circle: and if upon such a space, and at such a distance from the coast, we find nothing but what is confirmed by the actual appearance of the country, at the present moment, great allowance is to be made for those parts of the work which are less conspicuous, for the author did certainly not visit every place which he mentions; and there are manifest omissions in the text, as well as errors and corruptions."

The province of Canara, called by the author of the Periplus Limurike, follows in his description the pirate coast; after Limurike, he describes Pandion, corresponding with what is at present called Malabar Proper; this is succeeded by Paralia and Comari, and the description of the west coast of India is terminated by the pearl fishery and Ceylon. There were several small ports in Limurike frequented by the country ships; but the only mart frequented by vessels from Egypt was Musiris: it was likewise a great resort of native vessels from Ariake or Concan. The articles imported were nearly the same as those at Baragaza, but the exports from it were more numerous and valuable: this seems to have arisen from its lying nearer to the eastern and richer parts of India. The principal exports were, pearls in great abundance and extraordinary beauty; a variety of silk stuffs; rich perfumes; tortoise-shell; different kinds of transparent gems, especially diamonds; and pepper in large quantites, and of the best quality.

The port of Nelkundah, which, as we have already remarked, was the limit of our author's personal knowledge, was a place of very great trade; it was much frequented, principally on account of the betel and pepper, which were procured there on very reasonable terms: the pepper is distinguished, in the list of its imports, as the pepper of Cottonara. Besides this article and betel, the only exports were, pearls, ivory, silks, spikenard, precious stones, and tortoise-shell; the imports were chiefly specie, topazes, cloth, stibium, coral, glass, brass, tin, lead, wine, corn, &c.

The ports to the south of Nelkundah are described in a cursory manner in the Periplus; they were frequented principally by the country ships, which carried on a lucrative trade between them and the ports in the north of India. The exports of the island of Trapobane, or Ceylon, are particularized as consisting chiefly of pearls, gems, tortoise-shells, and muslins: cinnamon is not named; an almost decisive proof, if other proof were wanting, that the author of the Periplus had never visited this island. That trading voyages were carried on by the natives from the southern ports of India, not only to the northern ports of the western side of that country, but also to the eastern ports in the Bay of Bengal, and to the farther peninsula itself, we are expressly informed, as our author mentions vessels of great bulk adapted to the voyages made to the Ganges and the Golden Chersonese, in contradistinction to other and smaller vessels employed in the voyages to Limurike.

Of the remainder of the Periplus little notice is requisite, the account of the countries beyond Cape Comorin being entirely drawn from report, and consequently erroneous, both in respect to geography and commerce. In some particulars regarding the latter, however, it is surprisingly accurate: the Gangetic muslins are praised as the finest manufacture of the sort, and Gangetic spikenard is also noticed; the other articles of traffic in the ports on the Ganges were betel and pearls. Thina is also mentioned as a city, in the interior of a country immediately under the north, at a certain point where the sea terminates; from this city both the raw material and manufactured silks are brought by land through Bactria to Baragaza, or else down the Ganges, and thence by sea to Limurike: the routes we have already described. The means of approach to Thina are represented as very difficult; some merchants, however, came from it to a great mart which is annually held near it. The Sesatoe, who from the description of them are evidently Tartars, frequent this mart with their wives and children. "They are squat and thick-set, with their face broad and their nose greatly depressed. The articles they bring for trade are of great bulk, and inveloped in mats made of rushes, which, in their outward appearance, resemble the early leaves of the vine. Their place of assembly is between their own borders and those of China; and here spreading out their mats, they hold a fair for several days, and at the conclusion of it, return to their own country in the interior. Upon their retreat the Thinæ, who have continued on the watch, repair to the spot and collect the mats which the strangers left behind at their departure; from these they pick out the haulm, and drawing out the fibres, spread the leaves double, and make them into balls, and then pass the fibres through them. Of these balls there are three sorts, in this form they take the name of Malabathrum."

On this account Dr. Vincent very justly remarks, that we have here, upon the whole, a description of that mode of traffic, which has always been adopted by the Chinese, and by which they to this hour trade with Russia, Thibet, and Ava.

Many of the particulars which we have given on the subject of the Roman trade are supplied by Pliny, who wrote his natural history when Rome was in its most flourishing state under the reign of Vespasian. His works consist of thirty-seven books, the first six comprise the system of the world and the geography as it was then known. After examining the accounts of Polybius, Agrippa, and Artemidorus, he assigns the following comparative magnitudes to the three great divisions of the earth. Europe rather more than a third, Asia about a fourth, and Africa about a fifth of the whole. With few exceptions, his geographical knowledge of the east and of the north, the parts of the world of which the ancients were the most ignorant, was very inaccurate: he supposes the Ganges to be the north-eastern limit of Asia, and that from it the coast turned to the north, where it was washed by the sea of Serica, between which and a strait, which he imagined formed a communication from the Caspian to the Scythian ocean, he admits but a very small space. According to the system of Pliny, therefore, the ocean occupied the whole county of Siberia, Mogul Tartary, China, &c. He derived his information respecting India from the journals of Nearchus, and the other officers of Alexander; and yet such is his ignorance, or the corrupt state of the text, or the vitiated medium through which he received his information, that it is not easy to reconcile his account with that of Nearchus. Salmasius, indeed, charges him with confounding the east and west in his description of India. His geography, in the most important particular of the relative distances of places, is rendered of very little utility or authority, from the circumstance pointed out and proved by D'Anville, that he indiscriminately reckons eight stadia to the mile, without reference to the difference between the Greek and Roman stadium. He has, however, added two articles of information to the geographical and commercial knowledge of the east possessed before his time; the one is the account of the new course of navigation from Arabia to the coast of Malabar, which has been already described; the other is a description of Trapobane, or Ceylon, which, though inaccurate and obscure in many points, must be regarded as a real and important addition to the geographical knowledge of the Romans.

Pliny's geography of the north is the most full and curious of all antiquity. After describing the Hellespont, Moeotis, Dacia, Sarmatia, ancient Scythia, and the isles in the Euxine Sea, and proceeding last from Spain, he passes north to the Scythic Ocean, and returns west towards Spain. The coast of part of the Baltic seems to have been partly known to him; he particularly mentions an island called Baltia, where amber was found; but he supposes that the Baltic Sea itself was connected with the Caspian and Indian Oceans. Pliny is the first author who names Scandinavia, which he represents as an island, the extent of which was not then known; but by Scandinavia there is reason to believe the present Scandia is meant. Denmark may probably be rcognised in the Dumnor of this author, and Norway in Noligen. The mountain Soevo, which he describes as forming a vast bay called Codanus, extending to the promontory of the Cimbri, is supposed by some to be the mountains that run along the Vistula on the eastern extremity of Germany, and by others to be that chain of mountains which commence at Gottenburgh. The whole of his information respecting the north seems to have been drawn from the expeditions of Drusus, Varus, and Germanicus, to the Elbe and the Weser, and from the accounts of the merchants who traded thither for amber.

Tacitus, who died about twenty years after Pliny, seems to have acquired a knowledge of the north more accurate in some respects than the latter possessed. In his admirable description of Germany, he mentions the Suiones, and from the name, as well as other circumstances, there can be little doubt that they inhabited the southern part of modern Sweden.

The northern promontory of Scotland was known to Diodorus Siculus under the name of Orcas; but the insularity of Britain was certainly not ascertained till the fleet sent out by Agricola sailed round it, about eighty-four years after Christ. Tacitus, who mentions this circumstance, also informs us, that Ireland, which was known by name to the Greeks, was much frequented in his time by merchants, from whose information he adds, that its harbours were better known than those of Britain: this statement, however, there is much reason to question, as in the time of Cæsar, all that the Romans knew of Ireland was its relative position to Britain, and that it was about half its size.

The emperor Trajan, who reigned between A.D. 98 and A.D. 117, was not only a great conqueror, carrying the Roman armies beyond the Danube into Dacia, and into Armenia, Mesopotamia, and Assyria, and thus extending and rendering more accurate the geographical knowledge of his subjects; but he was also attentive to the improvement and commercial prosperity of the empire. He made good roads from one end of the empire to the other; he constructed a convenient and safe harbour at Centum Cellæ (Civita Vecchia), and another at Ancona on the Adriatic: he dug a new and navigable canal, which conveyed the waters of the Nahar-Malcha, or royal canal of Nebuchadnezzar, into the river Tigris; and he is supposed to have repaired or renewed the Egyptian canal between the Nile and the Red Sea. He also gave directions and authority to Pliny, who was appointed governor of Pontus and Bithynia, to examine minutely into the commerce of those provinces, and into the revenues derived from it, and other sources.

The emperor Adrian passed nearly the whole of his reign in visiting the different parts of his dominions: he began his journey in Gaul, and thence into Germany; he afterwards passed into Britain. On his return to Gaul, he visited Spain; on his next journey he went to Athens, and thence into the east; and on his second return to Rome, he visited Sicily; his third journey comprised the African provinces; his fourth was employed in again visiting the east; from Syria he went into Arabia, and thence into Egypt, where he repaired and adorned the city of Alexandria, restoring to the inhabitants their former privileges, and encouraging their commerce. On his journey back to Rome, he visited Syria, Thrace, Macedonia, and Athens. By his orders, an artificial port was constructed at Trebizond on a coast destitute by nature of secure harbours, from which this city derived great wealth and splendour.

The only writer in the time of Adrian, from whom we can derive any additional information respecting the geography and trade of the Romans, is Arrian. He was a native of Nicodemia, and esteemed one of the most learned men of his age; to him we are indebted for the journal of Nearchus's voyage, an abstract of which has been given. His accuracy as a geographer, is sufficiently established in that work, and indeed, in almost all the particulars respecting India, which he has detailed in his history of the expedition of Alexander the Great; and in his Indica, which may be regarded as an appendix to that history. He lived at Rome, under the emperors Adrian, Antoninus, and Marcus Aurelius, and was preferred to the highest posts of honour, and even to the consulship. In the year A.D. 170, he was appointed governor of Pontus, by Adrian, for the special purpose of opposing the Alani, who were invading that part of the empire. His situation and opportunities as governor, enabled him to derive the most accurate and particular information respecting the Euxine Sea, which he addressed in a letter to Adrian; this Periplus, as it is called, "contains whatever the governor of Pontus had seen, from Trebizond to Dioscurias; whatever he had heard from Dioscurias to the Danube and whatever he knew from the Danube to Trebizond."

The letter begins with the arrival of Arrian at Trebizond, at which place, the artificial port already noticed was then forming. At Trebizond he embarked, and surveyed the eastern coast of the Euxine Sea, visiting every where the Roman garrisons. His course led him past the mouth of the Phasis, the waters of which, he remarks, floated a long time on those of the sea, by reason of their superior lightness. A strong garrison was stationed at the mouth of this river, to protect this part of the country against the Barbarians; he adds, however, in his letter, that the new suburbs which had been built by the merchants and veterans, required some additional defence, and that he had, accordingly, for the greater security of the place, strengthened it with a new ditch: he ended his voyage at Sebastapolis, the most distant city garrisoned by the Romans. The description of the coasts of Asia, from Byzantium to Trebizond, and another of the interior, from Sebastapolis to the Bosphorus Cimmerius, and thence to Byzantium, is added to his voyage. The great object of this minute and accurate survey was to enable the emperor to take what measures he might deem proper, in case he designed to interfere in the affairs of the Bosphorus, as well as to point out the means of defence against the Alani, and other enemies of the Roman power.

We have contented ourselves with this short abstract of the Periplus of the Euxine, because we have already given all the important information it contains on the subject of the commerce of this sea. It is very inferior in merit to the Periplus of the Euxine, which has also been attributed to this Arrian, though Dr. Vincent, we think, has proved that it is the work of an earlier writer, and of a merchant.

As the Roman conquests extended, their geographical knowledge of course increased. In the reign of Antoninus Pius, their armies had forced a passage much further north in Britain than they had ever ventured before. One of the results of this success was a maritime survey, or rather two partial surveys of the north part of Britain, from which the geography of that part of the island was compiled by Ptolemy.

The maritime laws of the Rhodians, or those which passed under their name, seem to have been the basis and authority of the Roman maritime laws at this period; for we are told, that when a merchant complained to the emperor that he had been plundered by the imperial officers at the Cyclades, where he had been shipwrecked, the latter replied, that he indeed was lord of the earth, but that the sea was governed by the Rhodian laws, and that from them he would obtain redress. This part of the Rhodian law, however, had been but lately adopted by the Romans; for Antoninus is expressly mentioned as having enacted, among other laws, that shipwrecked merchandize should be the entire property of the lawful owners, without any interference or participation of the officers of the exchequer, and that those who were guilty of plundering wrecks should be severely punished.

One of the most important and complete surveys of the Roman empire (the idea of which, as has been already stated, was first formed by Julius Cæsar) was begun and finished in the reign of Antoninus, and is well known under the appellation of his Itinerary. It has, indeed, been objected to this date of the Itinerary, that it contains places which were not known in the time of Antonine, and names of places which they did not bear till after his reign; thus mention is made of the province of Arcadia in Egypt, and of Honorius in Pontus, so styled in honor of the sons of the emperor Theodosius. But the fact seems to be that alterations and additions were made to the Itinerary, and that occasionally, or perhaps under each subsequent emperor, new editions of it were published. From the maritime part of this Itinerary of Antoninus we derive a clear idea of the timidity or want of skill and enterprise of the Mediterranean seamen in their commercial voyages. All the ports which it was prudent or necessary, for the safety of the voyage, to touch at, in sailing from Achaia to Africa are enumerated; and of these there are no fewer than twenty, some of them at the heads of bays on the coasts of Greece, Epirus, and Italy, and within the Straits of Sicily as far as Messina. Their course was then to be directed along the east and south coasts of Sicily to the west point of it; from an island off this point they took their departure for the coast of Africa, a distance of about ninety miles.

These Itineraries undoubtedly were drawn up in as accurate a manner as possible; but till the time of Ptolemy they were of little service to geography or commerce, as, for a private individual to have one in his possession was deemed a crime little short of high treason. Geography as a science, therefore, had hitherto made little advances; indeed the discovery and example of Hipparchus, of reducing it to astronomical basis, seems to have been forgotten or neglected till the middle of the second century. The first after him, who attempted to fix geography on the base of science was Marinus, of Tyre, who lived a short time before Ptolemy; of his work we have only extracts given by this geographer. He divided the terms latitude and longitude, which, as we have already stated, were introduced by Artemidorus (A.C. 104) into degrees, and these degrees into their parts, though this improvement was not reduced generally to practice before Ptolemy, for we are informed by him, that Marinus had the latitude of some places and the longitude of others, but scarcely one position where he could ascertain both.

With regard to the extent of Marinus' geographical knowledge, or the accuracy of his details, we cannot form a fair judgment from the fragments of his works which remain. According to Ptolemy, he had examined the history of preceding ages, and all the information that had been collected in his own time, comparing and rectifying them as he proceeded in his own account.

It will be recollected that the Periplus of the Erythrean Sea did not trace the African coast lower down than Rhapta; but Marinus mentions Prasum, which, according to that hypothesis, which fixes it in the lowest southern latitude, must have been seven degrees to the south of Rhapta. So far, therefore, the knowlege of the ancients, in the time of Marinus, respecting the east coast of Africa extended; but, as neither he nor Ptolemy mentions a single place between Rhapta and Prasum, it is probable that the latter was not frequently or regularly visited for the purposes of trade, but that commercial voyages were still confined to the limit of Rhapta. We have just stated that Prasum, according to the most moderate hypothesis, must be fixed seven degrees to the south of Rhapta. Marinus, however, fixes it either in thirty-five degrees south, or under the tropic of Capricorn. He was led into this and similar errors by assigning too great a number of stadia to the degree. Ptolemy endeavours to correct him, and places Prasum in latitude 15, 30 south; it is remarkable that the Prasum of Ptolemy is precisely at Mosambique, the last of the Arabian settlements in the following ages, and the Prasum of Marinus, if under the tropic of Capricorn, is the limit of the knowledge of the Arabians on this coast of Africa.

Marinus, as quoted by Ptolemy, affirms that he was in possession of the journals of two expeditions under the command of Septimus Flaccus and Julius Maternus: the former of these officers set off from Cyrene, and the latter from Leptis; and, according to Marinus, they penetrated through the interior of Africa to the southward of the Equator, as far as a nation they styled Agesymba. The error of Marinus with respect to the valuation of the stadium, has led him to fix this nation in twenty-four degrees south latitude; if allowance, however, be made for his error, the Agesymba will still be placed under the Equator,—a great distance for a land expedition to have readied in the interior of Africa. Flaccus reported that the Ethiopians of Agesymba, were three months journeying to the south of the Garamantes, and the latter were 5400 of the stadia of Marinus, distant from Cyrene. According to the journal of Maternus, when the king of the Garamantes set off to attack the people of Agesymba, he marched four months to the south.

There are also some notices in Marinus of voyages performed along the coast of Africa, between India and Africa, and along part of the coast of India; he particularly mentions one Theophilus who frequented the coast of Azania, and who was carried by a south-west wind from Rhapta to Aromata in twenty days; and Diogenes, one of the traders to India, who on his return after he had come in sight of Aromata, was caught by the north-east monsoon, and carried down the coast during twenty-five days, till he reached the lakes from which the Nile issues. Marinus also mentions a Diogenes Samius, who describes the course held by vessels from the Indus to the coast of Cambay, and from Arabia to the coast of Africa. According to him, in the former voyage they sailed with the Bull in the middle of the heavens, and the Pleiades in the middle of the main yard; in the latter voyage, they sailed to the south, and by the star Canobus.

We now arrive at the name of Ptolemy, certainly the most celebrated geographer of antiquity. He was a native of Alexandria, and flourished in the reign of the emperor Marcus Antoninus. In the application of astronomy to geography, he followed Hipparchus principally, and he seems from his residence at Alexandria to have derived much information through the merchants and navigators of that city, as well as from its magnificent and valuable library. His great work, as it has reached us, consists almost entirely of an elementary picture of the earth, (if it may be so called,) in which its figure and size, and the position of places are determined. There is only a short notice of the division of countries, and it is very seldom that any historical notice is added. To this outline, it is supposed that Ptolemy had added a detailed account of the countries then known, which is lost.

His geography, such as we have described it, consists of eight books, and is certainly much more scientific than any which had been previously written on this science. In it there appears, for the first time, an application of geometrical principles to the construction of maps: the different projections of the sphere, and a distribution of the several places on the earth, according to their latitude and longitude. Geography was thus established on its proper principles, and intimately connected with astronomical observations and mathematical science. The utility and merit of Ptolemy's work seems to have been understood and acknowledged soon after it appeared. Agathemidorus, who lived not long after him, praises him for having reduced geography to a regular system; and adds, that he treats of every thing relating to it, not carelessly, or merely according to the ideas of his own, but to what had been delivered by more ancient authors, adopting from them whatever he found consonant to truth. Agathodæmon, an artist of Alexandria, observing the request in which his work was held, prepared a set of maps to illustrate it, in which all the places mentioned in it were laid down, with the latitudes and longitudes he assigned them. The reputation of his geography remained unshaken and undiminished during the middle ages, both in Arabia and Europe; and even now, the scientific language which he first employed, is constantly used, and the position of places ascertained by specifying their latitude and longitude.

It was not to be expected, however, that Ptolemy could accurately fix the longitude and latitude of places in the remoter parts of the then known world; his latitudes and longitudes are accordingly frequently erroneous, but especially the latter. This arose partly from his taking five hundred stadia for a degree of a great circle, and partly from the vague method of calculating distances, by the estimate of travellers and merchants, and the number of days employed in their journies by land, and voyages by sea. As he took seven hundred stadia for a degree of latitude, his errors in latitude are not so important; and though the latitude he assigns to particular places is incorrect, yet the length of the globe, according to him, or the distance from the extreme points north and south, then known, is not far from the truth. Thus the latitude of Thule, according to Ptolemy, is 64 degrees north, and the parallel through the cinnamon country 16° 24' south, that is, 80° 24' on the whole, a difference from the truth of not more than six or seven degrees. It is remarked by D'Anville, and Dr. Vincent coincides in the justice of the remark, that the grandest mistake in the geography of Ptolemy has led to the greatest discovery of modern times. Strabo had affirmed, that nothing obstructed the passage from Spain to India by a westerly course, but the immensity of the Atlantic ocean; but, according to Ptolemy's errors in longitude, this ocean was lessened by sixty degrees; and as all the Portuguese navigators were acquainted with his work, as soon as it was resolved to attempt a passage to India, the difficulty was, in their idea, lessened by sixty degrees; and when Columbus sailed from Spain, he calculated on sixty degrees less than the real distance from that country to India. Thus, to repeat the observation of D'Anville, the greatest of his errors proved eventually the efficient cause of the greatest discovery of the moderns.

Beside the peculiar merit of Ptolemy, which was perceived and acknowledged as soon as his work appeared, he possesses another excellence, which, as far as we know, was first pointed out and dwelt upon by Dr. Vincent. According to him, Ptolemy, in his description of India, serves as the point of connection between the Macedonian orthography and the Sanscrit, dispersing light on both sides, and showing himself like a luminary in the centre. He seems indeed to have obtained the native appellations of the places in India, in a wonderful manner; and thus, by recording names which cannot be mistaken, he affords the means of ascertaining the country, even though he gives no particulars regarding it. We have applied this remark to India exclusively, but it might be extended to almost all the names of places that occur in Ptolemy, though, as respects India, his obtaining the native appellations is more striking and useful.

Having offered these general remarks on the excellencies and errors of Ptolemy, we shall next proceed to give a short and rapid sketch of his geographical knowledge respecting Europe, Asia, and Africa. On the north-east of Europe he gives an accurate description of the course of the Wolga; and further to the south, he lays down the course of the Tanais, much nearer what it really is than the course assigned it by Strabo. He seems to have been acquainted with the southern shores of the Baltic from the western Dwina, or the Vistula, to the Cimbric Chersonesus: he also describes part of the present Livonia. The Chersonesus, however, he stretches two degrees too far to the north, and also gives it too great a bend to the east. He applies the name of Thule to a country situated to the north-east of Britain; if his usual error in longitude is rectified, the position he assigns Thule would correspond with that of Norway. Such seem to have been the limits of his Europe, unless, perhaps, he had some vague idea of the south of Sweden.

He begins his geographical tables with the British isles; and here is one of his greatest errors. According to him, the north part of Britain stretches to the east, instead of to the north: the Mull of Galloway is the most northern promontory, and the land from it bends due east. The Western Islands run east and west, along the north shore of Ireland, the west being the true north point in them. He is, however, on the whole, pretty accurate in his location of the tribes which at that period inhabited Scotland. Strabo had placed Ireland to the north of Britain, but in its true latitude. Ptolemy's map, which is the first geographical document of that island, represents it to the west of Britain, but five degrees further to the north than it actually is. He delineates its general shape, rivers, and promontories with tolerable accuracy, and some of his towns may be traced in their present appellations, as Dublin in Eblana. It has already been noticed that he was probably acquainted with the south of Sweden, and his four Scandinavian islands are evidently Zealand, Funen, Laland, and Falster. It is remarkable that his geography is more accurate almost in proportion as it recedes from the Mediterranean. The form which he assigns to Italy is much farther removed from the truth than the form of most of the other European countries which he describes. His fundamental error in longitude led him to give to the Mediterranean Sea a much greater extent than it actually possesses. According to him, it occupies nearly sixty-five degrees; and it is a singular circumstance, as well as a decisive proof of the influence of his authority, as well of the slow progress of accurate and experimental geography, that his mensuration of this sea was reputed as exact till the reign of Louis XIV., when it was curtailed of nearly twenty-five degrees by observation.

The principal points in the geography of Asia, as given by Ptolemy, respect the coasts of India, the route to the Seres, and the Caspian sea. His delineation of India is equally erroneous with his delineation of the British Isles: according to him, it stretches in a right line from west to east, a little to the south of a line drawn between the Ganges and the Indus. He possessed, however, information respecting places in the farther peninsula of India, the locality of several of which, by comparing his names with the Sanscrit, may be traced with considerable certainty. He assigns to the island of Ceylon a very erroneous locality, arising from his error respecting the form of India, and likewise an extent far exceeding the truth. He is the first author, however, who mentions the seven mouths of the Ganges. The route to the Seres, which he describes, has been already noticed: it is remarkable that the latitude which he assigns to his Sera metropolis, is within little more than a degree of the latitude of Pekin, which, in the opinion of Dr. Vincent, is one of the most illustrious approximations to truth that ancient geography affords. His description of Arabia is, on the whole, accurate; he has, however, greatly diminished the extent of the Arabian Gulf, and by at the same time increasing the size of the Persian, he has necessarily given an erroneous form to this part of Asia. The ancient opinion of Herodotus, that the Caspian was a sea by itself, unconnected with any other, which was overlooked or disbelieved by Strabo, Arrian, &c. was adopted by Ptolemy, but he erroneously describes it as if its greatest length was from east to west. The peninsula to which he gives the name of the Golden Chersonesus, and which is probably Malacca, he describes as stretching from north to south: to the east of it he places a great bay, and in the most distant part of it the station of Catigara. Beyond this, he asserts that the earth is utterly unknown, and that the land bends from this to the west, till it joins the promontory of Prasum in Africa, at which place this quarter of the world terminated to the south. Hence it appears that he did not admit a communication between the Indian and Atlantic oceans, and that he believed the Erythrean sea to be a vast basin, entirely enclosed by the land.

Strabo and Pliny believed that Africa terminated under the torrid zone, and that the Atlantic and Indian oceans joined. Ptolemy, as we have just seen, rejected this idea, and following the opinion of Hipparchus, that the earth was not surrounded by the ocean, but that the ocean was divided into large basins, separated from each other by intervening land, maintained, that while the eastern coast of Africa at Cape Prasum united with the coast of Asia at the bay of the Golden Chersonesus, the western coast of Africa, after forming a great gulf, which he named Hespericus, extended between the east and south till it joined India. The promontory of Prasum was undoubtedly the limit of Ptolemy's knowledge of the east coast of Africa: the limit of his knowledge of the west coast is not so easily fixed: some suppose that it did not reach beyond the river Nun; while others, with more reason, extend it to the Gulf of St. Cyprian, because the Fortunate Islands, which he assumed as his first meridian, will carry his knowledge beyond the Nun; and because, at the Gulf of St. Cyprian, the coast turns suddenly and abruptly to the east, in such a manner as may be supposed to have led Ptolemy to believe that it stretched towards and joined the coast of India.

Of some of the interior parts of Africa Ptolemy possessed clear and accurate information; regarding others, he presents us with a mass of confused notions. He clearly points out the Niger, though he fixes its source in a wrong latitude. In the cities of Tucabath and Tagana, which he places on its banks, may perhaps be recognized Tombuctoo and Gana. The most striking defect in his geography of the interior of Africa is, that he does not allow sufficient extent to the great desert of Sahara, while the southern parts are too much expanded. He places the sources of the Nile, and the Mountains of the Moon in south latitude thirteen, instead of north latitude six or seven; but the error of latitude is not so remarkable and unaccountable as the very erroneous latitude which he assigns to Cape Aromata, on a coast which was visited every year by merchants he must have seen at Alexandria. The most difficult point to explain in Ptolemy's central Africa is the river Gir, which he describes as equal in length to the Niger, and running in the same direction, till it loses itself in the same lake. What this river is, geographers have not agreed. It is mentioned by Claudian, as resembling the Nile in the abundance of its waters. Agethimedorus, a geographer of the third century, regards it and the Niger as the same river.

What then was the amount of the knowledge of the ancients, as it existed among the Romans, in the height of their power, respecting the form, extent, and surface of the globe? If we view a map drawn up according to their ideas, we are immediately struck with the form they assigned the world, and perceive with what propriety they called the extent of the world from east to west longitude or *length*, and the extent from north to south latitude, or *breadth*. In some maps, especially that drawn up from the celebrated Peutingerian Tables, which contain an itinerary of the whole Roman empire, thirty-five degrees of longitude occupy twenty-eight feet eight inches, whereas thirteen degrees of latitude are compressed within the space of one foot. It is easy to conceive how it happened that too much space is assigned between places situated east and west of each other, as the latitude of a place is much more easily determined than its longitude. At the same time, as the routes of the Roman armies generally were from east to west, the countries lying in that direction were better known than those lying to the north and south, though the longitudes, and general space assigned the world, in the former deviation, were erroneous. It was the opinion of most of the ancient geographers, that there was a southern continent or hemisphere, to correspond to and balance the northern; and this they formed by cutting off the great triangle to the south. The ancients also, while they curtailed those parts of the world with which they were unacquainted, extended the known parts.

The limit of the Roman geography of Europe to the north was the Baltic, beyond which they had some very imperfect and obscure notion of the south of Sweden, and perhaps of Norway. They were acquainted with the countries on the eastern boundary of Europe lying on the Danube and the Vistula, and the rivers Wolga and Tanais seem also to have been tolerably well known to them. Of the whole of the west of Europe they were well informed, with the exception of the general figure, and some part of the British isles.

With respect to Africa, the Romans seem to have been acquainted with one-third of it. The promontory of Prasum was the limit of their knowledge on the east coast: its limits on the western coast it is not so easy to fix. The western horn was the limit of the voyage of Hanno, which, according to some, is Cape Nun; and, according to others, Cape Three Points, in Guinea; and we have observed already, that the Gulf of St. Cyprian was probably the limit of Ptolemy's knowledge. The coasts of Africa on the Mediterranean, and on the Red Sea, were of course well known to the Romans; and some points of their information respecting the interior were clear and accurate, but, as for these, they trusted almost entirely to the reports of merchants, they were as frequently erroneous.

The northern, north-western, north-eastern, and east parts of Asia were almost utterly unknown to the Romans; but they possessed tolerably accurate information regarding the whole hither peninsula of India, from the Indus to the Ganges, and some partial and unconnected notices of the farther peninsula and of China.

5 The most probable opinion is, that they were made of fluat of lime, or Derbyshire spar.

CHAPTER IV

Historical Sketch Of The Progress Of Discovery And Of Commercial Enterprise, From The Time Of Ptolemy Till The Close Of The Fifteenth Century.

Although the period, which the present chapter embraces, extends to thirteen centuries, yet, as it is by no means rich or fruitful either in discovery or commercial enterprise, it will not detain us long. The luxuries and wealth of the east, which, in all ages of the world and to all nations have been so fascinating, had, as we have already seen, drawn to them the interest and the enterprise of the Romans, in the height of their conquests; and towards the east, with few exceptions, discovery and commerce pointed, during the whole of the period which this chapter embraces. Yet, notwithstanding this powerful attraction, geography made comparatively little progress: the love of luxury did not benefit it nearly so much as the love of science. The geography of Ptolemy, and the description of Greece by Pausanias, are, as Malte Brun justly remarks, the last works in which the light of antiquity shines on geography. We may further observe, that as circumstances directed the route to the east, during the middle ages, principally through the central parts of Asia, the countries thus explored, or visited, were among the least interesting in this quarter of the globe, and those of which we possess, even at the present day, very obscure and imperfect information.

The nations to whom geography and commerce were most indebted, during the period which this chapter embraces, were the Arabians,—the Scandinavians, —under that appellation comprehending the nations on the Baltic and in the north of Germany,—and the Italian states. Before, however, we proceed to notice and record their contributions to geography, discovery, and commerce, it will be proper briefly to attend to a few circumstances connected with those subjects, which occurred between the age of Ptolemy and the utter decline of the Roman empire.

We have already alluded to the intercourse which was begun between Rome and China, during the reign of Marcus Antoninus, for the purpose of obtaining silk. Of the embassy which preceded and occasioned this commercial intercourse, we derive all our information from the Chinese historians. A second embassy seems to have been sent in the year A.D. 284, during the reign of Probus: that the object of this also was commercial there can be no doubt; but the particulars or the precise object in view, and the result which flowed from it, are not noticed by the Chinese historians. There can be no doubt, however, that these embassies contributed to extend the geography and commerce of the Romans towards the eastern districts of Asia.

Of the attention which some of the Roman emperors, during the decline of the empire, paid to commerce, we possess a few notices which deserve to be recorded. The emperor Pertinax, whose father was a manufacturer and seller of charcoal, and who, himself, for some time pursued the same occupation, at that period an extensive and profitable one, preserved and exercised, during his reign, that sense of the value of commerce which he had thus acquired. He abolished all the taxes laid by Commodus on the ports, harbours, and public roads, and gave up his privileges as emperor, especially in all those points where they were prejudicial to the freedom and extension of commerce. It may indeed be remarked, that the very few good or tolerable princes who, at this period, filled the government of Rome, displayed their wisdom as well as their goodness by encouraging trade. Alexander Severus granted peculiar privileges and immunities to foreign merchants who settled in Rome: he lowered the duties on merchandises; and divided all who followed trade, either on a large or small scale, into different companies, each of which seems to have preserved the liberty of choosing their own governor, and over each of whom persons were appointed, conversant in each particular branch of trade, whose duty it was to settle all disputes that might arise.

Soon after this period the commerce of Rome in one particular direction, and that a most important one, received a severe blow. The Goths, who had emigrated from the north of Germany to the banks of the Euxine, were allured to the "soft and wealthy provinces of Asia Minor, which produced all that could attract, and nothing that could resist a barbarian conqueror." It is on the occasion of this enterprise, that we first became acquainted with the maritime usages and practices of the Goths; a branch of whom, under the name of Scandinavians, we shall afterwards find contributed so much to the extension of geography and commerce. In order to transport their armies across the Euxine, they employed "slight flat-bottomed barks, framed of timber only, without the least mixture of iron, and occasionally covered with a shelving roof on the appearance of a tempest." Their first object of importance was the reduction of Pityus, which was provided with a commodious harbour, and was situated at the utmost limits of the Roman provinces. After the reduction of this place, they sailed round the eastern extremity of the Euxine, a distance of nearly three hundred miles, to the important commercial city of Trebizond. This they also reduced; and in it they found an immense booty, with which they filled a great fleet of ships, that were lying in the port at the time of the capture. Their success encouraged and stimulated them to further enterprises against such of the commercial cities or rich coasts of the Roman empire, as lay within their grasp. In their second expedition, having increased their fleet by the capture of a number of fishing vessels, near the mouths of the Borysthenes, the Niester, and the Danube, they plundered the cities of Bithynia. And in a third expedition, in which their force consisted of five hundred sail of ships, each of which might contain from twenty-five to thirty men, they passed the Bosphorus and the Hellespont, and ravaged Greece, and threatened Italy itself.

The extent to which some branches of trade were carried by the Romans about this time, may be deduced from what is related of Firmus, whose ruin was occasioned by endeavouring to exchange the security of a prosperous merchant for the imminent dangers of a Roman emperor. The commerce of Firmus seems principally to have been directed to the east; and for carrying on this commerce, he settled himself at Alexandria in Egypt. Boasting that he could maintain an army with the produce of paper and glue, both of which articles he manufactured very extensively, he persuaded the people of Egypt that he was able to deliver them from the Roman yoke, and actually had influence sufficient to prevent the usual supplies of corn from being shipped from Alexandria to Rome. His destruction was the consequence. As an instance of his wealth and luxury, Vopiscus relates that he had squares of glass fixed with bitumen in his house. The Roman commerce suffered considerably during the reign of Dioclesian by the revolt of Britain, under Carausius, who, by his skill and superiority, especially in naval affairs, which enabled him to defeat a powerful Roman fleet fitted out against him, obtained and secured his independence. Carausius was murdered by Alectus: against the latter the emperor Constantine sailed with a powerful fleet, and having effected a landing in Britain, Alectus was defeated and slain. This fleet requires to be particularly noticed from two considerations. In the first place, it sailed with a side wind, and when the weather was rather rough,—circumstances so unusual, if not unprecedented, that they were deemed worthy of an express and peculiar panegyric: and, secondly, this fleet was not equipped and ready for sea till after four years' preparation, whereas, in the first Punic war, "within sixty days after the first stroke of the axe had been given in the forest, a fleet of 160 galleys proudly rode at anchor in the sea."

Soon after this event, we are furnished with materials, from which we may judge of the comparative opulence, commerce, and shipping of the several countries which bordered on the Mediterranean. Constantine and Licinius were contending for the Roman empire; and as the contest mainly depended on superiority at sea, each exerted himself to the utmost to fit out a formidable and numerous fleet. Licinius was emperor of the east: his fleet consisted of 380 gallies, of three ranks of oars; eighty were furnished by Egypt, eighty by Phoenicia, sixty by Ionia and Doria, thirty by Cyprus, twenty by Caria, thirty by Bithynia, and fifty by Africa. At this period there seems to have been no vessels larger than triremes. The naval preparations of Constantine were in every respect inferior to those of his rival: he seems to have got no ships from Italy: indeed, the fleets which Augustus had ordered to be permanently kept up at Misenum and Ravenna, were no longer in existence. Greece supplied the most if not all Constantine's vessels: the maritime cities of this country sent their respective quotas to the Piraeus; and their united forces only amounted to 200 small vessels. This was a feeble armament compared with the numerous and powerful fleets that Athens equipped and maintained during the Peloponnesian war. While this republic was mistress of the sea, her fleet consisted of 300, and afterwards of 400 gallies, of three ranks of oars, all ready, in every respect, for immediate service. The scene of the naval battle between Licinius and Constantine was in the vicinity of Byzantium: as this city was in possession of the former, Constantine gave positive orders to force the passage of the Hellespont: the battle lasted two days, and terminated in the complete defeat of Licinius. Shortly after this decisive victory, the Roman world was again united under one emperor, and the imperial residence and seat of government was fixed by Constantine at Byzantium, which thenceforth obtained the name of Constantinople.

In the middle of the fourth century Ammianus Marcellinus gives us some important and curious information respecting the Roman commerce with the East. According to him it was customary to hold an annual fair at Batnae, a town to the east of Antioch, not far from the banks of the Euphrates. Merchandize from the East was brought hither overland by caravans, as well as up the Euphrates; and its value at this fair was so great, that the Persians made an attempt to plunder it. To the same author we are indebted for some notices respecting the countries which lay beyond the eastern limits of the Roman empire, and also for the first clear and undoubted notice of rhubarb, as an extensive article of commerce for medicinal purposes.

Towards the end of the fourth century, the naval expeditions of the Saxons attracted the notice and excited the fears of the Britons and the Gauls: their vessels apparently were unfit for a long voyage, or for encountering either the dangers of the sea or of battle; they were flat-bottomed and slightly constructed of timber, wicker-work, and hides; but such vessels possessed advantages, which to the Saxons more than compensated for their defects: they drew so little water that they could proceed 100 miles up the great rivers; and they could easily and conveniently be carried on waggons from one river to another.

We have already noticed the itineraries of the Roman empire: of these there were two kinds, the *annotota* and the *picta*; the first containing merely the names of places; the other, besides the names, the extent of the different provinces, the number of their inhabitants, the names of the mountains, rivers, seas, &c.; of the first kind, the itinerary of Antoninus is the most celebrated: to it we have already alluded: to the second kind belong the Peutingarian tables, which are supposed to have been drawn up in the reign of Theodosius, about the beginning of the fifth century, though according to other conjectures, they were constructed at different periods.

The beginning of the tables is lost, comprising Portugal, Spain, and the west part of Africa; only the south-east coast of England is inserted. Towards the east, the Seres, the mouth of the Ganges, and the island of Ceylon appear, and routes are traced through the heart of India. Dr. Vincent remarks, that it is a very singular circumstance that these tables should have the same names in the coast of India as the Periplus, but reversed. Mention is also made in them of a temple of Augustus or the Roman emperor: these circumstances, Dr. Vincent justly observes, tend to prove the continuance of the commerce by sea with India, from the time of Claudius to Theodosius; a period of above 300 years. In these tables very few of the countries are set down according to their real position, their respective limits, or their actual size.

The law of the emperor Theodosius, by which he prohibited his subjects, under pain of death, from teaching the art of ship-building to the barbarians, was ineffectual in the attainment of the object which he had in view; nor did any real service to the empire result from a fleet of 1100 large ships that he fitted out, to act in conjunction with the forces of the western empire for the protection of Rome against Genseric, king of the Vandals. This fleet arrived in Sicily, but performed nothing; and Genseric, notwithstanding the law of Theodosius, obtained the means and the skill of fitting out a formidable fleet. The Vandal empire in Africa was peculiarly adapted to maritime enterprise, as it stretched along the coast of the Mediterranean above ninety days' journey from Tangier to Tripoli: the woods of mount Atlas supplied an inexhaustible quantity of ship timber; the African nations whom he had subdued, especially the Carthaginians, were skilled in ship-building and in maritime affairs; and they eagerly obeyed the call of their new sovereign, when he held out to them the plunder of Rome. Thus, as Gibbon observes, after an interval of six centuries, the fleets that issued from the port of Carthage again claimed the empire of the Mediterranean. A feeble and ineffectual resistance was opposed to the Vandal sovereign, who succeeded in his grand enterprise, plundered Rome, and landed safely in Carthage with his rich spoils. The emperor Leo, alarmed at this success, fitted out a fleet of 1113 ships, at the expense, it is calculated, of nearly five millions sterling. This fleet, with an immense army on board, sailed from Constantinople to Carthage, but it effected nothing. Genseric, taking advantage of a favourable wind, manned his largest ships with his bravest and most skilful sailors; and they towed after them vessels filled with combustible materials. During the night they advanced against the imperial fleet, which was taken by surprise; confusion ensued, many of the imperial ships were destroyed, and the remainder saved themselves by flight. Genseric thus became master of the Mediterranean; and the coasts of Asia, Greece, and Italy, were exposed to his depredations.

Towards the end of the fifth century, the Romans under Theodoric exhibited some slight and temporary symptoms of reviving commerce. His first object was to fit out a fleet of 1000 small vessels, to protect the coast of Italy from the incursions of the African Vandals and the inhabitants of the Eastern empire. And as Rome could no longer draw her supplies of corn from Egypt, he reclaimed and brought into cultivation the Pomptine marshes and other neglected parts of Italy. The rich productions of Lucania, and the adjacent provinces, were exchanged at the Marcilian fountain, in a populous fair, annually dedicated to trade: the gradual descent of the hills was covered with a triple plantation of divers vines and chestnut trees. The iron mines of Dalmatia, and a gold mine in Bruttium, were carefully explored and wrought. The abundance of the necessaries of life was so very great, that a gallon of wine was sometimes sold in Italy for less than three farthings, and a quarter of wheat at about five shillings and sixpence. Towards a country thus wisely governed, and rich and fertile, commerce was naturally attracted; and it was encouraged and protected by Theodoric: he established a free intercourse among all the provinces by sea and land: the city gates were never shut; and it was a common saying, "that a purse of gold might safely be left in the field." About this period, many rich Jews fixed their residence in the principal cities of Italy, for the purposes of trade and commerce.

The most particular information we possess respecting the geographical knowledge, and the Indian commerce of the ancients at the beginning of the sixth century, is derived from a work of Cosmas, surnamed Indico Pleustes, or the Indian navigator. He was originally a merchant, and afterwards became a monk; and Gibbon justly observes, that his work displays the knowledge of a merchant, with the prejudices of a monk. It is entitled *Christian Topography*, and was composed at Alexandria, in the middle of the fifth century, about twenty years after he had performed his voyage. The chief object of his work was to confute the opinions that the earth was a globe, and that there was a temperate zone on the south of the torrid zone. According to Cosmas, the earth is a vast plane surrounded by a wall: its extent 400 days' journey from east to west, and half as much from north to south. On the wall which bounded the earth, the firmament was supported. The succession of day and night is occasioned by an immense mountain on the north of the earth, intercepting the light of the sun. In order to account for the course of the rivers, he supposed that the plane of the earth declined from north to south: hence the Euphrates, Tigris, &c. running to the south, were rapid streams; whereas the Nile, running in a contrary direction, was slow and sluggish. The prejudices of a monk, are sufficiently evident in these opinions; but, in justice to Cosmas, it must be remarked, that he labours hard, and not unsuccessfully, to prove that his notions were all the same as those of the most ancient Greek philosophers; and, indeed, his system differs from that of Homer, principally in his assigning a square instead of a round figure to the plane surface, which they both supposed to belong to the earth. The cosmography of Homer, thus adopted by Cosmas and most Christian writers, modified in some respects by the cosmography they drew from the Scriptures, is a strong proof, as Malte Brun observes, of the powerful influence which the poetical geography of Homer possessed over the opinions even of very distant ages.

Having thus briefly detailed those parts of Cosmas's work, which are merely curious as letting us into the prevalent cosmography of his time, we shall now proceed to those parts which, as Gibbon remarks, display the knowledge of a merchant.

We have already noticed the inscription at Aduli for which we are indebted to this author, and the light which it throws on the commercial enterprise of the Egyptian sovereigns. According to Cosmas, the oriental commerce of the Red Sea, in his time, had entirely left the Roman dominions, and settled at Aduli: this place was regularly visited by merchants from Alexandria and Aela, an Arabian port, at the head of the eastern branch of the Red Sea. From Aduli, vessels regularly sailed to the East: here were collected the aromatics, spices, ivory, emeralds, &c. of Ethiopia, and shipped by the merchants of the place in their own vessels to India, Persia, South Arabia, and through Egypt and the north of Arabia, for Rome.

Cosmas was evidently personally acquainted with the west coast of the Indian peninsula. He enumerates the principal ports, especially those from which pepper was shipped. This article he describes as a source of great traffic and wealth. The great island of Sielidiba, or Ceylon, was the mart of the commerce of the Indian ocean. Its ports were visited by vessels from Persia, India, Ethiopia, South Arabia, and Tzinitza. If the last country is China, of which there can be little doubt, as he mentions that the Tzinitzae brought to Ceylon silk, aloes, cloves, and sandal-wood, and expressly adds that their country produced silk,—Cosmas is the first author who fully asserts the intercourse by sea between India and China. Besides the foreign vessels which frequented the ports of Ceylon, the native merchants carried on an extensive trade in their own vessels, and on their own account. In addition to pepper from Mali on the coast of Malabar, and the articles already enumerated from China, &c., copper, a wood resembling ebony, and a variety of stuffs, were imported from Calliena, a port shut to the Egyptian Greeks at the time of the Periplus; and from Sindu they imported musk, castoreum, and spikenard. Ceylon was a depôt for all these articles, which were exported, together with spiceries, and the precious stones for which this island was famous.

Cosmas expressly states that he was not in Ceylon himself, but that he derived his information respecting it and its trade from Sopatrus, a Greek, who died about the beginning of the sixth century. This, as Dr. Vincent observes, is a date of some importance: for it proves that the trade opened by the Romans from Egypt to India direct, continued upon the same footing from the reign of Claudius and the discovery of Hippalus, down to A.D. 500; by which means we came within 350 years of the Arabian voyage published by Renaudot, and have but a small interval between the limit of ancient geography and that of the moderns.

From this author we first learn that the Persians having overcome the aversion of their ancestors to maritime enterprise, had established a flourishing and lucrative commerce with India. All its principal ports were visited by Persian merchants; and in most of the cities there were churches in which the service was performed by priests, ordained by a Persian archbishop.

We shall conclude our notice of Ceylon, as described by Cosmas, from the account of Sopatrus, with mentioning a few miscellaneous particulars, illustrative of the produce and commerce of the island. The sovereignty was held by two kings; one called the king of the Hyacinth, or the district above the Ghants, where the precious stones were found; the other possessed the maritime districts. In Ceylon, elephants are sold by their height; and he adds, that in India they are trained for war, whereas, in Africa, they are taken only for their ivory. Various particulars respecting the natural history of Ceylon and India, &c. are given, which are very accurate and complete: the cocoa-nut with its properties is described: the pepper plant, the buffalo, the camelopard, the musk animal, &c.: the rhinoceros, he says, he saw only at a distance; he procured some teeth of the hippopotamus, but never saw the animal itself. In the palace of the king of Abyssinia, the unicorn was represented in brass, but he never saw it. It is extraordinary that he makes no mention of cinnamon, as a production of Ceylon.

The most important points respecting the state of Eastern commerce in the age of Cosmas, as established by his information, are the following: that Ceylon was the central mart between the commerce of Europe, Africa, and the west of India, and the east of India and China; that none of the foreign merchants who visited Ceylon were accustomed to proceed to the eastern regions of Asia, but received their silks, spices, &c. as they were imported into Ceylon; and that, as cloves are particularly specified as having been imported into Ceylon from China, the Chinese at this period must have traded with the Moluccas on the one hand, and with Ceylon on the other.

Cosmas notices the great abundance of silk in Persia, which he attributes to the short land carriage between it and China.

In our account of the very early trade of Carthage, a branch of it was described from Herodotus, which the Carthaginians carried on, without the use or intervention of words, with a remote African tribe. Of a trade conducted in a similar manner, Cosmas gives us some information; according to him, the king of the Axumites, on the east coast of Africa, exchanged iron, salt, and cattle, for pieces of gold with an inland nation, whom he describes as inhabiting Ethiopia. It may be remarked in confirmation of the accuracy, both of Herodotus and of Cosmas, in what they relate on this subject, and as an illustration and proof of the permanency and power of custom among barbarous nations, that Dr. Shaw and Cadamosto (in Purchas's Pilgrimage) describe the same mode of traffic as carried on in their times by the Moors on the west coast of Africa, with the inhabitants of the banks of the Niger.

In the middle of the sixth century, an immense and expensive fleet, fitted out by the Emperor Justinian for the purpose of invading the Vandals of Africa, gives us, in the detail of its preparation and exploits, considerable insight into the maritime state of the empire at this period. Justinian assembled at Constantinople 500 transports of various sizes, which it is not easy exactly to calculate; the presumption derived from the accounts we have is, that the smallest were 30 tons, and the largest 500 tons; and that the aggregate tonnage of the whole amounted to about 100,000 tons: an immense fleet, even compared with the fleets of modern times. On board of this fleet there were 35,000 seamen and soldiers, and 5000 horses, besides arms, engines, stores, and an adequate supply of water and provisions, for a period, probably, of two or three months. Such were the transports: they were accompanied and protected by 92 light brigantines, for gallies were no longer used in the Mediterranean; on board of these vessels were 2000 rowers. The celebrated Belisarius was the commander-in-chief, both of the land and sea forces. The course of this numerous and formidable fleet was directed by the master-galley in which he sailed; this was conspicuous by the redness of its sails during the day, and by torches fixed on its mast head during night. A circumstance occurred during the first part of the voyage, which instructs us respecting the mode of manufacturing the bread used on long voyages. When the sacks which contained it were opened, it was found to be soft and unfit for use; and on enquiring into the cause, the blame was clearly traced to the person by whose orders it had been prepared. In order to save the expense of fuel, he had ordered it to be baked by the same fire which warmed the baths of Constantinople, instead of baking it twice in an oven, as was the usual and proper practice. In the latter mode, a loss of one-fourth was calculated on and allowed; and the saving occasioned by the mode adopted was probably another motive with the person under whose superintendence the bread was prepared.

During the voyage from Methone, where fresh bread was taken on board to the southern coast of Sicily, from which, according to modern language, they were to take their departure for Africa, they were becalmed, and 161 days were spent in this navigation. An incident is mentioned relating to this part of the voyage, which points out the method used by the ancients to preserve their water when at sea. As the general himself was exposed to the intolerable hardship of thirst, or the necessity of drinking bad water, that which was meant for his use was put into glass bottles, which were buried deep in the sand, in a part of the ship to which the rays of the sun could not reach. Three months after the departure of the fleet from Constantinople, the troops were landed near Carthage; Belisarius being anxious to effect this as soon as possible, as his men did not hesitate to express their belief, that they were not able to contend at once with the winds, the waves, and the barbarians. The result of this expedition was the conquest of the African provinces, Sardinia, and Corsica.

The absurd and injudicious regulations of Justinian, respecting the corn trade of the empire have been already noticed; nor did his other measures indicate, either a better acquaintance with the principles of commerce, or more regard to its interests. The masters of vessels who traded to Constantinople were often obliged to carry cargoes for him to Africa or Italy, without any remuneration; or, if they escaped this hardship, enormous duties were levied on the merchandize they imported. A monopoly in the sale of silk was granted to the imperial treasurer; and, indeed, no species of trade seems to have been open and free, except that in cloth. His addition of one-seventh to the ordinary price of copper, so that his money-changers gave only 180 ounces of that metal, instead of 210, for one-sixth of an ounce of gold, seems rather to have been the result of ignorance than of fraud and avarice; since he did not alter the gold coin, in which alone all public and private payments were made. At this time, the geographical knowledge of the Romans, respecting what had formerly constituted a portion of their empire, must have declined in a striking manner, if we may judge from the absurd and fabulous account which Procopius gives of Britain. And the commercial relations of the Britons themselves had entirely disappeared, even with their nearest neighbours; since, in the history of Gregory of Tours, there is not a single allusion to any trade between Britain and France.

At the beginning of the seventh century we glean our last notice of any event connected with the commerce and maritime enterprise of the Romans; and the same period introduces us to the rising power and commerce of the Arabians.

Alexandria, though its importance and wealth as a commercial city had long been on the wane, principally by the removal of most of the oriental trade to Persia, was still the commercial capital of the Mediterranean, and was of the utmost importance to Constantinople, which continued to draw from it an annual supply of about 250,000 quarters of corn; but in the beginning of this century it was conquered by the Persians, and the emperor was obliged to enter into a treaty with the conquerors, by which he agreed to pay a heavy and disgraceful tribute for the corn which was absolutely necessary for the support of his capital. But a sudden and most extraordinary change took place in the character of Heraclius: he roused himself from his sloth, indolence and despair; he fitted out a large fleet; exerted his skill, and displayed his courage and coolness in a storm which it encountered; carried his armies into Persia itself, and succeeded in recovering Egypt and the other provinces which the Persians had wrested from the empire.

The very early commerce of the Arabians, by means of caravans, with India, and their settlements on the Red Sea and the coasts of Africa and India at a later period, for the purposes of commerce, have been already noticed. Soon after they became the disciples of Mahomet, their commercial and enterprizing spirit revived, if indeed it had ever languished; and it certainly displayed itself with augmented zeal, vigour, and success, under the influence of their new religion, and the genius and ambition of their caliphs. Persia, Syria, Egypt, Africa, and Spain, were successively conquered by them; and one of their first and most favourite objects, after they had conquered a country, was the amelioration or extension of its commerce. When they conquered Persia, the trade between that country and India was extensive and flourishing: the Persian merchants brought from India its most precious commodities. The luxury of the kings of Persia consumed a large quantity of camphire, mixed with wax, to illuminate their palaces; and this must have been brought, indirectly, through India, from Japan, Sumatra, or Borneo, the only places where the camphire-tree grows: a curious and striking proof of the remote and extensive influence of the commerce and luxury of Persia, at the time it was conquered by the Arabians. The conquerors, aware of the importance of the Indian commerce, and of the advantages which the Tigris and Euphrates afforded for this purpose, very soon after their conquest, founded the city of Bassora: a place, which, from its situation midway between the junction and the mouth of these rivers, commands the trade and navigation of Persia. It soon rose to be a great commercial city; and its inhabitants, directing their principal attention and most vigorous enterprize to the East, soon pushed their voyages beyond Ceylon, and brought, directly from the place of their growth or manufacture, many of those articles which hitherto they had been obliged or content to purchase in that island. Soon after the conquest of Persia was completed, the Caliph Omar directed that a full and accurate survey and description, of the kingdom should be made, which comprehended the inhabitants, the cattle, and the fruits of the earth.

The conquest of Syria added comparatively little to the commerce of the Arabians; but in the account which is given of this enterprize, we are informed of a large fair, which was annually held at Abyla, between Damascus and Heliopolis, where the produce and manufactures of the country were collected and sold. In the account given of the conquest of Jerusalem by the Arabians, we have also an account of another fair held at Jerusalem, at which it is probable the goods brought from India by Bassora, the Euphrates, and the caravans, were sold. As soon as the conquest of the western part of Syria was completed, the Arabians took advantage of the timber of Libanus, and of the maritime skill of the Phoenicians, which even yet survived: they fitted out a fleet of 1,700 barks, which soon rode triumphant in the Mediterranean. Cyprus, Rhodes, and the Cyclades, were subdued, and Constantinople itself was attacked, but without effect.

The conquest of Egypt, however, was of the most importance to the Arabian commerce, and therefore more especially demands our notice.—"In their annals of conquest," as Gibbon remarks, "the siege of Alexandria is perhaps the most arduous and important enterprize. The first trading city in the world was abundantly replenished with the means of subsistence and defence." But the Saracens were bold and skilful; the Greeks timid and unwarlike; and Alexandria fell into the possession of the disciples of Mahomet. As soon as the conquest of Egypt was completed, its administration was settled, and conducted on the most wise and liberal principles. In the management of the revenue, taxes were raised, not by the simple but oppressive mode of capitation, but on every branch from the clear profits of agriculture and commerce. A third part of these taxes was set apart, with the most religious exactness, to the annual repairs of the dykes and canals. At first, the corn which used to supply Constantinople was sent to Medina from Memphis by camels; but Omrou, the conqueror of Egypt, soon renewed the maritime communication "which had been attempted or achieved by the Pharaohs, the Ptolemies, or the Cæsars; and a canal, at least eighty miles in length, was opened from the Nile to the Red Sea. This inland navigation, which would have joined the Mediterranean and the Indian Ocean, was soon, however, discontinued, as useless and dangerous;" and about the year 775, A.D., it was stopped up at the end next the Red Sea.

The conquest of Africa, though not nearly so advantageous to the commerce of the Arabians, was yet of some importance to them in this point of view: it gradually extended from the Nile to the Atlantic Ocean. Tripoly was the first maritime and commercial city which their arms reduced: Bugia and Tangier were next reduced. Cairoan was formed as a station for a caravan; a city, which, in its present decay, still holds the second rank in the kingdom of Tunis. Carthage was next attacked and reduced; but an attempt was made by forces sent from Constantinople, joined by the ships and soldiers of Sicily, and a powerful reinforcement of Goths from Spain, to retake it. The Arabian conquerors had drawn a strong chain across the harbour; this the confederate fleet broke: the Arabians for a time were compelled to retreat; but they soon returned, defeated their enemies, burnt Carthage, and soon afterwards completed the conquest of this part of Africa.

The beginning of the eighth century is remarkable for their invasion of Spain, and for their second fruitless attack on Constantinople; during the latter, their fleet, which is said to have consisted of 1800 vessels, was totally destroyed by the Greek fire. With regard to their conquest of Spain, it was so rapid, that in a few months the whole of that great peninsula, which for two centuries withstood the power of the Roman republic at its greatest height, was reduced, except the mountainous districts of Asturia and Biscay, Here also the Arabians displayed the same attention to science by which they were distinguished in Asia: ten years after the conquest, a map of the province was made, exhibiting the seas, rivers, harbours, and cities, accompanied with a description of them, and of the inhabitants, the climate, soil, and mineral productions. "In the space of two centuries, the gifts of nature were improved by the agriculture, the manufactures, and the commerce of an industrious people." The first of the Ommiades who reigned in Spain, levied on the Christians of that country, 10,000 ounces of gold, 10,000 pounds of silver, 10,000 houses, &c. "The most powerful of his successors derived from the same kingdom the annual tribute of about six millions sterling. His royal seat of Cordova contained 600 mosques, 900 baths, and 200,000 houses: he gave laws to 80 cities of the first order, and to 300 of the second and third: and 12,000 villages and hamlets were situated on the banks of the Guadalquivir."

The religious prejudices, as well as the interests of the Arabians, led them to exclude the Christians from every channel through which they had received the produce of India. That they were precluded from all commercial intercourse with Egypt, is evident, from a fact noticed by Macpherson, in his Annals of Commerce. Before Egypt was conquered by the Arabians, writings of importance in Europe were executed on the Egyptian papyrus; but after that period, at least till the beginning of the ninth century, they are upon parchment.—This, as Macpherson observes, amounts almost to a proof, that the trade with Egypt, the only country producing papyrus, was interrupted.

In consequence of the supply of silks, spices, and other oriental luxuries which Constantinople derived from the fair at Jerusalem, (still allowed by the Arabians to be annually held,) not being sufficient for the demand of that dissipated capital, and their price in consequence having very much increased, some merchants were tempted to travel across Asia, beyond the northern boundary of the Arabian power, and to import, by means of caravans, the goods of China and India.

Towards the beginning of the ninth century, as we have already remarked, the commercial relations of the Arabians and the Christians of Europe commenced, and Alexandria was no longer closed to the latter. The merchants of Lyons, Marseilles, and other maritime towns in the south of France, in consequence of the friendship and treaties subsisting between Charlemagne and the Caliph Haroun Al Rasched, traded with their ships twice a year to Alexandria; from this city they brought the produce of Arabia and India to the Rhone, and by means of it, and a land carriage to the Moselle and the Rhine, France and Germany were supplied with the luxuries of the east. The friendship between the emperor and the caliph seems in other cases to have been employed by the former to the advancement of the commercial intercourse between Asia and Europe; for we are expressly informed, that a Jewish merchant, a favourite of Charlemagne, made frequent voyages to Palestine, and returned with pictures,—merchandize before unknown in the west.

Hitherto we have viewed the Arabians chiefly as fostering and encouraging commerce; but they also deserve our notice, for their attention to geographical science and discoveries. From the period of their first conquests, the caliphs had given orders to their generals to draw up geographical descriptions of the countries conquered; and we have already noticed some of these descriptions. In 833, A.D., the Caliph Almamon employed three brothers of the name of Ben Schaker, to measure a degree of latitude, first in the desert of Sangdaar, betweeen Racca and Palmyra, and afterwards near Cufa, for the purpose of ascertaining the circumference of the globe.

We now arrive at the era of a most important document, illustrative of the commerce of the eastern parts of India and of China, with which we are furnished by the Arabians: we allude to the "ancient Accounts of India and China, by two Mahomedan travellers, who went to those parts in the ninth century, translated from the Arabic by Renaudot." The genuineness and authenticity of these accounts were for a long time doubted; but De Guignes, from the Chinese annals, has completely removed all doubt on the subject.

The most remarkable circumstance connected with this journey is, that in the ninth century the Mahomedans should have been able to reach China; but our surprise on this point will cease, when we consider the extent of the Mahomedan dominions towards the east of Asia, the utmost limits of which, in this direction, approached very nearly the frontiers of China. If, therefore, they travelled by land, no serious difficulty would lie in their way; but Renaudot thinks it more probable, that they proceeded thither by sea.

According to these travellers, the Arabian merchants, no longer confining themselves to a traffic at Ceylon for the commodities of the east of Asia, traded to every part of that quarter of the globe, even as far as the south coast of China. The account they give of the traffic with this latter country, is very minute: "When foreign vessels arrive at Canfu, which is supposed to be Canton, the Chinese take possession of their cargoes, and store them in warehouses, till the arrival of all the other ships which are expected: it thus happens that the vessels which first arrive are detained six months. They then take about a third part of all the merchandize, as duty, and give the rest up to the merchants: of these the emperor is the preferable purchaser, but only for ready money, and at the highest price of the market." One circumstance is particularly noticed, which proves, that at this period the Arabians were numerous and respected in China; for a cadi, or judge, of their own religion, was appointed to preside over them, under the emperor. The Chinese are described as sailing along the coast as far as the Persian Gulf, where they loaded their vessels with merchandize from Bassora. Other particulars are mentioned, respecting their trade, &c., which agree wonderfully with what we know of them at present: they regarded gold and silver merely as merchandize: dressed in silk, summer and winter: had no wine, but drank a liquor made from rice. Tea is mentioned under the name of *sak*—an infusion of this they drank, and a large revenue was derived from the duty on it. Their porcelaine also is described and praised, as equally fine and transparent as glass. Every male child was registered as soon as born; at 18 he began to pay the capitation tax; and at 80 was entitled to a pension.

These Arabian travellers likewise supply us with some information respecting the trade of the Red Sea. The west side of it was in their time nearly deserted by merchant ships; those from the Persian Gulf sailed to Judda on the Arabian coast of it: here were always found many small coasting vessels, by means of which the goods from India, Persia, &c. were conveyed to Cairo. If this particular is accurate, it would seem to prove that at this period the canal between the Nile and the Red Sea, which had been rendered navigable by Omrou, was regularly used for the purposes of commerce.

In these accounts, the typhon, or whirlwind, so common in the Chinese seas, is mentioned under that appellation: the flying fish and unicorn are described; and we have notices of ambergrise, the musk, and the animal from which it is produced: the last is mentioned as coming from Thibet.

The next Arabian author, in point of time, from whom we derive information respecting geography and commerce, is Massoudi. He died at Cairo in 957: he was the author of a work describing the most celebrated kingdoms in Europe, Africa, and Asia; but the details respecting Africa, India, and the lesser Asia, are the most accurate and laboured. The account we shall afterwards give of the geographical knowledge of the Arabians, renders it unnecessary to present any abstract, in this place, of the geographical part of his work; we shall therefore confine ourselves to the notices interspersed respecting commerce. The Arabians traded to nearly every port of India, from Cashmere to Cape Comorin; and seem to have been protected and particularly favoured in their commercial pursuits. In the year 877 a great rebellion occurred in China, and the Arabian merchants had been massacred at Canfn. According to Massoudi, however, in his time this city had recovered from its disasters; confidence had revived; the Arabian merchants from Bassora, and other ports in Persia, resorted to it; and vessels from India and the adjacent islands. He also describes a route to China by land frequented by traders: this seems to have been through Korasin, Thibet, and a country he calls Ilestan. With regard to the Arabian commerce with Africa, the merchants settled at Omar traded to Sofala for gold, and to an island, which is supposed to be Madagascar, where they had established colonies.

Of the geographical knowledge displayed by the next Arabian traveller in point of date, [Ebor-]Ebn] Haukal, we shall at present take no notice, for the reason already assigned; but confine ourselves to his notices regarding commerce. According to him, the most wealthy merchants resided at Siraf, where they traded very extensively and successfully in the commodities of India and China. Hormus was the principal trading place in Karmania; Daibul in Sind: the merchants here traded to all parts. The countries near the Caspian were celebrated for their manufactures of silk, wool, hair, and gold stuffs. In Armenia, hangings and carpets, dyed with a worm or insect a beautiful colour, called *kermez*, were made. Samarcand was celebrated for the excellency of its paper. Trebezond was the principal trading place on the Black Sea. Alexandria is celebrated for the grandeur of its buildings; but its trade is not mentioned.

About the beginning of the eleventh century we derive our earliest notice of the commerce of Spain under its Arabian conquerors. The port of Barcelona was at this period the principal station for commercial intercourse with the eastern nations bordering on the Mediterranean; and as a proof of the character which its merchants held, it may be noticed, that their usages were collected into a code: by this code all vessels arriving at, or sailing from, Barcelona, are assured of friendly treatment; and they are declared to be under the protection of the prince, so long as they are near the coast of Catalonia. How much Spain was indebted to the Arabians for their early commerce may be judged of from the number of commercial and maritime terms in the Spanish language, evidently derived from the Arabic.

In the middle of the twelfth century, Al Edrissi composed at the court of Roger King of Sicily, whose subject he was, his Geographical Amusements. In this work we find little that relates to commerce: its geographical details will assist us when we give our sketch of the geographical knowledge of the Arabians.

In the work of [Ebor-]Ebn] Al Ouardi, which was drawn up in 1232, Africa, Arabia, and Syria are minutely described; but comparatively little is said on Europe, India, and the North of Asia.

The next Arabian geographer in point of time is Abulfeda: he wrote a very particular description of the earth, the countries being arranged according to climates, with the latitude and longitude of each place. In the introduction to this work he enters on the subject of mathematical geography, and describes the most celebrated mountains, rivers, and seas of the world. Abulfeda was a native of Syria; and this and the adjacent countries are described with most fullness and accuracy: the same remark applies to his description of Egypt and the north coast of Africa. The information contained in his work, respecting Tartary, China, &c., is not nearly so full and minute as might have been expected, considering the intercourse of the Arabians with those countries. Of Europe, and all other parts of Africa except Egypt and the north coast, he gives little or no information.

Within these very few years, some valuable notices have been received, through M. Burckhardt, and Mr. Kosegarten of Jena, of Ibn Batouta, an Arabian traveller of the fourteenth century. According to M. Burckhardt, he is, perhaps, the greatest land traveller that ever wrote his travels. He was a native of Tangier, and travelled for thirty years, from 1324 to 1354. He traversed more than once Egypt, Syria, Arabia, Persia, the coast of the Red Sea, and the eastern coast of Africa. Bochara, Balk, Samarcand, Caubul, India, and China, were visited by him: he even ventured to explore several of the Indian islands; crossed the mountains of Thibet, traversed India, and then, taking shipping, went to Java. He again visited China, and returned thence by Calicut, Yeman, Bagdad, and Damascus, to Cairo. After having visited Spain, he directed his travels to Africa; reached the capital of Morocco, and thence as far as Sodjalmasa. From this place he crossed the Desert with the slave merchants to Taghary—twenty-five days journey: he represents the houses here as built of rock salt, and covered with camel skins.

For twenty days more he crossed a desert without water or trees, and the sand of which was so loose, that it left no traces of footsteps. He now arrived at the frontier town of Soudan. After travelling for some time longer, he reached the banks of the Niger, which, according to the information he received, flowed into the Nile at the second cataract. He visited Tombuctoo and other places in this part of Africa, and finished his travels at Fez.

We shall now conclude our account of the Arabians, with a connected and condensed view of their geographical knowledge.

It is natural to suppose that they would be best acquainted with those countries which had embraced the faith of Mahomet; and that the prejudices and contempt with which his disciples have always regarded Christians, and, indeed, all who were of a different religion, would stand in the way of their seeking or acquiring information respecting those portions of the globe, the inhabitants of which were not of their faith. The exceptions to this are to be found principally in those countries, from which they derived the principal articles of their commerce; or which, though not proselytized, were conquered by them.

Hence, Europe in general was scarcely known to them beyond their dominions in Spain, and the adjacent parts of France. There are, however, exceptions to this remark; for we find, scattered through their geographical works, notices tolerably accurate and just respecting Ireland, Paris, Antharvat, which seems to be England, the Duchy of Sleswig, the City of Kiov, and some other places.

The whole of the north of Africa having been subdued, was thoroughly known by them; and they seem to have extended their arms, or at least their knowledge, as far into the interior as the banks of the Niger. On the east side, their arms had penetrated to Sofala; but on the west their knowledge does not appear to have reached beyond Cape Blanco, in the Bay of Arguin. The fortunate islands of the ancients were known to them, and the Pike of Teneriffe seems obscurely represented. Of the other islands and ports farther to the south on this side of Africa, it is impossible to ascertain their identity; or whether, as represented by the Arabians, they may not be regarded as among those fables in geography, in which all the ancient nations indulged. We may, however, trace some resemblance, in name or description, to the Canary Islands, the River Senegal, and the Rio d'Ouro. Malte Brun is of opinion, that their knowledge extended beyond Cape Boyador, for so long a time impassable by the Portugese.

On the eastern side of Africa, the Ethiopia of the Arabians seems to have terminated at Cape Corrientes: their power and religion were established from the Cape to the Red Sea. In their geographical descriptions of this part of Africa, we may trace many names of cities which they still retain. But they adopted the error of Ptolemy in supposing that the southern parts of Africa and Asia joined; for Edrisi describes an extensive country, extending from the coast of Africa to that of India, beyond the Ganges.

The island of Madagascar seems to be faintly pourtrayed by them; and it is certain that Arabian colonies and the Mahometan religion were established in it from a very early period. Massoudi mentions an island, two days' sail from Zanguebar, which he calls Phanbalu, the inhabitants of which were Mahometans; and it is worthy of remark, as Malte Brun observes, that in the time of Aristotle a large island in this Ocean was known under a similar name, that of Phebol. It is surprizing that the island of Ceylon, with which the Arabians had such regular and constant intercourse, should be placed by Edrisi near the coast of Africa.

But it was in Asia that the conquest, and commerce, and religion of the Arabians spread most extensively; and hence their geographical knowledge of this part of the globe is more full, accurate, and minute, than what they had acquired of the other portions. By their conquest of Persia, the ancient Bactriana, Transoxiana, &c. fell into their power; and according to their wise plan, they immediately made themselves acquainted with the geography, productions, &c. of these countries. From their writers we can glean many new and curious particulars, respecting the districts which lie to the north and east of the Gihon: whether in all respects they are accurate, cannot now be ascertained; for these districts, besides that they are comparatively little known to the moderns, have suffered so much from various causes, that their identity can hardly be determined.

On the west of Asia, near the Black Sea and the borders of Europe, the Arabian geographers throw much light; their information is minute and exact, and it reaches to the passes of Caucasus. Red Russia, it is well known, derives its appellation from the colour of the hair of its inhabitants. Now the Arabian geographers describe a Sclavonic nation, inhabiting a country near Caucasus, called *Seclab*, remarkable for the redness of their hair. Hence, it is probable that the modern inhabitants of Red Russia, who are Sclavonic, emigrated to it from this district of Caucasus.

Some notices appear of those parts, of Russia which border on Russia: Maschput, which is represented as a city of consequence, probably is Moscow. On the borders of the salt plains of Susith, a country is described, called Boladal Rus, evidently Russia, the inhabitants of which are represented as noted for their filth.

With the figure and extent of the Caspian Sea, the Arabian geographers were tolerably well acquainted: and they describe, so as to be recognized, several tribes inhabiting the borders of this sea, as well as the vicinity of the Wolga. One is particularly noticed and celebrated, being called the People of the Throne of Gold, the khan of whom lived at Seray, near the mouth of the Wolga. To the east of the Caspian, the Arabian conquests did not extend farther than those of Alexander and his immediate successors. Transoxiana was the limit of their dominions towards the north, in this part of the world.

Of many of the districts which the Arabians, conquered, in this part of Asia, they have furnished us with such accurate and full information, that modern discoveries have been able to add or correct very little. That they were acquainted with Thibet and China, has already appeared, from the account given of their commerce. Thibet they represent as divided into three parts, Thibet upper, central, and lower. At the beginning of the eighth century, Arabian ambassadors were sent to China: they passed through Cashgar. After this period, journies to China by the route of Samarcand were frequent. Besides Canfu, described by the Mahomedan travellers of Renaudot, other cities in China were visited by the Arabian merchants, most of which were in the interior; but the Arabian geographers seem to have been puzzled by the Chinese names. We learn, however, that the provinces of the north were distinguished from those of the south; the former were called Cathay and Tehar Cathar, or Cathay, which produces tea: its capital was Cambalu: the provinces in the south were called Tchin or Sin. The appellation of Cathay was that under which alone China was long known to the Europeans. Under the name of Sin, given to the southern districts, the Arabian geographers frequently comprehended all the country to the Ganges. The Arabians divided the present Hindostan into two parts; Sind and Hind: the first seems to have comprised the countries lying on the Indus; Hind lay to the east, and comprehended Delhi, Agra, Oude, Bengal, &c. The Decan, at least the western part of it, belonged to Sind. The coast of Coromandel, as well as the interior, was unknown to them. On the west or Malabar coast, their information was full and accurate; but it terminated at Cape Comorin.

While part of the forces of the Caliph Walid were employed in the conquest of Spain, another part succeeded in reducing Multan and Lahore; and the Arabian geographers, always ready to take advantage of the success of their arms, to promote geographical knowledge, describe their new eastern conquests, and the countries which bordered on them, in the most glowing language. The valley of Cashmere, in particular, affords ample matter for their panegyrics. The towns of Guzerat, Cambay, and Narwhorra are described: in the last resided the most powerful king of India; his kingdom extended from Guzerat and Concan to the Ganges. The city of Benares, celebrated as a school of Indian philosophy, and the almost impregnable fortress of Gevatior, are mentioned by them, as well as a colony of Jews in Cochin, and the Maldive islands: these they frequented to obtain cowries, which then, as now, were used as money.

It is supposed that the isle of Sumatra is described by them under the name of Lumery; for the peculiar productions are the same, and Sumatra was known under the name of Lambry in the time of Marc Paul, and Mandeville. Java is evidently meant by Al D'Javah: it is represented as rich in spices, but subject to volcanic eruptions; circumstances by which it is yet distinguished. A short period before the Portuguese reached these seas, Arabian colonists established themselves at Ternate and some of the other spice islands; and their language, religious opinions, and customs, may clearly be traced in the Philippine islands.

From the geographical discoveries, the travels by sea and land, and the commercial enterprize of the Arabians, we pass to those of the Scandinavians; under that appellation, including not only the Scandinavians, properly so called, who inhabited the shores of the Baltic and the coasts of Norway, but also those people who dwelt on the northern shores of the German Ocean; for they were of the same origin as the Baltic nations, and resembled them in manners and pursuits.

By an inspection of the map it will appear, that all these tribes were situated nearly as favorably for maritime enterprize as the nations which inhabited the shores of the Mediterranean; and though their earliest expeditions by sea were not stimulated by the same cause, commercial pursuits, yet they arose from causes equally efficient. While the countries bordering on the Mediterranean were blessed with a fertile soil and a mild climate, those on the Baltic were comparatively barren and ungenial; their inhabitants, therefore, induced by their situation to attend to maritime affairs, were further led to employ their skill and power by sea, in endeavouring to establish themselves in more favored countries, or, at least, to draw from them by plunder, what they could not obtain in their own.

We have already mentioned the maritime expeditions of the Saxons, which struck terror into the Romans, during the decline of their empire. The other Scandinavian nations were acted on by the same causes and motives. Neglecting the peaceful art of agriculture, inured to the sea from their earliest years, and the profession and practice of piracy being regarded as actually honourable by them, it is no wonder that their whole lives were spent in planning or executing maritime expeditions. Their internal wars also, by depriving many of their power or their property, compelled them to seek abroad that which they had lost at home. No sooner had a prince reached his eighteenth year, than he was entrusted by his father with a fleet; and by means of it he was ordered and expected to add to his glory and his wealth, by plunder and victory. Lands were divided into certain portions, and from each portion a certain number of ships were to be fully equipped for sea. Their vessels, as well as themselves, were admirably adapted to the grand object of their lives; the former were well supplied with stones, arrows, and strong ropes, with which they overset small vessels, and with grappling irons to board them; and every individual was skilful in swimming. Each band possessed its own ports, magazines, &c. Their ships were at first small, being only a kind of twelve-oared barks; they were afterwards so much enlarged, that they were capable of containing 100 or 120 men.

It is not our intention to notice the piratical expeditions of Scandinavians, except so far as they tended to discovery, or commerce, or were productive of permanent effects. Among the first countries to which they directed themselves, and where they settled permanently, were England and Ireland; the result of their settlement in England was the establishment of the Anglo-Saxon dominion power in that kingdom; the result of their expeditions to Ireland was their settlement on its eastern coasts. In the middle of the ninth century, the native Irish had been driven by them into the central and western parts of the country, while the Scandinavian conquerors, under the appellation of Ostmen, or Eastmen, possessed of all the maritime cities, carried on an extensive and lucrative commerce, not only with their native land, but also with other places in the west of Europe. Their settlements on the Shetland, Orkney, and western islands of Scotland, are only mentioned, because in these last the Scandinavians seem to have established and encouraged manufactures, the forerunner and support of commerce; for towards the end of the ninth century, the drapery of the Suderyans, (for so the inhabitants were called, as their country lay to the south of Shetland and Orkney,) was much celebrated and sought after.

About this period the Scandinavian nations began to mingle commerce and discovery with their piratical expeditions. Alfred, king of England, obliged to attend to maritime affairs, to defend his territories from the Danes, turned his ardent and penetrating mind to every thing connected with this important subject. He began by improving the structure of his vessels; "the form of the Saxon ships (observes Mr. Strutt, who derives his description from contemporary drawings) at the end of the eighth century, or beginning of the ninth, is happily preserved in some of the ancient MSS. of that date, they were scarcely more than a very large boat, and seem to be built of stout planks, laid one over the other, in the manner as is done in the present time; their heads and sterns are very erect, and rise high out of the water, ornamented at top with some uncouth head of an animal, rudely cut; they have but one mast, the top of which is also decorated with a bird, or some such device; to this mast is made fast a large sail, which, from its nature and construction, could only be useful when the vessel went before the wind. The ship was steered with a large oar, with a flat end, very broad, passing by the side of the stern; and this was managed by the pilot, who sat in the stern, and thence issued his orders to the mariners." The bird on the mast head, mentioned in this description, appears, from the account of Canute's fleet, given in Du Cange, to have been for the purpose of shewing the wind.

The same energy and comprehension of mind which induced and enabled Alfred to improve his navy so much, led him to favour geographical pursuits and commerce. In his Anglo-Saxon translation of Orosius, he has inserted the information he had obtained from two Scandinavians, Ohter and Wulfstan. In this we have the most ancient description, that is clear and precise, of the countries in the north of Europe. Ohter sailed from Helgoland in Norway, along the coast of Lapland, and doubling the North Cape, reached the White Sea. This cape had not before been doubled; nor was it again, till in the middle of the 16th century, by Chancellor, the English navigator, who was supposed at that time to be the original discoverer. Ohter also made a voyage up the Baltic, as far as Sleswig. Wulfstan, however, penetrated further into this sea than Ohter; for he reached Truse, a city in Prussia, which he represents as a place of considerable trade.

Alfred even extended his views to India, whether stimulated by religious views, or by the desire of obtaining its luxuries, is uncertain; perhaps both motives operated on his mind. We know that the patriarch of Jerusalem corresponded with him; and that the Christians of St. Thomas, in India, would probably be mentioned in these letters: we also know, that about a century before Alfred lived, the venerable Bede was possessed of pepper, cinnamon, and frankincense. Whatever were Alfred's motives, the fact is undoubted, that he sent one of his bishops to St. Thomas, who brought back aromatic liquors, and splendid jewels. Alfred seems to have been rich in the most precious commodities of the East; for he presented Asser, his biographer, with a robe of silk, and as much incense as a strong man could carry. After all, however, the commerce of England in his reign was extremely limited: had it been of any importance, it would have been more specially noticed and protected by his laws. It was otherwise, however, in the reign of Athelstan; for there is a famous law made by him, by which the rank and privileges of a thane are conferred on every merchant, who had made three voyages across the sea, with a vessel and cargo of his own. By another law passed in this reign, the exportation of horses was forbidden.

From this period till the conquest, England was prevented from engaging in commerce by the constant irruption of the Danes, and by the short duration of their sovereignty after they had succeeded in obtaining it. There are, however, even during this time, some notices on the subject; as appears from the laws of Ethelred: by these, tolls were established on all boats and vessels arriving at Billingsgate, according to their size. The men of Rouen, who brought wine and large fish, and those from Flanders, Normandy, and other parts of France, were obliged to shew their goods, and pay the duties; but the emperor's men, who came with their ships, were more favoured, though they were not exempt from duty.

From what relates to the geographical knowledge and the commerce of the Scandinavian inhabitants of England, we shall now pass on to the geographical discoveries and commerce of the other Scandinavian nations.

About the year 861, a Scandinavian vessel, probably on its voyage to Shetland or Orkney, discovered the Feroe islands. This discovery, and the flight of some birds, induced the Scandinavians to believe that there was other land in the vicinity of these islands. About ten years afterwards, Iceland was discovered by some Norwegian nobility and their dependants, who were obliged to leave their native country, in consequence of the tyranny of Harold Harfragre. According to some accounts, however, Iceland had been visited by a Norwegian pirate a few years before this; and if the circumstance mentioned in the Icelandic Chronicles be true, that wooden crosses, and other little pieces of workmanship, after the manner of the Irish and Britons, were found in it, it must have been visited before the Scandinavians arrived. The new colonists soon acquired a thorough knowledge of the size of the island; for they expressly state, that its circumference is 168 leagues, 15 to a degree, which corresponds with the most accurate modern measurement.

Iceland soon became celebrated for its learning; the history of the North, as well as its geography, is much indebted to its authors: nor were its inhabitants, though confined to a cold and sterile land very remote from the rest of Europe, inattentive to commerce; for they carried on a considerable trade in the northern seas,—their ships visiting Britain, Ireland, France, Germany, &c.; and there is even an instance of their having made a commercial voyage as far as Constantinople.

To them the discovery of Greenland and of America is due. The first took place about the beginning of the tenth century: a colony was immediately established, which continued till it was destroyed by a pestilence in the 14th century, and by the accumulation of ice, which prevented all communication between Iceland and Greenland.

The discovery of America took place in the year 1001: an Icelander, in search of his father who was in Greenland, was carried to the south by a violent wind. Land was discovered at a distance, flat, low, and woody. He did not go on shore, but returned. His account induced a Norwegian nobleman to fit out a ship to explore this new land; after sailing for some time, they descried a flat shore, without verdure; and soon afterwards a low land covered with wood. Two days' prosperous sailing brought them to a third shore, on the north of which lay an island: they entered, and sailed up a river, and landed. Pleased with the temperature of the climate, the apparent fertility of the soil, and the abundance of fish in the rivers, they resolved to pass the winter in this country; and they gave it the name of Vinland, from the quantity of small grapes which they found growing. A colony was soon afterwards formed, who traded with the natives; these are represented as of diminutive stature, of the same race as the inhabitants of the west part of Greenland, and as using leathern canoes. The merchandize they brought consisted chiefly of furs, sables, the skins of white rats, &c.; and they principally and most eagerly requested, in exchange, hatchets and arms. It appears from the Icelandic Chronicles, that a regular trade was established between this country and Norway, and that dried grapes or raisins were among the exports. In the year 1121, a bishop went from Greenland for the purpose of converting the colonists of Vinland to the Christian religion: after this period, there is no information regarding this country. This inattention to the new colony probably arose from the intercourse between the west of Greenland and Iceland having ceased, as we have already mentioned, and from the northern nations having been, about this period, wasted by a pestilence, and weakened and distracted by feuds. Of the certainty of the discovery there can be no doubt: the Icelandic Chronicles are full and minute, not only respecting it, but also respecting the transactions which took place among the colonists, and between them and the natives. And Adam of Bremen, who lived at this period, expressly states, that the king of Denmark informed him, that another island had been discovered in the ocean which washes Norway, called Vinland, from the vines which grew there; and he adds, we learn, not by fabulous hearsay, but by the express report of certain Danes, that fruits are produced without cultivation. Ordericus Vitalis, in his Ecclesiastical History, under the year 1098, reckons Vinland along with Greenland, Iceland, and the Orkneys, as under the dominion of the king of Norway.

Where then was Vinland?—it is generally believed it was part of America; and the objections which may be urged against this opinion, do not appear to us to be of much weight. It is said that no part of America could be reached in four days, the space of time in which the first discoverer reached this land, and in which the voyages from Greenland to it seem generally to have been made. But the west part of Greenland is so near some part of America, that a voyage might easily be effected in that time. In answer to the objection, that vines do not grow in the northern parts of America, where Vinland, if part of this continent, must be fixed, it may be observed, that in Canada the vine bears a small fruit; and that still further north, in Hudson's Bay, according to Mr. Ellis, vines grew spontaneously, producing a fruit which he compares to the currants of the Levant. The circumstances mentioned in the Icelandic Chronicles respecting the natives, that their canoes are made of skins; that they are very expert with their bows and arrows; that on their coasts they fish for whales, and in the interior live by hunting; that their merchandize consists of whalebone and furs; that they are fond of iron, and instruments made of it; and that they were small in stature, all coincide with what we know to be characterestic of the inhabitants of Labrador. It is probable, therefore, that this part of America, or the island of Newfoundland, was the Vinland discovered by the Icelanders.

The beginning and middle of the tenth century witnessed an increasing spirit of commerce, as well as considerable attention to geographical pursuits in other Scandinavian nations, as well as the Icelanders. Periodical public fairs were established in several towns of Germany, and other parts of the North: one of the most considerable articles of traffic at these fairs consisted of slaves taken in war. Sleswig is represented as a port of considerable trade and consequence; from it sailed ships to Slavonia, Semland, and Greece, or rather, perhaps, Russia. From a port on the side of Jutland, opposite to Sleswig, vessels traded to Frisca, Saxony, and England; and from another port in Jutland they sailed to Fionia, Scania, and Norway. Sweden is represented as, at this time, carrying on an extensive and lucrative trade. At the mouth of the Oder, on the south side of the Baltic, there seems to have been one, if not two towns which were enriched by commerce.

For most of these particulars respecting the commerce of the Baltic and adjacent seas, at this period, we are indebted to Adam of Bremen. He was canon of Bremen in the eleventh century: and from the accounts of the missionaries who went into Lapland, and other parts of the North, to convert the inhabitants to Christianity, the information he received from the king of Denmark, and his own observations, he drew up a detailed account of the Scandinavian kingdoms. His description of Jutland is full, and he mentions several islands in the Baltic, which are not noticed by prior writers. He also treats of the interior parts of Sweden, the coasts only of which had been previously made known by the voyages published by king Alfred. Of Russia, he informs us that it was a very extensive kingdom, the capital of which was Kiev; and that the inhabitants traded with the Greeks in the Black Sea. So far his information seems to have been good; but though his account of the south coasts of the Baltic is tolerably correct, yet he betrays great ignorance in most of what he says respecting the northern parts of the Baltic. In his work the name Baltic first Occurs. His geographical descriptions extend to the British isles; but of them he relates merely the fabulous stories of Solinus, &c. The figure of the earth, and the cause of the inequality of the length of the day and night, were known to Adam of Bremen.

About the middle of the twelfth century, Lubeck was founded; and it soon became a place of considerable trade, being the resort of merchants from all the countries of the North, and having a mint, custom-house, &c. We shall afterwards be called upon to notice it more particularly, when we come to trace the origin and history of the Hanseatic League. At present we shall only mention, that within thirty years after it was founded, and before the establishment of the League, Lubeck was so celebrated for its commerce, that the Genoese permitted its merchants to trade in the Mediterranean on board their vessels, on the same footing with their own citizens. The success of the Lubeckers stimulated the other inhabitants of this part of the Baltic shores; and the bishop of Lunden founded a city in Zealand, for the express purpose of being a place of trade, as its name, Keopman's haven, Chapman's haven, (Copenhagen,) implies. Towards the close of this century, Hamburgh is noticed as a place of trade.

The two cities of Lubeck and Hamburgh are generally regarded as having laid the foundation of the Hanseatic League. This League was first formed, solely to protect the carriage by land of merchandize between these cities; it is supposed to have been began about the middle of the thirteenth century. Other cities soon joined the League, and its objects became more multiplied and extensive; but still having the protection and encouragement of their commerce principally in view. The total number of confederated cities was between seventy and eighty. Lubeck was fixed upon as the head of the League: in it the assemblies met, and the archives were preserved. Inland commerce, the protection of which had given rise to the League, was still attended to; but the maritime commerce of the Baltic, as affording greater facilities and wealth, was that with which the League chiefly occupied itself. The confederated cities were the medium of exchange between the productions of Germany, Flanders, France, and Spain; and the timber, metals, fish, furs, &c. of the countries on this sea.

The conquest and conversion of the pagan countries between the Vistula and the Gulf of Finland, by the Teutonic knights, was favourable to the commercial views of the confederated cities; for the conquerors obliged the natives to confine their attention and labour exclusively to agriculture, permitting Germans alone to carry on commerce, and engage in trade. Hence Germans emigrated to these countries; and the League, always quicksighted to their own interests, soon connected themselves with the new settlers, and formed commercial alliances, which were recognized and protected by the Teutonic knights. Elbing, Dantzic, Revel, and Riga, were thus added to the League—cities, which, from their situation, were admirably calculated to obtain and forward the produce of the interior parts of Poland and Russia.

The northern countries of the Baltic shore, in a great measure inattentive to commerce, and distracted by wars, were supplied by the League with money, on condition that they should assign to them the sources of wealth which their mines supplied, and moreover grant them commercial privileges, immunities, and establishments. Lubeck was chiefly benefited and enriched by the treaties thus formed; for she obtained the working of the mines of Sweden and Norway, which do not seem to have been known, and were certainly not productively and effectively worked before this time. The League also obtained, by various means, the exclusive herring fishery of the Sound, which became a source of so much wealth, that the "fishermen were superintended, during the season, with as much jealousy as if they had been employed in a diamond mine."

Towards the close of the thirteenth century, the king of Norway permitted the League to establish a factory and the staple of their northern trade at Bergen. A singular establishment seems soon to have been formed here: at first the merchants of the League were permitted to trade to Bergen only in the summer months; but they afterwards were allowed to reside here permanently, and they formed twenty-one large factories, all the members of which were unmarried, and lived together in messes within their factories. Each factory was capable of accommodating about one hundred merchants, with their servants. Their importations consisted of flax, corn, biscuit, flour, malt, ale, cloth, wine, spirituous liquors, copper, silver, &c.; and they exported ship-timber, masts, furs, butter, salmon, dried cod, fish-oil, &c.

As the grand object of the League was to secure to themselves the profits arising from the mutual supply of the north and south of Europe, with the merchandize of each, they had agents in France, Spain, &c. as well as in the countries on the Baltic. England, at this period, did not carry on much commerce, nor afford much merchandize or produce for exportation; yet even in it the Hanseatic League established themselves. Towards the end of the thirteenth century they had a factory in London, and were allowed to export wool, sheep's skins, and tin, on condition that they kept in repair the gate of the city called Bishopsgate: they were also allowed the privilege of electing an alderman.

Bruges, which is said to have had regular weekly fairs for the sale of the woollen manufactures of Flanders so early as the middle of the tenth century, and to have been fixed upon by the Hanseatic League, in the middle of the thirteenth, as an entrepôt for their trade, certainly became, soon after this latter period, a city of great trade, probably from its connection with the Hanseatic League, though it never was formally admitted a member. We shall afterwards have occasion to notice it in our view of the progress of the Hanseatic League.

As the commerce of the League encreased and extended in the Baltic, it became necessary to fix on some depôt. Wisby, a city in the island of Gothland, was chosen for this purpose, as being most central. Most exaggerated accounts are given of the wealth and splendour to which its inhabitants rose, in consequence of their commercial prosperity. It is certain that its trade was very considerable, and that it was the resort of merchants and vessels from all the north of Europe: for, as the latter could not, in the imperfect state of navigation, perform their voyage in one season, their cargoes were wintered and lodged in magazines on shore. At this city was compiled a code of maritime laws, from which the modern naval codes of Denmark and Sweden are borrowed; as those of Wisby were founded on the laws of Oleren, (which will be noticed when we treat of the commerce of England during this period,) and on the laws of

Barcelona, of which we have already spoken; and as these again were, in a great measure, borrowed from the maritime code of Rhodes.

But to return to the more immediate history of the Hanseatic League,— about the year 1369 their power in the Baltic was so great, that they engaged in a successful war with the king of Denmark, and obliged him, as the price of peace, to deliver to them several towns which were favourably situated for their purpose.

The Hanseatic League, though they were frequently involved in disputes, and sometimes in wars, with France, Flanders, Holland, Denmark, England, and other powers, and though they undoubtedly aimed at, not only the monopoly, but also the sovereignty of the Baltic, and encroached where-ever they were permitted to fix themselves, yet were of wonderful service to civilization and commerce. "In order to accomplish the views of nature, by extending the intercourse of nations, it was necessary to open the Baltic to commercial relations; it was necessary to instruct men, still barbarous, in the elements of industry, and to familiarize them in the principles of civilization. These great foundations were laid by the confederation; and at the close of the fifteenth century, the Baltic and the neighbouring seas had, by its means, become frequented routes of communication between the North and the South. The people of the former were enabled to follow the progress of the latter in knowledge and industry." The forests of Sweden, Poland, &c. gave place to corn, hemp, and flax; the mines were wrought; and, in return, the produce and manufactures of the South were received. Towns and villages were erected in Scandinavia, where huts only were before seen: the skins of the bear and wolf were exchanged for woollens, linens, and silks: learning was introduced; and printing was scarcely invented before it was practised in Denmark, Sweden, &c.

It was at this period that the Hanse towns were the most flourishing; and that Bruges, largely partaking of their prosperity, and the sole staple for all their goods, rose to its highest wealth and consequence, and, in fact, was the grand entrepôt of the trade of Europe. The Hanse towns were at this time divided into four classes: Lubeck was at the head of the whole League; in it the meetings of the deputies from the other towns were held, and the archives of the League were kept. Under it were Hamburgh, Rostok, Wismar, and other nine towns situated in the north of Germany. Cologne was the chief city of the second class, with twenty-nine towns under it, lying in that part of Germany. Brunswick was the capital of the third class, having under it twelve towns, farther to the south than those under Lubeck. Dantzic was at the head of the fourth class, having under it eight towns in its vicinity, besides some smaller ones more remote. The four chief factories of the League were Novogorod in Russia, London, Bruges, and Bergen.

From this period till the middle of the sixteenth century, their power, though sometimes formidable, and their commerce, though sometimes flourishing, were both on the decline. Several causes contributed to this: they were often engaged in disputes, and not unfrequently in wars, with the northern powers. That civilization, knowledge, and wealth, to which, as we have remarked, they contributed so essentially, though indirectly, and without having these objects in view, disposed and enabled other powers to participate in the commerce which they had hitherto exclusively carried on. It was not indeed to be supposed, that either the monarchs or the subjects would willingly and cheerfully submit to have all their own trade in the very heart of their own country conducted, and the fruit of it reaped by foreign merchants. They, therefore, first used their efforts to gain possession of their own commerce, and then aspired to participate in the trade of other countries; succeeding by degrees, and after a length of time, in both these objects, the Hanseatic League was necessarily depressed in the same proportion.

The Dutch and the English first began to seek a participation in the commerce of the North. The chief cities which formed the republic of Holland had been among the earliest members or confederates of the League, and when they threw off the yoke of Germany, and attached themselves to the house of Bourbon, they ceased to form part of the League; and after much dispute, and even hostility with the remaining members of it, they succeeded in obtaining a part of the commerce of the Baltic, and commercial treaties with the king of Denmark, and the knights of the Teutonic order.

The commerce of the League was also curtailed in the Baltic, where it had always been most formidable and flourishing, by the English, who, in the beginning of the fifteenth century, gained admission for their vessels into Dantzic and the ports of Sweden and Denmark. The only port of consequence in the northern nations, to which the ships of the League were exclusively admitted, was Bergen, which at this period was rather under their dominion than under that of Norway. In the middle of the sixteenth century, however, they abandoned it, in consequence of disputes with the king of Denmark. About the same time they abandoned Novogorod, the czar having treated their merchants there in a very arbitrary and tyrannical manner. These, and other circumstances to which we have already adverted, made their commerce and power decline; and, towards the beginning of the seventeenth century, they had ceased to be of much consequence. Though, however, the League itself at this period had lost its influence and commerce, yet some cities, which had been from the first members of it, still retained a lucrative trade: this remark applies chiefly to Lubeck and Hamburgh; the former of these cities possessed, about the middle of the seventeenth century, 600 ships, some of which were very large; and the commerce by which Hamburgh is still distinguished, is in some measure the result of what it enjoyed as a member of the Hanseatic League.

We shall now turn our attention to the Italian states: Venice and Amalfi were the first which directed their labours to the arts of domestic industry, the forerunners and causes of commercial prosperity. New wants and desires being created, and a taste for elegance and luxury formed, foreign countries were visited. Muratori mentions several circumstances which indicate a revival of a commercial spirit; and, as Dr. Robertson remarks, from the close of the seventh century, an attentive observer may discern faint traces of its progress. Indeed, towards the beginning of the sixth century, the Venetians had become so expert at sea, that Cassiodorus addressed a letter to the maritime tribunes of Venice, (which is still extant,) in which he requests them to undertake the transporting of the public stores of wine and oil from Istria to Ravenna. In this letter, a curious but rather poetical account is given of the state of the city and its inhabitants: all the houses were alike: all the citizens lived on the same food, viz. fish: the manufacture to which they chiefly applied themselves was salt; an article, he says, more indispensable to them than gold. He adds, that they tie their boats to their walls, as people tie their cows and horses in other places.

In the middle of the eighth century, the Venetians no longer confined their navigation to the Adriatic, but ventured to double the southern promontory of Greece, and to trade to Constantinople itself. The principal merchandize with which they freighted their ships, on their return-voyage, consisted of silk, the rich produce of the East, the drapery of Tyre, and furs; about a century afterwards, they ventured to trade to Alexandria. Amalfi, Genoa, and Pisa followed their example; but their trade never became very considerable till the period of the crusades, when the treasures of the West were in fact placed in their hands, and thus fresh vigour was given to their carrying trade, manufactures, and commerce.

There are a few notices, however, respecting the commerce of Venice, and the other states of Italy, prior to the crusades, which it may be necessary very briefly to give. About the year 969, Venice and Amalfi are represented, by contemporary authors, as possessing an equal share of trade. The latter traded to Africa, Constantinople, and, it would appear, to some ports in the east end of the Mediterranean; and Italy, as well as the rest of Europe, entirely depended on these two states for their supply of the produce of the East. At the beginning of the eleventh century, the citizens of Amalfi seem to nave got the start of the Venetians in the favor and commerce of the Mahomedan states of the East: they were permitted to establish factories in the maritime towns, and even in Jerusalem; and those privileges were granted them expressly because they imported many articles of merchandize hitherto unknown in the East.

In the middle of the same century, Pisa rose into eminence for its commerce; it traded principally with the Saracen king of Sicily, and with Africa. The Genoese also, at this period, are represented as possessing a large portion of the trade of the Levant, particularly of Joppa.

As the most lucrative branch of commerce of all the Italian states was that in the productions of the East, and as these could only be obtained through Constantinople or Egypt, each state was eager to gain the favor of rulers of these places. The favor of the Greek emperor could be obtained principally by affording him succours against his enemies; and these the Venetians afforded in 1082 so effectually, that, in return, they were allowed to build a number of warehouses at Constantinople, and were favoured with exclusive commercial privileges. Dalmatia and Croatia were also ceded to them.

We now come to the period of the crusades, from which may be dated the rapid increase of the commerce and power of the Italian states. As none of the other European powers had ships numerous enough to convey the crusaders to

Dalmatia, whence they marched to Constantinople, the fleets of Venice, Pisa, and Genoa were employed for this purpose. But before they agreed to lend their fleets, they bargained, that on the reduction of any city favorable to commerce, they should be permitted to trade there without duty or molestation, and be favoured with every privilege and protection which they might desire. In consequence of this bargain, they obtained, in some places, the exclusive right over whole streets, and the appointment of judges to try all who lived in them, or traded under their protection.

A quarrel which took place between the Venetians and the Greek Emperor Manuel, in 1171, is worthy of notice, as being connected with the origin of the bank of Venice. The republic not being able to supply, from its own sources, the means of carrying on the war, was obliged to raise money from her citizens. To regulate this the chamber of loans was established: the contributors to the loan were made creditors to the chamber, and an annual interest of 4 per cent. was allotted to them. If this rate of interest was not compulsive, it is a sure criterion of a most flourishing state of trade, and of very great abundance of money; but there is every reason to believe if was compulsive.

At the beginning of the 13th century, Constantinople was conquered by the Venetians, and the leaders of the fourth crusade: this event enabled them to supply Europe more abundantly with all the productions of the East. In the partition of the Greek empire which followed this success, the Venetians obtained part of the Peloponnesus, where, at that period, silk was manufactured to a great extent. By this accession, to which was added several of the largest islands in the Archipelago, their sea coast extended from Venice to Constantinople: they likewise purchased the isle of Crete. The whole trade of the eastern Roman empire was thus at once transferred to the Venetians; two branches of which particularly attracted their attention,—the silk trade and that with India. The richest and most rare kinds of silk were manufactured at Constantinople; and to carry on this trade, many Venetians settled themselves in the city, and they soon extended it very considerably, and introduced the manufacture itself into Venice, with so much success, that the silks of Venice equalled those of Greece and Sicily. The monopoly of the trade of the Black Sea was also obtained by them, after the capture of Constantinople; and thus some of the most valuable articles of India and China were obtained by them, either exclusively, or in greater abundance, and at a cheaper rate than they could be procured by any other route. In consequence of all these advantages, Venice was almost the sole channel of commerce in this part of Europe, during the period of the Latin empire in Constantinople. This empire, however, was of very short continuance, not lasting more than 57 years.

In the interval, the merchants of Florence became distinguished for their commercial transactions, and particularly by becoming dealers in money by exchange, and by borrowing and lending on interest. In order to carry on this new branch of traffic, they had agents and correspondents in different cities of Europe; and thus the remittance of money by bills of exchange was chiefly conducted by them. Other Italian states followed their example; and a new branch of commerce, and consequently a new source of wealth, was thus struck out.

In the year 1261, the Greek emperor regained Constantinople through the assistance of the Genoese; and the latter, as usual, were amply repaid for their services on this occasion. Pera, the chief suburb of Constantinople, was allotted to them: here they had their own laws, administered by their own magistrates; and they were exempted from the accustomed duties on goods imported and exported. These privileges raised their commerce in this part of the world above that of the Venetians and Pisans; who, however, were still permitted to retain their factories. The Genoese soon began to aim at more extensive power and trade; and under the pretext that the Venetians were going to attack their new settlement, they obtained permission to surround it, and their factories in the neighbouring coasts, with fortifications. The trade of the Black Sea was under the dominion of the Greek emperor, who, by the possession of Constantinople, commanded its narrow entrance: even the sultan of Egypt solicited liberty to send a vessel annually to purchase slaves in Circassia and Lesser Tartary. The Genoese eagerly looked to participating in the valuable commerce of this sea; and this object they soon obtained. In return they supplied the Greeks with fish and corn. "The waters of the Don, the Oxus, the Caspian, and the Wolga, opened a rare and laborious passage for the gems and spices of India; and after three months march, the caravans of Carizme met the Italian vessels in the harbours of the Crimea." These various branches of trade were monopolized by the diligence and power of the Genoese; and their rivals of Venice and Pisa were forcibly expelled. The Greek emperor, alarmed at their power and encroachments, was at length engaged in a maritime war with them; but though he was assisted by the Venetians, the Genoese were victorious.

The Venetians, who were thus driven from a most lucrative commerce, endeavoured to compensate for their loss by extending their power and commerce in other quarters: they claimed and received a toll on all vessels navigating the Adriatic, especially from those sailing between the south-point of Istria and Venice. But their commerce and power on the Adriatic could be of little avail, unless they regained at least a portion of that traffic in Indian merchandize, which at this period formed the grand source of wealth. Constantinople, and consequently the Black Sea, was shut up from them: on the latter the Genoese were extending their traffic; they had seized on Caffa from the Tartars, and made it the principal station of their commerce. The Venetians in this emergency looked towards the ancient route to India, or rather the ancient depôt for Indian goods,— Alexandria: this city had been shut against Christians for six centuries; but it was now in the possession of the sultan of the Mamalukes, and he was more favourable to them. Under the sanction of the Pope, the Venetians entered into a treaty of commerce with the sultans of Egypt; by which they were permitted to have one consul in Alexandria, and another in Damascus. Venetian merchants and manufacturers were settled in both these cities. If we may believe Sir John de Mandeville, their merchants frequently went to the island of Ormus and the Persian Gulf, and sometimes even to Cambalu. By their enterprize the Indian trade was almost entirely in their possession; and they distributed the merchandize of the East among the nations of the north of Europe, through Bruges and the Hanseatic League, and traded even directly in their own vessels to England.

In the beginning of the fifteenth century, the annual value of the goods exported from Venice amounted to ten millions of ducats; and the profits on the home and outward voyages, were about four millions. Their shipping consisted of 3000 vessels, of from 10 to 200 amphoras burden, carrying 17,000 sailors; 300 ships with 8000 seamen; and 45 gallies of various sizes, manned by 11,000 seamen. In the dock-yard, 16,000 carpenters were usually employed. Their trade to Syria and Egypt seems to have been conducted entirely, or chiefly, by ready money; for 500,000 ducats were sent into those countries annually: 100,000 ducats were sent to England. From the Florentines they received annually 16,000 pieces of cloth: these they exported to different ports of the Mediterranean; they also received from the Florentines 7000 ducats weekly, which seems to have been the balance between the cloth they sold to the Venetians, and the French and Catalan wool, crimson grain, silk, gold and silver thread, wax, sugar, violins, &c., which they bought at Venice. Their commerce, especially the oriental branch of it, increased; and by the conquest of Constantinople by the Turks, the consequence of which was the expulsion of the Genoese, they were enabled, almost without a rival, to supply the encreasing demand of Europe for the productions of the East. Their vessels visited every port of the Mediterranean, and every coast of Europe; and their maritime commerce, about the end of the fifteenth century, was probably greater than that of all the rest of Europe. Their manufactures were also a great source of wealth; the principal were silk, cloth of gold and silver, vessels of gold and silver, and glass. The discovery of a passage to the East Indies by the Cape of Good Hope, the powerful league of Cambray, and other circumstances, weakened and gradually destroyed their commerce and power.

We have said that they supplied almost, without a rival, the demand in Europe for the produce of the East. That rival was Florence: the success of her merchants in a new branch of commerce has been already noticed. The profits they derived from lending money on interest, and from negociating bills of exchange, aided by their profits on their manufactures, for which, particularly those of silk and woollen, they were celebrated so early as the beginning of the fourteenth century, had rendered Florence one of the first cities of Europe, and many of its merchants extremely rich. In the year 1425, having purchased the port of Leghorn, they resolved, if possible, to partake in the commerce of Alexandria. A negociation was accordingly opened with the sultan: the result of which was, that the Florentines obtained some share in the Indian trade; and soon afterwards it appears that they imported spices into England. It is supposed, that the famous family of the Medici were extensively concerned in the Indian trade of Florence. Cosmo de Medici was the greatest merchant of the age: he had agents and money transactions in every part of Europe; and his immense wealth not only enabled him to gratify his love for literature and the fine arts, but also to influence the politics of Italy, and occasionally of the more remote parts of Europe. In the time of Lorenzo de Medici, about the close of the fifteenth century, the commercial intercourse between Florence and Egypt was greatly extended. Florence, indeed, was now in the zenith of her prosperity; after this period her commerce declined, principally from the discovery of the Cape of Good Hope.

In these brief notices of the commerce of the principal Italian states, Venice, Genoa, and Florence, in the days of their greatest glory, we have purposely omitted any reference to the other states, except stating a fact or two relating to Amalfi and Pisa, during that period, when they nearly rivalled the three great states. It will be proper, however, to subjoin to this account of Italian commerce, as it existed prior to the discovery of the Cape of Good Hope, some important facts respecting Amalfi, Pisa, Milan, Modena, &c., in order that our sketch, though necessarily brief, may not be deficient.

A great rivalship existed between Pisa and Amalfi in the twelfth century, arising chiefly from commercial jealousy; and this rivalship leading to war, Amalfi was twice taken and pillaged by the Pisans, who, indeed, during the zenith of their power, had repeatedly triumphed over the Saracens of Africa and Spain. Amalfi, however, soon recovered; but we possess no memorials of her commerce after this period, which deserve insertion here. Her maritime laws, the date of which is uncertain, seem to have been generally adopted by the Italian states.

Towards the end of the twelfth century, the power and commerce of Pisa were at their height: it partook, with Genoa and Venice, of the advantages derived from the trade of Constantinople. In the beginning of the next century, however, we find it became a mere auxiliary of Venice. Its subsequent wars with Genoa, and the factions which arose within its walls, reduced its commerce so low, about the middle of the fourteenth century, that nothing respecting it worthy of notice occurs after this period.

The wealth derived by Florence from a traffic in money has been already noticed. The example of this city was followed by Asti, an inland town of Piedmont, Milan, Placentia, Sienna, Lucca, &c. Hence the name of Lombard, or Tuscan merchant, was given to all who engaged in money transactions. The silk manufacture was the principal one in Italy; it seems to have been introduced by the Venetians, when they acquired part of the Greek empire. In the beginning of the fourteenth century, Modena was the principal seat of this manufacture; soon afterwards Florence, Lucca, Milan, and Bologna, likewise engaged in it.

Within the period to which the present chapter is confined, there are few traces of commerce in any other parts of Europe besides the Italian states and the Hanseatic League: the former monopolizing the commerce of the south of Europe and of Asia, and the latter that of the north of Europe, particularly of the Baltic, engrossed among them and the cities which were advantageously situated for intermediate depôts, nearly all the trade that then existed. There are, however, a few notices of commercial spirit and enterprize in other parts of Europe, during this period, which must not be omitted.

In Domesday-book a few particulars are set down relating to the internal and foreign trade of England. In Southwark the king had a duty on ships coming into a dock, and also a toll on the Strand. Gloucester must have enjoyed some manufactures of trade in iron, as it was obliged to supply iron and iron rods for the king's ships. Martins' skins were imported into Chester, either from Iceland or Germany. The navigation of the Trent and the Fosse, and the road to York, were carefully attended to.

If we may believe Fitz-Stephen, London, in the middle of the twelfth century, possessed a considerable portion of trade: among the imports, he mentions gold, spices, and frankincense from Arabia; precious stones from Egypt; purple drapery from India, palm oil from Bagdad: but it is certain that all these articles were obtained directly from Italian merchants. The furs of Norway and Russia were brought by German merchants, who, according to William of Malmsbury, were the principal foreign merchants who traded to England. The same author mentions Exeter, as a city much resorted to by foreign merchants; and that vessels from Norway, Iceland, and other countries, frequented the port of Bristol. Chester at this period also possessed much trade, particularly with Iceland, Aquitaine, Spain, and Germany. Henry I. made a navigable canal from the Trent to the Witham at Lincoln, which rendered this place one of the most flourishing seats of home and foreign trade in England. The Icelandic Chronicles inform us that Grimsby was a port much resorted by the merchants of Norway, Scotland, Orkney, and the Western Islands.

Previous to the reign of Henry II., the sovereigns and lords of manors in England claimed, as their right, the property of all wrecked vessels; but this monarch passed a law, enacting, that if any one human creature, or even a beast, were found alive in the ship, or belonging to her, the property should be kept for the owners, provided they claimed it in three months. This law, as politic as it was humane and just, must have encouraged foreign trade. In this reign the chief exports seem to have been lead, tin, and wool, and small quantities of honey, wax, cheese, and salmon. The chief imports were wine from the king's French dominions, woad for dying, spiceries, jewels, silks, furs, &c.

The laws of Oleron, an island near the coast of France belonging to England, are generally supposed to have been passed by Richard I.; both these, however, and their exact date, are uncertain: they were copied from the Rhodian law, or rather from the maritime laws of Barcelona.

Though it appears by official documents in the reign of king John, that the south coast of England, and the east coast only, as far as Norfolk, were esteemed the principal part of the country; yet, very shortly after the date of these documents, Newcastle certainly had some foreign trade, particularly with the northern nations of Europe for furs. In this reign are the first records of English letters of credit.

Some idea may be formed of the importation of wine at the beginning of the fourteenth century, by the following facts: in the year ending 20th Nov. 1299, the number of vessels that arrived in London and the other ports, (with the exception of the Cinque ports,) bringing cargoes of wine amounting to more than nineteen tuns, was seventy-three; and the number in the next year was seventy-one. It is probable, however, that we may double these numbers, since the Cinque ports, being exempted from the duty on wine, would import much more than any other equal number of ports. From a charter granted to foreign merchants in 1302, it appears that they came from the following countries to trade in England:—Germany, France, Spain, Portugal, Navarre, Lombardy, Tuscany, Provence, Catalonia, Aquitaine, Thoulouse, Quercy, Flanders, and Brabant. The very important privileges and immunities granted to them sufficiently proves, that at this period the commerce of England was mainly dependent on them. That there were, however, native merchants of considerable wealth and importance, cannot be doubted. In the year 1318, the king called a council of English merchants on staple business: they formed a board of themselves; and one was appointed to preside, under the title of mayor of the merchants, or mayor of the staple.

About the middle of this century, Dover, London, Yarmouth, Boston, and Hull, were appointed places for exchanging foreign money; and the entire management was given to William de la Pole. His name deserves particular notice, as one of the richest and most enlightened of the early merchants of England. His son, Michael, was also a merchant, and was created earl of Suffolk by Richard II. "His posterity flourished as earls, marquises, and dukes of Suffolk, till a royal marriage, and a promise of the succession to the crown, brought the family to ruin."

When Edward III. went to the siege of Calais, the different ports of England furnished him with ships. From the list of these it appears, that the whole number supplied was 700, manned by 14,151 seamen, averaging under twenty men for each vessel. Gosford is the only port whose vessels average thirty-one men. Yarmouth sent forty-three vessels; Fowey, forty-seven; Dartmouth, thirty-one; Bristol, twenty-four; Plymouth, twenty-six; London, twenty-five; Margate, fifteen; Sandwich, twenty-two; Southampton, twenty-one; Winchelsea, twenty-one; Newcastle, sixteen; Hull, seventeen.

In the year 1354 we have a regular account of such exports and imports as paid duty; from which it appears, that there were exported 31,651 sacks of wool, 3036 cwt. of woad, sixty-five wool-fells, 4774 pieces of cloth, and 8061 pieces of worsted stuff; and there were imported 1831 pieces of fine cloth, 397 cwt. of wax, and 1829 tuns of wine, besides linen, mercery, groceries, &c. As tin, lead, and several other articles are not enumerated, it may be inferred that they paid no duty. In the year 1372 there is the earliest record of direct trade with Prussia. As the woollen manufactures of England began to flourish, the importation of woollen cloths necessarily diminished; so that, in the act of 1378, reviving the acts of 1335 and 1351 for the encouragement of foreign merchants, though cloth of gold and silver, stuffs of silk, napery, linen, canvas, &c. are enumerated as imported by them, woollen cloth is not mentoned. The trade to the Baltic gradually increased as the ports in the north of England, particularly Newcastle, rose in wealth. In 1378 coals and grindstones were exported from this place to Prussia, Norway, Schonen, and other ports of the Baltic. Soon afterwards, in consequence of some disputes between the Prussians and English, a commercial treaty was formed between the Grand Master of Prussia and Edward III., by which it was agreed that the Prussian merchants in London should be protected, and that English merchants should have free access to every part of Prussia, to trade freely, as it used to be in ancient times. In order to carry this treaty into full effect on the part of the English, a citizen of London was chosen to be governor of the English merchants in Prussia and the other countries on the Baltic. Disputes, however, still arose, and piracies were committed on both sides. Meetings were therefore held at the Hague, to hear and settle the complaints of each party. From the statements then given in, it appears, that woollen clothes now formed a considerable part of the exports of England to the Baltic. That they were also exported in considerable quantity to the south of Europe, appears from other documents.

At the beginning of the fifteenth century the foreign commerce of England had considerably increased; for we are informed, that some merchants of London shipped wool and other goods, to the value of 24,000*l.*, to the Mediterranean; and nearly about the same time, the English merchants possessed valuable warehouses and an extensive trade at Bergen in Norway, and sent vessels of the size of 200 tons to Portugal. The freight of one of these is stated to have been worth 6000 crowns in gold. The improvement of the woollen manufactures may be inferred from the following circumstance: alum is very useful to fullers and dyers. About the year 1422, the Genoese obtained from the Greek emperor the lease of a hill in Asia Minor, containing alum: England was one of the chief customers for this article; but it undoubtedly was imported, not in English, but in Genoese vessels. In the year 1450 the Genoese delivered alum to the value of 400l. to Henry VI. Bristol seems to have been one of the most commercial cities in England. One merchant of it is mentioned as having been possessed of 2470 tuns of shipping: he traded to Finmark and Iceland for fish, and to the Baltic for timber and other bulky articles in very large ships, some of which are said to have been of the burden of 400, 500, and even 900 tons. Towards the latter end of the fifteenth century, the parliament, in order to encourage English shipping, (as hitherto the greatest part of the foreign trade of England had been carried on by foreign merchants in foreign vessels,) enacted a species of navigation law, and prohibited the king's subjects from shipping goods in England and Wales on board any vessel owned by a foreigner, unless when sufficient freight could not be found in English vessels.

Such are the most instructive and important notices respecting the state and progress of English commerce, which occur prior to the discovery of the Cape of Good Hope and America. We shall now proceed to give similar notices of the commerce of Scotland, Ireland, France, and the other countries of Europe; these, however, shall be very brief and few. In the middle of the twelfth century, Berwick, which then belonged to Scotland, is described as having more foreign commerce than any other port in that kingdom, and as possessing many ships. One of the merchants of this town was distinguished by the appellation of *the opulent.* Inverluth, or Leith, is described merely as possessing a harbour, but no mention is made of its trade. Strivelen had some vessels and trade, and likewise Perth. There was some trade between Aberdeen and Norway. There were no trading towns on the west coast of Scotland at this period; but about twenty years afterwards, a weekly market, and an annual fair were granted by charter to Glasgow.

It is probable that the foreign commerce of Scotland, being confined to the east coast, was principally carried on with Norway: with which country, indeed, Scotland had intimate connection; for we do not find any notice of foreign merchants from other countries trading to or settling in Scotland, till towards the end of the thirteenth century, when some Flemish merchants established a factory at Berwick. Wool, wool-fells, hides, &c. were the chief articles of export; salmon also was exported. Of the importance and value of the trade of this place we may form some idea, from the circumstance, that the custom duties amounted to upwards of 2,000l. sterling; and of 1,500 marks a year settled on the widow of Alexander prince of Scotland, 1,300 were paid by Berwick.

In the year 1428. foreign commerce attracted considerable attention in Scotland; and in order to encourage the native merchants to carry it on themselves, and by their own vessels, the parliament of Scotland seem, some time previous to this date, to have passed a navigation act; for in an act passed this year, the Scotch merchants were permitted for a year ensuing, to ship their goods in foreign vessels, where Scotch ones were not to be found, notwithstanding the statute to the contrary. Indeed, during the civil wars in England, between the houses of York and Lancaster, when the manufactures and commerce of that country necessarily declined, the commerce of Scotland began to flourish, and was protected and encouraged by its monarchs. The herring fishery was encouraged; duties were laid on the exportation of wool, and a staple for Scotch commerce was fixed in the Netherlands, In the year 1420 Glasgow began to acquire wealth by the fisheries; but until the discovery of America and the West Indies, it had little or no foreign trade. Towards the middle of the fifteenth century, several acts of parliament were passed to encourage agriculture, the fisheries, and commerce; the Scotch merchants had now acquired so much wealth and general respectability, that they were frequently employed, along with the clergy and nobles, in embassies. Even some of the Scotch barons were engaged in trade. In 1467 several acts were passed: among the most important enactments were those which related to the freight of ships, the mode of stowing it, the mode of fixing the average in case goods were thrown overboard, and the time of the year when vessels might sail to foreign countries.

The commerce of Ireland, when its ports were frequented by the Ostmen, has been already noticed. In the middle of the twelfth century, we are informed, that foreign merchants brought gold to Ireland, and that wheat and wine were imported from Bretagne into Wexford; but the exports in return are not particularized. About this period, some trade seems to have been carried on between Bristol and Dublin; and on the conquest of Ireland by Henry II., that monarch gave his city of Dublin to be inhabited by his men of Bristol. A charter granted by the same monarch, gives to the burgesses of that city free trade to England, Normandy, Wales, and the other ports of Ireland. From this time the commerce of Dublin seems to have flourished. It is certain, that at the middle of the fourteenth century the Irish stuffs were in such request abroad, that imitations of them were attempted by the Catalans, and they were worn as articles of luxury by the ladies of Florence. But of the mode in which they were conveyed to foreign countries, and the articles which were received in exchange for them, we have no certain information.

Though France possessed excellent ports in the Mediterranean, particularly Marseilles, which, as we have seen, in very early times was celebrated for its commerce, yet she, as well as less favoured ports of Europe, was principally indebted for her trade to the Lombards and other Italian merchants, during the middle ages. The political state of the country, indeed, was very unfavourable to commerce during this period; there are, consequently, few particulars of its commerce worth recording. About the beginning of the fourteenth century, Montpelier seems to have had a considerable trade; and they even sent ships with various articles of merchandize to London. Mention of Bourdeaux occurs about the same time, as having sent out, in one year, 1350 vessels, laden with 13,429 tuns of wine; this gives nearly 100 tuns in each vessel on an average. But Bourdeaux was in fact an English possession at this time. That commerce between France and England would have flourished and extended considerably, had it not been interrupted by the frequent and bitter wars between these countries, is evident from the consequences which followed the truce which was concluded between their monarchs in 1384. The French, and particularly the Normans, taking immediate advantage of this truce, imported into England an immense quantity of wine, fruits, spiceries, and fish; gold and silver alone were given in exchange. The Normans appear to have traded very extensively in spiceries; but it is uncertain, whether they brought them directly from the Mediterranean: they likewise traded to the east country or Baltic countries. About a century afterwards, that is in 1453, France could boast of her wealthy merchant, as well as Florence and England. His name was Jacques Coeur: he is said to have employed 300 factors, and to have traded with the Turks and Persians; his exports were chiefly woollen cloth, linen, and paper; and his imports consisted of silks, spiceries, gold, silver, &c.

In all our preceding accounts of the trade of Europe, the Italian and Flemish merchants make a conspicuous figure. Flanders was celebrated for its woollen manufactures, as well as for containing the central depôts of the trade between the south and north of Europe. Holland, which afterwards rose to such commercial importance, does not appear in the annals of commerce till the beginning of the fifteenth century. At this period, many of the manufacturers of Brabant and Flanders settled in Holland; and about the same time the Hollanders engaged in maritime commerce; but there are no particulars respecting it, that fall within the limits of the present chapter.

It remains to notice Spain. The commerce of Barcelona in its earliest stage has been already noticed. The Catalans, in the thirteenth century, engaged very extensively in the commerce of the Mediterranean, to almost every port of which they traded. The earliest navigation act known was passed by the count of Barcelona about this time; and laws were also framed, containing rules for the owners and commanders of vessels, and the clerks employed to keep their accounts; for loading and discharging the cargo; for the mutual assistance to be given by vessels, &c. These laws, and others, to extend and improve commerce, were passed during the reign of James I., king of Arragon, who was also count of Barcelona. The manufactures and commerce of this part of Spain continued to flourish from this time till the union of the crowns of Castile and Arragon, which event depressed the latter kingdom. In 1380, a Catalan ship was wrecked on the coast of Somersetshire, on her voyage from Genoa to Sluys, the port of Bruges: her cargo consisted of green ginger, cured ginger, raisins, sulphur, writing paper, white sugar, prunes, cinnamon, &c. In 1401, a bank of exchange and deposit was established at Barcelona: the accommodation it afforded was extended to foreign as well as native merchants. The earliest bill of exchange of which we have any notice, is one dated 28th April, 1404, which was sold by a merchant of Lucca, residing in Bruges, to a merchant of Barcelona, also residing there, to be paid by a Florence merchant residing in Barcelona. By the book of duties on imports and exports, compiled in 1413, it appears, that the Barcelonians were very liberal and enlightened in their commercial policy; this document also gives us a high idea of the trade of the city of Barcelona. A still further proof and illustration of the intelligence of the Barcelona merchants, and of the advantages for which commerce is indebted to them, occurs soon afterwards: for about the year 1432 they framed regulations respecting maritime insurance, the principal of which were, that no vessel should be insured for more than three quarters of her real value,—that no merchandize belonging to foreigners should be insured in Barcelona, unless freighted in a vessel belonging to the king of Arrogan: the words, *more or less*, inserted frequently in policies, were prohibited: if a ship should not be heard of in six months, she was to be deemed lost.

Little commerce seems to have been carried on from any other port of Spain besides Barcelona at this period: the north of Spain, indeed, had a little commercial intercourse with England, as appears by the complaints of the Spanish merchants; complaints that several of their vessels bound to England from this part of Spain had been plundered by the people of Sandwich, Dartmouth, &c. Seven vessels are particularly mentioned: one of which, laden with wine, wool, and iron, was bound for Flanders; the others, laden with raisins, liquorice, spicery, incense, oranges, and cheese, were bound for England. The largest of these vessels was 120 tons: one vessel, with its cargo, was valued as high as 2500l.

The following short abstract of the exports and imports of the principal commercial places in Europe, about the middle of the fifteenth century, taken from a contemporary work, will very properly conclude and sum up all we have to say on this subject.

Spain exported figs, raisins, wine of inferior quality, dates, liquorice, Seville oil, grain, Castile soap, wax, iron, wool, goat skins, saffron, and quicksilver; the most of these were exported to Bruges. The chief imports of Spain were Flemish woollen cloth and linen. This account, however, of the commerce of Spain, does not appear to include Barcelona. The exports of Portugal were wine, wax, grain, figs, raisins, honey, Cordovan leather, dates, salt, &c.; these were sent principally to England. The imports are not mentioned.

Bretagne exported salt, wine, cloth, and canvas.

The exports of Scotland were wool, wool-fells, and hides to Flanders; from which they brought mercery, haberdashery, cart-wheels, and barrows. The exports of Ireland were hides, wool, salmon, and other fish; linen; the skins of martins, otters, hares, &c. The trade of England is not described: the author being an Englishman, and writing for his countrymen, we may suppose, thought it unnecessary.

The exports of Prussia were beer, bacon, copper, bow-staves, wax, putty, pitch, tar, boards, flax, thread of Cologne, and canvas; these were sent principally to Flanders, from which were brought woollen cloths. The Prussians also imported salt from Biscay.

The Genoese employed large vessels in their trade; their principal exports were cloth of gold and silver, spiceries, woad, wool, oil, wood-ashes, alum, and good: the chief staple of their trade was in Flanders, to which they carried wool from England.

The Venetians and Florentines exported nearly the same articles as the Genoese; and their imports were nearly similar.

Flanders exported madder, wood, garlick, salt-fish, woollen cloths, &c. The English are represented as being the chief purchasers in the marts of Brabant, Flanders, and Zealand; to these marts were brought the merchandize of Hainault, France, Burgundy, Cologne, and Cambray, in carts. The commodities of the East, and of the south of Europe, were brought by the Italians: England sent her wool, and afterwards her woollen cloth.

From this view of the trade of Europe in the middle of the fifteenth century, it appears, that it was principally conducted by the Italians, the Hanse merchants, and the Flemings; and that the great marts were in Flanders. Towards the end of this century, indeed, the other nations of Europe advancing in knowledge and enterprize, and having acquired some little commercial capital, each began, in some degree, to conduct its own trade. The people of Barcelona, at a very early period, form the only exception to this remark; they not only conducted their own trade, but partook largely in conducting the trade of other nations.

From the remotest period to which we can trace the operations of commerce, we have seen that they were chiefly directed to the luxuries of Asia; and as the desire of obtaining them in greater abundance, and more cheaply and easily, was the incitement which led to the discovery of the Cape of Good Hope by the Portuguese, it will be proper, before we narrate that event, briefly to give such particulars respecting Asiatic commerce as occur within the period which this chapter embraces, and to which, in our account of the Arabians, we have not already alluded. This will lead us to a notice of some very instructive and important travels in the East; and the information which they convey will point out the state of the geography of Asia, as well as its commerce, during the middle ages.

The dreadful revolutions which took place in Asia in the twelfth and thirteenth centuries, and which threatened to extend to Europe, induced the European powers, and particularly the Pope, to endeavour to avert the evil, by sending embassies to the Mogul potentates. So frequent were these missions, that, in the beginning of the fourteenth century, a work was composed which described the various routes to Grand Tartary. What was at first undertaken from policy and fear, was afterwards continued from religious zeal, curiosity, a love of knowledge, and other motives. So that, to the devastations of Genghis Khan we may justly deem ourselves indebted for the full and important information we possess respecting the remote parts of Asia during the middle ages.

The accounts of India and China by the two Mahomedan travellers have been already noticed: between the period of their journey, and the embassies and missions to which we have just alluded, the only account of the East which we possess is derived from the work of Benjamin, a Jew of Tudela in Spain. It is doubted whether he visited all the places he describes: his object was principally to describe those places where the Jews resided in great numbers.

After describing Barcelona as a place of great trade, frequented by merchants from Greece, Italy, and Alexandria, and a great resort of the Jews, and giving a similar character of Montpelier and Genoa, he proceeds to the East. The inhabitants of Constantinople being too lazy to carry on commerce themselves, the whole trade of this city, which is represented as surpassing all others, except Bagdad, in wealth, was conducted by foreign merchants, who resorted to it from every part of the world by land and sea. New Tyre was a place of considerable traffic, with a good harbour: glass and sugar were its principal exports. The great depôt for the produce and manufactures of India, Persia, Arabia, &c., was an island in the Persian Gulf. He mentions Samarcand as a place of considerable importance, and Thibet as the country where the musk animal was found. But all beyond the Persian Gulf he describes in such vague terms, that little information can be gleaned. It is worthy of remark, that nearly all the Jews, whom he represents as very numerous in Thebes, Constantinople, Samarcand, &c., were dyers of wool: in Thebes alone, there were 2000 workers in scarlet and purple. After the conquest of the northern part of China by Genghis Khan, the city of Campion in Tangut seems to have been fixed upon by him as the seat of a great inland trade. Linens, stuffs made of cotton, gold, silver, silks, and porcelain, were brought hither by the Chinese merchants, and bought by merchants from Muscovy, Persia, Armenia, &c.

In the years 1245, 1246, the pope sent ambassadors to the Tartar and Mogul khans: of these Carpini has given us the most detailed account of his embassy, and of the route which he followed. His journey occupied six months: he first went through Bohemia, Silesia, and Poland, to Kiov, at that time the capital of

Russia. Thence he proceeded by the Dnieper to the Black Sea, till he arrived at the head quarters of the Khan Batou. To him we are indebted for the first information of the real names of the four great rivers which water the south of Russia, the Dnieper, the Don, the Volga, and the Jaik. He afterwards proceeded to the head quarters of another khan, on the eastern shores of the Caspian. After passing a country where the famous Prester John is said to have reigned, he reached the end of his journey, the head quarters of the khan of the Moguls. Besides the information derived from his own observations, he inserts in his narrative all he had collected; so that he may be regarded as the first traveller who brought to the knowledge of western Europe these parts of Asia; but though his travels are important to geography, they throw little light on the commerce of these countries.

Rubruquis was sent, about this time, by the king of France to the Mogul emperor: he passed through the Crimea, and along the shores of the Volga and the Caspian Sea; visited the Khans Sartach and Batou; and at length arrived at the great camp of the Moguls. Here he saw Chinese ambassadors; from whom, and certain documents which he found among the Moguls, he learnt many particulars respecting the north of China, the most curious of which is his accurate description of the Chinese language and characters. He returned by the same route by which he went. In his travels we meet with some information respecting the trade of Asia. The Mogul khans derived a considerable revenue from the salt of the Crimea. The alum of Caramonia was a great object of traffic. He is the first author, after Ammianus Marcellinus, who mentions rhubarb as an article of medicine and commerce. Among the Moguls he found a great number of Europeans, who had been taken prisoners: they were usually employed in working the mines, and in various manufactures. He is the first traveller who mentions *koumis* and arrack; and he gives a very particular and accurate description of the cattle of Thibet, and the wild and fleet asses of the plains of Asia. Geography is indebted to him for correcting the error of the ancients, which prevailed till his time, that the Caspian joined the Northern Ocean: he expressly represents it as a great inland sea,—the description given of it by Herodotus, but which was overlooked or disbelieved by all the other ancient geographers.

While the pope and the French monarch were thus endeavouring to conciliate the Moguls by embassies, the Emperor Frederic of Germany, having recovered Jerusalem, Tyre, and Sidon, formed an alliance with the princes of the East; and this alliance he took advantage of for the purposes of oriental commerce: for his merchants and factors travelled as far as India. In the last year of his reign, twelve camels, laden with gold and silver, the produce of his trade with the East, arrived in his dominions. The part of India to which he traded, and the route which was pursued, are not recorded.

Among the most celebrated travellers of the middle ages, was Marco Polo: he, his father, and uncle, after trading for some time in many of the commercial and opulent cities of Lesser Asia, reached the more eastern parts of that continent, as far as the court of the great khan, on the borders of China. For 26 years they were either engaged in mercantile transactions, or employed in negociations with the neighbouring states by the khan; they were thus enabled to see much, and to collect much important information, the result of which was drawn up by Marco Polo. He was the first European who reached China, India beyond the Ganges, and the greater number of the islands in the Indian Ocean. He describes Japan from the accounts of others: notices great and little Java, supposed to be Borneo and Sumatra; and is the first who mentions Bengal and Guzerat by their present names, as great and opulent kingdoms. On the east coast of Africa, his knowledge did not reach beyond Zanguebar, and the port of Madagascar opposite to it: he first made known this island to Europe. Such is a sketch of the countries described by Marco Polo; from which it will easily be perceived, how much he added to the geographical knowledge of Asia possessed at that period.

The information he gives respecting the commerce of the countries he either visited himself, or describes from the reports of others, is equally important. Beginning with the more western parts of Asia, he mentions Giazza, a city in the Levant, as possessed of a most excellent harbour, which was much frequented by Genoese and Venetian vessels, for spices and other merchandize. Rich silks were manufactured in Georgia, Bagdat, Tauris, and Persia, which were the source of great wealth to the manufacturers and merchants. All the pearls in Christendom are brought from Bagdat. The merchants from India bring spices, pearls, precious stones, &c. to Ormus: the vessels of this port are described as very stoutly built, with one mast, one deck, and one sail. Among the most remarkable cities of China, he particularly notices Cambalu, or Pekin, Nankin, and Quinsai. At the distance of 2,500 Italian miles from this last city, was the port of Cauzu, at which a considerable trade was carried on with India and the spice islands. The length of the voyage, in consequence of the monsoons, was a year. From the spice islands was brought, besides other articles, a quantity of pepper, infinitely greater than what was imported at Alexandria, though that place supplied all Europe. He represents the commerce and wealth of China as very great; and adds, that at Cambalu, where the merchants had their distinct warehouses, (in which they also lived,) according to the nation to which they belonged, a large proportion of them were Saracens. The money was made of the middle bark of the mulberry, stamped with the khan's mark. Letters were conveyed at the rate of 200 or 250 miles a day, by means of inns at short distances, where relays of horses were always kept. The tenth of all wool, silk, and hemp, and all other articles, the produce of the earth, was paid to the khan: sugar, spices, and arrack, paid only 3-1/2 per cent. The inland trade is immense, and is carried on principally by numerous vessels on the canals and rivers. Marco Polo describes porcelain, which was principally made at a place he calls Trigui; it was very low-priced, as eight porcelain dishes might be bought for a Venetian groat: he takes no notice of tea. He supposes the cowries of the Maldives to be a species of white porcelaine. Silver then, as now, must have been in great demand, and extremely scarce; it was much more valuable than gold, bearing the proportion to the latter, as 1 to 6 or 8. Fine skins also bore a very high price:

another proof of the stability of almost every thing connected with China. He was particularly struck with what he calls black stones, which were brought from the mountains of Cathay, and burnt at Pekin, as wood, evidently meaning some kind of coal. The collieries of China are still worked, principally for the use of the porcelaine manufactures.

Marco Polo seems to have regarded Bengal and Pegu as parts of China: he mentions the gold of Pegu, and the rice, cotton, and sugar of Bengal, as well as its ginger, spikenard, &c. The principal branch of the Bengal trade consisted in cotton goods. In Guzerat also, there was abundance of cotton: in Canhau, frankincense; and in Cambaia, indigo, cotton, &c. He describes the cities on the east and west coasts of India; but he does not seem either to have penetrated himself inland, or to have learnt any particulars regarding the interior from other persons. Horses were a great article of importation in all parts of India: they were brought from Persia and Arabia by sea. In the countries to the north of India, particularly Thibet, corals were in great demand, and brought a higher price than any other article: this was the case in the time of Pliny, who informs us, that the men in India were as fond of coral for an ornament, as the women of Rome were of the Indian pearls. In Pliny's time, corals were brought from the Mediterranean coast of France to Alexandria, and were thence exported by the Arabians to India. Marco Polo does not inform us by what means, or from what country they were imported into the north of India. The greater Java, which he represents as the greatest island in the world, carried on an extensive trade, particularly by means of the Chinese merchants, who imported gold and spices from it. In the lesser Java, the tree producing sago grows: he describes the process of making it. In this island there are also nuts as large as a man's head, containing a liquor superior to wine,—evidently the cocoa nut. He likewise mentions the rhinoceros. The knowledge of camphire, the produce of Japan, Sumatra, and Borneo, was first brought to Europe by him. The fishery of pearls between Ceylon and the main land of India is described; and particular mention is made of the large ruby possessed by the king of that island. Madagascar is particularly mentioned, as supplying large exports of elephants' teeth.

Marco Polo's description of the vessels of India is very full and minute: as he sailed from China to the Indian islands in one of these vessels, we may suppose it is perfectly accurate. according to him, they were fitted up with many cabins, and each merchant had his own cabin. They had from two to four masts, all or any of which could be lowered; the hold was divided not merely for the purpose of keeping distinct each merchant's goods, but also to prevent the water from a leak in one division extending to the rest of the hold. The bottoms of the vessels were double planked at first, and each year a new sheathing was added; the ships lasted only six years. They were caulked, as modern ships are; the timbers and planks fixed with iron nails, and a composition of lime, oil, and hemp, spread over the surface. They were capable of holding 5000 or 6000 bags of pepper, and from 150 to 300 seamen and passengers. They were supplied with oars as well as sails: four men were allotted to each oar. Smaller vessels seem to have accompanied the larger ones, which besides had boats on their decks.

When the power of the Romans was extinguished in Egypt, and the Mahomedans had gained possession of that country, Aden, which had been destroyed by the former in the reign of Claudius, resumed its rank as the centre of the trade between India and the Red Sea. In this situation it was found by Marco Polo. The ships which came from the East, did not pass the straits, but landed their cargoes at Aden; here the *trankies* of the Arabs, which brought the produce of Europe, Syria, and Egypt, received them, and conveyed them to Assab, Cosir, or Jidda: ultimately they reached Alexandria. Marco Polo gives a magnificent picture of the wealth, power, and influence of Aden in the thirteenth century.

When the Christians were expelled from Syria, in the beginning of the fourteenth century, and, in order to procure the merchandize of the east, were obliged to submit to the exactions of the sultan of Egypt; Sanuto, a Venetian, addressed a work to the Pope, in which he proposed to suppress the Egyptian trade by force. In this work are many curious particulars of the Indian trade at this time; and it is highly interesting both on this account, and from the clear-sighted speculations of the author. It appears to have produced a strong sensation; and though his mode of suppressing the Egyptian trade was not followed, yet, in consequence of it, much more attention was paid to Oriental commerce. According to him, the productions of the East came to the Venetians in two different ways. Cloves, nutmegs, pearls, gems, and other articles of great value, and small bulk, were conveyed up the Persian Gulf and the Tigris to Bassora, and thence to Bagdat; from which they were carried to some port in the Mediterranean. The more bulky and less valuable articles were conveyed by Arabian merchants to the Red Sea, and thence across the desert and down the Nile to Alexandria. He adds, that ginger and cinnamon, being apt to spoil on shipboard, were from ten to twenty per cent. better in quality, when brought by land carriage, though this conveyance was more expensive.

From the works of Sanuto, it appears that sugar and silk were the two articles from their trade in which the Saracens derived the greatest portion of their wealth. Cyprus, Rhodes, Amorea, and Marta (probably Malta), produced sugar; silk was the produce of Apulia, Romania, Crete, and Cyprus. Egypt was celebrated, as in old times, for the fineness of its flax; European flax was far inferior. The Egyptian manufactures of linen, silk, and linen and silk mixed, and also the dates and cassia of that country were exported to Turkey, Africa, the Black Sea, and the western ports of Europe, either in Saracen or Christian vessels. In return for these articles, the Egyptians received from Europe, gold, silver, brass, tin, lead, quicksilver, coral, and amber: of these, several were again exported from Egypt to Ethiopia and India, particularly brass and tin. Sanuto further observes, that Egypt was dependent on Europe for timber, iron, pitch, and other materials for ship building.

As his plan was to cut off all trade with the Saracens, and for that purpose to build a number of armed galleys, he gives many curious particulars respecting the expence of fitting them out; he estimates that a galley capable of holding 250 men, will cost 1500 florins, and that the whole expence of one, including pay, provisions, &c. for nine months, would be 7000 florins. The seamen he proposes to draw from the following places, as affording the most expert: Italy, the north of Germany, Friesland, Holland, Slavia, Hamburgh, Denmark, Sweden, and Norway.

In the year 1335, Pegoletti, an Italian, wrote a system of commercial geography; in this, the route taken by the merchants who brought produce and manufactures from China to Azof is particularly described. "In the first place," he says, "from Azof to Astracan it is twenty-five days journey with waggons drawn by oxen; but with waggons by horses, only ten or twelve. From Astracan to Sara, by the river, one day; from Sara to Saracanco, on the north-east coast of the Caspian Sea, eight days by water; thence to Lake Aral, twenty days' journey with camels. At Organci on this lake there was much traffic. To Oltrarra on the Sihon, thirty-five or forty days, also with camels; to Almaley with asses, thirty-five days; to Camexu, seventy days with asses; to a river, supposed to be the Hoangho, in China, fifty days with horses; from this river the traveller may go to Cassai, to dispose of his loading of silver there, and from this place he travels through the whole of Cathay with the Chinese money he receives for his silver; to Gambelecco, Cambalu, or Pekin, the capital of Cathay, is thirty days' journey." So that the whole time occupied about 300 days. Each merchant generally carried with him silver and goods to the value of 25,000 gold ducats; the expence of the whole journey was from 300 to 350 ducats. The other travellers of the fourteenth century, from whom we derive any information respecting Eastern geography and commerce, are Haitho, Oderic, and Sir John Mandeville; they add little, however, to the full and accurate details of Marco Polo, on which we can depend.

Haitho's work, comprehends the geography of the principal states of Asia; his information was derived from Mogul writings, the relation of Haitho I. king of Armenia, who had been at the head quarters of Mangu Khan, and from his own personal knowledge.

Oderic is the first missionary upon record in India; the date of his journey is 1334; among much that is marvellous, his relations contain some extraordinary truths. He went, in company with other monks, as far as China. There is little new or valuable till he reaches the coast of Malabar: of the pepper trade on this coast he gives a clear and rational account. He next describes Sumatra and the adjacent islands, and mentions the sago tree. Respecting China, he informs us, among other things which are fabulous, that persons of high rank keep their nails extremely long, and that the feet of the women are very small. He expresses great surprise and admiration at the wealth of the cities through which he passed on his return from Zartan to Pekin. Tartary and Thibet were visited by him, after leaving China; he mentions the high price of the rhubarb of the former country and the Dalai Lama of Thibet. In his voyages in India he sailed on board a vessel which carried 700 people,—a confirmation, as Dr. Vincent observes, of the account we have from the time of Agatharcides down to the sixteenth century,—which sailed from Guzerat and traversed the Indian Ocean.

Sir John Mandeville, an Englishman, in order to gratify his desire of seeing distant and foreign countries, served as a volunteer under the Sultan of Egypt and the Grand Khan of Cathai. He travelled through Turkey, Armenia, Egypt, Africa, Syria, Arabia, Persia, Chaldea, Ethiopia, Tartary, India, and China. There is, however, little information in his travels on our present subject. He represents the Venetians as not only trading regularly to Ormus, but sometimes even penetrating as for as Cambalu. Famagusta, in Cyprus, according to him, was one of the most commercial places in the world, the resort of merchants of all nations, Christians and Mahomedans.

Some curious and interesting particulars on the subject of Oriental commerce are scattered in the travels of Clavigo, who formed part of an embassy sent by Henry III. of Castile to Tamerlane, in 1403. Clavigo returned to Spain in 1406. He passed through Constantinople, which he represents as not one-third inhabited, up the Black Sea to Trebizond. Hence he traversed Armenia, the north of Persia, and Khorasan. Tauris, according to him, enjoyed a lucrative commerce: in its warehouses were an abundance of pearls, silk, cotton goods, and perfumed oils. Sultania also was a great mart for Indian commodities. Every year, between June and August, caravans arrived at this place. Cotton goods of all colours, and cotton yarn were brought from Khorasan; pearls and precious stones from Ormus; but the principal lading of the caravans consisted of spices of various kinds: at Sultania these were always found in great abundance, and of the best quality. From Tauris to Samarcand there were regular stations, at which horses were always ready to convey the orders of the khan or travellers. We are indebted to Clavigo for the first information of this new route of the commerce between India and Europe, by Sultania: it is supposed to have been adopted on the destruction of Bagdat by the Moguls; but we learn from other travellers that, towards the end of the fifteenth century, Sultania was remarkable for nothing besides the minarets of a mosque, which were made of metal, and displayed great taste and delicacy of workmanship.

Tamerlane lived in excessive magnificence and luxury at Samarcand; hither he had brought all his captives, who were expert in any kind of manufacture, especially in the silks of Damascus, and the sword cutlery of Turkey. To this city the Russians and Tartars brought leather, hides, furs, and cloth: silk goods, musk, pearls, precious stones, and rhubarb, were brought from China, or Cathay. Six months were occupied in bringing merchandize from Cambalu, the capital of Cathai, to Samarcand; two of these were spent in the deserts. Samarcand had also a trade with India, from which were received mace and other fine spices. Clavigo remarks, that such spices were never brought to Alexandria.

Schildeberger, a native of Munich, was taken prisoner by the Turks in 1394: he afterwards accompanied Tamerlane in his campaigns till the year 1406. During this period, and his subsequent connexion with other Tartar chiefs, he visited various parts of central Asia. But as he had not an opportunity of writing down at the time what he saw and learnt, his narrative is neither full, nor altogether to be depended upon for its accuracy. He was, besides, illiterate, And therefore it is often extremely difficult to ascertain, from his orthography, what places he actually means to name or describe. With all these drawbacks and imperfections, however, there are a few points on which he gives credible and curious information. He particularizes the silk of Strana, and of Schirevan; and adds, that from the last the raw silk is sent to Damascus, and there manufactured into the stuffs or damasks, for which it was already so celebrated. Fine silk was produced at Bursa, and exported to Venice and Lucca, for the manufacture of velvet. It ought to be mentioned, that he takes no notice of Saray and Astrakan, the latter of which was taken and destroyed by Tamerlane, in 1395. The wild asses in the mountainous deserts, and the dogs which were harnessed to sledges, are particularly mentioned by this traveller.

The interior parts of the north of Asia were visited, in 1420, by the ambassadors of the Emperor Tamerlane's son; and their journey is described in the Book of the Wonders of the World, written by the Persian historian, Emir Khond, from which it was translated into Dutch by Witsen, in his Norden Oste Tartarye. Their route was through Samarcand to Cathay. On entering this country, we are informed of a circumstance strikingly characteristic of Chinese policy and suspicion. Cathayan secretaries took down, in writing, the names of the ambassadors, and the number of their suite. This was repeated at another place, the ambassadors being earnestly requested to state the exact number of their servants; and the merchants, who were with him, having been put down by him under the description of servants, were, on that account, obliged to perform the particular duties under which they were described. Among the presents made by the emperor to the ambassadors, tin is mentioned. Paper-money seems, at this period, to have given place to silver, which, however, from several circumstances mentioned, must have been very scarce.

From the travels of Josaphat Barbaro, an ambassador from Venice, first to Tana (Azof), and then to Persia, some information may be drawn respecting the commerce of these parts of Asia, about the middle of the fifteenth century. He particularly describes the Wolga as being navigable to within three days' journey of Moscow, the inhabitants of which sail down it every year to Astrakan for salt. Astrakan was formerly a place of consequence and trade, but had been laid waste by Tamerlane. Russia is a fertile country, but extremely cold. Oxen and other beasts are carried to market in the winter, slaughtered, with their entrails taken out, and frozen so hard, that it is impossible to cut them up: they are very numerous and cheap. The only fruits are apples, nuts, and walnuts. Bossa, a kind of beer, is made in Russia. This liquor is still drank in Russia: it is made from millet, and is very inebriating. The drunkenness of the Russians is expressly and pointedly dwelt upon. Barbaro adds, that the grand duke, in order to check this vice, ordered that no more beer should be brewed, nor mead made, nor hops used. The Russians formerly paid tribute to Tartary; but they had lately conquered a country called Casan; to the left of the Wolga, in its descent. In this country a considerable trade is carried on, especially in furs, which are sent by way of Moscow to Poland, Prussia, and Flanders. The furs, however, are not the produce of Kasan, but of countries to the north-east, at a great distance.

Barbaro is very minute and circumstantial in his description of the manners, dress, food, &c. of the Georgians. He visited the principal towns of Persia. Schiraz contained 200,000 inhabitants. Yezd was distinguished and enriched by its silk manufactures.

CHAPTER V

Historical Sketch Of The Progress Of Discovery And Commerce,
From The Middle Of The Fifteenth To The Beginning Of The
Nineteenth Century.

The improvement of mankind in knowledge and civilization evidently depends on the union of three circumstances,—enlarged and increased desires, obstacles in the way of obtaining the objects of these desires, and practicable means of overcoming or removing these obstacles. The history of mankind in all ages and countries justifies and illustrates the truth of this remark; for though it is, especially in the early periods of it, very imperfect and obscure, and even in the later periods almost entirely confined to war and politics, still there are in it sufficient traces of the operation of all those three causes towards their improvement in knowledge and civilization.

That they operated in extending the progress of discovery and commerce is evident. We have already remarked that from the earliest periods, the commodities of the east attracted the desires of the western nations: the Arabians, Carthaginians, Greeks, and Romans of the ancient world; the Italian and Hanseatic states of the middle ages, all endeavoured to enrich themselves by trading in commodities so eagerly and universally desired. As industry and skill increased, and as the means as well as the desire of purchase and enjoyment spread, by the rise of a middle class in Europe, the demand for these commodities extended. The productions and manufactures of the north, as well as of the south of Europe, having been increased and improved, enabled the inhabitants of these countries to participate in those articles from India, which, among the ancients, had been confined exclusively to the rich and powerful.

On the other hand, even at the very time that this enlarged demand for Indian commodities was taking place in Europe, and was accompanied by enlarged means as well as extended skill and expedience in discovery and commerce,—at this very time obstacles arose which threatened the almost entire exclusion of Europeans from the luxuries of Asia. It may well be doubted, whether, if the enemies of the Christian faith had not gained entire possession of all the routes to India, and moreover, if these routes had been rendered more easy of access and passage, they could have long supplied the increased demands of improving Europe. But that Europe should, on the one hand, improve and feel enlarged desires as well as means of purchasing the luxuries of the east, while on the other hand, the practicability of acquiring these luxuries should diminish, formed a coincidence of circumstances, which was sure to produce important results.

As access to India by land, or even by the Arabian Gulf by sea, was rendered extremely difficult and hazardous by the enmity of the Mahometans, or productive of little commercial benefit by their exactions, the attention and hopes of European navigators were directed to a passage to India along the western coast of Africa. As, however, the length and difficulties of such a voyage were extremely formidable, it would probably have been either not attempted at all, or have required much longer time to accomplish than it actually did, if, in addition and aid of increased desires and an enlarged commercial spirit, the means of navigating distant, extensive, and unknown seas, had not likewise been, about this period, greatly improved.

We allude, principally, to the discovery of the mariners' compass. The first clear notice of it appears in a Provençal poet of the end of the twelfth century. In the thirteenth century it was used by the Norwegians in their voyages to and from Iceland, who made it the device of an order of knighthood of the highest rank; and from a passage in Barber's Bruce, it must have been known in Scotland, if not used there in 1375, the period when he wrote. It is said to have been used in the Mediterranean voyages at the end of the thirteenth or beginning of the fourteenth century.

With respect to the nations of the east, it is doubted whether they derived their knowledge of it from the Europeans, or the Europeans from them. When we reflect on the long and perilous voyages of the Arabians, early in the Christian era, we might be led to think that they could not be performed without the assistance of the compass; but no mention of it, or allusion to it, occurs in the account of any of their voyages; and we are expressly informed by Nicolo di Conti, who sailed on board a native vessel in the Indian seas, about the year 1420, that the Arabians had no compass, but sailed by the stars of the southern pole; and that they knew how to measure their elevation, as well as to keep their reckoning, by day and night, with their distance from place to place. With respect to the Chinese, the point in dispute is not so easily determined: it is generally imagined, that they derived their knowledge of the compass from Europeans: but Lord Macartney, certainly a competent judge, has assigned his reasons for believing that the Chinese compass is original, and not borrowed, in a dissertation annexed to Dr. Vincent's Periplus of the Erythrean Sea. At what period it was first known among them, cannot be ascertained; they pretend that it was known before the age of Confucius. That it was not brought from China to Europe by Marco Polo, as some writers assert, is evident from the circumstance that this traveller never mentions or alludes to it. The first scientific account of the properties of the magnet, as applicable to the mariner's compass, appears in a letter written by Peter Adsiger, in the year 1269. This letter is preserved among the manuscripts of the university of Leyden; extracts from it are given by Cavallo, in the second edition of his Treatise on Magnetism. From these extracts it is evident that he was acquainted with the attraction, repulsion, and polarity of the magnet, the art of communicating those properties to iron, the variation of the magnetic needle; and there are even some indications that he was acquainted with the construction of the azimuth compass.

Next in importance and utility to the mariners' compass, in preparing the way for the great discoveries by which the fifteenth century is distinguished, maps and charts may be placed. For though, in general, they were constructed on very imperfect and erroneous notions of the form of the world, and the relative size and situation of different countries, yet occasionally there appeared maps which corrected some long established error, or supplied some new information; and even the errors of the maps, in some cases, not improbably held out inducements or hopes, which would not otherwise have been entertained and realized, as we have already remarked, after D'Anville, that the greatest of Ptolemy's errors proved eventually the efficient cause which led to the greatest discovery of the moderns.

Malte Brun divides the maps of the middle ages into two classes: those in which the notions of Ptolemy and other ancient geographers are implicitly copied, and those in which new countries are inserted, which had been either discovered, or were supposed to exist.

In most of the maps of the first description, Europe, Asia, and Africa are laid down as forming one immense island, and Africa is not carried so far as the equator. One of the most celebrated of these maps was drawn up by Marin Sanuto, and inserted in his memorial presented to the pope and the principal sovereigns of Europe, for the purpose of persuading and shewing them, that if they would oblige their merchants to trade only through the dominions of the Caliphs of Bagdat, they would be better supplied and at a cheaper rate, and would have no longer to fear the Soldans of Egypt. This memorial with its maps was inserted in the Gesta Dei per Francos, as we are assured by the editor, from one of the original copies presented by Sanuto to some one of the princes. Hence, as Dr. Vincent remarks, it probably contains the oldest map of the world at this day extant, except the Peutingerian tables. Sanuto, as we have already noticed, in giving an abstract of the commercial information contained in his memorial, lived in 1324.

In the monastery of St. Michael di Murano, there is a planisphere, said to be drawn up in 1459, by Fra Mauro, which contains a report of a ship from India having passed the extreme point south, 2000 miles towards the west and southwest in 1420.

Ramusio describes a map, supposed to be this, which he states to have been drawn up for the elucidation of Marco Polo's travels.

On this map, so far as it relates to the circumnavigation of Africa, Dr. Vincent has given a dissertation, having procured a *fac-simile* copy from Venice, which is deposited in the British Museum; the substance of this dissertation we shall here compress. He divides his dissertation into three parts. First, whether this was the map noticed by Ramusio, and by him supposed to be drawn up to elucidate the travels of Marco Polo. On this point he concludes that it was the map referred to by Ramusio, but that his information respecting it is not correct. The second point to be determined is, whether the map procured from Venice was really executed by Mauro, and whether it existed previous to the Portuguese discoveries on the west coast of Africa. Manro lived in the reign of Alphonso the Fifth, that is between 1438 and 1480; the whole of this map, therefore, is prior to Diaz and Gama, two celebrated Portuguese navigators. Consequently, if it can be proved that the map obtained by Dr. Vincent is genuine, it must have existed previous to the Portuguese discoveries. The proof of the genuineness of the map is derived from the date on the planisphere, 1459; the internal evidence on the work itself; and the fact that Alphonso, or Prince Henry of Portugal, who died in 1463, received a copy of this map from Venice, and deposited it in the monastery of Alcobaca, where it is still kept. The sum paid for this copy, and the account of expenditure, are detailed in a MS. account in the monastery of St. Michael.

The third, and by far the most important part of Dr. Vincent's dissertation, examines what the map contains respecting the termination cf Africa to the south. On the first inspection of the map it is evident, that the author has not implicitly followed Ptolemy, as he professes to do. The centre of the habitable world is fixed at Bagdat. Asia and Europe he defines rationally, and Africa so far as regards its Mediterranean coast. He assigns two sources to the Nile, both in Abyssinia. On the east coast of Africa, he carries an arm of the sea between an island which he represents as of immense size, and the continent, obliquely as far nearly as the latitude and longitude of the Cape of Good Hope. This island he calls Diab, and the termination on the south, which he makes the extreme point of Africa, Cape Diab.

The great object of Mauro, in drawing up this map, was to encourage the Portuguese in the prosecution of their voyages to the south of Africa. This is known to be the fact from other sources, and the construction of the map, as well as some of the notices and remarks, which are inserted in its margin, form additional evidence that this was the case. Two passages, as Dr. Vincent observes, will set this in the clearest light. The first is inserted at Cape Diab; "here," says the author, about the year 1420, "an Indian vessel, on her passage across the Indian ocean was caught by a storm, and carried 2000 miles beyond this Cape to the west and south-west; she was seventy days in returning to the Cape." This the author regards as a full proof that Africa was circumnavigable on the south.

In the second passage, inserted on the margin, after observing that the Portuguese had been round the continent of Africa, more than 2000 miles to the south-west beyond the Straits of Gibraltar; that they found the navigation easy and safe, and had made charts of their discoveries; he adds, that he had talked with a person worthy of credit, who assured him he had been carried by bad weather, in an Indian ship, out of the Indian Ocean, for forty days, beyond Cape Sofala and the Green Islands, towards the west and south-west, and that in the opinion of the astronomer on board, (such as all Indian ships carry,) they had been hurried away 2000 miles. He concludes by expressing his firm belief that the sea surrounding the southern and south-eastern part of the world is navigable; and that the Indian Sea is ocean, and not a lake. We may observe, by the bye, that in another passage inserted in the margin, he expressly declares that the Indian ships had no compass, but were directed by an astronomer on board, who was continually making his observations.

It is evident that the two accounts are at variance, as the first asserts that the passage was round Cape Diab, at the termination of Africa, and the second that it was round Cape Sofala, fifteen degrees to the north of the extremity of this quarter of the world: but without attempting to reconcile this contradiction, it is abundantly evident that Mauro, by noticing the Portuguese navigators, as having reached 2000 miles to the south of Gibraltar, and adding that 2000 miles more of the coast of Africa had been explored by an Indian ship, meant to encourage the further enterprises of the Portuguese, by the natural inference that a very small space of unsailed sea must lie between the two lines, which were the limits of the navigation of the Portuguese and Indian vessel. The unexplored space was indeed much greater than Mauro estimated and represented it in his map to be; but, as Dr. Vincent remarks, his error in this respect manifestly contributed to the prosecution of the Portuguese designs, as the error of the ancient geographers, in approximating China to Europe, produced the discovery of America by Columbus.

We have dwelt thus long on the map of Mauro, as being by far the most important of the maps of the second description, or those in which were inserted real or supposed discoveries. The rest of this description require little notice.

A map of the date of 1346, in Castilian, represents Cape Bojada in Africa as known, and having been doubled at that period. A manuscript, preserved at Genoa, mentions that a ship had sailed from Majorca to a river called Vedamel, or Rui Jaura (probably Rio-do-Ouro,) but her fate was not known. The Genoese historians relate that two of their countrymen in 1291, attempted to reach India by the west; the fate of this enterprize is also unknown. The Canary Islands, the first discovery of which is supposed to have taken place before the Christian era, and which were never afterwards completely lost sight of, being described by the Arabian geographers, appear in a Castilian map of 1346. Teneriffe is called in this map Inferno, in conformity with the popular notion of the ancients, that these islands were the seat of the blessed. In a map of 1384, there is an island called Isola-di-legname, or the Isle of Wood, which, from this appellation, and its situation, is supposed by some geographers to be the island of Madeira. It would seem that some notions respecting the Azores were obscurely entertained towards the end of the fourteenth century, as islands nearly in their position are laid down in the maps of 1380.

In the library of St. Marc, at Venice, there is a map drawn by Bianco, in 1436. In it the ancient world is represented as forming one great continent, divided into two unequal parts by the Mediterranean, and by the Indian Ocean, which is carried from east to west, and comprises a great number of islands. Africa stretches from west to east parallel to Europe and Asia, but it terminates to the north of the equator. The peninsula of India and the Gulf of Bengal scarcely appear. The eastern part of Asia consists of two great peninsulas, divided by an immense gulf. Then appear Cathai, Samarcand, and some other places, the names of which are unintelligible. All the kingdoms of Europe are laid down except Poland and Hungary. To the west of the Canaries, a large tract of country is laid down under the appellation of Antitia; some geographers have maintained that by this America was indicated, but there does not appear any ground for this belief.

Having offered these preliminary and preparatory observations, we shall now proceed to the discoveries of the Portuguese. From the slight sketch which has already been given of the progress of geography and commerce, between the time of Ptolemy and the fifteenth century, it appears that the Portuguese had distinguished themselves less, perhaps, than any other European nation, in these pursuits; but, long before the beginning of the fifteenth century, circumstances had occurred, connected with their history, which were preparing the way for their maritime enterprizes. So early as the year 1250, the Portuguese had succeeded in driving the Moors out of their country; and, in order to prevent them from again disturbing them, they in their turn invaded Fez and Morocco, and having conquered Ceuta in 1415, fortified it, and several harbours near it, on the shores of the Atlantic. So zealous were the Portuguese in their enterprizes against the Moors, that the ladies of Lisbon partook in the general enthusiasm, and refused to bestow their hand on any man who had not signalized his courage on the coast of Africa, The spirit of the nation was largely participated by Prince Henry, the fifth son of John I., king of Portugal, who took up his residence near Cape St. Vincent, in the year 1406. The sole passion and object of his mind was to further the advancement of his country in navigation and discovery: his regard for religion led him to endeavour to destroy or diminish the power of the Mahometans; and his patriotism to acquire for Portugal that Indian commerce, which had enriched the maritime states of Italy. He sought every means and opportunity by which he could increase or render more accurate his information respecting the western coast, and the interior of Africa: and it is probable that the relations of certain Jews and Arabs, respecting the gold mines of Guinea, weighed strongly with him in the enterprizes which he planned, encouraged, and accomplished.

It is not true, however, that he was the inventor of the astrolobe and the compass, or the first that put these instruments into the hands of navigators, though he undoubtedly was an excellent mathematician, and procured the best charts and instruments of the age: the use and application of these, he taught in the best manner to those he selected to command his ships.

With respect to the compass, we have already stated all that is certainly known respecting its earliest application to the purposes of navigation. The sea astrolobe, which is an instrument for taking the altitude of the sun, stars, &c., is described by Chaucer, in 1391, in a treatise on it, addressed to his little son, Louis; and Purchas informs us, that it was formerly applied only to astronomical purposes, but was accommodated to the use of seamen by Martin Behaim, at the command of John II., king of Portugal, about the year 1487.

About the year 1418, when Prince Henry first began his plan of discovery, Cape Nun, in latitude 28° 40', was the limit of European knowledge on the coast of Africa. With this part of the coast, the Portuguese had become acquainted in consequence of their wars with the Moors of Barbary. In 1418, two of Henry's commanders reached Cape Boyada in latitute 26° 30'; but the Cape was not actually doubled till 1434. The Canary islands were visited during the same voyage that the Cape was discovered: Madeira was likewise visited or discovered; it was first called St. Laurence, after the saint of the day on which it was seen, and afterwards Madeira, on account of its woods. In 1420, the Portuguese set fire to these woods, and afterwards planted the sugar cane, which they brought from Sicily, and the vines which they brought from Cyprus. Saw mills were likewise erected on it.

About the year 1432, Gonzalos was sent with two small vessels to the coast of Africa on new discoveries. In 1434, Cape Boyada was doubled: in 1442, the Portuguese had advanced as far as Rio-do-Ouro, under the tropic of Cancer. On the return of the ships from this voyage, the inhabitants of Lisbon first saw, with astonishment, negroes of a jet black complexion, and woolly hair, quite different from the slaves which had been hitherto brought from Africa; for, before this time, they had seized, and sold as slaves, the tawny Moors, which they met with on the coast of Africa. In the year 1442, however, some of these had been redeemed by their friends, in exchange for negroes and gold dust. This last article stimulated the avarice of the Portuguese to greater exertions, than Prince Henry had been able to excite, and an African company was immediately formed to obtain it, slaves, &c.; but their commerce was exclusively confined to the coast of Africa, to the south of Sierra Leone. Dr. Vincent justly remarks, that Henry had stood alone for almost forty years, and had he fallen before these few ounces of gold reached his country, the spirit of discovery might have perished with him, and his designs might have been condemned as the dreams of a visionary. The importation of this gold, and the establishment of the African company in Portugal, to continue the remark of the same author, is the primary date, to which we may refer that turn for adventure which sprung up in Europe, which pervaded all the ardent spirits in every country for the two succeeding centuries, and which never ceased till it had united the four quarters of the globe in commercial intercourse.

In 1445, the Portuguese reached Senegal, where they first saw Pagan negroes: in 1448 and 1449, their discoveries extended to Cape Verd. The islands of that name were discovered in 1456. The exact extent of their discoveries from this time till 1463, when Prince Henry died, is not certainly known. According to some, Cape Verd, or Rio Grande, was the limit; according to others, one navigator reached as far as the coast of Guinea, and Cape Mesanado: some extend the limit even as far south as the equator. Assuming, however, Rio Grande as the limit of the discoveries made in Prince Henry's time, Rio Grande is in latitude 11 north, and the straits of Gibraltar in latitude 36 north; the Portuguese had therefore advanced 25 degrees to the south; that is 1500 geographical, or 1750 British miles, which, with the circuit of the coast, may be estimated at 2000 miles.

For nearly 20 years after the death of Prince Henry, little progress was made by the Portuguese in advancing to the south. At the time of the death of Alonzo, in 1481, they had passed the equator, and reached Cape St. Catherine; in latitude S. 2° 30'. The island of St. Thomas under the line, which was discovered in 1471, was immediately planted with sugar cane; and a fort, which was built the same year on the gold coast, enabled them to extend their knowledge of this part of Africa to a little distance inland. Portugal now began to reap the fruits of her discoveries: bees' wax, ostrich feathers, negro slaves, and particularly gold, were imported, on all of which the profits were so great, that John II., who succeeded Alonzo, immediately on his accession, sent out 12 ships to Guinea; and in 1483, two other vessels were sent, which in the following year reached Congo, and penetrated to 22° south. The river Zaire in this part of Africa was discovered, and many of the inhabitants of the country through which it flows embarked voluntarily for Portugal. Benin was discovered about the same time; here they found a species of spice, which was imported in great quantities into Europe, and sold as pepper: it was, however, nothing else but grains of paradise. The inhabitants of Benin must have had considerable traffic far into the interior of Africa, for from them the Portuguese first received accounts of Abyssinia. By the discovery and conquest of Benin and Congo, the Portuguese traffic in slaves was much extended, but at the same time it took another character for a short time; for the love of gold being stronger than the hope of gain they might derive from the sale of negroes, (for which, indeed, till the discovery of the West Indies there was little demand,) the Portuguese used to exchange the natives they captured for gold with the Moors, till John II. put an end to this traffic, under the pretence that by means of it, the opportunity of converting the negroes was lost, as they were thus delivered into the hands of Infidels. About eighty years after Prince Henry began his discoveries, John I. sent out Diaz with three ships: this was in 1486, and in the following year Covilham was sent by the same monarch in search of India, by the route of Egypt and the Red Sea.

The king displayed great judgment in the selection of both these persons. Diaz was of a family, several members of which had already signalized themselves by the discoveries on the coast of Africa. His mode of conducting the enterprize on which he was sent, proved at once his confidence in himself, his courage, and his skill; after reaching 24° south latitude, 120 leagues beyond any former navigator, he stood right out to sea, and never came within sight of the coast again, till he had reached 40 degrees to the eastward of the Cape, which, however, he was much too far out at sea to discover. He persevered in stretching still farther east, after he made land, till at length he reached the river Del Infante, six degrees to the eastward of the most southern point of Africa, and almost a degree beyond the Cape of Good Hope. He then resolved to return, for what reason is not known; and on his return, he saw the Cape of Good Hope, to which, on account of the storms he encountered on his passage round it, he gave the appellation of Cabo Tormentoso. John II., however, augured so well from the doubling of the extremity of Africa having been accomplished, that he changed its name into that of the Cape of Good Hope.

As soon as John II. ascended the throne, he sent two friars and a layman to Jerusalem, with instructions to gain whatever information they could respecting India and Prester John from the pilgrims who resorted to that city, and, if necessary, to proceed further to the east. As, however, none of this party understood Arabic, they were of little use, and in fact did not go beyond Jerusalem. In 1487, the king sent Covilham and Paayva on the same mission: the former had served in Africa as a soldier, and was intimately acquainted with

Arabic. In order to facilitate this enterprise, Covilham was entrusted with a map, drawn up by two Jews, which most probably was a copy of the map of Mauro, of which we have already spoken. On this map, a passage round the south of Africa was laid down as having been actually accomplished, and Covilham was directed to reach Abyssinia, if possible; and ascertain there or elsewhere, whether such a passage did really exist. Covilham went from Naples to Alexandria, and thence to Cairo. At this city he formed an acquaintance with some merchants of Fez and Barbary, and in their company went to Aden. Here he embarked and visited Goa, Calicut, and other commercial cities of India, where he saw pepper and ginger, and heard of cloves and cinnamon. From India he returned to the east coast of Africa, down which he went as low as Sofala, "the last residence of the Arabs, and the limit of their knowledge in that age, as it had been in the age of the Periplus." He visited the gold mines in the vicinity of this place: and here he also learnt all the Arabs knew respecting the southern part of Africa, viz. that the sea was navigable to the south-west (and this indeed their countrymen believed, when the author of the Periplus visited them); but they knew not where the sea terminated. At Sofala also Covilham gained some information respecting the island of the Moon, or Madagascar. He returned to Cairo, by Zeila, Aden, and Tor. At Cairo, he sent an account of the intelligence to the king, and in the letter which contained it, he added, "that the ships which sailed down the coast of Guinea, might be sure of reaching the termination of the continent, by persisting in a course to the south, and that when they should arrive in the eastern ocean, their best direction must be to enquire for Sofala and the island of the Moon."

"It is this letter," observes Dr. Vincent, "above all other information, which, with equal justice and equal honour, assigns the theoretical discovery to Covilham, as the practical to Diaz and Gama; for Diaz returned without hearing any thing of India, though he had passed the Cape, and Gama did not sail till after the intelligence of Covilham had ratified the discovery of Diaz." One part of the instructions given to Covilham required him to visit Abyssinia: in order to accomplish this object, he returned to Aden, and there took the first opportunity of entering Abyssinia. The sovereign of his country received and treated him with kindness, giving him a wife and land. He entered Abyssinia in 1488, and in 1521, that is, 33 years afterwards, the almoner to the embassy of John de Lima found him. Covilham, notwithstanding he was as much beloved by the inhabitants as by their sovereign, was anxious to return to Portugal, and John de Lima, at his request, solicited the king to grant him permission to that effect, but he did not succeed. "I dwell," observes Dr. Vincent, "with a melancholy pleasure on the history of this man,—whom Alvarez, the almoner, describes still as a brave soldier and a devout Christian;—when I reflect upon what must have been his sentiments on hearing the success of his countrymen, in consequence of the discovery to which he so essentially contributed. *They* were sovereigns of the ocean from the Cape of Good Hope to the straits of Malacca: *he* was still a prisoner in a country of barbarians."

It might have been supposed, that after it had been ascertained by Diaz that the southern promontory of Africa could be doubled, and by Covilham, that this was the only difficulty to a passage by sea to India, the court of Portugal would have lost no time in prosecuting their discoveries, and completing the grand object they had had in view for nearly a century: this, however, was not the case. Ten years, and another reign, and great debates in the council of Portugal were requisite before it was resolved that the attempt to prosecute the discovery of Diaz to its completion was expedient, or could be of any advantage to the nation at large. At last, when Emanuel, who was their sovereign, had determined on prosecuting the discovery of India, his choice of a person to conduct the enterprise fell on Gama. As he had armorial bearings, we may justly suppose that he was of a good family; and in all respects he appears to have been well qualified for the grand enterprise to which he was called, and to have resolved, from a sense of religion and loyalty, to have devoted himself to death, if he should not succeed. Diaz was appointed to a command under him, but he had not the satisfaction of witnessing the results of his own discovery; for he returned when the fleet had reached St. Jago, was employed in a secondary command under Cabral, in the expedition in which Brazil was discovered, and in his passage from that country to the Cape, four ships, one of which he commanded, perished with all on board.

As soon as the fleet which Gama was to take with him was ready for sea, the king, attended by all his court, and a great body of the people, formed a solemn procession to the shore, where they were to embark, and Gama assumed the command, under the auspices of the most imposing religious ceremonies. Nearly all who witnessed his embarkation regarded him and those who accompanied him "rather as devoted to destruction, than as sent to the acquisition of renown."

The fleet which was destined to accomplish one of the objects (the discovery of America is the other)—which, as Dr. Robertson remarks, "finally established those commercial ideas and arrangements which constitute the chief distinction between the manners and policy of ancient and modern times,"—consisted only of three small ships, and a victualler, manned with no more than 160 souls: the principal officers were Vasco de Gama, and Paul his brother: Diaz and Diego Diaz, his brother, who acted as purser: and Pedro Alanquer, who had been pilot to Diaz. Diaz was to accompany them only to a certain latitude.

They sailed from Lisbon on the 18th of July, 1497: in the bay of St. Helena, which they reached on the 4th of November, they found natives, who were not understood by any of the negro interpreters they had on board. From the description of the peculiarity in their mode of utterance, which the journal of the voyage calls sighing, and from the circumstance that the same people were found in the bay of St. Blas, 60 leagues beyond the Cape, there can be no doubt that they were Hottentots. In consequence of the ignorance or the obstinacy of the pilot, and of tempestuous weather, the voyage to the Cape was long and dangerous: this promontory, however, was doubled on the 20th of November. After this the wind and weather proving favourable, the voyage was more prosperous and rapid. On the 11th of January, 1498, they reached that part of the coast where the natives were no longer Hottentots, but Caffres, who at that period displayed the same marks of superior civilization by which they are distinguished from the Hottentots at present.

From the bay of St. Helena till they passed Cape Corrientes, there had been no trace of navigation,—no symptom that the natives used the sea at all. But after they passed this cape, they were visited by the natives in boats, the sails of which seem to have been made of the fibres of the cocoa-palm. A much more encouraging circumstance, however, occurred: some of the natives that came off in these boats were clothed in cotton, silk, and sattin,—evident proofs that intercourse, either direct or indirect, was practicable, and had in fact been held between this country and India. The language of these people was not understood; but from their signs it was inferred that they had seen ships as large as the Portuguese, and that they had come from the north.

This part of Africa lies between latitudes 19° and 18° south; and as Gama had the corrected chart of Covilham on board, in which Sofala was marked as the limit of his progress, and Sofala was two degrees to the south of where he then was, he must have known that he had now passed the barrier, and that the discovery was ascertained, his circumnavigation being now connected with the route of Covilham. This point of Gama's progress is also interesting and important in another respect, for we are here approaching a junction with the discoveries of the Arabians, the Egyptians, the Greeks, and the Romans.

At this place Gama remained till the 24th of February, repairing his ships and recruiting his men. On the 1st of March, he arrived off Mozambique; here evidences of a circumnavigation with India were strong and numerous. The sovereign of Mozambique ruled over all the country from Sofala to Melinda. The vessels, which were fitted out entirely for coasting voyages, were large, undecked, the seams fastened with cords made of the cocoa fibres, and the timbers in the same manner. Gama, in going on board some of the largest of those, found that they were equipped with charts and compasses, and what are called æst harlab, probably the sea astrolabe, already discovered. At the town of Mozambique, the Moorish merchants from the Red Sea and India, met and exchanged the gold of Sofala for their commodities, and in its warehouses, which, though meanly built, were numerous, pepper, ginger, cottons, silver, pearls, rubies, velvet, and other Indian articles were exposed to sale. At Mombaça, the next place to which Gama sailed, all the commodities of India were found, and likewise the citron, lemon, and orange; the houses were built of stone, and the inhabitants, chiefly Mahomedans, seemed to have acquired wealth by commerce, as they lived in great splendour and luxury.

On the 17th of March, 1498, Gama reached Melinda, and was consequently completely within the boundary of the Greek and Roman discovery and commerce in this part of the world. This city is represented as well built, and displaying in almost every respect, proofs of the extensive trade the inhabitants carried on with India, and of the wealth they derived from it. Here Gama saw, for the first time, Banians, or Indian merchants: from them he received much important information respecting the commercial cities of the west coast of

India: and at Melinda he took on board pilots, who conducted his fleet across the Indian Ocean to Calicut on the coast of Malabar, where he landed on the 22d of May, 1498, ten months and two days after his departure from Lisbon. He returned to Lisbon in 1499, and again received the command of a squadron in 1502; he died at Cochin in 1525, after having lived to witness his country sovereign of the Indian seas from Malacca to the Cape of Good Hope. "The consequence of his discovery was the subversion of the Turkish power, which at that time kept all Europe in alarm. The East no longer paid tribute for her precious commodities, which passed through the Turkish provinces; the revenues of that empire were diminished; the Othmans ceased to be a terror to the western world, and Europe has risen to a power, which the three other continents may in vain endeavour to oppose."

The successful enterprize of Gama, and the return of his ships laden not only with the commodities peculiar to the coast of Malabar, but with many of the richer and rarer productions of the eastern parts of India, stimulated the Portuguese to enter on this new career with avidity and ardour, both military and commercial. It fortunately happened that Emanuel, who was king of Portugal at this period, was a man of great intelligence and grasp of mind, capable of forming plans with prudence and judgment, and of executing them with method and perseverance; and it was equally fortunate that such a monarch was enabled to select men to command in India, who from their enterprize, military skill, sagacity, integrity, and patriotism, were peculiarly qualified to carry into full and successful execution all his views and plans.

The consequences were such as must always result from the steady operation of such causes: twenty-four years after the voyage of Gama, and before the termination of Emanuel's reign, the Portuguese had reached, and made themselves masters of Malacca. This place was the great staple of the commerce carried on between the east of Asia, including China, and the islands and the western parts of India. To it the merchants of China, Japan, the Moluccas, &c. came from the east, and those of Malabar, Ceylon, Coromandel and Bengal, from the west; and its situation, nearly at an equal distance from the eastern and western parts of India, rendered it peculiarly favorable for this trade, while by possessing the command of the straits through which all ships must pass from the one extremity of Asia to the other, it had the monopoly of the most extensive and lucrative commerce completely within its power.

From Malacca the Portuguese sailed for the conquest of the Moluccas; and by achieving this, secured the monopoly of spices. Their attempt to open a communication and trade with China, which was made about the same time, was not then successful: but by perseverance they succeeded in their object, and before the middle of the sixteenth century, exchanged, at the island of Sancian, the spices of the Moluccas, and the precious stones and ivory of Ceylon, for the silks, porcelain, drugs, and tea of China. Soon afterwards the emperor of China allowed them to occupy the island of Macao. In 1542 they succeeded in forming a commercial intercourse with Japan, trading with it for gold, silver and copper; this trade, however, was never extensive, and it ceased altogether in 1638, when they were driven from the Japanese territories.

As the commodities of India could not be purchased except with large quantities of gold, the Portuguese, in order to obtain it, as well as for other commercial advantages, prosecuted their discoveries on the east of Africa, at the same time that they were extending their power and commerce in India. On the east of Africa, between Sofala and the Red Sea, Arabian colonies had been settled for many centuries: these the Portuguese navigators visited, and gradually reduced to tribute; and the remains of the empire they established at this period, may still be traced in the few and feeble settlements they possess between Sofala and Melinda. In 1506 they visited and explored the island of Madagascar; in 1513, by the expulsion of the Arabs from Aden, the Red Sea was opened to their ships; and they quickly examined its shores and harbours, and made themselves acquainted with its tedious and dangerous navigation. In 1520 they visited the ports of Abyssinia, but their ambition and the security of their commerce were not yet completely attained; the Persian Gulf, as well as the Red Sea, was explored; stations were formed on the coasts of both: and thus they were enabled to obstruct the ancient commercial intercourse between Egypt and India, and to command the entrance of those rivers, by which Indian goods were conveyed not only through the interior of Asia, but also to Constantinople. By the conquest of Ormus, the Portuguese monopolised that extensive trade to the East, which had been in the hands of the Persians for several centuries. "In the hands of the Portuguese this island soon became the great mart from which the Persian empire, and all the provinces of Asia to the west of it, were supplied with the productions of India: and a city which they built on that barren island, destitute of water, was rendered one of the chief seats of opulence, splendour, and luxury in the eastern world."

The Venetians, who foresaw the ruin of their oriental commerce in the success of the Portuguese, in vain endeavoured to stop the progress of their rivals in the middle of the sixteenth century: the latter, masters of the east coast of Africa, of the coasts of Arabia and Persia, of the two peninsulas of India, of the Molucca islands, and of the trade to China and Japan, supplied every part of Europe with the productions of the east, by the Cape of Good Hope; nor was their power and commerce subverted, till Portugal became a province of Spain.

We have purposely omitted, in this rapid sketch of the establishment and progress of the Portuguese commerce in the East, any notice of the smaller discoveries which they made at the same time. These, however, it will be proper to advert to before we proceed to another subject.

In the year 1512, a Portuguese navigator was shipwrecked on the Maldives: he found them already in the occasional possession of the Arabians, who came thither for the cocoa fibres, of which they formed their cordage, and the cowries, which circulated as money from Bengal to Siam. The Portuguese derived from them immense quantities of these cowries, with which they traded to Guinea, Congo, and Benin. On their conquest, they obliged the sovereigns of this island to pay them tribute in cinnamon, pearls, precious stones, and elephants. The discovery and conquest of the Malaccas has already been noticed, and its importance in rendering them masters of the trade of both parts of India, which had been previously carried on principally by the merchants of Arabia, Persia from the West, and of China from the East. In Siam, gum lac, porcelain, and aromatics enriched the Portuguese, who were the first Europeans who arrived in this and the adjacent parts of this peninsula.

In the year 1511 the Portuguese navigators began to explore the eastern archipelago of India, and to make a more complete and accurate examination of some islands, which they had previously barely discovered. Sumatra was examined with great care, and from it they exported tin, pepper, sandal, camphire, &c. In 1513, they arrived at Borneo: of it, however, they saw and learned little, except that it also produced camphire. In the same year they had made themselves well acquainted with Java: here they obtained rice, pepper, and other valuable articles. It is worthy of remark, that Barros, the Portuguese historian of their discoveries and conquests in the East, who died towards the close of the sixteenth century, already foresaw that the immense number of islands, some of them very large, which were scattered in the south-east of Asia, would justly entitle this part, at some future period, to the appellation of the fifth division of the world. Couto, his continuator, comprehends all these islands under five different groups. To the first belong the Moluccas. The second archipelago comprises Gilolo, Moratai, Celebes, or Macassar, &c. The third group contains the great isle of Mindinao, Soloo, and most of the southern Philippines. The fourth archipelago was formed of the Banda isle, Amboyna, &c.; the largest of these were discovered by the Portuguese in the year 1511: from Amboyna they drew their supplies of cloves.

The Portuguese knew little of the fifth archipelago, because the inhabitants were ignorant of commerce, and totally savage and uncultivated. From the description given of them by the early Portuguese writers, as totally unacquainted with any metal, making use of the teeth of fish in its stead, and as being as black as the Caffres of Africa, while among them there were some of an unhealthy white colour, whose eyes were so weak that they could not bear the light of the sun;—from these particulars there can be no doubt that the Portuguese had discovered New Guinea, and the adjacent isles, to whose inhabitants this description exactly applies. These islands were the limit of the Portuguese discoveries to the East: they suspected, however, that there were other islands beyond them, and that these ranged along a great southern continent, which stretched as far as the straits of Magellan. It is the opinion of some geographers, and particularly of Malte Brun, that the Portuguese had visited the coasts of New Holland before the year 1540; but that they regarded it as part of the great southern continent, the existence of which Ptolemy had first imagined.

We have already alluded to the obstacles which opposed and retarded the commercial intercourse of the Portuguese with China. Notwithstanding these, they prosecuted their discoveries in the Chinese seas. In the year 1518, they arrived at the isles of Liqueou, where they found gold in abundance: the inhabitants traded as far as the Moluccas. Their intercourse with Japan has already been noticed.

From these results of the grand project formed by Prince Henry, and carried on by men animated by his spirit, (results so important to geography and commerce, and which mainly contributed to raise Europe to its present high rank in knowledge, civilization, wealth, and power,) we must now turn to the discovery of America, the second grand cause in the production of the same effects.

For the discovery of the new world we are indebted to Columbus. This celebrated person was extremely well qualified for enterprizes that required a combination of foresight, comprehension, decision, perseverance, and skill. From his earliest youth he had been accustomed to regard the sea as his peculiar and hereditary element; for the family, from which he was descended, had been navigators for many ages. And though, from all that is known respecting them, this line of life had not been attended with much success or emolument, yet Columbus's zeal was not thereby damped; and his parents, still anxious that their son should pursue the same line which his ancestors had done, strained every nerve to give him a suitable education. He was accordingly taught geometry, astronomy, geography, and drawing. As soon as his time of life and his education qualified him for the business he had chosen, he went to sea; he was then fourteen years old. His first voyages were from Genoa, of which city he was a native, to different ports in the Mediterranean, with which this republic traded. His ambition, however, was not long to be confined to seas so well known. Scarcely had he attained the age of twenty, when he sailed into the Atlantic; and steering to the north, ran along the coast of Iceland, and, according, to his own journal, penetrated within the arctic circle. In another voyage he sailed as far south as the Portuguese fort of St. George del Mina, under the equator, on the coast of Africa. On his return from this voyage, he seems to have engaged in a piratical warfare with the Venetians and Turks, who, at this period, disputed with the Genoese the sovereignty and commerce of the Mediterranean; and in this warfare he was greatly distinguished for enterprize, as well as for cool and undaunted courage.

At this period he was attracted to Lisbon by the fame which Prince Henry had acquired, on account of the encouragement he afforded to maritime discovery. In this city he married the daughter of a person who had been employed in the earlier navigations of the prince; and from his father-in-law he is said to have obtained possession of a number of journals, sea charts, and other valuable papers. As he had ascertained that the object of the Portuguese was to reach India by the southern part of Africa, he concluded, that, unless he could devise or suggest some other route, little attention would be paid to him. He, therefore, turned his thoughts to the practicability of reaching India by sailing to the west. At this time the rotundity of the earth was generally admitted. The ancients, whose opinions on the extent and direction of the countries which formed the terrestrial globe, still retained their hold on the minds even of scientific men, had believed that the ocean encompassed the whole earth; the natural and unavoidable conclusion was, that by sailing to the west, India would be reached. An error of Ptolemy's, to which we have already adverted, contributed to the belief that this voyage could not be very long; for, according to that geographer, (and his authority was implicitly acceded to,) the space to be sailed over was sixty degrees less than it actually proved to be,—a space equal to three-fourths, of the Pacific Ocean. From considering Marco Polo's account of his travels in the east of Asia, Columbus also derived great encouragement; for, according to him, Cathay and Zepango stretched out to a great extent in an easterly direction; of course they must approach so much the more towards the west of Europe. It is probable, also, that Columbus flattered himself, that if he did not reach India by a western course, he would, perhaps, discover the Atlantis, which was placed by Plato and Aristotle in the ocean, to the west of Europe.

Columbus, however, did not trust entirely to his own practical knowledge of navigation, or to the arguments he drew from a scientific acquaintance with cosmography: he heard the reports of skilful and experienced pilots, and corresponded with several men of science. He is said, in a particular manner to have been confirmed in his belief that India might be reached by sailing to the west, by the communications which he had with Paul, a physician of Florence, a man well known at this period for his acquaintance with geometry and cosmography, and who had paid particular attention to the discoveries of the Portuguese. He stated several facts, and offered several ingenious conjectures, and moreover, sent a chart to Columbus, on which he pointed out the course which he thought would lead to the desired object.

As Columbus was at the court of Lisbon, when he had resolved to undertake his great enterprise, and, in fact, regarded himself as in some degree a Portuguese subject, he naturally applied in the first instance to John II., requesting that monarch to let him have some ships to carry him to Marco Polo's island of Zepango or Japan. The king referred him to the Bishop of Ceuta and his two physicians; but they having no faith in the existence of this island, rejected the services of Columbus. For seven years afterwards he solicited the court of Spain to send him out, while, during the same period, his brother, Bartholomew, was soliciting the court of England: the latter was unsuccessful, but Columbus himself at length persuaded Isabella to grant 40,000 crowns for the service of the expedition. He accordingly sailed from Palos, in Andalusia, on the 3d of August, 1492; and in thirty-three days landed on one of the Bahamas. He had already sailed nine hundred and fifty leagues west from the Canaries: after touching at the Bahamas, he continued his course to the west, and at length discovered the island of Cuba. He went no farther on this voyage; but on his return home, he discovered Hispaniola. The variation of the compass was first observed in this voyage. In a second voyage, in 1492, Columbus discovered Jamaica, and in a third, in 1494, he visited Trinidad and the continent of America, near the mouth of the Orinoco. In 1502, he made a fourth and last voyage, in which he explored some part of the shores of the Gulph of Mexico. The ungrateful return he met with from his country is well known: worn out with fatigue, disappointment, and sorrow, he died at Valladolid, on the 20th of

May, 1506, in the fifty-ninth year of his age.

In the mean time, the completion of the discovery of America was rapidly advancing. In 1499, Ogeda, one of Columbus's companions, sailed for the new world: he was accompanied by Amerigo Vespucci: little was discovered on the voyage, except some part of the coast of Guana and Terra Firma. But Amerigo, having, on his return to Spain, published the first account of the New World, the whole of this extensive quarter of the globe was called after him. Some authors, however, contend that Amerigo visited the coasts of Guiana and Terra Firma before Columbus; the more probable account is, that he examined them more carefully two years after their discovery by Columbus. Amerigo was treated by the court of Spain with as little attention and gratitude as Columbus had been: he therefore offered his services to Portugal, and in two voyages, between 1500 and 1504, he examined the coasts of that part of South America which was afterwards called Brazil. This country had been discovered by Cabral, who commanded the second expedition of the Portuguese to India: on his voyage thither, a tempest drove him so far to the west, that he reached the shores of America. He called it the Land of the Holy Cross; but it was afterwards called Brazil, from the quantity of red wood of that name found on it.

For some time after the discovery of America it was supposed to be part of India: and hence, the name of the West Indies, still retained by the islands in the Gulph of Mexico, was given to all those countries. There were, however, circumstances which soon led the discoverers to doubt of the truth of the first conceived opinion. The Portuguese had visited no part of Asia, either continent or island, from the coast of Malabar to China, on which they had not found natives highly civilized, who had made considerable progress in the elegant as well as the useful arts of life, and who were evidently accustomed to intercourse with strangers, and acquainted with commerce. In all these respects, the New World formed a striking contrast: the islands were inhabited by savages, naked, unacquainted with the rudest arts of life, and indebted for their sustenance to the spontaneous productions of a fertile soil and a fine climate. The continent, for the most part, presented immense forests, and with the exception of Mexico and Peru, was thinly inhabited by savages as ignorant and low in the scale of human nature as those who dwelt on the islands.

The natural productions and the animals differed also most essentially from those, not only of India, but also of Europe. There were no lemons, oranges, pomegranates, quinces, figs, olives, melons, vines, nor sugar canes: neither apples, pears, plumbs, cherries, currants, gooseberries, rice, nor any other corn but maize. There was no poultry (except turkeys), oxen, sheep, goats, swine, horses, asses, camels, elephants, cats, nor dogs, except an animal resembling a dog, but which did not bark. Even the inhabitants of Mexico and Peru were unacquainted with iron and the other useful metals, and destitute of the address requisite for acquiring such command of the inferior animals, as to derive any considerable aid from their labour.

In addition to these most marked and decided points of difference between India and the newly discovered quarter of the globe, it was naturally inferred that a coast extending, as America was soon ascertained to do, many hundred miles to the northward and to the southward of the equator, could not possibly be that of the Indies. At last, in the year 1513, a view of the Grand Ocean having been attained from the mountains of Darien, the supposition that the New World formed part of India was abandoned. To this ocean the name of the South Sea was given.

In the mean time, the Portuguese had visited all the islands of the Malay Archipelago, as far as the Moluccas. Portugal had received from the Pope a grant of all the countries she might discover: the Spaniards, after the third voyage of Columbus, obtained a similar grant. As, however, it was necessary to draw a line between those grants, the Pope fixed on 27-1/2° west of the meridian of the island of Ferro. The sovereigns, for their mutual benefit, allowed it to 370 leagues west of the Cape Verd islands: all the countries to the east of this line were to belong to Portugal, and all those to the west of it to Spain. According to this line of demarcation, supposing the globe to be equally divided between the two powers, it is plain that the Moluccas were situated within the hemisphere which belonged to Spain. Portugal, however, would not yield them up, contending that she was entitled to the sovereignty of all the countries she could discover by sailing eastward. This dispute gave rise to the first circumnavigation of the globe, and the first practical proof that India could be reached by sailing westward from Europe, as well as to other results of the greatest importance to geography and commerce.

During the discussions which this unexpected and embarrassing difficulty produced, Francis Magellan came to the court of Spain, to offer his services as a navigator, suggesting a mode by which he maintained that court would be able to decide the question in its own favour. Magellan had served under Albuquerque, and had visited the Moluccas: and he proposed, if the Spanish monarch would give him ships, to sail to these islands by a westerly course, which would, even according to the Portuguese, establish the Spanish right to their possession. The emperor Charles, who was at this period king of Spain, joyfully embraced the proposal, although a short time previous, Solis, who had sailed in quest of a westerly passage to India, had, after discovering the Rio de la Plata, perished in the attempt.

It is maintained by some authors that Magellan's confidence in the success of his own plan arose from the information he received from a chart drawn up by Martin Behaim, in which the straits that were afterwards explored by Magellan, and named after him, were laid down; and that he carried the information he derived from it to Spain, and by means of it obtained the protection of Cardinal Ximenes, and the command of the fleet, with which he was the first to circumnavigate the world.

As this is a point which has been a good deal discussed, and as it is of importance, not only to the fame of Magellan, but to a right understanding of the actual state of geographical knowledge, with respect to the New World, at this era, it may be proper briefly to consider it.

The claim of Behaim rests entirely on a passage in Pigafetta's journal of the voyage of Magellan, in which it is stated that Magellan, as skilful as he was courageous, knew that he was to seek for a passage through an obscure strait: this strait he had seen laid down in a chart of Martin Behaim, a most excellent cosmographer, which was in the possession of the king of Portugal. In describing the nature of the maps and charts which, during the whole of the middle ages, were drawn up, we observed that it was very usual to insert countries, &c. which were merely supposed to exist. The question, therefore, is—allowing that a strait was laid down in a chart drawn up by Behaim, whether it was a conjectural strait or one laid down from good authority? That Behaim himself did not discover such a strait will be evident from the following circumstances: in the Nuremberg globe, formed by Behaim, it does not appear: there is nothing between the Azores and Japan, except the fabulous islands of Aulitia and St. Brandon; no mention of it is made in the archives of that city or in his numerous letters, which are still preserved. The date of the Nuremberg globe is 1492, the very year in which Columbus first reached the West Indies: Behaim therefore cannot be supposed to have contributed to this discovery. It is said, however, that he made a long voyage in 1483 and 1484: but this voyage was in an easterly direction, for it is expressly stated to have been to Ethiopia; probably to Congo, and the cargo he brought home, which consisted of an inferior kind of pepper, proves that he had not visited America. Besides, if he had visited any part of America in 1483 or 1484, he would have laid it down in his globe in 1492, whereas, as we have remarked, no country appears on it to the west of St. Brandon. We may, therefore, safely conclude that he did not himself discover any passage round the south point of America.

But all the other great discoveries of the Portuguese and Spaniards (except that of Diaz in 1486) were made between 1492, the date of the Nuremberg Globe, and 1506, the date of the death of Behaim, and between these periods, he constantly resided at Fayal. It is much more probable that he inserted this strait in his chart on supposition, thinking it probable that, as Africa terminated in a cape, so America would. That Magellan did not himself believe the strait was laid down in Behaim's chart from any authority is evident, from a circumstance mentioned by Pigafetta, who expressly informs us, that Magellan was resolved to prosecute his search after it to latitude 75°, had he not found it in latitude 52°. Now, as Behaim undoubtedly was the greatest cosmographer of the age, and had been employed to fit the astrolobe as a sea instrument, it is not to be supposed that, if he had good authority for the existence of a passage round South America, he would have left it in any chart he drew, with an uncertainty of 23 degrees.

Magellan sailed from Spain in 1519, with five ships: he explored the river Plate a considerable way, thinking at first it was the sea, and would lead him to the west. He then continued his voyage to the south, and reached the entrance of the straits which afterwards received his name, on the 21st October, 1520, but, in consequence of storms, and the scarcity of provisions, he did not clear them till the 28th of November. He now directed his course to the north-west: for three months and twenty days he saw no land. In 15 south, he discovered a small island; and another in 9 south. Continuing his course still in the same direction, he arrived at the Ladrones, and soon afterwards at the Phillippines, where he lost his life in a skirmish. His companions continued their voyage; and, on the twenty-seventh month after their departure from Spain, arrived at one of the Molucca islands. Here the Spaniards found plenty of spices, which they obtained in exchange for the cloth, glass, beads, &c., which they had brought with them for that purpose. From the Moluccas they returned home round the Cape of Good Hope, and reached Seville in September, 1552. Only one ship returned, and she was drawn up in Seville, and long preserved as a monument of the first circumnavigation of the globe. The Spaniards were surprised, on their return to their native country, to find that they had gained a day in their reckoning—a proof of the scanty knowledge at that time possessed, respecting one of the plainest and most obvious results of the diurnal motion of the earth.

The voyage of Magellan occupied 1124 days: Sir Francis Drake, who sailed round the world about half a century afterwards, accomplished the passage in 1051 days: the next circumnavigator sailed round the globe in 769 days; and the first navigators who passed to the south of Terra del Fuego, accomplished the voyage in 749 days. In the middle of the eighteenth century, a Scotch privateer sailed round the world in 240 days.

In the meantime, several voyages had been performed to the east coast of North America. The first voyages to this part of the new world were undertaken by the English: there is some doubt and uncertainty respecting the period when these were performed. The following seems the most probable account.

At the time when Columbus discovered America, there lived in London a Venetian merchant, John Cabot, who had three sons. The father was a man of science, and had paid particular attention to the doctrine of the spheres: his studies, as well as his business as a merchant, induced him to feel much interest in the discoveries which were at that period making. He seems to have applied to Henry VII.; who accordingly empowered him to sail from England under the royal flag, to make discoveries in the east, the west, and the north, and to take possession of countries inhabited by Pagans, and not previously discovered by other European nations. The king gave him two ships, and the merchants of Bristol three or four small vessels, loaded with coarse cloth, caps, and other small goods. The doubt respecting the precise date of this voyage seems to receive the most satisfactory solution from the following contemporary testimony of Alderman Fabian, who says, in his *Chronicle of England and France*, that Cabot sailed in the beginning of May, in the mayoralty of John Tate, that is, in 1497, and returned in the subsequent mayoralty of William Purchase, bringing with him three *sauvages* from Newfoundland. This fixes the date of this voyage: the course he steered, and the limits of his voyage, are however liable to uncertainty. He himself informs us, that he reached only 56° north latitude, and that the coast of America, at that part, winded to the east: but there is no coast of North America that answers to this description. According to other accounts, he reached 67-1/2° north latitude; but this is the coast of Greenland, and not the coast of Labrador, as these accounts call it. It is most probable that he did not reach farther than Newfoundland, which he certainly discovered. To this island he at first gave the names of Prima Vista and Baccaloas; and it is worthy of notice, that a cape of Newfoundland still retains the name of Bona Vista, and there is a small island still called Bacalao, not far from hence.

From this land he sailed to the south-west till he reached the latitude of Gibraltar, and the longitude of Cuba; if these circumstances be correct, he must have sailed nearly as far as Chesapeak Bay: want of provisions now obliged him to return to England.

Portugal, jealous of the discoveries which Spain had made in the new world, resolved to undertake similar enterprizes, with the double hope of discovering some new part of America, and a new route to India. Influenced by these motives, Certireal, a man of birth and family, sailed from Lisbon in 1500 or 1501: he arrived at Conception Bay, in Newfoundland, explored the east coast of that island, and afterwards discovered the river St. Lawrence. To the next country which he discovered, he gave the name of Labrador, because, from its latitude and appearance, it seemed to him better fitted for culture than his other discoveries in this part of America. This country he coasted till he came to a strait, which he called the Strait of Anian. Through this strait he imagined a passage would be found to India, but not being able to explore it himself, he returned to Portugal, to communicate the important and interesting information. He soon afterwards went out on a second voyage, to prosecute his discoveries in this strait; but in this he perished. The same voyage was undertaken by another brother, but he also perished. As the situation of the Strait of Anian was very imperfectly described, it was long sought for in vain on both sides of America; it is now generally supposed to have been Hudson's Strait, at the entrance of Hudson's Bay.

The Spaniards were naturally most alarmed at the prospect of the Portuguese finding a passage by this strait to India. Cortez, the conqueror of Mexico, undertook himself an expedition for this purpose; but he returned without accomplishing any thing. After him the viceroy, Mendoza, sent people, both by sea and land, to explore the coast as far as 53° north latitude; but neither party reached farther than 36 degrees. The Spanish court itself now undertook the enterprize; and in the year 1542, Cabrillo, a Portuguese in the service of that court, sailed from Spain. He went no farther than to 44 degrees north latitude, where he found it very cold. He coasted the countries which at present are called New California, as far as Cape Blanco: he discovered, likewise, Cape Mendocino; and ascertained, that from this place to the harbour De la Nadividad, the land continued without the intervention of any strait. In 1582, Gualle was directed by the king of Spain to examine if there was a passage to the east and north-east of Japan, that connected the sea of Asia with the South Sea. He accordingly steered from Japan to the E.N.E. about 300 leagues: here he found the current setting from the north and north-west, till he had sailed above 700 leagues, when he reckoned he was only 200 leagues from the coast of California. In this voyage he discovered those parts of the north-west coast of America which are called New Georgia and New Cornwall. At the beginning of the seventeenth century, the

Spaniards, alarmed at the achievements of Sir Francis Drake on this part of America, and still anxious to discover, if possible, the Straits of Anian, sent out Sebastian Viscaino from Acapulco: he examined the coasts as far as Cape Mendocino, and discovered the harbour of Montery. One of his ships reached the latitude of 43 degrees, where the mouth of a strait, or a large river, was said to have been discovered.

The expedition of Sir Francis Drake, though expressly undertaken for the purpose of distressing the Spaniards in their new settlements, must be noticed here, on account of its having contributed also, in some degree, to the geographical knowledge of the north-west coast of America. He sailed from Plymouth on the 15th November, 1577, with five vessels, (the largest only 100 tons, and the smallest 15,) and 164 men. On the 20th of August, 1578, he entered the Strait of Magellan, which he cleared on the 6th of September: "a most extraordinary short passage," observes Captain Tuckey, "for no navigator since, though aided by the immense improvements in navigation, has been able to accomplish it in less than 36 days." After coasting the whole of South America to the extremity of Mexico, he resolved to seek a northern passage into the Atlantic. With this intention, he sailed along the coast, to which, from its white cliffs, he gave the name of New Albion. When he arrived, however, at Cape Blanco, the cold was so intense, that he abandoned his intention of searching for a passage into the Atlantic, and crossed the Pacific to the Molucca islands. In this long passage he discovered only a few islands in 20° north latitude: after an absence of 1501 days, he arrived at Plymouth. The discoveries made by this circumnavigator, will, however, be deemed much more important, if the opinion of Fleurien, in his remarks on the austral lands of Drake, inserted in the Voyage of Marchand, in which opinion he is followed by Malte Brun, be correct; viz. that Drake discovered, under the name of the Isles of Elizabeth, the western part of the archipelago of Terra del Fuego; and that he reached even the southern extremity of America, which afterwards received, from the Dutch navigators, the name of Cape Horn. These are all the well authenticated discoveries made in the sixteenth and seventeenth centuries, on the north-west coast of America. Cape Mendocino, in about 40-1/2 degrees north latitude, is the extreme limit of the certain knowledge possessed at this period respecting this coast: the information possessed respecting New Georgia and New Cornwall was very vague and obscure.

In the beginning of the sixteenth century, the coasts of the east side of North America, particularly those of Florida, Virginia, Acadia and Canada, were examined by navigators of different countries. Florida was discovered in the year 1512, by the Spanish navigator, Ponce de Leon; but as it did not present any appearance of containing the precious metals, the Spaniards entirely neglected it. In 1524, the French seem to have engaged in their first voyage of discovery to America. Francis I. sent out a Florentine with four ships: three of these were left at Madeira; with the fourth he reached Florida. From this country he is said to have coasted till he arrived in fifty degrees of north latitude. To this part he gave the name of New France; but he returned home without having formed any colony. Towards the end of the sixteenth and beginning of the seventeenth centuries, the English began to form settlements in these parts of North America. Virginia was examined by the famous Sir Walter Raleigh: this name was given to all the coast on which the English formed settlements. That part of it now called Carolina, seems to have been first discovered by Raleigh.

The beginning of the seventeenth century was particularly distinguished by the voyage of La Maire and Schouten. The States General of Holland, who had formed an East India Company, in order to secure to it the monopoly of the Indian trade, prohibited all individuals from navigating to the Indian Ocean, either round the Cape of Good Hope or through the Straits of Magellan. It was therefore an object of great importance to discover, if practicable, any passage to India, which would enable the Dutch, without incurring the penalties of the law, to reach India. This idea was first suggested by La Maire, a merchant of Amsterdam, and William Schouten, a merchant of Horn. They had also another object in view: in all the maps of the world of the sixteenth century, a great southern continent is laid down. In 1606, Quiros, a Spanish navigator, had searched in vain for this continent; and La Maire and Schouten, in their voyage, resolved to look for it, as well as for a new passage to India. In 1615 they sailed from Holland with two ships: they coasted Patagonia, discovered the strait which bears the name of La Maire, and Staten Island, which joins it on the east. On the 31st of January next year, they doubled the southern point of America, having sailed almost into the sixtieth degree of south latitude; this point they named Cape Horn, after the town of which Schouten was a native. From this cape they steered right across the great southern ocean to the northwest. In their course they discovered several small islands; but finding no trace of a continent, they gave up the search for it, and steering to the south, passed to the east of the Papua Archipelago. They then changed their course to the west; discovered the east coast of the island, afterwards called New Zealand, as well as the north side of New Guinea. They afterwards reached Batavia, where they were seized by the president of the Dutch East India Company. This voyage was important, as it completed the navigation of the coast of South America from the Strait of Magellan to Cape Horn, and ascertained that the two great oceans, the Pacific and the Atlantic, joined each other to the south of America, by a great austral sea. This voyage added also considerably to maritime geography, "though many of the islands in the Pacific thus discovered have, from the errors in their estimated longitudes, been claimed as new discoveries by more recent navigators." In the year 1623, the Dutch found a shorter passage into the Pacific, by the Straits of Nassau, north-west of La Maire's Strait; and another still shorter, by Brewer's Straits, in the year 1643.

The success of the Portuguese and Spaniards in their discoveries of a passage to India by the Cape of Good Hope, and of America, induced, as we have seen, the other maritime nations to turn their attention to navigation and commerce. As, however, the riches derived from the East India commerce were certain, and the commodities which supplied them had long been in regular demand in Europe, the attempts to discover new routes to India raised greater energies than those which were made to complete the discovery of America. In fact, as we have seen, the east coast, both of South and North America, in all probability would not have been visited so frequently, or so soon and carefully examined, had it not been with the hope of finding some passage to India in that direction. But it was also supposed, that a passage to India might be made by sailing round the north of Europe to the east. Hence arose the frequent attempts to find out what are called the north-west and north-east passages; the most important of which, that were made during the sixteenth and seventeenth centuries, we shall now proceed to notice.

We have already mentioned the earliest attempts to find out the Straits of Anian; the idea that they existed on the northwest coast of America seems to have been abandoned for some time, unless we suppose, that a voyage undertaken by the French in 1535 had for its object the discovery of these straits: it is undoubted, that one of the objects of this voyage was to find a passage to India. In this voyage, the river St. Lawrence was examined as far as Montreal. In 1536, the English in vain endeavoured to find a north-west passage to India. The result of this voyage was, however, important in one respect; as it gave vise to the very beneficial fishery of the English on the banks of Newfoundland. The French had already engaged in this fishery.

In 1576, the idea of a north-west passage having been revived in England, Frobisher was sent in search of it, with two barks of twenty-five tons each, and one pinnace of ten tons. He entered the strait, leading into what was afterwards called Hudson's Bay: this strait he named after himself. He discovered the southern coast of Greenland; and picking up there some stone or ore which resembled gold, he returned to England. The London goldsmiths having examined this, they reported that it contained a large proportion of gold. This induced the Russian Company to send him out a second time, in 1577; but during this voyage, and a third in 1578, no discoveries of consequence were made. In the years 1585, 86, and 87, Captain Davis, who was in the service of an English company of adventurers, made three voyages in search of a north-west passage. In the first he proceded as far north as sixty-six degrees forty minutes, visited the southwest coast of Greenland, and gave his own name to the straits that separate it from America. At this time the use of a kind of harpoon was known, by which they were enabled to kill porpoises; but though they saw many whales, they knew not the right manner of killing them. In his second voyage an unsuccessful attempt was made to penetrate between Iceland and Greenland, but the ships were unable to penetrate beyond sixty-seven degrees north latitude. The west coast of Greenland was examined; but not being able to sail along its north coast, he stretched across to America, which he examined to latitude fifty-four. In his last voyage, Davis reached the west coast of Greenland, as far as latitude seventy-two. All his endeavours, however, to find a north-west passage were ineffectual.

In 1607, Hudson, an experienced seaman of great knowledge and intrepidity, sailed in search of this passage. He directed his course straight north, and reached the eighty-second degree of latitude, and the seventy-third degree of west longitude. During this voyage more of the eastern coast of Greenland was discovered than had been previously known. In his second voyage, which was undertaken in 1608, he endeavoured to sail between Nova Zembla and Spitzbergen, but unsuccessfully: of this and his first voyage we have very imperfect accounts. His third voyage was undertaken for the Dutch: in this he discovered the river in America which bears his name. His fourth and last voyage, in which he perished, and to which he owes his principal fame as a navigator, was in the service of the Russia Company of England. In this voyage he reached the strait which bears his name: his crew mutinied at this place, and setting him on shore, returned to England. As soon as the Russia Company learned the fate of Hudson, they sent one Captain Button in search of him, and also to explore the straits which he had discovered: in this voyage Hudson's Bay was discovered. Button's journal was never published: it is said, however, to have contained some important observations on the tides, and other objects of natural philosophy.

The existence of such a bay as Hudson's was described to be, induced the merchants of England to believe that they had at length found out the entrance to a passage which would lead them to the East Indies: many voyages were therefore undertaken, in a very short time after this bay had been discovered. The most important was that of Bylot and Baffin: they advanced through Davis's Straits into an extensive sea, which they called Baffin's Bay: they proceeded, according to their account, as far north as the latitude 78°. The nature and extent of this discovery was very much doubted at the time, and subsequently, till the discoveries of Captains Ross and Parry, at the beginning of the nineteenth century, proved that Baffin was substantially accurate and faithful.

Baffin's voyage took place in the year 1616: after this there was no voyage undertaken with the same object, till the year 1631, when Captain Fox sailed from Deptford. He had been used to the sea from his youth, and had employed his leisure time in collecting all the information he could possibly obtain, respecting voyages, to the north. He was besides well acquainted with some celebrated mathematicians and cosmographers, particularly Thomas Herne, who had carefully collected all the journals and charts of the former voyages, with a view to his business, which was that of a maker of globes. When Fox was presented to Charles I, his majesty gave him a map, containing all the discoveries which had been made in the north seas. He discovered several islands during the voyage, but not the passage he sought for; though he is of opinion, that if a passage is to be found, it must be in Sir Thomas Roe's Welcome,—a bay he discovered near an island of that name, in north latitude 64° 10', not far from the main land, on the west side of Hudson's Bay. He published a small treatise on the voyage, called The North-west Fox, which contains many important facts and judicious observations on the ice, the tides, compass, northern lights, &c. Captain James sailed on the same enterprise nearly at the same time that Fox did. His account was printed by King Charles's command, in 1633: it contains some remarkable physical observations respecting the intenseness of the cold, and the accumulation of ice, in northern latitudes; but no discovery of moment. He was of opinion, that no north-west passage existed.

The last voyage in the seventeenth century, in search of this passage, was undertaken in consequence of the representations of a Frenchman to Charles II. From the same cause proceeded the establishment of the Hudson's Bay Company by that monarch.

Canada was at this time colonized by the French; and a French settler there, De Gronsseliers, an enterprising and speculative man, after travelling in various directions, reached a country, where he received information respecting Hudson's Bay: he therefore resolved to attempt to reach this bay by sea. In the course of this undertaking he met with a few English, who had settled themselves near Port Nelson River: these he attacked, and by their defeat became master of the country. He afterwards explored the whole district, and returned to Quebec with a large quantity of valuable furs and English merchandize; but meeting with ill-treatment in Quebec, and afterwards at the court of France, he came to England, where he was introduced to the Count Palatine Rupert. The prince patronized all laudable and useful enterprises; and persuaded the king to send out Captain Gillam, and the Frenchman with him. The ship was loaded with goods to traffic for furs. They passed through Hudson's Straits to Baffin's Bay, as far as 75 degrees north latitude: they afterwards sailed as far to the south as 51 degrees, where, near the banks of a river, called after Prince Rupert, they built Charles Fort. This was the first attempt to carry on commerce in this part of America.

We must now return to the period of the first attempt to find out a north-east passage to India. A society of merchants had been formed in London for this purpose. Sebastian Cabot, either the son or the grandson of John Cabot, and who held the situation of grand pilot of England under Edward VI., was chosen governor of this society. Three vessels were fitted out: one of them is particularly noticed in the contemporary accounts, as having been sheathed with thin plates of lead. Sir Hew Willoughby had the chief command: Captain Richard Chanceller and Captain Durfovill commanded the other two vessels under him. Willoughby, having reached 72 degrees of north latitude, was obliged by the severity of the season to run his ship into a small harbour, where he and his crew were frozen to death. Captain Durfovill returned to England. Chanceller was more fortunate; for he reached the White Sea, and wintered in the Dwina, near the site of Archangel. While his ship lay up frozen, Chanceller proceeded to Moscow, where he obtained from the Czar privileges for the English merchants, and letters to King Edward: as the Czar was at this period engaged in the Livonian war, which greatly interrupted and embarrassed the trade of the Baltic, he was the more disposed to encourage the English to trade to the White Sea. We have already remarked, in giving an account of the voyage of Ohter, in King Alfred's time, that he had penetrated as far as the White Sea. This part of Europe, however, seems afterwards to have been entirely lost sight of, till the voyage of Chanceller; for in a map of the most northern parts of Europe, given in Munster's Geographia, which was printed in 1540, Greenland is laid down as joined to the north part of Lapland; and, consequently, the northern ocean appears merely as a great bay, enclosed by these countries. Three years afterwards, the English reached the coasts of Nova Zembla, and heard of, if they did not arrive at, the Straits of Waygats. The next attempts were made by the Dutch, who were desirous of reaching India by a route, in the course of which they would not be liable to meet with the Spaniards or Portuguese. They accordingly made four attempts between 1594 and 1596, but unsuccessfully. In the last voyage they reached Spitzbergen; but after striving in vain to penetrate to the north-east, they were obliged to winter on the north coast of Nova Zembla, in 76° latitude. Here they built a smaller vessel out of the remains of the one they had brought from Holland, and arrived the following summer at Kola, in Lapland.

In 1653, Frederic III, king of Denmark, sent three vessels to discover a north-east passage: it is said that they actually passed through Waygats' Straits; but that in the bay beyond these straits they found insurmountable obstacles from the ice and cold, and consequently were obliged to return.

The last attempt made in the seventeenth century, was by the English: it was proposed and undertaken by John Wood, an experienced seaman, who had paid particular attention to the voyages that had been made to the north. His arguments in favour of a north-east passage were, that whales had been found near Japan, with English and Dutch harpoons in them; and that the Dutch had found temperate weather near the Pole, and had sailed 300 leagues to the east of Nova Zembla. The first argument only proved, that there was sea between Nova Zembla and Japan; but not that it was navigable, though passable for whales: the other two positions were unfounded. Wood, however, persuaded the Duke of York to send him out in 1676. He doubled the North Cape, and reached 76 degrees of north latitude. One of the ships was wrecked off the coast of Nova Zembla, and Wood returned in the other, with an opinion that a north-east passage is impracticable, and that Nova Zembla is a part of the continent of Greenland.

But we must turn from these attempts to discover a northwest or north-east passage to India, which, from the accounts given of them, it will be evident, contributed very little to the progress of geographical knowledge, though they necessarily increased the skill, confidence, and experience of navigators.

While these unprofitable voyages were undertaken in the north, discoveries of consequence were making in the southern ocean. These may be divided into two classes; viz., such as relate to what is now called Australasia; and those which relate to the islands which are scattered in the southern ocean.

We have already stated that there is reason to believe some part of New Holland was first discovered by the Portuguese: two ancient maps in the British Museum are supposed to confirm this opinion; but the date of one is uncertain; the other is dated 1542, and certainly contains a country, which, in form and position, resembles New Holland, as it was laid down prior to the voyage of Tasman. But allowing this to be New Holland, it only proves, that at the date of this map it was known, not that it had been discovered by the Portuguese.

The Dutch, however, certainly made several voyages to it between 1616 and 1644: the western extremity was explored in 1616. The same year Van Dieman's Land was discovered. In the course of the ten following years, the western and northern coasts were visited. The southern coast was first discovered in 1627, but we have no particulars respecting the voyage in which it was discovered. In 1642, Tasman, a celebrated Dutch navigator, sailed from Batavia, and discovered the southern part of Van Dieman's Land and New Zealand. From this time to the beginning of the eighteenth century, little progress was made in exploring the coast of New Holland. Dampier, however, a man of wonderful talents, considering his education and mode of life, collected, during his voyage, some important details respecting the west coast. And among the numerous voyages undertaken by the Dutch East India Company towards the close of the seventeenth and beginning of the eighteenth century, to examine this vast country, which the Dutch regarded as belonging to them, there was one by Van Vlaming deserving of notice: this navigator examined with great care and attention many bays and harbours on the west side; and he is the first who mentions the black swans of this country.

Papua, or New Guinea, another part of Australasia, was discovered by the Portuguese in 1528. The passage that divides this country from New Britain was discovered by Dampier, who was also the first that explored and named the latter country in 1683. The discovery of Solomon Islands by the Spaniards took place in 1575: Mendana, a Spanish captain, sailed from Lima, to the westward, and in steering across the Pacific, he fell in with these islands. On a second voyage he extended his discoveries, and he sailed a third time to conquer and convert the natives. His death, which took place in one of these islands, put an end to these projects. They are supposed to be the easternmost of the Papua Archipelago, afterwards visited by Carteret, Bougainville, and other navigators. Mendana, during his last voyage, discovered a group of islands to which he gave the name of Marquesas de Mendoza.

This group properly belongs to Polynesia: of the other islands in this quarter of the globe, which were discovered prior to the eighteenth century, Otaheite is supposed to have been discovered by Quiros in 1606. His object was to discover the imagined austral continent; but his discoveries were confined to Otaheite, which he named Sagittaria, and an island which he named Terra del Esperitu Sancto, which is supposed to be the principal of the New Hebrides. The Ladrones were discovered by Magellan in 1521. The New Philippines, or Carolinas, were first made known by the accidental arrival of a family of their natives at the Philippines in 1686. Easter island, a detached and remote country, which, however, is inhabited by the Polynesian race, was discovered by Roggewein in 1686.

Having thus exhibited a brief and general sketch of the progress of discovery, from the period when the Portuguese first passed the Cape of Good Hope to the beginning of the eighteenth century, we shall next, before we give an account of the state and progress of commerce during the same period, direct our attention to the state of geographical science in the sixteenth and seventeenth centuries.

We have already stated that the astrolobe, which had been previously applied only to astronomical purposes, was accommodated to the use of mariners by Martin Behaim, towards the end of the fifteenth century. He was a scholar of Muller, of Koningsberg, better known under the name of Regiomontanus, who published the Almagest of Ptolemy. The Germans were at this time the best mathematicians of Europe. Walther, who was of that nation, and the friend and disciple of Regiomontanus, was the first who made use of clocks in his astronomical observations. He was succeeded by Werner, of Nuremberg, who published a translation of Ptolemy's Geography, with a commentary, in which he explains the method of finding the longitude at sea by the distance of a fixed star from the moon. The astronomical instruments hitherto used were, with the exception of the astrolobe, those which had been employed by Ptolemy and the Arabians. The quadrant of Ptolemy resembled the mural quadrant of later times; which, however, was improved by the Arabians, who, at the end of the tenth century, employed a quadrant twenty-one feet and eight inches radius, and a sextant fifty-seven feet nine inches radius, and divided into seconds. The use of the sextant seems to have been forgotten after this time; for Tycho Brahe is said to have re-invented it, and to have employed it for measuring the distances of the planets from the stars. The quadrant was about the same time improved by a method of subdividing its limbs by the diagonal scale, and by the Vernier. The telescope was invented in the year 1609, and telescopic sights were added to the quadrant in the year 1668. Picard, who was one of the first astronomers who applied telescopes to quadrants, determined the earth's diameter in 1669, by measuring a degree of the meridian in France. The observation made at Cayenne, that a pendulum which beat seconds there, must be shorter than one which beat seconds at Paris, was explained by Huygens, to arise from the diminution of gravity at the equator, and from this fact he inferred the spheroidal form of the earth. The application of the pendulum to clocks, one of the most beautiful and useful acquisitions which astronomy, and consequently navigation and geography have made, was owing to the ingenuity of Huygens. These are the principal discoveries and inventions, relating to astronomy, which were made prior to the eighteenth century, so far as they are connected with the advancement of the art of navigation and the science of geography.

The discoveries of Columbus and Gama necessarily overturned the systems of Ptolemy, Strabo, and the other geographers of antiquity. The opinion that the earth was a globe, which had been conjectured or inferred prior to the voyage of Magellan, was placed beyond a doubt by that voyage. The heavenly bodies were subjected to the calculations of man by the labours of Copernicus, Tycho Brahe, and Galileo. Under these circumstances it was necessary, and it was easy, to make great improvements in the construction of maps, in laying down the real form of the earth, and the relative situations of the countries of which it is formed, together with their latitudes and longitudes. The first maps which displayed the new world were those of the brothers Appian, and of Ribeiro: soon afterwards a more complete and accurate one was published by Gemma

Frisius. Among the geographers of the sixteenth century, who are most distinguished for their science, may be reckoned Sebastian Munster; for though, as we have already mentioned, he joins Greenland to the north of Lapland in his map, yet his research, labour, and accuracy were such, that he is compared by his contemporaries to Strabo. Ortelius directed his studies and his learning to the elucidation of ancient geography; and according to Malte Bran, no incompetent judge, he may yet be consulted on this subject with advantage.

But modern geography may most probably be dated from the time of Mercator: he published an edition of Ptolemy, in which he pointed out the imperfection of the system of the ancients. The great object at this time, was to contrive such a chart in plano, with short lines, that all places might be truly laid down according to their respective longitudes and latitudes. A method of this kind had been obscurely pointed at by Ptolemy; but the first map on this plan was made by Mercator, about the year 1550. The principles, however, on which it was constructed, were not demonstrated till the year 1559, when Wright, an Englishman, pointed them out, as well as a ready and easy way of making such a map. This was a great help to navigators; since by enlarging, the meridian line, as Wright suggested and explained, so that all the degrees of longitude might be proportional to those of latitude, a chart on Mercator's projection shews the course and distance from place to place, in all cases of sailing; and is therefore in several respects more convenient to navigators than the globe itself. Mercator, in his maps and charts, chose Corvo, one of the Azores, for his first meridian, because at that time it was the line of no variation of the compass.

We have already alluded to Regiomontanus, as a celebrated mathematician, and as having published the Almagest of Ptolemy. He seems, likewise, to have written notes on Ptolemy's Geography. In 1525, a later translation of Ptolemy was published, which contained these annotations. To Ptolemy's maps, tables, &c., are added a new set of maps on wooden plates, according to the new discoveries: from these we find, that in consequence of the voyages of the Portuguese, the charts of the coasts of Arabia, Africa, Persia, and India, are laid down with tolerable accuracy. Nothing is noticed regarding China, except that it may be reached by sea from India. America is called Terra Nova inventa per Christ. Columbus: this seems to be all the editor knew of it. That part of the work which relates to the north of Europe, is most grossly erroneous: Denmark, Norway, Sweden, and the Baltic, seem to have been little known. A great bay is laid down between Greenland and Lapland, which bay is bounded on the north by a ridge of mountains, thus retaining the error of Ptolemy with respect to this part of Europe. There are two maps of England and Scotland: in one they are represented as one island; in the other as different islands. These maps and charts must have been the work of the editor or translator, as Regiomontanus, whose annotations are subjoined, died before the discovery of America.

We have been thus particular in describing the principal maps of this work, as they prove how imperfect geography was, prior to the time of Mercator, and with how much justice it may be said that he is the father of modern geography. There were, however, some maps of particular countries, drawn up in the sixteenth century with tolerable accuracy, considering the imperfection of those sciences and instruments, by which alone perfect accuracy can be attained. George Lilly, son of William, the famous grammarian, published, according to Nicholson, (English Historical Library,) "the first exact map that ever was, till then, drawn of this island." This praise must, however, be taken with great qualification; for even so late as the beginning of the nineteenth century, the distance from the South Foreland to the Lands-end was laid down, in all the maps of England, half a degree more than it actually is. We may here remark, that Nicholson represents Thomas Sulmo, a Guernsey man, who died in 1545, as our oldest general geographer.

In some of the MSS. of Harding's Chronicle, written in the reign of Edward IV., there is a rude map of Scotland. In 1539, Alexander Lindsey, an excellent navigator and hydrographer, published a chart of Scotland and its isles, drawn up from his own observations, which were made when he accompanied James V. in 1539, on his voyage to the highlands and islands. This chart is very accurate for the age; and is much superior to that published by Bishop Lesley, with his history, in 1578.

The first map of Russia, known to the other nations of Europe, was published in 1558 by Mr. Anthony Jenkinson, agent to the English Russia Company, from the result of his enquiries and observations during his long residence in that kingdom.

These are the most important maps, either general or of particular countries, with which the sixteenth century supplies us.

The seventeenth century continued the impulse which was given to the science of geography by Mercator. As new discoveries were constantly in progress, errors in maps were corrected, vacant spaces filled up, more accurate positions assigned, and greater attention paid to the actual and relative sizes of different countries. Malte Brun justly reckons Cluverius, Riccioli, and Varenius, as amongst the most celebrated geographers of this century. Cluverius was a man of extensive and accurate erudition, which he applied to the illustration of ancient geography. Riccioli, an Italian Jesuit, devoted his abilities and leisure to the study of mathematics, and the sciences dependent upon it, particularly astronomy; and was thus enabled to render important service to the higher parts of geography. Varenius is a still more celebrated name in geographical science: he excelled in mathematical geography; and such was his fame and merit in the higher branches of physics, and his ingenuity in applying them to geography, that a system of universal geography, which he published in Latin, was deemed worthy by Newton, to be republished and commented upon. Cellarius bestowed much pains on ancient geography. That branch of the science which pays more especial regard to the distances of places, was much advanced by Sanson, in France; Blew, in Holland; and Buraeus, in Sweden.

We must now turn to the progress of commerce during the sixteenth and seventeenth centuries.

The discovery of a passage to India by the Cape of Good Hope, gave immediately a great impulse to commerce; whereas, it was a long time after the discovery of America before commerce was benefited by that event. This arose from the different state and circumstances of the two countries. The Portuguese found in India, and the other parts of the East, a race of people acquainted with commerce, and accustomed to it; fully aware of those natural productions of their country which were in demand, and who had long been in the habit of increasing the exportable commodities by various kinds of manufactures. Most of these native productions and manufactures had been in high estimation and value in Europe for centuries prior to the discovery of the Cape. The monarchs of the East, as well as their subjects, were desirous of extending their trade. There was, therefore, no difficulty, as soon as the Portuguese arrived at any part of the East; they found spices, precious stones, pearls, &c., or silk and cotton stuffs, porcelaine, &c., and merchants willing to sell them. Their only business was to settle a few skilful agents, to select and purchase proper cargoes for their ships. Even before they reached the remote countries of the East, which they afterwards did, they found depôts of the goods of those parts, in intermediate and convenient situations, between them and the middle and western parts of Asia and Europe.

It was very different in America: the natives here, ignorant and savage, had no commerce. "Even the natural productions of the soil, when not cherished and multiplied by the fostering and active hand of man, were of little account." Above half a century elapsed before the Spaniards reaped any benefit from their conquests, except some small quantities of gold, chiefly obtained from plundering the persons, the houses, and temples of the Mexicans and Peruvians. In 1545, the mines of Potosi were discovered; these, and the principal Mexican mine, discovered soon afterwards, first brought a permanent and valuable revenue to Spain. But it was long after this before the Spaniards, or the other nations of Europe, could be convinced that America contained other treasures besides those of gold and silver, or induced to apply that time, labour, and capital, which were requisite to unfold all the additions to the comforts, the luxuries, and the health of man, which the New World was capable of bestowing. When, however, European skill and labour were expended on the soil of America, the real and best wealth of this quarter of the world was displayed in all its importance and extent. In addition to the native productions of tobacco, indigo, cochineal, cotton, ginger, cocoa, pimento, drugs, woods for dying, the Europeans cultivated the sugar cane, and several other productions of the Old World. The only articles of commerce supplied by the natives, were furs and skins; every thing else imported from the New World consists at present, and has always consisted of the produce, of the industry of Europeans settled there.

But though it was long before Europe derived much direct benefit from the discovery of America, yet in one important respect this discovery gave a great stimulus to East India commerce. Gold and silver, especially the latter, have always been in great demand in the East, and consequently the most advantageous articles to export from Europe in exchange for Indian commodities. It was therefore absolutely necessary for the continuance of a commerce so much extended as this to India was, in consequence of the Portuguese discoveries, that increased means of purchasing Indian commodities should be given; and these were supplied by the gold and silver mines of America.

If these mines had not been discovered about the time when trade to India was more easy, expeditious, and frequent, it could not long have been in the power of Europe to have availed herself of the advantages of the Portuguese discoveries; gold and silver would have become, from their extreme scarcity, more valuable in Europe than in India, and consequently would no longer have been exported. But the supply of the precious metals and of Indian commodities increasing at the same time, Europe, by means of America, was enabled to reap all possible advantage from the Portuguese discoveries. The gold and silver of Mexico and Peru traversed the world, in spite of all obstacles, and reached that part of it where it was most wanted, and purchased the productions of China and Hindostan.

Yet, notwithstanding the effectual demand for East India commodities was necessarily increased by the increased supply of the precious metals, yet the supply of these commodities being increased in a much greater proportion, their price was much lowered. This lowering of price naturally arose from two circumstances: after the passage to India by the Cape, the productions and manufactures of the East were purchased immediately from the natives; and they were brought to Europe directly, and all the way, by sea. Whereas, before the discovery of the Cape, they were purchased and repurchased frequently; consequently, repeated additions were made to their original price; and these additions were made, in almost every instance, by persons who had the monopoly of them. Their conveyance to Europe was long, tedious, and mostly by land carriage, and consequently very expensive. There are no data by which it can be ascertained in what proportion the Portuguese lowered the price of Indian commodities; but Dr. Robertson's supposition appears well founded,— that they might afford to reduce the commodities of the East, in every part of Europe, one half. This supposition is founded on a table of prices of goods in India, the same sold at Aleppo, and what they might be sold for in England,— drawn up, towards the end of the seventeenth century, by Mr. Munn: from this it appears, that the price at Aleppo was three times that in India, and that the goods might be sold in England at half the Aleppo price. But as the expense of conveying goods to Aleppo from India, may, as Dr. Robertson observes, be reckoned nearly the same as that which was incurred by bringing them to Alexandria, he draws the inference already stated,—that the discovery of the Cape reduced the price of Indian commodities one half. The obvious and necessary result would follow, that they would be in greater demand, and more common use. The principal eastern commodities used by the Romans were spices and aromatics,—precious stones and pearls; and in the later periods of their power, silk; these, however, were almost exclusively confined to rare and solemn occasions, or to the use of the most wealthy and magnificent of the conquerors of the world. On the subversion of the Roman empire, the commodities of the East were for a short time in little request among the barbarians who subverted it: as soon, however, as they advanced from their ignorance and rudeness, these commodities seem strongly to have attracted their notice, and they were especially fond of spices and aromatics. These were used very profusely in their cookery, and formed the principal ingredients in their medicines. As, however, the price of all Indian commodities was necessarily high, so long as they were obliged to be brought to Europe by a circuitous route, and loaded with accumulated profits, it was impossible that they could be purchased, except by the more wealthy classes. The Portuguese, enabled to sell them in greater abundance, and at a much cheaper rate, introduced them into much more general use; and, as they every year extended their knowledge of the East, and their commerce with it, the number of ships fitted out at Lisbon every year, for India, became necessarily more numerous, in order to supply the increased demand.

Commerce in this case, as in every other, while it is acted upon by an extension of geographical knowledge, in its turn has an obvious tendency to extend that knowledge; this was the case with respect to India. The ancients had indeed made but small advances in their acquaintance with this country, notwithstanding they were stimulated by the large profits they derived from their eastern commerce; but this was owing to their comparative ignorance of navigation and the sciences on which it depends. As soon as the moderns had improved this art, especially by the use of the compass, and the Cape of Good Hope was discovered, commerce gave the stimulus, which in a very few years led the Portuguese from Calicut to the furthest extremity of Asia.

It is remarkable that the Portuguese were allowed to monopolize Indian commerce for so long a time as they did; this, however, as Dr. Robertson observes, may be accounted for, "from the political circumstances in the state of all those nations in Europe, whose intrusion as rivals the Portuguese had any reason to dread. From the accession of Charles V. to the throne, Spain was either so much occupied in a multiplicity of operations in which it was engaged by the ambition of that monarch, and of his son Philip II., or so intent on prosecuting its own discoveries and conquests in the New World, that although by the successful enterprize of Magellan, its fleets were unexpectedly conducted by a new course to that remote region of Asia, which was the seat of the most gainful and alluring branch of trade carried on by the Portuguese, it could make no considerable effect to avail itself of the commercial advantages which it might have derived from that event. By the acquisition of the crown of Portugal, in the year 1580, the kings of Spain, instead of the rivals, became the protectors of the Portuguese trade, and the guardians of all its exclusive rights. Throughout the sixteenth century, the strength and resources of France were so much wasted by the fruitless expeditions of their monarchs to Italy; by their unequal contest with the power and policy of Charles V., and by the calamities of the civil wars which desolated the kingdom upwards of forty years, that it could neither bestow much attention on commerce, nor engage in any scheme of distant enterprize. The Venetians, how sensibly soever they might feel the mortifying reverse of being excluded almost entirely from the Indian trade, of which their capital had been formerly the chief seat, were so debilitated and humbled by the league of Cambray, that they were no longer capable of engaging in any undertaking of magnitude. England, weakened by the long contests between the houses of York and Lancaster, and just beginning to recover its proper vigour, was restrained from active exertions during one part of the sixteenth century, by the cautious maxims of Henry VII., and wasted its strength, during another part of it, by engaging inconsiderately in the wars between the princes on the continent. The nation, though destined to acquire territories in India more extensive and valuable than were ever possessed by any European power, had no such presentiment of its future eminence there, as to take an early part in the commerce or transactions of that country, and a great part of the century elapsed before it began to turn its attention to the East.

"While the most considerable nations in Europe found it necessary, from the circumstances which I have mentioned, to remain inactive spectators of what passed in the East, the seven United Provinces of the Low Countries, recently formed into a small state, still struggling for political existence, and yet in the infancy of its power, ventured to appear in the Indian Ocean as the rivals of the Portuguese; and, despising their pretensions to an exclusive right of commerce with the extensive countries to the eastward of the Cape of Good Hope, invaded that monopoly which they had hitherto guarded with such jealous attention. The English soon followed the example of the Dutch, and both nations, at first by the enterprizing industry of private adventurers, and afterwards by the more powerful efforts of trading companies, under the protection of public authority, advanced with astonishing ardour and success in this new career opened to them. The vast fabric of power which the Portuguese had opened in the East, (a superstructure much too large for the basis on which it had to rest) was almost entirely overturned in as short time, and with as much facility, as it had been raised. England and Holland, by driving them from their most valuable settlements, and seizing the most lucrative branches of their trade, have attained to that pre-eminence of naval power and commercial opulence by which they are distinguished among the nations of Europe." (Robertson's India, pp. 177-9. 8vo. edition.)

Before, however, we advert to the commerce of the Dutch in India, it will be proper to notice those circumstances which gave a commercial direction to the people of the Netherlands, both before their struggle with Spain, and while the result of that struggle was uncertain. The early celebrity of Bruges as a commercial city has already been noticed; its regular fairs in the middle of the tenth century; its being made the entrepôt of the Hanse Association towards the end of the thirteenth. It naturally partook of the wealth and commercial improvement which Flanders derived from her woollen manufactures, and was in fact made the emporium of that country at the beginning of the fourteenth century; and within 100 years afterwards, the staple for English and Scotch goods. When the increased industry of the north of Europe induced and enabled its inhabitants to exchange the produce of their soil, fisheries, and manufactures, for the produce of the south of Europe, and of India, Bruges was made the great entrepôt of the trade of Europe. In the beginning of the sixteenth century its commercial importance began to decline, but the trade which left it, did not pass beyond the limits of the Netherlands; it settled in a great measure at Antwerp, which, as being accessible by sea, was more convenient for commerce than Bruges. This city, however, would not have fallen so easily or rapidly before its rival, had it not been distracted by civil commotions. From it the commerce of the Netherlands, and with it of the north of Europe, and the interchange of its commodities with those of the south of Europe and of Asia, gradually passed to Antwerp; and about the year 1516, most of the trade of Bruges was fixed here, the Portuguese making it their entrepôt for the supply of the northern kingdoms.

Even before this time the ships of the Netherlands seem to have been the carriers of the north of Europe; for in 1503, two Zealand ships arrived at Campveer, laden with sugars, the produce of the Canary Islands. Antwerp, however, continued till it was taken by the Spaniards, and its port destroyed by the blocking up of the Scheldt, to be most distinguished for its commerce, and its consequent wealth:—its situation, its easy access by sea, joined to the circumstance of its being made the Portuguese entrepôt for spices, drugs, and other rich productions of India, mainly contributed to its commerce. Merchants from every part of the north of Europe settled here, and even many of the merchants of Bruges removed to it, after the decline of their own city. Its free fairs for commerce, two of which lasted each time six weeks, attracted merchants from all parts, as they could bring their merchandize into it duty free, and were here certain of finding a market for it. In it also bills of exchange on all parts of Europe could be easily and safely negotiated. We have already mentioned the most wealthy merchants of England and France, in the fifteenth century: there existed at Antwerp, in the sixteenth, a firm of the name of Fugger, whose wealth was very great, and indicates the extent of their commercial dealings. From this firm the Emperor Charles V. had borrowed a very large sum, in order to carry on an expedition against Tunis. In the year 1534, Charles, being at Antwerp, Fugger invited him to an entertainment at his house, made a fire in his hall with cinnamon, and threw all the emperor's bonds into that fire. About eleven years afterwards, the same merchant gave an acquittance to Henry VIII. of England, for the sum of 152,180l. Flemish, which the king had borrowed of him. The Fuggers had a licence from the king of Portugal to trade to India; and they used to send their own factor in every ship that sailed thither, and were the owners of part of every cargo of pepper imported.

In the year 1541, it contained 100,000 inhabitants: soon afterwards the persecutions on account of religion in Germany, England, and France, drove many people thither, and of course increased both its population and wealth. If we may believe Huet, in his History of Dutch Commerce, it was, at this time, not uncommon to see 2500 ships at once lying in the Scheldt.

The picture, however, which Guicciardini draws of Antwerp in 1560, when it had reached the zenith of its prosperity and wealth,—being that of a contemporary author, and entering into detail,—is at once much more curious and interesting, and may be depended on as authentic. It is also valuable, as exhibiting the state of the manufactures, commerce, &c. of most of the nations of Europe at this period.

"Besides the natives and the French, who are here very numerous, there are six principal foreign nations, who reside at Antwerp, both in war and peace, making above 1000 merchants, including factors and servants, viz. Germans, Danes, and Easterlings—that is, people from the ports in the south shores of the Baltic, from Denmark to Livonia—Italians, Spaniards, English, and Portuguese of these six nations; the Spaniards are the most numerous. One of those foreign merchants, Fugger, of Augsburg, died worth above six millions of crowns; there are many natives there with from 200,000 to 400,000 crowns."

"They meet twice a day, in the mornings and evenings, one hour each time, at the English bourse, where, by their interpreters and brokers, they buy and sell all kinds of merchandize. Thence they go to the new bourse, or principal exchange, where, for another hour each time, they transact all matters relating to bills of exchange, with the above six nations, and with France; and also to deposit at interest, which is usually twelve per cent. per annum."

"They send to Rome a great variety of woollen drapery, linen, tapestry, &c.: the returns are in bills of exchange. To Ancona, English and Flemish cloths, stuffs, linen, tapestry, cochineal; and bring in return such spices and drugs as the merchants of Ancona procure in the Levant, and likewise silks, cotton, Turkey carpets, and leather. To Bologne they export serges, and other stuffs, tapestry, linen, merceries, &c. and bring in return for it, wrought silks, cloth of gold and silver, crapes, caps, &c. To Venice they send jewels and pearls, English cloth and wool, Flemish drapery, cochineal, &c. and a little sugar and pepper: thus, with respect to these two latter articles, sending to Venice what they formerly obtained from her. For, prior to the Portuguese discovery of the Cape, the merchants of Antwerp brought from Venice all sorts of India spices and drugs: and even so late as the year 1518, there arrived in the Scheldt, five Venetian ships, laden with spices and drugs, for the fair at Antwerp. In 1560, however, the imports from Venice consisted of the finest and choicest silks, carpets, cotton, &c. and colours for dyers and painters."

"To Naples they export great quantities of Flemish and English cloths and stuffs, tapestry, linens, small wares of metal, and other materials: and bring back raw, thrown and wrought silk, fine furs and skins, saffron and manna. The exports to Sicily are similar to those of the other parts of Italy: the imports from it are galls in great quantity, cinnamon, oranges, cotton, silk, and sometimes wine. To Milan, Antwerp exports pepper, sugar, jewels, musk, and other perfumes, English and Flemish woollen manufactures, English and Spanish woollinens, and cochineal. The imports are gold and silver, thread, silks, gold stuffs, dimities, rich and curious draperies, rice, muskets and other arms, high priced toys and small goods; and Parmesian cheese. The exports to Florence are nearly the same as to the other parts of Italy, but in addition, fans are specified. Besides the usual imports of silks and gold stuffs, there are also fine furs.

Household furniture is exported to Genoa, besides the usual articles: velvets, which were then the best in the world; satins, the best coral, mithridate, and treacle, are the principal or the peculiar imports. Genoa, is the port through which Antwerp trades with Mantua, Verona, Modena, Lucca, &c."

"Besides all these articles, Antwerp imports from Italy by sea, alum, oil, gums, leaf senna, sulphur, &c. and exported to it by sea, tin, lead, madder, Brazil wood, wax, leather, flax, tallow, salt fish, timber, and sometimes corn. The imports from Italy, including only silks, gold and silver, stuffs, and thread camblets and other stuffs, amount to three millions of crowns, or 600,000*l.* yearly.

"Antwerp exports to Germany precious stones and pearls, spices, drugs, saffron, sugars, English cloths, as a rare and curious article, bearing a high price: Flemish cloth, more common and not so valuable as English, serges, tapestry, a very large quantity of linen and mercery, or small wares of all sorts: from Germany, Antwerp receives by land carriage, silver, bullion, quicksilver, immense quantities of copper, Hessian wool, very fine, glass, fustians of a high price, to the value of above 600,000 crowns annually; woad, madder, and other dye stuffs; saltpetre, great quantities of mercery, and household goods, very fine, and of excellent quality: metals of all sorts, to a great amount; arms; Rhenish wine, of which Guicciardini speaks in the highest terms, as good for the health, and not affecting either the head or the stomach, though drunk in very large quantities:—of this wine 40,000 tuns were brought to Antwerp annually, which, at thirty-six crowns per tun, amounted to 1,444,000 crowns."

"To Denmark, Sweden, Norway, Eastland, Livonia, and Poland, Antwerp exports vast quantities of spices, drugs, saffron, sugar, salt, English and Flemish cloths, fustians, linens, wrought silks, gold stuffs, tapestries, precious stones, Spanish and other wines, alum, Brazil wood, merceries, and household goods. From these countries, particularly from Eastland and Poland, that is, the countries on the south shore of the Baltic, Antwerp receives wheat and rye to a large amount; iron, copper, brass, saltpetre, dye-woods, vitriol, flax, honey, wax, pitch, tar, sulphur, pot-ashes, skins and furs, leather, timber for ship building, and other purposes; beer, in high repute; salt meat; salted, dryed, and smoked fish; amber in great quantities, &c."

"To France, Antwerp sends precious stones, quicksilver, silver bullion, copper and brass, wrought and unwrought, lead, tin, vermillion; azure, blue, and crimson colours, sulphur; saltpetre, vitriol, camblets, and Turkey grograms, English and Flemish cloths, great quantities of fine linen, tapestry, leather, peltry, wax, madder, cotton, dried fish, salt fish, &c. Antwerp receives her returns from France, partly by land and partly by sea. By sea, salt to the annual value of 180,000 crowns; fine woad of Thoulouse, to the value annually of 300,000 crowns; immense quantities of canvass and strong linen, from Bretagne and Normandy; about 40,000 tuns of excellent red and white wines, at about twenty-five crowns per tun; saffron; syrup, or sugar, or perhaps capillaire; turpentine, pitch, paper of all kinds in great quantities, prunes, Brazil wood, &c. &c. By land, Antwerp receives many curious and valuable gilt and gold articles, and trinkets; very fine cloth, the manufacture of Rouen, Peris, Tours, Champagne, &c.; the threads of Lyons, in high repute; excellent verdigrise from Montpelier, merceries, &c."

"To England, Antwerp exports jewels and precious stones, silver bullion, quicksilver, wrought silks, cloth of gold and silver, gold and silver thread, camblets, grograms, spices, drugs, sugar, cotton, cinnamon, galls, linens, serges, tapestry, madder, hops in great quantities, glass, salt fish, small wares made of metal and wood, arms, ammunition, and household furniture. From England, Antwerp imports immense quantities of fine and coarse woollen goods; the finest wool; excellent saffron, but in small quantities; a great quantity of lead and tin; sheep and rabbit skins, and other kinds of fine peltry and leather; beer, cheese, and other sorts of provisions, in great quantities; also Malmsey wines, which the English import from Candia."

Guicciardini observes, that Antwerp exported but little to Scotland, as that country was principally supplied from England and France: some spiceries, sugars, madder, wrought silks, camblets, serges, linen, and merceries, are exported. In return, Antwerp received from Scotland vast quantities of peltry of various kinds, leather, wool, cloth of coarse quality, fine large pearls, but not of quite so good a water as the oriental pearls.

The exports to Ireland were nearly the same as to Scotland: the returns were skins and leather, some low-priced cloths, and other coarse and common articles of little value.

The exports to Spain consisted chiefly of copper, brass, and latten, wrought and unwrought; tin, lead; much woollen cloth, both Flemish and English; serges, tapestry, linens, flax-thread, wax, pitch, madder, tallow, sulphur, wheat, rye, salted meat and fish, butter, cheese, merceries, silver bullion and wrought, arms, ammunition, furniture, tools; and every thing also, he adds, produced by human industry and labour, to which the lower classes in Spain have an utter aversion. From Spain, Antwerp received jewels, pearls, gold and silver in great quantities; cochineal, sarsaparilla, guiacum, saffron; silk, raw and thrown; silk stuffs, velvets, taffeties, salt, alum, orchil, fine wool, iron, cordovan leather, wines, oils, vinegar, honey, molasses, Arabian gums, soap; fruits, both moist and dried, in vast quantities, and sugar from the Canaries.

The exports to Portugal were silver bullion, quicksilver, vermilion, copper, brass, and latten; lead, tin, arms, artillery and ammunition; gold and silver thread, and most of the other articles sent to Spain. From Portugal, Antwerp received pearls and precious stones, gold, spices, to the value of above a million of crowns annually; drugs, amber, musk, civet, great quantities of ivory, aloes, rhubarb, cotton, China root, (then and even lately much used in medicine,) and many other rare and valuable Indian commodities, with which the greatest part of Europe is supplied from Antwerp; also, sugars from St. Thomas, under the line, and the other islands belonging to the Portuguese on the African coast; Brazil wood, Guinea grains, and other drugs from the west coast of Africa; Madeira sugar and wines. Of the produce of Portugal itself, Antwerp imported salt, wines, oils, woad, seeds, orchil, fruits, &c. &c.

To Barbary, Antwerp exported woollen goods, linen, merceries, metals, &c.; and received from it sugar, azure or anil, gums, coloquintida, leather, peltry, and fine feathers.

From this sketch of the commerce of Antwerp, when it was at its height, we see, that it embraced the whole commerce of the world: and that in it centered all the commodities supplied by Asia, America, Africa, and the south of Europe on the one hand, and England, the Baltic countries, Germany, and France on the other. The account given by Guicciardini is confirmed by Wheeler, who wrote in 1601. He observes, that a little before the troubles in the Low Countries, the people of Antwerp were the greatest traders to Italy in English and other foreign merchandize; and also to Alexandria, Cyprus, and Tripoli in Syria; "beating the Italians, English, and Germans, almost entirely out of that trade, as they also soon did the Germans in the fairs of their own country." He adds, that the Antwerp merchants, being men of immense wealth, and consequently able to supply Spain for the Indies at long credit, set their own prices on their merchandize. Antwerp also supplied Germany, Spain, Portugal, and Eastland with the wares, which France was wont to supply them. He adds, "It is not past eighty years ago, (that would be about 1520,) since there were not, in London, above twelve or sixteen Low Country merchants, who imported only stone pots, brushes, toys for children, and other pedlar's wares; but in less than forty years after, there were, in London, at least one hundred Netherland merchants, who brought thither all the commodities which the merchants of Italy, Germany, Spain, France, and Eastland, (of all which nations there were, before that time, divers famous and notable rich merchants and companies,) used to bring into England out of their own country directly, to the great damage of the said strangers, and of the natural born English merchants."

Guicciardini informs us, that in his time the port of Armuyden, in the island of Walcheren, was the place of rendezvous for the shipping of Antwerp: in it have often been seen 500 large ships lying at one time, bound to, or returning from distant parts of the world. He adds, that it was no uncommon thing for 500 ships to come and go in one day; that 10,000 carts were constantly employed in carrying merchandize to and from the neighbouring countries, besides hundreds of waggons daily coming and going with passengers; and 500 coaches used by people of distinction. In his enumeration of the principal trades, it is curious that there were ninety-two fishmongers, and only seventy-eight butchers; there were 124 goldsmiths, who, it must be recollected, at that time acted as bankers, or rather exchangers of money. The number of houses was 13,500. With respect to the shipping, which, according to this author, were so numerous at the port of Antwerp, comparatively few of them belonged to this city, as most of its commerce was carried on by ships of foreign nations.

This circumstance, of its having but few ships of its own, may be regarded as one cause why, when it was taken and plundered by the Spaniards in the year 1585, it could not recover its former commerce, as the shipping removed with the nations they belonged to. The forts which the Dutch built in the Scheldt were, however, another and a very powerful cause. The trade of Holland rose on the fall of Antwerp, and settled principally at Amsterdam; this city had indeed become considerable after the decline of the Hanseatic confederacy; but was not renowned for its commerce till the destruction of Antwerp. The commerce of Holland was extended and supported by its fisheries, and the manufactures of Flanders and the adjoining provinces, which in their turn received support from its commerce. Guicciardini informs us, that there were in the Netherlands, in time of peace, 700 busses and boats employed in the herring fishery: each made three voyages in the season, and on an average during that period, caught seventy lasts of herring, each last containing twelve barrels of 9OO or 1000 herrings each barrel; the price of a last was usually about 6£. sterling: the total amount of one year's fishery, was about 294,000£. sterling. About sixty years after this time, according to Sir Walter Raleigh, the cod and ling fishery of Friesland, Holland, Zealand, and Flanders, (the provinces included by Guicciardini in the maritime Netherlands) brought in 100,000£. annually: and the salmon-fishing of Holland and Zealand nearly half that sum.

The woollen manufactures of the Netherlands had, about the time that Guicciardini wrote, been rivalled by those of England: yet he says, that, though their wool was very coarse, above 12,000 pieces of cloth were made at each of the following places; Amsterdam, Bois-le-duc, Delft, Haarlem, and Leyden. Woollen manufactures were carried on also at other places, besides taffeties and tapestries. Lisle is particularised by him as next in commercial importance to Antwerp and Amsterdam. Bois-le-duc seems to have been the seat of a great variety of manufactures; for besides woollen cloth, 20,000 pieces of linen, worth, on an average, ten crowns each, were annually made; and likewise great quantities of knives, fine pins, mercery, &c. By the taking of Antwerp, the Spanish or Catholic Netherlands lost their trade and manufactures, great part of which, as we have already observed, settled in the United Provinces, while the remainder passed into England and other foreign countries.

The destruction of the Hanseatic league, which benefited Amsterdam, seems also to have been of service to the other northern provinces of the Netherlands: for in 1510, we are informed by Meursius, in his History of Denmark, there was at one time a fleet of 250 Dutch merchant ships in the Baltic: if this be correct, the Dutch trade to the countries on this sea must have been very great. The circumstance of the Dutch, even before their revolt from Spain, carrying on a great trade, especially to the Baltic, is confirmed by Guicciardini; according to him, about the year 1559, they brought annually from Denmark, Eastland, Livonia, and Poland, 60,000 lasts of grain, chiefly rye, worth 560,000l. Flemish. They had above 800 ships from 200 to 700 tons burden: fleets of 300 ships arrived twice a year from Dantzic and Livonia at Amsterdam, where there were often seeing lying at the same time 500 vessels, most of them belonging to it. He mentions Veer in Zealand (Campveer) as at that time being the staple port for all the Scotch shipping, and owing its principal commerce to that circumstance.

The destruction of Antwerp brought to Amsterdam, along with other branches of commerce, the valuable trade which the former city had with Portugal for the produce and manufactures of India; these the Dutch merchants resold to all the nations of the north. As soon, however, as Philip II. had obtained possession of the throne of Portugal in 1580, he put a stop to all further commerce between Lisbon and the Dutch. The latter, having tasted the sweets of this commerce, resolved to attempt a direct trade to India. We have already mentioned the voyages of Barentz in search of a north-east passage; these proving unsuccessful, the Dutch began to despair of reaching India, except by the Cape of Good Hope; and this voyage they were afraid to undertake, having, at this time, neither experienced seamen nor persons acquainted with Indian commerce. A circumstance, however, occurred while Barentz was in search of a north-west passage, which determined them to sail to India by the Cape. One Houlman, a Dutchman, who had been in the Portuguese Indian service, but was then confined in Lisbon for debt, proposed to the merchants of Rotterdam, if they could liberate him, to put them in possession of all he knew respecting Indian commerce; his offer was accepted, and four ships were sent to India in 1594 under his command. The adventurers met with much opposition from the Portuguese in India, so that their voyage was not very successful or lucrative: they returned, however, in twenty-nine months with a small quantity of pepper from Java, where they had formed a friendly communication with the natives. The arrival of the Dutch in India,—the subjugation of Portugal by Spain, which circumstance dispirited and weakened the Portuguese, and the greater attention which the Spaniards were disposed to pay to their American than their Indian commerce, seem to have been the causes which produced the ruin of the Portuguese in India, and the establishment of the Dutch.

The Dutch pushed their new commerce with great vigour and zeal. In the year 1600 eight ships entered their ports laden with cinnamon, pepper, cloves, nutmegs, and mace: the pepper they obtained at Java, the other spices at the Moluccas, where they were permitted by the natives, who had driven out the Portuguese, to establish factories.

In consequence of a wild and ruinous spirit of speculation having seized the Dutch merchants, the government, in 1602, formed all the separate companies who traded to India, into one; and granted to this extensive sovereignty over all the establishments that might be formed in that part of the world. Their charter was for twenty-one years: their capital was 6,600,000 guilders (or about 600,000*l.*) Amsterdam subscribed one half of the capital, and selected twenty directors out of sixty, to whom the whole management of the trade was entrusted.

From this period, the Dutch Indian commerce flourished extremely: and the company, not content with having drawn away a large portion of the Portuguese trade, resolved to expel them entirely from this part of the world. Ships fitted, either to trade or to fight, and having on board a great number of soldiers, were sent out within a very few years after the establishment of the company. Amboyna and the Moluccas were first entirely wrested from the Portuguese: factories and settlements were in process of time established from Balsora, at the mouth of the Tigris in the Persian Gulf; along the coasts and islands of India, as far as Japan. Alliances were formed with many of the Indian princes: and in many parts, particularly on the coasts of Ceylon, and at Pulicat, Masulipatam, Negapatam, and other places along the coasts of Coromandel and Malabar, they were themselves, in fact, the sovereigns. The centre of all their Indian commerce was fixed at Batavia in Java, the greatest part of this island belonging to them. From this general sketch of the extent of country, which was embraced, either by their power or their commerce, it is evident that the Indian trade was almost monopolized by them; and as they wisely employed part of the wealth which it produced, to establish and defend their possessions, they soon became most formidable in this part of the world, sending out a fleet of 40 or 50 large ships, and an army of 30,000 men.

They were not, however, content, but aimed at wresting from the Portuguese almost the only trade which remained to them; viz. their trade with China. In this attempt they did not succeed; but in the year 1624, they established themselves at Formosa. Soon after this, the conquest of China by the Tartars, induced or compelled an immense number of Chinese to leave their native country and settle in Formosa. Here they carried on a very extensive and lucrative trade; and Formosa became the principal mart of this part of Asia. Vessels from China, Japan, Siam, Java, and the Philippines, filled its harbours. Of this commerce the Dutch availed themselves, and derived great wealth from it, for about forty years, when they were driven out of the island. In 1601, the Dutch received permission to trade to Japan, but this privilege was granted under several very strict conditions, which were, however, relaxed in 1637, when they discovered a conspiracy of the Spaniards, the object of which was to dethrone the emperor, and seize the government. The jealousy of the Japanese, however, soon revived; so that by the end of the seventeenth century, the lucrative commerce which the Dutch carried on with this island for fine tea, porcelaine, lacquered or Japan ware, silk, cotton, drugs, coral, ivory, diamonds, pearls, and other precious stones, gold, silver, fine copper, iron, lead, and tin; and in exchange for linen, and woollen cloths, looking-glasses, and other glass ware; and the merchandize of India, Persia, and Arabia, was almost annihilated.

Before proceeding to narrate the events which arose from the arrival of the English in the East Indies, and the effects produced on the Dutch power and commerce there, by their arrival, it will be proper to take a short notice of the commerce of the Dutch to the other parts of the world. As their territories in Europe were small and extremely populous, they were in a great measure dependent on foreign nations for the means of subsistence: in exchange for these, they had few products of their manufactures to give. The sources of their wealth, therefore, as well as of the means of their existence, were derived from the exchange of their India commodities, and from their acting as the great carriers of Europe. From these two circumstances, their cities, and especially Amsterdam, became the great mart of Europe: its merchants had commercial transactions to an immense amount with all parts of the world. In consequence of the vastness and extent of their commerce, they found great payments in specie very inconvenient. Hence arose the bank of Amsterdam. It is foreign to our purpose, either to describe the nature of this bank, or to give a history of it;

but its establishment, at once a proof, and the result of the immense commerce of Amsterdam, and the cause of that commerce becoming still more flourishing, and moreover, as the principal of those establishments, which have changed the character of the commerce of Europe, could not be passed over without notice. It was formed in the year 1609.

In this year, the Dutch had extended their trade to the west coast of Africa so much, that they had about 100 ships employed in the gold coast trade. About the same time, they formed a colony in North America, in that province now called New York. In 1611, having formed a truce with Spain, they resolved to venture into the Mediterranean, and endeavour to partake in the lucrative trade with the Levant: for this purpose, they sent an ambassador to Constantinople, where he concluded a favourable treaty of commerce. But by far the most extensive and lucrative commerce which the Dutch possessed in Europe, was in the Baltic: there they had gradually supplanted the Hanseatic League, and by the middle of the seventeenth century, nearly all the commodities of the countries lying on, or communicating with this sea, were supplied to the rest of Europe by the Dutch. In the year 1612, they first engaged in the whale fishery at Greenland. In 1648, taking advantage of the civil troubles in England, and having by this time acquired a powerful influence at the Russian court, they interfered with the trade of the English Russian Company at Archangel; and this new branch of trade they pushed with their national industry and perseverance, so that in 1689 they had 200 factors in this place.

In the year 1621 the Dutch formed a West India Company: their first objects were to reduce Brazil and Peru: in the latter they were utterly unsuccessful. By the year 1636 they had conquered the greater part of the coast of Brazil: they lost no time in reaping the fruits of this conquest: for in the space of thirteen years, they had sent thither 800 ships of war and commerce, which were valued at 4-1/2 millions sterling; and had in that time taken from Spain, then sovereign of Portugal, 545 ships. In the year 1640 the Portuguese shook off the Spanish yoke, and from this event may be dated the decline of the Dutch power in Brazil: in 1654 they were entirely expelled from this country.

In the year 1651, they colonized the Cape of Good Hope; and in the same year, began the obstinate and bloody maritime, war between Holland and England. This arose principally from the navigation act, which was passed in England in 1650: its object and effect was to curtail the commerce between England and Holland, which consisted principally of foreign merchandize imported into, and English merchandize exported from, England in Dutch vessels. In this war, the Dutch lost 700 merchant ships in the years 1652 and 1653. In 1654, peace was made. The object of the navigation act, at least so far as regarded the Dutch acting as the carriers of the English trade, seems to have been completely answered, for in 1674, after a great frost, when the ports were open, there sailed out of the harbour of Rotterdam above 300 sail of English, Scotch, and Irish ships at one time. The example of the English being followed by the nations of the north, the Dutch carrying trade was very much reduced. Between the years 1651 and 1672, when Holland was overrun by the French, their commerce seems to have reached the greatest extent, which it attained in the seventeenth century; and perhaps, at no subsequent period, did it flourish so much. De Witt estimates the increase of their commerce and navigation from the peace with Spain in 1648 to the year 1669, to be fully one-half. He adds, that during the war with Holland, Spain lost the greater part of her naval power: that since the peace with Spain, the Dutch had obtained most of the trade to that country, which had been previously carried on by the Easterlings and the English;—that all the coasts of Spain were chiefly navigated by Dutch shipping: that Spain had even been forced to hire Dutch ships to sail to her American possessions; and that so great was the exportation of goods from Holland to Spain, that all the merchandize brought from the Spanish West Indies, was not sufficient to make returns for them.

The same author informs us, that in the province of Holland alone, in 1669, the herring and cod fisheries employed above one thousand busses, from twenty-four to thirty lasts each; and above 170 smaller ones: that the whale fishery was increased from one to ten; that the cod and herring, when caught, were transported by the Hollanders in their own vessels throughout the world; thus obtaining, by means of the sea alone, through their own industry, above 300,000 lasts of salt fish.

As the Dutch commerce was decidedly and undoubtedly more extensive than that of all the rest of Europe, about the middle of the seventeenth century, it may be proper, before we conclude our notice of it at this time, to consider briefly the causes which cherished it into such full growth and vigour. These causes are explained in a very judicious and satisfactory manner by Sir William Temple, in his observations on the Netherlands. He remarks, that though the territory of the Dutch was very small, and though they laboured under many natural disadvantages, yet their commerce was immense; and it was generally esteemed that they had more shipping belonging to them than there did to all the rest of Europe.

They had no native commodities towards the building or equipping their ships; their flax, hemp, pitch, wood, and iron, coming all from abroad, as wool does for clothing their men, and corn for feeding them. The only productions or manufactures of their own, which they exported, were butter, cheese, and earthern wares. They have no good harbours in all their coast; even Amsterdam is difficult of approach, from the dangerous entrance of the Texel, and the shallowness of the Zuider Zee.

What then were the causes which, in spite of these disadvantages, rendered Holland so commercial? In the first place, great multitudes in small compass, who were forced to industry and labour, or else to want. In the second place, the emigration of men of industry, skill, and capital, driven into Holland from Germany, France, and England, by persecution and civil wars. In the third place, the security to property established by the government of the United States; and akin to this, general liberty of conscience in religious matters. The great fairs in the Netherlands may be regarded as another cause. These Sir W. Temple regards as the principal causes of the foundation of their trade. He next enquires into the chief advancers and encouragers of trade in that country.

These he considers to have been low interest, which caused money to be easily obtained, not only for the purposes of commerce, but also to make canals, bridges, &c. and to drain marshes. The use of their banks, which secures money, and makes all payments easy and trade quick,—the sale by registry, which makes all purchases safe,—the severity of justice, especially with regard to forging bills,—the convoys of merchant ships, which gives trade security, the nation credit abroad, and breeds up seamen,—the lowness of their custom duties and freedom of their ports, which rendered their cities magazines as well as markets,—order and exactness in managing their trade,—each town affecting some particular commerce or staple, and so improving it to the greatest height; as Flushing, the West India trade; Middleburgh, French wines; Terveer, the Scotch staple; Dort, the English staple and Rhenish wines; Rotterdam, the English and Scotch trade at large, and French wines; Leyden, the manufacture of all sorts of stuffs, silk, hair, gold, and silver; Haerlem, linen, mixed stuffs, and flowers; Delft, beer and earthen ware; Swaardam, ship building; Sluys, herring fishery; Friezeland, the Greenland trade; and Amsterdam, the East India, Spanish, and Mediterranean trade. Sir W. Temple mentions other two causes, the great application of the whole province to the fishing trade, and the mighty advance the Dutch made towards engrossing the whole commerce of the East Indies. "The stock of this trade," he observes, "besides what it turns to in France, Spain, Italy, the Straits, and Germany, makes them so great masters in the trade of the northern parts of Europe, as Muscovy, Poland, Pomerania, and all the Baltic, where the spices, that are an Indian drug and European luxury, command all the commodities of those countries which are so necessary to life, as their corn; and to navigation, as hemp, pitch, masts, planks, and iron."

The next question that Sir William Temple discusses is, what are the causes which made the trade of Holland enrich it? for, as he remarks, "it is no constant rule that trade makes riches. The only and certain scale of riches arising from trade in a nation is, the proportion of what is exported for the consumption of others, to what is imported for their own. The true ground of this proportion lies in the general industry and parsimony of a people, or in the contrary of both." But the Dutch being industrious, and consequently producing much,— and parsimonious, and consequently consuming little, have much left for exportation. Hence, never any country traded so much and consumed so little. "They buy infinitely, but it is to sell again. They are the great masters of the Indian spices, and of the Persian silks, but wear plain woollen, and feed upon their own fish and roots. Nay, they sell the finest of their own cloth to France, and buy coarse out of England for their own wear. They send abroad the best of their own butter into all parts, and buy the cheapest out of Ireland or the north of England for their own use. In short, they furnish infinite luxury which they never practise, and traffic in pleasures which they never taste." "The whole body of the civil magistrates, the merchants, the rich traders, citizens, seamen and boors in general, never change the fashion of their cloaths; so that men leave off their cloaths only because they are worn out, and not because they are out of fashion. Their great consumption is French wine and brandy; but what they spend in wine they save in corn, to make other drinks, which is brought from foreign parts. Thus it happens, that much going constantly out, either in commodity or in the labour of seafaring men, and little coming in to be consumed at home, the rest returns in coin, and fills the country to that degree, that more silver is seen in Holland, among the common hands and purses, than brass either in Spain or in France; though one be so rich in the best native commodities, and the other drain all the treasures of the West Indies." (Sir W. Temple's Observations on the Netherlands, Chapter VI.)

Having thus sketched the progress and nature of Dutch commerce, during that period when it was at its greatest height, and brought our account of it down to the commencement of the eighteenth century, we shall next proceed to consider the English commerce from the time of the discovery of the Cape and America, till the beginning of the same century.

From the sketch we have already given of English commerce prior to the end of the fifteenth century, it is evident that it was of very trifling extent and amount, being confined chiefly to a few articles of raw produce, and to some woollen goods. The improvement of the woollen manufacture, the establishment of corporations, and the settlement of foreign merchants, as well as the gradual advancement of the English in the civilization, skill, and industry of the age,—in the wants which the first occasions, and in the means to supply those wants afforded by the two latter,—these are the obvious and natural causes which tended to improve English commerce. But its progress was slow and gradual, and confined for a long time to countries near at hand; it afterwards ventured to a greater distance. Companies of merchant adventurers were formed, who could command a greater capital than any individual merchant. Of the nature and extent of their foreign commerce at the close of the fifteenth century we are informed by an act of parliament, passed in the 12 Hen. VII. (1497.)

From this act it appears, that England traded at this time with Spain, Portugal, Bretagne, Ireland, Normandy, France, Seville, Venice, Dantzic, Eastland, Friesland, and many other parts. The woollen cloth of England is particularly specified as one of the greatest articles of commerce. In a licence granted by Henry VII. to the Venetians, to buy and sell at London, and elsewhere in England, Ireland, and Calais, woollen cloth, lead, tin, and leather, are enumerated as the chief exports. From this document it also appears, that there resided in or traded to England, the following foreign merchants: Genoese, Florentines, Luccans, Spaniards, Portuguese, Flemings, Hollanders, Brabanters, Burgundians, German, Hanseatic, Lombards, and Easterlings.

From these two documents, the nature and extent of English commerce at this period may be inferred: its exports were sent as far north as the southern countries of the Baltic, and to all the rest of Europe, as far south and east as Venice; but this export trade, as well as the import, seems to have been almost entirely carried on by foreign capital and ships; the merchant adventurers having yet ventured very little from home.

In 1511, English commerce, in English ships, extended into the Levant, chiefly from London, Bristol, and Southampton. Chios, which was still in the possession of the Genoese, was the port to which they traded. This branch of trade flourished so much in a few years, that in 1513 a consul, or protector of all the merchants and other English subjects in Chios, was appointed. The voyages were gradually lengthened, and reached Cyprus, and Tripoli, in Syria. The exports were woollen goods, calf-skins, &c.; and the imports were silks, camblets, rhubarb, malmsey, muscadel, and other wines: oils, cotton wool, Turkey carpets, galls, and Indian spices. The commerce was in a small degree carried on by English ships, but chiefly by those of Candia, Ragusa, Sicily, Genoa, Venice, Spain, and Portugal. The voyages to and from England occupied a year, and were deemed very difficult and dangerous. So long as Chios remained in the possession of the Genoese, and Candia in that of the Venetians, England traded with these islands; but ceased to trade when the Turks conquered them. From 1553, to 1575, the Levant commerce was quite discontinued by England, though during that period, the French, Genoese, Venetians, and Florentines, continued it, and had consuls at Constantinople.

The small and temporary trade with the Genoese and Venetian possessions in the Levant, seems to have been attended with such profit, and to have opened up such further prospects of advantage, as to have given rise to a direct trade with Turkey, and the formation of the Turkey Company. The enlightened ministers of Elizabeth effected these objects: they first sent out an English merchant to the Sultan, who obtained for his countrymen all the commercial advantages enjoyed by the Venetians, French, Germans, and Poles. Two years afterwards, in 1581, the Turkey Company was established. Sir William Monson, in his Naval Tracts, assigns the following as the causes and reasons why England did not sooner embark in the Turkey trade for Persian and Indian merchandize: 1. That there was not sufficient shipping; 2. the hostility of the Turks; and, lastly, England was supplied with Levant goods by the Venetian ships, which came annually to Southampton. He adds, "the last argosser that came thus from Venice was unfortunately lost near the isle of Wight, with a rich cargo, and many passengers, in the year 1587." The Turkey Company carried on their concern with so much spirit, that the queen publicly thanked them, with many encouragements to go forward for the kingdom's sake: she particularly commended them for the ships they then built of so great burden. The commodities of Greece, Syria, Egypt, Persia, and India, were now brought into England in greater abundance, and sold much cheaper than formerly, and yet the returns of this trade are said to have been, at its commencement, three to one.

It is not our object, nor would it be compatible with our limits, to trace the progress of commerce minutely, in any of its branches, but rather to point out, as it were, its shootings in various directions; and any special causes which may have given vigour to its growth, or have retarded it. In conformity with this plan, we shall only notice some of the more marked and important eras of our Levant trade, prior to the commencement of the eighteenth century. The trade to the Levant, in its infancy, like all other trades, at a time when there was little capital and commercial knowledge, required the formation of a company which should possess exclusive privileges. Charters were granted to such a company for a term of years, and renewed by Elizabeth. In 1605 king James gave a perpetual charter to the Levant Company: the trade was carried on with encreasing vigour and success: our woollen manufactures found a more extensive market: the Venetians, who had for many years supplied Constantinople and other ports of the Levant, were driven from their markets by the English, who could afford to sell them cloths cheaper; and English ships began to be preferred to those of Venice and other nations, for the carrying trade in the Mediterranean. According to Sir W. Monson, England exported broad cloth, tin, &c. enough to purchase all the wares we wanted in Turkey; and, in particular, 300 great bales of Persian raw silk yearly: "whereas a balance of money is paid by the other nations trading thither. Marseilles sends yearly to Aleppo and Alexandria at least 500,000*l.* sterling, and little or no wares. Venice sends about 400,000*l.* in money, and a great value in wares besides: the Low Countries send about 50,000*l.*, and but little wares; and Messina 25,000*l.* in ready money: besides great quantities of gold and dollars from Germany, Poland, Hungary, &c.; and all these nations take of the Turks in return great quantities of camblets, grograms, raw silk, cotton wool and yarn, galls, flax, hemp, rice, hides, sheep's wool, wax, corn, &c."

The first check which the Levant trade received was given by the East India Company: about the year 1670 the Levant Company complained that their trade in raw silk was much diminished; they had formerly imported it solely from Turkey, whereas then it was imported in great quantities direct from India. In 1681, the complaints of the one company, and the defence of the other, were heard before the Privy Council. The Levant Company alleged, that for upwards of one hundred years they had exported to Turkey and other parts of the Levant, great qualities of woollen manufactures, and other English wares, and did then, more especially, carry out thither to the value of 500,000*l.*; in return for which they imported raw silks, galls, grograms, drugs, cotton, &c.; whereas the East India Company exported principally gold and silver bullion, with an inconsiderable quantity of cloth; and imported calicoes, pepper, wrought silks, and a deceitful sort of raw silk; if the latter supplants Turkey raw silk, the Turkey demand for English cloth must fail, as Turkey does not yield a sufficient quantity of other merchandize to return for one fourth part of our manufactures carried thither.

The East India Company, on the other hand, alleged that the cloth they exported was finer and more valuable than that exported by the Turkey Company, and that, if they were rightly informed, the medium of cloths exported by that company, for the last three years, was only 19,000 cloths yearly: it is admitted, however, that before there was any trade to China and Japan, the Turkey Company's exportation of cloth did much exceed that of the East India Company. With respect to the charge of exporting bullion, it was alleged that the Turkey Company also export it to purchase the raw silk in Turkey. The East India Company further contended, that since their importation of raw silk, the English silk manufacturers had much encreased, and that the plain wrought silks from India were the strongest, most durable, and cheapest of any, and were generally re-exported from England to foreign parts.

We have been thus particular in detailing this dispute between these companies, partly because it points out the state of the Levant Company and their commerce, at the close of the seventeenth century, but principally because it unfolds one of the principal causes of their decline; for, though some little notice of it will afterwards occur, yet its efforts were feeble, and its success diminished, chiefly by the rivalry of the East India Company.

The Levant trade, as we have seen, was gradually obtained by the English from the hands of the Venetians and other foreign powers. The trade we are next to notice was purely of English origin and growth;—we allude to the trade between England and Russia, which began about the middle of the sixteenth century. The discovery of Archangel took place, as we have already related, in 1553. Chanceller, who discovered it, obtained considerable commercial privileges from the Czar for his countrymen. In 1554, a Russian Company was established; but before their charter, the British merchants had engaged in the Russian trade. The first efforts of the company seem to have been confined to attempts to discover a north-east passage. Finding these unsuccessful, they turned their attention to commerce: they fortunately possessed a very enterprising man, peculiarly calculated to foster and strengthen an infant trade, who acted as their agent. He first set on foot, in 1558, a new channel of trade through Russia into Persia, for raw silk, &c. In the course of his commercial enquiries and transactions, he sailed down the Volga to Nisi, Novogorod, Casan, and Astracan, and thence across the Caspian Sea to Persia. He mentions that, at Boghar, which he describes as a good city, he found merchants from India, Persia, Russia, and Cathay,—from which last country it was a nine months journey to Boghar. He performed his journey seven different times. It appears, however, that this channel of trade was soon afterwards abandoned, till 1741, when it was resumed for a very short time, during which considerable quantities of raw silk were brought to England by the route followed by the Russian agent in the sixteenth century. The cause of this abandonment during the sixteenth century seems to have been the length and danger of the route; for we are informed that one of the adventures would have proved exceedingly profitable, had not their ships, on their return across the Caspian, with Persian raw silk, wrought silks of many kinds, galls, carpets, Indian spices, turquois stones, &c., been plundered by Corsair pirates, to the value of about 40,000*l.* The final abandonment of this route, in the eighteenth century, arose partly from the wars in Persia, but principally from the extension of India commerce, which being direct and by sea, would, of course supply England much more cheaply with all eastern goods than any land trade. Beside the delay, difficulty, and danger of the route from the Volga, already described, the route followed in the sixteenth century, till the merchants reached the Volga, was attended with great difficulty. The practice was to transport the English goods, which were to be exchanged, in canoes, up the Dwina, from Archangel to Vologda, thence over land, in seven days, to Jeroslau, and thence down the Volga, in thirty days, to Astracan.

The Russians having conquered Narva, in Livonia in 1558, the first place they possessed in the Baltic, and having established it as a staple port, the following year, according to Milton, in his brief history of Muscovia, the English began to trade to it, "the Lubeckers and Dantzickers having till then concealed that trade from other nations." The other branches of the Baltic trade also encreased; for it appears by a charter granted by Elizabeth, in 1579, to an Eastland Company, that trade was carried on between England and Norway, Sweden, Poland, Lithuania, Prussia, Pomerania, Dantzic, Elbing, Konigsberg, Copenhagen, Elsinore, and Finland. This company was established in opposition to the Hanseatic merchants; and it seems to have attained its object; for these merchants complained to the Diet of the Empire against England, alleging, that of the 200,000 cloths yearly exported thence, three-fourths went into Denmark, Sweden, Poland, and Germany; the other fourth being sent to the Netherlands and France.

It was not to be supposed that our commerce with Archangel and Narva would long remain without a rival. The Dutch, aware of its importance, prevented by their influence or presents, the Czar from renewing the Russian Company's privileges. As this trade was become more extensive, and carried off, besides woollen goods, silks, velvets, coarse linen cloth, old silver plate, all kinds of mercery wares, serving for the apparel of both sexes, purses, knives, &c. Elizabeth used her efforts to re-establish the company on its former footing; and a new Czar mounting the throne, she was successful.

The frequent voyages of the English to the White Sea made them acquainted with Cherry Island, of which they took possession, and where they carried on for a short time the capture of morses: the teeth of these were regarded as nearly equal in quality and value to ivory, and consequently afforded a lucrative trade; oil was also obtained from these animals. Lead ore is said to have been discovered in this island, of which thirty tons were brought to England in 1606. The Russian Company, however, soon gave up the morse fishery for that of whales. They also carried on a considerable trade with Kola, a town in Russian Lapland, for fish oil and salmon: of the latter they sometimes brought to England 10,000 at one time. But in this trade the Dutch likewise interfered.

The fishery for whales near Spitzbergen was first undertaken by the company in 1597. In 1613, they obtained from King James an exclusive charter for this fishery; and under this, fitting out armed ships, they expelled fifteen sail of French, Dutch, and Biscayners, besides some private English ships. But the Dutch persevered, so that next year, while the Russian Company had only thirteen ships at the whale fishery, the former had eighteen. The success of their whale fishery seems to have led to the neglect of their Russian trade, for, in 1615, only two vessels were employed in it, instead of seventeen great ships formerly employed. From this period, the commerce carried on between Russia and England, by the Russian Company, seems gradually to have declined.

The commerce between England and the other parts of Europe, during the sixteenth and seventeenth centuries, presents little that calls for notice; as the manufactures and capital of England encreased, it gradually encreased, and was transferred from foreign to English vessels. The exports consisted principally of woollen goods, prepared skins, earthen-ware, and metals. The imports of linens, silks, paper, wines, brandy, fruits, dye-stuffs, and drugs. The woollen cloths of England were indeed the staple export to all parts of England during the whole of the sixteenth and seventeenth centuries: as our cotton, earthen-ware, and iron manufactures sprung up and encreased, they supplied other articles of export;— our imports, at first confined to a few articles, afterwards encreased in number and value, in proportion as our encreased industry, capital, and skill, enlarged our produce and manufactures, and thus enabled us to purchase and consume more. A very remarkable instance of the effect of skill, capital, and industry, is mentioned by Mr. Lewis, a merchant, who published a work entitled, *The Merchant's Map of Commerce*, in 1641. "The town of Manchester," he says, "buys the linen yarn of the Irish in great quantity, and, weaving it, returns the same again, in linen, into Ireland to sell. Neither doth her industry rest here, for they buy cotton wool in London, that comes first from Cyprus and Smyrna, and work the same into fustians, vermilions, dimities, &c., which they return to London, where they are sold, and from thence not seldom are sent into such foreign parts where the first materials may be more easily had for that manufacture." How similar are these two instances to that which has occurred in our own days, when the cotton-wool, brought from the East Indies, has been returned thither after having been manufactured, and sold there cheaper than the native manufactures.

But though there are no particulars relative to the commerce between England and Europe, which call for our notice, as exhibiting any thing beyond the gradual extension of commercial intercourse already established; yet in the sixteenth and seventeenth centuries, there were other commercial intercourses into which England entered, that deserve attention. These may be classed under three heads: the trade to Africa, to America, and India.

I. The trade to Africa.—The first notice of any trade between England and Africa occurs in the year 1526, when some merchants of Bristol, which, at this period, was undoubtedly one of our most enterprising cities, traded by means of Spanish ships to the Canaries. Their exports were cloth, soap, for the manufacture of which, even at this early period, Bristol was celebrated, and some other articles. They imported drugs for dyeing, sugar, and kid skins. This branch of commerce answering, the Bristol merchants sent their factors thither from Spain. The coast of Africa was, at this period, monopolized by the Portuguese. In 1530, however, an English ship made a voyage to Guinea for elephants' teeth: the voyage was repeated; and in 1536, above one hundred pounds weight of gold dust, besides elephants' teeth, was imported in one ship. A few years afterwards, a trade was opened with the Mediterranean coast of Africa, three ships sailing from Bristol to Barbary with linens, woollen cloth, coral, amber, and jet; and bringing back sugar, dates, almonds, and molasses. The voyages to Guinea from the ports of the south and southwest of England, particularly Portsmouth, Plymouth, and Bristol, were frequently repeated: the returns were uniformly gold dust and elephants' teeth. But it does not appear that other ports followed the example of these, that these sent many ships, or that the commerce became very regular and lucrative, till the west coast of Africa was resorted to for slaves.

This infamous trade was first entered upon by the English in the year 1562. Mr. John Hawkins, with several other merchants, having learnt that negroes were a good commodity in Hispaniola, fitted out three ships, the largest 120, the smallest forty tons, for the coast of Guinea. Here they bought slaves, which they sold in Hispaniola for hides, sugar, ginger, and pearls. The other branches of the African trade continued to flourish. In 1577, English merchants were settled in Morocco; Spanish, Portuguese, and French merchants had been settled there before. In this year, Elizabeth, always attentive to whatever would benefit commerce, sent an ambassador to the Emperor of Morocco, who obtained some commercial privileges for the English. In 1588, the first voyage to Benin was made from London, by a ship and a pinnace: in 1590, a second voyage was made from the same port with the same vessels. Their exports were linen, woollen cloths, iron manufactures, bracelets of copper, glass beads, coral, hawks' bells, horses' tails, hats, &c. They imported Guinea pepper, elephants' teeth, palm oil, cotton cloth, and cloth made of the bark of trees.

An African Company had been formed in Elizabeth's reign; but neither this, nor two others succeeded; their ruin was occasioned by war, misconduct, and the interference of what were called interlopers. In 1672, a fourth company was established, whose efforts at first seem to have been great and successful. They bought the forts the former companies had erected on the west coast: instead of making up their assortments of goods for export in Holland, as the former companies had been obliged to do, they introduced into England the making of sundry kinds of woollen goods not previously manufactured. They imported large quantities of gold dust, out of which 50,000 guineas were first coined in one year, 1673. Their other imports were red wood for dyes, elephants' teeth, wax, honey, &c. The value of the English goods exported to them averaged annually 70,000*l*. This company was broken up at the Revolution.

II. Though the Portuguese and Spaniards were very jealous of the interference of any nation with their East India commerce; yet they were comparatively easy and relaxed with regard to their American possessions. Accordingly, we find that, in 1530, there was some little trade between England and Brazil: this is the first notice we can trace of any commercial intercourse between this country and the New World. The first voyage was from Plymouth: in 1540 and 1542 the merchants of Southampton and London also traded to Brazil. We are not informed what were the goods imported; but most probably they were Brazil wood, sugar, and cotton. The trade continued till 1580, when Spain, getting possession of Portugal, put a stop to it.

The next notice of any trading voyage to America occurs in 1593, when some English ships sailed to the entrance of the St. Lawrence for morse and whale fishing. This is the first mention of the latter fishery, or of whale fins, or whale bones by the English. They could not find any whales; but on an island they met with 800 whale fins, the remains of a cargo of a Biscay ship which had been wrecked here.

In 1602, the English had suspended all intercourse with America for sixteen years, in consequence of the unsuccessful attempts of Raleigh. But, at this time, the intercourse was renewed: a ship sailed to Virginia, the name then given to the greater part of the east coast of North America; and a traffic was carried on with the Indians for peltry, sassafras, cedar wood, &c. Captain Gosnol, who commanded this vessel, was a man of considerable skill in his profession, and he is said to have been the first Englishman who sailed directly to North America, and not, as before, by the circuitous course of the West Indies and the Gulf of Florida. In the subsequent year there was some traffic carried on with the Indians of the continent, and some of the uncolonized West India islands.

Prior to the year 1606 several attempts had been made to colonize different parts of the new world by the English, but they all proved abortive. In this year, however, a permanent settlement was established near James River, within the Chesapeake. It is not our plan to detail all the particular settlements, or their progress to maturity; but merely to point out the beginnings of them, as evidence of our extending commerce, and to state such proofs as most strikingly display their improvement and the advantages the mother country derived from them. In conformity with this plan, we may mention that sugar plantations were first formed in Barbadoes in 1641: this, as Mr. Anderson, in his History of Commerce, justly observes, "greatly hastened the improvement of our other islands, which soon afterwards followed it in planting sugar to very great advantage. And, as it was impossible to manage the planting of that commodity by white people in so hot a climate, so neither could sufficient numbers of such be had at any rate. Necessity, therefore, and the example of Portugal gave birth to the negro slave trade to the coast of Guinea and it is almost needless to add, that such great numbers of slaves, and also the increase of white people in those islands, soon created a vast demand for all necessaries from England, and also a new and considerable trade to Madeira for wines to supply those islands." The immediate consequence of the spread of the sugar culture in our West India islands was, that the ports of London and Bristol became the great magazines for this commodity, and supplied all the north and middle parts of Europe; and the price of the Portuguese-Brazil sugars was reduced from 8*l.* to 2*l.* 10*s.* per cwt.

The rapid growth of the English colonies on the continent and in the islands of America, during the seventeenth century, is justly ascribed by Sir Josiah Child, to the emigration thither, occasioned by the persecution of the Puritans by James I. and Charles I.; to the defeat of the Royalists and Scotch by Cromwell; and, lastly, to the Restoration, and the consequent disbanding of the army, and fears of the partizans of Cromwell. It may be added, that most of the men who were driven to America from these causes, were admirably fitted to form new settlements, being of industrious habits, and accustomed to plain fare and hard work.

The American plantations, as they were called, increased so rapidly in commerce that, according to the last author referred to, they did, even in the year 1670, employ nearly two-thirds of all our English shipping, "and therefore gave constant sustenance, it may be, to 200,000 persons here at home." At this period New England seems to have directed its chief attention and industry to the cod and mackerel fisheries, which had increased their ships and seamen so much as to excite the jealousy of Sir Josiah Child, who, however, admits that what that colony took from England amounted to ten times more than what England took from it. The Newfoundland fishery, he says, had declined from 250 ships in 1605, to eighty in 1670: this he ascribes to the practice of eating fish alone on fast days, not being so strictly kept by the Catholics as formerly. From Carolina, during the seventeenth century, England obtained vast quantities of naval stores, staves, lumber, hemp, flax, and Indian corn. About the end of this century, or at the very commencement of the next, the culture of rice was introduced by the accident of a vessel from Madagascar happening to put into Carolina, which had a little rice left; this the captain gave to a gentleman, who sowed it.

The colony of Virginia seems to have flourished at an earlier period than any of the other English colonies. In the year 1618, considerable quantities of tobacco were raised there; and it appears, by proclamations of James I. and Charles I., that no tobacco was allowed to be imported into England, but what came from Virginia or the Bermudas.

The colony of Pennsylvania was not settled by Pen till the year 1680: he found there, however, many English families, and a considerable number of Dutch and Swedes. The wise regulations of Pen soon drew to him industrious settlers; but the commerce in which they engaged did not become so considerable as to demand our notice.

III. The commercial intercourse of England with India, which has now grown to such extent and importance, and from which has sprung the anomaly of merchant-sovereigns over one of the richest and most populous districts of the globe, began in the reign of Elizabeth. The English Levant Company, in their attempts to extend their trade with the East, seem first to have reached Hindostan, in 1584, with English merchandize. About the same time the queen granted introductory letters to some adventurers to the king of Cambaya; these men travelled through Bengal to Pegu and Malacca, but do not seem to have reached China. They, however, obtained much useful information respecting the best mode of conducting the trade to the East.

The first English ship sailed to the East Indies in the year 1591; but the voyage was rather a warlike than a commercial one, the object being to attack the Portuguese; and even in this respect it was very unfortunate. A similar enterprize, undertaken in 1593, seems, by its success, to have contributed very materially to the commercial intercourse between England and India; for a fleet of the queen's ships and some merchant ships having captured a very large East India carrack belonging to the Spaniards or Portuguese, brought her into Dartmouth: if she excited astonishment at her size, being of the burthen of 1600 tons, with 700 men, and 36 brass cannon, she in an equal degree stimulated and enlarged the commercial desires and hopes of the English by her cargo. This consisted of the richest spices, calicoes, silks, gold, pearls, drugs, China ware, ebony wood, &c., and was valued at 150,000*l.*

The increasing commercial spirit of the nation, which led it to look forward to a regular intercourse with India, was gratified in the first year of the seventeenth century, when the queen granted the first charter to an East India Company. She seems to have been directly led to grant this in consequence of the complaints among her subjects of the scarcity and high price of pepper; this was occasioned by the monopoly of it being in the power of the Turkey merchants and the Dutch, and from the circumstance that by our war with Portugal, we could not procure any from Lisbon. The immediate and principal object of this Company, therefore, was to obtain pepper and other spices; accordingly their ships, on their first voyage, sailed to Bantam, where they took in pepper, to the Banda isles; where they took in nutmeg and mace, and to Amboyna, where they took in cloves. On this expedition the English established a factory at Bantam. In 1610, this Company having obtained a new charter from James I., built the largest merchant ship that had ever been built in England, of the burthen of 1100 tons, which with three others they sent to India. In 1612 the English factory of Surat was established with the permission of the Great Mogul; this was soon regarded as their chief station on the west coast of India. Their first factory on the coast of Coromandel, which they formed a few years afterwards, was at Masulipatam: their great object in establishing this was to obtain more readily the cloths of Coromandel, which they found to be the most advantageous article to exchange for pepper and other spices. For at this time their trade with the East seems to have been almost entirely confined to these latter commodities. In 1613, the first English ship reached a part of the Japan territories, and a factory was established, through which trade was carried on with the Japanese, till the Dutch persuaded the emperor to expel all Europeans but themselves.

The year 1614 forms an important era in the history of our commercial intercourse with India; for Sir Thomas Roe, whom James sent ambassador to the Mogul, and who remained several years at his court, obtained from him important privileges for the East India Company. At this time, the following European commodities were chiefly in repute in India; knives of all kinds, toys, especially those of the figures of beasts, rich velvets and satins, fowling pieces, polished ambers and beads, saddles with rich furniture, swords with fine hilts inlaid, hats, pictures, Spanish wines, cloth of gold and silver, French shaggs, fine Norwich stuffs, light armour, emeralds, and other precious stones set in enamel, fine arras hangings, large looking glasses, bows and arrows, figures in brass and stone, fine cabinets, embroidered purses, needlework, French tweezer cases, perfumed gloves, belts, girdles, bone lace, dogs, plumes of feathers, comb cases richly set, prints of kings, cases of strong waters, drinking and perspective glasses, fine basons and ewers, &c. &c. In consequence of the privileges granted the East India Company by the Mogul, and by the Zamorine of Calicut, their factories were now numerous, and spread over a large extent of coast.

If we may trust the controversial pamphlets on the East India Company which were published in 1615, it appears that up to this year they had employed only twenty-four ships; four of which had been lost; the largest was 1293 tons, and the smallest 150. Their principal imports were still pepper, cloves, mace, and nutmegs, of which 615,000 lbs. were consumed in England, and the value of 218,000*l.* exported: the saving in the home consumption of these articles was estimated at 70,000*l.* The other imports were indigo, calicoes, China silks, benzoin, aloes, &c. Porcelain was first imported this year from Bantam. The exports consisted of bays, kersies, and broad cloths, dyed and dressed, to the value of 14,000*l.*; lead, iron, and foreign merchandize, to the value of 10,000*l.*; and coin and bullion, to the value of 12,000*l.*; the outfit, provisions, &c. of their ships cost 64,000*l.*

The Dutch, who were very jealous of the successful interference of the English in their eastern trade, attacked them in every part of India; and though a treaty was concluded between the English and the Dutch East India Company, yet the treachery and cruelty of the Dutch, especially at Amboyna, and the civil wars into which England was plunged, so injured the affairs of the English East India Company, that at the death of Charles I. its trade was almost annihilated. One beneficial consequence, however, resulted from the hostility of the Dutch; the English, driven from their old factories, established new ones at Madras and in Bengal.

Before, however, this decline of the English trade to India, we have some curious and interesting documents relating to it particularly, and to the effects produced on the cost of East Indian commodities in Europe generally, by the discovery of the Cape of Good Hope. These are supplied by Mr. Munn, in a treatise he published in 1621; in favour of the East India trade. We have already given the substance of his remarks so far as they relate to the lowering the price of Indian commodities, but as his work is more particularly applicable to, and illustrative of the state of English commerce with India, at this time, we shall here enter into some of his details.

According to them, there were six million pounds of pepper annually consumed in Europe, which used to cost, when purchased at Aleppo, brought over land thither from India, at the rate of two shillings per lb.; whereas it now cost, purchased in India, only two-pence halfpenny per lb.: the consumption of cloves was 450,000 lbs.; cost at Aleppo four shillings and nine-pence per lb., in India nine-pence: the consumption of mace was 150,000 lbs.; cost at Aleppo the same per lb. as the cloves; in India it was bought at eight-pence per lb.: the consumption of nutmegs was 400,000 lbs.; the price at Aleppo, two shillings and four-pence per lb.; in India only four-pence; the consumption of indigo was 350,000 lbs.; the price at Aleppo four shillings and four-pence per lb.; in India one and two-pence, and the consumption of raw silk was one million lbs., the price of which at Aleppo was twelve shillings per lb., and in India eight shillings. It will be remarked that this last article was purchased in India, at a rate not nearly so much below its Aleppo price as any of the other articles; pepper, on the other hand, was more reduced in price than any of the other articles. The total cost of all the articles, when purchased at Aleppo, was 1,465,000 *l.*; when purchased in India, 511,458 *l.*; the price in the latter market, therefore, was little more than one-third of their Aleppo price. As, however, the voyage from India is longer than that from Aleppo, it added, according to Mr. Munn's calculation, one-sixth to the cost of the articles beyond that of the Turkey voyage. Even after making this addition, Mr. Munn comes to the conclusion we have formerly stated, "that the said wares by the Cape of Good Hope cost us but about half the price which they will cost from Turkey."

Mr. Munn also gives the annual importation of the principal Indian goods into England, by the East India Company, and the price each article sold for in England; according to this table, the quantity of pepper was 250,000 lbs., which, bought in India for twopence halfpenny, sold in England for one shilling and eightpence:—150,000 lbs. of cloves, which bought in India for ninepence, sold in England for six shillings:—150,000 lbs. of nutmegs, bought for four-pence, sold for two shillings and sixpence:—50,000 lbs. of mace, bought for eightpence, sold for six shillings:—200,000 lbs. of indigo, bought for one shilling and twopence, sold for five shillings:—107,140 lbs. of China raw silk, bought for seven shillings, sold for twenty shillings:—and 50,000 pieces of calico, bought for seven shillings a piece, sold for twenty-six shillings.

In a third table he gives the annual consumption of the following India goods, and the lowest prices at which they used to be sold, when procured from Turkey or Lisbon, before England traded directly to India. There was consumed of pepper, 400,000 lbs., which used to be sold at three shillings and sixpence per lb.; of cloves, 40,000, at eight shillings; of mace, 20,000, at nine shillings; of nutmegs, 160,000, at four shillings and sixpence; and of indigo, 150,000, at seven shillings. The result is, that when England paid the lowest ancient prices, it cost her 183,500*l.* for these commodities; whereas, at the common modern prices, it costs her only 108,333*l.* The actual saving therefore to the people of England, was not near so great as might have been expected, or as it ought to have been, from a comparison of the prices at Aleppo and in India.

There are some other particulars in Mr. Munn's Treatise relating to the European Trade to the East at this period, which we shall select. Speaking of the exportation of bullion to India, he says that the Turks sent annually 500,000*l.* merely for Persian raw silk; and 600,000*l.* more for calicoes, drugs, sugar, rice, &c.: their maritime commerce was carried on from Mocha; their inland trade from Aleppo and Constantinople. They exported very little merchandize to Persia or India. Marseilles supplied Turkey with a considerable part of the bullion and money which the latter used in her trade with the East,—sending annually to Aleppo and Alexandria, at least 500,000*l.* and little or no merchandize. Venice sent about 400,000*l.* and a great value in wares besides. Messina about 25,000*l.*, and the low countries about 50,000*l.*, besides great quantities of gold and dollars from Germany, Poland, Hungary, &c. With these sums were purchased either native Turkish produce and manufactures, or such goods as Turkey obtained from Persia and other parts of the East: the principal were camblets, grograms, raw silk, cotton wool and yarn, galls, flax, hemp, rice, hides, sheeps' wool, wax, corn, &c. England, according to Mr. Munn, did not employ much bullion, either in her Turkey or her India trade; in the former she exported vast quantities of broad cloth, tin, &c. enough to purchase nearly all the wares she wanted in Turkey, besides three hundred great bales of Persian raw silk annually. In the course of nineteen years, viz. from their establishment in 1601 to 1620, the East India Company had exported, in woollen cloths, tin, lead, and other English and foreign wares, at an average of 15,383*l.* per annum, and in the whole, 292,286*l.* During the same period they had exported 548,090*l.* in Spanish silver. The East India Company employed in 1621, according to this author, 10,000 tons of shipping, 2500 mariners, 500 ship carpenters, and 120 factors. The principal places to which, at this period, we re-exported Indian goods, were Turkey, Genoa, Marseilles, the Netherlands, &c.; the re-exportations were calculated to employ 2000 more tons of shipping, and 500 more mariners.

From a proclamation issued in 1631, against clandestine trade to and from India, we learn the different articles which might be legally exported and imported: the first were the following: perpalicanos and drapery, pewter, saffron, woollen stockings, silk stockings and garters, ribband, roses edged with silver lace, beaver hats with gold and silver bands, felt hats, strong waters, knives, Spanish leather shoes, iron, and looking glasses. There might be imported, long pepper, white pepper, white powder sugar, preserved nutmegs and ginger preserved, merabolans, bezoar stones, drugs of all sorts, agate heads, blood stones, musk, aloes socratrina, ambergris, rich carpets of Persia and of Cambaya, quilts of satin taffety, painted calicoes, Benjamin, damasks, satins and taffeties of China, quilts of China embroidered with silk, galls, sugar candy, China dishes, and porcelain of all sorts.

Though several articles of Chinese manufacture are specified in the proclamation, yet we have no notice of any direct trade to China till nearly fifty years after this time, viz. in the year 1680. In this year the East India Company sent out eleven ships, including two to China and the Moluccas; their general burden was between 500 and 600 tons: in these ships there was a stock of nearly 500,000*l.* Besides the articles imported from India enumerated in the proclamation of 1631, there now appear cowries, saltpetre, muslins, diamonds, &c.

In 1689 the East India Company published a state of their trade, from which it appeared that in the last seven years they had built sixteen ships from 900 to 1300 tons each,—that they had coming from India eleven ships and four permission ships, the value of their cargoes being above 360,000*l.*: that they had on their outward voyage to Coast and Bay, seven ships and six permission ships, their cargoes valued at 570,000*l.*: that they had seven ships for China and the South Seas, whose cargoes amounted to 100,000*l.* That they had goods in India unsold, to the amount of 700,000*l.* About this period, Sir John Child, being what would now be called governor general of India, and his brother, Sir Jonah, leading member of the Court of Committees, the policy was introduced through their means, on which the sovereign power, as well as the immense empire of the East India Company was founded; this policy consisted of the enlargement of the authority of the Company over British subjects in India, and in attaining political strength and dominion, by retaliating by force of arms, on those Indian princes who oppressed their settlements.

In the year 1698, in consequence of complaints against the East India Company, and their inability to make any dividend, they thought it necessary to give in a statement of their property in India. In this they asserted that they had acquired, solely at their own expence, revenues at Fort St. George, Fort St. David, and Bombay, as well as in Persia, and elsewhere, to the amount of 44,000*l.* per annum, arising from customs and licenses, besides a large extent of land in these places; they had also erected forts and settlements in Sumatra, and on the coast of Malabar, which were absolutely necessary to carry on the pepper trade; they had a strongfort in Bengal, and many factories, settlements, &c. in other places. The result of the complaints against the Company was, that a new company was established this year; the two companies, however, united in the beginning of the eighteenth century.

We shall conclude our account of the state of English commerce during the sixteenth and seventeenth centuries, with some more general and miscellaneous topics.

I. Exports. In the year 1534, the total value of our exports did not exceed 900,000*l.* of the present value of our money: the balance of trade was estimated at 700,000*l.*: this arose principally from the very great exportation of woollen goods, tin, leather, &c., on which an export duty was laid, bringing in 246,000*l.*; whereas, the duty on imports did not produce more than 1700*l.* In the year 1612, according to Missenden, in his Circle of Commerce, the exports to all the world amounted to 2,090,640*l.*, and the imports to 2,141,151*l.*; on the latter, however, the custom duties are charged; the custom duties on the exports were 86,794*l.*; the impost paid outwards on woollen goods, tin, lead, pewter, &c. 10,000*l.*; and the merchants' gains, freight, and other charges, to 300,000*l.*:—if these be added to the value of the exports, the total amount will be 2,487,435*l.*,— from which the imports, including custom duty on them, being deducted, leaves 346,283*l.*,—which Missenden regards as the balance gained that year by the nation. The principal articles of export have been enumerated: the principal articles of import were silks, Venice gold and silver stuffs, Spanish wines, linen, &c. At this time, London paid nearly three times as much for custom duties as all the rest of England together. In the year 1662, according to D'Avenant, the inspector general of the customs, our imports amounted to 4,016,019*l.*, and our exports only to 2,022,812*l.*; the balance against the nation being nearly two millions. In the last year of the seventeenth century, according to the same official authority, there was exported to England from all parts, 6,788,166l.: of this sum, our woollen manufactures were to the value of 2,932,292l.; so that there was an increase of our exports since 1662, of 4,765,534l. The yearly average of all the merchandize imported from, and exported to the north of Europe, from Michaelmas, 1697, to Christmas, 1701, is exhibited in the following table:

Annual Countries.	Imported from.		Exported to		.Loss	
Denmark and Sweden	76,215l	*1.*	39,543l.	*1.*	36,672l.	*1.*
East Country	181,296		149,893		31,403	
Russia	112,252		58,884		53,568	
Sweden	212,094		57,555		154,539	
					———	
Total annual average loss					*275,982l.*	*1.*

II. Ships. In the year 1530, the ship which first sailed on a trading voyage to Guinea, and thence to the Brazils, was regarded as remarkably large; her burden amounted to 250 tons. And in Wheeler's Treatise of Commerce, published in 1601, we are informed, that about 60 years before he wrote (which would be about 1541), there were not above four ships (besides those of the royal navy) that were above 120 tons each, in the river Thames; and we learn from Monson, in his Naval Tracts, that about 20 years later, most of our ships of burden were purchased from the east countrymen, or inhabitants of the south shores of the Baltic, who likewise carried on the greatest trade of our merchants in their own vessels. He adds, to bid adieu to that trade and those ships, the Jesus of Lubec. a vessel then esteemed of great burden and strength, was the last ship bought by the queen. In 1582, there were 135 merchant vessels in England, many of them of 500 tons each: and in the beginning of King James's reign, there were 400, but these were not so large, not above four of these being of 400 tons. In 1615, it appears, that the East India Company, from the beginning of their charter, had employed only 24 ships, four of which had been lost. The largest was 1293 tons; one 1100, one 1060, one 900, one 800, and the remainder from 600 to 150. In the same year, 20 ships sailed to Naples, Genoa, Leghorn, and other parts of the Mediterranean, chiefly laden with herrings; and 30 from Ireland, to the same ports, laden with pipe staves: to Portugal and Amsterdam, 20 ships for wines, sugar, fruit, and West India drugs: to Bourdeaux, 60 ships for wines: to Hamburgh and Middleburgh, 35 ships: to Dantzic, Koningsberg, 30 ships: to Norway 5;—while the Dutch sent above 40 large ships. The Newcastle coal trade employed 400 sail;—200 for London, and 200 for the rest of England. It appears, that at this time many foreign ships resorted to Newcastle for coals: whole fleets of 50 sail together from France, besides many from Bremen, Holland, &c. The Greenland fishery employed 14 ships.

The following calculation of the shipping of Europe in 1690, is given by Sir William Petty. England, 500,000 tons; the United Provinces, 900,000; France, 100,000; Hamburgh, Denmark, Sweden, Dantzic, 250,000; Spain, Portugal, Italy, 250,000: total 2,000,000. But that this calculation is exceeding loose, so far as regards England at least, is evident from the returns made to circular letters of the commissioners of customs: according to these returns, there belonged to all the ports of England, in January 1701-2., 3281 vessels, measuring 261,222 tons, and carrying 27,196 men, and 5660 guns. As we wish to be minute and enter into detail, while our commerce and shipping were yet in their infancy, in order to mark more decidedly its progress, we shall subjoin the particulars of this return.

Ports.	Vessels.	Tons.	Men.
London	560	84,882	10,065
Bristol	165	17,338	2,359
Yarmouth	143	9,914	668
Exeter	121	7,107	978
Hull	115	7,564	187
Whitby	110	8,292	571
Liverpool	102	8,619	1,101
Scarborough	100	6,860	606

None of the other ports had 100 vessels: Newcastle had sixty-three, measuring 11,000 tons; and Ipswich thirty-nine, measuring 11,170; but there certainly is some mistake in these two instances, either in the number of the ships, or the tonnage. The small number of men employed at Hull arose from eighty of their ships being at that time laid up.

III. During the sixteenth and seventeenth centuries, the great rivals of the English in their commerce were the Dutch: they had preceded the English to most countries; and, even where the latter had preceded them, they soon insinuated themselves and became formidable rivals: this was the case particularly with respect to the trade to Archangel. Some curious and interesting particulars of this rivalry are given by Sir Walter Raleigh, in his Observations concerning the Trade and Commerce of England with the Dutch and other foreign Nations, which he had laid before King James. In this work he maintains that the Dutch have the advantage over the English by reason of the privileges they gave to foreigners, by making their country the storehouse of all foreign commodities; by the lowness of their customs; by the structure of their ships, which hold more, and require fewer hands than the English; and by their fishery. He contends that England is better situated for a general storehouse for the rest of Europe than Holland: yet no sooner does a dearth of corn, wine, fish, &c. happen in England, than forthwith the Hollanders, Embedners, or Humburghers, load 50 or 100 ships, and bring their articles to England. Amsterdam, he observes, is never without 700,000 quarters of corn, none of it the growth of Holland; and a dearth of only one year in any other part of Europe enriches Holland for seven years. In the course of a year and a half, during a scarcity in England, there was carried away from the ports of Southampton, Bristol, and Exeter alone, nearly 200,000*l.*: and if London and the rest of England were included, there must have been 2,000,000 more. The Dutch, he adds, have a regular trade to England with 500 or 600 vessels annually, whereas we trade, not with fifty to their country. After entering into details respecting the Dutch fishery, by means of which, he says, they sell herrings annually to the value of upwards of one million and a half sterling, whereas England scarcely any, he reverts to the other branches of Dutch commerce, as compared with ours. The great stores of wines and salt, brought from France and Spain, are in the Low Countries: they send nearly 1,000 ships yearly with these commodities into the east countries alone; whereas we send not one ship. The native country of timber for ships, &c. is within the Baltic; but the storehouse for it is in Holland; they have 500 or 600 large ships employed in exporting it to England and other parts: we not one. The Dutch even interfere with our own commodities; for our wool and woollen cloth, which goes out rough, undressed, and undyed, they manufacture and serve themselves and other nations with it. We send into the east countries yearly but 100 ships, and our trade chiefly depends upon three towns, Elbing, Koningsberg, and Dantzic; but the Low Countries send thither about 3,000 ships: they send into France, Spain, Portugal, and Italy, about 2,000 ships yearly with those east country commodities, and we, none in that course. They trade into all cities and port towns of France, and we chiefly to five or six.

The Low Countries have as many ships and vessels as eleven kingdoms of Christendom have; let England be one. For seventy years together, we had a great trade to Russia (Narva), and even about fourteen years ago, we sent stores of goodly ships thither; but three years past we sent out four thither, and last year but two or three ships; whereas the Hollanders are now increased to about thirty or forty ships, each as large as two of ours, chiefly laden with English cloth, herrings, taken in our seas, English lead, and pewter made of our tin. He adds, that a great loss is suffered by the kingdom from the undressed and undyed cloths being sent out of the kingdom, to the amount of 80,000 pieces annually; and that there had been annually exported, during the last fifty-three years, in baizes, northern and Devonshire kersies, all white, about 50,000 cloths, counting three kersies to one cloth.

Although there is undoubtedly much exaggeration in the comparative statement of the Dutch and English commerce and shipping in the details, yet it is a curious and interesting document, as exhibiting a general view of them. Indeed, through the whole of the seventeenth century, the most celebrated and best informed writers on the commerce of England dwell strongly on the superior trade of the Dutch, and on their being able, by the superior advantages they enjoyed from greater capital, industry, and perseverance, aided by the greater encouragement they gave to foreigners as well as their own people, to supply the greatest part of Europe with all their wants, though their own country was small and unfertile. A similar comparative statement to that of Raleigh is given by Child in 1655; he asserts that in the preceding year the Dutch had twenty-two sail of great ships in the Russia trade,—England but one: that in the Greenland whale fishery, Holland and Hamburgh had annually 400 or 500 sail,—and England but one last year: that the Dutch have a great trade for salt to France and Portugal, with which they salt fish caught on our coasts; that in the Baltic trade, the English have fallen off, and the Dutch increased tenfold. England has no share in the trade to China and Japan: the Dutch a great trade to both countries. A great part of the plate trade from Cadiz has passed from England to Holland. They have even bereaved us of the trade to Scotland and Ireland. He concludes with pointing out some advantages England possesses over Holland: In the Turkey, Italian, Spanish, and Portuguese trades, we have the natural advantage of our wool:—our provisions and fuel, in country places, are cheaper than with the Dutch;—our native commodities of lead and tin are great advantages:—of these, he says, as well as of our manufactures, we ship off one-third more than we did twenty years ago; and he adds, that we have now more than double the number of merchants and shipping that we had twenty years ago. He mentions a circumstance, which seems to indicate a retrograde motion of commerce, viz., that when he wrote most payments were in ready money; whereas, formerly, there were credit payments at three, six, nine, twelve, and even eighteen months. From another part of his work, it appears that the tax-money was brought up in waggons from the country.

The gradual advancement of a nation in knowledge and civilization, which is in part the result of commerce, is also in part the cause of it. But besides this advancement, in which England participated with the rest of Europe, during the sixteenth and seventeenth centuries, there were other circumstances peculiar to this country, some of which were favourable, and others unfavourable to the increase of its commerce.

Among the favourable circumstances may be reckoned the taking away of the exclusive privileges of the steelyard merchants by Edward VI., by which native merchants were encouraged, private companies of them formed, and the benefits of commerce more extensively diffused:—the encouragement given by Elizabeth, particularly by her minister Cecil, to commerce; this was so great and well directed, that the customs which had been farmed, at the beginning of the reign, for 14,000*l.* a year, towards its close were fanned for 50,000*l.*;—the pacific character of James I., and the consequent tranquillity enjoyed by England during his reign;—the strong and general stimulus which was given to individual industry, by the feeling of their own importance, which the struggle between Charles I. and the Parliament naturally infused into the great mass of the people;—the increased skill in maritime affairs, which was produced by our naval victories under Cromwell;—the great vigour of his government in his relations with foreign powers; and the passing of the navigation act. The Restoration, bringing a great fondness for luxury and expence, naturally produced also exertions to gratify that fondness. If to these and other causes of a similar nature, we add the introduction of East India commodities direct to England, and the import trade to the West Indies and America, the emigration of the industrious Flemings during the Spanish wars in the Low Countries, and of the French after the revocation of the edict of Nantz, we shall have specified most of the efficient circumstances, which, in conjunction with the progress of mankind in industry and civilization, were beneficial to our commerce.

The causes and circumstances which were unfavourable to it during the same period are much fewer in number; and though some of them were powerful, yet, even these, for the most part, when they ceased to operate, gave birth to a reaction favourable to commerce. The more general causes may be sought for in the erroneous notions entertained respecting commerce, in consequence of which monopolies were granted, especially in the reign of James I.; and laws were made to regulate what would have gone on best, if it had been left to itself. The civil wars, and the emigration occasioned by them, and the religious persecutions in the time of Mary, Elizabeth, and Charles, may be regarded as the most remarkable particular causes and circumstances, which were injurious to commerce.

We must again lay down the position, that in what respects the improvement of a country in industry and wealth, whether agricultural manufacturing, or commercial, the same circumstances may often be viewed in the light both of effect and cause. This position will be clearly illustrated by a very common and plain case. The trade in a certain district improves, and of course requires more easy and expeditious communication among different parts of this district: the roads are consequently made better, and the waggons, &c. are built on a better construction; these are the effects of an improved trade: but it is plain that as by the communication being thus rendered quicker, the commodities interchanged can be sold cheaper, a greater quantity of them will be sold; and thus better roads, which in the first instance proceeded from an improvement in trade, will, when made, improve the trade still more.

We have introduced these observations as preparatory to our notice of the establishment of the Bank of England. This undoubtedly was the effect of our increased commercial habits, but it was as undoubtedly the cause of those habits becoming stronger and more general: it supposed the pre-existence of a certain degree of commercial confidence and credit, but it increased these in a much greater ratio than they existed before: and if England owes its very superior wealth to any other causes besides its free government, its superior industry, and improvements in machinery, those causes must be sought for in the very extensive diffusion of commercial confidence and credit. The funding system, which took place about the same, time that the Bank of England was established, may be regarded as another powerful cause of the increase of our commerce: we do not mean to contend that the national debt is a national blessing, but it is certain that the necessity of paying the interest of that debt produced exertions of industry, and improvements in manufactures, which would not otherwise, have been called forth; while, on the other hand, the funds absorbed all the superfluous capital, which, otherwise, as in Holland, must have had a bad effect on commerce, either by reducing its profits very low, or by being transferred to other countries; and the interest, which so many individuals felt in the stability of the funds, induced them most steadily and strongly to support government.

The commerce of Scotland and Ireland during the sixteenth and seventeenth centuries, supplies us with very few materials. In the year 1544, Scotland must have had no inconsiderable foreign trade, as in the war which took place at this time between that country and England, twenty-eight of the principal ships of Scotland, laden with all kinds of rich merchandize, were captured by the English, on their voyage from France, Flanders, Denmark, &c.; and in the same year, when the English took Leith, they found more riches in it than they had reason to expect. While Scotland and England were at peace, however, the former was principally supplied through the latter with the commodities which Antwerp, during the sixteenth century, dispersed over all Europe. The exports of Scotland to Antwerp, &c. were indeed direct, and consisted principally, as we have already remarked from Guicciardini, of peltry, leather, wool, indifferent cloth, and pearls.

The earliest account which occurs of the Scotch carrying on commerce to any port out of Europe, is in the year 1589, when three or four Scotch ships were found at the Azores by the earl of Cumberland. In the year 1598, it appears, from a letter of king James to Queen Elizabeth, that some Scotch merchants traded to the Canaries. There is evidence that the Scotch had some commerce in the Mediterranean in the beginning of the seventeenth century; for in the "Cabala," under the year 1624, the confiscation of three Scotch ships at Malaga is noticed, for importing Dutch commodities. The principal articles of export from Scotland to foreign countries consisted of coarse woollen stuffs and stockings, linen goods, peltry, leather, wool, pearls, &c. The principal imports were wine and fruits from France, wine from Spain and Portugal, the finer woollen goods from England, timber, iron, &c. from the Baltic, and sugars, spices, silks, &c. from Antwerp, Portugal, &c.

The following statement, with which we shall conclude our account of Scotch commerce, is interesting, as exhibiting a view of the commercial intercourse by sea between England and Scotland, from the commencement of the inspector general's accounts in 1697, to the Union in 1707.

	England received from Scotland Merchandize to the value of	Scotland received from England Merchandize to the value of
1697	£91,302	£73,203
1698.	124,835	58,043
1699.	86,309	66,303
1700.	130,087	85,194
1701.	73,988	56,802
1702.	71,428	58,688
1703.	76,448	57,338
1704.	54,379	87,536
1705.	57,902	50,035
1706.	50,309	60,313
1707.	6,733	17,779

The earliest notices of Irish trade, to which we have already adverted, particularly mention linen and woollen cloth, as two of the most considerable articles of export from that country. Hides, wool, fish of different kinds, particularly salmon, and the skins of martins, otters, rabbits, sheep, kids, &c. are also specified, as forming part of her early export. From Antwerp in the middle of the sixteenth century she received spices, sugar, silks, madder, camblets, &c. Pipe staves were a considerable article of export in the beginning of the seventeenth century; they were principally sent to the Mediterranean. In 1627 Charles issued a proclamation respecting Ireland, from which we learn that the principal foreign trade of Ireland was to Spain and Portugal, and consisted in fish, butter, skins, wool, rugs, blankets, wax, cattle, and horses; pipe staves, and corn; timber fit for ship-building, as well as pipe staves, seem at this period to have formed most extensive and valuable articles of export from Ireland. In the middle of this century, Irish linen yarn was used in considerable quantities in the Manchester manufactures, as we have already noticed. The importation into England of fat cattle from Ireland seems to have been considerable, and to have been regarded as so prejudicial to the pasture farmers of the former country, that in 1666 a law was passed laying a heavy duty on their importation. This statute proving ineffectual, another was passed in 1663, enacting the forfeiture of all great cattle, sheep, swine, and also beef, pork, or bacon, imported from Ireland. Sir W. Petty remarks, that before this law was passed, three-fourths of the trade of Ireland was with England, but not one-fourth of it since that time. Sir Jonah Child, in his Discourse on Trade, describes the state of Ireland as having been much improved by the soldiers of the Commonwealth settling there; through their own industry, and that which they infused into the natives, he adds, that Ireland was able to supply foreign markets, as well as our plantations in America, with beef, pork, hides, tallow, bread, beer, wood, and corn, at a cheaper rate than England could afford to do. Though this country, as we have seen, exported linen goods at a very early period, yet this manufacture cannot be regarded as the staple one of Ireland, or as having contributed very much to her foreign commerce, till it flourished among the Scotch colonists in Ulster towards the middle of the seventeenth century. As soon as they entered on it with spirit, linen yarn was no longer exported to Manchester and other parts of England, but manufactured into cloth in Ireland, and in that state it formed the chief article of its commerce. The woollen manufactures of Ireland, which were always viewed with jealousy by England, and were checked in every possible manner, gradually gave way to the restraints laid on them, and to the rising and unchecked linen manufacture, and of course ceased to enter into the exports.

The commerce of Scotland during the sixteenth and seventeenth centuries was kept low, by ignorance and want of industry, by the disturbed state of the country, by disputes between the king and nobility, and, till the union of the crowns, by wars with England. The commerce of Ireland had still greater difficulties to struggle with; among which may be mentioned the ignorant oppression of the English government in every thing that related to its manufactures or trade.

The commerce of France, during the sixteenth century, presents few particulars worthy of notice; that, which was carried on between it and England, was principally confined to the exportation of wines, fruit, silk and linen, from France; and woollen goods, and tin and lead, from England. There seems to have been a great exchange between the woollens of England and the linens of Bretagne. The French, however, like all the other nations of Europe at this period, were ignorant of the principles, as well as destitute of the enterprize and capital essential to steady and lucrative commerce; and amply deserve the character given of them by Voltaire, that in the reign of Francis I., though possessed of harbours both on the ocean and Mediterranean, they were yet without a navy; and though immersed in luxury, they had only a few coarse manufactures. The Jews, Genoese, Venetians, Portuguese, Flemings, Dutch, and

English, traded successively for them. At the very close of this century we have a very summary account of the commerce of France by Giovani Bolero. France, says he, possesses four magnets, which attract the wealth of other countries;—corn, which is exported to Spain and Portugal;—wine, which is sent to Flanders, England, and the Baltic;—salt, made by the heat of the sun on the Mediterranean coast, and also on that of the ocean, as far north as Saintoigne; and hemp and cloth, of which and of cordage great quantities are exported to Lisbon and Seville:—the exportation of the articles of this fourth class, he adds, is incredibly great.

In the middle of the seventeenth century, the finer manufactures of woollen and silken goods having been carried to great perfection in France, her exports in these articles were greatly increased. In the political testament of Richelieu, we are informed that a considerable and lucrative trade in these articles was carried on with Turkey, Spain, Italy, &c., and that France had driven, in a great measure, out of those markets the serges of Milan, the velvets of Genoa, and the cloth of gold of Italy.

Early in the reign of Louis XIV., Colbert directed his attention to the improvement of manufactures and commerce; and though many of his plans were frustrated from the operation of causes over which he had no control, and principally because he went before the age in which he lived, yet there can be no doubt that to him France was indebted for the consolidation, extension, and firm footing of her commerce. Immediately before the revocation of the edict of Nantes, her commerce was at its greatest heighth, as the following estimates of that she carried on with England and Holland will prove. To the former country the exportation of manufactured silks of all sorts is said to have been to the value of 600,000*l.*;—of linen, sail-cloth, and canvass, about 700,000*l.*;—in beaver hats, watches, clocks, and glass, about 220,000*l.*;—in paper, about 90,000*l.*;—in iron ware, the manufacture of Auvergne, chiefly, about 40,000*l.*;—in shalloons, tammies, &c. from Picardy and Champagne, about 150,000*l.*;—in wines, about 200,000*l.*; and brandies, about 80,000*l.* The exports to Holland, shortly before the revocation of the edict of Nantes, in silks, velvets, linen, and paper, are estimated at 600,000*l.*; —in hats, about 200,000*l.*;—in glass, clocks, watches, and household furniture, about 160,000*l.*;—in small articles, such as fringes, gloves, &c., about 200,000*l.*;—in linen, canvass, and sail cloth, about 160,000*l.*; and in saffron, dye-wood, woollen yarn, &c., about 300,000*l.*

In the year 1700 a council of commerce was constituted in France, consisting of the principal ministers of state and finance, and of twelve of the principal merchants of the kingdom, chosen annually from Paris, Rouen, Bourdeaux, Lyons, Marseilles, Rochelle, Nantes, St. Maloe, Lisle, Bayonne, and Dunkirk.

From the first report of this board, we gain some information of the state of French commerce at this time; according to it, the French employed in their West India and Guinea trade only 100 vessels, whereas the English employed 500. The principal articles they drew from these islands were sugar, indigo, cotton, cocoa, ginger, &c. The exclusive trades formed in 1661, when France was little versed in commerce and navigation, are deprecated: the chief of them were, that granted to Marseilles for the sole trade to the Levant;—the East India Company;—the prohibiting foreign raw silk to be carried to Paris, Nismes, Tours, &c., till it had passed through Lyons;—the Canada and Guinea Companies, besides various farms or monopolies of certain merchandize in trade: the principal of these last was lead from England, with which, made into shot, the persons who had the monopoly supplied not only France, but, through France, Spain, Portugal, Switzerland, the Levant, and the French West Indies.

The report contains some information respecting the comparative commerce of France, and the other nations of Europe. The Spaniards, it is observed, though they possess within their own country wool, silk, oil, wine, &c., and are in no want of good ports, both on the ocean and Mediterranean, nevertheless neglect all these advantages. Hence it happens that the raw silk of Valencia, Murcia, and Grenada, is exported to France: the wool of Castile, Arragon, Navarre, and Leon, to England, Holland, France, and Italy; and these raw articles, when manufactured, are sent back to Spain, and exchanged for the gold and silver of the American mines. France also supplies Peru and Mexico, through Spain, receiving in return, cochineal, indigo, hides, &c., besides a balance of eighteen or twenty million of livres, and by the flotas, seven or eight million more. The report adds, on this head, that latterly the English and Dutch have interfered with some branches of this trade with Spain; and it also complains that the former nation carry on the Levant trade to much more advantage than the French, their woollen cloths being better and cheaper. The English also carry to the Levant, lead, pewter, copperas, and logwood, together with a great deal of pepper;—with these, and the money received on the coasts of Portugal, Spain and Italy, for the dry fish and sugar they sell there on their outward voyage, they purchase their homeward cargoes. This superiority of England over France in the Levant trade, is ascribed in the report to the monopoly enjoyed by Marseilles.

The report, in relation to the commerce of France with the northern nations of Europe, observes, that it appears from the custom books, that the Dutch had possession of almost the whole of it. The Dutch also are accused of having, in a great measure, made themselves masters of the inland trade of France. In order to secure to this latter country the direct trade with the north of Europe, certain plans are suggested in the report; all of which were objected to by the deputies from Nantes, principally, it would seem, on the ground, that the Dutch trade to the Baltic was so well settled, that it governed the prices of all the exports and imports there, and that the Dutch gave higher prices for French goods than could be obtained in the Baltic for them, while, on the other hand, they sold at Amsterdam Baltic produce cheaper than it could be bought in the Baltic. One objection to a direct trade between France and the Baltic affords a curious and instructive proof of the imperfect state of navigation at this time, that is, at the beginning of the eighteenth century. The deputy from Marseilles urged that the voyage from Dantzic, or even from Copenhagen to Marseilles, was too long for a ship to go and come with certainty in one season, considering the ice and the long nights; and that therefore, there is no avoiding the use of entrepots for the trade of Marseilles. Mr. Anderson, in his History of Commerce, very justly observes, "that the dread of a long voyage from the north to the south parts of Europe, contributed, in a great measure, to make Antwerp, in former times, the general magazine of Europe."

The decline of the commerce of the Italian states, in consequence of the discovery of the Cape of Good Hope, has been already mentioned; their efforts however to preserve it were vigorous, and we can trace, even in the middle of the sixteenth century, some Indian commerce passing through Venice. Indeed in the year 1518, Guicciardini informs us that there arrived at Antwerp, five Venetian ships laden with the spices and drugs of the East: and 1565, when the English Russia Company sent their agents into Persia, they found that the Venetians carried on a considerable trade there; they seem to have travelled from Aleppo, and to have brought with them woollen cloths, &c. which they exchanged for raw silks, spices, drugs, &c. The agents remarked, that much Venetian cloth was worn in Persia: in 1581, Sir William Monson complains that the Venetians engrossed the trade between Turkey and Persia, for Persian and Indian merchandize. In 1591, when the English Levant Company endeavoured to establish a trade over land to India, and for that purpose carried some of their goods from Aleppo to Bagdat, and thence down the Tigris to Ormus and to Goa, they found that the Venetians had factories in all these places, and carried on an extensive and lucrative trade. It is difficult to perceive how Indian commodities brought by land to Europe, could compete with those which the Portuguese brought by sea. The larger capital, more numerous connexions, greater credit, and skill of the Venetians, must however have been much in their favour in this competition.

We have noticed that, even so late as the beginning of the eighteenth century, a voyage from Marseilles to the Baltic and back again, was thought by French navigators an impracticable undertaking in the course of one year; and yet a century earlier, viz. in 1699, Venice sent at least one ship annually for Archangel: the first instance we believe of a direct commercial intercourse between the northern and southern extreme seas of Europe.

We must turn to the northern nations of Europe, Sweden, Denmark and Russia, and glean what few important materials we can respecting their commerce during the sixteenth and seventeenth centuries. We have already seen that the commerce of the Scandinavian nations of the middle ages was by no means despicable, though it was chiefly confined to Britain and Iceland, and among themselves: the establishment of the Hanseatic League, some of the cities composing which lay in the Baltic, gradually made the Scandinavian nations better known, and by creating a demand for their produce, stimulated them to industry and commerce. In a poor country, however, with a sterile soil and ungenial climate; where winter prevented intercourse by sea, for several months every year, capital must increase very slowly, and commerce, reciprocally the cause and effect of capital, equally slow. Besides the piratical habits of the early Scandinavians, were adverse to trade; and these habits shed their influence even after they were discontinued. But though the Scandinavian nations were long in entering into any commercial transactions of importance, yet they contributed indirectly to its advancement by the improvements they made in ship-building, as well as by the ample materials for this purpose which their country supplied. Their ships indeed were constructed for warfare, but improvements in this description of ships naturally, and almost unavoidably, led to improvements in vessels designed for trade. In 1449, a considerable commerce was carried on between Bristol, and Iceland, and Finmark, in vessels of 400, 500, and even 900 tons burden, all of which, there is reason to believe, were built in the Baltic; and, about six years afterwards, the king of Sweden was the owner of a ship of nearly 1000 tons burden, which he sent to England, with a request that she might be permitted to trade.

Gustavus I. who reigned about the beginning of the sixteenth century, seems to have been the first Swedish king who directed the attention and industry of his subjects to manufactures and commerce; but, in the early part of his reign, the inhabitants of Lubec had the monopoly of the foreign trade of Stockholm. This sovereign, in 1540, entered into a commercial treaty with Francis I., King of France; the principal article of which was, that the Swedes should import their wine, salt, &c. directly from France, instead of obtaining them indirectly from the Dutch. The conquest of Revel by Sweden, and the consequent footing obtained in Livonia, in 1560, greatly increased its commerce and wealth; while important improvements were introduced into its manufactures of iron a few years afterwards by the Flemings, who fled there on the destruction of Antwerp. Prior to their arrival, most of the Swedish iron was forged in Dantzic and Prussia; but they not only taught the Swedes how to forge it, but also how to make iron cannon, and other iron, copper, and brass articles. The Swedes had from an early period, been sensible of the real riches of their territory, and how much their timber, iron, pitch, and tar, were converted for maritime and other purposes. The pitch and tar manufacture especially had long constituted a very considerable part of their commerce. In 1647, Queen Christiana very unwisely granted a monopoly of these articles, which was productive of the usual effects, injury to commerce, without a correspondent benefit to those who held it. In the beginning of the eighteenth century, the tar company in Sweden not only put a very high price on their goods, but refused to sell them, even for ready money, unless they were exported in Swedish vessels. In consequence of this, England began at this period to encourage the importation of tar, pitch, hemp, and naval timber, from her American colonies.

The commerce of Denmark, besides its common origin with that of the rest of Scandinavia, seems, in the middle ages, to have been chiefly nourished by two circumstances:—The trade which Iceland carried on, and the establishment of Bergen, first as the staple of the German merchants, and afterwards as the chief factory of the Hanse merchants. In 1429, it was also established by the king of Denmark, as the sole staple for the fish trade. In 1553, its trade began to decline, in consequence, it is said, of its being deserted by the Hanseatics. The historian of the Hanseatic League adds, that "whereas the ancient toll of the Sound had been only a golden rose-noble on every sail, which was always understood to be meant on every ship; the court of Denmark had for some time past put a new and arbitrary construction on the word sail, by obliging all ships to pay a rose-noble for every sail on, or belonging to each ship". In consequence of this, the Vandalic-Hanse Towns, or those on the south shores of the Baltic, deserted the Bergen trade.

The same sovereign, however, who increased the tolls of the Sound, counterpoised the bad effects of this measure, by the encouragement he gave to manufactures and commerce; in this he was seconded by the Danish gentry, who began to carry on merchandize and factorage themselves, and also established manufactories. Copenhagen at this time was the staple for all Danish merchandize, especially corn, butter, fish, &c.

The commercial history of this country, towards the close of the sixteenth century, is remarkable for having given rise to the earliest dispute, of which we have any notice, respecting, the carrying of naval stores, of contraband of war, in neutral bottoms, to any enemy. It seems that the English merchants endeavoured to evade the custom duties in the Danish ports, particularly on their skins, woollen goods, and tin; on which they were siezed. On a remonstrance however from Elizabeth, they were restored, when the king of Denmark, on his part, complained that the English committed piracies on his subjects; for now, says Camden, there began to grow controversies about such matters, that is, the carrying naval stores, &c. to the Spaniards.

The commercial history of Denmark, during the period to which we are at present confined, presents no other circumstance sufficiently striking or interesting to detain us; for the establishments of this country in the East Indies are too trifling to deserve or require notice in a work whose limits and objects equally confine it to those points which are of primary importance.

The locality of Russia, cut off from the sea till a comparatively late period, except the almost inaccessible sea on which Archangel stands; the ignorance and barbarism of its inhabitants, and its wars with the Tartars, necessarily prevented and incapacitated this immense empire from engaging in any commercial intercourse with the rest of Europe till the beginning of the sixteenth century, when it became independent, and began to be powerful. Novogorod, indeed, which was in fact a republic under the jurisdiction of a nominal sovereign, enjoyed in the fifteenth century, a great trade, being then the mart between Russia and the Hanseatic cities. On its conquest by the Russians in the beginning of the next century, the Hanseatic merchants deserted it, though it continued for a considerable period afterward the largest and most commercial city in Russia. In 1509, Basilicus IV. conquered the city and territory of Pleskow and Smolensko, and consolidated the Russian empire, by reducing all the petty principalities into which it had been previously divided. Pleskow, situated near the head of the lake Czudskoc, soon became a celebrated emporium, and before the end of this century was frequented by merchants from Persia, Tartary, Sarmatia, Livonia, Germany, Britain, and other countries.

The accidental discovery of the White Sea by the English, in 1553, has been already narrated: this led to the first intercourse by sea between Russia and the rest of Europe, for previously, whatever of their produce was exported, was carried in Livonian ships. In the following year, the facilities of Russia with Asia were encreased by the conquest of the city and kingdom of Astracan: by this conquest the entire navigation of the Wolga became theirs, and by crossing the Caspian, they carried their commercial transactions into Persia. The spirit of conquest was now alive among them, and exerting itself both to the east and west; for in 1558 they conquered Narva, in Livonia, and by means of it formed a communication with the rest of Europe by the Baltic sea. To this city the Hanseatic merchants removed their mart from Revel. The conquest of Samoieda and Siberia near the close of the sixteenth century, contributed to encrease the exportable commodities of Russia by their furs, salmon, sturgeon, &c.

In the mean time the Russian commerce in the Caspian was increasing: the Persian vessels brought into Astracan dyed silks, calicoes, and Persian stuffs, and returned with cloth, sables, martens, red leather, and old Russia money. The trade from Archangel also increased in a still more rapid manner, principally, as we have already seen, with the English and Dutch. In the year 1655, the exports were valued at the 660,000 rubles, two rubles at that period being equal to one pound sterling. The principal articles were potash, caviare, tallow, hides, sables, and cable yarn; the other articles of less importance, and in smaller quantities, were coarse linen, feathers for beds, tar, linen yarn, beet, rhubarb, Persian silk, cork, bacon, cordage, skins of squirrels, and cats; bees' wax, hogs' birstles, mice and goats' skins, swan and geese down, candles, &c.

Peter the Great became emperor in 1689; he soon unfolded and began to execute his vast plans of conquest, naval power, and commerce. He gained for his country a passage into the Black Sea, by reducing Asoph, at the mouth of the Don, and he soon established a navy on this sea. His personal exertions in Holland and England, to make himself acquainted with ship-building, are well known. The event of his reign, however, which most completely changed the relative situation of Russia, and established her as a commercial nation, was the conquest from Sweden of Livonia, Ingria, and Carelia. Scarcely were these provinces secured to him, when he built, first Cronstadt, and then St. Petersburgh. The erection of this city, and the canals he constructed in the interior for the purpose of facilitating the transportation of merchandize from the more southerly and fertile districts of his empire to the new capital, soon drew to it the greater portion of Russian commerce. Archangel, to which there had previously resorted annually upwards of one hundred ships from England, Holland, Hamburgh, &c. declined; and early in the eighteenth century Petersburgh, then scarcely ten years old, beheld itself a commercial city of great importance.

Having now brought the historical sketch of the progress of discovery and of commercial enterprise down to the commencement of the eighteenth century, it will be necessary, as well as proper, to contract the scale on which the remainder of this volume is to be constructed. For, during nearly the whole of the period which intervenes between the commencement of the eighteenth century and the present time, the materials are either so abundant or so minute, that to insert them all without discrimination and selection, would be to give bulk, without corresponding interest and value, to the work.

So far as discovery is concerned, it is evident, from the sketch of it already given, that nearly the entire outline of the globe had been traced before the period at which we are arrived: what remained was to fill up this outline. In Asia, to gain a more complete knowledge of Hither and Farther India, of China, of the countries to the north of Hindostan, of the north and north-east of Asia, and of some of the Asiatic islands. In Africa, little besides the shores were known; but the nature of the interior, with its burning sands and climate, uninhabitable, or inhabited by inhospitable and barbarous tribes, held out little expectation that another century would add much to our knowledge of that quarter of the world; and though the perseverance and enterprise of the eighteenth century, and what has passed of the nineteenth, have done more than might reasonably have been anticipated, yet, comparatively speaking, how little do we yet know of Africa! America held out the most promising as well as extensive views to future discovery; the form and direction of her north-west coast was to be traced. In South America, the Spaniards had already gained a considerable knowledge of the countries lying between the Atlantic and the Pacific, but in North America, the British colonists had penetrated to a very short distance from the shores on which they were first settled; and from their most western habitations to the Pacific, the country was almost entirely unknown.

The immense extent of the Pacific Ocean, which presented to navigators at the beginning of the eighteenth century but few islands, seemed to promise a more abundant harvest to repeated and more minute examination, and this promise has been fulfilled. New Holland, however, was the only portion of the world of great extent which could be said to be almost entirely unknown at the beginning of the eighteenth century; and the completion of our knowledge of its form and extent may justly be regarded as one of the greatest and most important occurrences to geography contributed by the eighteenth century.

The truth and justice of these observations will, we trust, convince our readers, that, in determining to be more general and concise in what remains of the geographical portion of our works, we shall not be destroying its consistency or altering the nature of its plan, but in fact preserving both; for its great object and design was to trace geographical knowledge from its infancy till it had reached that maturity and vigour, by which, in connection with the corresponding increased civilization, general information and commerce of the world, it was able to advance with rapid strides, and no longer confining itself to geography, strictly so called, to embrace the natural history of those countries, the existence, extent, and form of which it had first ascertained.

The great object and design of the commercial part of this work was similar; to trace the progress of commercial enterprises from the rudest ages of mankind, the changes and transfers it had undergone from one country to another, the causes and effects of these, as well as of its general gradual increase, till, having the whole of Europe under its influence, and aided by that knowledge and civilization with which it had mainly contributed to bless Europe, it had gained its maturity and vigour, and by its own expansive force pushed itself into every part of the globe, in which there existed any thing to attract it.

At the beginning of the eighteenth century, commerce had not indeed assumed those features, or reached that form and dimensions by which it was distinguished at the end of this century; but as its dimensions gradually enlarge, it will be necessary to be less particular and more condensed.

Our plan indeed of being more minute in the early history of geographical science and commercial enterprise, is founded on an obvious as well as a just and important principle. In the infancy of geography and commerce, every fact is important, as reflecting light on the knowledge and state of mankind at that period, and as bearing on and conducing to their future progress; whereas when geography and commerce have been carried so far as to proceed in their course as it were by their own internal impulse, derived from the motion they have been acquiring for ages, their interest and importance is much diminished from this cause, as well as from the minuteness of the objects to which,—all the great ones having been previously occupied by them,—they must necessarily be confined.

Several circumstances co-operated to direct geographical discovery, during the eighteenth century, principally towards the north and north-east of Asia, and the north-west of America. The tendency and interest of the Russian empire to stretch itself to the east, and the hope still cherished by the more commercial and maritime nations of Europe, that a passage to the East Indies might be discovered, either by the north-east round Asia, or by the north-west, in the direction of Hudson's Bay, were among the most powerful of the causes which directed discovery towards those parts of the globe to which we have just alluded.

The extent of the Russian discoveries and conquests in the north and north-east of Asia, added much to geographical knowledge, though from the nature of the countries discovered and conquered, the importance of this knowledge is comparatively trifling. About the middle of the seventeenth century, they ascertained that the Frozen Ocean washed and bounded the north of Asia: the first Russian ship sailed down the river Lena to this sea in the year 1636. Three years afterwards, by pushing their conquests from one river to another, and from one rude and wandering tribe to another, they reached the eastern shores of Asia, not far distant from the present site of Ochotsk. Their conquests in this direction had occupied them nearly sixty years; and in this time they had annexed to their empire more than a fourth part of the globe, extending nearly eighty degrees in length, and in the north reaching to the 160° of east longitude; in breadth their conquests extended from the fiftieth to the seventy-fifth degree of north latitude. This conquest was completed by a Cossack; another Cossack, as Malte Brun observes, effected what the most skilful and enterprising of subsequent navigators have in vain attempted. Guided by the winds, and following the course of the tides, the current and the ice, he doubled the extremity of Asia from Kowyma to the river Anadyn. Kamschatcka, however, which is their principal settlement in the east of Asia, was not discovered till the year 1690; five years afterwards they reached it by sea from Ochotsk, but for a long time it was thought to be an island. The Kurile Islands were not discovered till the beginning of the eighteenth century.

The direction of discovery to this part of the world, as well as the plan by which it might be most advantageously and successfully executed, was given by Peter the Great, and affords one proof, that his mind was capacious, though his manners, morals, and conduct, might be those of a half-civilized tyrant. Peter did not live to carry his plan into execution: it was not, however, abandoned or neglected; for certainly the Russian government, much more than any other European government, seems to pursue with a most steady and almost hereditary predilection, all the objects which have once occupied its attention and warmed its ambition. On his death, his empress and her successors, particularly Anne and Elizabeth, contributed every thing in their power to carry his plan into full and complete execution. They went from Archangel to the Ob, from the Ob to the Jenesei. From the Jenesei they reached the Lena, partly by water and partly by land; from the Lena they went to the eastward as far as the Judigirka: and from Ochotsk they went by the Kurile Islands to Japan.

One of the most celebrated men engaged in the Russian discoveries in the early part of the eighteenth century was Behring: he was a Dane by birth, but in the service of Catherine, the widow of Peter the Great, who fixed upon him to carry into execution one of the most favourite plans of her husband. During Peter's residence in Holland, in the year 1717, the Dutch, who were still disposed to believe that a passage might be discovered to the East Indies in the northern parts of America, or Asia, urged the Emperor to send out an expedition to determine this point. There was also another point, less interesting indeed to commercial men, but on which geographers had bestowed much labour, which it was stated to the Emperor might be ascertained by the same expedition; this was, whether Asia and America were united, or divided by a sea, towards their northern extremities.

When Peter the Great returned to Russia, he resolved to attempt the solution of these problems; and with his own hand drew up a set of instructions for the proposed voyage; according to these, the vessels to be employed were to be built in Kamschatka; the unknown coasts of Asia and America were to be explored, and an accurate journal was to be kept.

It is not known whether the Emperor was induced to plan this expedition solely on the representations which were made to him in Holland, or from a belief that the close vicinity of the two continents of Asia and America had already been ascertained, or at least rendered highly probable, by some of his own subjects. It is certain that the Russians and the Cossacks in their service had reached the great promontory of Asia opposite to America; and it is said that the islands lying in Behring Straits, and even the continent beyond them, were known to them by report.

Peter, however, did not live to accomplish his design; and, as we have already noticed, his widow Catherine fixed upon Behring to conduct the expedition. After building a vessel in Kamschatka, he sailed in 1728: his first object was to examine the coast of this part of Asia. He was the first who ascertained Kamschatka to be a peninsula, and he framed an accurate chart of it, which is still regarded as one of the best extant. After reaching a Cape in north latitude 67° 18', and being informed by the inhabitants that beyond it the coast bended to the west, he resolved to alter his course to the south. This was accordingly done, but he did not discover the opposite coast of America; several circumstances were noticed, however, which indicated that there was land to the east, at no great distance, such as floating pine branches and other species of plants, unknown on the coast of Asia; these were always driven ashore when easterly winds prevailed. The inhabitants also informed him, that, in very clear weather, they were able, from the top of their highest mountains, to descry land to the east.

Encouraged by these circumstances, Behring resolved to undertake a second voyage from Kamschatka: in this voyage he was accompanied by a Russian, named Tchirikoff. They steered east, and first sought for land, which was said to have been discovered between the latitude of 40° and 50°; but finding none, they separated, and steering further north, the Russian discovered the continent of America in about 56-1/2°, and Behring 2° further north. On his return, the latter was wrecked in the island which bears his name, where he died.

About four years after the death of this navigator, which happened in 1741, the sea between Asia and America was visited by some Russian merchants, who obtained permission from the government to make discoveries, hunt and trade; the vessels employed for this purpose were formed of a few boards fastened together with leathern thongs; yet in these were discovered the Aleutian Islands. Soon afterwards another group of islands were discovered; and then a third group, the Black Fox Islands, which are near the American continent. It was not, however, till the year 1760, that the Russians learnt that Ochotsk was only separated from America by a narrow strait; and it is said that in 1764, a Russian mercantile company sent out some vessels, which passed through a strait to some inhabited islands in 64° north latitude; these were supposed to belong to the continent of America; but if a strait was discovered by these adventurers, there must be an error in the latitude, as in 64° there is no opening known to exist.

It was reserved for an English navigator to ascertain the truth of the report which the Russians had received from the inhabitants of Ochotsk, that their country was separated from America only by a narrow strait.

This was done during the third and last voyage of Captain Cook; the principal design of which was to ascertain the existence and practicability of a passage between the Pacific and Atlantic oceans, either to the north-east or north-west. For this purpose he carefully examined the north- west coast of America, beginning this examination in the latitude of 44° 33' north. Previously to this voyage an act of Parliament was passed, granting a reward of 20,000l. to any person who should discover any northern passage by sea between the

Atlantic and Pacific Oceans, in any parallel to the northward of the 52° of northern latitude. This voyage of Cook began in 1778; on the 9th of August, in that year, he ascertained the position and latitude of the western extremity of America, and soon afterwards he determined the width of that strait which divides the two continents. He then steered to the north, and continuing up the strait till he was in the latitude 70° 41', he found himself close to the edge of the ice which "was as compact as a wall," and ten or twelve feet high. He was of course obliged to return to the south, and in this part of his voyage he observed, on the American side, a low point in latitude 70° 29', to which he gave the name of Icy Cape. After the death of Cook, Captain Clarke entered the strait on the Asiatic side, and reached the latitude of 70° 33'; he afterwards got sight of the land on the American side in latitude 69° 34'. Such were the results of the last voyage of Captain Cook, respecting the proximity of Asia and America, and the nature of the strait by which they were divided.

Although the Spaniards seemed to be most interested in whatever concerned the west coast of America, yet they made no attempt to explore it from the commencement of the seventeenth century till the year 1774. In 1769, indeed, being alarmed at the evident design of the Russians to settle in the north-west coast, they formed establishments at St. Diego and Montory. In 1774 they traced the American coast from latitude 53° 53' to latitude 55°, and it is said discovered Nootka Sound. In the following year an expedition was sent from St. Blas, which proceeded along the north-west coast, and reached to latitude 57° 58'.

The voyage of Cook roused the Russian government to further exertions; and they accordingly fitted out an expedition to explore the sea between Asia and America: the command of it was given to an Englishman of the name of Billings, who had served as a petty officer under Captain Cook. He was, however, by no means qualified for his situation, and abandoned the enterprise in the latter end of July, having proceeded only a few leagues beyond Cape Barrenoi: the whole amount of the information procured during this voyage being confined to a few of the Aleutian Islands, and some points in the coast of America and Asia.

A few years afterwards the Empress Catherine sent out a secret expedition; the principal object of which was to ascertain the situation of the islands between the two continents. Little is known respecting this expedition, except that some observations were made on Behring's Straits, which, however, were not passed. The distance between the continents was estimated at forty-eight miles.

About the same time, the great profits which it was expected would be derived from the fur trade on the north-west coast of America, induced several commercial vessels to visit it; and during their voyages, nearly all the parts of it which had not been visited by Cook, were examined as far as the inlet which was named after him, in latitude 61° 15'. This extent of coast was found to consist of a vast chain of islands; and the appearance and nature of it revived the hope which Cook's last voyage had extinguished, that in this part of the coast there might be a practicable passage from the Pacific to the Atlantic ocean.

This hope was again extinguished in the opinion of most people, by the result of two of the most celebrated voyages which have been performed since the death of Captain Cook: we allude to the voyages of La Perouse, and of Vancouver: the former sailed with two frigates from Brest on the 1st of August, 1785: the object of this voyage was very comprehensive and important, being no less than to fill up whatever had been left deficient or obscure by former navigators, and to determine whatever was doubtful, so as to render the geography of the globe as complete and minute as possible: he was directed to supply the island in the South Seas with useful European vegetables. At present we shall confine our notice of this voyage to what relates to the more immediate object of this part of our work, the coast of North-west America.

The north-west coast of America was made by La Perouse, in latitude sixty degrees north: from this latitude he carefully traced and examined it to the Spanish settlement of Monterey.—an extent of coast of which Cook had had only a transient and imperfect view. Of this he constructed a chart, which at the time was justly regarded as extremely accurate and complete, but was subsequently rendered much more so by the survey of particular points and bays made by the vessels engaged in the fur trade, and especially by that which was constructed by Vancouver, from a close and careful examination of the numerous channels with which this coast abounds, principally performed in boats, and therefore descending into very minute details.

The accessions made by him to geography in other parts of the globe, as well as his unfortunate fate, will be afterwards related.

In the year 1790, a dispute arose between Britain and Spain, respecting Nootka Sound: on the adjustment of this dispute, the British government determined to send out an officer to secure possession of the settlement, and also to determine the question respecting the existence of a navigable passage between the Atlantic and Pacific Oceans. Captain Vancouver was selected for these purposes: his instructions were, after accomplishing his mission at Nootka Sound, to examine that part of the coast occupied by the chain of islands, discovered by the vessels in the fur trade, "and to ascertain, with the greatest exactitude, the nature and extent of every communication by water which might seem to tend to facilitate commercial relations between the north-west coast and the countries on the east of the continent, inhabited by British subjects or claimed by Great Britain;" and in particular to search for the strait of John de Fuca, and to examine if Cook's River had not its source in some of the lakes frequented by the Canadian traders, or by the servants of the Hudson's Bay Company.

He sailed from England with a sloop and brig on the 1st of April, 1791. He began his examination of the west coast of America, in latitude 39° 27' north, and continued it as far as Nootka: finding that the Spaniards raised difficulties to the restoration of this settlement, he proceeded to carry into execution the other objects of this voyage. During three summers, he surveyed the north-west coast of America as far as Cook's River, with a diligence, attention, and accuracy which could not have been surpassed. Every opening which presented itself was explored, and never left till its termination was determined; so that on a very careful and minute inspection of every creek and inlet of a coast consisting almost entirely of creeks and channels, formed by an innumerable multitude of islands, he thought himself justified in pronouncing, that there is no navigable passage between the Pacific and Atlantic Oceans, unless there may be a possibility of sailing through the strait between Asia and America, and navigating the Frozen Ocean. The surveys which were made during this voyage, may justly be said to have rendered perfect the geography of that part of the north-west coast of America to which it extended, and indeed to have completed the whole geography of this coast, which, from the multitude of its creeks, inlets, islands, &c., presents formidable as well as petty and troublesome difficulties in the way of its accurate and complete survey. Captain Vancouver, however, was extremely fortunate in the weather which attended him during the whole of the three summers which he spent on this coast.

Upwards of twenty years elapsed after the voyage of Vancouver, before another attempt was made to find out a passage from the north Pacific into the Atlantic Ocean. This attempt proceeded from Russia: not however from the government, but an individual. Count Romanzoff, a Russian nobleman, is well known for his liberal and judicious encouragement of every thing which can promote useful knowledge, especially in what relates to the improvement and benefit of his country. His first design was to fit out an expedition to explore the north-west passage by Hudson's Bay or Davis' Straits; but learning that the British government were making preparations to attempt it by that route, he changed his plan, and resolved to fit out an expedition to attempt the discovery of a passage from the eastward.

A ship was accordingly built and equipped, and the command given to Lieutenant Kotzebue. He sailed from Russia in the autumn of 1815, and on the 19th of June in the following year he reached Kamschatka. This he left on the 15th of July and on the 20th of that month, Behring's Islands were seen to the northward of Cape Prince of Wales. A tract of low land was ascertained to be an island about seven miles long, and a mile across, in the widest part: beyond it was a deep inlet running eastward into the continent. Lieutenant Kotzebue, animated and encouraged by this appearance, proceeded in a northerly direction, and found that the land continued low, and tended more to the eastwards. On the 1st of August the entrance into a broad inlet was discovered, into which the current ran very rapidly. The opening of this inlet was known before, and is indeed laid down in the charts attached to Marchand's Voyage round the World; but Kotzebue is certainly the first person who explained it. As it was perfectly calm when he reached this inlet, he resolved to go on shore, and examine from some eminence the direction of the coast. "We landed," he observes, "without difficulty, near a hill, which I immediately ascended; from the summit I could no where perceive land in the strait: the high mountains to the north either formed islands, or were a coast by themselves; for that the two coasts could not be connected together was evident, even from the very great difference between this very low and that remarkably high land. It was my intention to continue the survey of the coast in the boats, but a number of baydares coming to us along the coast from the east, withheld me." He afterwards had an interview with the Americans who came in these baydares: he found that they prized tobacco very highly, and that they received this and other European goods from the natives of the opposite coast of Asia. It was probably the first time in their lives that these Americans had seen Europeans. They were of the middle size; robust and healthy; ugly and dirty; with small eyes, and very high cheek bones: "they bore holes on each side of their mouths, in which they wear morse bones, ornamented with blue glass beads, which give them a most frightful appearance. Their dresses, which are made of skins, are of the same cut as the Parka, in Kamtschatka; only that there they reach to the feet, and here hardly cover the knee: besides this, they wear pantaloons, and small half boots of seal skins."

The latitude of this place, or rather of the ship's anchorage, at the time this survey was made, was 66° 42' 30", and the longitude 164° 12' 50". There were several circumstances which induced Kotzebue to hope that he had at length found the channel which led to the Atlantic: nothing was seen but sea to the eastward, and a strong current ran to the north-east. Under these circumstances, thirteen days were occupied in examining the shores of this opening; but no outlet was discovered, except one to the south-east, which seemed to communicate with Norton Sound, and a channel on the western side, which of course could not be the one sought for. Kotzebue, however, remarks, "I certainly hope that this sound may lead to important discoveries next year; and though a north-east passage may not with certainty be depended on, yet I believe I shall be able to penetrate much farther to the east, as the land has very deep indentures." The name of Kotzebue's Sound was given to this inlet. Next year he returned to prosecute his discovery; but in consequence of an accident which happened to the ship, and a very dangerous blow which he received at the same time, he abandoned the attempt.

That there is an opening, either by Kotzebue's Inlet or near to it, to the Frozen Ocean, is probable, not only from the circumstances we have mentioned of an opening and a strong current to the north-east having been observed, but also from other circumstances noticed in the account of this voyage. This current brings large quantities of drift wood into Kotzebue's Sound: and in the breaking up of the ice in the sea of Kamschatka, the icebergs and fields of ice do not drift, as in the Atlantic, to the south, nor do they drive to the Atlantic islands, but into the strait to the north. The direction of the current was always north-east in Behring's Straits; and it was so strong and rapid, as to carry the ship fifty miles in twenty-four hours; that is, above two miles an hour. On the Asiatic side of the strait it ran at the rate of three miles an hour; and even with a fresh north wind, it ran equally strong from the south. The inference drawn by Kotzebue is as follows: "The constant north-east direction of the current in Behring's Straits, proves that the water meets with no opposition, and consequently a passage must exist, though perhaps not adapted to navigation. Observations have long been made, that the current in Baffin's Bay runs to the south; and thus no doubt can remain that the mass of water which flows into

Behring's Straits takes its course round America, and returns through Baffin's Bay into the Ocean."

In 1819 the Russian government sent out another expedition, whose object was to trace the continent of America to the northward and eastward. In July, 1820, they reached Behring's Straits, and were supposed to have passed them in that year; in the winter they returned to some of the Russian settlements on the coast of America: what they have since done or discovered is not known.

Such is the result of what has hitherto been discovered by sea, with respect to the contiguity of Asia and America, the northern parts of these continents, and the probability of a passage from the Pacific to the Atlantic.

Very lately some attempts have been made to reach the north-eastern extremity of Asia by land. "In February, 1821, Baron Wrangel, an officer of great merit and of considerable science, left his head-quarters in the Nishney Kolyma, to settle by astronomical observations the position of Shatatzkoi Noss, or the North-east Cape of Asia, which he found to lie in latitude 70° 5' north, considerably lower than it is usually placed in the maps. Having crossed this point, he undertook the hazardous enterprize of crossing the ice of the Polar Sea, on sledges drawn by dogs, in search of the land said to have been discovered in 1762 to the northward of the Kolyma, He travelled directly north eighty miles, without perceiving any thing but a field of interminable ice, the surface of which had now become so broken and uneven, as to prevent a further prosecution of his journey. He had gone far enough, however, to ascertain that no such land had ever been discovered." (Quarterly Review, No. LII. p. 342.)

Another attempt, still more extraordinary and hazardous, has lately been made to explore the north-east of Asia, and particularly to determine whether the two continents of Asia and America do not unite at the North-east Cape, or in some other point. This enterprize was undertaken by Henry Dundas Cochrane, a commander in the British navy; who received assurances from the Russian government that he should not be molested on his journey; that he should receive any assistance, protection, and facilities he should require; and that he might join an expedition sent by the Russian government toward the Pole, if he should meet it, and accompany it as far as he might be inclined. He left Petersburgh in the beginning of the summer of 1820, and in one hundred and twenty-three days reached the Baikal, having traversed eight thousand versts of country, at the rate of forty-three miles a day. He seems afterwards to have gone as far as the Altai Mountains, on the frontiers of China. As, however, his principal object was to explore the extreme north-east of Asia, he went down the Lena, and reached Jakutzk on the 16th of October, 1820. On the Kolyma, where he arrived on the 30th of December, in longitude 164°, he met the Russian polar expedition. From Jakutzk to this place he travelled four hundred miles, without meeting a single human being. At the fair held at Tchutski, whither he next directed his steps, he received much information respecting the northeast of Asia. He ascertained the existence of this cape; all doubts, he says, being now solved, not by calculation, but by ocular demonstration. Its latitude and longitude, are well ascertained: he places this cape half a degree more to the northward than Baron Wrangel; but it is doubtful whether he himself reached it, and if he did, whether he had the means of fixing its latitude, or whether he depends entirely on the information he received at the fair of Tchutski. His expressions, in a letter to the President of the Royal Society, are, "No land is considered to exist to the northward of it. The east side of the Noss is composed of bold and perpendicular cliffs, while the west side exhibits gradual declivities; the whole most sterile, but presenting an awfully magnificent appearance." From the fair he seems to have returned to Kolyma, and thence proceeded to Okotsk, a dangerous, difficult, and fatiguing journey of three thousand versts, a great part performed on foot, in seventy days. From this last place he proceeded to Kamschatka, where it is supposed he was obliged to terminate his investigations, in consequence of an order or intimation from the Russian government not to proceed further.

We must next direct our attention to what has been done since the commencement of the eighteenth century, toward discovering a passage in the north-east of America, from the Atlantic to the Pacific Ocean.

One of the conditions on which the Hudson's Bay Company obtained their charter, in the year 1670, from Charles II., was, that they should prosecute their discoveries; but so far from doing this, they are accused, and with great appearance of reason, of not only suffering their ardour for discovery to cool, but also of endeavouring to conceal, as much as possible, the true situation and nature of the coast about Hudson's Bay, partly in order to secure more effectually their monopoly, and partly from the dread they entertained, that if a passage to the Pacific were discovered by this route, government would recal their charter, and grant it to the East India Company. They were indeed roused, but very ineffectively, from their torpor, by one of their captains intimating, that if they refused to fulfill the terms of their charter, by making discoveries, and extending their trade, he would himself apply to the crown. In order to silence him, they sent him and another captain out in two vessels, in 1719 or 1720; but they both perished, it is supposed, near Marble Island, without effecting any thing.

Two years afterwards they sent out another ship under the command of a person, who, destitute of the requisite knowledge and enterprize, was totally unfit for such an undertaking: the result was such as might have been anticipated—nothing was effected. An interval of twenty years passed over, and the company again sank into apathy on the subject of a north-west passage, when the attention of government was directed to the subject by the enthusiasm of an Irish gentleman of the name of Dobbs. Having well considered what preceding navigators had ascertained, and especially the remarkable circumstance particularly noticed by Fox, that the farther he removed from Sir Thomas Roe's Welcome the smaller was the height to which the tide rose, and who thence inferred, that if a passage were practicable, it must be in this direction, this gentleman applied to the company to send out a vessel. Accordingly, a vessel was sent; but all that is known of this voyage, and probably all that was done, amounts merely to this, that the vessel reached 62° 30' north latitude: here they saw a number of islands, and of white whales, and ascertained that the tide rose ten or twelve feet, and came from the north.

Mr. Dobbs next applied to government, who at his request sent out two vessels under Captain Middleton. But Middleton, who had been in the service of the company for many voyages, returned after having sailed up the Welcome to Wager's River, and looked into, or perhaps sailed round, a bay, which he named Repulse Bay. Mr. Dobbs accused him of having misrepresented or concealed his discoveries; and there seems good ground for such an accusation, which indeed was confirmed by the evidence of his officers, and not explicitly denied by himself. Government was undoubtedly of opinion that the voyage of Middleton had not determined the non-existence or impracticability of a passage; for the next year an act of parliament was passed, granting a reward of 20,000*l.* to the person or persons who should discover a northwest passage through Hudson's Straits to the western and southern ocean of America.

Stimulated by the hope of obtaining this large sum, a company was formed, who raised 10,000*l.*, in shares of 100*l.*, with which they fitted out two ships; the Dobbs, commanded by Captain More; and the California, by Captain Smith. They sailed from London on the 20th of May, 1746. When they reached the American coast near Marble Island, they made some observations on the tides, which they found flowed from the north-east, and consequently followed the direction of the coast; they likewise ascertained that the tide rose to the height of ten feet. While they were in their winter quarters at Port Jackson, they received little or no assistance from the servants of the Hudson's Bay Company. On resuming their voyage, and reaching the vicinity of Knight's Island, the needles of their compasses lost their magnetic quality, which they did not recover till they were kept warm. Proceeding northwards, they examined Wager's Strait; but in consequence of a difference of opinion between the commanders, they returned to England. The only points ascertained by this voyage were, that Wager's Strait was a deep bay, or inlet, and that there existed another inlet, which, however, they did not explore to the termination, named by them Chesterfield's Inlet. The fresh buffalo's flesh, which was sold to them by the Esquimaux, was probably the flesh of the musk ox.

After this voyage nothing was done, either by the Hudson's Bay Company, government, or individuals, towards the exploring of a passage in the north, till the year 1762, when the company, coinciding with the opinion that was then prevalent, that Chesterfield's Inlet ought to be examined, as affording a fair prospect of a passage into the Pacific Ocean, sent a vessel to determine this point. The report of the captain, on his return, was, that he had sailed up the inlet in a westerly direction for more than one hundred and fifty miles, till he found the water perfectly fresh; but he acknowledged that he did not go farther, or reach the head of it. As the result of this voyage was deemed unsatisfactory, still leaving the point which it had been its object to determine doubtful, the same captain was again sent out, in company with another ship, with express directions to trace the inlet to its western limits, if practicable. They ascertained that the fresh water, which had been discovered in the former voyage, was that of a river, which was the outlet of a lake, and this lake they explored; it was twenty-four miles long, and six or seven broad; they likewise found a river flowing into the lake from the west, but they were prevented from exploring it to any great distance by falls, that intercepted the progress of their boats. These particulars are detailed in Goldson's Observations on the Passage between the Atlantic and Pacific Oceans; the voyages themselves were never published, do not seem to be generally known, and have escaped the notice of Forster, the author of the History of Voyages and Discoveries in the North. Forster is likewise silent respecting an expedition that was equipped and sent out by some gentlemen of Virginia in 1772, to attempt a north-west passage. The captain on his return reported that he reached a large bay in latitude 69° 11', which he supposed hitherto unknown; that from the course of the tides, he thought it probable there might be a passage through it, but that as this bay was seldom free from ice, the passage could seldom if ever be practicable.

In the year 1770 the Hudson's Bay Company, more alive to the prospect of gain than to the interests of discovery and geographical science, having received some information from the Indians that copper might be obtained in great quantity far to the west of Fort Prince of Wales, resolved to dispatch Mr. Hearne, belonging to that fort, in search of it. This gentleman made four different excursions for this purpose, but it was only during the fourth that he reached to any great distance from the fort. In this excursion he penetrated to what he conceived to be the mouth of the Coppermine River, in the Frozen Ocean, about the latitude of 72° north. According to his account, Chesterfield Inlet is not the north-west passage, and the American continent stretches very considerably to the north-west of Hudson's Bay. The whole extent of his journey was about thirteen hundred miles. It was however doubted, whether what he deemed to be the mouth of the Coppermine River was actually such. It is certainly singular, that though he staid there for twenty-four hours, he did not actually ascertain the height to which the tide rose, but judged at that circumstance from the marks on the edge of the ice. There are other points in the printed account, as well as discrepancies between that and his MS., which tended to withhold implicit belief from his assertion, that he had reached the Frozen Ocean.

In the year 1789 the North-west Company having received information from an Indian, that there was at no great distance from Montreal, to the northward, a river which ran into the sea, Mr. M'Kenzie, one of the partners of that company, resolved to ascertain the truth of this report, by going himself on an expedition for that purpose. He set out, attended by a few Indians; and after traversing the desert and inhospitable country in which the posts of the company are established, he reached a river which ran to the north. He followed the course of this river till he arrived at what he conceived to be the Frozen Ocean, were he saw some small whales among the ice, and determined the rise and fall of the tide. This river was called after him, Mackenzie's River, and to the island he gave the name of Whale Island. This island is in latitude 69° 14'.

In 1793 Mr. M'Kenzie again set out on an inland voyage of geographical and commercial discovery, taking with him the requisite astronomical instruments and a chronometer. His course he directed to the west. After travelling one hundred miles on foot, he and his companions embarked on a river, running westward, which conveyed them to an inlet of the Pacific Ocean. Here he observed the rise and fall of the tide, and saw porpoises and sea otters. The claim of the discovery of the Frozen Ocean by a north-west route, to which Mr. M'Kenzie lays claim, has been questioned, as well as Mr. Hearne's claim. It has been remarked, that he might have ascertained beyond a doubt whether he had actually reached the sea, by simply dipping his finger into the water, and ascertaining whether it was salt or not. The account he gives of the rise of the tides at the mouth of Mackenzie River serves also to render it very doubtful whether he had reached the ocean; this rise he does not estimate greater than sixteen or eighteen inches. On the whole, we may conclude, that if Mr. Hearne actually traced the Coppermine River to its entrance into the sea, or Mr. M'Kenzie the river that bears his name, they have not been sufficiently explicit in their proofs that such was really the case.

At the time when the British government sent out Captain Cooke on his last voyage of discovery, Lieutenant Pickersgill was also sent out by them, to examine the western parts of Baffin's Bay, but he never entered the bay. Government were equally unfortunate in their choice of Lieutenant Young, who was sent with the same object the following year: he reached no farther than the seventy-second degree of latitude; and instead of sailing along the western side of the bay, which is generally free from ice, he clung to the eastern side, to which the ice is always firmly attached. Indeed, if Dr. Douglas's character of him was just, he was ill fitted for the enterprize on which he was sent; for his talents, he observes, were more adapted to contribute to the glory of a victory, as commander of a line-of-battle ship, than to add to geographical discoveries by encountering mountains of ice, and exploring unknown coasts.

Notwithstanding the unsuccessful issue of all these attempts to discover a north-west passage, the existence and practicability of it still were cherished by many geographers, who had particularly studied the subject. Indeed, nothing had resulted from any of the numerous voyages to the Hudson's or Baffin's Bay, which in the smallest degree rendered the existence of such a passage unlikely. Among those scientific men who cherished the idea of such a passage with the most enthusiasm and confidence, and who brought to the investigation the most extensive and minute knowledge of all that had been done, was Mr. Dalrymple, hydrographer to the Admiralty. "He had long been of opinion, that not only Greenland, but all the land seen by Baffin on the northern and eastern sides of the great bay bearing his name, was composed of clusters of islands, and that a passage through the *Fretum Davis*, round the northern extremity of Cumberland Island, led directly to the North Sea, from the seventy to the seventy-first degree of latitude." This opinion of Mr. Dalrymple was grounded, in part at least, on the authority of an old globe, one of the first constructed in Britain, preserved in the library of the Inner Temple: this globe contains all the discoveries of our early navigators. Davis refers to it; and Hackluyt, in his edition of 1589, describes it "as a very large and most exact terrestrial globe, collected and reformed according to the newest, secretest, and latest discoveries, both Spanish, Portugal, and English, composed by Mr. Emmeric Molyneaux, of Lambeth, a rare gentleman in his profession, being therein for diverse years greatly supported by the purse and liberality of the worshipful merchant Mr. William Sanderson."

Mr. Dalrymple prevailed on the Hudson's Bay Company to send out Mr. Duncan, a master in the navy, who had displayed considerable talent on a voyage to Nootka Sound. This gentleman was very sanguine of success, and very zealous in the cause in which he was employed. But this attempt also was unsuccessful: Mr. Duncan, after a considerable lapse of time, reaching no farther than Chesterfield Inlet.

The attention of scientific men, and of the public at large, was called again to this important problem in the geography of the northern seas, by some elaborate and well informed articles in the Quarterly Review, which are generally supposed to be written by Mr. Barrow, the under secretary of the Admiralty, who also published an abstract of voyages to the Northern Ocean.

The British government, influenced by a very laudable love of science, and perhaps regarding the discovery of a north-west passage as of the same importance to commerce as the reviewer evidently did, resolved to send an expedition for the purpose of attempting the discovery. Accordingly, on the 8th of April 1818, two ships, the Isabella and Alexander, well fitted by their construction, as well as strengthened and prepared in every possible manner for such a voyage, sailed from the Thames. Captain Ross had the principal command. It is not our design here to follow them during their voyage to their destination: suffice it to say, that on the 18th of August, exactly four months after they sailed from the Thames, the ships passed Cape Dudley Digges, the latitude of which they found to agree nearly with that assigned to it by Baffin, thus affording another proof of the accuracy of that old navigator, whose alleged discoveries have been latterly attempted to be wrested from him, or rather been utterly denied. The same day they passed an inlet, to which Baffin had given the name of Wolstenholme Sound. Captain Ross, in his account of his voyage, says it was completely blocked up with ice; but in the view taken of it, and published by him, there is a deep and wide opening, completely free from ice. In fact, on this occasion, as well as others of more consequence, to which we shall presently advert, Captain Ross, unfortunately for the accomplishment of the object on which he was sent, contented himself with conjecture where proof was accessible; for all he remarks respecting this sound is, that it seemed to be eighteen or twenty leagues in depth, and the land on the east side appeared to be habitable. When it is considered that in these high and foggy latitudes much deception of sight takes place, it ought to be the absolute and undeviating rule of the navigator to explore so far, and to examine so carefully and closely, that he may be certain, at least, that his sight does not deceive him. The same negligence attended the examination of Whale Sound: all the notice of it is, that they could not approach it in a direct line, on account of ice; it was, in fact, never approached nearer than twenty leagues. Captain Ross does not seem to have been fully sensible of the nature of the object on which he was sent out. If there existed a passage at all, it must be in a strait, sound, or some other opening of the sea: it could exist no where else. Every such opening, which exhibited the least appearance, or the smallest symptoms of stretching far, especially if it stretched in the proper direction, ought to have been practically and closely examined, not merely viewed at a distance in a foggy atmosphere. As for the impediments, they were what were to be expected, what the ships were sent out to meet and overcome; and till persevering and even highly hazardous efforts had proved that they could not be overcome, they ought not to have been suffered to weigh the least with the captain or his men, and especially not with the former.

But to proceed: about midnight on the 19th of August, the sound described by Baffin to be the largest of all the sounds he discovered, and called by him Sir Thomas Smith's Sound, was distinctly seen; and the two capes which formed its entrance were called by Captain Ross after the two ships Isabella and Alexander. "I considered," he informs us, "the bottom of this sound to be about eighteen leagues distant, but its entrance was completely blocked up by ice." Here again, a sound which seemed to promise fair to lead them into the great Polar Sea was left undiscovered, and in fact unapproached; for at the distance of eighteen leagues, in that deceptive climate, nothing could be really known of its real state or practicability. Had Captain Ross made the attempt; had he spent but a couple of days, and actually encountered serious obstacles, even though he had not experienced that those obstacles were insurmountable, he would have had some excuse; but it is impossible not to censure him for approaching no nearer than eighteen leagues to a sound such as this, and pronouncing at this distance that the ice blocked it up completely. His reasoning to support his belief that this sound afforded no passage, and to defend his not having explored it, is weak and inconclusive; but we shall not examine it, because the commander to whom such an expedition is entrusted, should never reason, where he can prove by actual observation and experiment. It is unsafe in him to reason, because he will most assuredly be tempted to make his line of conduct bend to his hypothesis and reasoning.

Captain Ross returned down the western side of Baffin's Bay. On the 21st an opening was seen, which answered to the description of Alderman Jones Sound, given by Baffin; but here again the ice and fog prevented them from approaching near; as if the fog might not have cleared up in a day or two, and the ice might not either have been drifted off in as short a space, or, if it could not, have been passed by the crew, so far, at least, as to have gained a nearer and better view of this sound.

Baffin describes this sound as a large inlet, and adds, that the coast tended to the southward, and had the appearance of a bay. This is confirmed by Captain Ross; for he informs us that the land was observed to take a southerly direction. On the 28th of August the sea became more clear of ice, and no bottom was found with three hundred fathoms of line: in the afternoon of that day they succeeded in getting completely clear of the ice, and once more found themselves in the open sea. Baffin and Davis both mention that the northern parts of Baffin's Bay were clear of ice when they were there, so that it is probably generally the case. On the 29th a wide opening was descried in the land; this they entered on the following day. "On each side was a chain of high mountains; and in the space between, W. S.W., there appeared a yellow sky, but no land was seen, nor was there any ice on the water, except a few icebergs; the opening therefore took the appearance of a channel, the entrance of which was judged to be forty-five miles; the land on the north side lying in an E.N.E. and W.S.W. direction, and the south side nearly east and west." "As the evening closed, the wind died away, the weather became mild and warm, the water much smoother, and the atmosphere clear and serene."

Even those who are little acquainted with the symptoms which in this high latitude indicate an open sea, must be struck with the wide difference between these circumstances and those which had met the navigators in almost every other part of their voyage, since they had approached the place where a passage might possibly exist and be found. Yet, even at this time and place, when expectation must have been high, and not without good reason, and when we are expressly informed by Captain Ross that much interest was excited by the appearance of the sound, the attempt to ascertain, by close and accurate investigation, whether this sound was really closed at its extremity, or led into another sea, was given up, after having sailed into it during the night, and till three o'clock the following day. It is unnecessary here to examine the reasons which induced Captain Ross to leave this sound without putting the question of its nature and termination beyond a doubt, by an accurate and close survey. He says, that at three o'clock he distinctly saw the land round the bottom of the bay, forming a connected chain of mountains with those which extended along the north and south sides. No person seems to have been on deck when this land was seen by the captain, and orders in consequence given to put the ships about, except Mr. Lewis, the master, and another. So that in this latitude, where the sight at all times is mocked with fogs and other circumstances which mislead it, and where, therefore, it is absolutely necessary that as many eyes as possible should be employed, that these should get as near the object as possible, that it should be viewed for a considerable length of time, and under as many aspects, and from as many points as possible—not a subordinate or incidental design of the voyage, but that for which it was expressly made, was abandoned, and on the sole responsibility of the captain and two other persons.

It is evident, too, that the entrance to many inland seas seems, when viewed from a distance, to be blocked up by connected land. It is well observed by the reviewer, whom we have already quoted, that there is not a reach in the Thames that to the eye does not appear to terminate the river; and in many of them (in the Hope, for instance) it is utterly impossible to form a conjecture, at the distance of only two or three miles, what part of the land is intersected by the stream.

Although, however, this voyage was abandoned when it ought not to have been, and consequently failed in its peculiar and important object, yet some access to geographical knowledge was gained by it. The existence of Baffin's Bay is confirmed, though its width and form are different from those which were previously assigned it in the maps; and thus this enterprising and deserving navigator has at length justice done to him.

Other branches of science were benefited and extended by this voyage, however unsuccessful it proved in its grand and leading object; and some of the accessions were of a very interesting nature. We allude principally to the observations made on the swinging of the pendulum,—the variation and dip of the magnetic needle,—especially by the influence of the iron in and about the ship,—and on the temperature of the sea at different depths.

Soon after the return of this expedition, an order in council was issued, which empowered and authorized the Board of Longitude to adopt a graduated scale of rewards, proportioned to the progress of discovery made to the westward in these high northern latitudes, from Hudson's or Baffin's Bay, in the direction of the Pacific Ocean. The first point of this graduated scale is the meridian of the Coppermine River of Hearne, and whatever ship reaches this is entitled to a reward of 5000l. Government were so convinced that Captain Ross's voyage had increased the probability of a north-west passage, that they determined to lose no time in making another attempt to discover it; and in order to afford every chance of success to this second attempt, they also determined, not only to send out a maritime expedition, to follow out the route which Captain Ross had so unaccountably and provokingly abandoned, but also to send out a land expedition, to co-operate in the same grand object.

The latter, under the command and direction of Lieutenant Franklin, was ordered to proceed from Fort York, on the shores of Hudson's Bay, to the mouth of the Coppermine River; and from thence along the shores of the Polar Sea, either to the east or to the north, as circumstances might determine: they were expressly to have in view the determination of the question regarding the position of the northeastern extremity of the continent of America. As the route of this land expedition lay for a great part of it through those districts within which the Hudson's Bay Company were accustomed to travel and trade, their co-operation and assistance was requested and obtained. The exact results of this land expedition are not yet fully and clearly known; but it is generally understood, that after having undergone infinite hardships and sufferings, they have been enabled to confirm Hearne and Mackenzie's discoveries or conjectures respecting the Coppermine River, and to ascertain other points connected with the geography and natural history of these remote and almost inaccessible regions, though the most important and leading points of the expedition have not been settled. [6]

In consequence of Captain Ross having penetrated into Baffin's Bay, an object only accomplished once before by Baffin himself, and which for two hundred years had been frequently again fruitlessly attempted, the Greenland ships which left England during the season immediately following Captain Ross's return, were induced, in order to reach a fresh and unfished sea, to pursue the course that he had opened for them. The circumstance that fourteen of them were wrecked, proves, unless the season had been uncommonly tempestuous, that Captain Ross must have conducted his expedition with considerable care and skill, notwithstanding he missed an excellent opportunity of either discovering a north-west passage, or of adding one more opening to those which were proved not to contain it.

The second sea expedition, to which we have already alluded, was under the direction of Captain Parry, who had sailed along with Captain Ross in the first expedition; he was therefore possessed of much knowledge and experience, which would prove essentially useful and directly applicable to the object he was about to undertake. Two ships were fitted out with all necessary preparations for such a voyage, the Hecla bomb, and Griper gun-brig, and they sailed from the Thames early in the month of May 1819. Of the high importance and value to navigators of the chronometer, Captain Parry had a striking and undoubted proof in the early part of his voyage. On the 24th of May he saw a small solitary crag, called Rockall, not far from the Orkney Islands. "There is," he observes, in this part of his journal, "no more striking proof of the infinite value of chronometers at sea, than the certainty with which a ship may sail directly for a single rock, like this, rising like a speck out of the ocean, and at the distance of forty-seven leagues from any other land."

About the middle of July he reached the latitude of 73°, after having made many fruitless attempts to cross the ice that fills the central portion of Davis's Strait and Baffin's Bay. the instructions of Captain Parry particularly pointed out the sound which Captain Ross had left unexplored, and which there could be no doubt was the Sir James Lancaster's Sound of Baffin, to be most carefully and minutely examined, as the one by which it was most probable a north-west passage might be effected, or which, at least, even if not navigable, on account of the ice, would connect the Pacific and Atlantic Oceans. On the seventh day after entering this sound, he succeeded in reaching open water; but this was not reached without infinite difficulty and labour, as the breadth of the barrier of ice was found to be eighty miles; through this they penetrated by the aid of sailing, tracking, heaving by the capstan, and sawing, being able to advance, even with the assistance of all the methods, only at the rate of half a mile an hour, or twelve miles a day.

For some days after this, their patience was tried, and nearly exhausted, by contrary winds, but on the 3d of August a favourable and fresh breeze arose from the eastward. Advantage was immediately taken of it. "We all felt," says Captain Parry, "it was that point of the voyage which was to determine the success or failure of the expedition, according as one or other of the opposite opinions respecting the termination of the sound should be corroborated. It is more easy to imagine than to describe (he continues) the almost breathless anxiety which was now visible in every countenance, while, as the breeze increased to a fresh gale, we ran quickly up the sound. The masts' heads were crowded by the officers and men during the whole afternoon; and an unconcerned observer (if any could have been unconcerned on such an occasion) would have been amused by the eagerness with which the various reports from the crow's-nest were received, all, however, hitherto favourable to our most sanguine hopes."

The weather, most fortunately at this interesting and important period, continued remarkably clear; and the ships having reached the longitude of 83° 12', the two shores of the sound were ascertained to be still at least fifty miles asunder, and what was still more encouraging, no land was discerned to the westward. In fact, there seemed no obstacle; none of those mountains with which, according to Captain Ross, the passage of the sound was eternally blocked up, nor even any ice, an object of a less serious and permanent nature. Other circumstances were also encouraging; the whole surface of the sea was completely free from ice, no land was seen in the direction of their course, and no bottom could be reached with one hundred and seventy fathoms of line, so that "we began," observes Captain Parry, "to flatter ourselves that we had fairly entered the Polar Sea, and some of the most sanguine among us had even calculated the bearing and distance of Icy Cape, as a matter of no very difficult or improbable accomplishment. This pleasing prospect was rendered the more flattering, by the sea having, as we thought, regained the usual oceanic colour, and by a long swell which was rolling in from the southward and eastward." The first circumstance that threw a damp over their sanguine expectations, was the discovery of land a-head; they were however renewed by ascertaining that this was only a small island: but though the insurmountable obstacle of a land termination of the sound was thus removed, another appeared in its place; as they perceived that a floe of ice was stretched from the island to the northern shore. On the southern shore, however, a large inlet was discovered, ten leagues broad at its entrance, and as no land could be seen in the line of its direction, hopes were excited that it might lead to a passage into the Polar Sea, freer from ice than the one above described. At this period of the voyage a singular circumstance was remarked: during their passage down Sir James Lancaster's Sound, the compass would scarcely traverse, and the ship's iron evidently had great influence over it: both these phaenomena became more apparent and powerful, in proportion as their westerly course encreased. When they were arrived in the latitude of 73°, the directive power of the needle became so weak, that it was completely overcome by the attraction of the iron in the ship, so that the needle might now be said to point to the north pole of the ship. And by an experiment it was found, that a needle suspended by a thread, the movements of which were of course scarcely affected by any friction, always pointed to the head of the ship, in whatever direction it might be.

To this inlet, which Captain Parry was now sailing down, he gave the name of the Prince Regent. The prospect was still very flattering: the width increased as they proceeded, and the land inclined more and more to the south-westward. But their expectations were again destroyed: a floe of ice stretched to the southward, beyond which no sea was to be descried. Captain Parry therefore resolved to return to the wide westerly passage which he had quitted. On the 22d of August, being in longitude 92-1/4°, they opened two fine channels, the one named after the Duke of Wellington; this was eight leagues in width, and neither land nor ice could be seen from the mast head though the weather was extremely clear; this channel tended to the N.N.W. The other stretched nearly west: and though it was not so open, yet as it was more directly in the course which it was their object to pursue, it was preferred by Captain Parry. By the 25th they had reached 99° west longitude, about 20 degrees beyond Lancaster Sound. On the 30th they made the S.E. point of Melville Island. By the 4th of September they had passed the meridian of 110° west longitude, in latitude 74° 44' 20": this entitled them to the first sum in the scale of rewards granted by parliament, namely 5000*l*; as at this part of their course they were opposite a point of land lying in the S.E. of Melville Island; this point was called Bounty Cape. On the 6th of September they anchored, for the first time since they had left England, in a bay, called after the two ships.

During the remainder of the season of 1819, which however contained only twenty more days, in which any thing could be done, Captain Parry prosecuted with much perseverance, and in the midst of infinite difficulties and obstacles, a plan which had suggested itself to him some time before; this was to conduct the ships close to the shore, within the main body of the ice; but their progress was so extremely slow, that, during the remainder of the year they did not advance more than forty miles. On the 21st Captain Parry abandoned the undertaking, and returned to the bay which was called after the two ships. Here they lay ten months; and the arrangements made by Captain Parry for the safety of the vessels, and for the health, comfort, and even the amusement of the crew, were planned and effected with such admirable good sense, that listlessness and fatigue were strangers, even among sailors, a class of men who, above all others, it would have been apprehended, would have soon wearied of such a monotonous life. The commencement of winter was justly dated from the 14th of September, when the thermometer suddenly fell to 9°. On the 4th of November the sun descended below the horizon, and did not appear again till the 8th of February. A little before and after what in other places is called the shortest day, but which to them was the middle of their long night, there was as much light as enabled them to read small print, when held towards the south, and to walk comfortably for two hours. Excessive cold, as indicated by the thermometer, took place in January: it then sunk from 30° to 40° below Zero: on the 11th of this month it was at 49°; yet no disease, or even pain or inconvenience was felt in consequence of this most excessive cold, provided the proper precautions were used; nor did any complaint arise from the extreme and rapid change of temperature to which they were exposed, when, as was often the case, they passed from the cabins, which were kept heated up to 60° or 70°, to the open air, though the change in one minute was in several instances 120° of temperature.

Cold, however, as January was, yet the following month, though, as we have already observed, it again exhibited the sun to them, was much colder; on the 15th of February the thermometer fell to 55° below Zero, and remained for fifteen hours not higher than 54°. Within the next fifteen hours it gradually rose to 34°. But though the sun re-appeared early in February, they had still a long imprisonment to endure; and Captain Parry did not consider it safe to leave their winter quarters till the 1st of August, when they again sailed to the westward: their mode of proceeding was the same as that which they had adopted the preceding year, viz. crawling along the shore, within the fast ice; in this manner they got to the west end of Melville Island. But all their efforts to proceed further were of no avail. Captain Parry was now convinced, that somewhere to the south-west of this there must be an immoveable obstacle, which prevented the ice dispersing in that direction, as it had been found to do in every other part of the voyage.

At last, on the 16th of August, further attempts were given up, and Captain Parry determined to return to the eastward, along the edge of the ice, in order that he might push to the southward if he could find an opening. Such an opening, however, could not be found; but by coasting southward, along the west side of Baffin's Bay, Captain Parry convinced himself that there are other passages into Prince Regent's Inlet, besides that by Lancaster Sound. The farthest point in the Polar sea reached in this voyage was latitude 71° 26' 23", and longitude 113° 46' 43:5". On the 26th of September they took a final leave of the ice, and about the middle of November they arrived in the Thames.

In every point of view this voyage was extremely creditable to Captain Parry; it is not surpassed by any for the admirable manner in which it was conducted, for the presence of mind, perseverance, and skill of all the arrangements and operations. It has also considerably benefited all those branches of science to which the observations and experiments of Captain Ross and his companions were directed, and to which we have already adverted. Perhaps in no one point has it been of more use to mariners, than in proving the minute accuracy of going to which chronometers have been brought.

As this expedition very naturally encouraged the hope that a north-west passage existed, and might be discovered and effected, and as Captain Parry was decidedly of this opinion, government very properly resolved to send him out again; he accordingly sailed in the spring of the year following that of his return. He recommended that the attempt should be made in a more southern latitude, and close along the northern coast of America, as in that direction a better climate might be expected, and a longer season by at least six weeks; and this recommendation, it is supposed, had its weight with the admiralty in the instructions and discretionary powers which they gave him.

We must now direct our attention to the southern polar regions. Geographers and philosophers supposed that in this portion of the globe there must be some continent or very large island, which would serve, as it were, to counterbalance the immense tracts of land which, to the northward, stretched not only as near the pole, as navigation had been able to proceed, but also west and east, the whole breadth of Europe and Asia.

The second voyage of Captain Cook was planned and undertaken for the express purpose of solving the question respecting the Terra Australis which occupied the older maps. He sailed on this voyage in July 1772, having under his command two ships, particularly well adapted and fitted up for such a service, the Resolution and Adventure; he was accompanied by a select band of officers, most of whom were not only skilful and experienced navigators, but also scientific astronomers and geographers; there were also two professed astronomers, two gentlemen who were well skilled in every branch of natural history, and a landscape painter.

On the 12th of December, Captain Cook entered the loose and floating ice, in latitude 62° 10'; on the 21st he met with icebergs in latitude 67°; and by the end of the month he returned to latitude 58°. On the 26th of January in the following year, he again penetrated within the Antarctic circle, and on the 30th, had got as far as latitude 71° 16'. This was the utmost point to which he was able to penetrate; and he was so fully persuaded, not only of the impracticability of being able to sail further to the south, but also of remaining in that latitude, that he returned to the northward the very same day, deeming it, as he expresses it, a dangerous and rash enterprize to struggle with fields of ice. "I," he continues, "who had ambition not only to go farther than any one before, but as far as it was possible for man to go, was not sorry to meet with this interruption." The existence of a southern continent was thus considered by Captain Cook, and all other geographers, as disproved to an almost absolute certainty.

In this voyage Captain Cook also obtained a correct knowledge of the land discovered by La Roche in 1675, and gave to it the name of New Georgia; he discovered, too, Sandwich land, which was then supposed to be the nearest land to the South Pole; he ascertained the extent of the Archipelago, of the New Hebrides, which had been originally seen by Quiros, and superficially examined by Bougainville. New Caledonia, and many of the islands among the groupe to which he gave the name of the Friendly Islands, were also among the fruits of this voyage.

The French government had sent out an expedition, about the same time that Captain Cook sailed in quest of a southern continent, on a similar pursuit. A French navigator some time before had stated that he had discovered land, having been driven far to the south, off the Cape of Good Hope. This supposed land the expedition alluded to was also to look after. The person selected to conduct it, M. De Kerguelen, does not seem to have been well chosen or qualified for such an enterprize; for after having discovered land, situated in 49° south latitude, and 69° east longitude from Greenwich, he returned rather precipitately to France, without having explored this land, concluding very rashly, and without any sufficient grounds, that the Terra Australis was at length ascertained to exist, and its exact situation determined. He was received and treated in France as a second Columbus: but as the French court seems to have had some doubts on the extent and merit of his alleged discoveries, notwithstanding the reception which it gave him, he was sent out a second time, with two ships of war of 64 and 32 guns each, and 700 men, to complete his discovery and take possession of this new continent. But he soon ascertained, what indeed he might and ought to have ascertained in his first voyage, that what he deemed and represented to be the Terra Australis was only a dreary and inhospitable island, of small size, so very barren and useless, that it produces no tree or even shrub of any kind, and very little grass. On such an island, in such a part of the globe, no inhabitants could be looked for; but it is even almost entirely destitute of animals; and the surrounding sea is represented as not more productive than the land. The French navigator was unable to find safe anchorage in this island, though it abounded in harbours; to this miserable spot he gave his own name. It was afterwards visited by Captain Cook, in his third voyage, and also by Peyrouse.

As the southern ocean, in as high a latitude as the climate and the ice rendered accessible and safe, had been as it were swept carefully, extensively, and minutely, by Captain Cook, and some subsequent navigators, without discovering land of any considerable extent, it was naturally supposed that no southern continent or even large island existed.

In the year 1819, however, this disbelief was partly destroyed by an unexpected and singular discovery. Mr. Smith, who commanded a vessel trading between Rio Plato and Chili, was naturally desirous to shorten, as much as possible, his passage round Cape Horn. With this object in view, he ran to a higher latitude than is usual in such voyages; and in latitude 62° 30' and in longitude 60° west, he discovered land. This was in his voyage out to Chili; but as he could not then spare the time necessary to explore this land, he resolved to follow the same course on his return voyage, and ascertain its extent, nature, &c. This he accordingly did; and likewise on a subsequent voyage. "He ran in a westward direction along the coasts, either of a continent or numerous islands, for 200 or 300 miles, forming large bays, and abounding with the spermaceti whale, seals, &c. He took numerous soundings and bearings, draughts and charts of the coast." He also landed and took possession of the country in the name of his sovereign, and called his acquisition New South Shetland. He represents the climate as temperate, the coast mountainous, apparently uninhabited, but not destitute of vegetation, as he observed firs and pines in many places; and on the whole, the country appeared to him very much like the coast of Norway.

It may seem extraordinary that land of this extent should not have been discovered by any former navigator; but the surprise will cease, when we reflect that though Captain Cook penetrated much further to the south than the latitude of New South Shetland, yet his meridian was 45 degrees farther to the west, and that he thus left a large expanse of sea unexplored, on the parallel of 62° between that and Sandwich land, the longitude of which is 22° west. He indeed likewise reached 67° south latitude: but this was in longitude from 137° to 147° west. Now the longitude of New South Shetland being 60° west, it is evident that Captain Cook in his first attempt, left unexplored the whole extent of longitude from 28°, the longitude of Sandwich land, to 60°, the longitude of New South Shetland; and in his second attempt, he was still further from the position of this new discovered land. Peyrouse reached no higher than 60° 30' latitude, and Vancouver only to 55°. Thus we clearly see that this land lay out of the track, not only of those navigators, whose object being to get into the Pacific by the course best known, pass through the Straits of Magellan and Le Maire, or keep as near Cape Horn as possible, but also of those who were sent out expressly to search for land in a high southern latitude.

The intelligence of the discovery of New South Shetland, and that its coasts abounded in Spermaceti whales, and in seals, quickly and powerfully roused the commercial enterprise both of the British and the Americans. In the course of a short time, numerous ships of both these nations sailed to its coasts; but from their observations and experience, as well as from a survey of it which was undertaken by the orders of one of His Majesty's naval officers, commanding on the southwest coast of America, it was soon ascertained that it was a most dangerous land to approach and to continue near. Its sterility and bleak and forbidding appearance, from all the accounts published respecting it, are scarcely equalled, certainly are not surpassed, in the most inhospitable countries near the North Pole; while ships are suddenly exposed to most violent storms, from which there is little chance of escaping, and in which, during one of the seal-catching seasons, a great number were lost.

There are, however, counterbalancing advantages: the seals were, at least during the first seasons, uncommonly numerous, and taken with very little trouble or difficulty, so that a ship could obtain a full cargo in a very short time; but, in consequence of a very great number of vessels which frequented the coasts for the purpose of taking these animals, they became soon less numerous, and were captured with less ease. The skins of these seals fetched a very high price in the China market; the Chinese, especially in the more northern parts of that vast and populous empire, use these skins for various articles of their dress; and the seal skins of New South Shetland being much finer and softer than those which were obtained in any other part of the world, bore a proportionably higher price in the China market. But the English could not compete with the Americans in this lucrative trade; for in consequence of the charter of the East India Company, the English ships were obliged to bring their cargoes of skins to England; here they were sold, and as none but the East India Company could export them to China, and consequently none except the Company would purchase; they in fact had the monopoly of them, and obtained them at their own price. The English indeed might take them directly from New South Shetland to Calcutta, whence they might be exported in country ships to China; but even in this case, which was not likely to happen, as few vessels, after having been employed in catching seals off such a boisterous coast, were prepared or able to undertake a voyage to Calcutta; much unnecessary expence was incurred, additional risk undergone, and time consumed. To these disadvantages in the sale of their seal skins, the Americans were not exposed; they brought them into some of their own ports, and thence shipped them directly and immediately to China.

The last navigator whom we noticed as having added to our knowledge respecting New Holland, was Dampier, who in this portion of the globe, not only discovered the Strait that separates New Guinea from New Britain, but also surveyed the north-west coast of New Holland; and, contrary to the Dutch charts, laid down De Witt's land as a cluster of islands, and gave it as his opinion that the northern part of New Holland was separated from the lands to the southward by a strait. Scarcely any thing was added to the geography of this portion of the globe, between the last voyage of Dampier, and the first voyage of Cook. One of the principal objects of this voyage of our celebrated navigator, was to examine the coast of New Holland; and he performed this object most completely, so far as the east coast was concerned, from the 38th degree of latitude to its northern extremity; he also proved that it was separated from New Guinea, by passing through the channel, which he called after his ship, Endeavour Strait. In the year 1791, Captain Vancouver explored 110 leagues of the south-west coast, where he discovered King George's Sound, and some clusters of small islands. In the same year two vessels were dispatched from France in search of La Peyrouse; in April 1792, they made several observations on Van Dieman's Land, the south cape of which they thought was separated from the main land; they also discovered a great harbour. In the subsequent year 1793, they again made the coast of New Holland, near Lewin's Land, and they ascertained that the first discoveries had been extremely accurate in the latitudes which they had assigned to this part of it.

In consequence of the British forming a settlement at Botany Bay, much additional information was gained, not only regarding the interior of New Holland, in the vicinity of the settlement, but also regarding part of its coast: the most interesting and important discovery relative to the latter was made towards the end of the year 1797, by Mr. Bass, surgeon of His Majesty's ship Reliance. He made an excursion in an open boat to the southward of Port Jackson, as far as 40 degrees of south latitude, and visited every opening in the coast in the course of his voyage: he observed sufficient to induce him to believe that Van Dieman's Land was no part of New Holland. Soon after the return of Mr. Bass, the governor of the English colony sent out him and Captain Flinders, then employed as a lieutenant of one of His Majesty's ships on the New South Wales station, with a view to ascertain whether Mr. Bass's belief of the separation of Van Dieman's Land was well founded. They embarked on board a small-decked boat of 25 tons, built of the fir of Norfolk island. In three months they returned to Port Jackson, after having circumnavigated Van Dieman's Land, and completed the survey of its coasts. The strait that separates it from New Holland was named by the governor, Bass's Strait. The importance of this discovery is undoubted. In voyages from New Holland to the Cape of Good Hope, considerable time is gained by passing through it, instead of following the former course. In the year 1800, Captain Flinders was again sent out by the governor, to examine the coast to the northward of Port Jackson; of this nothing more was known but what the imperfect notices given of it by Captain Cook supplied. In this voyage he completely examined all the creeks and bays as far to the northward as the 25th degree of latitude, and more particularly Glasshouse and Harvey's Bays. The English government at length resolved that they would wipe off the reproach, which, as Captain Flinders observes, was not without some reason attributed to them, "that an imaginary line of more than

250 leagues of extent, in the vicinity of one of their colonies, should have been so long suffered to remain traced upon the charts, under the title of UNKNOWN COAST," and they accordingly appointed him to the command of an expedition fitted out in England for this purpose.

Before giving an account of this voyage of Captain Flinders, we shall abridge, from the Introduction prefixed to it, his clear and methodical account of the progressive discoveries which have been made on the coast of New Holland, and of what was still to be explored. He particularly dwelt on the advantages that would result from a practicable passage through Torres' Strait; if this could be discovered, it would shorten the usual route by the north of New Guinea, or the Eastern Islands, in the voyage to India and China. The immense gulf of Carpentaria was unknown, except a very small portion of its eastern side. The lands called after Arnheim and Van Dieman also required and deserved a minute investigation, especially the bays, shoals, islands, and coasts of the former, and the northern part of the latter. The north-west coast had not been examined since the time of Dampier, who was of opinion that the northern portion of New Holland was separated from the lands to the northward by a strait. The existence of such a strait, Captain Flinders completely disproved.

With respect to the south coast, at least 250 leagues were unexplored. Captain Flinders had examined with considerable care and minuteness the east coast and Van Dieman's Land; but there were still several openings which required to be better explored.

Such were the principal objects which Captain Flinders had in view in his voyage; and no person could have been found better qualified to accomplish these objects. On the 18th of July, 1801, he sailed from England in the Investigator, of 334 tons: there were on board, beside the proper and adequate complement of men, an astronomer, a naturalist, a natural history painter, a landscape painter, a gardener, and a miner. As soon as he approached the south coast of New Holland, he immediately began his examination of the coasts, islands, and inlets of that large portion of it, called Nuyts' Land; he particularly examined all that part of the coast, which lies between the limit of the discoveries of Nuyts and Vancouver, and the eastern extremity of Bass' Straits, where he met a French ship, employed on the same object. In the month of July, 1802, he left Port Jackson, whither he had gone to refit, and sailing through Torres' Straits in 36 hours, he arrived in the Gulf of Carpentaria in the latter end of the season. In the course of this part of his voyage, he examined Northumberland and Cumberland islands, and the great barrier reefs of coral rock; and every part of the eastern side of the Gulf of Carpentaria; not a cape, creek, bay, or island on this coast of the gulf escaped his notice and examination. It was his intention to have pursued the same mode of close and minute examination: "following the land so closely, that the washing of the surf upon it should be visible, and no opening nor any thing of importance escape notice;" but he was prevented by ascertaining that the vessel was in such a crazy state, that, though in fine weather she might hold together for six months longer, yet she was by no means fit for such an undertaking. After much deliberation what conduct he ought to pursue under these circumstances, as it was impossible, with such a vessel, he could at that season return to Port Jackson by the west route, in consequence of the monsoon (and the stormy weather would render the east passage equally improper) he resolved to finish the survey of the Gulf of Carpentaria. This occupied him three months: at the end of this period he was obliged, by the sickness of his crew, to sail for Timor, which he reached on the 31st of March, 1803.

As the Investigator was no longer fit for service, she was condemned. Captain Flinders resolved, as he could not finish the survey, to return to England, in order to lay his journals and charts before the Admiralty: he accordingly embarked on board the Porpoise store ship, which, in company with the Cato and Bridgwater, bound to Batavia, sailed in August, 1803. The Porpoise and Cato were wrecked on a reef of rocks nearly 800 miles from Botany Bay: most of the charts, logs, and astronomical observations were saved; but the rare plants, as well as the dried specimens, were lost or destroyed. On the 26th of August, Captain Flinders left the reef in the cutter, and after a passage of considerable danger, reached Port Jackson on the 8th of September. As he was extremely anxious to lodge his papers as soon as possible with the Lords of the Admiralty, he embarked from Port Jackson in a vessel, something less than a Gravesend passage boat, being only 29 tons burden. Even in such a vessel, Captain Flinders did not lose sight of the objects nearest his heart: he passed through Torres' Straits, examined Pandora's entrance, explored new channels among the coral reefs, examined Prince of Wales Island, crossed the Gulf of Carpentaria, and after anchoring at some islands on the western side of the gulf, directed his route to Timor: here he refitted his vessel, and then sailed for the Isle of France, where it was absolutely necessary he should touch, in order that she might undergo a repair, as she was very leaky. Though he possessed passports from the French government, he was detained at the Isle of France, under the absurd pretence that he was a spy. All his books, charts, and papers were seized; and he himself was kept a prisoner in a miserable room for nearly four months. He was afterwards removed to the garden prison, a situation not so uncomfortable and prejudicial to his health as that from which he was taken; at length, in consequence of an application from the Royal Society to the National Institute, the French government sent an order for his liberation; but it was not received, or, at least, it was not acted upon till the year 1810; for it was not till that year that Captain Flinders was permitted to leave the Isle of France: he arrived in England on the 24th of October of that year.

There are few voyages from which more important accessions to geographical knowledge have been derived, than from this voyage of Captain Flinders, especially when we reflect on the great probability that New Holland will soon rank high in population and wealth. Before his voyage, it was doubtful, whether New Holland was not divided into two great islands, by a strait passing between Bass' Straits and the Gulf of Carpentaria. Captain Flinders has put an end to all doubts on this point: he examined the coast in the closest and most accurate manner: he found indeed two great openings; these he sailed up to their termination; and, consequently, as there were no other openings, and these were mere inlets, New Holland can no longer be supposed to be divided into two great islands, but must be regarded as forming one very large one; or, rather, from its immense size, a species of continent. He made another important and singular discovery, viz. that there are either no rivers of any magnitude in New Holland, or that if there be such, they do not find their way to the sea coast. This country seems also very deficient in good and safe ports: in his survey of the south coast, he found only one. He completed the survey of the whole eastern coast; of Bass's Straits and Van Dieman's Land, observing very carefully every thing relative to the rocks, shoals, tides, winds, currents, &c. Coral reefs, which are so common in most parts of the Pacific, and which, owing their origin entirely to worms of the minutest size, gradually become extensive islands, stretch along the eastern coast of New Holland. These were examined with great care by Captain Flinders: he found that they had nearly blocked up the passage through Torres' Straits, so that it required great care and caution to pass it with safety. But one of the most important results of this voyage respects the survey of the Gulf of Carpentaria; previously the extent and bearings of this gulf were not known; but from Captain Flinders's geography we have received an accurate and full survey of it. Its extent was ascertained to be 5 1/2 degrees of longitude, and 7 degrees of latitude; and its circuit nearly 400 leagues. On the coast of this gulf he found a singular trade carried on. Sixty proas, each about the burden of 25 tons, and carrying as many men, were fitted out by the Rajah of Boni, and sent to catch a small animal which lives at the bottom of the sea, called the sea slug, or *biche de mer.* When caught, they are split, boiled, and dried in the sun, and then carried to Timorlaot, when the Chinese purchase them: 100,000 of these animals is the usual cargo of each proa, and they bring from 2000 to 4000 Spanish dollars.

Notwithstanding the English had had settlements in New Holland for upwards of 26 years, little progress had been made in exploring the interior of the country even in the immediate vicinity of Botany Bay. It was supposed that a passage across the Blue Mountains, which are within sight of that settlement, opposed insurmountable obstacles. At length, about the end of the year 1813, the Blue Mountains were crossed for the first time, by Mr. Evans, the deputy surveyor of the colony. He found a fertile and pleasant district, and the streams which took their rise in the Blue Mountains, running to the westward; to one of the most considerable of these he gave the name of Macquarrie river; the course of this river he pursued for ten days. On his return to the colony, the governor, Mr. Macquarrie ordered that a road should be made across the mountains; this extended 100 miles, and was completed in 1815. Mr. Evans soon afterwards discovered another river, which he called the Lachlan.

As it was of great consequence to trace these rivers, and likewise to examine the country to the west of the Blue Mountains more accurately, and to a greater distance than it had been done, the governor ordered two expeditions to be undertaken. Lieutenant Oxley, the surveyor-general of the colony had the command of both. It does not fall within our plan or limits to follow him in these journeys; we shall therefore confine ourselves to an outline of the result of his discoveries. He ascertained that the country in general is very unfertile: the Lachlan he traced, till it seemed to loose itself in a multitude of branches among marshy flats. "Perhaps," observes Lieutenant Oxley, "there is no river, the history of which is known, that presents so remarkable a termination as the present: its course, in a strai*unknown?*—and what comparison, in point of extent and importance, do they bear to what was *known* to the ancients? In Asia, the interior of the vast kingdom of China is very imperfectly known, as well as Daouria and other districts on the confines of the Chinese and Russian empires; central Asia in general, and all that extensive, populous, and fertile region which extends from the southern part of Malaya, nearly under the equator, in a northerly direction, to the fortieth degree of latitude, are still not explored, or but very partially so, by European travellers. This region comprehends Aracan, Ava, Pegu, Siam, Tsiompa, and Cambodia. The south and east coasts of Arabia still require to be more minutely and accurately surveyed. In the eastern archipelago, Borneo, Celebes, and Papua, are scarcely known. Though all these bear but a small proportion to the vast extent of Asia, yet some of them, especially the country to the north of the Malay peninsula, and the islands in the eastern archipelago, may justly be regarded as not inferior, in that importance which natural riches bestows, to any part of this quarter of the globe.

Still, however, we possess some general notice, and some vague reports of all these countries; but it is otherwise with respect to the unknown portions of Africa. The whole of this quarter of the world, from the Niger to the confines of the British settlement at the Cape of Good Hope, may, with little limitation, be considered as unknown. Travellers have indeed penetrated a short distance from the western coast into the interior, in some parts between the latitude of the Niger and the latitude of the extreme northern boundary of the Cape settlement: and a very little is known respecting some small portions of the districts closely adjoining to the eastern coast; but the whole of central Africa is still unexplored, and presents difficulties and dangers which it is apprehended will not be speedily or easily overcome. To the north of the Niger lies the Sahara, or Great Desert; of this, probably, sufficient is known to convince us that its extent is such, that no country that would repay a traveller for his fatigue and risk, is situated to the north of it. To the east of the Niger, however, or rather along its course, and to the north of its course, as it flows to the east, much remains to be explored; many geographical details have been indeed gathered from the Mahomedan merchants of this part of Africa, but these cannot entirely be trusted. The course and termination of the Niger itself is still an unsolved problem.

Captain Scoresby, a most intelligent and active captain in the whale fishery trade, has very lately succeeded in reaching the eastern coasts of Greenland, and is disposed to think that the descendants of the Danish colonists, of whose existence nothing is known since this coast was blocked, up by ice at the beginning of the fifteenth century, still inhabit it. The northern shores of Greenland, and its extent in this direction are still unknown.

Notwithstanding the zeal and success with which the government of the

United States prosecute their discoveries to the west of the Mississippi, there is still much unexplored country between that river and the Pacific Ocean. It is possible that lands may lie within the antarctic circle, of which we have hitherto as little notion as we had of South Shetland ten years ago; but if there are such, they must be most barren and inhospitable. It is possible also, that, notwithstanding the care and attention with which the great Pacific has been so repeatedly swept, there may yet be islands in it undiscovered; but these, however fertile from soil and climate, must be mere specks in the ocean.

But though comparatively little of the surface of the globe is now utterly unknown, yet even of those countries with which we are best acquainted, much remains to be ascertained, before the geography of them can justly be regarded as complete. Perhaps we are much less deficient and inaccurate in our knowledge of the natural history of the globe, than in its geography, strictly so called; that is, in the extent, direction, latitudes and longitudes, direction and elevation of mountains, rise, course, and termination of rivers, &c. How grossly erroneous geography was till very lately, in some even of its most elementary parts, and those, too, in relation to what ought to have been the most accurately known portion of Europe, may be judged from these two facts,—that till near the close of the last century, the distance from the South Foreland, in Kent, to the Land's End, was laid down in all the maps of England nearly half a degree greater than it actually is; and that, as we have formerly noticed, "the length of the Mediterranean was estimated by the longitudes of Ptolemy till the eighteenth century, and that it was curtailed of nearly twenty-five degrees by observation, no farther back than the reign of Louis XIV."

To speak in a loose and general manner, the Romans, at the height of their conquests, power, and geographical knowledge, were probably acquainted with a part of the globe about equal in extent to that of which we are still ignorant; but their empire embraced a fairer and more valuable portion than we can expect to find in those countries which remain to reward the enterprise of European travellers. The fertile regions and the beautiful climate of the south of Europe, of the north of Africa, and above all of Asia Minor, present a picture which we can hardly expect will be approached, certainly will not be surpassed, under the burning heats of central Africa, or even the more mitigated heats of the farther peninsula of India. The short and easy access of all portions of the Roman Empire to the ocean, gave them advantages which must be denied to the hitherto unexplored districts in the interior of Asia and Africa. The farther peninsula of India is infinitely better situated in this respect.

At that very remote period, when sacred and profane history first displays the situation, and narrates the transactions of the human race, the countries, few in number, and comparatively of small extent, that were washed by the waters of the Mediterranean, comprised the whole of the earth which was then known. Asia Minor, which possessed the advantage of lying not only on this sea, but also on the Euxine, and which is moreover level in its surface, and fertile in its soil, seems to have been the first additional portion of the earth that became thoroughly known. The commercial enterprize of the Phoenicians, and their colonists the Carthaginians,—the conquests of Alexander the Great, and of the Romans, gradually extended the knowledge of the earth in all directions, but principally in the middle regions of Europe, in the north of Africa, and in Asia towards the Indus. At the period when the Roman empire was destroyed, little more was known; and during the middle ages, geography was feebly assisted and extended by a desire to possess the luxuries of the East, (which seems to have been as powerful and general with the conquerors of the Romans as with the Romans themselves,) by the religious zeal of a few priests, and by the zeal for knowledge which actuated a still smaller number of travellers.

The desire of obtaining the luxuries of the East, however, was the predominating principle, and the efficient cause of the extension of geography. Actuated by it, the passage of the Cape of Good Hope was accomplished; the eastern limits of Asia were reached; America was discovered, and even the Frozen Seas were braved and carefully examined, in the hope that by them a speedier passage might be found to the countries which produced these luxuries. At length the love of conquest, of wealth, and of luxury, which alone are sufficiently gross and stimulating in their nature to act on men in their rudest and least intellectual state, and which do not loose their hold on the most civilized, enlightened, and virtuous people, was assisted by the love of science; and though when this union took place, little of the globe was unknown, as respected its grand outline, and the general extent and relative situation of the seas and lands which compose its surface, yet much remained to be accomplished in determining the details of geography; in fixing accurately and scientifically the situation of places; in exhibiting the surface of the land, as it was distinguished by mountains, plains, lakes, rivers, &c.; in gaining a full and accurate knowledge of the natural history of each country, and of the manners, customs, institutions, religion, manufactures and commerce of its inhabitants.

Before we give a sketch of the progress of commercial enterprize during the last hundred years, it will be proper to notice the advancement of geographical science during the same period, and the assistance which was thus afforded, as well as from other sources, to those who travelled both by sea and land, for the purpose of discovering or exploring foreign and distant countries. This part of our subject seems naturally to divide itself into three parts; viz. the improvement of maps, which was equally advantageous to sea and land travellers; those particulars which rendered navigation more safe, easy, and expeditious; and those particulars which bestowed the same benefit on land travellers.

The science of geography dates its origin, as we have already mentioned, from Mercator, though he was unable to point out and explain the law, according to which the projection which bears his name might be laid down on fixed principles: this was effected by an Englishman of the name of Wright. Mathematical geography, strictly so called, seems to have owed its origin to the discussion respecting the flattening of the Poles, which took place, in the beginning of the eighteenth century, among Newton, Huygens, and Cassini, and which was afterwards continued by some of the most distinguished mathematicians and natural philosophers of France and England. Still, however, the construction of maps derived little advantage from the application of strict science to geography, till Delisle, in France, and Haase, in Germany, directed their attention and talents to this particular subject: their efforts were indeed great, but in some measure unavailing, in consequence of the want of sufficient materials. The same impediment lay in the way of Busching, notwithstanding he brought to the task the characteristic patience and research of a German. To him, however, and the more illustrious D'Anville, accurate delineations and descriptions of the countries of the globe may first justly be ascribed.

D'Anville possessed excellent and ample materials, in authentic relations, and plans and delineations made on the spot: with these he advanced to the task, calling to his aid mathematical principles. He first exhibited in his maps the interior of Asia free from that confusion and error by which all former maps had obscured it; and struck out from his map of Africa many imaginary kingdoms. Ancient geography, and the still more involved and dark geography of the middle ages, received from him the first illumination; and if subsequent geographers have been able to add to and correct his labours, it has been chiefly owing to their possessing materials which did not exist in his time.

Busching confined himself entirely to modern geography; and though his minuteness is generally tiresome and superfluous, yet we can pardon it, for the accuracy of his details: he was patronized and assisted in his labours by all the governments, of the north, who gave him access to every document which could further his object.

Since the time of D'Anville and Busching, the description of countries, and the construction of maps, have proceeded with a rapidly encreasing decree of accuracy. In ancient geography, Gosselin, Rennell, Vincent, and Malte Brun, are among the most celebrated names. Two Germans, Voss and Munnert, have directed their labours to illustrate and explain the geographical details and hints of the Greek poets. It would be almost endless to enumerate those to whom modern geography, and the construction of modern maps are principally indebted. Gaspari and Zimmerman, among the Germans, have thrown into a philosophical and interesting form the labours and heavy details which were supplied them by less original but more plodding men. The English, though, as Malte Brun observes, they are still without a system of geography which deserves the name, are rich in excellent materials, which have been supplied by the extent of their dominions and their commerce in various parts of the globe; by their laudable and happy union of conquest, commerce, and science; and by the advantage which Dalrymple, Arrowsmith, and other geographers have derived from these circumstances. The French, Russians, Spaniards, Danes, and indeed most nations of Europe, sensible of the vast importance of accurate maps, especially such as relate to their respective territories, have contributed to render them much more accurate than they formerly were; so that at present there is scarcely any part of the globe, which has been visited by sea or land, of-which we do not possess accurate maps; and no sooner has the labour of any traveller filled up a void, or corrected an error, than the map of the country which he has visited becomes more full and accurate.

The most direct and perfect application of mathematical and astronomical science to the delineation of the surface of the globe, so as to ascertain its exact form, and the exact extent of degrees of latitude in different parts of it, has been made by the English and French; and much to their honour, by them in conjunction. The first modern measurement of degrees of latitude was made by an Englishman of the name of Norwood: he ascertained the difference of latitude between London and York in 1635, and then measured their distance: from these premises he calculated, that the length of a degree was 122,399 English yards. At this time there was no reason to suppose that the earth was flattened at the Poles. Shortly afterwards, it having been discovered that the weights of bodies were less at the equator than at Paris, Huygens and Cassini directed their attention, as we have already stated, to the subject of the figure of the earth. In 1670 Picard measured an arc of the meridian in France; and in 1718, the whole area extending through France was measured by Cassini and other philosophers. The results of this measurement seemed to disprove Newton's theory, that the curvature of the earth diminished as we recede from the equator. To remove all doubts, an arc near the equator was measured in Peru, by some French and Spanish astronomers; and an arc near the arctic circle by some French and Swedish astronomers; the result was a confirmation of Newton's theory, and that the equatorial diameter exceeded the polar by about 1/204 part of the whole.

Since this period, arcs of the meridian have been measured in several countries. In 1787 it was determined by the British and French governments to connect the observatories of Greenwich and Paris by a series of triangles, and to compare the differences of latitudes and longitudes, ascertained by astronomical observations, with those ascertained by actual measurement. The measurement in England was extended to a survey of the whole kingdom; and the accurate maps thus obtained have been since published. Arcs of the meridian have also been measured lately from Dunkirk to Barcelona,—in Lapland, by which an error in the former measurement there was corrected;—and in India.

We have been thus particular in our notice of this subject, because it is evident that such measurements must lie at the foundation of all real improvements in the construction of maps.

Let us next turn our attention to the improvements in navigation which have taken place during the last and present centuries; these seem to consist, principally, in those which are derived from physical science, and those which are derived from other sources.

The grand objects of a navigator are the accurate knowledge of where he exactly is, in any part of his course, and how he ought to steer, in order to reach his destination in the shortest time. The means of ascertaining his latitude and longitude, of calculating how far he has sailed, and at what rate he is sailing, and the direction of his course with reference to the port to which he is desirous to proceed, are what he principally requires. We do not intend, by any means, to enter at any length, or systematically, on these subjects; but a brief and popular notice of them seems proper and necessary in such a work as this.

Astronomy here comes essentially to the aid of navigation: we have already seen how, even in the rudest state of the latter, it derived its chief assistance from this sublime science, confined as it then was to a knowledge of the position of a few stars. Astronomy enables the navigator to ascertain his latitude and longitude, and to find the variation of the compass. The principal difficulty in ascertaining the latitude at sea, arose from the unsteady motion of the ship: to remedy this, several instruments were invented. We have already alluded to the astrolobe; but this, as well as the others, were imperfect and objectionable, till such time as Hadley's quadrant was invented, the principle and uses of which were first suggested by Newton.

To ascertain the longitude was a much more difficult task: there are evidently two methods of doing this,—by time-keepers or chronometers, and by making the motions of the celestial bodies serve instead of time-keepers. About the middle of the seventeenth century, Huygens proposed the pendulum clock for finding the longitude at sea; but it was unfit for the purpose, for many and obvious reasons. Watches, even made with the utmost care, were found to be too irregular in their rate of going, to be depended upon for this purpose. In the reign of Queen Anne the celebrated act was passed, appropriating certain sums for encouraging attempts to ascertain the longitude. Stimulated by this, Mr. Harrison invented his time-keeper, which on trial was found to answer the purpose with such tolerable accuracy, that he was deemed worthy to receive the sum awarded by parliament: it went within the limit of an error of thirty miles of longitude, or two minutes of time, in a voyage to the West Indies. Since this period, chronometers have been much improved, and excellent ones are very generally used: perhaps the most trying circumstances in which any were ever placed, existed during the voyage for the discovery of a northwest passage by Captain Parry; and then most of those he had with him were found to be extremely accurate.

It is evident, however, that chronometers are liable to a variety of accidents, and that in very long voyages the means of verifying their rate of going seldom occur. Hence the lunar method, or the method of ascertaining the longitude by means of the motions of the moon, is more useful and valuable. Here again, the profoundest researches of Clairaut, Euler, D'Alembert, and La Place, were brought practically to bear on navigation. Guided and aided by these, Tobias Mayer, of Gottingen, compiled a set of solar and lunar tables, which were sent to the lords of the admiralty, in the year 1755; they gave the longitude of the moon within thirty seconds. They were afterwards improved by Dr. Maskelyne and Mr. Mason, and still more lately by Burg and Burckhardt; the error of these last tables will seldom exceed fifteen seconds, or seven miles and a half. The computations, however, necessary in making use of these tables, were found to be very laborious and inconvenient; to obviate this difficulty, the nautical almanack, suggested by Dr. Maskelyne, was published, which is now annually continued. The longitude is thus ascertained to such a nicety, as to secure the navigator from any danger arising from the former imperfect modes of finding it; "he is now enabled to make for his port without sailing into the parallel of latitude, and then, in the seaman's phrase, running down the port, on the parallel, as was done before this method was practised. Fifty years ago, navigators did not attempt to find their longitude at sea, unless by their reckoning, which was hardly ever to be depended on."

Not long after the mariner's compass was employed, its variation was noticed; as it is obvious that, unless the degree and direction of this variation are accurately known, the compass would be of little service in navigation, the attention of navigators and philosophers was carefully directed to this point; and it was ascertained that the quantity of this variation is subject to regular periodical changes. By means, therefore, of a table indicating those changes, under different latitudes and longitudes, and of what are called variation charts, the uncertainty arising from them is in a great measure done away. Another source of error however existed, which does not seem to have been noticed till the period of Captain Cook's voyages: it was then found, "that the variation of the needle differed very sensibly on the same spot, with the different directions of the ship's head." Captain Flinders attributed this to the iron in the ship, and made a number of observations on the subject; these have been subsequently added to and corrected, so that at present the quantity of variation from this cause can be ascertained, and of course a proper allowance made for it. It does not appear that any material improvement has been made in the construction and use of the log,—that useful and necessary appendage to the compass,— since it was invented about the end of the sixteenth century.

These are the most important improvements in nautical knowledge and science, which renders navigation at present so much more safe and expeditious than it formerly was; there are, however, other circumstances which tend to the same object; the more full, accurate, and minute knowledge of the prevalent winds at different times of the year, and in various parts of the ocean; the means of foretelling changes of weather; and, principally, a knowledge of the direction and force of the currents must be regarded as of essential advantage to the seaman. When to these we add, the coppering of ships, which was first practised about the year 1761, and other improvements in their built and rigging, we have enumerated the chief causes which enable a vessel to reach the East Indies in two-thirds of the time which was occupied in such a voyage half a century ago.

Nor must we forget that the health of the seamen has, during the same period, been rendered infinitely more secure; so that mortality and sickness, in the longest voyages, and under great and frequent changes of climate, and other circumstances usually affecting health, will not exceed what would have occurred on land during the same time.

The great advantages which the very improved state of all branches of physical science, and of natural history, bestow on travellers in modern times, are enjoyed, though not in an equal degree, by navigators and by those who journey on land. To the latter they are indeed most important, and will principally account for the superiority of modern travels over those which were published a century ago, or even fifty years since. It is plain that our knowledge of foreign countries relates either to animate or inanimate nature: to the soil and geology, the face of the surface, and what lies below it; the rivers, lakes, mountains, climate, and the plants; or to the natural history, strictly so called:— and to the manners, institutions, government, religion, and statistics of the inhabitants. Consequently, as the appropriate branches of knowledge relating to these objects are extended, travellers must be better able, as well as more disposed, to investigate them; and the public at large require that some or all of them should at least be noticed in books of travels. The same science, and many of the same instruments, which enable the seaman to ascertain his latitude and longitude, and to lay down full and accurate charts of the shores which he visits, are also useful to the land-traveller; they both draw assistance from the knowledge of meteorology which they may possess, to make observations on the climate, and from their acquaintance with botany and natural history, to give an account of the plants and animals. But it is evident that so far as the latter are concerned, as well as so far as relates to the inhabitants, the land traveller has more opportunities than he who goes on a voyage.

But there are other advantages enjoyed by modern travellers besides those derived from superior science: foreign languages are at present better and more generally understood; and it is unnecessary to point out how important such an acquisition is, or rather how indispensible it is to accurate information. The knowledge of the languages of the East which many of the gentlemen in the service of the East India Company, and the missionaries, possess has been of infinite service in making us much better acquainted with the antiquities, history, and present state of those countries, than we could possibly have otherwise been. There is at present greater intercourse among even remote nations; and prejudices, which formerly operated as an almost insurmountable barrier, are now either entirely destroyed, or greatly weakened: in proof of this, we need only refer to the numerous travellers who have lately visited Egypt,--a country which it would have been extremely dangerous to visit half a century ago. At the same distance of time, natives of Asia or Africa, especially in their appropriate costume, were seldom or never seen in the streets of London, or, if seen, would have been insulted, or greatly incommoded by the troublesome curiosity of its inhabitants; now there are many such, who walk the streets unmolested, and scarcely noticed.

Commerce, which has derived such advantages from the progress of geographical knowledge, has in some measure repaid the obligation, by creating a much greater, more intimate, and more frequent mutual intercourse among nations; and by doing away with those prejudices and antipathies which formerly closed many countries effectually against Christian and European travellers: and to the zeal and perseverance of modern travellers, assisted as they are by commercial intercourse, we may reasonably hope that we shall, before long, be indebted for a knowledge of the interior of Africa. Those countries still imperfectly known in the south-east of Asia will, probably, from their vicinity to our possessions in Hindostan, be explored from that quarter. The encreasing population of the United States, and the independence of South America, will necessarily bring us acquainted with such parts of the new world as are still unknown. But it is difficult to conjecture from what sources, and under what circumstances, the empires of China and Japan will be rendered more accessible to European travellers: these countries, and some parts of the interior of Asia, are cut off from our communication by causes which probably will not speedily cease to operate. The barriers which still enclose all other countries are gradually yielding to the causes we have mentioned; and as, along with greater facilities for penetrating into and travelling within such countries, travellers now possess greater capabilities of making use of the opportunities thus enjoyed, we may hope that nearly the whole world will soon be visited and known, and known, too, in every thing that relates to inanimate and animate nature.

The progress of commerce during the last hundred years, the period of time to which we are at present to direct our attention, has been so rapid, its ramifications are so complicated, and the objects it embraces so various and numerous, that it will not be possible, within the limits to which we must confine ourselves, to enter on minute and full details respecting it; nor would these be consonant to the nature of our work, or generally interesting and instructive.

During the infancy of commerce, as well as of geographical science, we deemed it proper to be particular in every thing that indicated their growth; but the reasons which proved the necessity, or the advantage, of such a mode of treating these subjects in the former parts of this volume, no longer exist, but in fact give way to reasons of an opposite nature--reasons for exhibiting merely a general view of them. Actuated by these considerations, we have been less minute and particular in what relates to modern geography, than In what relates to ancient; and we shall follow the same plan in relation to what remains to be said on the subject of commerce. So long as any of the causes which tended to advance geography and commerce acted obscurely and imperfectly--so long as they were in such a weak state that the continuance of their progress was doubtful, we entered pretty fully into their history; but after a forward motion was communicated to them, such as must carry them towards perfection without the possibility of any great or permanent check, we have thought it proper to abstain from details, and to confine ourselves to more general views. Guided by this principle which derives additional weight from the vastness to which commerce has reached within the last hundred years, we shall now proceed to a rapid and general sketch of its progress during that period, and of its present state.

From the first and feeble revival of commerce in the middle ages, till the discovery of the Cape of Good Hope, the Italian republics, and the Hanseatic League, nearly monopolized all the trade of Europe; the former, from their situation, naturally confining themselves to the importation and circulation of the commodities supplied by the East, and by the European countries in the south of Europe, and the districts of Africa then known and accessible; while the latter directed their attention and industry to those articles which the middle and north of Europe produced or manufactured.

The discovery of the Cape of Good Hope gave a different direction to the commerce of the East, while at the same time it very greatly extended it; but as it is obvious that a greater quantity of the commodities supplied by this part of the world could not be purchased, except by an increase in the produce and manufactures of the purchasing nations, they also pushed forward in industry, experience, skill, and capital. The Portuguese and Spaniards first reaped the fruits of the discovery of the Cape of Good Hope; subsequently the Dutch; and at the period at which this part of our sketch of commerce commences, the English were beginning to assume that hold and superiority in the East, by which they are now so greatly distinguished. The industry of Europe, especially of the middle and northern states, was further stimulated by the discovery of America, and, indirectly, by all those causes which in the fifteenth and sixteenth centuries tended to increase information, and to secure the liberty of the mass of the people. The invention of printing; the reformation; the destruction of the feudal system, at least in its most objectionable, degrading, and paralizing features; the contentions between the nobility and the sovereigns, and between the latter and the people; gave a stimulus to the human mind, and thus enlarged its capacities, desires, and views, in such a manner, that the character of the human race assumed a loftier port.

From all these causes commerce benefited, and, as was natural to expect, it benefited most in those countries where most of these causes operated, and where they operated most powerfully. In Holland we see a memorable and gratifying instance of this: a comparatively small population, inhabiting a narrow district, won and kept from the overwhelming of the ocean, by most arduous, incessant, and expensive labour,--and the territory thus acquired and preserved not naturally fertile, and where fertile only calculated to produce few articles,--a people thus disadvantageously situated, in respect to territory and soil, and moreover engaged in a most perilous, doubtful, and protracted contest for their religion and liberty, with by far the most potent monarch of Europe,--this people, blessed with knowledge and freedom, forced to become industrious and enterprizing by the very adverse circumstances in which they were placed, gradually wrested from their opponents--the discoverers of the treasures of the East and of the new world, and who were moreover blessed with a fertile soil and a luxurious climate at home,--their possessions in Asia, and part of their possessions in America. Nor did the enterprising spirit of the Dutch confine itself to the obtaining of these sources of wealth: they became, as we have already seen, the carriers for nearly the whole of Europe; by their means the productions of the East were distributed among the European nations, and the bulky and mostly raw produce of the shores of the Baltic was exchanged for the productions and manufactures of France, England, Germany, and the Italian states.

From the middle of the eighteenth century, the commerce of the Dutch began to decline; partly in consequence of political disputes among themselves, but principally because other nations of Europe now put forth their industry with effect and perseverance. The English and the French, especially, became their great rivals; first, by conducting themselves each their own trade, which had been previously carried on by the Dutch, and, subsequently, by the possessions they acquired in the East. The American war, and soon afterwards the possession of Holland by the French during the revolutionary war, gave a fatal blow to the remnant of their commerce, from which it has not recovered, nor is likely at any time to recover, at least nearly to its former flourishing state. For, as we have remarked, the Dutch were flourishing and rich, principally because other nations were ignorant, enslaved, and destitute of industry, skill, and capital.

England took the place of the Dutch in the scale of commercial enterprise and success: the contest between them was long and arduous; but at length England attained a decided and permanent superiority. She gradually extended her possessions in the East; and after expelling the French from this part of the world, became in reality the only European sovereign power there.

The manufactures of England, those real and abundant causes and sources of her immense commerce, did not begin to assume that importance and extent to which they have at present reached, till the middle, or rather the latter part of the eighteenth century; then her potteries, her hardware, her woollens, and above all her cotton goods, began to improve. Certainly the steam engine is the grand cause to which England's wealth and commerce may be attributed in a great degree; but the perfection to which it has been brought, the multifarious uses to which it is applied, both presuppose skill, capital, and industry, without which the mere possession of such an engine would have been of little avail.

At the termination of the American war, England seemed completely exhausted: she had come out of a long and expensive contest, deprived of what many regarded as her most valuable possessions, and having contracted an enormous debt. Yet in a very few years, she not only revived, but flourished more than ever; it is in vain to attribute this to any other causes but those alone which can produce either individual or national wealth, viz. industry, enterprize, knowledge, and economy, and capital acquired by means of them. But what has rendered Britain more industrious, intelligent, and skilful than other nations?-- for if we can answer this question, we can satisfactorily account for her acquisition of capital; and capital, industry, and skill existing, commerce and wealth must necessarily follow.

Britain enjoys greater political freedom, and greater security of property than any other European nation; and without political freedom, the mass of the people never can be intelligent, or possess either comprehensive views or desires; and where views and desires are limited, there can be no regular, general, and zealous industry. Unless, however, security of property is enjoyed, as well as political liberty, industry, even if it could spring up under such circumstances, must soon droop and decay. It is a contradiction in terms to suppose that comprehensive views and desires can exist and lead to action, when at the same time it is extremely doubtful whether the objects of them could be realized, or, if realized, whether they would not immediately be destroyed, or torn from those whose labour, and skill, and anxious thought had acquired them.

But there are other causes to which we must ascribe the extension of British manufactures and commerce; of these we shall only enumerate what we regard as the principal and the most powerful: the stimulus which any particular improvement in manufactures gives to future and additional improvements, or rather, perhaps, the necessity which it creates for such additional improvements; the natural operation of enlarged capital; the equally natural operation of encreased wealth among the various classes of the community; the peculiar circumstances in which Britain has been placed since the termination of the war which deprived her of her American colonies; and, lastly, her national debt. A short view of each of these particulars will, we believe, sufficiently account for the present unparalleled state of British manufactures and commerce.

The direct effect of improvement in the mode of manufacturing any article, by the introduction of a more powerful machinery, is to encrease the quantity, and to lower the price of that article. Hence it follows, that those who manufacture it on the old plan must be undersold, unless they also adopt such machinery; and as knowledge, both speculative and practical, has greater chance to improve in proportion as it is spread, from this cause, as well as from the more powerful cause of rival interests, wherever improvements in manufactures have begun and been extended, they are sure to advance.

That this is not theoretical doctrine requires only an appeal to what has been effected, and is yet effecting in Britain, to prove. A very curious, interesting, and instructive work might be written on the improvements in the cotton machinery alone, which have been made in this country during the last forty years: we mean interesting and instructive, not merely on account of the tacts relative to mechanical ingenuity which it would unfold, but on account of the much higher history which it would give of the mechanism of the human mind, and of the connections and ramifications of the various branches of human knowledge. In what state would the commerce of Great Britain have been at this time, if the vast improvements in the machinery for spinning cotton had not been made and universally adopted?--and how slowly and imperfectly would these improvements have taken place, had the sciences been unconnected, or greater improvements, which at first were unseen or deemed impracticable, not been gradually developed, as lesser improvements were made. The stimulus of interest, the mutual connection of various branches of science, and above all the unceasing onward movement of the human mind in knowledge, speculative as well as practical, must be regarded as the most powerful causes of the present wonderful state of our manufactures, and, consequently, of our commerce.

2. The natural operation of enlarged capital is another cause of our great commerce. There is nothing more difficult in the history of mankind--not the history of their wars and politics, but the history of their character, manners, sentiments, and progress in civilization and wealth--[as->than] to distinguish and separate those facts which ought to be classed as causes, and those which ought to be classed as effects. There can be no doubt that trade produces capital; and, in this point of view, capital must be regarded as an effect: there can be as little doubt, that an increase of capital is favourable to an increase of commerce, and actually produces it; in this point of view, therefore, capital must be regarded as

a cause. As in the physical world action and reaction are equal, so are they, in many respects, and under many circumstances, in the moral and intellectual world; but, whereas in the physical world the action and reaction are not only equal but simultaneous, in the moral and intellectual world the reaction does not take place till after the immediate and particular action from which it springs has ceased.

To apply these remarks to our present subject, it is unnecessary to point out in what manner trade must increase capital; that capital, on the other hand, increases trade, is not, perhaps, at first sight, quite so obvious; but that it must act in this manner will be perceptible, when, we reflect on the advantages which a large capital gives to its possessor. It enables him to buy cheaper, because he can buy larger quantities, and give ready money; buying cheaper, he can sell cheaper, or give longer credit, or both; and this must ensure an increase of trade. It enables him immediately to take advantage of any improvement in the mode of manufacturing any article; and to push the sale of any article into countries where it was before unknown. Such are some of the more important effects on commerce of large capital; and these effects have been most obviously and strikingly shewn in the commercial history of Britain for the last thirty years, and thus give a practical confirmation to the doctrine, that capital, originally the creature of trade, in its turn gives nourishment, rigour, and enlarged growth to it.

3. Encreased wealth among the various classes of the community, may be viewed In the same light as capital; it flows from increased trade, and it produces a still further increase of trade. The views, and desires, and habits of mankind, are like their knowledge, they are and must be progressive: and if accompanied, as they generally are, by increased means, they must give birth to increased industry and skill, and their necessary consequences, increased trade and wealth.

Had the views, desires, and habits of mankind, and especially of the inhabitants of Europe and the United States, continued as they were fifty years ago, it is absolutely impossible that one half of the goods manufactured in Great Britain could have been disposed of; and unless these additional and enlarged views, desires, and habits, had been accompanied with commensurate means of gratifying them, our manufactures and commerce could not have advanced as they have done. Minutely and universally divided as human labour is, no one country can render its industry and skill additionally productive, without, at the same time, the industry and skill of other countries also advance. No one nation can acquire additional wealth, unless additional wealth is also acquired in other nations. Before an additional quantity of commodities can be sold, additional means to purchase them must be obtained; or, in other words, increased commerce, supposes increased wealth, not only in that country in which commerce is increased, but also in that where the buyers and consumers live.

4. Since the termination of the American war, Britain has been placed in circumstances favourable to her commerce: the human mind cannot long be depressed; there is an elasticity about it which prevents this. Perhaps it is rather disposed to rebound, in proportion to the degree and time of its restraint. It is certain, however, that the exhaustion produced by the American war speedily

gave place to wonderful activity in our manufactures and commerce; and that, at the commencement of the first French revolutionary war, they had both taken wonderful and rapid strides. The circumstances, indeed, of such a country as Britain, and such a people as the British, must be essentially changed,--changed to a degree, and in a manner, which we can hardly suppose to be brought about by any natural causes,--before its real wealth can be annihilated, or even greatly or permanently diminished. The climate and the soil, and all the improvements and ameliorations which agriculture has produced on the soil, must remain: the knowledge and skill, and real capital of the inhabitants, are beyond the reach of any destroying cause: interest must always operate and apply this knowledge and skill, unless we can suppose, what seems as unlikely to happen as the change of our climate and soil, the annihilation of our knowledge and skill, or that interest should cease to be the stimulating cause of industry; unless we can suppose that political and civil freedom should be rooted out, and individual property no longer secure.

Circumstances, however, though they cannot destroy, must influence, beneficially or otherwise, the wealth and commerce of a country; and it may happen that circumstances apparently unfavourable may become beneficial. This was the case with Britain: during the American war, her manufactures and commerce languished; during the French wars they increased and throve most wonderfully. The cause of this difference must be sought for principally in the very artificial and extraordinary circumstances in which she was placed during the French war: and of these circumstances, the most powerfully operative were her foreign loans; her paper circulation; the conquests and subsequent measures of Bonaparte on the continent; and her superiority at sea. Foreign loans necessarily rendered the exchange unfavourable to Britain; an unfavourable exchange, or, in other words, a premium on bills, in any particular country, enabled the merchant to sell his goods there at a cheaper rate than formerly, and consequently to extend his commerce there. The paper circulation of Britain,-- though a bold and hazardous step, and which in a less healthy and vigorous state of public credit and wealth than Britain enjoyed could not have been taken, or, if taken, would not have produced nearly the beneficial effects it did, and would have left much more fatal consequences than we are at present experiencing,-- undoubtedly tended to increase her commerce; and the very stimulus which it gave to all kinds of speculation has been favourable to it. The ruinous consequences of such speculation, though dreadful, are comparatively of short duration; whereas it is impossible that speculation should be active and vigorous, with commensurate means, without improving manufactures, and opening new channels for commerce; and these effects must remain. In what manner the measures of Bonaparte on the continent, and our superiority at sea, were favourable to our commerce, it is unnecessary to explain.

Lastly. It only remains to explain how our national debt has been beneficial to our commerce. Necessity, if it is not absolutely overpowering, must act as a stimulus to industry as well as interest: the desire to avoid evil, and the desire to obtain good, are equally powerful motives to the human mind. In the same manner as an increase of family, by creating additional expense, spurs a man to additional industry; so the certainty that he must pay additional taxes produces the same effect. Individuals may contrive to shift the burden from themselves, and pay their taxes by spending less; but there can be no doubt that the only general, sure, and permanent fund, out of which additional taxes can be paid, must arise from the fruits of additional industry. We wish to guard against being taken for the advocates for taxation, as in any shape a blessing: we are merely stating what we conceive to be its effect. But we should no more regard taxation as a blessing, because it increased commerce, than we should regard it as a blessing to a man, that, from any cause, he was obliged to work fourteen hours a day instead of twelve. In both cases, increased labour might be necessary, but it would not the less be an evil.

The only other nation, the commerce of which has increased very materially and rapidly, is the United States of America; and if we trace the chief and most powerful causes of their commercial prosperity, we-shall still further be confirmed in the opinion, that at least some of the causes which we have assigned for the extension of British commerce are the true ones; and that, in fact, commerce cannot generally or permanently increase where these causes do not exist, and that where they do they must encourage and extend it

It is not our intention to enter into a detail of the causes of American prosperity, except so far as they are connected with its commerce. They may, however, be summed up in a few words. An inexhaustible quantity of land, in a good climate, obtained without difficulty, and at little expence; with the produce of it, when obtained and cultivated, entirely at the disposal and for the exclusive advantage of the proprietor. The same with regard to all other labour; or, in other words, scarcely any taxes: and with respect to labour in general, great demand for it, and extremely high wages. These are causes of increased population and of prosperity, and indirectly of commerce, peculiar to America. It requires no illustration or proof to comprehend how the increased produce of a new soil must supply increased articles for commerce. While Britain, therefore, finds increased articles for her commerce, from her improvements in the machinery applicable to manufactures, by means of which the same quantity of human labour is rendered infinitely more productive,--the United States finds materials for her increased commerce, in the increasing stock of the produce of the soil.

Political and civil liberty, and the consequent security of property, are causes of commercial prosperity, common to the United States and Britain.

It may also be remarked, that the circumstances of Europe, almost ever since the United States have had a separate and independent existence, have been favourable to its commerce. The long war between Britain and France afforded them opportunities for increasing their commerce, which they most sedulously and successfully embraced and improved. They became, in fact, the carriers for France, and in many cases the introducers of British produce into the continent.

There is only another circumstance connected with the United States to which we deem it necessary to advert in this brief and general developement of the causes of their commercial prosperity: we allude to the wonderful facilities for internal commerce afforded them by their rivers, and especially by the Mississippi and its branches. There can be no doubt that easy, speedy, cheap, and general inter-communication to internal trade,--whether by means of roads and canals, as in England, or by means of rivers as in America, is advantageous to foreign commerce, both directly and indirectly. It is advantageous directly, in so far as it enables the manufacturer with great facility, and at little expence, to transmit his goods to the places of exportation; and to ascertain very quickly the state of the markets by which he regulates his purchases, sales, and even the quantity and direction of his labour. It is advantageous indirectly, in so far as by stimulating and encouraging internal trade, it increases wealth, and with increased wealth comes the increased desire of obtaining foreign produce, and the increased means to gratify that desire.

We deemed it proper to preface the details we shall now give on the subject of the present state of commerce with these general remarks on the principal causes which have enlarged it, in those two countries in which alone it flourishes to a very great extent. But, as we have already remarked, commerce cannot extend in one country, without receiving an impulse in other countries. While, therefore, British and American commerce have been increasing, the general commerce of the whole civilized world, and even of parts hardly civilized, have been increasing; but in no country nearly to the extent to which it has reached in Britain and the United States, because none are blessed with the political advantages they enjoy, or have the improved machinery and capital of the one, or the almost inexhaustible land of the other.

In the details which we are now about to give, we shall confine ourselves to the statement of any particular circumstance which may have been favourable or otherwise to the commerce of any country during the last hundred years, and to an enumeration of the principal ports and articles of import and export of each country. We shall not attempt to fix the value of the imports and exports in toto, or of any particular description of them, because there are in fact no grounds on which it can be accurately fixed. We shall, however, in the arrangement of the order of the goods exported, place ihose first which constitute the most numerous and important articles.

1. The countries in the north of Europe, including Russia, Sweden, Norway, Denmark, and the countries generally on the south shores of the Baltic. From the geographical situation of these countries, and their consequent climate, the chief articles of the export commerce must consist in the coarsest produce of the soil. These, and the produce of their mines, are the sources of their wealth, and consequently of their commerce.

The principal exports of Norway consist of timber, masts, tar, potash, hides, (chiefly those of the goat,) iron, copper, cobalt, tallow, salted provisions, and fish. Corn, principally from the southern shores of the Baltic, is the most considerable article of import. The only event in the modern history of this country, which can affect its commerce, is its annexation to Sweden; and whether it will be prejudicial or otherwise, is not yet ascertained.

Denmark consists of the islands in the Baltic, and the peninsula lying in the north-west of Germany, comprizing Jutland, Sleswig, and Holstein. The face of the country, both insular and continental, presents a striking contrast to that of Norway, being flat, and fertile in corn and cattle. Denmark possesses a large extent of sea coast, but the havens do not admit large vessels. The communication between the insular and continental possessions, the German ocean and the Baltic, and consequently the commerce of Denmark, was much facilitated by the canal of Keil, which was finished in 1785. Prior to the year 1797, the commerce was much injured by numerous restraints on importation. During the short wars between this country and Britain, it suffered considerably. At present it cannot rank high as a commercial kingdom. Denmark and the Duchies, as they are called, export wheat, rye, oats, barley, rape seed, horses, cattle, fish, wooden domestic articles, &c.; and import chiefly woollen goods, silks, cottons, hardware, cutlery, paper, salt, coals, iron, hemp, flax, wines, tobacco, sugar, and other colonial produce.

Sweden in general is a country, the wealth, and consequently the objects of commerce of which, are principally derived from its mines and woods. Its principal ports are Stockholm and Gothenburgh. The political event in the history of this country which gave the most favourable impulse to its commerce in modern times, is the alteration in its constitution after the death of Charles XII.; by this the liberties of the people were encreased, and a general stimulus towards national industry was given: agriculture was improved, the produce of the mines doubled, and the fishery protected. More lately, the revolution in 1772, and the loss of Finland, have been prejudicial to Sweden. The principal exports are, iron, copper, pine-timber, pitch, tar, potash, fish, &c.; the principal imports are, corn, tobacco, salt, wines, oils, wool, hemp, soap, cotton, silk and woollen goods, hardware, sugar, and other colonial produce.

The most important commercial port on the southern shore of the Baltic is Dantzic, which belongs to Prussia. This town retained a large portion of the commerce of the Baltic after the fall of the Hanseatic League, and with Lubec, Hamburgh, and Bremen, preserved a commercial ascendency in the Baltic. It suffered, however, considerably by the Prussians acquiring possession of the banks of the Vistula, until it was incorporated with the kingdom in 1793. Dantzic exports nearly the whole of the produce of the fertile country of Poland, consisting of corn, hides, horse-hair, honey, wax, oak, and other timber; the imports consist principally of manufactured goods and colonial produce. Swedish Pomerania, and Mecklenburgh, neither of which possess any ports of consequence, draw the greater part of their exports from the soil, as salted and smoked meat, hides, wool, butter, cheese, corn, and fruit; the imports, like those of Dantzic, are principally manufactured goods and colonial produce.

The immense extent of Russia does not afford such a variety, or large supply of articles of commerce, as might be expected: this is owing to the ungenial and unproductive nature of a very large portion of its soil, to the barbarous and enslaved state of its inhabitants, and to the comparatively few ports, which it possesses, and the extreme distance from the ocean or navigable rivers of its central parts. We have already mentioned the rise of Petersburgh, and its rapid increase in population and commerce. The subsequent sovereigns of Russia have, in this as in all other respects, followed the objects and plans of its founder; though they have been more enlightened and successful in their plans of conquest than in those of commerce. The most important advantage which they have bestowed on commerce, arises from the canals and inland navigation which connects the southern and the northern provinces of this vast empire. The principal commerce of Russia is by the Baltic. Petersburgh and Riga are the only ports of consequence here; from them are exported corn, hemp, flax, fir timber, pitch, tar, potash, iron and copper, hides, tallow, bristles, honey, wax, isinglass, caviar, furs, &c. The principal imports consist of English manufactures and colonial produce, especially coffee and sugar, wines, silks, &c. The commerce of the Black Sea has lately increased much, especially at Odessa. The principal exports are, corn, furs, provisions, &c.; its imports, wine, fruit, coffee, silks, &c. Russia carries on a considerable internal trade with Prussia, Persia, and China, especially, with the latter. Nearly the whole of her maritime commerce is in the hands of foreigners, the Russians seeming rather averse to the sea; and the state of vassalage in the peasants, which binds them to the soil, preventing the formation of seamen. Latterly, however, she has displayed considerable zeal in posecuting maritime discoveries; and as she seems disposed to extend her possessions in the north-west coast of America, this will necessarily produce a commercial marine.

2. The next portion of Europe to which we shall direct our attention consists of Germany, the Netherlands, and France.

Germany, though an extensive and fertile country, and inhabited by an intelligent and industrious race of people, possesses few commercial advantages from its want of ports: those on the Baltic have been already mentioned; those on the German Ocean are Hamburgh and Embden, of which Hamburgh is by far the most important, while, to the south, the only port it possesses is Trieste. It is, however, favoured in respect to rivers: the Elbe, Weser, Rhine, and Danube, with their tributary streams affording great facilities, not only for inland commerce, but also for the export and import of commodities. The chief political disadvantage under which Germany labours, affecting its commerce, arises from the number of independent states into which it is divided, and the despotic nature of most of its governments. As might be expected from such a large tract of country, the productions of Germany are various. Saxony supplies for exportation, wool of the finest quality, corn, copper, cobalt, and other metals, thread, linen-lace, porcelain, &c. Hanover is principally distinguished for its mines, which supply metals for exportation. The chief riches of Bavaria arise from its corn and cattle: these, with pottery, glass, linen, and silk, are the exports of Wurtemburgh. Prussia Proper affords few things for exportation: the corn of her Polish provinces has been already mentioned, as affording the principal export from Dantzic. Silesia supplies linen to foreign countries. Austria, and its dependant states, export quicksilver, and other metals, besides cattle, corn, and wine.

The commerce of the Netherlands, including Holland, though far inferior in extent and importance to what it formerly was, is still not inconsiderable. Indeed, the situation of Holland, nearly all the towns and villages of which have a communication with the sea, either by rivers or canals, and through some part of the territory of which the great rivers Rhine, Meuse, and Scheld empty themselves into the sea, must always render it commercial. The principal ports of the Netherlands are Amsterdam, Rotterdam, and Antwerp. The exports of the Netherlands consist either of its own produce and manufactures, or of those which are brought to it from the interior of Germany: of the former, butter, cheese, madder, clover-seed, toys, &c. constitute the most important; from Germany, by means of the Rhine, vast floats of timber are brought. The principal imports of the Netherlands, both for her own use and for the supply of Germany, consist of Baltic produce, English goods, colonial produce, wines, fruits, oil, &c.

There is perhaps no country in Europe which possesses greater advantages for commerce than France: a large extent of sea coast, both on the Atlantic and the Mediterranean; excellent harbours; a rich soil and genial climate, adapted to a great variety of valuable productions; and some manufactures very superior in their workmanship,--all these present advantages seldom found united. Add to these her colonial possessions, and we shall certainly be surprized that her commerce should ever have been second, to that of any other country in Europe. Prior to the revolution it was certainly great; but during and since that period it was and is vastly inferior to the commerce of Great Britain, and even to that of the United States.

The extent of sea coast on the Atlantic is 283 leagues, and on the Mediterranean eighty leagues: the rivers are numerous, but none of the first class. The canal of Languedoc, though from its connecting the Atlantic and the Mediterranean it would naturally be supposed highly advantageous to commerce, is not so; or rather, it is not turned to the advantage to which it might be applied. In England such a canal would be constantly filled with vessels transporting the produce of one part to another. It is not, however, so; and this points to a feature in the French character which, in all probability, will always render them indisposed, as well as unable, to rival Britain, either in manufactures or commerce. Besides the want of capital, which might be supplied, and would indeed be actually supplied by industry and invention, the French are destitute of the stimulus to industry and invention. As a nation, they are much more disposed to be content with a little, and to enjoy what they possess without risk, anxiety, or further labour, than to increase their wealth at such a price.

The principal commercial ports of France on the Atlantic are Havre, St. Maloes, Nantes, Bourdeaux, and Bayonne: Marseilles is the only commercial port of consequence in the Mediterranean. The principal exports of France are wines, brandy, vinegar, fruit, oil, woollen cloth of a very fine quality, silk, perfumery, &c.: the imports are Baltic produce, the manufactures of England; fruits, drugs, raw wool, leather, &c. from Spain, Italy, and the Mediterranean states.

3. The next division of Europe comprehends Spain, Portugal, Italy, and

Greece.

Spain, a country highly favoured by nature, and at one period surpassed by no other kingdom in Europe in civilization, knowledge, industry, and power, exhibits an instructive and striking instance of the melancholy effects of political degradation. Under the power of the Arabians, she flourished exceedingly; and even for a short period after their expulsion, she retained a high rank in the scale of European kingdoms. The acquisition of her East Indian and American territories, and the high eminence to which she was raised during the dominion of Charles V. and his immediate successors,--events that to a superficial view of things would have appeared of the greatest advantage to her,--proved, in fact, in their real and permanent operation, prejudicial to her industry, knowledge, and power. It would seem that the acquisition of the more precious metals, which may be likened to the power of converting every thing that is touched into gold, is to nations what it was to Midas,--a source of evil instead of good. Spain, having substituted the artificial stimulus of her American mines in the place of the natural and nutritive food of real industry, on which she fed during the dominion of the Moors, gradually fell off in commercial importance, as well as in political consequence and power. The decline in her commerce, and in her home industry, was further accelerated and increased by the absurd restrictions which she imposed on the intercourse with her colonies. All these circumstances concurring, about the period when she fell into the power of the house of Bourbon,--that is, about the beginning of the eighteenth century,--she sunk very low in industry and commerce, and she has, since that period, continued to fall.

And yet, as we have observed, she possesses great natural advantages: a sea coast on the Atlantic and Mediterranean of considerable extent; a great variety of climate and soil, and consequently of productions,--she might become, under a wise and free government, distinguished for her political power and her commerce.

On the Atlantic, the first port towards the north is Saint Sebastian; then succeeds Bilboa, St. Andero, Gijon, Ferrol, and Corunna; but though some of these, especially Ferrol and Corunna, possess excellent harbours, yet the poverty of the adjacent country prevents them from having much trade. To the south of Portugal is Seville, on the Guadalquiver, sixteen leagues from the sea; large vessels can ascend to this city, but its commerce was nearly destroyed by the transfer of the colonial trade to Cadiz. This last town, one of the most ancient commercial places in the world, is highly favoured both by nature and art as a port; and before the French revolutionary war, and the separation of the American colonies from the mother state, was undoubtedly the first commercial city in Spain. The exports of the northern provinces consist principally in iron, wool, chesnuts and filberts, &c.; the imports, which chiefly come from England, Holland, and France, are woollen, linen, and cotton goods, hardware, and salted fish.

On the Mediterranean, Malaga may be regarded as the third commercial city in Spain, though its harbour is not good; the other ports in this sea, at which trade is carried on to any considerable extent, are Carthagena, Alicant, and

Barcelona, which ranks after Cadiz in commercial importance, and now that the colonial trade is destroyed, may be placed above it. The principal exports from these Mediterranean towns are wines, dried fruits, oils, anchovies, wool, barilla, soap, kermes, antimony, vermilion, brandy, cork, silk, &c. Barcelona formerly exported an immense number of shoes to the colonies. The imports consist chiefly of Baltic produce, the articles enumerated as forming the imports of the north of Spain, and some articles from Italy and Turkey.

Portugal, not nearly so extensive as Spain, nor blessed with such a fertile territory, is before her in commerce: she possesses two sea-ports of the first consideration, Lisbon and Oporto; and five of the second class. There are few cities that surpass Lisbon in commerce. The principal trade of Portugal is with England; from this country she receives woollens and other manufactures; coals, tin, salted cod, Irish linen, salt provisions, and butter: her other imports are iron from the north of Spain; from France, linens, silks, cambrics, fine woollens, jewellery; from Holland, corn, cheese, and drugs for dying; from Germany, linens, corn, &c.; and from Denmark, Sweden, and Russia, Baltic produce. The principal exports of Portugal are wine, oil, fruits, cork, &c.

The Italian States, the origin of the commerce of the middle ages, are no longer remarkable for their trade; the principal ports for commerce are Leghorn, Naples, Venice, Genoa, Messina, and Palermo. The exports of Leghorn are silk, raw and manufactured; straw hats, olive oil, fruits, marble, &c.: its chief trade, however, consists in the importation of English merchandize, which it distributes to all parts of the Mediterranean, receiving in return their produce to load the British ships on their home voyage. The greatest import to Naples consists in European manufactured goods, and salt fish; its exports are those of Leghorn, with capers, wool, dye stuffs, manna, wax, sulphur, potash, macaroni, &c. Venice has declined very much, from the influence of political circumstances: her exports are olives, looking-glasses, rice, coral, Venice treacle, scarlet cloth, and gold and silver stuffs; the imports are similar to those of Leghorn and Naples. The exports and imports of Genoa, consisting principally of those already enumerated, do not require particular notice. Sicily, a very rich country by nature, and formerly the granary of Rome, has fallen very low from bad government: her exports are very various, including, beside those already mentioned, barilla, a great variety of dying drugs and medicines, goat, kid, and rabbit skins, anchovies, tunny fish, wheat, &c.: its chief imports are British goods, salted fish, and colonial produce.

The principal trade of Greece is carried on by the inhabitants of Hydra, a barren island. The commerce of the Hydriots, as well as of the rest of Greece, was very much benefited by the scarcity of corn which prevailed in France in 1796, and subsequently by the attempts of Bonaparte to shut British manufactures from the continent. These two causes threw the greatest part of the coasting trade of the Mediterranean into their hands. The chief articles of export from Greece are oil, fruits, skins, drugs, volonia, and gall nuts, cotton and wool. The imports are principally English goods, and colonial produce, tin, lead, &c.

We have already dwelt on the causes which produced the immense commercial superiority of England; and we shall, therefore, now confine ourselves to an enumeration of its principal ports, and the principal articles of its export and import. London possesses considerably above one-half of the commerce of Great Britain; the next town is undoubtedly Liverpool; then may be reckoned, in England, Bristol, Hull, Newcastle, Sunderland, Yarmouth, &c.; in Scotland, Greenock, Leith, Aberdeen, Dundee, &c.; in Ireland, Cork, Dublin, Limerick, Belfast, Waterford, &c. From the last return of the foreign trade of Great Britain it appears, that by far the most important article of export is cotton manufactures and yarn, amounting in real or declared value to nearly one-half of the whole amount of goods exported; the next articles, arranged according to their value, are woollen manufactures, refined sugar, linen manufactures, iron, steel and hardware, brass and copper manufactures, glass, lead, and shot, &c. &c.; of colonial produce exported, the principal articles are coffee, piece goods of India, rum, raw sugar, indigo, &c. &c. The principal imports of Great Britain are cotton wool, raw sugar, tea, flax, coffee, raw silk, train oil and blubber, madder, indigo, wines, &c. &c. The principal imports into Ireland consist of old drapery, entirely from Great Britain; coals, also entirely from Great Britain; iron wrought and unwrought, nearly the whole from Great Britain; grocery, mostly direct from the West Indies; tea, from Britain, &c. &c. In fact, of the total imports of Ireland, five-sixths of them are from Great Britain; and of her exports, nine-tenths are to Great Britain. The principal articles of export are linen, butter, wheat, meal, oats, bacon, pork, &c. &c.

On the 30th September, 1822, there belonged to the United Kingdom 24,642 vessels, making a total of 2,519,044 tons, and navigated by 166,333 men; of the vessels employed in the foreign trade, including their repeated voyages, in the year ending the 5th of January 1823, there were about 12,000, of which upwards of 9,000 were British and Irish, and the rest foreign vessels. The coasting trade of England is calculated to employ 3000 vessels. We have already stated the proportion which the trade of Ireland to Britain bore to her trade with the rest of the world; this point may be still further elucidated by the following fact: that the number of vessels, (including their repeated voyages,) which entered the ports of Ireland, from all parts of the world, in the year ending the 5th of January, 1823, was 11,561, and that all these, except 943, came from Great Britain.

From this rapid view of the commerce of the European states, it appears that, with the exception of Great Britain, by far the largest portion and greatest value of the exports of each country consist in the produce of the soil, either in its raw and natural state, or after having undergone a change that requires little industry, manual labour, or mechanical agency. Britain, on the contrary, derives her exports almost entirely from the produce of her wonderful mechanical skill, which effects, in many cases, what could alone be accomplished by an immense population, and in a few cases, what no manual labour could perform.

In reviewing the commerce of the remaining parts of the world, we shall find the articles that constitute it almost exclusively the produce of the soil, or, where manufactured, owing the change in their form and value to the simplest contrivances and skill. We shall begin with Asia.

Turkey possesses some of the finest portions of this quarter of the globe; countries in which man first emerged into civilization, literature, and knowledge; rich in climate and soil, but dreadfully degraded, oppressed, and impoverished by despotism. The exports from the European part of Turkey are carpets, fruit, saffron, silk, drugs, &c.: the principal port is Constantinople. From Asiatic Turkey there are exported rhubarb and other drugs, leather, silk, dye stuffs, wax, sponge, barilla, and hides: nearly the whole foreign trade is centered in Smyrna, and is in the hands of the English and French, and Italians. The imports are coffee, sugar, liqueurs, woollen and cotton goods, lead, tin, jewellery, watches, &c.

China, from the immense number of its population, and their habits, possesses great internal commerce; but, with the exception of her tea, which is taken away by the English and Americans, her export trade is not great. She also carries on a traffic overland with Russia, to which We have already alluded, and some maritime commerce with Japan. Besides tea, the exports from China are porcelain, silk, nankeens, &c.; the imports are the woollen goods, and tin and copper of England; cotton, tin, pepper, &c. from the British settlements in India; edible birds' nests, furs, &c.

The trade of Japan is principally with China: the exports are copper, lackered ware, &c.; the imports are raw silk, sugar, turpentine, drugs, &c. The trade of the Birman empire is also principally with China, importing into it cotton, amber, ivory, precious stones, betel nuts, &c., and receiving in return raw and wrought silk, gold leaf, preserves, paper, &c. European broad cloth and hardware, Bengal muslins, glass, &c. are also imported into this country.

But by far the most important commerce that is carried on in the eastern parts of Asia, consists in that which flows from and to Calcutta, Bombay, and Madras. In fact, the English country trade there, as it is called, is of great value, and embraces a very great variety of articles. Bombay is the grand emporium of the west of India, Persia, and Arabia; here the productions of those countries are exchanged against each other, and for the manufactures, &c. of England. The principal articles of export from Bombay to these places, as well as to England, are cotton piece goods, sugar, and saltpetre, received from Bengal; pepper from Sumatra; coffee from the Red Sea. The imports from Europe are woollens, tin, lead, &c. A very lucrative trade is carried on from Bombay to China, to which it exports cotton in very great quantity, sandal wood, &c., and receives in return sugar, sugar-candy, camphire, nankeens, &c. There is also considerable traffic between Bombay and Bengal, Ceylon, Pegu, and the Malay archipelago. The exports of Ceylon are cinnamon, arrack, coir, cocoa nuts: the imports are grain, piece goods, and European merchandize. The commerce of the eastern coast of Hindostan centers in Madras: the exports from this place are principally piece goods, grain, cotton, &c.; the imports, woollen manufactures, copper, spirits, pepper, and other spices. The trade of Bengal may be divided into four branches: to Coromandel and Ceylon, the Malabar coast, Gulph of Persia and

Arabia, the Malay archipelago and China and Europe. The principal exports by the port of Calcutta are piece goods, opium, raw silk, indigo, rice, sugar, cotton, grain, saltpetre, &c.: the principal imports are woollen goods, copper, wine, pepper, spices, tea, nankeen, camphire, &c.

A considerable trade is carried on in the Malay archipelago from Prince of Wales Island, which, since it was settled by the English, has become the emporium of this trade.--Batavia, Bencoolen, and Achen; the principal articles of export from these islands are cloves, nutmegs, camphire, pepper, sago, drugs, bichedemer, birds' nests, gold dust, ivory, areca nuts, benzoin, tin, &c.: the imports are tea, alum, nankeens, silks, opium, piece goods, cotton, rice, and European manufactures. Manilla is the depôt of all the productions of the Philippines, intended to be exported to China, America, and Europe. The exports of these islands are birds' nests, ebony, tobacco, sugar, cotton, cocoa, &c. The commerce of New Holland is still in its infancy, but it promises to rise rapidly, and to be of great value: a soil very fertile, and a climate adapted to the growth of excellent grain, together with the uncommon fineness of its wool, have already been very beneficial to its commerce.

The external commerce of Persia is principally carried on by the foreign merchants who reside at Muscat, on the Persian Gulph: into this place are imported from India, long cloths, muslins, silks, sugar, spices, rice, indigo, drugs, and European manufactures; the returns are copper, sulphur, tobacco, fruits, gum-arabic, myrrh, frankincense, and all the drugs which India does not produce.

The Red Sea, washed on one side by Asia, and on the other by Africa, seems the natural transit, from this consideration, of the commerce of the former quarter of the globe to that of the latter. Its commerce is carried on by the Arabians, and by vessels from Hindostan: Mocha and Judda are its principal ports. The articles sent from it are coffee, gums and drugs, ivory, and fruit: the imports are the piece goods, cotton, and other produce of India; and the manufactures, iron, lead, copper, &c. of Europe.

Egypt, in which anciently centered all the commerce of the world, retains at present a very small portion of trade: the principal exports from Alexandria consist in the gums and drugs of the east coast of Africa, Arabia, Persia, and India; rice, wheat, dates, oil, soap, leather, ebony, elephants' teeth, coffee, &c. The imports are received chiefly from France and the Italian States, and England; and consist in woollen and cotton goods, hardware, copper, iron, glass, and colonial produce. The commerce of the Barbary States is trifling: the exports are drugs, grain, oil, wax, honey, hides and skins, live bullocks, ivory, ostrich feathers, &c.; the imports, colonial produce, (which indeed finds its way every where,) cutlery, tin, woollen and linen goods, &c. The exports of the rest of Africa are nearly similar to those enumerated, viz. gums, drugs, ivory, ostrich feathers, skins, gold dust, &c. From the British settlement at the Cape are exported wine, wheat, wool, hides, &c.

The United States claim our first notice in giving a rapid sketch of the commerce of America: we have already pointed out the causes of their extraordinary progress in population and wealth. American ships, like English ones, are found in every part of the world: in the South Sea Islands, among people just emerging into civilization and industry; among the savages of New Zealand; on the north-west coast of America; and on the dreadful shores of New South Shetland. Not content with exporting the various productions of their own country, they carry on the trade of various parts of the globe, which, but for their instrumentality, could not have obtained, or ever have become acquainted with each other's produce.

The exports from America, the produce of their own soil, are corn, flour, timber, potash, provisions, and salt fish from the northern States; corn, timber, and tobacco from the middle States; and indigo, rice, cotton, tar, pitch, turpentine, timber, and provisions, to the West Indies, from the southern States. The imports are woollen, cotton goods, silks, hardware, earthen-ware, wines, brandy, tea, drugs, fruit, dye-stuffs, and India and colonial produce. By far the greatest portion of the trade of the United States is with Great Britain. The principal ports are Boston, New York, Philadelphia, Baltimore, and New Orleans.

The British settlements in America export, chiefly from Quebec and Halifax, corn, potash, wheel timber, masts, lumber, beaver and other furs, tar, turpentine, and salted fish from Newfoundland. The imports are woollen and cotton goods, hardware, tea, wine, India goods, groceries, &c.

The exports of the West India Islands are sugar, coffee, rum, ginger, indigo, drugs, and dye stuffs. The imports are lumber, woollen and cotton goods, fish, hardware, wine, groceries, hats, and other articles of dress, provisions, &c.

Brazil, and the late Spanish settlements in America, countries of great extent, and extremely fertile, promise to supply very valuable articles for commerce; even at present their exports are various, and chiefly of great importance. Some of the most useful drugs, and finest dye stuffs, are the produce of South America. Mahogany and other woods, sugar, coffee, chocolate, cochineal, Peruvian bark, cotton of the finest quality, gold, silver, copper, diamonds, hides, tallow, rice, indigo, &c. Carthagena, Porto Cabello, Pernambucco, Bahia, Rio de Janeiro, and Buenos Ayres, are the principal ports on the east coast of South America; and Valparaiso, Calloa (the port of Lima), Guayaquil, Panama, and Acapulco, on the west coast.

Our sketch of commerce would be incomplete, did it not comprehend a short notice of the manner in which the trade of great part of Asia and Africa is conducted, by means of caravans. This is, perhaps, the most ancient mode of communication between nations; and, from the descriptions we possess, the caravans of the remotest antiquity were, in almost every particular, very similar to what they are at present. The human race was first civilized in the East. This district of the globe, though fertile in various articles which are well calculated to excite the desires of mankind, is intersected by extensive deserts; these must have cut off all communication, had not the camel,--which can bear a heavy burden, endure great famine, is very docile, and, above all, seems made to bid defiance to the parched and waterless desert, by its internal formation, and its habits and instinct,--been civilized by the inhabitants. By means of it they have, from the remotest antiquity, carried on a regular and extensive commerce.

The caravans may be divided into those of Asia and those of Africa: the great centre of the former is Mecca: the pilgrimage to this place, enjoined by Mahomet, has tended decidedly to facilitate and extend commercial intercourse. Two caravans annually visit Mecca; one from Cairo, and the other from Damascus. The merchants and pilgrims who compose the former come from Abyssinia; from which they bring elephants' teeth, ostrich feathers, gum, gold dust, parrots, monkies, &c. Merchants also come from the Senegal, and collect on their way those of Algiers, Tunis, &c. This division sometimes consists of three thousand camels, laden with oils, red caps, fine flannels, &c. The journey of the united caravans, which have been known to consist of 100,000 persons, in going and returning, occupies one hundred days: they bring back from Mecca all the most valuable productions of the East, coffee, gum arabic, perfumes, drugs, spices, pearls, precious stones, shawls, muslins, &c. The caravan of Damascus is scarcely inferior to that of Cairo, in the variety and value of the produce which it conveys to Mecca, and brings back from it, or in the number of camels and men which compose it. Almost every province of the Turkish empire sends forth pilgrims, merchants, and commodities to this caravan. Of the Asiatic caravans, purely commercial, we know less than of those which unite religion and commerce; as the former do not travel at stated seasons, nor follow a marked and constant route. The great object of those caravans is to distribute the productions of China and Hindustan among the central parts of Asia. In order to supply them, caravans set out from Baghar, Samarcand, Thibet, and several other places. The most extensive commerce, however, carried on in this part of Asia, is that between Russia and China. We have already alluded to this commerce, and shall only add, that the distance between the capitals of those kingdoms is 6378 miles, upwards of four hundred miles of which is an uninhabited desert; yet caravans go regularly this immense distance. The Russians and Chinese meet on the frontiers; where the furs, linen and woollen cloth, leather, glass, &c. of Russia, are exchanged for the tea, porcelain, cotton, rice, &c. of China. This intercourse is very ancient. There are also caravans of independent Tartars, which arrive on the Jaik and Oui, and bring Chinese and Indian commodities, which they interchange for those of Russia.

Tombuctoo is the great depot of central Africa: with it the maritime states of Egypt, Tripoli, Algiers, Tunis, and Morocco carry on a very extensive and lucrative trade by means of caravans. They take 129 days in travelling to Tombuctoo from the borders of the desert, but only fifty-four are spent in actual travelling. There is also another caravan which sets off from Wedinou, and after collecting salt at West Tagossa, proceeds to Tombuctoo. This goes as far as the White Mountains, near Cape Blanco, and is occupied five or six months in its journey. The merchandize carried by these caravans is German linens, Irish linens, muslins, woollen cloth, coral beads, pearls, silk, coffee, tea, sugar, shawls, brass nails, &c. &c. In exchange they bring back chiefly the produce of Soudan, viz. gold dust, gold rings, bars of gold, elephants' teeth, gum, grains of paradise, and slaves. There are also several caravans that trade between Cairo and the interior of Africa, which are solely employed in the traffic of slaves. There can be no doubt that caravans arrive at Tombuctoo from parts of Africa very distant from it, and not only inaccessible, but totally unknown, even by report, to Europeans, and even to the inhabitants of North Africa.

What a picture does modern commerce present of the boundless desires of man, and of the advancement he makes in intellect, knowledge, and power, when stimulated by these desires! Things familiar to use cease to attract our surprise and investigation; otherwise we should be struck with the fact, that the lowest and poorest peasant's breakfast-table is supplied from countries lying in the remotest parts of the world, of which Greece and Rome, in the plenitude of their power and knowledge, were totally ignorant. But the benefits which mankind derives from commerce are not confined to the acquisition of a greater share and variety of the comforts, luxuries, or even the necessaries of life. Commerce has repaid the benefits it has received from geography: it has opened new sources of industry; of this the cotton manufactures of Britain are a signal illustration and proof:--it has contributed to preserve the health of the human race, by the introduction of the most valuable drugs employed in medicine. It has removed ignorance and national prejudices, and tended most materially to the diffusion of political and religious knowledge. The natural philosopher knows, that whatever affects, in the smallest degree, the remotest body in the universe, acts, though to us in an imperceptible manner, on every other body. So commerce acts; but its action is not momentary; its impulses, once begun, continue with augmented force. And it appears to us no absurd or extravagant expectation, that through its means, either directly, or by enlarging the views and desires of man, the civilization, knowledge, freedom and happiness of Europe will ultimately be spread over the whole globe.

---

6 Since this part of our work was written, the narrative of Lieutenant Franklin has been published: from this it appears, that he was engaged in this arduous undertaking during the years 1819, 1820, 1821, and 1822; that the route he followed to the Coppermine River was to the east o the routes of M'Kenzie and Hearne; that he reached the river three hundred and thirty-four miles north of Fort Enterprize; and the Polar Sea in lat. 67° 47' 50"; and in longitude 115° 36' 49" west; that he sailed five hundred and fifty miles along its shores to the eastward, and then returned to Port Enterprize.

CATALOGUE OF VOYAGES AND TRAVELS

Preliminary Observations on the Plan and Arrangement pursued in drawing up this Catalogue

IT is obvious, that whoever undertakes to draw up a catalogue of books on any particular subject, must proceed on one or other of these two plans,—either to give a complete catalogue of all the works published on that subject, or a select catalogue of what seems to him the best works. It is scarcely necessary to point out the objection to the first plan, arising from the impracticability of making any catalogue absolutely complete; but it may be said, though not absolutely complete, it may, by sufficient information and diligence, be rendered nearly so. Let us suppose, then, that by unwearied assiduity and research, aided and guided by the requisite knowledge, a catalogue is rendered as perfect as it practically can be made,—is the utility of such a catalogue enhanced in a proportion any thing approaching to the labour, research, and time expended upon it; or, rather, would not such a catalogue be much less useful than one within smaller compass, drawn up on the plan of selection?

On all subjects there are more bad or indifferent works published than good ones. This remark applies with peculiar justice and force to modern works of voyages and travels. A very extensive catalogue, therefore, must contain a large portion of bad or indifferent books, which are not worth the purchasing, the consulting, nor the perusing; consequently, if such works appear in a catalogue drawn up for the purpose of guiding those who purpose to travel in particular countries, to write on the subject of them, or merely to read respecting them for the sake of information, it is plain that such a catalogue cannot be trusted as a safe and judicious guide; as if the persons consulting it select for themselves, there is an equal chance of selecting useless books as good ones; and if they attempt to peruse all, they must waste a great deal of time.

It may be said, however, that this objection can easily be obviated, by distinguishing such works as are bad or indifferent from such as are good, either by a short notice, or by a particular mark. The first plan necessarily must increase the size of the catalogue; and it really appears a piece of superfluous labour to introduce works not worthy to be perused, and then, either by a notice or mark, to warn the reader from the perusal of them. Is it not much more direct to omit such works altogether?

As the object in view in the present catalogue is to render it useful to the generality of readers, and not valuable to the bibliographer, those works are omitted which have no other recommendation but their extreme scarcity. For such works are of course accessible only to very few, and when obtained, convey little interest or information.

A select catalogue then appears to be the most useful, and of course must occupy less room. But to this objections start up, which it will be proper to consider.

In the first place, What is the criterion of good works of voyages and travels? The antiquarian will not allow merit to such as pass over, or do not enter, *con amore*, and at great length, into the details of the antiquities of a country: the natural historian is decidedly of opinion, that no man ought to travel who is not minutely and accurately acquainted with every branch of his favourite science, and complains that scarcely a single work of travels is worthy of purchase or perusal, because natural history is altogether omitted in them, or treated in a popular and superficial manner. Even those who regard man as the object to which travellers ought especially to direct their attention, differ in opinion regarding the points of view in which he ought to be studied in foreign countries. To many the travels of Johnson and Moore seem of the highest merit and interest, because these authors place before their readers an animated, philosophical, and vivid picture of the human character; whereas other readers consider such works as trifling, and contend that those travels alone, which enter into the statistics of a country, convey substantial information, and are worthy of perusal.

Whoever draws up a catalogue, therefore, must, in some measure, consult the judgment, taste, and peculiar studies of all these classes of readers, and endeavour to select the best works of travels in all these branches.

But there is a second objection to a select catalogue to be considered. The information and research of the person who draws it up may be inadequate to the task, or his judgment may be erroneous. This observation, however, applies to a complete catalogue—indeed the first part of it,—the information and research requisite, in a greater degree to a complete than to a select catalogue; and with respect to the judgment required, it will be equally required in a complete catalogue, if the bad and indifferent works are distinguished from the good ones; and if they are not, such a catalogue, we have already shewn, can only lead astray into unnecessary or prejudicial reading.

Whoever draws up a catalogue, or gives to the public a work on any particular subject, is bound to make it as good as he can; but, after all, he must not expect that there will be no difference of opinion about his labours. Some will think (to confine ourselves to the catalogue) that he has admitted books that ought not to have found a place in it; whereas others will impeach his diligence, his information, or his judgment, because he has omitted books which they think ought to have entered into it. All, therefore, that a person who engages to draw up a catalogue can do, is to exercise and apply as much research and judgment as possible, and to request his readers, if they find general proofs of such research and judgment, to attribute the omission of what they think ought to have been inserted, or the insertion of what they think ought to have been omitted, to difference of opinion, rather than to a deficiency in research or judgment.

It may be proper to remark, with regard to the principle of selection pursued, that many works are admitted which do not bear the title of travels; this has been done, wherever, though not under that title, they are the result of the actual travels and observations, or enquiries of the authors. The form into which information respecting the agriculture, manufactures, commerce, antiquities, natural history, manners, &c. of foreign countries is cast, or the title under which it is communicated to the world, is obviously of little consequence, provided the information is not merely compiled by a stranger to the country, and is accurate and valuable. Such works, however, as are avowedly written for scientific purposes, and for the exclusive use of scientific men, and are consequently confined to scientific researches and information conveyed in the peculiar language of the science, are omitted.

So much for the plan on which this catalogue has been drawn up. Before we proceed to explain the arrangement pursued, it may be proper to make a few remarks on some intermediate points. One advantage of a select catalogue over a complete one is, that it occupies less room. With the same object in view, only the title in the original language is given where there is no translation of the work into the English or French; only translations into English or French are noticed, where such exist, and not the original work; and all the articles are numbered, so that a short and easy reference may be made from one article to another.

Room is thus evidently saved, and not, in our opinion, by any sacrifice of utility. For German or Spanish scholars it is unnecessary to translate the titles of German or Spanish books, and for the mere English scholar it is useless. Translations into the French are noticed in preference to the original, because this language is at present familiar to every literary man in Britain, and French works can easily be obtained; and the German or Spanish scholar, who wishes to obtain and peruse the original, can be at no loss to procure it from the translated title. The advantage of numbering the articles will be immediately explained in treating of the arrangement.

The catalogue is arranged in the following manner:

After noticing a few of the most useful works which contain instructions to travellers, in the first place, Collections and Histories of Voyages and Travels are placed: next follow Voyages round the World;—Voyages and Travels which embrace more than one quarter of the World;—Travels in Europe generally;—Travels in more than one Country of Europe;—Travels in each particular Country of Europe. It is in this particular department of the Catalogue that the plan of reference by numbers is more especially necessary and useful; for the Index to the Catalogue being drawn up with reference to the numbers, not only those travels which are confined to one country,—France, for instance,—may easily be found, but also all those travels which comprehend France along with other countries.

The same arrangement is pursued in the other parts of the world,—Asia, Africa, America, Australasia, and Polynesia. The articles are arranged as nearly as possible in the chronological order in which the voyages and travels were performed in each particular country, and the countries are placed according to their geographical relation to one another.

I.
INSTRUCTIONS FOR TRAVELERS

1. L'Utilité des Voyages qui concernent la Connoissance des Inscriptions, Sentences, Dieux, Larés, Peintures anciennes, Bas Reliefs, &c. Langues, &c.; avec un Memoire de quelques Observations générales qu'on peut faire pour ne pas voyager inutilement. Par Ch. C. Baudelot Dairval. 2 vol. 12mo. Paris 1656.—The Rouen edition is much inferior. This is an excellent work.

2. C. Linnæus on the Benefit of Travelling in one's own Country. (In Stillingfleet's Tracts.) This was published in Latin, separately, and in the Amoenitates Academicæ, in the Select, ex Amoenit.; and in the Fundamenta Botanices of Gilibert.

3. Instructio Peregrinatoris, Dissertatio. Præside C. Linnæo. 1759, 4to.

4. Mémoire Instructif sur la Manière de rassembler, de préparer, de conserver, et d'envoyer les diverses Curiosités d'Histoire Naturelle. Par Turgot. 1758. 8vo.—This work is also appended to "Avis pour le Transport par Mer des Arbres, des Plantes vivaces, des Semences, et de diverses autres Curiosités d'Histoire Naturelle. Par L.H. Duhamel." Published at Paris, 1753. 12mo.

5. Directions in what Manner Specimens of all Kinds may be collected, preserved, &c. By J.R. Forster. London, 1771.—This tract, worthy of its well-informed and able author, was published along with his Catalogue of North American Animals.

6. The Naturalist's and Traveller's Companion. By J.C. Lettsom, M.D. London, 1799 8vo.

7. Analysis of the Natural Classification of Mammalia, for the Use of Travellers. Introduction to the Ornithology of Cuvier, for the Use of Travellers. Introduction to Conchology, for the Use of Travellers. By T.E. Bowdich. Paris, 1821-2. 8vo.

8. Instructions for Travellers. By Dean Tucker. 1757. 4to.

9. Essay to direct and extend the Enquiries of patriotic Travellers. By Count Berchtold.—The second volume contains a Catalogue of Travels in Europe; the first alone relates to the subject of the title. 2 vols. 8vo. 1789.

10. Essay on the Study of Statistics; intended to assist the Enquiries of inexperienced Travellers. By D. Boileau. 12mo. 1807.

11. Fried. J. Freyherr von Gunderode Gedanken uber Reisen. Frankfort, 1781. 8vo.

12. Apodenick, oder die kunst zu Reisen von Posselt. Leipsic, 1795. 8vo.—This is an excellent work.

13. Uber den Worth und Nutzen der Fussreisen. Hanover, 1805. 8vo.—We notice this work, because it points out the superior advantages possessed by foot travellers, in exploring the natural beauties and natural history of a country.

II
COLLECTIONS AND HISTORIES OF VOYAGES AND TRAVELS

14. The principal Navigations, Voyages, Traffiques, and Discoveries of the English Nation, made by Sea or Over-land, to the remote and farthest distant Quarters of the Earth. By Richard Hakluyt, 3 vols. fol. 1598, 1599, 1600.—This work is often incomplete; the completeness of it may be ascertained by its containing the voyage to Cadiz, which was suppressed by order of Queen Elizabeth, after the disgrace of the Earl of Essex. The first volume of this collection contains Voyages to the North and North-east: The True State of Iceland; The Defeat of the Spanish Armada: The Victory at Cadiz, &c. The second volume contains Voyages to the South and South-east Parts of the World: and the third to North America, the West Indies, and round the World. It has lately been republished.

15. S. Purchas, his Pilgrims and Pilgrimages, 5 vols. folio, 1625-26.—The first volume contains Voyages by the Ancient Circumnavigators of the Globe: Voyages along the Coasts of Africa to the East-Indies, Japan, China, Philippines, and the Persian and Arabian Gulphs. Vol. 2. contains Voyages and Relations of Africa, Ethiopia, Palestina, Arabia, Persia, Asia. Vol. 3. Tartary, China, Russia, North-west America, and the Polar Regions. Vol. 4. America and the West Indies. Vol. 5. Early History of the World; of the East Indies; Egypt; Barbary, &c. &c.

16. A General Collection of Voyages and Travels. Published by Astley. 4 vols. 4to. 1745.

17. A Collection of Voyages and Travels, some now first printed from original MSS.; others now first published in English. By Churchill. 6 vols. folio. 1732.

18. Navigantium atque Itinerantium Bibliotheca. Harris's Collection of Voyages and Travels, from Hakluyt, Purchas, Ramusio, &c. The whole work revised and continued, by Dr. John Campbell. 2 vols. fol. 1744.

19. A General Collection of the best and most interesting Voyages and Travels, in all Parts of the World. By John Pinkerton. 1808-1814. 17 vols. 4to.

20. A General History and Collection of Voyages and Travels, arranged in systematic Order. By Robert Kerr. Edin. 1811-22. 18 vols. 8vo.

21. Relation de divers Voyages curieux, qui n'ont point encore été publiés, et qu'on a traduits ou tirés des Originaux des Voyageurs Français, Espagnols, Allemands, &c. &c. Par M. Thevenot. Paris, 1696. 2 vol. fol.—This work is seldom found complete: the marks of the complete and genuine edition are given in the Bibliothèque des Voyages, vol. i. pp. 82, 83. To this work the following is a proper supplement:

22. Recueil des Voyages de M. Thevenot. Paris, 1681. 8vo.

23. Recueil des Voyages qui ont servi a l'Etablissement et au Progrès de la Campagne des Indes Orientates Hollandaises. Par Constantin.—The best editions are those of Amsterdam, 1730, and of Paris and Rouen, 1705; each in 10 vol. 12mo.

24. Recueil des Voyages au Nord, &c. Amsterdam, 1717. 8 vol. 12mo.

25. Lettres Edifiantes et Curieuses. Paris, 1780, 1781. 24 vols. 12mo.

26. Mémoires Orientales. Paris, 1789. 12mo.

27. Collection Portative de Voyages, traduit de différentes Langues Orientales et Europiennes. Par Langles. Paris, 3 vols. 18mo.

28. Histoire Générale des Voyages. Par Prevot. Paris, 20 vols. 4to.—This work is valuable for its excellent engravings, maps, plans, &c., but in other respects its value has fallen, in consequence of the following abridgment of it:

29. Abrégé de l'Histoire Générate des Voyages de Prevot. Par La Harpe. Paris, 1780-1786. 23 vols. 8vo.—The last five volumes contain voyages and travels not given by Prevot. This work also has been continued by Comeyras in 1798-1801, in 9 vols. 8vo.

30. Abrégé de l'Histoire Générale des Voyages. Par La Harpe. 2 vols. 12mo. Paris, 1820.—This abridgment is executed with considerable judgment; it is necessarily confined to the most novel and curious parts of the narratives and descriptions.

31. Annales des Voyages. Par Malte Brun. 25 vols. 8vo. Paris, 1814-1817.

32. Nouvelles Annales des Voyages. Par Malte Brun et Eyries.—Twelve volumes are already published: four volumes are published annually. Perhaps the very high character of Malte Brun would lead us to expect a more severe and judicious selection than some parts of this work exhibit; but, on the whole, it is valuable.

33. Journal des Voyages, Découvertes et Navigations Modernes, ou Archives Géographiques du 19me Siècle.—This work began in Nov. 1818, and is published monthly. Like all collections of this kind, the value of it would have been encreased, and the bulk much diminished, if the selection had been more scrupulous.

34. Delle Navigationi e Viaggi raccolti da M.G.B. Ramusio. Venet.—The most complete and accurate edition of this book consists of vol. 1. of the edition of 1588; vol. 2. of 1583; the third of 1565; and the Supplement of 1606.

35. J.R. Forster und M.C. Sprengel, Beytrage zur Volker-und Landerkunde. Leipsic, 1781—94. 13 vols. 8vo.

36. Magazin von merkerurdigen Reisebeschreibungen, aus fremden Sprachen ubersizt. Von J.R. Forster. Berlin, 1790—1802. 24 vols. 8vo.

37. Bibliothek der neuesten und wichtigstien Reisebeschreibungen. Von M.C. Sprengel. Weimar, 1801. &c. 22 vols. 8vo.—There are many other collections in German; the best of which are noticed by Ersch, in his Literatur der Geschichte und deren Hulfswissenschaften. Leipsic, 1813.

38. Samling af de beste og nyeste Reise-beskriveler. Copen. 1790—5. 12 vols. 8vo.

39. Danskes Reise-iagttagelser. Copen. 1798—1800. 4 vols. 8vo.

40. Versamnelling der gedenkwaardegsten Reisen nae oost en West Indien door de Bry. Leyden, 1707—10. 30 vols. 8vo.

41. El Viagero Universal. Madrid, 1800.—This work was published originally in small parts, which form a great many volumes in 8vo.

42. Novus Orbis Regionum et Institutorum Veteribus incognitarum. Basle, 1532. fol. Paris, 1582. fol.

43. Collectiones Peregrinationum in Indiam Orientalem et Occidentalem. Francfort, 1590—1634. 7 vols. fol., or 9 vols. fol.—The first edition, when complete, is by far the most valuable. Several dissertations have been published on this work, which is generally called Les Grands et Petits Voyages. In 1742 the Abbé de Rothelin published Observationes sur des Grands et Petits Voyages. In 1802 Camus published Mémoire sur la Collection des Grands et Petits Voyages; and Debure, in his Bibliographe, has devoted upwards of one hundred pages to this work. Whoever wishes to ascertain exactly the best edition, should consult these authors, and the Bibliotheque des Voyages, vol. 1. 57.

III
VOYAGES AND TRAVELS ROUND THE WORLD

Boucher de la Richarderie, the author of the Bibliothèque Universelle des Voyages, makes some just remarks on the nature and extent of those voyages to which this appellation is usually applied. He observes that for the most part, by a Voyage round the World, is understood a voyage ither by the Atlantic Ocean or the Indian Sea to the Pacific or Great Southern Ocean, the visiting the isles in the last, exploring the Antarctic Seas, and returning by the route opposite to that by which the ship went out. This certainly is a voyage round the world, though probably scarcely any part of Asia, Africa, or America has been explored or visited, except for the purposes of refitting or provisioning the ship. But when these quarters of the globe, and especially the unknown parts of them, have been visited, the application of the term, though not perhaps so correct verbally, is more justly made. There is a third class of voyages thus denominated, which, though they embrace the four quarters of the globe, do not extend to the South Sea, or the Australasian Lands. All these three classes are comprehended in the following catalogue, and we have deemed it right also to follow the author of the Bibliothèque in dividing them into two parts, ancient voyages round the world, and modern voyages: the first comprehend voyages of the first class, and were performed from the middle of the sixteenth to the middle of the seventeenth century.

44. Il Viaggio fatto dagli Spanuoli attorno il Mondo, 1536. 4to.—This is the first edition of the Voyages of Pigafetta, who sailed with Magellan in his celebrated Voyage round the World, but it is incomplete. The genuine and complete work was published for the first time from a MS. in the Ambrosian Library of Milan, with notes, by Amoretti, under the following title:

45. Primo Viaggio, intorno al Globo terraqueo fatto dal Casaglieri Ant. Pigafetta. Milan, 1800. 4to.—The same editor published a French translation, with a description of the Globe of Behaim. Magellan's Voyage is published in the first volume of Harris's Collection.

46. C. Ortoga resumen del primero Viage hecho ad rededor del Mundo. Per H. Magellanes. Madrid, 1769. 4to.

47. The Famous Voyage of Sir Francis Drake, to which is added the Prosperous Voyage of Mr. Thomas Candish. London, 1741. 8vo. also in Harris, vol. 1. The second voyage of Candish is in Purchas.

48. The principal Navigations, Voyages, Traffique and Discoveries of the English Nation. London, 1599. 2 vols. folio.

49. The Discoveries of the World, from their original to 1555, translated from the Portuguese, by R. Hackluyt. London, 1610. 4to.

50. Funnell's Voyage round the World. London, 1607. 8vo. In Harris, vol. 1.

51. Description du penible Voyage fait autour de l'Univers. Par O. du Nord. Amsterdam, 1602, in folio.—This is translated from the Dutch. An English translation is given in Harris, vol.1.

52. Voyage de Jacques l'Hermite autour du Monde. Amsterdam, 1705-12.—This also is translated from the Dutch.

53. Dampier's New Voyage round the World. London, 1711. 3 vols. 8vo.—The French translation in 5 vols. 12mo. contains also the voyages of Wafer, Wood, Cowley, Robert, and Sharp. Dampier's and Cowley's are in Harris, vol. 1.

54. A Voyage round the World. By Captain G. Shelvocke. London, 1757. 8vo. This is also in Harris, vol. 1.

55. Voyage round the World, by Wood Rogers. London, 1728, 8vo. In Harris, vol. 1.

56. Voyage round the World, by Lord Anson. By Walter, corrected by Robins. London, 1749. 4to.

57. Hawksworth's Account of the Voyages for making Discoveries in the Southern Hemisphere, performed by Byron, Wallis, Carteret, and Cook, 1773. 3 vols. 4to.

58. Captain Cook's Voyage towards the South Pole, and round the World, 1777. 2 vols. 4to.

59. Captains Cook, Clarke, and Gore's Voyage to the Pacific Ocean. By Cook and King, with an introduction by Bishop Douglas, 1784. 3 vols. 4to.

60. G. Forster's Voyage round the World, with Captain Cook, during 1772-75-77. 2 vols. 4to.

61. Bougainville's Voyage round the World, translated from the French. By J.R. Forster, 1772. 4to.

62. Voyage round the World, more particularly to the North-west Coast of America, in 1785-88. By Captain Dixon, 1789. 4to.

63. Captain Portlock's Account of the same Voyage; 1789. 4to.

64 A Voyage round the World in 1785-88. By De la Perouse, translated from the French. 2 vols. 4to. and Atlas of Prints, 1799.

65. Account of a Voyage in search of La Peyrouse, translated from the French of Labellaidiere. 2 vols. 8vo. and Atlas in 4to. 1800.

66. Marchand's Voyage round the World, 1790-92. 2 vols. 4to. Translated from the French.

67. A Voyage of Discovery into the North Pacific Ocean, and round the World in 1790-5. By G. Vancouver, 3 vols. 4to. and an Atlas. 1798.

68. A Missionary Voyage to the South Pacific Ocean in 1796-8. 4to. 1799.

69. Flinder's Voyage to Terra Australis in 1801-3. 2 vols. 4to. with an Atlas, 1814.

70. Liansky's Voyage round the World, 1803-5, performed by order of Alexander the First. 4to.

71. Langsdorffe's Voyages and Travels in various Parts of the World, 1803-7. 2 vols. 4to. Translated from the German.

72. Krusenstern's Voyage round the World, 1803-6. 2 vols. 4to. Translated from

the German.

73. A Voyage of Discovery into the South Sea, and Behring's Straits, in 1815-18. By Kotzebue. 3 vols. 8vo. 1821. Translated from the German, but badly.

74. Voyage Pittoresque autour du Monde. Par Choris. Livraison, 1-9. Paris, 1821.—This splendid work illustrates Kotzebue's Voyage, by engravings of the savages of the different parts he visited; their arms, dresses, diversions, &c. On this account alone, however, we should not have given it a place here; but it is recommended to the natural historian, by the descriptions which Cuvier has added to the engravings of animals; and to the craniologist, by the observations of Gall, on the engravings of human skulls.

75. Peregrinacion que ha hecho de la mayor partè del Mundo. Par D.P.S. Cubero. Sarragoss. 1688. folio.

76. Giro del Mondo del G.F. Gemelli Carreri. Naples, 1699. 7 vols. 8vo.

IV
TRAVELS COMPRISING DIFFERENT QUARTERS
OF THE GLOBE

77. Letters from Barbary, France, Spain, and Portugal. By an English Officer (Jardine), 1794. 2 vols. 8vo.

78. Cor. de Jong Reisen naer de Cap de Goede Hop, Ierland en Norwégen. Haarlem, 1802. 8vo.

79. Friedrich, Briefe au einen freund, eine reise von Gibraltar nach Tanger und von da durch Spanien, und Frankreich, Zurich, nach Deutschland, betreffend. (In the Historical Magazine of Gottingen, 4th year. 1st cahier.)

80. Voyage to the Levant in 1700, by Tournefort. Translated from the French, 3 vols. 8vo.—These travels bear too high a character to be particularly pointed out. They comprise the Archipelago, Constantinople, the Black Sea, Armenia, Georgia, the Frontiers of Persia and Asia Minor; and are rich and valuable in the rare junction of antiquarian and botanical knowledge.

81. Le Bruyn's Voyage to the Levant, and Travels into Muscovy, Persia, and the East Indies. Translated from the French. 1720. 8 vols. fol.

82. Description of the North and Eastern Parts of Europe and Asia. Translated from the German of Baron Strahlenberg. 1738, 4to.

83. Historical Account of the British Trade over the Caspian Sea, with a Journey of Travels from London, through Russia, Germany, and Holland. By James Hanway. 1754. 2 vols. 4to.

84. Bell of Antermony's Travels from St. Petersburgh in Russia to several Parts of Asia. Glasgow, 1763. 2 vols. 4to.

85. Memoirs of B.H. Bruce, containing an Account of his Travels in Germany, Russia, Tartary, and the Indies. 1782. 4to.

86. A Journey from India to England, in the year 1797. By John Jackson. 1799. 8vo.

87. Histoire des Découvertes faites par divers Voyageurs. Pallas, Gmelin, Guldenstedt, et Lepechin, dans plusieurs Contrées de la Russe et de la Perse. La Haye, 1779. 2 vol. 4to. & 6 8vo.

88. Nouvelles Relations du Levant. Par Poullet. Paris, 1688. 2 vols. 12mo.—This is a scarce and valuable work, especially that part of it which relates to Asiatic Turkey, Georgia, and Persia: there is likewise in it a particular account of the commerce of the English and Dutch in the Levant at this period.

89. Le Voyage du Sieur Duloir. Paris, 1654. 4to.—This work, beside much historical information respecting Turkey, and the Siege of Babylon in 1639, contains many particulars regarding the Religion, &c. of the Turks. It comprises the Archipelago, Greece, European Turkey and Asia Minor. It is likewise particular in the description of antiquities.

90. Les Voyages de Jean Struys en Moscovie, en Tartarie, en Perse, aux Indes. Traduits du Hollandais. Amsterdam. 4to. 1681. Rouen, 3 vols. 12mo. 1730.—The Travels of Struys, who was actuated from his earliest youth with

an insatiable desire to visit foreign countries, are especially interesting from the account he gives of Muscovy and Tartary at this period.

91. Voyages très Curieux et très Renommés, faits en Moscovie, Tartarie et Perse. Par Adam Olearius. Traduits d'Allemagne. Amsterdam, fol.

92. Voyages en différent Endroits d'Europe et d'Asie. Par le P. Avril. Paris, 1692. 4to.—The object of this voyage, which was commenced in 1635, principally consisted in the discovery of a new route to China. Turkey, Armenia, European and Asiatic Russia. Tartary, &c. are comprised in these Travels.

93. Voyage en Turquie et en Perse. Par M. Otter. Paris, 1748. 2 vols. 12mo.— The chief merit of this work consists in the exactitude of its descriptions of places, and in the determination of their distances and true positions, which are further illustrated by maps.

94. Beschreibung der Reise eines Polnishchen Herrn Bothschafters gen Constantinople und in die Tartary. Nuremberg, 1574. 4to.

95. Sal. Schweiger Reise-beschriebung aus Deutschland nach Constantinopel und Jerusalem. Nuremberg, 1608. 4to.

96. Reise van Erfurt nach dem gelobten land, auch Spanien, Franckreich, Holland und England. Erfurt, 1605. 4to.

97. Muntzer von Babenbergh, Reise von Venedig nach Jerusalem, Damascus und Constantinopel, 1556. Nurembergh. 4to.

98. Brand, Reisen durch Brandenburgh, Preussen, Curland, Liefland, Plescovien und Muscovien. Nebst, A. Dobbins Beschriebung von Siberien, &c. Wesel, 1702. 8vo.

99. Itinera Sex a diversis Saxoniæ; Ducibus et Authoribus, diversis Temporibus, in Italiam, Palæstinam et Terram Sanctum. Studio Balt. Mincii. Wirtemberg, 1612. 12mo.

100. Edwin Sandy's Travels into Turkey, Palestine, Egypt, and Italy, begun in 1610. fol. 1658.

101. Travels through Europe, Asia, and into several parts of Africa, containing Observations especially on Italy, Turkey, Greece, Tartary, Circassia, Sweden and Lapland. By De la Mottraye. 1723. 2 vols. fol. Veracity and exactness, particularly so far as regards the copying of inscriptions, characterise these travels. They are also valuable for information respecting the mines of the North of Europe.

102. Travels of Thevenot into Turkey, Persia, and India. Translated from the French, 1687. fol. The 4th edition of the original in 3 vols. is very rare; the more common one is that of Amsterdam in 5 vols. 12mo. These travels comprise Egypt, Arabia, and other places in Africa and Asia, besides those places indicated in the title page. The chief value of them consists in his account of the manners, government, &c. of the Turks. This author must not be confounded with the Mel. Thevenot, the author of a Collection of Voyages.

103. A View of the Levant, particularly of Constantinople, Syria, Egypt and Greece. By Ch. Parry. 1743. fol. 1770. 3 vols. 4to. This work is much less

known than it deserves to be: the author of the bibliotheque des Voyages justly remarks, that the circumstance of its having been twice translated into German is a pretty certain indication that it is full of good matter.

104. Description of the East, and some other Countries: Egypt, Palestine, Arabia, Syria, Greece, Thrace, France, Italy, Germany. Poland, &c. by Dr. Richard Pococke. 3 vols. fol. 1743-8. The merits of this work in pointing out and describing the antiquities of Egypt and the East are well known.

105. Travels through Europe, Asia, and Africa. By Lithgow. Edinburgh, 1770. 8vo.—This is one of the best editions of a book, the chief interest of which consists in the personal narrative of the author.

106. Travels in the Ottoman Empire, Egypt, and Persia. By Olivier. Translated from the French, 1802. 4to.

107. Dr. Ed. Dan. Clarke's Travels in various Countries of Europe, Asia, and Africa. 6 vols. 4to. Vol. 1. Russia, Turkey, Tartary. Vol. 2. & 3. Greece, Egypt, and the Holy Land. Vol. 4. The same Countries, and a Journey from Constantinople to Vienna, and an Account of the Gold Mines of Transylvania and Hungary. Vols. 5. & 6. Scandinavia.—There is no department of enquiry or observation to which Dr. C. did not direct his attention during his travels: in all he gives much information in a pleasant *huel*, is exactly the prefix to the names of many of the mines in Cornwall.

108. Chateaubriand's Travels in Greece, Palestine, Egypt, and Barbary, 1806-7. 2 vols. 8vo.--Those who admire this author's manner and style will be gratified with these travels: and those who dislike them, may still glean much information on antiquities, manners, customs, religion, &c.

109. Travels of Mirza Abu Taleb Khan in Asia, Africa, and Europe. Translated by Charles Stewart. 1814. 3 vols. 12mo.--These travels, of the genuineness of which there can be no doubt, derive their chief interest, as depicting the character and feelings of the author, and the impressions made on his mind by what he saw and heard.

110. Les Observations de plusieurs Singularités et Choses mémorables trouvées en Greece, en Asie, Inde, Arabie, Egypte, &c. Par Pierre Belon.--Various editions from 1550 to 1585. 4to. Belon is supposed to have travelled between 1547 and 1550. His work is rich in botany and natural history, especially considering the period in which he lived; and the accompanying plates are very accurate.

111. Voyage à Constantinople, en Perse, en Egypte, dans l'année 1546, et les années suivantes. Par G. Lues d'Aramon, Ambassadeur de France à Constantinople. Paris, 1739. 3 vols. 4to.--This relates chiefly to the manners and customs; other pieces are contained in these volumes, which relate, in a manner more minute than important and edifying, the various journies in France, of the Kings of France, from Louis the Young to Louis XIV. inclusive.

112. Les Navigations, Pérégrinations, et Voyages, faits en Turquie. Par Nicholas Nicholai, Antwerp, fol. 1576.--This also is instructive, relative to the manners, &c. of many parts of Europe, Africa, and Upper Asia: the plates

are engraved on wood, after the designs of Titian.

113. Relations des Voyages de M. de Breves, tant en Grèce, Terre Sainte. Egypte, qu'aux Royaumes de Tunis et Alger. Paris, 1628. 4to. De Breves was ambassador from Henry IV. to the Porte, and sent afterwards on a special mission to Tunis and Algiers. What he relates regarding these states is the most curious and valuable part of his work.

114. Les Voyages et Observations du Sieur Laboulaye-le-Goux, où sont décrits les Religion, Gouverment, et Situation, des Etats et Royaumes d'Italie, Grèce, Natolie, Syrie, Perse, Palestine, &c.; Grand Mogul, Indes Orientales des Portugais, Arabie, Afrique, Hollande, Grande Bretagne, &c. Paris, 1657. 4to.--This work bears a high character for veracity and exactness; and is very minute in its account of the casts and religions of India. Prefixed to it is a short critical notice of travellers who preceded him, written with great judgment and candour.

115. Voyage de Paul Lucas au Levant. Paris, 1704. 2 vols. 12mo.

116. Voyage de Paul Lucas, dans la Grèce, l'Asie Mineure, la Macedoine, et l' Afrique. Paris, 1712. 2 vols. 12mo.--The credit and veracity of this author, which was long suspected, has, in many of his most suspicious parts, been confirmed by modern travellers.

117. Mèmoire du Chevalier D'Arvieux: contenant ses Voyages à Constantinople, dans l'Asie, la Palestine, l'Egypte, la Barbarie, &c. Paris, 1735. 6 vols. 12mo.--This author was well qualified from his knowledge of the oriental languages, and from the official situations he filled, to gain an accurate and minute knowledge of the people among whom he resided. His account of his sojourn among the Bedouin Arabs is particularly curious.

118. Viaggi di P. della Valle dall Anno 1614, fin al' 1626. Venice, 1671. 4 vols. 4to.--These travels comprehend Turkey, Egypt, Palestine, Persia, and the East Indies. They are written in a pleasant, lively manner; what relates to Persia is most valuable. They have been translated into French, English, and German.

119. Schultz, Reisen durch Europa, Asien, und Africa. Halle, 1771-75. 5 vols. 8vo.

120. Læflingii Petri iter Hispanicum. Stockholm, 1758. 8vo.--This work, originally published in Swedish, was translated by C. Linnæus into German, under the following title: Reise nach den Spanischen Landern in Europa und Amerika, 1751--56. Berlin, 1776. 8vo. It is chiefly valuable for its natural history information.

121. Voyage en Amérique, en Italie, en Sicile, et en Egypte, 1816--19. 2 vols. 8vo.

122. The true Travels of Captain J. Smith in Europe, Asia, Africa, and America, from 1593 to 1629. London, 1664. fol.--This work, like most of the old travels, derives its principal value from enabling us to compare the countries visited, and their inhabitants, with their present state; and its principal interest from the personal adventures of the author. To such works, as well as to minute biography, time gives a value and utility, which they do not

intrinsically possess.

123. Itinerarium Portugalensium e Lusitania in Indiam et inde in Occidentem et demum ad Aquilonem, ab. Arch. Madrignan. 1508. fol.--Originally published in Portuguese.

124. Josten, Reisebeschreibung durch die Turkey, Ungern, Polen, Reussen, Bohemen, &c. neue Jerusalem, Ost und West Indien. Lubec, 1652. 4to.

125. Graaf, Reisen naer Asia, Africa, America, en Europa. Amsterdam, 1686. 8vo.

126. Historia y Viage del Mundo en los cincos Partes; de la Europa, Africa, Asia, America y Magellanica. Par Levallos. Madrid, 1691. 4to.

127. John Ovington's Voyage to Surat, with a Description of the Islands of Madeira and St. Helena. London, 1698. 8vo.

128. Le Bruyn's Voyage to the Levant. Translated from the French. London, 1702. fol.--This work bears a similar character as the preceding travels of the author already noticed. The plates are excellent.

129. Irwin's Adventures in a Voyage up the Red Sea; and a Route through the Thebaid hitherto unknown, in the year 1779. London, 4to. and 8vo.--Chiefly valuable for the information which his personal adventures necessarily gives of the manners, &c. of the Arabians.

130. Memoirs and Travels of Count Beniousky. London, 1790. 2 vols. 4to.--Amidst much that is trifling, and more that is doubtful, this work contains some curious and authentic information, especially relating to Kamschatka and Madagascar: what he states on the subject of his communications with Japan, is very suspicious.

131. Travels in Africa, Egypt, and Syria. By W.G. Browne. London, 1799. 4to.--A most valuable work, and except in some few peculiarities of the author, a model for travellers: it is particularly instructive in what relates to Darfour.

132. Travels in Asia and Africa. By A. Parsons. 4to. 1809.--These travels were performed in 1772--78: they indicate good sense, and are evidently the result of attentive and careful observation and enquiry. From Scanderoon to Aleppo; over the desert to Bagdat: a voyage from Bussora to Bombay, and along the west coast of India; from Bombay to Mocha; and a journey from Suez to Cairo, are the principal contents.

133. Travels. By John Lewis Burckhardt. Vol.1. Nubia; vol. 2. Syria and the Holy Land; vol.3, in the Hedjaz. 1823. 4to.--Few travellers have done more for geography than this author: antiquities, manners, customs, &c., were examined and investigated by him, with a success which could only have been ensured by such zeal, perseverance, and judgment as he evidently possessed.

134. Lord Valentia's Travels in India. Ceylon, the Red Sea, Abyssinia, and Egypt. 1802-6. 3 vols. 4to.--It is not possible for a person to travel so long, in such countries, without collecting information of a novel and important kind: such there is in this work on antiquities, geography, manners, &c.; but it might all have been comprised in one third of the size.

135. Travels along the Mediterranean and Parts adjacent, 1816-17-18, extending

as far as the second Cataract of the Nile, Jerusalem, Damascus, Balbec, &c. By Robert Richardson, M.D. 1822. 2 vols. 8vo.--Much information may be gleaned from these volumes; but there is a want of judgment, taste, and life in the narrative.

136. Travels in Morocco, Tripoli, Cyprus, Egypt, Arabia, Syria, and Turkey. 1803-7. By Ali Bey. 3 vols. 4to.--This traveller procured access to many places, in his assumed character, to which Christians were not permitted to go: from this cause the travels are instructive and curious; but they certainly disappointed the expectations of the public.

137. Ludovici Patricii Romani Itinerarium Novum Ethiopiæ, Egypti, utriusque Arabiæ, Persidis, Syriæ, ac Indiæ ultra citraque Gangem. Milan, 1511. fol.-- This work is supposed to have been written originally in Italian. In the Spanish translation, published in Lisbon, 1576, the author's name is given, Barthema. This a very curious and rare work. It has been translated into German and Dutch.

138. Baumgarten, Peregrinatio in Egyptum, Arabiam, Palestinam, et Syriam. Nuremberg, 1621. 4to.

139. Voyages au Levant, 1749-52. Par Fréd. Hasselquist. Paris, 1769. 1 vol. 12mo.--This, originally published in Swedish by Linnæus, and translated into German and Dutch, is uncommonly valuable to the natural historian.

140. Itinéraire de Paris a Jérusalem, et de Jérusalem à Paris, en allant par la Grèce. Par Chateaubriand. 3 vols. 8vo. Paris, 1810.

141. Le Nouveau Monde, et Navigations faites par Améric. Vespuce, dans les Pays nouvellement trouvés, tant en Ethiopie qu'en Arabie. Paris, 4to.-- Translated from the Italian: both are rare. The claims and merits of Vespucius may be judged of from the following works: Canovai Elogio di Amerigo Vespucci. Florence, 1798.; Tiraboschi Storia dell Litt. vol. 1. p. 1. lib. 1. c. 6.; the Letters of Americo in Ramusio, 1. 138.; Bandini Vita del Amerigo, and an article in the North American Review, for 1822.

142. Voyage d'un Philosophe (M. Poivre). Paris, 1797. 18mo.--This little work, which embraces remarks on the arts and people of Asia, Africa, and America, deserves the title it bears better than most French works which claim it.

143. Langstadt, Reisen nach Sud-America, Asien, und Africa. Hildesheim, 1789. 8vo.

144. Recueil de divers Voyages faites en Afrique et Amérique. Paris, 1674. 4to.

145. Voyages du Cheval. Marchais en Guinée, Isles voisines, et à Cayenne. Par Labat. Paris, 1780. 4 vols. 12mo.

146. Voyage en Guinée et dans les Isles Caraïbes. Par Isert. 1793. 8vo. Translated from the German.

147. Voyage on the Coast of Africa, in the Straits of Magellan, Brazil, &c. in 1695-97. Translated from the French of Froger. London, 1698. 8vo.

148. Hans Sloane's Voyage to Madeira, Barbadoes, St. Christophers, &c. London, 2 vols. folio. 1707.--This work, generally known under the title of Sir Hans Sloane's History of Jamaica, is a rich mine of natural history, aad contains upwards of 1200 engravings of plants, &c.

149. The Four Years' Voyage of Captain G. Roberts to the Islands Canaries, Cape Verde, and the Coast of Guinea, and Barbadoes. 1725. 8vo.

150. Voyage to Guinea, Brazil, the West Indies, Madagascar, &c. By John Atkins. 1737. 8vo.

151. Voyage aux Indes Orientales, Maldives, Moluccas, et Brésil. Par Fr. Pyrard. Paris, 1619-8vo.--These voyages, which occupied the author from 1600 to 1611, are uncommonly well written, accurate, faithful, and circumstantial, especially regarding the Maldives, Cochin, Travancore, and Calicut. There is appended a particular and methodical description of the animals and plants of the East Indies.

152. Curiosités de la Nature et de l'Art, apportés dans deux Voyages dans Indes: Indes Occ. 1698-9; Ind. Orient. 1701-2. Par C. Biron, Chirurgeon Major. Paris, 1703. 12mo.--Valuable for its natural history, and its account of the implements and arts of the inhabitants.

153. The History of Travels in the West and East Indies. By Eden and Willis. 1577. 4to.

154. Reise nach Ost und West Indien. Von R.C. Zimmerman. Hamburgh, 1771. 8vo.

155. Variorum in Europa Itinerum deliciae. Collectae ab. A. Clytaeo. Bremen, 1605. 8vo.

156. Ponz Viage fuera de España in Europa. Madrid, 1785. 2 vols. 12mo.

157. Moryson's Travels through Europe. 1617. fol.--A very curious work.

158. Itinera through the twelve Dominions of Germany, Bohemia, Prussia, Sweden, Turkey, France, Britain, &c. 1617. fol.

159. Ray's Observations, made in a Journey through Part of the Low Countries, Germany, Italy, and France. 1738. 2 vols. 8vo.--Valuable for its botanical researches.

160. Travels in Hungary, Macedonia, Austria, Germany, the Low Countries, and Lombardy. By E. Browne, M.D. 1685. fol.--Natural history, the mines, mineral waters, as well as manners and customs, are described in this work, which bears a good character. The author was physician to Charles II., to Bartholomew Hospital, and afterwards President of the College of Physicians.

161. Bishop Burnet's Letters on Switzerland and Italy. 1686. 8vo.

162. Travels through Holland, Germany, Switzerland, and Italy. By De Blainville. 1749. 3 vols. 4to.

163. Smollet's Travels through France and Italy. 1766. 2 vols. 8vo.

164. Barretti's Journey from London to Genoa, through Portugal, Spain, and France. 1770. 2 vols. 8vo.

165. Dr. Moore's View of the Customs and Manners of France, Germany, and Switzerland. 2 vols. 8vo.

166. Stolberg's (Count) Travels in Germany, Italy, and Sicily. 1794. 2 vols. 4to.

167. Dr. C.J. Smith's Sketch of a Tour on the Continent in 1786-7. 3 vols. 8vo. 1807.--The travels of this celebrated botanist are not by any means confined to his favourite science, but comprehend well-drawn and interesting

sketches of manners, as well as notices of the antiquities, fine arts, &c. Holland, the Netherlands, France, and Italy, were the scene of his travels.

168. Beaumont's Travels from France to Italy, through the Lepantine Alps. 1800. fol.

169. Travels in Sicily, Greece, and Albania. By the Rev. T.S. Hughes. 1820. 2 vols. 4to.--Classical, antiquarian, and descriptive of the state of society, political, civil, religious, and domestic; bearing marks of much information and enquiry, a sound judgment and good education.

170. Letters from the Mediterranean. By Ed. Blaquiere. 1814. 2 vols. 8vo.--The information in these volumes chiefly relates to the civil and political state of Sicily, Malta, Tunis, and Tripoli.

171. The Diary of an Invalid, 1817--1819. By H. Matthews. 8vo. 1820.--Light and pleasant sketches of manners, and other popular information, on Portugal, Italy, Switzerland, and France.

172. Travels through Holland, Germany, and Part of France, in 1819. By W. Jacob, Esq. 4to. 1820.--Agriculture, Statistics, and Manufactures.

173. Journal du Voyage de Montaigne en Italie, par la Suisse et l'Allemagne, en 1580-81. Paris, 1774. 4to.--Italy and the Tyrol are particularly the objects of those travels, which are interesting, much more on account of the name of the author, and of the insight they afford into his temper and feelings, than from the information they convey.

174. Lettres du Baron de Busbec. Paris, 1748. 3 vols. 12mo.--These are written from Turkey, whither the author was sent as ambassador by Ferdinand King of Hungary, and from France, where he resided in an official character. The original is in Latin. There is a translation in English; but this comprises only the embassy to Turkey. They are rich in political information, and in depicting the manners, &c. of the people he visited, especially those inhabiting the neighbourhood of the Don, &c.

175. Relations Historiques des Voyages en Allemagne, Angleterre, Holland, Boheme, et Suisse. Par C. Patin. Lyon, 1674. 16mo.--This author was son of the celebrated physician, Guy Patin, and distinguished for his knowledge of medals: his travels principally relate to antiquities.

176. Relation d'un Voyage de Paris, en Espagne, en Portugal, et en Italie, 1769, 1770. Par M. Silhouette. Paris, 1770. 4 vols. 12mo.--This is the minister of finance, whose measures of economy were so much ridiculed by the Parisians, and from whom the portraits, called Silhouettes, took their name: his travels indicate considerable acquaintance with the arts and political affairs.

177. Lettres sur différens Sujets, écrites pendant le Cours d'un Voyage en Allemagne, en Suisse, dans la France Meridionelle, et en Italie. Par Bernouilli. Basle and Berlin, 1777. 3 vols. 8vo.--The author of these letters, one of the celebrated family of mathematicians of that name, has borrowed the greater part of his work that relates to natural history from a Spanish work, entitled, "Cartas familiares del Abbatè Juan Andres," of which there is an edition published in Madrid, in 6 vols. small 4to. Bernouilli has, however,

added much information and interest to his letters, by his description and account of collections of paintings.

178. Tableau de l'Angleterre et de l'Italie. Par Archenholz. Strasburgh, 1788. 3 vols. 12mo.--This work is translated from the German.

179. Voyage de Deux Français en Allemagne, en Danemarck, en Suède, en Russe, et en Pologne, 1790-1. Par Portia de Piles. Paris, 1796. 5 vols. 12mo.--This is a valuable work for all kinds of statistical information.

180. Voyage Philosophique et Pittoresque sur les Rives du Rhin, à Leige, dans la Flandre, le Brabant, la Hollande, augmentée d'une Voyage en Angleterre, et en France. Par G. Forster. Paris, 5 vols. 8vo.--The author (whose acquirements in natural history, and in general science and philosophical research, as well as whose peculiar temper, are well known from his connection with Captain Cook during his second voyage, and his works on this voyage) has here produced an interesting and instructive work; particularly so far as relates to his favourite study: it is also interesting as depicting the political state of the countries he visited, and his strong, ardent, and sanguine views at the commencement of the French Revolution.

181. Voyages en Sicile dans la Grande Grèce et au Levant. Par le Baron de Riedesel. Paris, 1802. 8vo.--This edition comprises all his travels, which were previously published separately. The travels in Sicily are the most valuable.

182. Voyages de Guibert dans diverses Parties de la France et de la Suisse, 1775. 1785. Paris, 1805. 8vo.--The celebrated author of the "Essai sur la Tactique" was employed to visit the different military hospitals in France; his journeys with this object, as well as when he went to join his regiment, were the occasion of these travels, in which there is much animated description of nature, and several well-drawn portraits of public men.

183. Voyage en Allemagne, dans le Tyrol et en Italie. 4 vols. 8vo. Paris, 1818.--This work is translated from the German of Mad. de la Recke, by Madame de Montelieu, and possesses much of that pleasing narrative and description which characterize female writers of talent.

184. Pauli Hertneri Itinera Germaniæ, Galliæ, Italitæ. Basle, 1611. 4to.

185. Joh. Bernouilli Reisen durch Brandenburgh, Pommern, Preussen, Curland, Russland, und Pohlen, 1777-8. Leips. 1779-80. 6 vols. 8vo.

186. Sulzer Reisen nach Schweitz, und Hieris, und Nice. 1775. 8vo.--This author is well known for his "Universal Theory of the Fine Arts;" and these travels, as well as those in the middle states of Europe, and among the Alps, which he also published, are worthy of him.

187. Bauman, Reise durch Deutschland und Walschland. Augsb. 1782. 8vo.--These travels in Germany and Italy contain observations on a subject little attended to by travellers; but one which they might much benefit: we mean domestic economy, or the different modes, plans, &c. pursued by different nations in domestic life, as regards food, houses, clothing, &c.

188. Fred. Nicholai, Beschriebung einer Reise durch Deutschland und de Schweitz, 1781. Berlin, 1783. 12 vols. 8vo.--This work is swelled beyond all due proportion with political disquisitions; but though bold and severe, it is a just picture.

189. Italien und Deutschland. Von C.P. Moritz. Berlin, 1790.--Manners, literature, and arts are the topics of this work. The same author published "Travels of a German in England."

190. Reisen durch Deutschland, Danemarck, Schweden, Italien, 1797--99. Von Kuttner. Leip. 4 vols. 8vo.--Statistical and political information, derived from authentic and official sources, especially as relates to Austria and Saxony, distinguishes this work.

191. Streifzuge durch Inner Oestreich, &c. Vien. 1800. 4to.--The quicksilver mines of Idria, the manners, &c. of the people of Trieste and Venice, and the principal objects of arts and industry in all the countries described, give to this work a merit greater than its brevity would seem to deserve.

192. Briefe woehrend meinis Aufenhalts en England und Portugal. Hamb. 1802. 8vo.--This work, by Mad. Barnard, is written with that peculiar charm and vivacity of style, which it would seem females only can attain. There are in it curious notices of Berlin, Hanover, and Cuxhaven, besides those on England and Portugal.

193. Bemerkungen gesammelt auf einer Reise durch Holland, und einin Theil Franchreichs, 1801. Von J.F. Droysen. Goetting. 1803. 8vo.--Literary establishments and societies, especially those of Paris, and the state of mathematical, physical, and chemical science, are particularly attended to by this author.

194. Arndt, Reisen durch einer Theil Deutschlands, Ungaren, Italien, und Franckreichs, 1798, 1799. 4 vols. 8vo. Leip. 1804.

195. Reisen durch das Osterreich, Illyrien, Dalmatien, und Albanien, 1818. 2 vols. 8vo. Meissen, 1822.

196. Reisen durch einen Theil Deutschlands, die Schweitz, Italien, und Griechenland. 8vo. Gotha, 1822.

197. Bemerkungen auf einer Reise aus Nord Deutschland, uber Francfort, nach dem sudlichen Franckreich. 1819. 8vo. Leips. 1822.

198. Lettere Scritte della Sicilia e della Turkia. Dall. Abbote D. Sestini, 1774-78. Florence, 1780. 3 vols. 8vo.--These travels, which have been translated into French, are very full on the agriculture of Sicily, and on its internal and external commerce.

199. Fred. Snedorfs Samlede Skrivter. Copenh. 1794. 4 vols. 8vo.--Of this work only the first volume relates to our present subject, containing letters from Germany, Switzerland, France and England. The author, who travelled at two different times into these countries, pays particular attention to political and literary persons, whose character he draws with great spirit, candour, and acuteness. As he travelled at the commencement of the French Revolution, his sketches of political characters and events are especially interesting and valuable. The universities of England and Germany also attract a deal of his attention, and on these he offers some judicious remarks.

V

VOYAGES AND TRAVELS IN THE ARCTIC SEAS AND COUNTRIES

200. Chronological History of Voyages into the Polar Regions. By John Barrow, 1819. 8vo.

201. History of North-Eastern Voyages of Discovery. By Captain Jos. Burney, 1819. 8vo.--These two works nearly exhaust the subject on which they treat: the character of their authors sufficiently warrants their accuracy and completeness.

202. J.R. Forster's History of Voyages and Discoveries made in the North, 1786. 4to.--This work is not confined to voyages and discoveries in the Arctic regions; but comprises those made in the central regions of Asia in the middle ages, as well as those in the northern parts of America. Its character is like that of all Forster's productions, to some of which we have already had occasion to advert.

203. Russian Voyages of Discovery for a North-west Passage. By Muller. London. 4to. 1800.--The following work, though relating rather to discoveries in the sea between Asia and America, than to attempts for a north-east or north-west passage, may be placed here, as a continuation of the work of Muller, which comes no farther down than the expedition of Behring, in 1741.

204. Account of the Russian Discoveries between Asia and America. By William Coxe, 1780. 8vo.--This work is interesting, not merely from the particular subject which the title indicates, but also on account of the sketch it contains of the conquest of Siberia, and of the Russian commerce with China.

205. Historia Navigationis Mar. Frobisberi, 1577. Nuremburg, 1580. 8vo.

206. Descriptio novi Freti, recens inventi, ab Hen. Hudson. Amsterdam, 1613. 4to.

207. Captain James's Voyage for the Discovery of the Northwest Passage, in 1632. London, 1633. 4to.--This narrative contains some remarkable physical observations on the cold and ice; but no hint of any discovery of importance.

208. Henry Ellis's Voyage for the Discovery of a North-west Passage, in 1746-7. London, 1748. 2 vols. 8vo.--Some important facts and remarks relating to Hudson's Bay are given in this voyage.

209. Account of a Voyage for the Discovery of a North-west Passage, by Hudson's Straits, in 1746-7, in the California. By the Clerk of that Ship. 2 vols. 8vo. 1748.--This relates to the same voyage as the work of Ellis.

210. Hearne's Journey from Prince of Wales' Fort, in Hudson's Bay, to the Northern Ocean. 1795. 4to.

211. Mackenzie's Voyage from Montreal, through the Continent of North America to the Frozen and Pacific Oceans, in the Years 1789 and 1793. 4to.--Besides the interesting details in these voyages, respecting the

countries travelled over, and the manners of the inhabitants, they are important, particularly Mackenzie's, as having effected the discovery of the Polar Sea by land, and as introductory to the following work:

212. Voyage of Discovery for a North-west Passage. By Captain Ross, 1819. 4to.--Although the end was not accomplished, nor that done which might have been, yet this volume is valuable for its scientific details on natural history and meteorology.

213. Voyage for the Discovery of a North-west Passage from the Atlantic to the Pacific. By Captain Parry, 1821. 4to.--Geography, natural history, and especially the sciences connected with, and contributing to the improvement of navigation and geographical knowledge, together with a most interesting narrative of sound judgment, presence of mind, perseverance and passive courage, characterize this volume.

214. Narrative of a Journey from the Shores of Hudson's Bay to the Mouth of the Copper Mine River, &c. By Captain. J. Franklin, 1823. 4to.--A work of intense and indeed painful interest, from the sufferings of those who performed this journey; of value to geography by no means proportional to those sufferings; but instructive in meteorology and natural history.

215. Geschicte der Schiffahrten zur endeckung des Nordeest-lichen Wegs nach Japan und China. Von J.C. Adelung. Halle, 1768. 4to.--Some of the above works, as well as others relating to attempts to discover a north-west and north-east passage, are inserted in Harris and Churchill's Collections.

216. Les Trois Navigations faites par les Hollandois au Septentrion. Par Gerard de Ver. Paris, 1610. 8vo.--This contains Barentz's Voyages.

217. Histoire des Peches, des Découvertes, &c. des Hollandois, dans la Mer du Nord. Paris, 1801. 3 vols. 8vo.--This work, translated from the Dutch, is full of curious matter, not only respecting the fish and fisheries of the North Sea, but also respecting Greenland, Spitzbergen, Nova Zembla, and on subjects of natural history.

218. Beschriebung des Alten und Neuen Grenland, nebist einem begrift der Reisen die Frobisher, &c. Nuremberg, 1679. 4to.

219. A Voyage towards the North Pole. By Lord Mulgrave, in 1773. 4to.

220. An Account of the Arctic Regions. By W. Scoresby, 1820. 2 vols. 8vo.--This, together with a voyage to Greenland, published subsequently by the same author, is full of most valuable information on the meteorology and natural history of this part of the World, besides containing interesting particulars on the Whale Fishery.

221. Déscription et Histoire Générale du Gröenland. Par Egede, traduite du Danois. Genève, 1763. 8vo.--In 1788-9, Egede published two other works on Greenland in Danish, which complete his description of this country.

222. Crantz's History of Greenland, translated from the High Dutch, 1767. 2 vols. 8vo.--A continuation of this history was published by Crantz, in German, 1770, which has not been translated.

VI
EUROPE

LAPLAND AND THE SCANDINAVIAN COUNTRIES

223. Canuti Leemii de Lapponibus. Copenhagen, 1767. 2 vols. 4to.--This work, containing a rich mine from which travellers in Lapland, particularly Acerbi, have drawn valuable materials, is seldom met with complete and with all the plates: there should be 100 of them.

224. Histoire de la Lapponie, traduite du Latin de M. Schaeffer. Paris, 1678. 4to.

225. Journal d'un Voyage au Nord, 1736-7. Amsterdam, 1746. 12mo.--This work, though principally and professedly an account of the labours of Maupertuis, to ascertain the figure of the earth, is interesting to the general reader, from the descriptions it gives of the manners, &c. of the natives of Lapland, &c.

226. Mémoires sur les Samoyedes et les Lappous. Copenhagen, 1766. 8vo.

227. Voyage dans le Nord de l'Europe, 1807. Par La Motte. 4to. Paris.--Norway and part of Sweden were visited by this traveller on foot, and he gives details of scenery, &c. which only a foot traveller could procure.

228. The natural History of Iceland. By Horrebow, 1758. folio.

229. Von Troil's Letters from Iceland. 1780. 8vo.--This translation is not nearly so accurate as that into French, published in Paris, 1781. 8vo.

230. Travels in Iceland during the Summer of 1810. By Sir G. Mackenzie, 1811. 4to.--Almost every topic on which a traveller is expected to give information is here treated of: the history, religion, natural history, agriculture, manners, &c.; and all evidently the result of much previous knowledge, good sense, and information collected on the spot.

231. Hooker's Journal of a Tour in Iceland in 1809. 2 vols. 8vo.--Natural History, especially Botany; the travels of this author, Mackenzie, and Henderson, would seem to leave nothing to be desired on the subject of this extraordinary island and its inhabitants.

232. Journal of a Residence in Iceland, 1814-15. By Henderson. 2 vols. 8vo.--The state of society, manners, domestic habits, and religion, are here treated of; but there is too much minuteness, and a tediousness and dryness of style and manner.

233. Voyage en Islande. Par Olafsen et Povelsen. Paris, 1801. 5 vols. 8vo.--This work, translated from the Danish, though tedious and prolix, supplies many curious particulars respecting the natural history of the country and the manners of the people.

234. OEconomische Reise durch Island. Von Olavius. Leip. 4to.

235. Landt's Description of the Feroe Islands. Translated from the Danish. 8vo.--This work, which was published at Copenhagen in 1800, is the only accurate account of these islands since the Feroe Reserata of Debes in 1673; but it is too minute and long for the subjects it describes.

236. Coxes's Travels in Poland, Russia, Sweden and Denmark. 5 vols. 8vo.--The substantial merits of this work are well known.

237. Acerbi's Travels through Sweden, Finland, and Lapland, to the North Cape, in 1798-9. 2 vols. 4to. 1801.--These travels are interesting and attractive; but they bear evident marks of having been made up by an editor. The author has been attacked by Rihs, a Swede, for misrepresenting the Swedes, and for having borrowed largely without acknowledgment from Leemius; and by his fellow-traveller, Skieldebrand, with having appropriated the views and designs which he made. The latter published in French a Picturesque Tour to the North Cape.

238. Lachesis Lapponica, or a Tour in Lapland. By Linnæus, 1811. 2 vols. 8vo.--These travels were performed in 1732, when Linnæus was very young. Botany of course forms the principal subject; but the work is also instructive and interesting from the picture it exhibits of the character of the author, and of the manners of the Laplanders.

239. Travels through Norway and Lapland. By Baron Von Buch; with Notes by Professor Jameson, 1818. 4to.--This work, translated from the German, contains much new and valuable information, chiefly on mineralogy and geology.

240. Thomson's Travels in Sweden, during the Autumn of 1812. 4to.--Mineralogy, geology, satistics, and politics form the chief topics: the work is carelessly written.

241. Travels through Sweden, Norway, and Finmark, to the North Cape, 1820. By A. de Capell Brocke. 4to. 1823. Picturesque.

242. Nouveau Voyage vers le Septentrion. Amsterdam, 1708. 12mo.--The customs, religion, character, domestic life, &c. of the Norwegians and Laplanders are here sketched in an interesting and pleasant manner.

243. Lettres sur le Danemark. Par Mallet. Genève, 1767. 2 vols. 8vo.--This work is worthy of the author, whose introduction to the History of Denmark is so advantageously known to English readers, by Bishop Percy's excellent translation of it. It gives an excellent and faithful picture of this country in the middle of the eighteenth century, and comprises also the southern provinces of Norway.

244. Voyage en Allemagne et en Suède. Par J.P. Catteau. Paris, 1810. 3 vols. 8vo.--Sensible and judicious on arts, manners, literature, literary men, statistics and economics; but more full and valuable on Sweden than on Germany. Indeed few authors have collected more information on the North of Europe than M. Catteau; his Tableau des Etats Danois, and his Tableau Général de la Suède, are excellent works, drawn up with great accuracy and judgment. The same may be said of his Tableau de la Mer Baltique; in which every kind of information relative to the Baltic, its shores, islands, rivers, ports, produce, ancient and modern commerce, is given.

245. Voyage en Norwège, traduit de l'Allemand de J. Fabricius. Paris, 1803. 8vo.--This too is an excellent work, especially in what regards the natural history and economics of the country.

246. Reise en die Marschlander au der Nordsee. Von J.N. Tetens. Leip. 1788. 8vo.--Holstein, Jutland, and Sleswick, countries in which we possess few

travels, are accurately described in this work.

247. Reise durch einige Schwedische Provinzen. Von J.W. Schmidt. Hamburgh, 1801.--These travels contain curious particulars respecting the Nomadic Laplanders.

248. Arndt, Reise durch Schweden, 1804. 4 vols. 8vo. Berlin, 1806.

There are several travels by Linnæus (besides the one published by Sir J. Smith, already noticed) and his pupils into different provinces of Sweden, relating to their natural history, which botanists will value highly; but we omit them, as interesting only to them. They are written in Swedish, but German translations have appeared of most of them. There are also valuable travels by Germans, especially Huelfer and Gilberg, which give full and accurate details of the copper mines, and the processes pursued in them; but these also we omit for a similar reason.

RUSSIA AND POLAND.

Whatever object has once been pursued by a Russian sovereign, seems to descend as a hereditary pursuit to his successors. This is true, not only of their plans of conquest, but also of their means of improving their country; but it is evident of all countries, and especially of such a vast extent of country as Russia exhibits, where new districts are from time to time added, the very limits of which are scarcely known, that no sure and regular means of improvement can be adopted, until the actual state and the capabilities of each district are fully known. The Empress Catherine gave great attention and encouragement to these enquiries: a number of men, well qualified for the undertaking, were sent to investigate the state of each district, especially its natural history, and the addition to the national strength and wealth which might be drawn from it. When the name of Pallas is mentioned as one of the scientific men employed for this purpose, and empowered to direct the enquiries of his associates, and to revise them, in it a sufficient pledge is given of the accuracy and value of their labours.

249. Michalonis Lithuani de Moribus Tartarorum, Lithuanorum et Moschorum Fragmenta. Basle, 1615. 4to.--We notice this work as exhibiting a lively picture of the manners of these nations at this period. The same reason induces us to notice the following. Indeed, the chief interest of these old works, and it is no languid one, is derived from being introduced into the midst of ancient manners and people.

250. Ulfedii Legatio Moscovitica. Franck. 1617. 4to.--This work, which particularly notices the Tartar tribes at that time subject to Russia, proves, by a comparison with what Pallas relates of them, that their manners, customs, and acquirements had been quite stationary for nearly 150 years.

251. State of Russia. By Captain Perry. London, 1716. 8vo.--Captain Perry, who visited Russia in 1706-12, at the request of Peter the Great, to assist in the formation of a fleet, navigable canals, &c., has in this work given an accurate

account of this vast empire; the first indeed that may be said to have introduced a knowledge of it into England.

252. View of the Russian Empire during the reign of Catherine II. By the Rev. W. Tooke. 3 vols. 8vo.--As this work is drawn up from a personal knowledge of the country, and aided by access to the best authorities, we have admitted it into the Catalogue, though not exactly falling within the description of travels. It is full of matter, physical, statistical, political, commercial, &c.; but heavily written, and displaying rather extent and accuracy of research, than a perspicuous and profound mind.

The following are the principal works by Pallas and his associates, or works undertaken with similar objects. They require no particular criticism, after the general notice we have given of them.

253. Reisen durch verschiedene Provinzen des Russischen Reichs, 1768. 1773. Peters. 3 vols. 4to.

254. Bemerkungen auf einer Reise in die Sudlichen Statthalterschaften des Russischen Reichs, 1793, 1794.--Of these travels by Pallas, the last is more particularly devoted to science, and therefore is interesting to general readers. Both have been translated into French, and the travels in 1793-4, into English.

255. Georgi Bemerkungen auf einer Reise im Russischen Reichs, 1772--1774. Peters. 1755. 2 vols. 4to.

256. Georgi Beschriebung alter Nation des Russischen Reichs. Leipsic. 2 vols. 4to.

257. Georgi Geographische, Physicalische und Naturhistorische, Beschriebung des Russischen Reichs. Koning. 3 vols. 4to.--This work of uncommon labour and research, treats of the geography, physical, and natural history of Russia, divided into zones, each of which will be separately described, when the work is completed.

258. Gmelin, Reisen durch Russland. Peters. 1770-4. 3 vols. 4to.--Of the Travels of Lepechin, the other associate of Pallas, which were performed 1768-1771, and published in Russian, there is a German translation. Altenburgh, 1774. 3 vols. 4to., of which we have not been able to procure the exact title.

259. Reise von Volhynien nach Cherson en Russland, 1787. Von J.C. Mæller. Hamb. 8vo.

260. Bemerkungen uber Russland en rucksicht auf wissen-schaften Kunst, Religion. Von J.J. Bollerman. Erfurt. 1788. 8vo.

261. Mineralogische, Geographische, und andere vermischte, Nachrechten von der Altaischen Gebirgen. Von H.M. Renovanz. Freyberg. 1789. 4to.

262. Tableau Historique et Statistique de l'Empire Russie à la fin du 18me siècle. Par H. Storch. Paris, 1800. 2 vols. 8vo.--This work, by the author of the Picture of Petersburgh, well known to the English reader, is admitted here for the same reason which gave insertion to Tooke's Russia. It is, however, we believe, not yet complete according to the original plan of the author; and the French translation only comprises what relates to the physical and civil state of the inhabitants. Storch's Work, in conjunction with that of

Georgi, on the geography and natural history of Russia, will comprise all that is interesting respecting this vast country.

263. Polonia, sive de Situ, Populis Moribus, &c. Poloniæ a Mart. Cromero. Cologne. 1578. 4to.

264. Sarmatiæ Europeæ Descriptio. ab Alex. Gaguin. Spire, 1581. fol.

265. Reise durch Pohlnische Provinzen. Von J.H. Carosi. Leip. 8vo.--These travels are chiefly mineralogical.

266. Nachrichten uber Pohlen. Von J.J. Kausch. Saltz. 1793. 8vo.

267 Letters, Literary and Political, on Poland. 1823. 8vo.--Rather feebly written, and too minute on uninteresting points; in other respects valuable, as relating to a country of which we know comparatively little.

TURKEY, GREECE, DALMATIA, &c.

The countries of Europe, the travels into which we have hitherto enumerated, do not present very various and numerous objects of research. In Scandinavia the natural historian, especially the mineralogist, will be chiefly interested. The vast extent of the Russian empire also affords objects of curious and novel research to the botanist and zoologist, few to the mineralogist. The Salt Mines of Poland afford the principal objects of investigation to scientific travellers in this country. Manners, habits, political institutions, and religion, of course, are interesting in all; and to those whose studies and enquiries lead them to investigate the differences in the different families of the human race, the opportunities afforded them by the Gothic Nations of Scandinavia; the Slavonic nations of Russia and Poland; and the totally distinct and singular races which inhabit Lapland and Finland, must be valuable and useful.

When we enter Turkey, the scene changes, or rather expands. Within its European, as well as its Asiatic empire, travellers of all descriptions, however various their objects, will find rich and ample materials. Situated in a mild climate, with great variety of soil, in it are found plants remarkable for their uses in medicine and the arts, or for their beauty: its mountainous districts contain treasures for the mineralogist; and to the politician and student of human nature, it exhibits the decided effects of the Mahometan religion, and of Asiatic despotism. But what principally distinguishes it from the other countries which have hitherto occupied us, must be sought in its ruins of Grecian magnificence and taste: in the traces and evidences it affords of ancient times, manners, and acquirements: in the hold it possesses over our feelings, and even over our judgment, as being classic ground--the soil which nourished the heroes of Marathon and the bard of Troy.--The language, the manners, the customs, the human form and countenance of ancient Greece, are forcibly recalled to our recollection.

The travels in this part of the world have been so numerous, that we must be strict and limited in our selection, having regard principally to those which exhibit it under its various aspects with the greatest fidelity, at various periods.

268. Nicholai Clenard Epistola de Rebus Mahomediis, in Itinere scriptis. Louvain, 1551. 8vo.

269. Petrus Gyllius de Bosphoro Thracio. Elzerer, 1561. 4to.--This is one of the first travellers who describes the antiquities of this part of Turkey: manners and natural history, such as it was in his time, also come under his notice. Dallaway praises him.

270. Sandy's (Geo.) Travels, containing the State of the Turkish Empire, of Greece, Egypt, and the Holy Land. 1673. fol.--Sandys was an accomplished gentleman, well prepared by previous study for his Travels, which are distinguished by erudition, sagacity, and a love of truth, and are written in a pleasant style.

271. Ricault's History of the Present State of the Ottoman Empire. 1689. 8vo.--Ricault was secretary to the English Embassy at the Porte in 1661. The Mahometan religion, the seraglio, the maritime and land forces of Turkey are particularly noticed by him. An excellent translation into French, with most valuable notes, by Bespier, was published at Rouen, in 1677. 2 vols. 12mo.

272. Lady Mary Wortley Montague's Letters.--A great number of editions of these Letters have been published. In 1805, her Works were published in 5 vols. 12mo., containing Letters which had not previously appeared. The character of her work, which principally relates to Turkey, is well known.

273. Porter's Observations on the Religion, Laws, Government, and Manners of the Turks. 1768. 2 vols. 12mo.--Sir James Porter was British ambassador at the Porte; his work is faithful and accurate, and is chiefly illustrative of the political state, manners, and habits of the Turks.

274. Eton's Survey of the Turkish Empire. 1801. 8vo.--This work is divided into four parts: government, finances, religion, arts, manners, commerce, and population; state of the provinces, especially Greece; causes of the decline of Turkey; and British commerce with Turkey. As it is the result of personal observation, and of excellent opportunities, it falls within our notice. Many of the opinions, however, and some of the statements of the author, have been controverted, particularly by Thornton in his Present State of Turkey. 2 vols. 8vo. 1809. In a note to the preface, Mr. Eton enumerates the best authors who have written on Turkey.

275. History of the Russian Embassy to Constantinople. By M. Reimers, Secretary to the Embassy, 1804. 3 vols. 4to.--This work is translated from the German. Though the title in its original language would lead the reader to suppose that it principally related to the Russian provinces traversed by the embassy on its going and return, this is not the case: the Turkish empire, and chiefly Constantinople, form the most extensive and important division of these volumes; in all that relates to the Turks there is much curious information; the work is also interesting from the picture it exhibits of the manner in which the embassy, consisting of a caravan of 650 persons,

travelled. They were six months in going from one capital to the other.

276. Tour in 1795-6 through the Crimea. By Maria Guthrie. 1800. 2 vols. 4to.--This work contains a lively description of the various tribes that inhabit the Crimea; their manners, institutions, and political state; the antiquities, monuments, and natural history, and remarks on the migrations of the Asiatic tribes. That part of the work which relates to antiquities was written by her husband, Dr. Guthrie.

277. Walpole's Memoirs relative to European and Asiatic Turkey. Edited from MS. journals.

278. Travels in various Countries of the East, being a Continuation of the Memoirs. 2 vols. 4to. 1817 and 1820.--The information in these volumes is very various, classical, antiquarian, and statistical: on natural history, manners, religion, politics; and most of it valuable.

279. Wheeler and Spon's Travels into Greece, 1681. fol--This work relates chiefly to the antiquities of Greece and Asia Minor, and is valuable for its plates of them, and of medals, inscriptions, &c.

280. A Journey into Greece, &c. By Wheeler, 1688. fol.--This work (which embraces, in some degree, the same countries as the former, but which takes in also Dalmatia) is also devoted to antiquities, descriptions, and medals, and bears a good character in these respects.

281. Travels in Asia Minor, &c. By Richard Chandler, 1775-6. 2 vols. 4to.--These are valuable travels to the antiquarian. The author, guided by Pausanias, as respects Greece, Strabo for that country and Asia Minor, and Pliny, has described with wonderful accuracy and perspicuity the ruins of the cities of Asia Minor, its temples, theatres, &c.

282. Savary's Letters on Greece. Translated from the French, 8vo.--Rhodes and Candia are most particularly described in this volume,--islands of which we previously had meagre accounts.

283. Fortis' Travels in Dalmatia. 4to.--The geology, natural history, and antiquities of this country, with curious and instructive notices on the singular races which inhabit it, form the subject of this volume, which is translated from the Italian.

284. Travels in Hungary. By Rob. Townson, M.D. 1796. 4to.--This is a valuable work to the natural historian, particularly the mineralogist: it also contains a very particular account of the Tokay wines.

285. Travels in the Ionian Islands, Albania, Thessaly, and Greece, 1812-13. By Dr. Holland. 4to. 1815.--Classical, antiquarian, and statistical information is here intermixed with valuable remarks on the natural history, manners, political state, &c. of the countries visited, especially Albania.

286. Dodwell's Classical and Topographical Tour through Greece, 1801. 1805 and 6. 2 vols. 4to. 1819.--This work displays great research, aided and directed by much preparatory knowledge, and a sound judgment and good taste.

287. Hobhouse's Journey through Albania and other Provinces of Turkey, to Constantinople, in 1809-10. 4to. 1813.--Classical, antiquarian, and statistical, with sketches of manners, national character, &c.

288. Tableau Général de l'Empire Ottoman.--Of this splendid and celebrated work 2 volumes folio were published in 1787, which comprised the religious code of Turkey. The 3d volume was published in 1821, divided into two parts: the first part on the political, military, civil, and judicial code; the second part on the state of the Ottoman empire. This completes the plan of the author D'Ohsson. Under all the heads, into which he has divided his work, he has introduced authentic and curious notices of the agriculture, arts, manners, domestic life, &c. of the Turks. The third volume was published under the superintendence of his son.

289. Voyage dans la Grèce Asiatique. Par Sestini. Paris, 1789, 8vo.--This work, translated from the Italian, comprises an account of the environs of Constantinople, the peninsula of Cyzicum, formerly an island in the Propontis, to which it was united by Alexander the Great; and the districts of Brusa and Nice. The antiquities of the peninsula, but especially the botany of the countries he visited, are treated of in a masterly manner.

290. Voyage de Vienne à Belgrade. Par N.E. Kleeman, 1768--1770. Neufchâtel, 1780. 8vo.--This work, translated from the German, comprehends an account of the Crimea, and of the Tartar tribes who inhabit it, full, minute, and accurate.

291. Traité sur le Commerce de la Mer Noire. Par M. de Peysonnel. Paris, 1783. 2 vols. 8vo.--Besides the commerce of the Crimea, its soil, agriculture, and productions, and its political state before it was annexed to Russia, are treated of in these volumes.

292. Description Physique de la Tauride. La Haye. 8vo.--This work, translated from the Russian, is intended to complete the survey of the Russian empire: it relates chiefly to natural history in all its three branches.

293. Voyage en Crimea, 1803. Par J. Reuilly. Paris, 1806. 8vo.--The author was assisted by the celebrated Pallas, who, at this time, lived in the Crimea. The physical as well as political state of this country are comprised in this work.

294. Les Ruins des plus beaux Monumens de la Grèce, considérés du côté de l'Histoire et du côté de l'Architecture. Par M. Le Roi. Paris, 1770. fol.

295. Voyage Littéraire de la Grèce, ou Lettres sur les Grecs Anciens et Modernes, avec un parallèle de leurs Moeurs. Par M. Guys. Paris, 1783. 4 vols. 8vo.

The peculiar nature of these two works is sufficiently indicated by their respective title: they are both interesting.

296. Voyage en Grèce et en Turquie. Par Sonnini. Paris, 1801. 4to.--This work, which is translated into English, is rich in natural history, commerce, and manners, particularly regarding some of the islands of the Archipelago, Rhodes, Macedonia, the Morea, and Asia Minor.

297. Voyage en Morea, à Constantinople, en Albania, &c. 1799--1801. Par Pouqueville.

298. Voyage dans la Grèce. Par Pouqueville. vol. 1. 4to. Paris, 1820.--The first work has been translated into English: they are both full of information, especially respecting Albania, though more accurate investigations, or

perhaps different views and opinions, have induced subsequent travellers to differ from him in some respects.

299. Bartholdy, Voyage en Grèce, 1803-4. 2 vols. 8vo. Paris, 1807.

300. Moeurs, Usages, Costumes des Ottomans. Par Castellan. Paris, 1812. 6 vols.12mo.--The value of this work is enhanced by the illustrations supplied by Langles from oriental authors.

301. Lettres sur la Grèce. Par Castellan. Paris, 1810. 8vo.--The Hellespont and Constantinople are the principal subjects of these letters, which are lively and amusing in their pictures of manners and life. The same character applies to his "Lettres sur l'Italie." Paris, 1819. 3 vols. 8vo.

302. Voyage à l'Embouchure de la Mer Noire. Par Andreossy. Paris, 1818. 8vo.-- A valuable work on physical geography, and to the engineer and architect, and such as might have been expected from the professional pursuits and favourable opportunities of the author.

303. Lettres sur le Bosphore, 1816--19. 8vo. 1821.

304. Voyage Pittoresque et Historique de l'Istrie et de la Dalmatie, rédigé d'après l'Itinéraire de L.F. Cassas, peintre. Par J. Lavallée. Paris, 1802. fol.--This splendid work, as its title indicates, principally relates to antiquities: there are, however, interspersed notices on manners, commerce, &c. Zara, celebrated for its marasquin, is particularly described.

305. Scrofani, Reise en Griechenland, 1794-5. Leip. 1801. 8vo.--The German translation of this work, originally published in Italian, is superior to the original, and to the French translation, by the addition of valuable notes by the translator, and the omission of irrelevant matter. Scrofani pays particular attention to commercial details respecting the Ionian Isles, Dalmatia, the Morea, &c.

The Germans were celebrated for their skill in metallurgy, and their knowledge of mineralogy, at a period when the rest of Europe paid little attention to these subjects; and German travels in countries celebrated for their mines are, therefore, valuable. Of the German travels in Hungary and Transylvania, the greater part are mineralogical. We shall select a few.

306. Born, Briefe uber Mineralogische gegenstande auf einer Reise durch den Temeswarer Bannat, &c. Leip. 1774. 8vo.--This mineralogical tour in Hungary and Transylvania by Born, and published by Ferber, possesess a sufficient guarantee of its accuracy and value from the names of the author and editor. It is, however, not confined to mineralogy, but contains curious notices on some tribes inhabiting Transylvania and the adjacent districts, very little known: it is translated into French.

307. Ferber, Physikalisch-metallurgische Abhandlunger uber die Gebirge and Bergewecke in Ungarn. Berlin, 1780. 8vo.

308. Balthazar Hacquet, Reise von dem Berge Terglou in Krain, au den Berg Glokner in Tyrol, 1779--1781. Vienne, 1784. 8vo.

309. Neueste Reisen, 1788--1795, durch die Daceschen und Sarmateschen Carpathen. Von B. Hacquet. Nuremb. 1796. 4 vols. 8vo.

310. Briefe uber Triestes, Krain, Kærnthen, Steyermark, und Saltzburgh. Franck.

1793. 8vo.

311. Briefe uber das Bannet. Von Steube, 1793. 8vo.

312. F. Grisselini, Lettere di Venetea, Trieste, Carinthia, Carnioli e Temeswar. Milan, 1780. 4to.--Natural history and manners are here described.

GERMANY.

This large district of Europe offers, not only from its extent, but also from numerous causes of diversity among its parts,--some established by nature, and others introduced by man--various numerous and important objects to the research and observation of the traveller. Its mines,-- the productions of its soil and its manufactures,--the shades of its expressive, copious, and most philosophical language,--from the classical idiom of Saxony, to the comparatively rude and uncultivated dialect of Austria,--the effects on manners, habits, feeling, and intellectual and moral acquirements, produced by the different species of the Christian religion professed,--and the different forms of government prevailing in its different parts;--all these circumstances, and others of a more evanescent and subtle, though still an influential nature, render Germany a vast field for enquiry and observation.

The travels in this country, especially by its native inhabitants, are so numerous, that we must content ourselves with a scrupulous and limited selection;--referring such of our readers as wish to consult a more copious catalogue, to "Ersch's Literatur der Geschichte und deren Hulfswissenschaften." We shall follow our usual plan, selecting those travels which give the best idea of the country, at remote, intervening, and late periods.

313. Martini Zeilleri, Itinerarium Germaniæ nov-antiquæ. Strasb. 1632. 4to.

314. Christ. Dorrington's Reflections on a Journey through some Provinces of Germany in 1698. Lond. 1699. 8vo.

315. The German Spy. By Thomas Ledyart. 1740. 8vo.

316. Keysler's Travels through Germany, Bohemia, Hungary, Switzerland, Italy, and Lorrain. Translated from the German, 1756. 2 vols. 4to.--Keysler, though a German, was educated at St. Edmund's Hall: he travelled with the Count of Gleich and other noblemen. His favourite study was antiquities; but his judgment, in those parts of his travels which relate to them, has been questioned. His work, though heavy, is interesting from the picture it exhibits of Germany, &c. in the middle of the 18th century.

317. Adams's Letters on Silesia, during a Tour in 1800-2. Philadelphia, 3 vols. 8vo.--Mr. Adams was ambassador from the United States to Berlin: his work contains some interesting information, especially on the manufactures of Silesia.

318. Cogan's Journey up the Rhine, from Utrecht to Frankfort. 2 vols. 8vo. 1794.--The style of this work is lively and interesting: its pictures of manners and scenery good; and it contains a learned disquisition on the origin of printing. Dr. Cogan resided the greater part of his life in Holland.

319. Travels in the North of Germany. By Thomas Hodgskin, Esq. 2 vols. 8vo.

1820.--That part, of Germany between the Elbe and the frontiers of Holland is here described: the topic is rather new; and Mr. H. has given us much information on the agriculture, state of society, political institutions, manners, &c.; interspersed with remarks, not in the best taste, or indicating the soundest judgment or principles.

320. Letters from Mecklenberg and Holstein, 1820. By G. Downes. 8vo.--This being a part of Germany seldom visited, every thing relating to it is acceptable. Mr. Downes's work is, however, not so full and various as might have been expected: on manners and German literature it is most instructive.

321. An Autumn near the Rhine, or Sketches of Courts, Scenery, and Society, in Germany, near the Rhine, 1821. 8vo.--The title indicates the objects of this volume, which bespeaks an observant and intelligent mind.

322. Travels from Vienna, through Lower Hungary. By Dr. Bright. 1817. 4to.-- Agriculture and statistics form the principal topics of this volume, which would have been equally valuable and much more interesting if the matter had been more compressed.

323. Historical and Statistical Account of Wallachia and Moldavia. By W. Wilkinson. 1820. 8vo.--Mr. Wilkinson, from his situation as British Consul, has been enabled to collect much information on these portions of Europe, chiefly such as the title indicates, and also of a political nature.

324. Voyages de Reisbeck en Allemagne. Paris, 1793. 2 vols. 8vo.--This work was originally published in German, under the title of Briefe eines reisenden Franzosen durch Deutschland: there is also an English translation. The travels took place in 1782: and the character of a French traveller, in the German original, was assumed, to secure the author from the probable effects of his severe remarks on the government, manners, and customs of Germany. To these subjects, and others connected with man, his agriculture, commerce, and other pursuits, Baron Reisbeck has chiefly confined his attention: perhaps the truth and impartiality of his strictures would be more readily acknowledged, if they were not so strongly impregnated with a satirical feeling.

325. Journal d'un Voyage en Allemagne, 1773. Par M. Guibert. Paris, 1802. 2 vols. 8vo.--The celebrated author of the "Essai General sur la Tactique," naturally directed his attention during his travels to military affairs, and to an examination and description of the sites of famous battles. But this work by no means is confined to such topics; and the remarks with which it abounds on more interesting subjects, are so evidently the fruit of an acute and original mind, that they equally command our attention, and instruct us.

326. Voyage en Hanovre, 1803-4. Par M.A.B. Mangourit. Paris, 1805. 8vo.-- Politics, religion, agriculture, commerce, mineralogy, manners, and customs, are discussed in this volume; and in general with good sense and information. Hamburgh, Hanover, its government, universities, and especially its mines, are particularly described.

327. Voyage dans quelques Parties de la Basse-Saxe, pour la Recherche des

Antiquités Slaves ou Wendes, 1794. Par J. Potocky. Hambro. 1795. 4to.

328. Journal d'un Voyage dans les Cercles du Rhin. Par Collini. Paris, 1777. 8vo.--Chiefly mineralogical.

329. Voyage sur le Rhin, depuis Mayence jusqu'à Dusseldorf. Newied, 1791. 8vo.--This tour contains some curious details on the subject of the wines of the Rhingau.

330. Voyage en Autriche, &c. Par De Serres. Paris, 1814. 4 vols. 8vo.--An immense mass of geographical and statistical information, in a great measure drawn from German authors, on Austria, Hungary, and Bohemia.

331. Viaggio sul Reno e ne suoi contorni di P. Bertolo. 1795. 8vo.--These travels, performed in the autumn of 1787, are elegantly written, rather than very instructive. They contain, however, some valuable notices respecting the volcanic appearances in the district of Andernach.

332. Briefe auf einer reise durch Deutschland, 1791. Leignitz, 1793. 2 vols. 8vo.--Arts, manufactures, and economy, are the principal topics of these letters.

333. Die Donnau reise. Ratesbonne. 1760. 8vo.--These travels describe the banks of the Danube, and the streams which flow into it.

334. Donnau Reise von Regensburgh bis Wein. Montag. 1802. 8vo.--The same remark applies to this work, only, as the title indicates, it is confined to the river and its streams, from Ratisbon to Vienna.

335. Reise durch Ober-Deutschland, OEsterreich, Nieder Bayern, Ober Schwaben, Wirtemberg, Baden, &c. Saltz. 1778. 8vo.

336. Litterarische reisen durch einen theil von Bayern, Franken und die Schweitz, 1780-2.; Von Zapf. Aug. 1782. 8vo.--The same author published another literary tour among the convents of Swabia, and Switzerland, and Bavaria; and in other parts of Franconia, Bavaria, and Swabia, in 1782. These tours are strictly literary; that is, have regard to MSS. and scarce editions, and are not scientific.

337. Reise durch einige Deutsche Provinzen, von Hollenberg. Stendal, 1782. 8vo.--Architecture and mechanics are the topics of these travels.

The following travels relate to the Hartz:

338. Geographische und Historische, Merkwurdigkeften des Ober Hartz. Leip. 1741. 8vo.

339. Reise nach dem Oberhartz. Von J.C. Sulzer.--Inserted in a collection of travels published by J. Bernouilli.

340. Reise nach dern Unterhartz. 1783. Von Burgsdorf.--In the natural history collection of Berlin.

341. Reise durch Ober Saxen und Hessen, von J. Apelbad. Berlin, 1785. 8vo.--Apelbad, a learned Swede, published a Collection of Voyages in different Parts of Europe, in Swedish, Stockholm, 1762, 8vo; and Travels in Saxony, in the same language, Stockholm, 1757, 8vo. There seems to have been another of the same surname, Jonas Apelbad, who published in Swedish, Travels in Pomerania and Brandenberg, Stockholm, 1757, 8vo. The work, of which we have given the title in German, was translated by Bernouilli, who has greatly enhanced the merits and utility of the original by his remarks.

Bernoulli's Collection of Travels,--Samlung kleiner reise beschriebungen, Leips. 1781-7, 18 vols. 8vo., contains many interesting short narratives and descriptions, particularly relating to Germany.

342. Reise durch die Norischen Alpen. Von Hacquet. Leips. 8vo. 1791.--These travels, like the former by the same author, which we have mentioned, are chiefly botanical and mineralogical.

343. Ausfluge nach dern Schnee-Berg in Unter-OEsterreich. Vienna, 1800. 8vo.--Botany, mineralogy, and what the Germans call economy, and technology, are principally attended to in this work.

344. Wanderrungen und Spazierfahrten in die gegenden um Wien. Vienna, 1802-4. 5 vols. 8vo.--The title of this work would not lead the reader to expect what he will find; valuable notices on mineralogy, agriculture, arts, and manufactures, in the midst of light and lively sketches of manners, places of amusement, &c.

345. Reise durch Sacksen. Von N.G. Leske. Leips. 1785. 4to.--Natural history and economy.

346. Beobachtungen uber Natur und Menschen. Von F.E. Lieberoth. Frankfort, 1791. 8vo.

347. Economische und Statische reisen durch Chur-Sacksen, &c. Von H. Engel. Leips. 1803. 8vo.

348. Bemerkungen einer Reisenden durch die Prussischen Staaten. Von J.H. Ulrich. Altenb. 1781. 8vo.

349. Briefe uber Schlesien Krakau, und die Glatz. 1791. Von J.L. Zoellner. Berlin, 1793. 2 vols. 8vo.

350. Reise durch einer Theil Preussen, Hambro, 1801. 2 vols. 8vo.--This work was drawn up by two travellers: one of whom supplied the statistical remarks, and the other, who traversed Prussia on foot, the remarks on entomology, amber, the sturgeon fishery, and other branches of natural history and economics.

351. Wanderrungen durch Rugen. Von Carl. Nernst. Dusseld. 1801. 8vo.--This island affords interesting notices on manners, ancient superstitions, particularly the worship of Ertha, besides statistical and geographical remarks.

352. Rhein-Reise. Von A.J. Von Wakerbert. Halberstadt, 1794. 8vo.

353. Ansichten des Rheins. Von Jno. Vogt. Bremen, 1805. 8vo.--This is a strange mixture of the picturesque, the romantic, and the instructive: the instructive parts contain historical and topographical notices of the cities on the Rhine, and curious details on its most famous wines.

354. Historische Jaarbocken, von oud nieven Friesland door Foeke Siverd. Leowarden, 1769. 8vo.--We insert the title of this work, though not strictly within our plan, because it gives an accurate account of a part of Germany, the dialect of which more resembles old English than any other German dialect; and in which there still lurk many very curious traditions, customs, and superstitions, which throw much light on our Saxon ancestors.

SWITZERLAND.

Perhaps no country in the world, certainly no district within such a small circuit, presents so many interesting objects to a traveller as Switzerland. Be he natural historian, and geologist, drawn by habit, feeling, and taste, to the contemplation of all that is grand, romantic, and picturesque in natural scenery, or attached to the study of man in that state, in which civilization and knowledge have brought with them the least intermixture of artifice, luxury, and dissoluteness--in Switzerland, he will find an ample and rich feast. It does not often happen that one and the same country attracts to it the abstract and cold man of science, the ardent imagination of the poet, and the strong, enthusiastic, and sanguine sympathies of the philanthropist.

355. Descriptio Helvetiæ, a Marso, 1555-9. 4to.--Marsus was ambassador from the Emperor and King of Spain, Charles V., to the Swiss, and gives a curious picture of their manners at this period.

356. Helvetia Profana et Sacra. 1642. 4to.--This work by Scotti, which is written in English, depicts the manners of the Swiss a century after Marsus.

357. Travels through the Rhætian Alps. By Beaumont, 1782, fol.--Travels through the Pennine Alps, by the same, 1788. small folio, both translated from the French.

358. Travels in Switzerland, and in the country of the Grisons, by the Rev. W. Coxe, 1791. 3 vols. 8vo.--These travels were performed in 1776, and again in 1785 and 1787, and bear and deserve the same character as the author's travels in Russia, &c., of which we have already spoken. Mr. Coxe gives a list of books on Switzerland at the end of his 3d volume, which may be consulted with advantage. There is a similar list at the end of his travels in Russia, &c.

359. A Walk through Switzerland, in Sept. 1816. 12mo.--The scenery and manners sketched with much feeling, taste, and judgment, in an animated style.

360. Journal of a Tour and Residence in Switzerland. By L. Simond. 1822. 2 vols. 8vo.--A description of Switzerland and the Swiss, which brings them in a clearer and stronger point of view, to the presence and comprehension of the reader than most travels in this country: though the range of observation and remark is not so extensive in this work, as in the author's work on Great Britain; in every other respect it is equal to it. The second volume is entirely historical.

The following French works particularly and accurately describe the natural history and the meteorology of the Swiss mountains and glaciers; the names of at least two of their authors must be familiar to our readers, as men of distinguished science.

361. Histoire Naturelle des Glaciers de Suisse. Paris, 1770. 4to. Translated from the German of Gruner.

362. Nouvelle Description des Glaciers. Par M. Bourrit. Geneva, 1785. 3 vols. 8vo.--This work of Bourrit is chiefly confined to the Valais and Savoy, and

its most important contents are given in the following work by the same author.

363. Nouvelle Description des Glaciers de la Savoie, particulièrement de la Vallèe de Chamouny et du Mont Blanc. 1785, 8vo.--This work contains an account of the author's successful attempt to ascend the summit of Mont Blanc. There are several other works of Bourrit on the Glaciers and Mountains of Savoy: the latest and most complete is the following:

364. Descriptions des Cols ou Passages des Alpes. Geneva, 1803. 2 vols. 8vo.

365. Voyage dans les Alpes, précédé d'un Essai sur l'Histoire Naturelle des Environs de Geneva. Par Saussure. Geneva, 1787--1796. 8 vols. 8vo.

366. Relation abrégée d'un Voyage à la Cime du Mont Blanc, en Aout, 1787. Par Saussure, Geneva. 8vo.

367. Voyage Minéralogique en Suisse. Lausanne, 1783-4. 8vo.

368. Voyage Minéralogique dans le Gouvernement de l'Argh, et ne partie du Valais. Lausanne, 1783. 8vo.--The first of these works by Razoumousky, and the other by Behoumwesky, are valuable, as noticing those parts which Saussure has not noticed.

369. Lettres sur quelques Parties de la Suisse, &c. Par J.A. de Luc. Paris, 1785. 8vo. Geological.

370. Voyage de J.M. Roland en Suisse, 1787: incribed in the 3d vol. of her works. Paris, 1800.--This celebrated, but mistaken and unfortunate woman, has thrown into her narrative much information on the manners of the Swiss, anecdotes of Lavater, &c. besides giving a most lively account of her visit to the glaciers.

371. Descriptions des Alpes Grecques et Cottiennes. Par Beaumont. 2 vols. 4to.--Part of this work is historical; the remainder embraces natural history, mineralogy, statistics, and manners.--The same character applies to No. 357.

372. Histoire Naturelle du Jurat et de ses Environs. Par le Comte de Razoumousky. Lausanne, 1789. 2 vols. 8vo.--The lakes of Neufchàtel, Morat, and Bienne, and part of the Pays de Vaud, are described in this work, which contains valuable information in meteorology, commerce, &c. besides natural history.

373. Journal du dernier Voyage de Dolomieu dans les Alpes. Par J.C. Bruien-Neergard. Paris, 1803. 8vo.--The French government directed Dolomieu to examine the Simplon; he was accompanied by the author, a young Dane, his pupil. Dolomieu died soon after his return: this work, therefore, is not nearly so full as it would have been, had he lived to give his observations to the public.

374. Lettre sur le Valais. Par M. Eschasseraux. Paris, 1806. 8vo.--This work, written in a pleasing style, gives important information on the manners and natural history of this most interesting part of Switzerland.

375. Voyage dans l'Oberland Bernois. Par J.R. Wyss. Leipsic, 1818. 8vo.--This work, translated from the German, is chiefly picturesque.

376. Fodere, Voyage aux Alpes Maritimes. Paris, 1820. 2 vols. 8vo.--Agriculture, natural history, and the state of medicine, are the principal topics.

377. Briefe aus der Schweitz, &c. Von Andreæ. Zurich, 1776. 4to.--Natural history, and a particular description of the celebrated bridge of Schaffhausen, and its mechanism, are what recommend this volume. Bernouilli, in his travels in Switzerland, has copied Andreæ in what relates to mineralogy and cabinets of natural history; but he has added some interesting descriptions of paintings.

378. Kleine reisen durch einige Schweizer-Cantons. Bâle, 1780. 8vo.

379. Letters on a Pastoral District, (the Valley of Samen in Fribourg). By Bonstellen (in German). Zurich, 1792. 8vo.

380. Physikalesch-Politische Reisen, aus der Dinarischen durch die Julischen, &c. in die Norischen. Alpen, 1781-83. Von B. Hacquet. Leipsic, 1784. 8vo.

381. Malerische Reise in die Italianische Schweitz. Von J.H. Mayer. Zurich, 1793. 8vo.--Mayer, in this work, as well as in travels in Italy, has been very happy in picturesque description.

382. Meine Wanderungen durch die Romanische Schweitz, Unterwaller und Savoyen. 1791. Tubingen, 1793. 8vo.

383. Kleine Fuss-reisen durch die Schweitz. Zurich, 1804. 2 vols. 8vo.--Parts of Switzerland are here described, which are seldom visited, and can be thoroughly known only by foot travellers.

384. Anleitung auf die nuzlichste und genussvollste art die Schweitz zu Bereisen. Von J.C. Ebel. Zurich, 1804-5. 4 vols. 8vo.--This most excellent work affords every kind of information which a person proposing to travel, or reside in Switzerland, would wish to acquire. It has been translated into French under the title of Manuel du Voyageur en Suisse. Zurich, 1818. 3 vols. 8vo. This contains all the additions of the 3d German edition.

ITALY.

As the traveller descends the Alps, the first regions of Italy into which he passes present him with mountains subdued in size, and gradually passing from magnificence to grandeur and beauty; then the rich and luxuriant plains of Lombardy meet him with their improved agriculture, and in some places curious geology. He next advances to those parts of Italy which are rich in the finest monuments of art, and associated with all that is interesting in the period of the revival of literature; with Dante, Boccacio, Petrarch, Ariosto, Tasso, and the Medici. The proofs of commercial wealth, united with magnificence and taste, present themselves to him in the palaces of Genoa, Venice, and Florence; and he hears, on every side, the most classical tongue of modern Europe.

Rome, with which, in conjunction with Greece, the associations of his frank and enthusiastic youth have been deeply formed, next rises to view: to the classical scholar, the antiquarian, the man of taste and virtue, the admirer of all that is most perfect in human conception, as brought into existence by the genius of Michael Angelo, and Raphael, this city affords rich and ample materials for study and description, though it is unable to excite that grandest feeling of the human breast, which is raised by the land of

Leonidas and of Socrates. Greece fought for liberty! Rome for conquest! The philosophy of Rome is less original, less pure and disinterested, less practical than that of Greece.

Through all this part of Italy the geologist finds materials for examination and conjecture, in the ridge of the Appennines: and these, rendered still more interesting, accompany him into the Neapolitan territory, both continental and insular.

Such are the principal subjects to which travellers have directed their attention in Italy; and the travels which chiefly relate to these subjects, and treat of them in the best manner, we shall select.

385. Les Observations Antiques du Seigneur Symion, Florentin, en son dernier Voyage d'Italie, 1557. Lyons, 1558. 4to--The principal merit of this work consists in the description and engravings of several remains of antiquity, which no longer exist.

386. An Itinerary of a Voyage through Italy, 1646, 1647. By John Raymond. 1648. 12mo.

387. Misson's New Voyage to Italy, 1704. 4 vols. 8vo.--This work is translated from the French; and contains the first general account of this country which appeared, but in many places incorrect and prejudiced. Addison's remarks on Italy are published with this edition of Misson; they are classical; and in fact a commentary made on the spot, on the descriptions of Virgil. Subsequent travellers, however, in some places differ from him in opinion, and in others question his accuracy and judgment.

388. Grosley's Observations on Italy. 2 vols. 8vo.--Chiefly political and anecdotal; in some parts of doubtful authority: translated from the French.

389. Sharp's Letters on Italy. 1769. 4 vols. 8vo.--Barretti's Account of the Manners and Customs of Italy. 1770. 2 vols. 8vo.--These works are noticed principally because they afford a curious and instructive proof of the very different views which may be taken of the same objects, according to the extent and accuracy of the knowledge, and the preconceived opinions and feelings of the observer. Barretti's work is certainly more accurate than that of Sharp, but in opposing him, he has sometimes gone into the opposite extreme: from comparing both, perhaps the reality may often be extracted. Manners and national character are their chief topics.

390. View of Society and Manners in Italy. By Dr. Moore, 1781. 2 vols. 8vo.-- The peculiar felicity of description and style with which this author paints manners, render these travels, as well as his others, extremely interesting.

391. Observations on Mount Vesuvius, Mount Etna, and other Volcanoes. By Sir W. Hamilton. Naples, 1776. 2 vols. folio.--London, 1772. 8vo.

392. Travels in the Two Sicilies. By H. Swinburne, 1790. 4 vols. 8vo.

393. Denon's Travels in Sicily and Malta, translated from the French. 8vo.-- Denon, an artist, accompanied Swinburne in his excursions to the vicinity of Naples, and into Sicily. These works are historical, geographical, and antiquarian, but heavily written.

394. Spallanzani's Travels in the Two Sicilies, and some parts of the Apennines,

1798. 4 vols. 8vo.--Translated from the Italian. Natural history forms the principal subject of these volumes, which are worthy of the author, who was esteemed one of the first natural historians of His age.

395. Boisgelin's Ancient and Modern Malta. 3 vols. 4to. translated from the French.--Only the first part of this work is descriptive, and it certainly contains an interesting account of Malta and the Maltese; the rest of the work is historical.

396. Brydon's Tour through Sicily and Malta. 2 vols. 8vo. 1776.--Liveliness of description of scenery and manners, couched in an easy and elegant style, has rendered these volumes extremely popular, notwithstanding they do not display much learning or knowledge, and are even sometimes superficial and inaccurate.

397. Boswell's Account of Corsica. 1768. 8vo.--Interesting details respecting Paoli, as well as on the island and its inhabitants.

398. Eustace's Classical Tour through Italy. 4 vols. 8vo.

399. Classical Tour through Italy and Sicily. By Sir R.C.Hoare, Bart. 1819. 4to.-- Mr. Eustace's work is very full and minute in the subject which the title indicates; it is written in good taste, but in rather a prolix style; his statements, however, are not always to be depended on, especially where his political or religious opinions interfere. Sir R. Hoare's work is meant as a supplement to Mr. Eustace's.

400. Remarks on Antiquities, Arts and Letters, during an excursion in Italy, in 1802-3. By Joseph Forsyth. 1816. 8vo.--This is an admirable work, giving in a short compass much information, and indicating strong powers of mind, and a correct taste.

401. Sketches Descriptive of Italy, 1816-17. 4 vols. 12mo. 1820.

402. Letters from the North of Italy. By W.S. Rose, 1819. 2 vols. 8vo.--Free and judicious remarks on the political degradation of this fair portion of Italy, with notes on manners, the state of society, &c.

403. Three Months passed in the Mountains East of Rome, in 1819. By Maria Graham, 8vo.--An interesting and well-written picture of manners and character, together with notices on the productions of the soil, &c.

404. Voyage to the Isle of Elba. By A.T. de Berneaud, 1814. 8vo.--This work, translated from the French, contains a very accurate survey of this island.

405. Tour through Elba. By Sir R.C. Hoare, bart. 1814. 4to.--Only seventeen pages are devoted to the journal, the remainder of the books consists of 8 views and a map: and a sketch of the character of Buonaparte.

406. Le Voyage et Observations de plusieurs Choses qui se peuvent remarquer en Italie. Par le Sieur Adelier. Paris, 1656. 8vo.--Interesting, from exhibiting a well-drawn picture of the manners of Italy at this period: with greater attention to natural history than was usual when Adelier wrote.

407. Voyage en Italie. Par M. de Lalande. Geneve, 1790. 7 vols. 8vo.--This large work embraces a vast variety of subjects, and in general they are treated in a masterly manner; manners, government, commerce, literature, the arts, natural history, antiquities, sculpture, paintings, &c. His narration of the

building of St. Peters is very full, curious, and interesting.

408. Voyage en Italie. Par. M. Duclos. Paris, 1791. 8vo.--Chiefly remarks on the government and political situation of the various states of Italy, with anecdotes and facts relating to these topics; expressed with an open and unshrinking boldness, not to have been expected from one who was the historiographer of France at the period when Duclos travelled, 1766-7.

409. Lettres Historiques et Antiques de Charles de Brosses. Paris, 1799. 3 vols. 8vo.--These letters by the celebrated De Brosses, author of L'Histoire des Navigations aux Terres Australes, and other works, hardly are equal to the literary reputation of the author; they paint with considerable force, though sometimes in too strong colours, the imperfections, follies, and vices of the Italians; and display good taste and judgment respecting the fine arts.

410. Voyage en Italie. De M. L'Abbé Barthelemi. Paris, 1802. 8vp.--The author of the travels of Anacharsis has here exhibited himself in the midst of his favourite pursuits; the precious remains of antiquity are described with an accuracy seldom equalled, and in a style which renders the description attractive, even to those who are not particularly conversant or interested in these topics. The work is grounded on letters written to Count Caylus; and contains, in an Appendix, some remarks of Winkelman, Jacquier, &c. This work has been translated into English. The travels of De Brosses and Barthelemi were performed in the middle of the eighteenth century.

411. Voyage dans le Montaniata et le Siennois. Par G. Santi. Lyons, 1802. 2 vols. 8vo.--This work, translated from the Italian, relates to mineralogy, botany, agriculture, and statistics.

412. Voyage sur la Scène des six derniers livres de L'Eneide. Par C.V. de Bonstetten. Geneva, 1805. 8vo.--The first part of this work, the nature of which is expressed by the title, is much superior to the travels of Addison, in extent of classical research, in originality of views, and in clearness of description: in this part there are also interesting particulars respecting Latium. In the second part, the author principally dwells on the Campagna, the causes of its depopulation, and its agriculture; this introduces some excellent observations on the agriculture of the ancient Romans, and the connection between it and their manners and religion; other topics are introduced, and treated in an able manner.

413. Voyages Physiques et Lithologiques dans la Campagna. Par Scipion Brieslack. Paris, 1800. 2 vols. 8vo.--Facts and conjectures on the formation of the Campagna, and on the soil of the territory and neighbourhood of Rome; on the extinct craters betwixt Naples and Canna, and on that of Vesuvius, render this work instructive and interesting to the geologist, while the picture of the Lazaroni must render this portion of his work attractive to the general reader.

414. Voyage en Sicile et dans la Grande-Grèce. Par le Baron de Riedesel, Paris, 1773. 12mo.--This work, translated from the German, is formed of letters addressed to Winkelman, describing minutely, and with great taste, learning, and accuracy, the magnificent views with which the scene of his travels

abounds, and contrasting them in ruins with their original perfection, as delineated in ancient authors. Interspersed are remarks on the manners and character of the inhabitants.

415. Lettres sur la Sicile et sur Malta, de M. le Comte de Borch, 1777. Turin, 1782. 2 vols. 8vo.--The object of the author is to supply the omissions and correct the mistakes of Brydon.

416. Voyage aux Isles Lipari, 1781. Par D. Dolomieu. Paris, 1788, 8vo..--The character of Dolomieu sufficiently points out the nature and value of this work. A Supplement was published the same year, under the title of Mémoire sur les Isles Ponces. Par Dolomieu. Paris. 8vo.

417. Voyage Historique Littéraire et Pittoresque dans les Isles et Possessions ci-devant Venétiennes du Levant. Par A. Grasset-Saint-Sauveur, jun. Paris, 1800. 3 vols. 8vo.--The author was French Consul at the Ionian Islands for many years; and hence he had opportunities which he seems to have employed with diligence and judgment, of gathering materials for this work, which, besides what its title indicates, enters fully into the agriculture, navigation, commerce, manners, &c.

418. Histoire Géographique, Politique, et Naturelle, de la Sardignie. Par D.A. Azami. Paris, 1801. 2 vols. 8vo.--Of this island we know less than of any other part of Europe; it has been seldom explored, and still seldomer described. There is certainly no work we are acquainted with, that gives such a complete and accurate account of this island and its inhabitants as Azami's.

419. Moeurs' et Coutumes des Corses. Par G. Faydel. Paris, 1798. 8vo.--Agriculture and natural history, rather popular than scientific; commerce and other similar topics are treated of in this work, though the title would lead us to expect only description of manners and customs.

420. Voyage Antique à l'Etna, en 1819. Par Gourbillon. 1820.--Chiefly relating to the natural history, and meteorology of the mountain.

421. Historisch Kritische Nachrichten von Italien. Von J.J. Volkman. Leipsic, 1770--1778. 3 vols. 8vo.--Manners, customs, politics, commerce, the state of the arts and sciences are treated of in these volumes.

422. Zusætze zu der Neusten Reise Beschriebung von Italien. Von J. Bernouilli. Leip. 1777--1782. 3 vols. 8vo.

423. Darstellungen aus Italien. Von F.J.L. Meyer. Berlin, 1792. 8vo.--This is a romantic work for a German; the author actually luxuriates in the recollections called up by the country of Michael Angelo, Raphael, Palladio, &c., and in his contemplation of the scenes of the convulsions of nature, and of the most striking incidents in the classical and middle ages. Independently of this extravagance of style, this work is valuable, especially in what relates to the Tyrol, where indeed his style is more simple. It is translated into French.

424. Briefe uber Calabrien und Sicilien. Von J.H. Bartels. Gottingen, 1789-1792. 3 vols. 8vo.--This is an excellent work on a part of the continent of Italy little known; the physical constitution of the country, natural productions,

agriculture, manners, &c. are treated of in a sensible and pleasant manner.

425. Brieven over Italien. Door W.R. Jansen. Lugden, 1793. 8vo.--We notice this work, principally because it relates to the state of medicine, as well as the natural history of Italy.

426. Eichholz, neue Briefe uber italien. 4 vols. 8vo. Zurich, 1806.

427. Reise nach Dalmatien und Ragusa. Von. E.F. Germar, 8vo. Leip. 1817.

428. Viaggio Geologico sur diversi Parti Meriodinali dell Italia. Milan, 1804. 8vo.--This work, by Pini, a naturalist of reputation, is instructive in the geology of the country between Modena and Florence, of the Campagna, and of part of Naples; there are also remarks on the antiquity and extent of the Italian Volcanoes.

429. Viaggio da Milano ai tre Laghi Maggiore, di Lugano, e di Como. Del C. Amoretti. Milan, 1803. 4to.--Mineralogy, and especially the various species of marble, zoology, and manners and customs, are here described, as well as the celebrated lakes mentioned in the title.

430. Spallanzani Lettere al Sig. Marchese Luchesini, Sopre le Coste dell Adriatico. Paris, 1789. 4 vols. 4to.

FRANCE

The author of the Bibliothèque des Voyages remarks, that no country in Europe has been so imperfectly described by travellers as France: certainly, if we compare the descriptions they give of it with the descriptions given by travellers of other countries, there appears good ground for this observation. And yet France offers a rich harvest for travellers of almost all kinds: the customs and usages of the people; the general character so strongly stamped on the whole nation, and the various shades of it in different provinces; the effects that have been produced by the different events of their history, and especially by their revolution; all these things present to the traveller, who studies human nature, rich and ample materials. To the geologist, the mineralogist, and botanist, especially to the former, France also is an interesting country, especially since Cuvier and other learned men in this department of science, have displayed the stores of important facts which France offers on this subject: her agriculture, and especially her vine districts, present a source of interest of a different kind; while, in the southern provinces, her antiquities, though not numerous, attract by their beauty the man of taste.

431. Matthæi Quadt Delicicæ Gallicæ, seu Itinerarium per Universam Galliam. Frankfort, 1603. fol.

432. Deliciæ Galliae, seu Itinerarium in Universam Galliam, a Gasp. Ens. Cologne, 1609. 8vo.

433. A Tour through the Western, Southern, and Interior Provinces of France. By N.W. Wraxall. London, 1772. 8vo.--This work bears all the characters of Mr. Wraxall's other productions: slight and superficial so far as manners are concerned: offering no information on agriculture, statistics, or natural history; with, however, some interesting historical details. It is noticed here,

because the travels in France are so few, that even those of moderate merit must be admitted.

434. Travels through France: to which is added, a Register of a Tour into Spain in 1787-89. By Arthur Young. 2 vols. 4to. 1792.--This is a most valuable and useful work; for though the professed object of Mr. Young was agriculture, yet it abounds in well-drawn pictures of manners and national character, and it derives additional interest from having been performed at the commencement of the revolution.

435. Journal during a Residence in France, from the beginning of August to the middle of December 1792. By Dr. John Moore. 2 vols. 8vo.--This work may be regarded in some measure as historical; yet it may also properly be placed here as exhibiting a strong picture of manners and feelings, as well as of events, at this interesting period.

436. Tour through several of the Midland and Western Departments of France, in the Summer of 1802. By the Rev. H. Hughes. London, 1802. 8vo.

437. Bugge's Travels in France. 1798-99. 12mo.--This work was written originally in Danish, and was afterwards translated into French. The author, a celebrated astronomer and professor of mathematics at Copenhagen, was sent to Paris to attend a committee on weights and measures. His travels are particularly interesting from the account they give of the different scientific and literary establishments in France.

438. Anglo-Norman Antiquities considered, in a Tour through Normandy. By A.C. Ducarel. Fol. 1767.--A valuable work on this particular subject.

439. Narrative of a Three Years' Residence in France, principally in the Southern Departments. 1802-5. By Anne Plumptree. 3 vols. 8vo.--Some useful information on the productions, scenery, and manners of this part of France, may be collected from these volumes.

440. Travels through the South of France, 1807-8. By Lieut.-Col. Pinckney. 4to.--These travels were performed in a part of France not often visited. They give light and amusing sketches of the manners, customs, and state of society there; but there is a manifest tendency to exaggeration in them.

441. Account of a Tour in Normandy. By Dawson Turner. 1821. 2 vols. 8vo.--Architectural antiquities form the chief topic; historical notices and manners are also given: all indicating a well-informed and intelligent mind.

442. Letters written during a Tour through Normandy, Brittany, and other Parts of France, in 1818. By Mrs. C. Stothard. 4to. 1821.--Much information on the manners, habits, &c. of the inhabitants of Brittany, a part of France not much visited by travellers; besides local and historical descriptions.

443. Itinerary of Provence and the Rhine. 1819. By J. Hughes. 8vo.--A useful book, and some parts of it very interesting.

444. Voyage Littéraire de la France. Par Deux Bénédictins. (D.D. Martine et Durand.) Paris, 1730. 2 vols. 4to.--This work relates to monuments and inscriptions, of which it gives an accurate account.

445. Voyage Géographique et Pittoresque des Départements de la France. Paris, 1794-97, 11 vols. fol.

446. Voyage dans les Départements de la France. Par La Vallée, pour le Texte; Brun père, pour la Partie Géographique; Brun fils, pour celle de Dessein. Paris, 1790--1800. 100 cahiers, 8vo.

447. Voyage en France, enrichi de belles Gravures. Paris, 1798. 4 vols. 18mo.-- These works, in conjunction with the following, though not strictly within our plan, as being not the result of the observations of the authors themselves, are noticed here, because they give the most full and satisfactory information respecting France, geographical, descriptive, statistical, &c. Statistique Générale et Particulière de la France. Par une Société des Gens de Lettres. Paris, 1805. 7 vols. 8vo.

448. Collection des Statistiques de chaque Département, imprimée par Ordre du Ministère du l'Intérieure, au nombre de trente-quatre.

449. Recherches Economiques et Statistiques sur le Departement de la Loire Inférieure. Par J.R. Heuet. Nantes, 1804. 8vo.

450. Statistique Elémentaire de la France. Par J. Peuchet. Paris, 1805. 8vo.

451. Essai sur les Volcans éteints du Vivarais. Par Faujas de Saint Fond. Paris, 1778. fol.

452. Histoire Naturelle du Dauphiné. Par le Méme. Grenoble, 1781. 4to.--These works, the result of travels in the district to which they allude, are valuable to the mineralogist and geologist.

453. Voyage en Provence. Par M. l'Abbé Papou. Paris, 1787. 2 vols. 12mo.--The objects of these travels are historical, literary, and picturesque.

454. Observations faites dans les Pyrénées. Par Ramond. Paris, 1789. 8vo.

455. Voyage au Mont Perdu, et dans les Partes adjacentes des Hautes Pyrennées. Par Raymond. Paris, 1801. 8vo.--Although these works principally relate to the formation, natural history, and meteorology of the Pyrennees, yet the dryness of scientific observation and research is most agreeably relieved by a lively picture of manners, as well as by the interesting personal adventures of the author in his attempts to reach the summit of the mountains. There is an English translation of the former of these works.

456. Voyage en 1787-88, dans la ci-devant Haute et Basse Auvergne. Par Le Grand D'Aussy. Paris, 1795. 3 vols. 8vo.

457. Tableau de la ci-devant Provence D'Auvergne. Par Rabine Beauregard, et P.M. Gault. Paris, 1802. 8vo.--No district in France presents such a variety of interesting objects as Auvergne; its inhabitants, in their language, dress, manners, and mode of life; its agriculture, its natural history, and its antiquities of the classical and middle ages. Le Grand D'Aussy treats well of all but the last, and this is supplied by the other work; its agriculture is more fully considered in the following:

458. Voyage Agronomique en Auvergne. Paris, 8vo. 1803.

459. Description du Département de l'Oise. Par Cambri. Paris, 1803. 2 vols. 8vo.--Agriculture, roads, canals, manufactures, commerce, antiquities, are treated of in this work in such a satisfactory manner, that the author of the Bibiothèque expresses a wish that all the departments were described as well as this, and the department of Finisterre by the same author, and Auvergne

by Le Grand D'Aussy.

460. Voyage Agronomique dans la Senatorerie de Dijon. Par N. Francais de Neufchâteau. Paris, 1806. 8vo.

461. Voyage dans le Jura. Par Lequinio. Paris, 1801. 8vo.--Much information in agriculture, natural history, &c. is given by this author, in an unpleasant style, and with little regard to method.

462. Voyage de Paris à Strasbourg. Paris, 1802. 8vo.--Relates to the agriculture and statistics of the departments through which the author travelled, and particularly the Lower Rhine.

463. Voyage dans la ci-devant Belgique, et sur la Rive Gauche du Rhin. Par Briton, et Brun père et fils. Paris, 1802. 2 vols. 8vo.--Commerce, manufactures, arts, manners, and mineralogy, enter into these volumes. Sometimes, however, rather in a desultory and superficial style.

464. Voyage dans les Départements nouvellement réunis, et dans le Départemens du Bas Rhin, du Nord, du Pas de Calais, et de la Somme. 1802. Par A.G. Camus. Paris, 2 vols. 8vo.--Camus was sent by the French government to examine the archives and titles of the new departments: the Institute at the same time deputed him to examine into the state of science, literature, and manufactures: on the latter topics, and on the state of the hospitals, the work is full of details. The information he collected respecting the archives, he does not give.

465. Briefe eines Sudlanders, von Fischer. Leipsic, 1805. 8vo.--Besides descriptions of the principal cities in France, this work contains an account of the fisheries of the Mediterranean; the arsenal of Toulon; the department of Vaucluse; the Provencal language, &c. The same author has published Travels in the Pyrennees, drawn up from the works of most scientific travellers among these mountains.

466. Reise durch eine theil des Westlichen Franckreichs. Leipsic, 1803. 8vo.-- This is also by the same author, and contains an excellent statistical description of Britanny, a full account of Brest and its maritime establishments, and of the famous lead mines of Poulavoine, and of Huelgeat. The first part of this word, *huel*, is exactly the prefix to the names of many of the mines in Cornwall.

467. Reise door Frankryk. Door Van der Willigen. Haarlem, 8vo.

468. Reisen durch die Sudlichen, Westlichen und Nordlichen, Provinzen. Von Frankreich. 1807-9. und 1815. Frank. 2 vols. 8vo. 1816.—French literature, the Spanish revolution in 1808, and the Basque language, are chiefly treated of.

469. Remarques faites dans un Voyage de Paris jusqu'à Munich. Par Depping. Paris, 1814. 8vo.—A most judicious and instructive book, noticing all that is really interesting in this route, and nothing else, and thus conveying much information in a small compass.

THE NETHERLANDS.

This portion of Europe presents to the traveller fewer varieties for his research and observation than any other part of Europe: in almost every other part the mineralogist and geologist find rich materials for the increase of their knowledge or the formation of their theories; and the admirer of the beautiful, the picturesque, or the sublime, is gratified. The Netherlands are barren to both these travellers; yet in some respects it is a highly interesting country: and the interest it excites, chiefly arises from circumstances peculiar to it. The northern division discovers a district won from the sea by most laborious, persevering, and unremitted industry, and kept from it by the same means. The middle division recalls those ages, when it formed the link between the feeble commerce of the south of Europe, and of Asia and of the Baltic districts. Antwerp, Ghent, and Bruges then were populous and rich above most cities in Europe. The whole of the Netherlands, especially Flanders, may be regarded as the birth-place of modern agriculture, which spread from it to England, where alone it flourishes in a vigorous and advanced state, but still in some points not to be compared to that of the country from which it came. Such, with the admirable paintings of the Dutch School, are the chief objects that attract the traveller to the Netherlands, independently of the desire to tudy human nature, which here also will find ample materials.

470. Descrizione di Ludovico Guicciardini di tutti Paesi Bassi. Antwerp, 1501. fol.—This work, which was translated into Latin, French, and Dutch, was written by the nephew of the historian; it is the result of his own travels in the Netherlands, and contains a full description of them, particularly of their principal towns, and their commerce.

471. Observations on the United Provinces. By Sir W. Temple. 8vo. & 12mo.— Sir W. Temple was embassador at the Hague in 1668: his little work contains much information on the history, government, manners, religion, commerce, &c. of the United Provinces.

472. Travels in Flanders and Holland in 1781. By Sir Joshua Reynolds. Confined to pictures.

473. Tour through the Batavian Republic during the last part of the year 1800. By R. Fell. 1801. 8vo.—This work gives an interesting picture of Holland and the Dutch at this period, besides historical and political details and observations on its connexion with France.

474. Neue Beschriebung des Burgundischen und Neiderlan dischen Kreises. Von Mart. Leiller. Ulm, 1649. 8vo.

475. Statische-Geographische, Beschriebung der Semtlichen Esterreichischen Niederlande. Von Crome. Dessau, 1785. 8vo.

476. Neueste Reisen durch die Sieben Vereinigten-Provinzen. Von Volkman. Leip. 1783. 8vo.—This is a valuable work, comprising the arts, manufactures, agriculture, economy, manners, &c. of the United Provinces.

477. Briefe uber die Vereinigten Niederlande. Von Grabner. Gothen, 1792. 8vo.

478. Lettres sur la Hollande Ancienne et Moderne. Par Beaumarchais. Frankfort,

1738. 8vo.—A good description of Holland and the Dutch, by a sensible and observant author*Quarterly Review, No. 48. page 325.*)

682. Marco Polo Reisen en der Orient, 1272-1295. 8vo. Ronneburgh, 1802.— This translation is accompanied by a learned commentary by the Editor, F.B. Peregrin.

683. Sauveboeuf, Mémoires des ses Voyages en Turque, en Perse, et en Arabic. 2 vols. 8vo, Paris, 1807.

VOYAGES AND TRAVELS IN DIFFERENT PARTS OF ASIA

684. Voyages célèbres et remarquables, faits de Perse aux Indes Orientates. Par J.A. De Mandeso. Amsterdam, folio, 1727.—This work, originally published in German, exhibits a curious picture of Indostan, the Mogul empire, Siam, Japan, China, &c., as they existed in the seventeenth century.

685. Les Voyages et Missions de P. Alex. de Rhodes. Paris, 1682. 4to.—This is one of the most valuable of the missionary travels in Asia, comprising Goa, Malacca, Macao, Cochin China, Tonkin, &c.

686. Amenitatum exoticarum fasciculi. Autore E. Koempfer. Lemgo, 1712. 4to.—This work relates principally to Persia, and the easternmost parts of Asia: M. Langles justly characterizes it as a rich mine of information of all kinds respecting this portion of the world.

687. Samlung der murkwurdigsten Reisen in den Orient. Von E. Panlus. Jena, 1792-1798. 10 vols. 8vo.—This collection contains many scarce and curious articles, and is illustrated by learned and judicious notes.

688. Asiatic Researches. 12 vols. 8vo. 1801. 1818.—Though many of the articles in this valuable work do not strictly and immediately come under the description of travels, yet even these are so essentially necessary to a full acquaintance with the most interesting parts of Asia, that we have deemed it proper to insert the title of this work. A valuable translation of most of the volumes has been published in Paris, enriched by the oriental literature of M. Langles; the astronomical and physical knowledge of M. Delambre; and the natural history knowledge of Cuvier, Lamark, and Olivier.

689. De la Roque, Voyage de Syrie et du Mont Liban. 2 vols. 12mo. Paris, 1722.

690. Voyage de l'Arabie heureuse par l'Océan Oriental. 12mo. Paris, 1716.

691. Voyage de M. d'Arvieux dans la Palestine, avec Description de l'Arabie, par Abulfeda. Mémoires du Chevalier d'Arvieux, contenant ses Voyages à Constantinople, dans l'Asie, la Palestine, l'Egypte, la Barbarie, &c. Paris, 6 vols. 12mo. 1735.—These are all valuable works, containing much and accurate information on almost every topic of physical, statistical, commercial, political and moral geography; the result of long personal observation, enquiry, and experience. The travels of la Roque into Arabia are particularly full respecting the history of coffee in Asia and Europe. The Voyage de M. d'Arvieux was published separately from his Mémoires, and previously to it, by la Roque, and is very interesting not only from the simplicity of its style and manner, but also from the vivid picture which it exhibits of the Bedouins.

692. Voyage en Syrie et en Egypte, 1783-1785. Par Volney. Paris, 1800. 2 vols. 8vo.—The character of this work, of which there is an English translation, is too well known to be insisted upon here. What relates to Syria is the most detailed and important, and has been less superseded by subsequent travellers.

693. A Journey from Aleppo to Jerusalem, in 1697. By H. Maundrel.

694. The Natural History of Aleppo, and parts adjacent. By Alex. Rumel. 2 vols. 4to. 1794.—This excellent work was translated into German by Gmelin, with valuable annotations.

695. Mariti's Travels through Cyprus, Syria, and Palestine. 3 vols. 8vo.—The original work in Italian consists of 5 volumes. On all that relates to Cyprus, this work is particularly interesting and full; there is also much information regarding it in Sonnini's Travels.

696. Kinnear's Journey though Asia Minor, Armenia, and Koordestan, 1812-14. 8vo.—This work will be particularly interesting to those who wish to trace the marches of Alexander, and the retreat of the ten thousand, on which points of history Mr. Kinnear has made some judicious remarks.

697. Beaufort's Karamania. 1818. 8vo.—A valuable addition to the maritime geography and antiquities of a part of Asia Minor not often described.

698. Reisebescriebung von Arabien. Von C. Niebuhr. Copenhagen, 1772. 4to.

699. Reisebescriebung nach Arabien. Von C. Niebuhr. Copenhagen 1774-1778. 2 vols. 4to.

700. Recueil des Questions proposées à une société des Savans, qui, par ordre de S.M. Danoise, font le Voyage de l'Arabie. Par M. Michaelis. Frankfort, 1753. 4to.

701. Pet. Forskal Descriptiones Animalium, Avium, &c. &c. in Itinere Orientale observatorum. Hafnioe, 1775. 4to.

702. Pet. Forskal Icones rerum naturalium, quas in Itinere Orient, depingi curavit. Hafnioe, 1776. 4to.—Every thing preparatory to, and connected with the travels of Niebuhr and his associate, was judiciously and well planned and executed: the selection of Michaelis to draw up the enquiries and observations to be made; those he actually proposed: and the learned men sent out, who were respectively conversant in physics, natural history, geography, and the connected and auxiliary branches of science. Hence resulted most admirable works on Arabia: those of Niebuhr, together with Michaelis, have been translated into French, in 4 vols. 4to. The English translation, besides omitting the most valuable and scientific parts, is, in other respects, totally unworthy of the original.

703. Il Viaggio dell Ambrosio Contarini, Ambasciatore della Signiora di Venetia, al Uxam Cassan, Re de Persia. Ven. 1543, 12mo.

704. Relacion de Don Juan de Persia, en III Libros. Vallad. 1604. 4to.

705. Chardin, Voyages en Persie, et autres lieux de l'Orient. Amsterd. 3 vols. 4to. 1711.—It may justly be said of these travels, that by means of them, Persia was made better known in every thing relating to its civil, military, religious, intellectual, moral, scientific, and statistical condition, than any other part of Asia, at the period when they were published. Very few travellers are more to be depended upon than Chardin.

706. Tavernier, Voyages en Turquie, en Perse, et aux Indes. 6 Vols. 12mo. Rouen, 1713.—The credit of this traveller, which had been for some time suspected, is recovering itself since it has been ascertained that many points in which he was supposed to have been inaccurate or credulous, are well

founded. As his object was commercial, especially for the purchase of diamonds, his travels may be consulted with advantage on the subject of the diamond mines, the traffic in these precious stones, and the various monies of Asia, and other topics not to be found in other travellers.

707. Observations made on a Tour from Bengal to Persia. By W. Franklin. 1790. 8vo.—The most original and valuable portion of this work relates to Persia, especially the province of Farsistan; it contains also much information respecting Goa, Bombay, &c, M. Langles translated it into French, and added a learned memoir on Persepolis.

    The same orientalist, M. Langles, has added to the value and interest of his translation of G. Forster's Journey from Bengal to England, by his judicious and instructive notes.

708. Waring's Tour to Sheeraz. 1807. 4to.—This work is chiefly confined to the manners, laws, religion, language, and literature of the Persians; on all of which it is instructive and interesting.

709. Morier's Two Journeys through Persia, Armenia, and Asia Minor. 1808-1816. 2 vols. 4to.—The opportunities which M. Morier possessed from his residence in Persia being much superior to those of a mere traveller, his work is justly regarded as one of authority on the civil, political, domestic, and commercial circumstances of the Persians.

710. Sir W. Ousely's Travels in Persia. 1810-12. 4to.—The connexion between England and Persia, formed, or rather strengthened, in consequence of the vicinity of our East India possessions to that country, has much extended our knowledge of it, and this work has contributed not a little to that knowledge.

711. Kotzebue's Narrative of a Journey into Persia, in the Suite of the Imperial Embassy, in 1817. 8vo.—It is always desirable to have travels performed in the same country, especially if it be one remote and little known, by persons of different nations: thus, different views of the same circumstances are given, and the truth is elicited. These travels are interesting in this and other points of view.

712. Ker Porter's Travels in Georgia, Persia, Armenia, Ancient Babylonia, &c. 2. vols. 4to.—A severer judgment, by suppressing much that is minute and uninteresting, and dwelling more on important matters, and a knowledge of natural history, would have enhanced the value of these travels, which, however, are much more creditable to the author than his Travels in Russia.

713. Reise in den Kaukasies und nach Georgien, 1807-8. 2 vols. 8vo. Halle, 1812.—These travels were undertaken by command of the Russian government, and are similar in design to those of Pallas; there is an English translation, but it is indifferently executed.

714. Reisen nach Georgien und Imerethi. Von J.A. Guldenstadt. 8vo. Berlin, 1813.—This work is edited by Klaproth, and is chiefly mineralogical.

715. Lettres sur la Caucase et la Georgie, et un Voyage en Perse en 1812. 8vo.

THE EAST INDIES.

The histories of the discoveries and conquests of the Portuguese in the East Indies are interspersed with various and numerous particulars regarding the political state of that country, and the manners, customs, religion, &c. of the inhabitants. The following French work is valuable in this respect.

716. Histoire de Portugal; contenant les Entreprises, &c. des Portugais, tant en la Conquête des Indes Orientales par eux découvertes, qu'en Guerres d'Afrique et autres Exploits: nouvellement mise en Français. Par S. Goullard. Paris, 1581. 4to.

717. Navigatio et Itinerarium in Orientalem Indiam, &c. Autore Joanne Linschot. Amsterd. 1614. folio.

718. Premier Livre de l'Histoire de la Navigation aux Indes Orientales, par les Hollandois. Amsterd, folio, 1558.

719. Le Second Livre. Amsterd. 1609, folio.

720. Relatio de Rebus in India Orientale, a Patribus. Soc. Jesu. 1598-1599, peractis, Mayence, 1601. 8vo.—The preceding works give an interesting picture of the East Indies during the 16th century.

721. Beschrievyng van oude niewe Ostinden. Von. F. Valyntin. Amster. 1724-1726. 8 vol. fol.—This work appears to be little known, except in Holland; the author resided upwards of twenty years in India, and has most industriously, though not always with a good taste, or scrupulous judgment, collected much minute information on its natural, civil, and religious state.

722. Alex. Hamilton's Account of the East Indies, 2 vols. 8vo. 1744.

723. Grose's Travels to the East Indies, 1772. 2 vols. 8vo.

724. Zend Avesta. Par Anquetil du Perrin. Paris, 1771. 3 vols. 4to.—M. Anquetil has prefixed to his translation of this supposed work of Zoroaster, an account of his travels in the East Indies, in which there is much valuable information, especially on antiquarian subjects. The Germans have translated and published separately, this part of M. Anquetil's work.

725. Voyages dans les Mers de l'Inde. Par M. Legentil, 1781. 5 vols. 8vo.—M. Legentil's object was to observe the transit of Venus, in 1761 and 1769. His work, besides entering into the subject of Indian astronomy, gives many important details on antiquities and natural history.

726. Description Historique et Geographique de l'Inde. Par J. Tieffenthaler. Recherches Historiques et Geographiques sur l'Inde. Par Anquetil du Perrin. Publiées par J. Bernouilli. Berlin, 1785. 3 vols. 4to.—The most curious and original portion of this work is that which relates to the Seiks, by the missionary Tieffenthaler.

727. Forrest's Voyage from Calcutta to the Menguy Archipelago, 1792. 2 vols. 4to.—This work is justly of great authority, for its details in maritime geography,

728. Stavorinus's Voyages to the East Indies, comprising an account of all the possessions of the Dutch in India, and at the Cape of Good Hope, 3 vols. 8vo. 1798.

729. Fra. Paolino's Voyage to the East Indies. With notes by J. Reinold Forster. 8vo. 1800.—A translation of this valuable work, which originally appeared in Italian, was published in Paris, in 1805, by Anquetil du Perrin, in 3 Vols. 8vo. There are few works which throw more light than this does, on the religious antiquities of India.

730. Rennel's Memoir of a Map of Indostan. 2 Vols. 4to. 1793.—For geographical research, this work justly bears the highest character.

Particular parts of the East Indies are specially described in the following works:

731. Nouvelle Relation d'un Voyage fait aux Indes Orientales. Par M. Dellen. Amsterd. 1699. 12mo.—Malabar, Calecut, and Goa, are particularly noticed by this author, who, being a medical man, is full and instructive on the poisonous animals, and the diseases.

732. Voyage de Francois Bernier, contenant la Description des Etats du Grand Mogul. Amsterd. 1725. 2 Vols. 12mo.—This author was also a medical man, and from that circumstance obtained favour from the Mogul, and an opportunity of visiting parts of Asia, at that time little known, particularly Cachemere, of which he gives a full and interesting description.

733. Voyage aux Indes Orientales, 1802-6, revu et augmenté de notes. Par Sonnini. 2 Vols. 8vo. Paris, 1810.—The notes by Sonnini sufficiently point out the nature and character of this work.

734. Voyage dans la Peninsule Occidentale de l'Inde, et dans l'Isle de Ceylon. 2 Vols. 8vo. Paris, 1811.—This work is translated from the Dutch of Haafner; and as latterly few, except the English, have published accounts of India, it is for this reason interesting.

735. A Journey from Madras, through Mysore, Canara, and Malabar. By F. Buchanan. 1811, 4to.—Much information, not well arranged or agreeably communicated, on the most valuable productions of these districts, on their climate, manufactures, and the manners, religion, &c. of their inhabitants.

736. Heyne's Tracts, historical and statistical, on India; with Journals of several Tours: and an account of Sumatra. 1814, 4to. A work not so well known, as from its information, particularly statistical, it deserves to be.

737. Forbes's Oriental Memoirs. 1813, 4 Vols. 4to.—It is to be regretted that this very splendid and expensive work was not published in a cheaper form, as it abounds in most striking pictures of the manners, customs, &c. of India.

738. Major Symes's Account of an Embassy to the Kingdom of Ava, in 1795. 4to 1800—Little was known in Europe respecting Pegu and Ava before the travels of Hunter, and Loset and Erkelskrom were published; these travels, translated respectively from the English and German, were published together in Paris, in 1793. From these, and Major Symes's works, much may be gathered respecting the manners, religion, and government of the inhabitants of this part of Asia; but unfortunately, these travellers do not instruct us on the topics of natural history. We are indebted for most that we know respecting Siam, to a notion that was put into Louis XIV.'s mind, that the King of Siam was desirous of becoming a convert to Christianity. Under this idea, Louis sent an embassy and missionaries, from whom

proceeded the following works: in which, allowing for a little exaggeration, in order to flatter the vanity of the French monarch, there is a deal of curious and valuable information of all kinds.

739. Premier Voyage de Siam des P.P. Jésuites. Redigé par Tachard.—Second Voyage du P. Tachard, Paris, 1686-89. 2 Vols. 12mo.

740. Histoire Naturelle et Civile de Siam. Par Gervaise. Paris, 1688, 4to.

741. Description du Royaume de Siam. Par M. de la Loubere, Envoyé Extraordinaire du Roi auprès du Roi de Siam. Amsterd. 1714. 2 Vols. 12mo.

742. Barrow's Voyage to Cochin China, 1792-93. 4to. 1806. This is perhaps the most valuable of Mr. Barrow's works, as it relates to a country not previously known, except by the accounts of the missionaries, and which has been scarcely visited since Mr. Barrow's time.

743. Relation Nouvelle et Curieuse du Royaume de Tonquin, et de Laos. Traduite de l'Italien du P. de Marini. Paris, 1666, 4to. This work is full of a variety of topics connected with the civil, political, military, agricultural, and commercial state of Tonquin; nor is it deficient in what relates to the natural history, and the manners, religion, &c. of the inhabitants,

744. Histoire Naturelle et Civile du Tonquin. Par l'Abbé Richard. Paris, 1788. 2 Vols. 12mo.—The first volume of this work, which describes Tonquin and its inhabitants, is drawn from the accounts of the missionary St. Phalte, and from other sources, with considerable neatness and judgment; the second volume is confined to a history of the missions thither.

745. Exposé Statistique du Tunkin. London, 2 Vols. 8vo. 1811. This work is drawn up from the papers of M. de la Bessachere, who resided 18 years in Tunkin; and it is rich in new and curious information on the physical properties of the country, and the national character.

746. Letters on the Nicobar Islands. By the Rev C.G. Haensel, Missionary of the United Brethren. 1812. 8vo.—This short account is written with great simplicity and appearance of truth, and conveys much information on the inhabitants, as well as the soil, climate, &c. of these islands.

747. A Description of Prince of Wales Island. By Sir Home Popham. 1806, 8vo.

748. Sir George Leith's Account of the Settlement, Produce, and Commerce of Prince of Wales Island. 8vo. 1805.

INDIAN ISLANDS.

749. Historical Relation of Ceylon. By Robert Knox. 1681. folio.—This work, though published so long ago, and by one who was a prisoner, still retains its character, as the fullest and most interesting account of the inhabitants of Ceylon in the English language. The voluminous work of Valyntyn, in Dutch, which we have already noticed, may be advantageously consulted on this island, as well as on all parts of India formerly possessed by the Dutch.

750. John C. Wolfe's Life and Adventures in Ceylon. 1785. 8vo.—This work, translated from the Dutch, amidst much that is merely personal, contains some curious notices on Ceylon and its inhabitants. To the English translation is appended an account by Erkelskrom, which is valuable, as describing the island

at the period when it passed from the Dutch to the English.

751. Davy's Account of the Interior of Ceylon. 1821, 4to.—This is an excellent work, though like many other works of excellence, too bulky; its chief and peculiar merit and recommendation consist in its details on the natural history of Ceylon.

752. Marsden's History of Sumatra. 1783. 4to.—This is a most excellent work in the plan and execution, embracing almost every topic connected with the island and its inhabitants.

753. Voyage to the Isle of Borneo. By Capt. Beckman. 1718, 8vo.—Of this large island, so little known, this volume, and an article inserted in the Transactions of the Batavian Society of Java, gives us many interesting particulars; there are also some notices of it in Forrest's Voyage.

754. The Narrative of Captain Woodward, with a Description of the Island of Celebes. 1804, 8vo.—Woodward was an American captain who was taken prisoner by the Malays of Celebes: this work is the result of his observations and experience during his captivity; but it is confined to the western division of the isle: of this, however, it gives many particulars, respecting the produce, animals, inhabitants, &c. Stavorinus's works may also be consulted regarding Celebes.

755. Crawfurd's History of the Indian Archipelago. 1820. 3 vols. 8vo.—This is a valuable work, particularly in what relates to the actual commerce and commercial capabilities of these islands: it also treats of the manners, religion, language, &c. of the inhabitants; but on some of these points not with the soundest judgment, or the most accurate information.

756. Raffles's History of Java. 1817. 2 vols. 4to.—Had this work been compressed into a smaller compass, by a judicious abridgment of the historical part, its value as well as interest would have been enhanced; these, however, are not small, as it gives by far the fullest and most accurate account of Java, and its inhabitants, that has appeared; and as the author, from his residence and high official situation, possessed every advantage, its accuracy may be depended on. When the natural history illustrations of Java, by Mr. Horsfield, are completed, they will, in conjunction with this work, and the Transactions of the Batavian Society, leave nothing to be desired on the subject of this part of Asia.

757. E. Koempfer's Geschichte und Beschriebung von Japan. Lemgo, 1777-79. 2 vols. 4to.—This edition of Koempfer's celebrated work on Japan contains several things which are not to be found in the English translation.

758. Histoire du Japan. Par Charlevoix. Paris, 1754, 6 vols. 12mo.—This is the best edition of Charlevoix's work, many parts of which, especially what relates to natural history, are drawn from Koempfer. Charlevoix has added important details on the administration of justice in Japan, and on the moral character of the Japanese; but the bulk of the work is swelled by tiresome ecclesiastical details.

759. Travels in Europe, Asia, and Africa. By Thunberg. 1794, 4 vols. 8vo.—This work relates principally to Japan; and it may justly be remarked, that few

parts of the world have met with sucn admirable describers as Japan has done, in Koempfer and Thunberg. Certainly the natural history of no part, so rich in this respect, has been so fully and scientifically investigated. A French translation of this work was published in Paris in 1796, in 2 vols. 4to. enriched by the notes of Langles and La Marck.

760. Golownin's Narrative of his Captivity in Japan, 1811-13. 2 vols. 8vo.— Japan is a country so little accessible, that every work on it is acceptable. This work does not add very much to what Koempfer and Thunberg have told, but perhaps quite as much as the author, under his circumstances, could collect or observe. The same remarks apply to his Recollections of Japan. 1 vol. 8vo.

The history of the missions in the East Indies, Japan, and China, which were published in the Italian, Spanish, German, and French languages, towards the end of the sixteenth, and the beginning of the seventeenth century, is interspersed with some curious and valuable information regarding these countries; the titles and character of the principal of these may be found in the Bibliothèque, vol. 5. p. 264, 272, &c.

761. Voyage to China and the East Indies, by Rel. Osbeck; with a Voyage to Surat, by Torreens; and an Account of the Chinese Husbandry, by Ekelberg. Translated from the German by J.R. Forster. To which is added a Fauna et Flora Sinensis. 1777, 2 vols. 8vo.—Travels, embracing scientific natural history, by competent persons, are so rare and valuable, that the titles of such should not be omitted: the nature of this work is sufficiently indicated by the title, and its merit by its having been translated by Forster.

762. Sonnerat, Voyage aux Indes Orientals et à la Chiné, 1774. 1781. Paris, 1806. 4 vols. 8vo.—This work is particularly full and minute on the theography of the Hindoos: besides the East Indies and China, it embraces Pegu, the Cape of Good Hope, Ceylon, Malacca, &c. A translation of part of it into English was printed at Calcutta.

763. Nouvelles Mémoires sur l'État present de la Chine. Par Le Comte. Paris, 1701, 3 vols. 12mo—The best account of China previous to Duhalde's work, though in many particulars extremely partial to the Chinese.

764. Mémoires concernant l'Histoire, les Sciences, et les Arts des Chinois. Par les Missionaires de Pekin. Paris, 1775, &c. 15 vols. 4to.—In this voluminous work is contained a wonderful deal of information on China; the continuation of the work was put a stop to by the French Revolution: it is by far the best the Jesuits have produced on China; and if there are materials for perfecting it, they ought to be given to the public.

765. Description Geographique, Historique, Chronologique, Politique, et Physique de la Chiné et de Tartarie Chinoise. Par Duhalde. Le Hague, 1736, 4 vols. 4to.—Of this work there is an English translation. Duhalde has drawn his materials from a variety of sources, especially from the printed and manuscript accounts of the missionaries; but he has failed to exercise a sound judgment, and a scrupulous examination into the truth of many facts

and opinions which he has admitted into his work.

But though the public are certainly much indebted to the missionaries for the information they have given respecting this singular country, yet there are obvious circumstances which rendered their accounts suspicious in some points, and defective in others, so that the publication of the accounts of the Dutch and British Embassies added much to our stock of accurate knowledge regarding China. The following is the title of the French translation of part of the Dutch Embassy:

766. Voyage de la Campagne des Indes Orientales vers l'Empire de la Chiné, 1794-5. Tiré du Journal de Van Braam. Philadelphe. 1797, 4to.—There is also an English translation.

767. Sir George Staunton's Account of the Embassy of the Earl of Macartney to China. 2 vols. 4to. 1797.

768. John Barrow's Travels to China. 4to. 1804.

These works, especially the latter, together with Lord Macartney's own journal in the second volume of his life, contain a deal of information, considering the jealousy of the Chinese; some additions, corrections, and different views of the same circumstances, as well as a further insight into the manners of the Chinese, as indicated by their conduct, will be found in the two following works which relate to the Embassy of Lord Amherst. The first is by the naturalist to the Embassy.

769. Abel's Narrative of a Journey in the Interior of China. 1816-17. 4to.

770. Ellis's Journal of the Proceedings of the late Embassy to China. 4to.

771. Relation du Naufrage sur la Côte de l'Isle de Quælpeart, avec la Description de Coree. Paris, 1670, 12mo.—This work, translated from the Dutch, besides the interest which personal adventures in a foreign country, and under unusual circumstances, always inspires, gives much information regarding the manners of the inhabitants, and the ceremonies, &c. of the court of Corea,—a part of Asia very little known.

772. Captain Hall's Voyage of Discovery to the West Coast of Corea, and the Great Loo-choo Island. 4to.—A work not less valuable for its maritime geography and science, than for the pleasing interest which it excites on behalf of the natives of Loo-choo, and the favourable impression it leaves of Captain Hall, his officers and seamen.

TARTARY, &C.

773. Noord-Oost Tartarie. Par Nic. Witsen. Amsterd. 1705, 2 vols. folio.—Forster, an excellent and seldom too favourable a judge, speaks highly of this work.

774. Nomadische Streifereisen unter den Kalmuken. Von B. Borgman. Riga, 1805-6, 4 vols. 8vo.—The author of this work resided some time with the Kalmucks, at the command of the Emperor of Russia; and he seems to have employed his time well, in gaining information respecting the past and present state of their country, and their manners, intellectual, moral, and religious state.

THIBET, &C.

775. Antonio de Andrada novo Descubrimento de Grao Catayo ou dos Regnos de Tibet. Lisbon, 1626, 4to.—This work has been translated into French, Italian, Flemish, and Spanish; it contains the narrative of the first passage of the Himalaya Mountains. (See Quarterly Review, No. 48. page 337, &c.)

776. Turner's Account of an Embassy to the Court of the Teesho Lama, in Thibet. 1800, 4to.—This work is full of information and interest: it relates to the soil, climate, and produce of Thibet; the moral character, and especially the singular religion of the inhabitants, and their institutions, manufactures, disorders, &c.

777. Kirkpatrick's Account of Nepaul in 1793. 4to.—This is one of the best accessions to our information respecting this part of Asia which has been produced by our establishments in India.

778. Account of the Kingdom of Nepaul. By Francis Hamilton, (formerly Buchanan). 1819, 4to.—The same character applies to this as to the other work by the same author.

779. Fraser's Journal of a Tour through part of the Snowy Ridge of the Himalaya Mountains. 1820. 4to.—Notwithstanding Mr. Fraser's ignorance of natural history, in a country quite new, and full of most interesting objects in this science, and that he had no means of measuring heights, or ascertaining the temperature or pressure of the air; and notwithstanding a want of method, and a heaviness and prolixity in the style, this book possesses great interest, from the scenes of nature and pictures of manners which it exhibits.

780. Elphinstone's Account of Caubul and its Dependencies. 1815. 4to.—The interest and value of this work arises more from the subject of it, than from the manner in which it is executed; respecting such countries, however, as Caubul, and others as little known and remote, we are glad of all accessions of information.

ASIATIC RUSSIA.

781. Reisen durch Siberien, 1733-1743. Von J.G. Gmelin. Gott. 4 vols. 8vo.—This work is worthy of the name which it bears: it is full and particular on the physical and moral geography of Siberia, but especially on its mines and iron foundries.

782. Voyage en Siberie, 1761. Par Chappe d'Auteroche. Paris, 1768. 3 vols. 4-to.—This work gave rise to a severe attack on it, under the title of Antidote. D'Auteroche's object on his travels was principally scientific, but he has entered fully into the character of the inhabitants, and especially those of the capital, and into the character, and intellectual and moral state of the Russians in general.

783. Relation d'un Voyage aux Monts d'Altai en Siberie, 1781. Par Patrin. Peters. 1785, 8vo.—Mineralogical.

784. Recherches Historiques sur les Principales Nations Établies en Siberie. Paris, 1801. 8vo.—This work, translated from the Russian of Fischer, displays a great deal of research, and is not unworthy of an author who

imitated Pallas, Gmelin, Müller, &c.

785. Recherches sur les Principales Nations en Siberie. Traduit du Russe de Stollenweck. 8vo.

786. Description de Kamschatcha. Par Krascheninnikof. Amsterd. 1770. 2 vols. 8vo.—The soil, climate, productions, minerals, furs, habitations, manners, employments, religious ceremonies and opinions, &c., and even the dialect spoken in different parts, are here treated of.

787. Journal Historique du Voyage de M. Lesseps. Paris, 1790. 2 vols. 8vo.— Lesseps sailed with Le Peyrouse, but left him in Kamschatcha, and travelled by land to France with despatches from him; his narrative gives a lively picture of the inhabitants of the northern parts of Asiatic and European Russia. The work has been translated into English; there is also a German translation by Forster.

788. Sauer's Account of Billing's Geographical and Astronomical Expedition to the Northern Parts of Russia, 1785-94. 4to.—An account of this expedition was also published in Russian by Captain Saretschewya, one of the officers engaged in it. Parts of the continent, and islands and seas little known, are described in these two works, but they are deficient in natural history.

789. Holderness's Notes relating to the Manners and Customs of the Crim Tartars. 1823. 8vo.—Mrs. Holderness resided four years in the Crimea, and she seems to have employed her time well, having produced an instructive book on the manners, domestic life, &c., not only of the Crim Tartars, but likewise of the various colonists of the Crimea.

IX. AMERICA

Those works which relate to the discovery of America, derive their interest rather from their historical nature than from the insight they give into the physical and moral state of this portion of the globe. In one important particular; America differs from all the other quarters of the world, very early travels in Asia or Africa unfold to us particulars respecting races of people that still exist, and thus enable us to compare their former with their present state, whereas nearly all the original inhabitants of America have disappeared.

Referring therefore our readers to the historians of the discovery and conquest of America, and to the Bibliothèque des Voyages, for the titles and nature of those works which detail the voyages of Columbus, Vespucius, &c., we shall confine ourselves chiefly to such works as enter more fully into a description of the country and its colonized inhabitants.

790. Journal des Observations Physiques, Mathematiques, et Botaniques, faites par le P. Feuillée, sur les Côtes de l'Amerique Méridionale et dans les Indes Occidentales. Paris, 1714. 2 vols. 4to.

791. Suite du Journal. Paris, 1715. 4to.—Excellent works on the subjects indicated in the title.

792. Notizias Americanas sobre las America Meridionel y la Septentrionel-Oriental. Par Don Ant. de Ulloa. Madrid, 1772. 4to.—This work, which must not be confounded with the conjoint work of Ulloa and Juan, is rich in valuable matter, physical, political, and moral; it was translated into German by M. Diez, Professor of Natural History at Gottingen, who has added learned and judicious observations.

793 Voyages intéressans dans differentes Colonies Françaises, Espagnoles, Anglaise. Paris, 1788. 8vo.—The most original and interesting portions of this work relate to Porto Rico, Curaçoa, Granada, the Bermudas, &c.; there are also valuable remarks on the climate and diseases of St. Domingo.

794. Catesby's Natural History of Carolina, Florida, and the Bahama Islands. 1734-43. 2 vols. folio.

795. Appendix to ditto. 1748. folio.—The celebrated naturalist, George Edwards, published an edition of this splendid work, with the appendix, in Latin and French, in 2 vols. folio. 1764-71.

796. Peter Kalm's Travels in North America, translated by R. Forster. 1772. 2 vols. 8vo.—Chiefly geological and mineralogical; in other respects not interesting.

797. Adair's History of the American Indians. 1775. 4to.—The speculations of this writer are abundantly absurd; but there are interspersed some curious notices of the Indians, collected by the author, while he resided and traded with them.

798. Travels through Carolina, Georgia, Florida, &c. By W. Bertram. 1792. 2 vols. 8vo.—A most interesting work to lovers of natural history, especially

botany, a study to which Bertram was enthusiastically attached. There is an account of Mr. Bertram in the American Farmer's Letters.

799. An Account of the Countries adjoining to Hudson's Bay. By Ar. Dobbs. 1744. 12mo.

800. The State of Hudson's Bay. By Ed. Humphraville. 1790. 8vo.

801. Account of Prince of Wales Island, in the Gulph of St. Lawrence. By J. Stewart. 1808. 8vo.—A good deal of information on the soil, agriculture, productions, climate, &c.: the zoology imperfect.

802. Hall's Travels in Canada and the United States, 1816-17. 8vo.

803. Howison's Sketches of Upper Canada. 8vo. 1821.

> Hall's is a pleasant and lively work, unfolding many of the peculiarities of the manners, customs, &c., of Canada and the adjacent parts of the United States. Howison's is the work of an abler man: it is rich in valuable information to emigrants; and is, moreover, highly descriptive of scenery and manners. The part relative to the United States is superficial.

804. Collection des Plusieures Relations du Canada, 1632-1672. 43 vols. 12mo.

805. Charlevoix's Travels in North America, translated from the French. 1772. 2 Vols. 4to.—The physical and moral state of the inhabitants are the principal objects of this work.

806. Carver's Travels through the Interior Parts of North America, 1766-68. 8vo.—There is much information in this work respecting that part of America, which has lately attracted so much attention from its vicinity to the supposed north-west passage; it is in all other respects, except natural history, an interesting and instructive work.

807. Long's Voyage and Travels of an Indian Interpreter. 1774. 3 vols. 4to. Volney characterizes this work as exhibiting a most faithful picture of the life and manners of the Indians and Canadian traders.

808. Weld's Travels through North America, 1795-7. 2 vols. 8vo.—Travels in the United States derive their interest and value from a variety of sources: the inhabitants of these states under their government, and the peculiar circumstances in which they are placed, must be a subject of deep attention and study to the moralist, the philosopher, the politician, and the political economist, while the country itself presents to the naturalist many and various sources of information and acquisitions to his knowledge. The travels of Mr. Weld, and most of those which we shall have to enumerate, were undertaken for the purpose of ascertaining what advantages and disadvantages an emigrant would derive from exchanging Europe for America. Thus led to travel from the principal motive of self-interest, it might be imagined that these travellers would examine every thing carefully, fully, most minutely, and impartially: in all modes except the last, it has certainly been done by several travellers; but great caution must be used in reading all travels in the United States, because the picture drawn of them is too often overcharged, either with good or evil. Mr, Weld's is a respectable work; and like all travels, even a few years back, in a country so rapidly changing and improving, from this cause as well as its information on

statistics, toil, climate, morals, manners, &c. may be consulted with advantage. It is to be regretted that he, as well as most other travellers in America, was not better prepared with a scientific knowledge of natural history. Canada, as well as the United States, is comprized in Mr. Weld's travels.

809. Mellish's Travels through the United States of America, 1816-17. 2 vols. 8vo.—This is perhaps as impartial and judicious an account of the United States as any that has lately appeared.

810. Lettres d'un Cultivateur Americain, 1770-86. Par M. St. John de Crevecoeur. Paris, 1787. 3 vols. 8vo.—We give the French edition of this work in preference to the English, because it is much fuller. This work of a Frenchman, long settled in the Anglo-American colonies, gives, in an animated and pleasing manner, much information on the manners of America at this period, the habits and occupations of the new settlers, and on the subject of natural history.

811. Voyages dans les États Unis, 1784. Par J.F.D. Smith. Paris, 1791. 2 vols. 8vo.— Virginia, Maryland, the two Carolinas, and Louisiana, parts of North America, not so often visited by travellers as the northern states, are here described with considerable talent, and in a pleasing style. We are not acquainted with the English work, of which this professes to be a translation.

812. Nouveau Voyage dans les États Unis, 1788. Par Brissot. Paris, 3 vols. 8vo.—Statistics, religion, manners, political economy, agriculture, commerce, manufactures, the arts and sciences, are here treated of in a sensible, but rather an uninteresting manner.

813. La Rochefoucault's Travels to the United States of America, 1799. 2 vols. 4to.—Agriculture, statistics, manufactures, commerce, national and domestic habits, form the chief topic of these volumes, which, allowing for some prejudices, present a fair picture of America at this period.

814. Tableau du Climat et du Sol des États Unis. Par C.F. Volney. 1803. 2 vols. 8vo.—Though physical geography and statistics form the principal portion of this valuable work, yet it is by no means uninstructive on the subject of national and domestic character; and it enters fully into the condition of savage life.

Particular histories and descriptions have been published of several of the United States; we shall merely notice such as are the result of personal observation, and as give interesting and instructive information respecting their past or present state.

815. Belknap's History of New Hampshire, 1792. Boston, 3 vols. 8vo.—The two first volumes are historical, but many things in them are instructive to those who wish to trace the formation of character: the third volume relates to climate, soil, produce,&c.

816. The History of Virginia, by a Native and Inhabitant of the place. R.B. Beverley. 1722. 8vo.—The first part is purely historical; in the second, the author gives an account of the productions of the country; the third relates to the manners, &c. of the Indians; the fourth is political. There are, besides, many pertinent remarks on the physical geography of Virginia, and on its climate and diseases.

817. Notes on Virginia. By Thos. Jefferson. 1788. 8vo.—Politics, commerce, manufactures, and navigation, are here treated of in a satisfactory and instructive manner, but with rather too much the air of philosophy.

818. Michaux's Travels to the West of the Alleghany Mountains. 1805. 8vo.— These travels are instructive regarding the manners, commerce, soil, climate, and especially botany.

819. Lewis and Clarke's Travels up the Missouri to the Pacific Ocean, 1804-6. 4to.

820. Pike's Exploratory Travels through the Western Territory of North America. 4to.

821. James's Account of an Expedition to the Rocky Mountains, 1819-20. 3 vols. 8vo.

822. Schoolcraft's Travels to the Sources of the Mississippi. 1820. 8vo.

823. Nuttall's Travels into the Arkansa Territory. 1819. 8vo.—These travels describe a vast portion of America to the west of the Alleghany Mountains, especially the valley of the Mississippi, and its tributary streams. They are rather prolix and heavily written. Mr. James's work is richest in natural history.

824. A Concise Natural History of East and West Florida. By Bernard Romans. New York, 1766. 12mo.—The climate, productions, and diseases of Florida are here treated of by this author, who was a medical man, and had good opportunities of observation and experience.

825. Description de la Louisiane. Par L.P. Hennepin, Paris, 1688. 12mo.—This author first made Europe acquainted with Louisiana; but his work is meagre on every topic, except the manners, &c. of the natives.

826. Histoire de la Louisiane. Par M. Le Page du Prats. Paris, 1758. 3 vols. 12mo.—During a residence of 15 years, this author seems to have paid particular attention to geology, mineralogy, and other branches of natural history, and has given the results of his observations in these volumes.

827. Travels through that part of North America called Louisiana. Translated and illustrated with notes by R.B. Forster. 1771-2. 2 vols. 8vo.—The author of this work was a M. Bossu; who also published, a few years afterwards, Nouveaux Voyages dans l'Amerique Septentrionale. Amsterdam. 8vo.—The first of these works is chiefly interesting from the minute details into which it enters respecting the Illinois territory. Mr. Forster's translation contains a catalogue of American plants.

828. Voyage en Californie. Par l'Abbé Chappe D'Auteroche. Paris, 1778. 4to.—The city of Mexico, as well as California, is here described in an interesting manner. As concerns the latter, this work may be regarded as a standard one.

829. The History of Mexico; to which are added, Dissertations on the Land, Animals, &c. Translated from the Italian of Clavigero, by C. Cullen. 1787. 2 vols. 4to.—Besides natural history, there is in this work much learned research on the ancient history of Mexico.

THE WEST INDIES.

830. Histoire Generale des Antilles. Par le P. Dututie. 1667-1671. 4 vols. 4to.—

This work is very full in all the branches of natural history, and is by no means uninstructive on intellectual and moral geography.

831. Voyages aux Antilles, &c., 1767-1802. Par J.B. Le Blond. Paris, 1813. 8vo.—Statistics, climate, geology, mineralogy, diseases, and manners, are the principal topics of this work, and are treated of with ability and interest.

832. Voyages aux Isles de Trinidad, &c. Par J.J.D. Laraysee. Paris, 1813. 2 vols. 8vo.—The first volume relates to Trinidad: the second to Tobago, Cumana, Guiana, and Margarita. The soil, climate, productions, and occasionally the natural history and geology of these parts are here treated of.

833. Baudin Voyage aux Isles Teneriffe la Trinite, Porto Rico, &c. 2 vols. 8vo. Paris, 1810.—To these travels Sonnini has added some valuable notes.

834. Voyage d'un Suisse dans differentes Colonies de l'Amerique. 1783. 8vo.— Martinique and St. Domingo are particularly described, and the mineralogy of the latter fully entered into.

835. Bryan Edwards' History of the British Colonies in the West Indies, and the French Colony in St. Domingo. 1801. 3 vols. 8vo.—This work justly bears an excellent character, and is very full and minute on almost every topic connected with these islands.

836. Histoire de St. Domingue. Par le P. Charlevoix. Paris, 1722. 2 vols. 4to.—This work, drawn up chiefly from the memoirs of the missionaries, treats of the political, military, and moral state of the island, and more briefly of its produce, animals, &c.—This briefness is compensated in the following work:

837. Essai sur l'Histoire Naturelle de St. Domingue. Par le P. Nicolson. Paris, 1766. 8vo.

838. Ed. Long's History of Jamaica. 3 vols. 4to. 1774.—A work of sterling merit, and if read in conjunction with the following to supply the natural history of the island, will leave little to be known respecting this important island.

839. Pat. Brown's Civil and Natural History of Jamaica. 1756. folio.

840. Ligon's History of Barbadoes. 1695. 8vo.

841. Labat Voyage aux Isles de l'Amerique. La Haye, 1724. 6 vols. 12mo.—This is esteemed the best work of Labat, and it certainly is very instructive in all that relates to Martinique, Guadaloupe, St. Vincent, St. Thomas, St. Lucia, St. Eustatius, &c.

842. Voyage à la Martinique. Par Chauvalson. Paris, 1763. 4to.—Natural history, meteorology, agriculture, and manners.

843. Account of St. Michael, one of the Azores. By Dr. Webster.—This work, which is published in America, contains an interesting description of St. Michael, particularly in what relates to its natural history and geology.

SOUTH AMERICA.

844. Preliminar al Tomo primero de las Memorias Historico-Physicas, Critico-Apologeticas, de la America Meridional. Par D.J.E. Lamo Zaputa. Cadiz, 1759. 8vo.

845. Reise eineger Missionarien in Sud America. Von C. Gott. Von Murr. Nurem. 1785. 8vo.

846. Depon's Travels in South America, 1801-4. 2 vols. 8vo.—The Caraccas, Venezuela, Guyana, Cumana, are the principal objects of this work; the rural economy, the political and commercial situation of these parts at this period, and the manners of the Spanish Americans are here treated of in a superior manner.

847. Nouvelle Description de la France Equinoctiale. Par Pierre Barrere. Paris, 1743. 12mo.

848. Essai sur l'Histoire Naturelle de la France Equinoctiale. Par P. Barrere. Paris, 1749. 2 vols. 8vo.—The former of these works is chiefly confined to a description of the natives, their weapons, manners, mode of life, &c.: the latter work is full on the natural history of Guyana.

849. Bancroft's Essay on the Natural History of Guyana. 1769. 8vo.—Besides natural history, this work may be consulted with advantage on the manners, &c. of the natives.

850. Stedman's Narrative of a Five-Years' Expedition against the Revolted Negroes of Surinam, 1772-7. 2 vols. 4to.—There is an air of romance in several parts of this work, which, though it adds to its interest, raises suspicions of its accuracy and faithfulness, and that it has been in the hands of a trading editor; still it is a work from which a lively picture may be obtained of Surinam and its inhabitants.

851. Tableau de Cayenne. Paris, 1793. 8vo.—Climate, produce, mode of culture, manners and nautical observations form the principal topics of this work.

852. Narrative of a Voyage to Brazil. By Th. Lindley. 1804. 8vo.—This work contains much information regarding the political, commercial, and domestic state of the Brazilians, with some notices on natural history. As Brazil used to be visited by our ships before we obtained the Cape, on their voyage to the East Indies and China, much information may be gained from several voyages to the latter, especially from the accounts of Lord Macartney's Embassy by Staunton and Barrow.

853. Luccock's Notes on Rio Janeiro, and the Southern Parts of Brazil. 1820. 4to.—Mr. Luccock resided eleven years in Brazil, and he seems to have been a careful observer; his work gives much new and important information on agriculture, statistics, commerce, mines, manners, &c., but it is heavily written.

854. Koster's Travels in the Brazils. 1816. 4to.—This work, together with Luccock's, Henderson's, and Mawe's, comprize a body of information on Brazil, nearly complete on all points except natural history, and that must be sought in Prince Maximilian's Travels.

855. History of Paraguay. By Charlevoix. 1760. 2 vols. 8vo.—This work is full on the plants, animals, fruits, &c., of this country; and is particularly interesting from the account it gives of the celebrated and singular Jesuit establishment in Paraguay.

856. Voyages dans l'Amerique Meridionale, 1781-1801. Par Don F. de Azara. 4 vols. 8vo. Paris, 1809.—The author, who was commissioner of the lines of the Spanish frontier in Paraguay, gives in this work much information on the climate, soil, &c. of countries little known; and the value of it is

enhanced by the notes of Cuvier and Sonnini on natural history.

857. Relation de la Voyage dans les Provinces de la Plata. 8vo. Paris, 1819.

858. Historia de Abifponibus. Autore Dobutzhoffen. Vienna, 1784. 8vo.—This work has lately been translated into English: had it been carefully and judiciously abridged it would have been acceptable, but it is tiresome from its extreme minuteness on uninteresting points.

859. Historia del Descubriniento y Conquesta del Peru. Par August de Zarate. Anvers, 1555. 8vo.—This work is not merely historical, but it also embraces many interesting particulars on physical geography, and the manners, religion, &c., of the Peruvians.

860. Histoire des Incas, traduit de l'Espagnole de Garcilasso de la Vega. Amsterdam, 1737. 2 vols. 4to.—The interest of this work arises from its accuracy and fullness on the laws, government, religion, &c., of the ancient Peruvians. To this French translation is added a history of the conquest of Florida.

861. A Voyage to the South Sea along the Coasts of Chili and Peru, 1712-14. By Mr. Frezier. 1717. 4to.—The object for which Mr. Frezier was sent related to the defence of Peru and Chili; but he also enters fully into an account of the mines and the mode of working them, and into a description of manners, domestic life, &c.

862. Journal du Voyage fait à l'Equateur. Par M. de la Condamine. Paris, 1751. 4to.—Besides the detail of astronomical observations, this work is interesting from the personal narrative of the labours of the academician, and instructive on several points of physical and moral geography.

863. Humboldt, Voyage aux Régions Equinoctiales du Nouveau Continent, 1799-1804. 6 vols. 8vo.

864. Humboldt, Relation Historique de son Voyage aux Régions Equinoctiales du Nouveau Continent. 2 vols. 4to.

865. Humboldt, Essai Politique sur le Royaume de la Nouvelle Espagne, Paris, 5 vols. 8vo. 1811.—Perhaps no traveller ever equalled Humboldt in the possession and exercise of such an union of qualifications requisite to render travels instructive and interesting; nor would it be easy to name any travels which have so completely exhausted the subject of them, as those, the titles of which we have given, if taken in connexion with the more purely scientific appendages to them.

866. A Voyage to South America. By Don George Juan and Don Ant. de Ulloa. 1758. 2 vols. 8vo.—Peru, Chili, Carthagena, Porto Bello, and Panama, are described in these volumes with great talent and science with regard to their natural history, climate, and productions; and together with the civil, political, and domestic life of the inhabitants, and various other topics.

867. Helm's Travels from Buenos Ayres by Potosi to Lima, 1806. 12mo.— Natural history, and chiefly geology and mineralogy, with a very particular account of the mines of Potosi.

868. Compendio della Istoria Geografica, Naturale e Civile de Chili. Bologna, 1776. 8vo.

869. Chiliduga sive res Chilenses. Opera Bern. Havestad. Munster, 1777-79.

8vo.—Natural history, the character of the inhabitants, their music and language are here treated of in a superior manner.

870. Molina's Geographical, Natural, and Civil History of Chili, 1809. 2 vols. 8vo.—An excellent work, which fulfils what the title promises.

POLYNESIA

871. An Historical Collection of the several Voyages and Discoveries in the South Pacific Ocean. By Alex. Dalrymple. 1770. 2 vols. 4to.

872. Captain James Burney's Chronological History of the Voyages and Discoveries in the South Seas. 5 vols. 4to. 1803-16.—Both these works are by men well qualified by science, learning, research, and devotedness to their object, to perform well what they undertook on any subject connected with geography and discovery.

873. Keate's Account of the Pelew Islands. 1788. 4to.

874. A Missionary Voyage to the South Pacific Ocean. By Captain Wilson. 1799. 4to.—Otaheite is the principal subject of this work.

875. Mariner's Account of the Tonga Islands in the South Pacific. 1817. 2 vols. 8vo.—This is a very full, accurate, and interesting picture of the manners and character of a singular people, drawn from long and attentive observation on the spot.

AUSTRALASIA

876. Histoire des Navigations aux Terres Australes. Par le President de Brosses. Paris, 1756. 2 vols. 4to—This work is more highly prized on the continent than with us: it certainly is not equal to some of our histories of voyages either in judgment, accuracy of information, or extensive views.

877. Relation de deux Voyages dans les Mers Australes et des Indes. 1771-73. Par M. de Kerguelen. Paris, 1781. 8vo.

878. Voyage à la Nouvelle Guinée. Par Sonnerat. Paris, 1776. 4to.—Natural history, and especially zoology and ornithology.

879. Voyage de Découvertes aux Terres Australes. 1800-4. Par Peron. 2 vols. 4to. Paris, 1811.

880. Captain Th. Forrest's Voyage to New Guinea and the Moluccas, 1774-6. Dublin, 1779. 4to.—This work supplies what is wanting in Sonneret's, as it is full on the physical and moral character of the inhabitants, and on their language, mode of life, and trade.

881. Governor Phillips's Voyage to Botany Bay. 1789. 4to.

882. Collins' Account of the English Colony in New South Wales. 1801. 2 vols. 4to.

883. Wentworth's Statistical, Historical, and Political Description of New South Wales, and Van Dieman's Land. 1819. 8vo.

884. Oxley's Journey of Two Expeditions into the Interior of New South Wales. 1820. 4to.—These British colonies are improving so rapidly that no description can long be full and accurate. Mr. Wentworth's work is, we believe, as good an account as we have; and Mr. Oxley's is interesting from giving an authentic description of the interior of this singular country. A perusal and comparison of the best works that have been published regarding it from the date of that of Collins to the present time, would exhibit a rapidity of improvement, of which there are few examples.

885. Some Account of New Zealand. By John Savage. 1808. 8vo.—A judicious and instructive work on the manners, religion, and character of the natives. Further information on these points, and likewise on the productions of New Zealand, may be gathered from Captain Cruise's Ten Months' Residence there, just published.

Echo Library
www.echo-library.com

Echo Library uses advanced digital print-on-demand technology to build and preserve an exciting world class collection of rare and out-of-print books, making them readily available for everyone to enjoy.

Situated just yards from Teddington Lock on the River Thames, Echo Library was founded in 2005 by Tom Cherrington, a specialist dealer in rare and antiquarian books with a passion for literature.

Please visit our website for a complete catalogue of our books, which includes foreign language titles.

The Right to Read

Echo Library actively supports the Royal National Institute for the Blind's Right to Read initiative by publishing a comprehensive range of Large Print (16 point Tiresias font as recommended by the RNIB) and Clear Print (14 point Tiresias font) titles for those who find standard print difficult to read.

Customer Service

If there is a serious error in the text or layout please send details to feedback@echo-library.com and we will supply a corrected copy. If there is a printing fault or the book is damaged please refer to your supplier.

Lightning Source UK Ltd.
Milton Keynes UK
UKOW042147030113

204395UK00001B/29/A